The Psychology of Emotions

EMOTIONS, PERSONALITY, AND PSYCHOTHERAPY

Series Editors:
Carroll E. Izard, *University of Delaware, Newark, Delaware*
and
Jerome L. Singer, *Yale University, New Haven, Connecticut*

Recent volumes in the series

THE COGNITIVE FOUNDATIONS OF PERSONALITY TRAITS
Shulamith Kreitler and Hans Kreitler

THE EMOTIONAL BRAIN: Physiology, Neuroanatomy, Psychology, and Emotion
P. V. Simonov

GUIDED AFFECTIVE IMAGERY WITH CHILDREN AND ADOLESCENTS
Hanscarl Leuner, Gunther Horn, and Edda Klessmann

IMAGERY AND VISUAL EXPRESSION IN THERAPY
Vija Bergs Lusebrink

LANGUAGE IN PSYCHOTHERAPY: Strategies of Discovery
Edited by Robert L. Russell

THE PSYCHOBIOLOGY OF EMOTIONS
Jack George Thompson

THE PSYCHOLOGY OF EMOTIONS
Carroll E. Izard

QUANTIFYING CONSCIOUSNESS: An Empirical Approach
Ronald J. Pekala

SAMPLING NORMAL AND SCHIZOPHRENIC INNER EXPERIENCE
Russell T. Hurlburt

SHYNESS: Perspectives on Research and Treatment
Edited by Warren H. Jones, Jonathan M. Cheek, and Stephen R. Briggs

THE TRANSFORMED SELF: The Psychology of Religious Conversion
Chana Ullman

The Psychology of Emotions

Carroll E. Izard
University of Delaware
Newark, Delaware

Plenum Press • New York and London

Library of Congress Cataloging-in-Publication Data

Izard, Carroll E. (Carroll Ellis), 1923-
The psychology of emotions / Carroll E. Izard.
p. cm. -- (Emotions, personality, and psychotherapy)
Includes bibliographical references and index.
ISBN 0-306-43865-8
1. Emotions. I. Title. II. Series.
BF531.I96 1991
152.4--dc20 91-21729
CIP

10 9 8 7 6 5 4 3 2

ISBN 0-306-43865-8

A Division of Plenum Publishing Corporation
233 Spring Street, New York, N.Y. 10013

Printed in the United States of America

To
Connor, Flynn, and Olivia

Preface

In the 13 years since the publication of *Human Emotions*, the amount of scientific information on the subject has probably more than doubled. The relevant books and journal articles published in this period number in the thousands. The quantity of scientific information on emotions has now reached the point where it is difficult for students or professionals to get a good picture of the array of concepts and exciting facts that are scattered on the shelves of university libraries.

Neuroscience has increased our knowledge of the brain mechanisms, hormones, and neurotransmitters that subserve emotions. Developmental psychologists have added information on developmental changes in emotions, their role in attachment and temperament, and the ways in which the development of emotions and cognition are interrelated. Social psychologists have presented studies on the communicative functions of emotion expressions, and the influences of emotions on social interactions and relationships. Cognitive and social–cognitive psychologists have increased our knowledge of the cognitive determinants of emotions and emotion–cognition relations. Personality psychologists have begun to analyze traits in terms of discrete emotions. Clinical psychologists have found relations among psychological disorders and types of emotion experiences and examined ways of applying the new knowledge of emotions in psychotherapy.

This newly enriched fund of knowledge has made it possible to write this textbook on emotions. The book is intended to give students an understanding of the activation (causal processes), expression, experience, and functions of each of the basic emotions. The general perspective is evolutionary–developmental, and the chief contributors of information are emotion researchers in developmental, personality, social, and clinical psychology, though there are significant portions from neuroscience, cognitive science, psychophysiology, and other domains.

The theoretical perspective is that of discrete emotions theories. In particular, the book presents a fairly broad sample of the ideas and findings of researchers who conceptualize the emotional life and the influence of emotions on thought and action as explainable in terms of separate, distinct emotions such as joy and sadness, anger and fear, shame and shyness, each having unique neural, expressive, and experiential/motivational characteristics. This does not mean that cognition and action are typically motivated by a single emotion. More often than not, behavior is influenced by multiple emotions.

The theoretical perspective can also be described as biosocial rather than constructivist. Some important aspects of biosocial theories are the recognition of genetic influences on emotion, noncognitive determinants of emotions, and the organization of emotions as a separate system. Foreknowledge of the fact that this book is influenced by an evolutionary–developmental approach and guided by principles of biosocial, discrete emotion theories should help in understanding the content.

Although the material for this text came largely from theory and research in the tradition of the evolutionary–developmental, biosocial, and discrete emotions theories, the suggested readings at the end of each chapter provide ideas and findings from a variety of other theoretical approaches. These include those that focus on appraisal, evaluative, and attributional processes as determinants of emotions. The readings contain interesting material for lectures or student assignments (oral reports, term papers) that will broaden the student's understanding of the emotions.

Carroll E. Izard

Acknowledgments

Many scientists in several different disciplines or specialties have contributed to this volume through their basic research and integrative writing. Among these contributors are my current and former graduate students and postdoctoral fellows. Without the wisdom and hard work of many devoted researchers, a textbook like this would not be possible.

My undergraduate psychology students have also contributed directly and indirectly to the book. Each chapter on a discrete emotion contains a student's biographical account of an intense emotional experience. These intelligent and sensitive accounts of emotions in personally meaningful situations provide excellent insights into the ways that emotions influence our thoughts and actions in daily life and sometimes change the course of events dramatically. Some also show how a single, emotionally strong experience may endure and have long-lasting effects.

I am indebted to the Department of Psychology at the University of Delaware for creating and sustaining a model academic climate for research and writing. Further, exchanges with my colleagues have improved my understanding of various topics that are presented in the book. I am also grateful to the many mothers and children who participate in our longitudinal projects on emotional development. Two people deserve special mention: Dr. O. Maurice Haynes, my research associate, has greatly increased the efficiency and effectiveness of my laboratory, and Sharon L. Antonio, executive secretary for the laboratory, has given charm and warmth, as well as a highly skilled performance to the efforts of my research group and the preparation of the manuscript for this book.

As always, my greatest debt is to Barbara Sinquefield Izard, whose beauty, grace, and love add immeasurably to my life and work. Her professional life had a direct impact on this book. She co-teaches my undergraduate seminar on human emotions. Her background in theater enables her to use dramatic literature to illustrate the integration of emotion experience, emotion expression, and actions and to demonstrate the functions of emotions in lifelike situations. By enriching our course she has enriched this book.

I am very grateful to all those who have helped. Without their effort and dedication the book would not have been possible.

Contents

Chapter 13

Chapter 14

1

On the Origins and Functions of Emotions

The psychology of emotions is just now coming of age. It seems strange that something so obviously central to human existence could have remained outside the mainstream of psychology for more than a century, virtually the lifespan of scientific psychology. The significance of emotions for self-confidence, social commitment, creative endeavors, and courageous actions has been recognized by keen observers of the human sphere for as long as there have been written records, yet until the 1980s most of psychology ignored them. One could argue that psychology in its first 100 years was a paradox, a science that neglected its most important subject matter. How could anyone maintain that human beings in relationships and in action in the real world would ever be understood without the scientific study of emotions?

Over the years there has been a wide range of scientific opinion regarding the nature and importance of the emotions. Some scientists have maintained that emotion concepts are unnecessary for the science of behavior. For example, Duffy (1962), as well as others (e.g., Lindsley, 1957), suggested that the concept of activation, or arousal, has more explanatory power and is less confusing than emotion concepts. Others (Izard, 1971, 1972; Tomkins, 1962, 1963) have maintained that the emotions constitute the primary motivational system of human beings. Some say that emotions are only transient phenomena, while others maintain that people are always experiencing some emotion to some extent or that there is no action without affect (e.g., Schachtel, 1959). Some scientists have maintained that for the most part emotions disrupt and disorganize behavior, and are primarily a source of human problems (e.g., Arnold, 1960a, 1960b; Lazarus, 1968; Young, 1961). Others have argued that the emotions play an important role in organizing, motivating, and sustaining behavior (Izard, 1971, 1972; Leeper, 1948; Mowrer, 1960; Rapaport, 1942; Schachtel, 1959; Tomkins, 1962, 1963).

Some scientists have taken the position that the emotions are primarily a matter of visceral functions—activities of organs innervated by the autonomic nervous system (Wenger, 1950). In 1974, the twenty-sixth International Congress of Physiological Sciences held in Baku, USSR, was entirely devoted to emotions and visceral functions (Gasanov, 1974). Other scientists have emphasized the importance of the externally observable behavior of the face and the role of the somatic nervous system—the part of the nervous system under voluntary control (Ekman, Friesen, & Ellsworth, 1972; Gellhorn, 1964, 1970; Izard, 1971, 1977; Tomkins, 1962, 1963).

Most clinical psychologists and psychiatrists describe problems of adjustment and types of psychopathology as emotional problems (e.g., Dunbar, 1954). On the other hand, Mowrer (1960, 1961) maintains that it is not the emotions that are at fault in problems of adjustment and psychopathology but the person's thoughts, attitudes, and actions. Some have argued that the emotions should be subordinate to cognition (and reason) and have maintained that when they are not something is wrong. Others have held that the emotions trigger and guide cognitive processes (that they always influence reasoning) and that the more important questions relate to the quality and intensity of the emotions involved. Some maintain that we alleviate psychopathological problems and human problems in general by deconditioning or extinguishing inappropriate emotional responses or by bringing emotion under control. Others maintain that psychopathological and other human problems are best treated by freeing the emotions to interact naturally and easily with the other subsystems of the personality—homeostatic processes, drives, perceptions, cognitions, motor acts.

Psychologists, as well as philosophers and educators, vary in their opinions regarding the place of emotions in life and human affairs. Some say we are essentially rational beings—our "reasons for being" are primarily cognitive-intellectual. Witness our occupation as students for 12 to 20 or more years of life. For almost everyone in our society and in many other societies, education continues from early childhood through the years of growth to maturity; and education is most widely considered as the process of learning facts and theories, the amassing of information. Other psychologists, however, despite their respect for cognitive-intellective activities and their own devotion to the accumulation of knowledge, feel that people are essentially emotional or emotional-social beings. They say that our "reasons for being" are affective or emotional in nature. They note that we surround ourselves with the people and things to which we are emotionally attached. They feel that learning through experiences (both private and social) is as important or more important than the acquisition of facts and theories.

Early views of the importance of the emotions in individual behavior and social relationships were given by a leading personality theorist (Leeper, 1948) and by a prominent learning theorist (Mowrer, 1960). Mowrer stated that "the emotions play a central role, indeed an indispensable role, in those changes in behavior or performance which are said to represent 'learning' " (Mowrer, 1960, p. 307). Mowrer went on to decry the widespread tendency in Western civilization to look upon the emotions with distrust and contempt and to elevate the intellect (reason, logic) above them. "If the present analysis is sound, the emotions are of quite extraordinary importance in the total economy of living organisms and do not at all deserve being put into opposition with 'intelligence' " (Mowrer, 1960, p. 308).

It may not be possible to write an adequate textbook that takes account of all the numerous theories in the field. The present text adopts a view that is best described as a discrete emotions approach. In this framework, an effort is made to delineate the characteristics and functions of each emotion separately and of interactions and relations among emotions. Equally importantly, it considers relations among emotion, cognition, and action. The discrete emotions approach is followed by numerous theorists and investigators whose work will be reviewed in this text. All the major theories that follow the discrete emotions approach share common assumptions. Chief among these is the idea that emotions organize and motivate significant aspects of individual behavior, personality development, and social relationships. A representative theory from this group will be presented in some detail in Chapter 2.

The discrete emotions approach differs in emphasis from the dimensional approach, which organizes emotion expressions and emotion states along dimensions such as pleasantness–unpleasantness and tension–relaxation. Although this approach will not be treated in depth, data will be presented that describe each emotion in terms of such dimensions.

Even though opinions of scientists vary widely regarding the nature and significance of emotions, the theoretical and research contributions of the past 20 years have established the emotions as a legitimate area of scientific inquiry. Despite the varying opinions of scientists, virtually all people, in keeping with the discrete emotions approach, readily admit that they experience joy, sadness, anger, and fear and that they know the differences among these emotions in how they feel and how they affect them. But how many people have reflected carefully on the basic questions? What really are the emotions? What are the processes by which they occur and influence us? How do they influence our lives? We shall begin to answer these questions by considering the origins of motivation and emotion.

On the Origins of Motivation and Emotion

Motivations of all types, including basic drives that insure survival and the emotions that enhance the quality of life, emerged and changed during the course of evolution, as did other structures and functions. Some thoughts on the origins and development of the various types of human motivations, particularly the central motivations we call emotions, will provide some perspective for this rapidly growing field of psychology.

Origins of Survival Motivations

When animal life first emerged on the earth, it undoubtedly carried a rudimentary "motivational," or drive, system. In the first single-celled animals the drive system was purely electrochemical. These simple life forms adapted and survived long before the emergence of the capacity for the cognitive evaluation of stimuli. They successfully engineered transactions with the environment by means of a basic motivational system for mediating approach and avoidance reactions without cognitive appraisal.

We know from contemporary research on gustation that a lowly virus can do a sort of back flip to avoid noxious substances (T. R. Scott, personal communication, November, 1988). It is also likely that single-celled animals have a corresponding mechanism for motivating approach. Mechanisms that motivate approach to nutritive substances and avoidance of toxic substances are essential to life. Some neuroscientists speak of the neurobehavioral aspect of the animals' approach–avoidance responses as a hedonic process—one in which an appropriate course of action is determined through decision-making and instrumental action. There are several concepts for explaining motivation that have their roots in the idea of approach and avoidance. For example, Freud developed his theory of motivation and personality around the concepts of pleasure (approach) and pain (avoidance). His concepts of sex and aggression are derived from this pleasure–pain principle.

The basic motivations are those that insure survival and physical well-being. In dire circumstances they drive one to work for one's very life—to find food, water, and shelter, and to eliminate waste products from one's body. In circumstances in which these needs are easily satisfied, the activities associated with them become mundane and occupy relatively little time (Maslow, 1971). Nevertheless, when adverse conditions and a scarcity of resources threaten survival or comfort, hunger elicits emotion. It is at these times that drives and emotions working in combination become very powerful.

Origins of Emotions

Drives such as sex and hunger are necessary for survival, and it is easy to understand why we have them. But why do people have emotions? Are they also essential for survival? It is relatively easy to see why animal life developed reflexes and instincts. Reflexes are specific adaptive responses to particular stimuli. Instincts motivate complex patterns of behavior that in some cases accompany an animal through an entire life cycle. Human beings are born with less reflexes, though a few of them, like the eye blink, remain adaptive throughout life. But reflexes and instincts are rigid and stimulus dependent; when decision-making and flexibility in strategy or performance are required, they are not enough.

Yet reflexes and instincts provide precise ways of responding and adapting to a limited set of environmental objects or events. The same can be said of the motivations we call drives—hunger, thirst, pain avoidance, sexual desire, and elimination of bodily waste. These motivational systems are necessary for survival. They are sometimes called survival needs, for along with the regulatory chemical, or homeostatic, system, they see to our sustenance and physical well-being.

But why did emotions evolve? As our evolutionary forebears became more and more complex, a longer period of maturation and learning was required for the young of the species to become capable of foraging for food and fending for their lives. In order for the young to survive, there had to develop a strong bond or attachment between a principal caregiver (usually mother) and the offspring. Although we do not know how it came about in evolution, we know from contemporary research that the "cement" binding human mother and infant consists of emotions. All it takes to demonstrate this is for mother to break the bonds of attachment, to leave the one-year-old infant alone in a strange room for only a few minutes. Most infants will respond to such separation with strong emotion (Ainsworth, Blehar, Waters, & Wall, 1978; Shiller, Izard, & Hembree, 1986). If the mother–infant bond is broken for a longer period or permanently, all infants respond with a similar pattern of negative emotions and in some cases severe depression or marasmus (Bowlby, 1969; Spitz, 1965).

Surely one of the reasons that emotions evolved was to insure social bonding between infant and caregiver. In the ecological niche of the human infant, the cognitive, social, and motor skills necessary for its very survival are vested in the caregivers. Without strong motivation for the caregiver to keep the infant in her arms or nearby, the infant could not survive. The infant depends upon the mother for sustenance, nurturing, warmth, hygiene, and protection from danger. In accordance with all that we know about human nature, the infant is also dependent on parental affection for health and psychological well-being. Even adults have a difficult time coping with life's challenges if they feel unloved. Feeling unloved and unlovable is a probable major determinant of psychological disorders, particularly depression. (In the final chapter, we shall see how the child's long dependency period and the mother–infant attachment has contributed to the evolution of the emotion complex we call love.)

Another reason emotion evolved was to ensure a means of communication between infant and mother and to facilitate communication between adults. Numerous studies of emotional development have shown that long before the infant either comprehends or speaks a single word, it already has a remarkable repertoire of signals to communicate its internal states (Izard, Huebner, Risser, McGinnes, & Dougherty, 1980). For example, biological needs such as hunger and pain are made apparent through the physical distress expression. Involvement with the social or physical world is signalled by expressions of interest and joy, while frustration is demonstrated through expressions of anger.

This system of social communication based upon emotion expressions is

FIGURE 1-1. Facial expressions of the basic emotions and the affect of pain or physical distress in young infants.

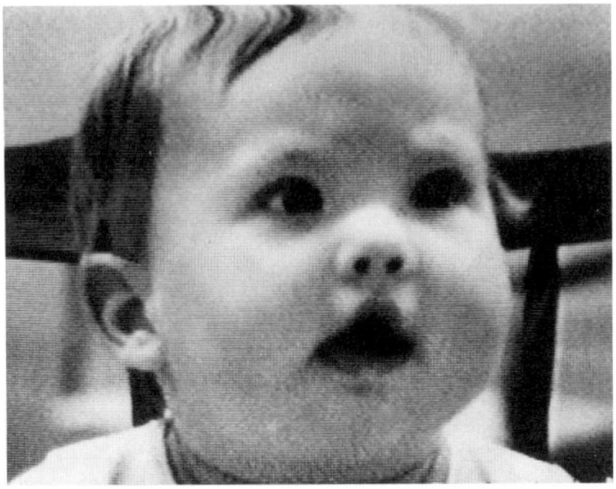

FIGURE 1-1. Interest.

FIGURE 1-1 (cont.). Joy.

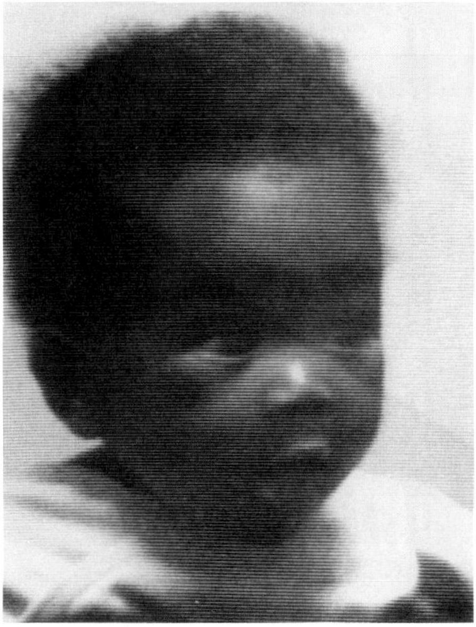

FIGURE 1-1 (cont.). Surprise.

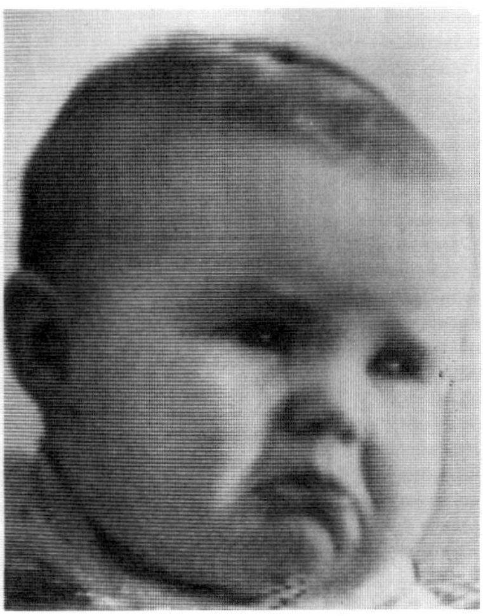

FIGURE 1-1 (cont.). Sadness.

FIGURE 1-1 (cont.). Anger.

vital, for without it there would be no mother–infant attachment. Research has indicated that the parents of Down's syndrome infants, whose emotion expressions are dampened, may become confused or depressed at the lack of facial and other emotion communication (Emde, Katz, & Thorpe, 1978).

Emotions are essential to our survival and existence as human beings. Without emotions—without the ability to feel joy and sadness, anger and guilt—we would really not be human beings at all. Emotions help define humanness. Equally important is the human being's ability to experience emotions vicariously

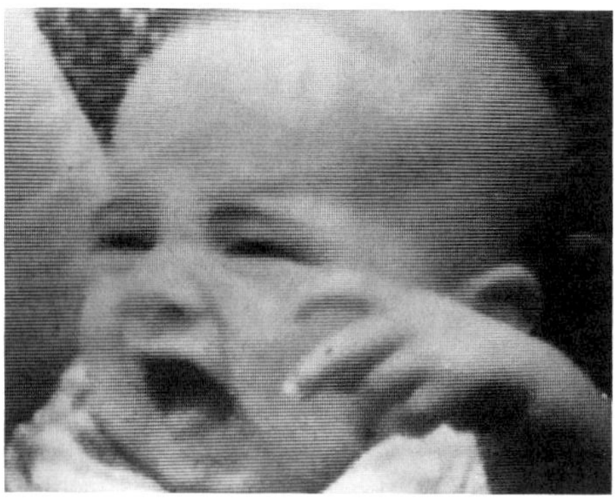

FIGURE 1-1 (cont.). Disgust.

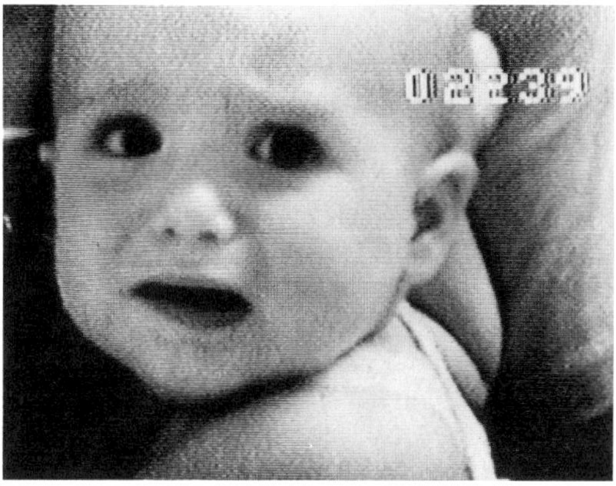

FIGURE 1-1 (cont.). Fear.

through empathy and the ability to label and discuss emotions. In the evolution of the human species, emotions emerged to provide new types of motivation and new action tendencies as well as a greater variety of behaviors to cope with the environment and life's demands.

From Physiological Drive to Emotion: Hunger, Taste, and Disgust

No one can say for sure how through evolution we came to have the various emotions that we now experience. We can speculate that when the first, simple forms of life emerged they had mechanisms that enabled them to respond to stimulation from the environment by accepting or rejecting, approaching or avoiding.

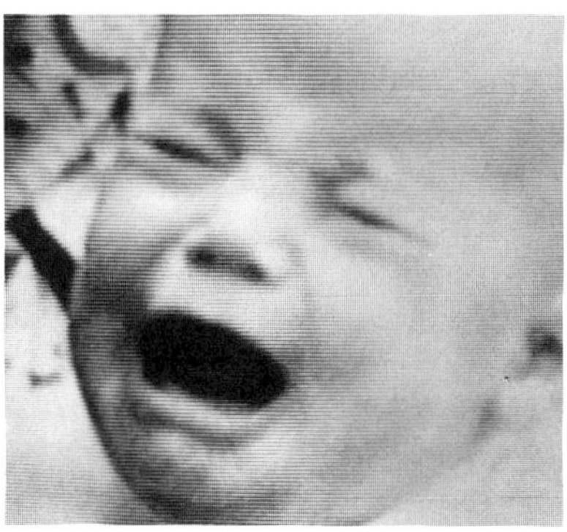

FIGURE 1-1 (cont.). Pain/distress.

Some emotions may have evolved from sensory processes and physiological drives related to basic approach and avoidance behavior. This seems to be the case for the emotion of disgust. Food rejection on the basis of taste is the earliest and simplest example of disgust. The lowly virus's back flip to avoid a noxious stimulus may be the rudimentary prototype of the disgust response human beings make to distasteful substances. The human newborn, even those born without the cerebral hemispheres of the brain, can reject bitter substances by the gustofacial response we know as the disgust expression (Steiner, 1973). Although in the neonate a simple taste is the effective and unlearned stimulus for disgust, through learning and experience we come to respond with disgust to a wide variety of phenomena. Once children can understand the concept of contamination (at about age 7), they can learn to experience disgust toward any food that they perceive to be spoiled, whether it is actually spoiled or not (Rozin & Fallon, 1987).

As you grow older, you come to respond with disgust to things that you have neither tasted nor smelled and that may have no relation to food and drink whatsoever. You might respond with disgust to dirty clothes or filthy language. At times, you can and do become disgusted with certain people and perhaps even with yourself.

The origin of the emotion of disgust is traceable to the sense of taste and the hunger drive, but tracing the origins of the other emotions is not so simple. We are not sure *how* they evolved, though we can suggest some reasons *why* they evolved.

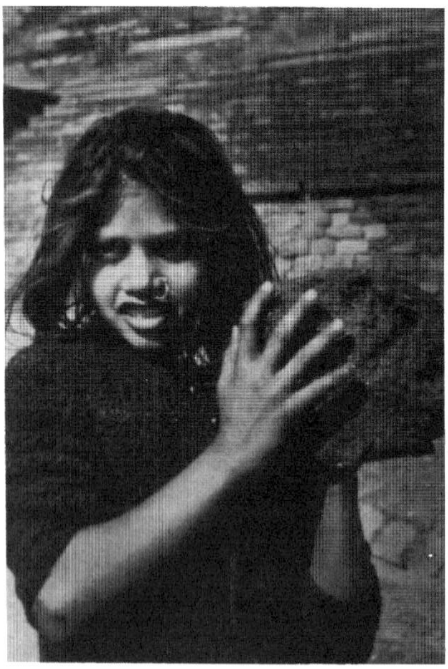

FIGURE 1-2. A smile of joy on the face of a beautiful Indian girl working with an object (fresh cow dung) that might elicit disgust in Westerners. Her smile for the people who attracted her attention has an innate neural substrate, but her affective–cognitive responses to the object have their basis in her experience in a culture where handmade dung cakes are readily marketable as a fuel supplement.

Types of Motivation

Motivation usually involves some type of stimulation and some type of sensory or motor process. That is, one or more of the basic senses—sight, hearing, touch, taste, smell—is activated, or there is some event that elicits sensory feedback. The simplest type of stimulation is that which emanates from a physical object. The light reflected by a ball informs you about its shape and color, though neither may have much motivational significance. But if it happens to be a ball coming at you at high speed and you are responsible for catching it in your glove or returning it with your racquet, the sensory information obtained from it as it approaches you is motivating your behavior as well as directing it precisely. Of course, if you are playing a ball game, many types of motivation other than simple sense data from the object are involved—your desire to experience the joy of triumph, your fear of looking foolish or of failing, the fun of doing something vigorous and exciting.

Reflexes and Automatic Behavior

A reflex is the simplest form of behavior. It is motivated by direct stimulation. Some inborn reflexes virtually disappear except in extreme conditions, while others remain useful throughout the life span. A puff of air will produce a rapid reflexive eye blink at any age. This very efficient way of closing the eye fissure helps keep uncomfortable and potentially dangerous foreign bodies from injuring the delicate tissue of the eyeball.

Reflexes are automatic responses that require no evaluation or appraisal of the stimulus; no decision about how to behave is involved. For this reason, human beings have a relatively small number of reflexes, for they are adaptive only in relation to events requiring no evaluation or judgment, and few such events impinge on human beings. Virtually everything can be responded to differently depending upon its context and the way one perceives or appraises it.

People speak of tennis players as athletes with great reflexes. When you are at the net, and your opponent standing only 20 feet away sends a ball toward you at 50 miles per hour, you have little time for evaluation and judgment. However, a player who consistently makes good volleys in such situations is not operating on reflexes. He has, instead, mastered the eye, body, hand, and arm movements involved in the volley and practiced until he can perform them automatically.

There are numerous examples of seemingly reflexive movements, which are in fact automatic responses, in the game of a great tennis player: snapping the wrist when serving, adjusting to a backhand grip for a high-bouncing ball, shortening the stroke for play on a fast surface, turning a hip to the net and pointing the free hand upward toward the ball while making an overhead smash. The more appropriate movements you can execute automatically, the more time and cognitive resources you have available to develop strategy. Smart players are those who automatically perform many of the movements requisite to good strokes. Obviously, the athletic talent necessary to make the movements with precision and timing is another consideration. Not everyone possesses the body, nervous system, and emotional makeup of a Chris Evert or a Jimmy Connors. Their skills are so sharp and precise that they make complex behavior look like reflex.

Instincts

Instincts are more complex than reflexes. They are often motivated by hormonal changes within the body. The most interesting examples of instincts, as we shall see, are drawn from animal life. Unlike reflexes, instincts are difficult or impossible to identify in human beings. A reflex, like the eye blink or pupil dilation, is a fixed response to a specific stimulus. Reflexes are stimulus bound; a standard response occurs whenever the appropriate stimulus impinges. Animal instincts also involve fixed responses that occur in a complex set called a fixed action pattern. They are also relatively stimulus bound, but less so than a reflex. Once a reflex is activated, it proceeds automatically. Instinctive behavior on the other hand can be interrupted and modified, so some appraisal or judgment may be involved. Nevertheless, instinctive behavior remains within a fixed pattern, one that is associated with the animal's life cycle. Here is an example of instinct in action as it steers an animal through a very narrow course, almost literally between the jaws of death.

> A young male salticid spider which, after molting for the last time, approaches a female must neither mistake another species for his own, nor must he perform the signaling of his specific courtship dance in any other way than the one to which his female responds; otherwise, he would be eaten by her immediately. He has no opportunity in his short life to gain any information about what a female of his own species looks like, nor what movements he must perform to inhibit her feeding reactions and to stimulate her specific mating responses. (Lorenz, 1965, p. 25)

The initial flight of a swift provides an even more remarkable example of instinctive behavior. It is almost beyond comprehension that such a complex set of behaviors is fundamentally guided by information in the animal's genes. It can be understood only from an evolutionary perspective and with an appreciation of the gains accumulated over millions of years of development.

> A young swift reared in a narrow cave in which it cannot extent its wings (far less beat them up and down), in which it cannot attain a sharp retinal image as the farthest point of the cave is much nearer than its shortest focusing distance, and in which it cannot gain any experience on parallactic shifting of retinal images, nevertheless proves to be perfectly able on the very moment it leaves the nest cavity to assess distances by the parallactic shift of the object's images. It can also cope, in its rapid flight, with all the intricacies of air resistance, upcurrents, turbulence, and air pockets and can "recognize" and catch prey, and finally effect a precise landing in a suitable place. The information implicitly contained in the adaptive molding of all these forms of behavior to the environmental givens to which they

> indubitably do fit would fill many volumes. The description of the innate distance computers alone would contain whole textbooks of stereometry and that of the responses and activities of flying, an equal number of data on aerodynamics. (Lorenz, 1965, pp. 25–26).

Most psychologists today do not believe humans have instincts comparable to those of lower animals. Freud spoke of a life instinct and a death instinct, but few contemporary behavioral scientists accept the validity of these concepts. Some speak of a mother instinct. Such a notion could account for the nurturant and protective behavior directed toward the young. Although a case can be made for the maternal instinct, or at least for mother–infant attachment, much of maternal or caregiver behavior seems to be learned rather than inborn, and there is great variation in its form and quality across individuals and cultures.

McDougall (1908), one of the great early psychologists, believed that human beings possess instincts; but in his theory, he proposed that every instinct was accompanied by a particular emotion that provided the motive power. McDougall may have been on the right track. The role of reflexes and instincts in the lives of lower animals may in fact be subsumed by emotions in human beings. As we shall see, the nature of emotion is in some ways similar to that of reflex or instinct. The biggest difference is that emotions, though powerful as motivators, are fixed only in regard to action tendencies. They are not stimulus bound, nor are they tied to fixed action patterns or overt action; and unlike reflexes or instincts, emotions do not characterize one particular phase of the life cycle. Emotions are with us always, from the moment of birth until death.

Drives

Drives are the physiological needs basic to all animal life. They include hunger, thirst, elimination of waste, comfort (or pain avoidance), and sex. These drives are sometimes referred to as survival needs because their satisfaction is necessary to sustain life. Underlying drives is a system of silent automatic processes that regulate blood flow, breathing, and body temperature as well as maintain homeostasis—the chemical balance necessary for health and well-being. The drives and homeostatic processes are essential for life, but how important are they as sources of motivation for day-to-day activities? Some psychologists believe that the basic drives or physiological needs like hunger and thirst, sex and pain avoidance are not very important sources of motivation in human beings (Maslow, 1971). Indeed, people who can readily obtain these necessities are not often motivated by drives. The great variety and complexity of human behavior, as well as the different cultures it produces, attest to that. It is a fruitless intellectual exercise to attempt accounting for the complex technical, scientific, literary, and artistic accomplishments of human beings entirely in terms of sublimated sexual impulses or any other derivative of biological drives or tissue needs.

Once we have acknowledged the power of emotions in social bonding, such as in the mother–infant attachment, we must know that human motivators go beyond mere survival needs. To explain such things as values, goals, courage, commitment, empathic behavior, altruism, pity, pride, compassion, and love, we must look to the emotions of human experience.

Emotions

Understanding the very complex concept of human emotion will be the pervasive aim of this text, and no simple definition can do justice to the concept. All of Chapter 2 will be dedicated to defining emotion and presenting some guidelines for identifying and understanding a basic emotion. For immediate convenience, here is a handy though incomplete description:

> An emotion is experienced as a feeling that motivates, organizes, and guides perception, thought, and action.

All aspects of this description are critical to understanding the nature of emotion. Emotion motivates. It mobilizes energy, and, in some cases, the energy buildup is sensed as an action tendency. Emotion guides mental and physical activity, channeling energy in selective directions. For example, you do not usually run away when you are angry, nor do you attack when frightened. Emotion also acts as a regulator or filter for our senses. When you are happy, you see the world through the proverbial rose-colored glasses, find joy in the scent of a flower or in most anything, and walk through life with a springy step.

Combining Feeling and Thought: Affective–Cognitive Structures

When emotion becomes linked to a mental image, symbol, or thought, there emerges a feeling–thought bond, an affective–cognitive structure. Because emotion in adult life is very frequently associated with mental imagery or thought, it is important to understand the notion that frequent association of specific emotions with specific imagery leads to the formation of affective–cognitive structures. Note, also, that although the thought processes or cognitive aspect of such phenomena may seem to be the more crucial of the two elements, it is in fact the emotional component that provides the motivation.

Affective–cognitive structures can also involve drive–cognition or drive–emotion–cognition combinations. You can see that the concept is rather complex, but it is vital to have some understanding of it to further understand the complexities of human motivation. Sometimes it is possible to break down the motivational components of a behavior and to recognize that a drive, an emotion, and/or mental imagery or thought played a part. For example, feelings of discouragement or sadness may touch off imagery and thoughts of comforting oneself. A person with an eating disorder may turn to food for this purpose. And if there is any level of hunger present at the time, the emotion and imagery working in tandem with the drive can amplify the behavior, producing an eating binge.

An affective–cognitive structure can be very simple, as when it is the positive emotion feeling of a young infant that has been linked to an image of its mother's face. It can also be very complex, as the one that motivated binging. It may take the form of a value, a goal, or an ideal, and a set of affective–cognitive structures may become an ideology or a philosophy of life. In any form, affective–cognitive structures are extremely important determinants of human behavior. Remember that the motivational force of an affective–cognitive structure lies in the affect—a drive, emotion, or drive–emotion combination. Most frequently, it is a basic emotion or combination of such emotions.

An incident in the life of a popular high school football player illustrates the power of emotion in cognition and action.

Time once stood still for Charlie. He was a gifted athlete, an outstanding high school running back having an especially good year. Then in the fourth game of the season, his right knee was injured. Charlie had to stop playing and begin a treatment and rehabilitation program.

> After five weeks, the doctor said I could play again but warned me that there was a weakness in the knee and that it was more vulnerable to injury than before. He also said that if I re-injured it, I wouldn't be able to play football or any other sport ever again.

The doctor's words jarred Charlie's mind. His face fell and his body slumped. He felt numb. But in a moment he clenched his teeth and stood erect, all the while pushing back the tears.

> When I left the doctor's office, I walked straight home to my room. I had to decide what I would do. It was my life and I would have to live every day with the consequences of my decision, so I didn't want to talk to anyone until I knew what it would be.

Charlie had physical courage; he had shown that on the footfall field over and over again. But physical courage did not seem to help with this decision. If he decided to continue football, some would say that he was foolish. If he stopped, others would say he was a quitter or didn't care about the team.

> I thought about it all afternoon. Finally I told myself that I wasn't going to play football anymore, and although I knew I had decided what was best for me, tears welled up in my eyes. I suddenly realized all that being a football player had meant to me. It had come easily, and until then I had taken all the benefits for granted. What really made me sad was realizing that I would lose that special companionship that comes with being a member of the team. I kept imagining myself wandering around the football field all alone, but then even this thought got fuzzy and I couldn't focus my mind on anything. It was as if I'd lost interest in everything. Life seemed so grey and gloomy.
>
> I wanted to tell my father first. That was the toughest thing of all. My dad was my number one fan, always telling his friends about how I'd done in the last game. Waiting for him to come home from work felt like forever. Minutes seemed like hours. It was as if everything had stopped, except my tears which I tried to fight.

This experience convinced Charlie that emotions make the world go around. Not only his world, but the whole wide world of human beings and human affairs.

You might disagree. You might believe that ideas are what count—that you just think of what it is you want to do, make a plan, set your goal, and go for it. But a plan or a goal is merely a set of cold and empty words if there is no emotion invested in it. If you have a goal but have no feelings about it, how likely are you to strive for it?

You might also agree feelings are necessary but that Freud was right—that sexual urges and feelings of aggression motivate all of human thought and action. But can sex and aggression really explain the music of Mozart, the poetry of William Butler Yeats, the plays of Shakespeare, or the singing of Billie Holiday? Can it wholly account for a man's life-threatening dive into the icy Potomac to save the life of a plane-crash victim or countless other gallant deeds and acts performed by individuals? Freud thought that sex and aggression drive people and motivate all human behavior; but even the sexual drive and aggressive behavior is influenced by emotion—you feel sexier when your partner elicits interest and joy, and you fight harder when you are angry.

The power of emotional commitment is far greater than that of sex, hunger, or thirst, and the power of each of these increases when combined with emotion. A person who gives you joy and shares your sorrows is in the long run far more important to you than an individual you do not know and who has never aroused your feelings.

Love, self-respect, pride, honor, affection, courage, commitment, and conscience are all based on emotions. Without emotion there would be no human values, for to value something is to invest in it emotionally with love, pride, interest, and joy. Each of us begins life as a highly emotional being without language or mobility. The very life of the human infant depends upon its ability to sense and to feel, and to express its feelings with clarity and force. We know that during the first year of life, the infant lacks language for verbal communication and must express its needs and feelings with the face, with vocal tones, and with patterned movements that hold meaning for the caregiver (see Figure 1-1).

Some Characteristics of Emotions

Though we have already given a compact description of just what comprises an emotion, it must be remembered that there is no simple definition of emotion. There are good reasons for this. First, there are many emotions, each of which has distinct properties. For example, anger creates action tendencies to strike out, fear, to flee or think of self-protection. Second, an emotion is a highly complex phenomenon that typically activates neural, cognitive, and motor processes. Put another way, it involves collaboration of mind and body—the whole person. Chapter 2 is devoted to a detailed definition and analysis of emotion. Let us consider some of the characteristics of emotions that help in defining and understanding them.

Emotions Can Function as States and as Traits

Do emotions come and go, or are they always with us? To what extent are emotions situational and momentary, and to what extent are they stable characteristics of the individual? Clearly, they are both. Since the work of Cattell and Scheier (1961) and Spielberger (1966), many investigators describe emotion phenomena as having two forms: state and trait. Application of this typology to the traditional concept of anxiety has provided the most widely known examples of this research. There has been a great deal of theorizing and research aimed at distinguishing the meanings and effects of "state anxiety" and "trait anxiety." The terms *state* and *trait* are distinguished primarily in terms of time—the duration of an emotion experience; they do not imply differences in the quality of the experience. It is also conceded that state emotion has a greater range of intensity than trait emotion. In this book the term *emotion state* (e.g., anger state) refers to a particular emotion process of limited duration. Emotion states may last from seconds to hours and vary widely in intensity. In extraordinary conditions an emotion state of high intensity may continue for an extended period of time, but chronically tense emotion or frequent episodes of intense emotion may indicate psychopathology.

The term *emotion trait* (e.g., anger trait) refers to the tendency of the individual to experience a particular emotion with frequency in his or her day-to-day life. A complementary concept is that of *emotion threshold* (Izard, 1971). If a person has a low threshold for anger, he or she probably experiences anger frequently and thus would score high on a measure of trait anger. Later chapters will discuss the evidence and arguments relating to a number of emotion traits.

Emotions Have Genetic and Environmental Determinants

The early work of Darwin (1872/1965, 1877) and the more recent work of Ekman, Friesen, and Ellsworth (1972) and Izard (1971) have shown that certain emotions, referred to in this book as *fundamental emotions*, have the same expressions and experiential qualities in widely different cultures from virtually every continent of the globe, including isolated preliterate cultures having had virtually no contact with Western civilization. The data presented in Tables 1-1 and 1-2 provide a sound basis for inferring that the fundamental emotions are subserved in innate neural programs. However, the fact that there are genetically based mechanisms for the fundamental emotions does not mean that no aspect of an emotion can be modified through experience. Almost anyone can learn to inhibit or modify the innate emotion expressions. While the innate expression of anger involves baring of the teeth as in preparation for biting, many people clinch their teeth and compress their lips as though to soften or disguise the expression. People of different social backgrounds and cultures may learn quite different facial movements for modifying innate expressions. In addition to learning modifications of emotion expressions, sociocultural influences and individual experiences play

TABLE 1-1

Percentage of Subjects Who Agreed on the Emotion Category of Photographs Selected to Represent Fundamental Emotions

	Cultural (national) group											
	American[a]	English[a]	German[a]	Swedish[a]	French[a]	Swiss[a]	Greek[a]	Japanese[a] (Tokyo)	Mexican[b]	Brazilian[c]	Chilean[c]	Argentinian[c]
$N =$	89	62	158	41	67	36	50	60	616	82	90	168
Interest–excitement	84.5	79.2	82.0	83.0	77.5	77.2	66.0	71.2	—	—	—	—
Enjoyment–joy	96.8	96.2	98.2	96.5	94.5	97.0	93.5	93.8	97	97	90	94
Surprise–startle	90.5	81.0	85.5	81.0	84.2	85.5	80.2	79.2	54	82	88	93
Distress–anguish	74.0	74.5	67.2	71.5	70.5	70.0	54.5	66.8	61	83	90	85
Disgust–contempt	83.2	84.5	73.0	88.0	78.5	78.2	87.5	55.8	61	86	85	79
Anger–rage	89.2	81.5	83.2	82.2	91.5	91.8	80.0	56.8	86	82	76	72
Shame–humilation	73.2	59.5	71.8	76.2	77.2	70.0	71.0	41.2	—	—	—	—
Fear–terror	76.0	67.0	84.0	88.8	83.5	67.5	67.8	58.2	71	77	78	68
Average	83.4	77.9	80.6	83.4	82.2	79.6	75.1	65.4	71.7	84.5	84.5	81.8

[a]From Izard, 1971.
[b]The Mexican data were obtained by Dicky and Knower (1941).
[c]The data from Brazil, Chile, and Argentina were obtained by Ekman, Friesen, & Ellsworth (1972). Ekman *et al*. also obtained data from a Japanese sample on the same six emotions they studied in South American, and they obtained somewhat higher percentages of agreement than those obtained by Izard.

TABLE 1-2
Identification of Emotion Photographs from Orally Presented Emotion Stories by Visually Isolated Preliterate Observers in New Guinea and Borneo

Emotion category described in the story	Percentage choice of the emotion expected in terms of agreement with the judgements of Western literate culture observers: Adults (N = 189)	Children (N = 130)
Happiness	92	92
Surprise	68	98
Sadness	79	81
Disgust	81	85
Anger	84	90
Fear		
Distinguished from anger/disgust	83	93
Sadness from surprise	43	—

[a]Table adapted from Ekman, Friesen, and Ellsworth, 1972, p. 161.

an important role in determining what will trigger an emotion and what a person will do as a result of emotion.

As used in this book, the terms *innate* and *learned* do not imply an absolute dichotomy. In the wake of the long-standing controversy over the nature of intelligence, Murphy (1958) remarked that "nothing is innate, nothing is acquired." Most behavioral scientists tend to agree with Murphy in the sense that virtually any response or behavior pattern requires some practice or experience. Innate emotion expressions come as close as anything to being an exception to Murphy's rule. For example, the prototypical distress expression (crying) appears at birth. The work of Dumas (1932, 1948), Fulcher (1942), Goodenough (1932), Thompson (1941), and Eibl-Eibesfeldt (1972) indicate that congenitally blind children express emotion in the same way as seeing children, although the expressions of the born-blind tend to deteriorate in quality with increasing age. The decrease in the quality of the expressions of the blind may be mainly a result of disuse, since changes in the expressive movements around the eyes are the most profound.

Although the role of learning, nurturance, and environment is acknowledged, the point of view represented in this text allows for genetic determination of emotion traits that are traits or characteristics of personality. The presence of the same traits in monozygotic twins reared apart (Nichols, 1978) is remarkable testimony to the robustness of genetic determinants of personality characteristics.

Emotions Are Not Simply Positive or Negative

Scientists as well as laypersons agree that there are both positive and negative emotions. While this very broad classification of emotions is generally correct and useful, the concepts of positiveness and negativeness as applied to the emotions require some qualification. Emotions such as anger, fear, and shame cannot be considered categorically negative or bad. Anger is sometimes positively correlated with survival, and more often with the defense and maintenance of personal integrity and the correction of social injustice. Fear is also correlated with survival and, together with shame, helps with the regulation of destructive aggression and the maintenance of social order. Unwarranted or overdetermined anger or fear usually has negative organismic and social consequences, but so may the emotion of joy if it is associated with derisive laughter or is combined with excitement and ulterior motives and becomes what Lorenz (1966) called "militant enthusiasm."

Instead of saying that emotions are simply positive or negative, it is more accurate to say that there are some emotions that tend to lead to psychological entropy and others that tend to facilitate constructive behavior, or the converse of entropy. Whenever a given emotion is positive or negative in this sense depends on intraindividual and person–environment processes as well as on more general ethological and ecological considerations. For example, fear of certain elements in the environment (e.g., flying in airplanes, antibiotics, school) may have purely deleterious effects. The positive emotion of interest–excitement may play a role in activities as widely different as sexual assault and creative endeavor. Nevertheless, for convenience the terms *positive* and *negative* will be used to divide emotions into classes that are less likely and more likely, respectively, to have undesirable consequences.

How Emotions Affect Us: An Overview

Your emotions affect your body, mind, and virtually every aspect of your existence. In the chapters that follow we shall see how specific emotions affect various aspects of biological, psychological, and social functioning. This section presents a very general picture of the scope of the effects of emotions on our lives.

Emotions and the Body

Electrophysical changes occur in the muscles of the face during emotions (Rusalova, Izard, & Simonov, 1975; Schwartz, Fair, Greenburg, Freedman, & Klerman, 1974). Changes occur in the electrical activity of the brain, in the circulatory system, and the respiratory system (Simonov, 1975). In strong anger or fear the heart rate may increase as much as 40 to 60 beats per minute (Rusalova *et al.*, 1975). These dramatic changes in body functions during strong emotion suggest that virtually all of the neurophysiological systems and subsystems of the body are involved in greater or lesser degree in emotion states. Such changes inevitably affect the perceptions, thoughts, and actions of the person. These bodily changes may also contribute to medical and mental health problems. Emotion activates the autonomic nervous system, which changes the flow of glandular secretions and neurohumors. The mind and body are tuned for action. If the emotion-relevant cognitions and actions are blocked, psychosomatic symptoms may result (Dunbar, 1954). But we do not have to experience a psychosomatic symptom to realize that emotion affects the body and various physiological systems of the body. (For a detailed discussion of emotions in relation to physiological systems see Thompson's *The Psychobiology of Emotions*, 1988.)

Recall an occasion when you were gripped by fear and your insides went wild—your heart pounded, your breath rushed in and out, your hands shook, and your legs were wobbly. You can probably remember other times when your anger mounted and your pounding heart sent blood rushing to your face and to the muscles of action. This was likely accompanied by a strong urge to strike out at the instigator of your rage to release the tension from tightly drawn muscles. Recall also times when you experienced overwhelming sadness, when your body seemed strangely dense or ponderous, while your muscles remained slackened and impotent. Your face and chest may have ached, tears flowed, or were stifled with effort, as your body was racked with sobs.

Recall an occasion when you felt charged with electricity, your body vibrating as blood pumped to the tips of your toes, the top of your head, and every place in between. You wanted to dance and shout and jump about, for you were experiencing great joy. Or think of a time when you were captivated by an object, a task, or a person, and your body seemed solely oriented toward the target of your interest. The expressive behavior in posture and body movements can enable observers to identify specific emotions (Sogon & Matsutani, 1989).

During the experience of any emotional extreme, the physiological changes are so dramatic that they are not easily ignored. However, the less intense bodily changes that accompany mild or moderate emotions—the kind that characterize most of your daily life—often remain undetected and just below the threshold of conscious awareness. That you are often unaware of bodily changes during mild emotion does not mean that such bodily processes are unimportant. Although the body responds to milder emotion less intensely, these responses may be very long lasting. *Mood* is the term used to describe emotion that endures. Mild to moderate negative emotion or mood persisting over a long period of time may eventually contribute to physical or mental disorders. Recent advances in neuroscience have suggested that even the immune system, the body's way of protecting itself from disease, is influenced by emotion or mood (Marx, 1985). If you remain hostile, anxious, or depressed, even moderately for an extended period of time, you are more likely to catch cold, contract influenza, or develop gastrointestinal disorders. Of course, these conditions are caused by viruses, but some disease-causing viruses are almost always present. They are more likely to multiply and render adverse effects upon your body when the immune system is weakened by the chronic stress of enduring negative emotions.

Emotions in Personality Development and Relationships

The emotions or patterns of emotions that a person experiences at a given time influences virtually everything the person does—work, study, play. When deeply interested in a subject, one is eager to study it and to pursue it in depth. If one is disgusted with a subject, one wants to reject it. Consider for a moment the difference in the educational experiences of students who are lucky enough to pursue many courses that interest and excite them and students who study primarily out of fear of failure and rejection.

Emotions and Personality Development. Two factors are important in considering emotion and personality development. The first is the person's genetic endowment in the sphere of the emotions. A person's genetic makeup probably plays an important role in establishing emotion traits or the thresholds for the various emotions. The second factor is the individual's experiences and learning relating to the emotion sphere, in particular the way emotion expressions and emotion-related behavior are socialized. Observations of Russian infants (ages 6 months to 2 years) who were reared in the same social environment (an institution that provided a great deal of attention, warmth, affection, and educational opportunities) showed wide individual differences in emotion thresholds and emotion-related activities (Izard, 1977). Anyone who doubts the significance of genetic influences on differences in emotion experiencing, emotion expression, and emotion responsivity, need only observe such children for a few hours.

However, when an infant has a low threshold for a particular emotion and experiences and expresses it frequently, this will inevitably lead to particular kinds of responses from other infants and from the surrounding adults. These interacting forces inevitably produce distinct and significant personality characteristics.

The individual's emotion traits also significantly influence social development, especially in infancy and childhood. The infant who has frequent temper tantrums, the one who frightens easily, and the one who often wears a smile will each invite and receive different responses from peers and adults. Social interactions and hence social development will differ widely depending upon the emotions most frequently experienced and expressed by the infant. Emotional responsiveness not only affects personality characteristics and social development but intellectual development as well. The infant who is distressed much of the time will be much less inclined to explore and manipulate the environment than the child who has a low threshold for interest and enjoyment. Tomkins (1962) has maintained that the emotion of interest is as essential to intellectual development as exercise is to physical development.

Emotions and Sex. As early as 1935, Beach showed that copulation and fear are incompatible phenomena. His subjects were rats, but the fact that this generalizes to human beings is well established in clinical literature as well as by common sense. The sex drive virtually always interacts with some emotion. The sex drive interacting with anger and contempt may result in sadism or rape. The sex drive interacting with guilt may produce impotence or masochism. In love and marriage the sex drive can interact with excitement and joy and produce peak experiences of sensory pleasure and emotion.

Emotion, Marriage, and Parenthood. An individual's emotion expressiveness and responsitivity will be a factor in courtship and marriage, but research in other areas suggests that two factors may be operative. A person may select a mate whose emotion experiences and expressiveness complement his or her own. Or an individual may select a mate who has a similar emotion profile—similar thresholds for experiencing and expressing the various emotions.

Just as the emotions affect sex life and marriage, so too do they affect parenthood. A parent's threshold for excitement, joy, disgust, or fear will play a significant role in his or her response to the child's interest, joy, disgust, or fear.

Emotion, Perception, and Cognition

A very general and fundamental principle of human behavior is that emotions energize and organize thought and action. When you feel any emotion intensely, you can, with a moment's reflection, recognize a surge of energy. Emotions do not simply create general arousal or a vague sense of strength and energy. A specific emotion sets up a specific action tendency—the first sign that emotion is working to organize your thought and action. Emotions directly influence what we see and hear. For example, while experiencing joy you see the world through rose-colored glasses. Fear tends to create tunnel vision, causing you to see only the object that frightens you or perhaps only a single route of escape. When experiencing intense fear this may be all that you perceive and all that will register in your consciousness. Likewise, in anger a person is more likely to have angry thoughts and memories, while in the experience of intense feelings of interest one is curious and desirous of exploration and learning.

In a study conducted many years ago, subjects were treated either courteously or discourteously by an authority figure (Izard, Nagler, Randall, & Fox, 1965). They were made happy by the experimenter acting in a friendly manner or made angry by his hostility. The subjects were then shown pairs of emotion expressions in a stereoscope. (This device permits a person to view one picture with the left eye and another with the right eye; however, what registers in the consciousness of the viewer is a single picture, which may be either the picture seen by the left eye, the picture seen by the right eye, or a combination of the two.) The experimenters presented happy expressions and angry expressions randomly on the right and left sides, and subjects reported what they saw. Those made angry by the experimenter's hostile manner saw significantly more anger expressions in the stereoscope, and those who were made happy by the experimenter's friendly approach saw significantly more happy expressions. This demonstrated how an emotion state can actually determine what is perceived and registered in consciousness. There have been a number of such experiments, and we shall learn more about them later.

Summary

The study of emotions is a recent development in the field of psychology. Thus far, emotions have been regarded by scientists in widely different ways, ranging from the idea that emotions are wholly irrelevant to the science of behavior to the approach of this text—that they constitute the primary motivational system for human beings.

The origins of emotion lie in evolution. Some emotions may have emerged from physiological drives such as hunger and from basic approach–avoidance mechanisms. All emotions have adaptive functions developed through the course of evolution. Robust cross-cultural and developmental research support the thesis, first proposed by Darwin, that the expressions of the basic emotions are innate and universal.

Reflexes, which are automatic responses to direct stimulation, require no evaluation or appraisal of the stimulus. Instincts are more complex, often motivated by hormonal changes in the body, and fundamentally guided by information in the animal's genes. Reflexes and instincts play much greater roles in the lives of lower animals than in human beings, in whom emotions are the predominant motivations.

A complex definition of emotion must take into account physiological, expressive, and experiential components. The emotions occur as a result of changes in the nervous system, and these changes may be brought about by either internal or external events. When emotions become linked to a mental image, symbol, or thought, the result is a thought–feeling bond, or an affective–cognitive structure. Affective–cognitive structures can also involve drive–cognition or drive–emotion–cognition combinations.

Intense emotion states have captured the attention of scientists and nonscientists alike, but the science of emotions must go beyond the study of transient states. There are stable individual differences in the frequency with which people experience the various emotions, and these differences may be studied in terms of emotion traits or emotion thresholds.

It is convenient to classify emotions as either positive or negative on the basis of their sensory or experiential characteristics. However, any emotion (e.g., joy, fear) may be positive or negative if the criteria for classification are based on the adaptiveness or dysadaptiveness of the emotion in a particular situation.

Emotions affect the whole person, and each emotion affects the person differently. Emotion affects the level of electrical activity in the brain, the amount of tension in the muscles of the face and body, the visceral-glandular system, circulatory system, and the respiratory system. Changes in emotions can alter the appearance of our world from bright and cheerful to dark and gloomy, our thinking from creative to morbid, and our action from awkward and inappropriate to skillful and effective.

Individual differences in infants' thresholds for the various emotions change the frequency with which they express these emotions, and this greatly influences the responses they invite from those around them. In turn, the way others respond to the emotion expressions of infants and children will influence their expressive style and hence their personalities.

It is a general and fundamental principle of human behavior that emotions energize and organize perception, thought, and action tendencies. Emotion directly influences what is perceived through the senses and thus affects all subsequent information processing and actions.

Suggested Readings

Forgas, J. P., & Bower, G. H. (1987). Mood effects on personality–perception judgments. *Journal of Personality and Social Psychology*, *53*(1), 53–60.

Effects of emotion on perception (impression formation) and memory.

Izard, C. E. (1989). The structure and functions of emotions: Implications for cognition, motivation, and personality. In I. S. Cohen (Ed.), *The G. Stanley Hall Lecture Series* (Vol. 9, pp. 35–73). Washington, D.C.: American Psychological Association.

A discussion of the components of emotions and a summary of their functions.

Malatesta, C. Z. (1990). The role of emotions in the development and organization of personality. In R. Thompson (Ed.), *Socioemotional Development* (pp. 1–56). Nebraska Symposium on Motivation.

The role of emotions in personality and personality development.

Plutchik, R. (1980). Emotion in the context of evolution. In *Emotion: A psychoevolutionary synthesis* (pp. 119–127). New York: Harper & Row.

How emotions evolved, and their role in adaptation.

2

Defining Emotions and Their Relations to Cognition, Action, and Personality

Emotion Theories and Personality Theories Relating to Emotion

Although McDougall's theory (1908) linked emotions and conation, and his work and Freud's (1938) laid the groundwork for relating emotions, motivations, and behavior, one of the current problems in psychology is that most theories of personality, of behavior, and of emotion have been created independently of one another. The majority of personality theories have typically not concerned themselves with the problem of emotion. Most personality theorists make use of one or more concepts of motivation, but they have very infrequently made use of discrete emotion concepts as motivational variables. On the other hand, investigators in the field of emotions have typically been concerned with one or more components of the emotion process—its neurophysiology, its expression, or its phenomenology—and with only a few exceptions they have done little to relate their findings to personality or the behavior of the organism as a whole. This chapter presents a synopsis of some of the major approaches to the study of emotions, discusses the relevance of a given approach to the study of other functions of the organism or to personality as a whole, and presents material that helps in defining and understanding an emotion.

Psychoanalytic Conceptions of Emotion

Freud (1930, 1936, 1938) and psychoanalytic theory occupy a special place in the history of psychology and behavioral sciences for many reasons: heuristic conceptions of the unconscious, dream dynamics, conscience development, and the concepts of defense mechanism, repression, regression, resistance, transference, infantile sexuality, and infantile amnesia. The reason most relevant to this chapter, however, is Freud's pioneering analysis of personality functioning, which opened up the field of human motivation, made it a significant part of modern psychology, and launched the psychodynamic tradition (Boring, 1950). Of greatest interest here is Freud's conception of affects, but these must be viewed in the context of his more general theory of motivation.

The core of the classical psychoanalytical theory of motivation is Freud's theory of instinctual drives. As in other areas of psychoanalysis, Freud developed and changed his ideas in this realm several times. An accurate and systematic synthesis is difficult, and even Freudian scholars have not always developed the same picture. Rapaport's (1960) integrative summary is perhaps the most widely accepted, and it is the principal source of the following synopsis.

Rapaport cautions his readers to beware of the exaggerated claims and often overlooked limitations of the explanatory power of instinctual drives. For example, instinctual drives do not explain a range of behaviors, such as defenses and cognitive synthesis and differentiation, that are determined by the ego. Nor do they explain the role of external stimulation in behavior or functions of consciousness that result from attention to external stimuli.

An instinctual drive, or motive, is defined by Rapaport as an appetitive internal or intrapsychic force that is (1) peremptory, (2) cyclic, (3) selective, and (4) displaceable. These characteristics define the appetitive nature of drives, or motives. Curiosity and exploratory behaviors are a function, in part, of external stimulations, and their determinants do not show cyclicity, selectivity, and displaceability.

Rapaport maintains that the four defining characteristics of the appetitive nature of instinctual drives are continuous dimensions rather than dichotomous categories. Thus drives vary in the extent to which they are peremptory, cyclic, selective, and displaceable. Instinctual drives have four other defining characteristics: (1) pressure, or the amount of force and demand for work it represents; (2) aim, or discharge of energy that results in satisfaction; (3) object, or that which makes satisfaction possible; and (4) source, or underlying somatic process.

It is difficult to present a consistent treatment of affect in terms of classical psychoanalytic theory since Freud and his followers used the term rather loosely and prescribed various roles for it as the theory developed. In his early work, Freud thought affect, or emotion, was the only driving force in mental life, and at various times in his later writings he "still spoke of affects or emotions as the intrapsychic factors which give rise to fantasies, wishes, and symptoms" (Rapaport, 1960, p. 191). Although the term *affect* was largely replaced by the concept of energy, or cathexis, the standard psychoanalytic view is that an instinctual drive is represented in mental life as both idea and affect, and both the idea and the affect are considered peremptory.

After reviewing psychoanalytic and other contributions, Rapaport reached the following conclusion:

> Of the various theories, the following theory of the mechanism of emotions emerges as not conflicting with known facts: an incoming percept initiates an unconscious process which mobilizes unconscious instinctual energies; if no free pathway of activity is open for

> these energies—and this is the case when instinctual demands conflict—they find discharge through channels other than voluntary motility; these discharge-processes—"emotional expression," and "emotion felt"—may occur simultaneously or may succeed one another, or either may occur alone; as in our culture open pathways for instincts are rare, emotional discharges of varying intensity constantly occur; thus in our psychic life, besides the "genuine" emotions described in textbooks—rage, fear, and so on—an entire hierarchy of emotions exists, ranging from the most intense to mild, conventionalized, intellectualized emotions. (Rapaport, 1961, p. 37)

The psychoanalytic literature often, though not always, distinguishes among the following aspects of affect: the energy component of the instinctual drive representation (the "charge" of affect), the discharge process, and perception of the final discharge (feeling or felt emotion). The discharge and feeling components are considered merely expressions, the communicative value of which was not generally recognized in psychoanalysis until the work of Schachtel (1959). However, Rapaport had noted that "affect as signals are just as indispensable a means of reality-testing as thoughts" (Rapaport, 1953, p. 196). The affect charge corresponds to the quantitative or intensity dimension of affect, and the discharge processes are perceived or felt in qualitatively different tones.

Freudian theory and psychoanalysis in general are concerned primarily with negative affects arising from conflict, hence the prominent role of repression as a defense mechanism. Since affects are by their nature phenomena of consciousness, they are not subject to repression. Only the ideational aspect of an instinctual drive can be denied entry into consciousness. When repression is successful, there is a separation of the ideational and affective components of drive such that the instinct representations are denied their preconscious cathexes and their associated verbal images. In short, the instinctual drive, or motive, can no longer be symbolized semantically. Repression thus may prevent conflict at one level (e.g., between libidinal interest and superego sanction) and the risk of neurotic or psychosomatic symptom formation at another. If repression fails, conflict occurs between the unconscious and preconscious systems, and a qualitatively distinct and symbolizable affect may emerge in consciousness. Since this affect is negative and associated with conflict-related ideation, it can constrict ego functions and contribute to mental health problems (cf. Singer, 1990).

Freud's concept of motive as an ideational-affective representation in consciousness is similar to the concepts of ideo-affective organization (Tomkins, 1962, 1963) and affective–cognitive structure (Izard, 1971, 1972). Affective–cognitive structures are conceived not as representations of instinctual drives but as the structures or orientations of consciousness that result from the interaction of emotion (the primary motivational condition) and cognition.

Another Freudian notion, the wish or wish impulse, bears an even closer resemblance to the concept of affective–cognitive structure. Freud first discussed the wish ("craving fulfillment") as the motive power of the dream. In the unconscious the wish impulse is an instinctual demand, and in the preconscious it becomes a dream-wish or wishfilling fantasy. "The wish, the affective organizing principle, uses the mechanisms of condensation, displacement, symbolism, and secondary elaboration to express itself—that is the latent content of the dream—in a form acceptable to consciousness" (Rapaport, 1961, p. 164). A difference between the Freudian wish impulse and the differential emotions theory concept of affective–cognitive structure is that the latter sees the affects rather than the ideational process as the organizing and motivational factor. Both theories agree that some kind of combination or bond of affect and cognition constitutes a significant factor in human motivation.

In his forthright rejection of instinctual drive theory, Holt (1976) developed a convincing conceptualization of affect and motivation. He placed emphasis on the importance of external stimulation and perceptual-cognitive processes, but he also recognized the significance of the experiential and expressive phenomena of the emotions.

Holt (1967), along with Kubie (1974), Rubinstein (1967), Peterfreund (1971) and others, holds that the concept of instinctual drive as psychic energy or appetitive internal force is completely without supporting evidence. He maintains that while sex, aggression, fear, or other affective phenomena may be innately determined ("though extensively modifiable") reactions, their arousal is largely dependent on awareness of external (sometimes limited or special classes of) *press*—the motivationally relevant aspects of a person's environment (Murray, 1938), defined in terms of consensually established meanings.

In moving toward a new theory of motivation, Holt (1976) builds on the early Freudian notion of *wish* and interprets it as "a cognitive–affective concept, framed in terms of meanings and potentially pleasant or unpleasant outcomes of possible courses of action" (p. 179). In Klein's (1976) model the main feature of the motivational system is the "perceptual-evaluative mismatch." A mismatch is explained as a conscious, preconscious, or unconscious comparison of a perceptual (input) and a centrally generated pattern *and* a comparison of the value judgments attached to the two patterns. Phenomenologically this amounts to a comparison between an existing and a potential state of affairs, a process similar to the appraisal, monitoring, and evaluative processes discussed in the cognitively oriented theories of emotion (Arnold, 1960a; Lazarus, 1974, 1984; Pribram, 1970; Schachter, 1971). Thus, a wish—the key motivational phenomenon—is initiated by a mismatch, "a cognitive–affective state something like dissatisfaction" (Holt, 1976, p. 182). A moderate degree of mismatch arouses mild pleasure and interest, while an extensive and sudden mismatch arouses startle and unpleasure. Holt's notion that different degrees of mismatch arouse different affects is similar to Singer's (1974) attempt to account for differential affect activation in terms of differential success in the assimilation of cognitive information.

Helen Lewis's work on the role of shame and guilt in personality, psychopathology, and psychotherapy draws from psychoanalytic theory, experimental psychology, and a wealth of personal experience as a practitioner and teacher of psychotherapy. In her most famous work, *Shame and Guilt in Neurosis* (1971), she began by elucidating the long-standing problems in distinguishing between shame and guilt as separate and important motivational conditions. She showed how the problem began when Freud failed to distinguish between the ego and self and explained the superego solely in terms of instinctual drives (especially the working of the death instinct), emphasizing the role of the affective state of guilt. Within this framework, Freud saw no place for shame in superego functioning, nor did he see a role for shame in depression.

Witkin (1949) and his colleagues developed an experimental procedure for distinguishing between different styles of perceptual-cognitive functioning: field dependence and field independence, a way of conceptualizing the degree to which a person relies on external or internal stimulation as a guide to thought and action. Lewis demonstrated the relationship between these perceptual-cognitive styles, styles of superego functioning, and the different relationship of shame and guilt in these processes. Her work shows the usefulness of studying shame and guilt as emotions that motivate superego functions.

Lewis described how reflection on or anticipation of shame functions as a defense against the loss of self-boundaries and as a force fostering the sense of a separate identity. On the other hand, she recognized that shame as an emotion state temporarily wrecks consciousness and the self and is the opposite of self-autonomy. Her research has shown that shame is strongly associated with self-directed hostility in field-dependent patients.

The individual's field-dependent or field-independent style of perceptual-cognitive functioning is one determinant of the mode of functioning of a superego, with shame being a greater force in the superego of field-dependent patients and guilt a greater force in the field-independent.

Lewis also clarified the positive functions of shame by showing how it plays a role in maintaining personal dignity and worth and affectional bonds. Her distinctions between the phenomenology of shame and guilt support her contention that shame as an affective state of the superego leads to depression and hysteria, while guilt leads to obsessive disorders and paranoia. Lewis hypothesized some potentially important sex differences in emotionality, maintaining that women are more prone to shame and hence to depression and hysteria.

The Dimensional Approach: Arousal, Activation, and Dimensions of Emotion and Behavior

Spencer (1890) was one of the early scientists to conceptualize emotions or feelings as dimensions or states of consciousness, and hence as dimensions of personality and behavior. Wundt (1896) extended the Spencerian tradition and proposed that the sphere of consciousness described by emotion or feelings could be accounted for by three dimensions: pleasantness–unpleasantness, relaxation–tension, and calm–excitement. Wundt's dimensions were revived by Woodworth (1938) and Schlosberg (1941) and their colleagues in a long line of successful research on the dimensions of emotion expression.

Emotion as Organismic Arousal. Building on the conceptions of Spencer and

Wundt, Duffy (1934, 1941, 1951, 1962) proposed that all behavior can be explained in terms of a single phenomenon, organismic arousal, a concept having apparent similarity to Wundt's dimension of relaxation–tension. Duffy (1962) maintained that behavior varies in only two dimensions, direction and intensity. She defined direction in terms of selectivity of response, a selectivity based on the expectancies and goal orientation of the organism and the relationships among the perceived stimuli. An individual goes toward or away from a situation depending on its incentive value or threat value. She considered her concept of directionality or "response to relationships" to be the same as Tolman's (1932) "cognitive maps" and Hebb's (1955) "cue functions."

Intensity was defined as general organismic arousal or energy mobilization, and level of arousal "as the extent of release of potential energy stored in the tissues of the organism, as this is shown in activity or response" (Duffy, 1962, p. 17). According to Duffy, emotion is simply a point or range of points toward the high end of the arousal dimension. Hence, emotion as such can vary only in intensity, there being no allowance for discrete types of emotion experience.

Duffy's ideas were among the influential forces that tended to exclude emotion concepts from psychological theory and research in the first half of the twentieth century. However, her conceptions helped to pave the way for activation theory which in turn helped facilitate the currently blossoming area of brain–behavior research. In recent years investigators in the latter group have initiated important lines of investigation on brain–emotion relationships.

Neural Activation, Emotion, and Behavior. Following Moruzzi and Magoun's discovery of certain functions of the brain stem reticular formation, or reticular activating system (RAS), Lindsley (1951, 1957) developed his activation theory of emotion and behavior. His theoretical formulation attempted to replace Duffy's (1962) broad and difficult-to-measure concept of organismic arousal with a concept of activation, defined as neural excitation of the RAS and concomitant changes in electroencephalographic patterns in the cortex. His explanation of emotion presupposes antecedent emotion stimuli, either external and conditioned or internal and unconditioned. Such stimuli initiate impulses activating the brain stem, which, in turn, sends impulses to the thalamus and cortex. A hypothetical activating mechanism transforms these impulses into behavior characterized by "emotional excitement" and into cortical EEG patterns characterized by low amplitude, high frequency, and asynchrony.

When impulses initiated by a reduction of emotional stimuli influence the thalamus directly, synchronized, high-amplitude, low-frequency EEG patterns may be established. Under these conditions, Lindsley predicts observable behavior opposite to that seen in "emotional excitement": namely, "emotional apathy." Lindsley acknowledged that his theory could not elucidate the nature of discrete emotions. His primary concern was with the relationship between certain antecedent conditions, changes in electrical activity of the brain (as measured by the EEG), and observed behavior.

More recent researchers in areas relating to arousal have abandoned the notion that there is only one kind of arousal. They have also linked types of arousal to particular personality traits. For example, Zuckerman (1979) holds that each personality trait is based on its own type of arousal. In his early work, he defined sensation seeking as the optimal kind of arousal for a given person. Zuckerman (1984) has shown that the trait of sensation seeking has some distinct neurochemical underpinnings as well as distinct cognitive and behavioral manifestations. Sensation seeking correlates with the impulsive, but not the sociable, aspects of extraversion. It also correlates with risky activities such as drug abuse and skydiving and with the choice of risky occupations. In general, people high on Zuckerman's sensation-seeking trait measure seek ways of increasing arousal through exciting experiences.

Dimensions of Emotion Expression. Since 1872, when Darwin published his famous work *The Expression of the Emotions in Man and Animals*, the complex field of facial expression of emotion has been treated by some investigators as virtually a discipline unto itself. Some of these workers made invaluable contributions to the analysis and understanding of facial expression but often did not integrate their important findings into the psychology of personality and social behavior.

The approach to the study of facial expressions with which we are concerned here was initiated when Woodworth (1938) proposed the first really successful system for classifying the facial expressions of discrete emotions. He showed that many facial expressions could be reliably categorized by use of the following six-step linear scale: (1) love, happiness, mirth; (2) surprise; (3) fear, suffering; (4) anger, determination; (5) disgust; (6) contempt.

After applying the Woodworth classification scheme to various series of photographs of facial expressions, Schlosberg (1941) proposed that facial expressions could be more adequately described by considering the Woodworth scale as a circular surface with two axes or dimensions: pleasantness–unpleasantness (P–U) and acceptance–rejection (A–R). Later, Schlosberg added a third dimension, sleep–tension, and thus came very close to adopting and verifying empirically the usefulness of the three dimensions of feeling originally proposed by Wundt in 1896.

Schlosberg's approach was similar to that in a psychophysical experiment where judgments are based on physical dimensions. His instructions required subjects to make their ratings on the basis of observable physical characteristics of the photographed expressions. In his earlier experiments Schlosberg had his subjects rate each photograph of a facial expression on two 9-point scales: pleasantness–unpleasantness and acceptance–rejection.

From each picture, the average rating was computed for each dimension. With P–U and A–R scales represented by perpendicular lines intersecting at scale point 5, the circular surface can be represented by a circle connecting the ends of the P–U and A–R axes. Any given picture (expression) can be represented as a point on the space within a quadrant of the circle. By drawing a line from the origin (intersection of P–U and A–R) through the plotted point to the rim of the circle, one can determine the circular scale value and the emotion category of the particular expression (see Figure 2-1). The correlation between the circular scale values obtained via the category sorting technique and those determined or predicted by the dimensional ratings was .76. Thus facial expressions represented in still photographs can be relatively accurately classified into discrete emotion categories on the basis of the P–U and A–R dimensional ratings.

Schlosberg and his colleagues (Engen, Levy, & Schlosberg, 1958) added the dimension of sleep–tension (S–T) because they became impressed by the work of Duffy and Lindsley and with evidence suggesting that dimension of "activation" was important in emotion. With a specially developed series of facial expressions

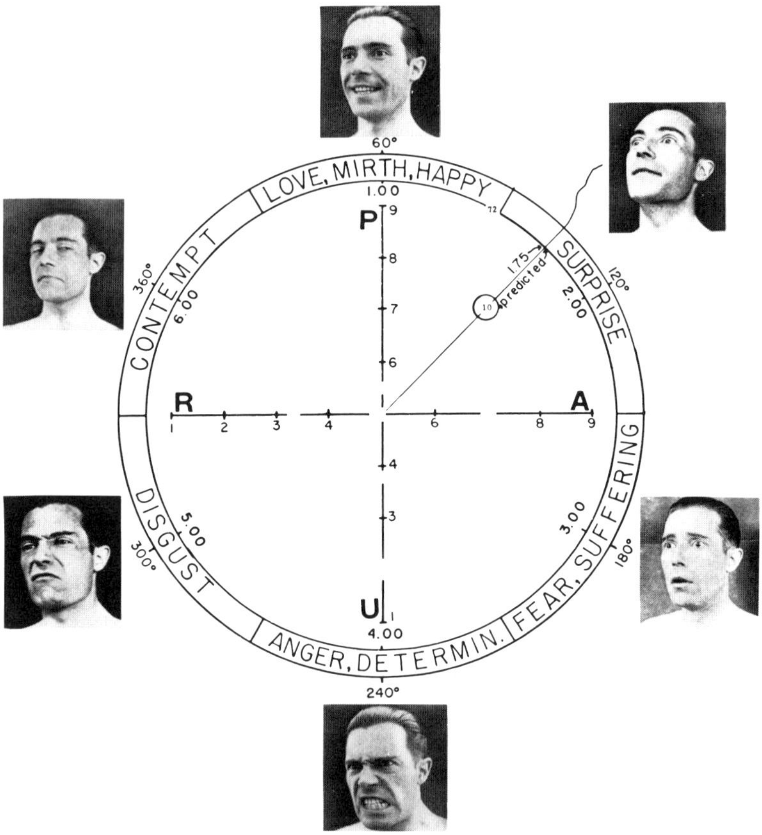

FIGURE 2-1. Predicting emotion categories from ratings on the dimensions of pleasantness–unpleasantness and acceptance–rejection. (Adapted from Woodworth & Schlosberg, 1954.)

(the Lightfoot series) they demonstrated test–retest reliabilities of .94, .87, and .92 ($N = 225$) for the P–U, A–R, and S–T dimensions, respectively. Triandis and Lambert (1958) applied Schlosberg's three dimensions in a cross-cultural study and showed that they were as valid for Greek subjects as for Americans. However, later investigators (e.g., Abelson & Sermat, 1962; Ekman, 1964) showed that the acceptance–rejection and sleep–tension dimensions were highly correlated (thus not independent dimensions) and raised the question of their meaningfulness as separate dimensions of emotion expression. Several other investigators made contributions to the dimensional approach to the study of facial expressions and emotion (Hofstatter, 1955–1956; Izard & Nunnally, 1965; Plutchik, 1962). Some of this research led to the development of new dimensions, such as control, or deliberative–impulsive (Osgood, 1966), attention–inattention (Frijda & Phillipszoon, 1963), and self-assured–insecure (Frijda, 1970).

Osgood's extensive analysis of live expressions yielded three dimensions that he interpreted in terms of his semantic dimensions of linguistic signs. He concluded that his expression dimensions of pleasantness, activation, and control correspond to the semantic dimensions of evaluation, activity, and potency. Osgood's interpretation may be an important one for students of emotion–cognition interactions.

The dimensional approach to the study of emotions remains active. For examples of recent research see J. A. Russell (1980, 1983) and Tellegen (1985).

Cognitive Theories of Emotion and Personality

At least two broad classes of theories may be classified as cognitive: self-theories and theories that view cognition as a cause and component of emotion. The central and overriding variable in self-theory is the self-concept. The individual's perceptions of and cognitions about the self as organized in the holistic and integrated phenomenon called the self-concept is given extensive explanatory powers (Rogers, 1951; Snygg & Combs, 1949). For these theorists, behavior is a function of perception, in particular the perception of self.

Self-Theory, Feeling, and Emotion. The more the perception or cognition relates to the center, or core, of the self, the more likely it is to involve feeling or emotion. When the self-concept is attacked the individual becomes fearful and defensive; when the self-concept is accepted and approved the individual is likely to feel interested and joyful.

Self-theories consistently emphasize the importance of the "feeling content" as opposed to the strictly semantic content of the verbal expressions of the individual. They hold that it is particularly important for psychotherapists to understand and respond in terms of this principle when treating individuals with psychological problems. A similar principle has been adopted by several current approaches to psychotherapy and personal growth (e.g., T-groups, encounter groups, gestalt therapy). The impressive volume of research in the framework of self-theory deals with the emotion or feeling in general terms and seldom makes use of discrete-emotion concepts.

Emotion as a Function of Cognition. Several contemporary theories treat emotion essentially as response or as a complex of responses determined by cognitive processes. These theories, which are deeply rooted in Western civilization, seem to have stemmed from some pervasive ideas about human nature that can be traced through Aristotle, Thomas Aquinas, Diderot, Kant, and other philosophers. These ideas are (1) man is first and foremost a rational being; (2) rationality is basically good, emotionality basically bad; (3) reason (cognitive processes) should be used as a control and as a substitute for emotion. Current theories have gone far beyond these early notions.

The most senior and comprehensive theory of emotion and personality in this influential tradition is that of Arnold (1960a, 1960b). For Arnold, emotion results from a sequence of events described by the concepts of perception and appraisal.

Arnold used the term *perception* to mean simple apprehension of an object. To apprehend something is to know what it is like as an object, independent of any effect on the perceiver. Before emotion can enter into the picture, the object must be perceived and appraised as having an effect on the perceiver. Emotion is distinct from appraisal, though it may include it as an integral or necessary part. To be precise, the emotion proper is the nonrational attraction or repulsion that follows upon the appraisal of something as good or bad for the perceiver.

Appraisal itself is characterized as direct, immediate, and intuitive, not the result of reflection or deliberation. It immediately follows and completes perception and can be recognized as a separate process only upon reflection.

> The sequence perception—appraisal—emotion is so closely knit that our everyday experience is never the strictly objective knowledge of a thing; it is always a knowing-and-liking, or a knowing-and-disliking. . . . The intuitive appraisal of the situation initiates an action tendency that is felt as emotion, expressed in various bodily changes, and that eventually may lead to overt action. (Arnold, 1960a, p. 177)

Emotion has important residual or continuing effects. The action tendencies that follow an emotion organize and bias later perception and appraisal; the emotion "fascinates us and takes us captive" (Arnold, 1960a, p. 182). Further, the intuitive appraisal and emotion response tend to have constancy, so that the object or situation so appraised and responded to tends to evoke this appraisal and response "for all times to come" (Arnold, 1960a, p. 184). In addition, appraisal and emotion response to a given object tend to be generalized to the whole class of objects.

Other Cognitive Theories of Emotion. Schachter and his colleagues (Schachter, 1966, 1971; Schachter & Singer, 1962) have proposed that emotion results from physiological arousal and a cognitive appraisal or evaluation of the situation that elicited the arousal. In short, some event, situation, or condition creates physiological arousal in the individual, and the individual has a need to appraise or evaluate the context of the arousal—the situation that elicited it. The type or quality of emotion that an individual experiences depends not on the sensation arising from the physiological arousal but on how the individual evaluates the situation or condition in which it occurs. The evaluation ("cognizing or sizing up") of the contextual situation enables the individual to label the arousal sensations as joy or anger, fear or sadness, or whatever is appropriate to the situation as it is appraised. According to Schachter's position, the same physiological arousal may be experienced as joy or anger (or as any other emotion), depending on the cognitions available in the situation. Mandler (1975) and Lazarus (1982) present similar views of emotion activation.

In one well-known experiment, Schachter and Singer (1962) tested their theory by injecting epinephrine to induce arousal in three groups and injecting a placebo in a fourth. Then they manipulated the "appropriate explanation" or cognitive input by giving accurate, inaccurate, or no information as to the effects of the drug to independent groups. Immediately after the injection and explanation, all of the misinformed group and half of the subjects in each of the other groups were exposed to a stooge who modeled euphoric actions and verbalizations; the other half of each of the three groups were exposed to a stooge who modeled angry actions and verbalizations. They found that subjects who were given misinformation or no information about their arousal state were more likely to imitate the stooge's mood and behavior, whether it was euphoric or angry. Subjects who were given accurate explanations of the effects of epinephrine were relatively immune to the influence of the stooge. Among the subjects exposed to the euphoric model, the misinformation and no-information groups reported significantly higher happiness scores than did the correctly informed group, but they did not differ from the placebo group. Of those exposed to the anger model, the groups having received no information to explain their drug-induced arousal symptoms were rated significantly higher on "angry behavior" than the other groups; but again the placebo group did not conform to Schachter's model. It was no different from either the misinformed or the noninformed group on the anger self-report scale.

Schachter's theory and research inspired considerable theorizing and research, but it has been criticized on methodological grounds by a number of other investigators (e.g., Izard, 1971; Manstead & Wagner, 1981; Plutchik & Ax, 1967). More significant than these criticisms is the fact that two experiments representing the first reported replications of the Schachter–Singer experiment failed to support its findings. (Marshall, 1976; Maslach, 1979). Maslach showed that unexplained hypnotically suggested autonomic arousal tended to create a mental set to interpret internal conditions (feelings) negatively. Subjects were not equally likely to report anger or joy depending on the actions of the confederate. Marshall used the same drug-arousal technique as Schachter and Singer and found results similar to those of Maslach.

More recent cognitive or social-cognitive theories of emotion are closer to biosocial theories in attributing motivational and adaptive functions to emotions. They differ in placing a greater emphasis on the role of cognition as cause of emotion. However, virtually all theories recognize that cognitive processes can be a link in the chain of events that activate emotion.

The special contribution of cognitive theories is in delineating emotion-specific cognitions—the particular kinds of thoughts that lead to specific emotions. In doing this they have also sharpened our understanding of emotion–cognition relations, especially our knowledge of the kinds of thoughts associated with each emotion.

Weiner (1985) explains the cognitive antecedents of emotions in terms of causal ascriptions. The cause of an emotion is a function of the person's attributions about causality or about the cause of the eliciting event. He proposes three dimensions of causality: locus (internal–external), stability (stable–unstable), and controllability (controllable–uncontrollable). Thus, for example, if someone intentionally moves into a queue ahead of you, you would see the act as internally motivated and controllable, and you would probably feel angry. If the person was pushed roughly into the line by someone running by, you would interpret the cause as external and uncontrollable, and you might feel pity or sadness.

Even more elaborate schemes of causal dimensions have been proposed (Ellsworth & Smith, 1988; Roseman, 1984; Smith & Ellsworth, 1985). For example, these theorists hold that the explanatory power of the control dimension is complemented by a responsibility dimension. They maintain that attributions of responsibility and control are important in differentiating surprise (other-responsibility/control) and guilt (self-responsibility/control).

Some researchers in the cognitive theory tradition have focused on studies attempting to specify the sequence of steps in the emotion activation process. Their studies attempt to show that appraisals/attributions are truly antecedents of emotion. Because an emotion can follow an internal or external event within milliseconds, establishing cognitive processes as antecedents is extremely difficult. Nevertheless, regardless of the place of cognitions in the causal chain, they doubtless occur and become part of the total phenomenology surrounding the emotion. Thus, cognitive theorists and investigators continue to make significant contributions to the psychology of emotions.

Emotions as Derivatives of Biological Processes and Mixtures of Emotions as Personality Traits

Plutchik (1962, 1980) views the emotions as adaptive devices that have played a role in individual survival at all evolutionary levels. The basic prototypical dimensions of adaptive behavior and the emotions or affective–cognitive structures related to them are given below:

Prototypical Adaptive Pattern	*Primary Emotion*
1. Incorporation—ingestion of food and water	Acceptance
2. Rejection—riddance reaction, excretion, vomiting	Disgust
3. Destruction—removal of barrier to satisfaction	Anger
4. Protection—primarily the response to pain or threats of pain or harm	Fear
5. Reproduction—responses associated with sexual behavior	Joy
6. Deprivation—loss of pleasurable object that has been contacted or incorporated	Sadness
7. Orientation—response to contact with new or strange object	Startle
8. Exploration—more or less random activities in exploring environment	Expectation or curiosity

Plutchik defines emotions as a patterned bodily reaction corresponding to one of the underlying adaptive biological processes common to all animals. He sees the primary emotions as transient and as usually, though not necessarily, triggered by external stimuli. There are physiological and overt expressive patterns of activity associated with each primary emotion and with each secondary emotion (mixture of two or more primary emotions). Plutchik (1954) interpreted a number of research findings to support the notion that the blocking or impeding of adequate motor responses in conflict or frustration gives rise to chronic muscular tension, often a characteristic of maladjustment.

Plutchik maintains that his emotion theory contains a number of implications for the study of personality and psychotherapy. He suggests that personality traits can be studied and analyzed in terms of emotions that represent two or more primary emotions that may be in conflict. Plutchik thinks that understanding the way emotions mix increases understanding of many important emotion phenomena. For example, he writes the following formulas: pride = anger + joy; love = joy + acceptance; curiosity = surprise + acceptance; modesty = fear + acceptance; hate = anger + surprise; guilt = fear + joy or pleasure; sentimentality = acceptance + sorrow.

Social regulators (superego phenomena) can be understood in Plutchik's system as mixtures of fear and other emotions, for example, anxiety, as a mixture of fear and expectancy. Thus, for example, analyzing situations that lead to fear and determining one's expectations in regard to these situations increases understanding of the dynamics of anxiety.

A Cognitive–Affective Approach

According to Singer (1973, 1974), the intimate relation between affect and cognition is rooted in the infant's early efforts at accommodation to its novel and ever-changing environment. He assumes, with Tomkins (1962) and Izard (1971), that environmental novelty activates the interest affect, which in turn sustains efforts at exploration and accommodation. Mastery or successful accommodation reduces excitement and activates joy, whereas a complex mass of unassimilable material may produce startle, sadness, or fear. Thus, affective and cognitive processes are intertwined from the very beginning of life.

A significant outcome of Singer's research has been his innovative application of his knowledge about imagery and affects to the practice of psychotherapy (Singer, 1974). He emphasizes the use of imagery and action (e.g., role-playing) in helping the patient achieve affect differentiation and thus a better basis for control of emotions, thought, and action. Singer adds valuable insights on the effectiveness of developing the patient's imagery and fantasy capacities as a means of increasing his or her feeling of competency and self-control. For example, he successfully treated voyeurism by having the patient cross-up his fantasy life. The patient developed a series of noxious images and learned to substitute disgust-evoking images of skin-diseased male nudes for guilt-ridden attempts to peep at partially dressed women in neighboring apartments. Positive emotion imagery involving women was used to counteract heterosexual fear and homosexual tendencies. These techniques were used in the framework of extended psychodynamic therapy, which provided the necessary understanding for their skillful application.

Differential Emotions Theory

Differential emotions theory draws from a rich intellectual heritage and claims kinship with the classical works of Duchenne, Darwin, Spencer, Kierkegaard, Wundt, James, Cannon, McDougall, Dumas, Dewey, Freud, Rado, and Woodworth and with the more contemporary works of Jacobson, Sinnott, Mowrer, Gellhorn, Harlow, Bowlby, Ekman, and many others. All of these scientists, representing several different disciplines and points of view, have in common a belief in the central importance of the emotions in motivation, social communication, cognition, and action. However, the contemporary writer who has contributed most to the conceptual foundations of the theory presented here is Silvan Tomkins, whose brilliant two-volume work *Affect, Imagery, Consciousness* is cited frequently throughout this volume.

Differential emotions theory takes its name from its emphasis on discrete emotions as distinct experiential/motivational processes that influence cognition and action differentially. The theory is based on five key assumptions: (1) ten fundamental emotions (which will be discussed in detail in later chapters) constitute the principal motivational system for human beings; (2) each fundamental emotion has particular organizing and motivational functions and unique experiential properties; (3) fundamental emotions such as joy, sadness, anger, and shame lead to different inner experiences and have different effects on cognition and action; (4) emotion processes interact with and exert influence on homeostatic, drive, perceptual, cognitive, and motor processes. (5) In turn, homeostatic, drive, perceptual, cognitive, and motor processes influence emotions.

Emotions as the Principal Motivational System

Differential emotions theory assumes that emotion is a determinant in behaviors as widely different as rape and unpremeditated murder on the one hand and personal sacrifice and courageous ventures on the other. The emotions are viewed not only as the principal motivational system but, even more fundamentally, as the personality processes that give meaning and significance to human existence. The emotions are considered important both for behavior and for sensing, experiencing, and being.

The Six Subsystems of Personality

Personality is a complex organization of six subsystems: the homeostatic, drive, emotion, perceptual, cognitive, and motor systems. Each system has a degree of autonomy or independence, but all are complexly interrelated. The homeostatic and drive systems are of primary importance in biological maintenance, reproduction and the regulation of body functions.

The homeostatic system is really a network of interrelated subsystems that operate automatically and unconsciously. Chief among these are the endocrine and cardiovascular systems, which are of importance to personality mainly through frequent interactions with the emotion system. Homeostatic mechanisms are considered auxiliary to the emotion system, but the hormones, neurohumors, enzymes, and other regulators of metabolism are important in regulating and sustaining emotion once it has been activated.

The drive system is based on tissue changes and deficits that create signals and provide information about bodily needs. The most common drives are hunger, thirst, sex, and comfort, or pain avoidance. Drives are obviously important when survival is at stake. Under normal circumstances (after survival and comfort needs are met) the drives (with the exception of sex and pain avoidance) are of little psychological importance, becoming significant mainly as they influence or are influenced by the emotions. The important exceptions, sex and pain avoidance, are drives that have some of the characteristics of emotion. These drives inevitably recruit and interact with emotions, and it is the subsequent drive–emotion interactions that often make sex and pain avoidance important for personality and behavior.

The four systems most important in personality, social interaction, and higher-order human functioning are the emotion, perceptual, cognitive, and motor systems. These four systems jointly form the basis for uniquely human behavior.

Effective behavior derives from the harmonious interactions of these four systems. Ineffective behavior and maladjustment result when systemic interaction breaks down or becomes faulty.

The Emotions and the Emotion System

An important assumption of differential emotions theory is that the discrete emotions of human experience are important variables for psychology and the life sciences. It also assumes that the 10 fundamental emotions, the drives, and the numerous affective–cognitive structures make the study of human motivation extremely complex.

Those concerned with the application of psychology, whether in industry, education, or clinic, sooner or later have to come to grips with specific discrete emotions. The people they work with feel specifically happy, angry, fearful, sad, disgusted, or excited, not simply "emotional." Recent practice is moving away from the use of such general terms as "emotional problem," "emotional disturbance," and "emotional disorder." A current trend is for the practitioner to try to analyze and treat the various discrete affects and affective patterns as distinct motivational phenomena in the life of the individual.

Definition of an Emotion. Differential emotions theory defines emotion as a complex process with neural, neuromuscular/expressive, and experiential aspects. At the neural level emotion is defined primarily in terms of patterns of electrochemical activity n the central nervous system. The cutaneous nerves in the face and the proprioceptors in the facial muscles also participate in emotion at the neurophysiological level. It is assumed that emotion proper is a function of the somatic nervous system (controller of voluntary actions) and that the somatically activated emotion recruits the autonomic nervous system (controller of involuntary functions such as hormonal release and heart rate), which in turn may amplify or sustain the emotion over time.

At the expressive or neuromuscular level emotion is primarily facial activity and facial patterning. Secondarily, it is bodily (postural–gestural, visceral–glandular, and sometimes vocal) response.

At the experiential level emotion is essentially motivating experience or experience that has immediate meaning and significance for the person. The experiencing of emotion can constitute a process in consciousness completely independent of cognition.

When neurochemical activity, via innate programs, produces patterned facial and bodily activities, and the feedback from these activities is transformed into conscious form, the result is an emotion feeling/experience that is both a motivating and meaningful cue-producing experience. Experientially, positive emotions have inherent characteristics that tend to enhance one's sense of well-being and to instigate and sustain approach toward, and constructive interactions or relations with, the involved persons, situations, or objects. Negative emotions, which tend to be sensed as noxious and difficult to tolerate, instigate avoidance of and/or nonconstructive interactions or relations. As already indicated, while certain emotions tend to be positive and others negative in import, these terms cannot be applied rigidly to the various emotion experiences without considering them in ecological perspective.

Before we leave the discussion of the components that help define emotion, it is important to note that emotion is not simply a response. It is not merely a part of what we do as the result of some stimulus event or situation, for emotions are stimuli for, or causes of, what we do. In fact, it is highly likely that emotions can be more or less self-generating. This seems particularly true of interest, the positive emotion that guides so much of the activity in our daily lives. In any case, once an emotion is activated, whether by sensory data (e.g., pain) or by cognitive processes (e.g., appraisal, attribution), even if it is in response to an event, it then becomes an organizing and driving force in subsequent thought and action. In turn, the thought and action along with the storehouse of your memories influence emotion.

The Emotions as a System. Differential emotions theory refers to the emotions as a separate, though interactive and interdependent, system of personality because on the basis of both innate and learned characteristics, emotions are interrelated in dynamic and relatively stable ways (cf. Cicchetti, 1990). Largely because of the nature of the underlying innate mechanisms, some of the emotions are organized in a kind of hierarchical relationship. Darwin (1872) noted that attention may graduate into surprise, and surprise into a "frozen astonishment" resembling fear. Similarly Tomkins (1962) has argued that the stimulation gradients that activate interest, fear, and startle represent a hierarchy, with the gradient for eliciting interest being the least steep and that for startle the steepest. A novel sound might elicit the interest of an infant or child. If in its first presentation the strange sound were quite loud, it might elicit fear. If the sound were extremely loud and sudden, it might evoke startle.

Another characteristic of the emotions that contributes to their organization as a system is the apparent polarity between some pairs of emotions. Observation and arguments for polarity extend from Darwin (1872) to Plutchik (1962). Joy and sadness, anger and fear are often considered as opposites. Other possible polar opposites are interest and disgust, shame and contempt. Like the concepts of positive and negative, the concept of polarity should not be considered as defining inflexible relationships between emotions, and the apparent opposition does not always denote an either-or relationship. Opposites are sometimes associated with or elicited by each other, as evidenced by the often observed "tears of joy."

Certain emotions other than the pairs of polar opposites tend to have fairly regular relationships, at least under certain circumstances. Interest may oscillate with fear as the organism explores some unknown (potentially exciting, potentially dangerous) object or situation. Contempt may graduate into or oscillate with joy and excitement to produce something like Lorenz's (1966) "militant enthusiasm." Regular or frequent occurrence of two or more fundamental emotions that interact with a particular set of cognitions may produce an affective–cognitive structure or orientation with traitlike characteristics. The descriptive term *affective–cognitive orientation* seems a particularly useful way of conceptualizing certain personality traits. For example, the interest–fear combination may be frequently associated with cognitions about risking and escaping danger for fun and thrills and result in the affective–cognitive orientation (or trait) of sensation seeking. However, the interest–fear combination may be associated with the risk taking involved in exploration for the sake of discovery, and in this case the affective–cognitive orientation could be intellectual curiosity.

Several other factors help to define the emotions as a system. All emotions have certain characteristics in common. All emotions, as contrasted with drives, are noncyclical. One does not become interested or disgusted or ashamed two or three times a day in rhythm with ingestion, digestion, and metabolic processes. Emotions have virtually unlimited generality and flexibility as motivational factors. While only food and drink will satisfy the hunger and thirst drives, a person can learn to be joyful or contemptuous or afraid in response to a seemingly infinite variety of things.

All emotions influence or regulate the drives and other personality subsystems. One of the important and frequent functions of emotion is to regulate—to act as amplifier or attenuator of other emotions, drives, and affective–cognitive structures. For example, drives that are not reduced to a level within the tolerance limits of the organism tend to instigate and recruit emotions, which in turn amplify the drive. The emotion of interest–excitement may bring the sex drive to high pitch; the emotions of disgust, fear, or sadness may modulate, mask, or reduce, or completely inhibit the sex drive.

The Auxiliary Systems. Two other biological systems function in an auxiliary relationship to the emotion system: the brain stem reticular system (which controls changes in levels of neural activation) and the autonomically innervated glandular–visceral system (which controls such activities as hormone secretion, heart rate, respiration rate, etc.). The glandular–visceral system helps prepare the body for emotion-determined and -directed action and helps sustain the emotion and emotion-related actions. The reticular formation serves as regulator or control for the neural component of emotion, acting as an amplifier or attenuator.

The emotion system rarely functions in complete independence of other systems. Some emotion or pattern of emotions is always present and interacting with the perceptual, cognitive, and motor systems, and effective personality functioning depends on balance and integration of activities of the different systems. In particular, since emotion of any substantial intensity tends to organize action of the individual as a whole, all physiological systems and organs are involved to some extent. The influence of emotion is readily observable in changes in the cardiovascular, respiratory, and other physiological subsystems of the glandular–visceral network.

The Causes of Emotion. The cause of an emotion can be described in terms of neural, affective, or cognitive processes. At the neural level of analysis the generation of emotion can be explained as the activity of certain neurotransmitters and brain mechanisms that mediate the evaluation of incoming information. At the affective level emotion activation can be explained in terms of sensory-perceptual processes, and at the cognitive level in terms of certain thought processes. There is considerably more research on the cognitive activation of emotions than on the other two types of emotion activation. Nevertheless, it is important to note that there are both cognitive and noncognitive (neural, affective) activators of emotion. Because the types of activators will be discussed in more detail later they will be simply listed here, along with some examples.

1. Neural and neuromuscular activators
   a. Naturally occurring hormones and neurotransmitters
   b. Drugs
   c. Expressive behavior (e.g., facial expression, posture)
   d. Changes in cerebral blood temperature and subsequent neurochemical processes
2. Affective activators
   a. Pain
   b. Sex
   c. Fatigue
   d. Another emotion
3. Cognitive activators
   a. Appraisal
   b. Attribution
   c. Memory
   d. Anticipation

Differential emotions theory emphasizes the point that emotions can occur as a direct function of neurochemical and affective processes independently of cognition. The foregoing list of neural, neuromuscular, and affective causes of emotions are noncognitive activators. The theory emphasizes that specific emotion expressions and corresponding specific emotion feelings are innately linked and that their dissociation is learned. It follows that facial expression and its sensory feedback play a significant role in the emotion process and in emotion regulation. For a detailed discussion of these principles, the reader is referred to Izard and Malatesta (1987; Izard, 1990).

Complex Patterns of Emotions in a Critical Life Event

Although this text will emphasize the discreteness of human emotions and each will be discussed individually in the following chapters, in reality a critical life event or crisis often brings out many emotions. Sometimes one emotion urges you in one direction, while another emotion is telling you to do something else. The complex interplay of many emotions was evident in Marie's life when she was 17.

> I was rather unhappy and rather dissatisfied at this point in my life. I was sure that my mother was a paranoid schizophrenic. Nothing I did made her happy; or, better put, everything I did made her mad. In order to gain some control over my existence, I took up some rebellious hobbies such as smoking, drinking, and "hanging out," one of my mother's more unique forbidden pleasures. To top it off, not long after all this began I delivered the ultimate slap to my mom's face—premarital sex.
>
> I met Jeff three months before I turned 17. I thought I was in love, and for my maturity level at that time I suppose I was. Our decision to sleep with one another was mutual, and I think that on my part, at least, it was originally more an act of love than one of rebellion; however, it began to make me feel good that I was doing something that would turn my mother green if she ever found out. At the same time I felt guilty, because I knew it was wrong to feel such satisfaction in revenge against someone you love. I suppose the underlying problem here was that I wasn't sure anymore that I DID love my mother. My feelings for her had gone from unconditional love, even worship of her, to doubt that I even liked her as a person. It was a terrible conflict, and I often felt sadness as I thought about the past, anger as I thought about the present, and guilt as I wondered how I could be so inhuman as to even consider that I didn't love my own mother. At any rate, Jeff quickly became the center of my life because he fit in with my "burnout" friends, and he was a symbol to me of my antiparental control crusade.

In the account of her crisis, Marie does not mention her heart pounding when she is angry, or a heaviness in her face and chest when she is sad. We often do not attend to the inner world of our bodies when we experience intense emotion, but changes do occur, and they constitute an important factor in emotion. Marie's account also does not include description of facial expressions. This is not unusual. She is relating heartfelt experiences. She describes her feelings and her concerns, the things that are acutely fixed in her mind. Although facial expressions are perhaps the most meaningful part of our communications with loved ones when under stress, we are rarely conscious of our expressive movements. They are not what we are thinking about when we reflect upon a heated conflict with a parent or other loved ones. The "messages" in a facial expression are potent, and whether or not we are keenly aware of them, they are often the most prominent messages in an interpersonal encounter. That facial expressions of genuine emotions are automatic and unconscious does not detract from their importance.

> We had been sleeping together for a few months when I began thinking how "neat" it would be having Jeff's baby growing inside me—to create something so beautiful with our love. "And," I thought, "Mom would really get a kick out of THAT!" One night, at the end of a particularly harrowing week of frustrated anger and disgust with my mother's whole attitude, Jeff came over while no one else was home. He hadn't brought any protection with him, but I shrugged this off, figuring he would just withdraw before the crucial moment. But as we proceeded, I made a conscious decision. Somehow I knew he wouldn't pull out unless I reminded him to. Yet, fully aware that I was in the middle of my cycle (peak time for making babies), I remained silent, because THIS was the utmost in rebellion. And I felt in control for the first time in a long time.

Two weeks later I missed my first period. I was a little nervous, but I figured it was just a freak thing. After missing my second period I began to feel real fear. But strangely I also felt a kind of warm anticipation at the prospect of carrying the child of the man I loved. This, I thought, created a bond between us that no one could break; that is, no one except Jeff, who, upon hearing of my possible pregnancy, decided that he felt tied down and didn't want to see me anymore.

Telling my parents that I was pregnant was the second hardest thing I've ever had to do. I was terrified, and more than that, ashamed. There was no longer any desire, even need, to turn against them, to purposely hurt them in return for all they'd put me through. I no longer wanted no part of them; I needed them, now more than ever before.

It was Marie's feelings that inspired her thoughts and guided her actions. While she was only minimally aware of the bodily changes involved in her emotions and probably completely unaware of her facial expressions, she was keenly in touch with her feelings. When she said she was angry or disgusted, frightened and lost, she was responding to the feelings involved in these emotions. For her, the feeling was the emotion, the experience that wholly claimed her mind and dictated her thoughts and actions.

I told them that they would have to be more open-minded than they had ever been in their lives. I knew that I would have to be the strong one now, and I was prepared to accept any blows that were forthcoming. The emotions flew. My mother stared in disbelief, began to cry, and accused me of having done this to deliberately hurt them. My father sat very still in his favorite recliner. In was pure agony—to see the two people who loved me most in the world suffering so at my hand. I felt horribly ashamed and I wished to God that I could somehow take away their pain and making everything all better. But all I could do was try to comfort them. As I held my mom's head on my shoulder to let her cry, my dad came over and put his arms around both of us. From that moment on, all our relationships would drastically change.

After a few days my parents recovered from the initial shock and jumped into some decision-making. The first choice they made was that I was giving the baby up for adoption. They had our parish priest come over to talk to me about the Catholic agency they had chosen. I sat nodding and looking agreeable while vowing to myself that somehow I would investigate every alternative before giving my baby away. But deep in my heart I knew that adoption would be the best thing for him, and that the hard part was going to be overcoming my powerful desire to keep him.

Throughout the pregnancy I went through numerous changes. For one thing, I no longer had any desire whatsoever to go out with my friends to any of our usual hangouts. It wasn't that I was ashamed—I just sort of grew out of it all in a period of weeks. I quit smoking also, and began taking extreme care in my diet. The most important thing, however, was the sudden and drastic change in both my perception of my parents and theirs of me. They would tell friends that I was "17 going on 25," marvelling at how much and how quickly I had matured as a result of the situation. And my mom and I actually became close. She went out of her way to make me maternity blouses, even surprising me with a special one that took her extra time to create. We talked about what to expect, and we shared our fears and concerns. Most importantly, it was she who held my hand through 13 hours of grueling labor. It was quite a turnaround in a short 9 months.

Both my parents sat with me in recovery. I nearly cried when they brought in my son, because he looked quite a bit like my dad. The scene was remarkable: Mom and I were exhausted from the ordeal, but we were all happily aware of the bond that had formed between her and me. Dad promised to bring me a coke as soon as I had the energy to

> swallow it. I fell asleep seconds after they left, at peace with myself, and happy and excited about the new life that had come from inside me.
>
> The day came to sign the papers and I endured the formalities without crying. By then, my emotions were pretty drained; I had gone through just about every one during the previous weeks. There was uncertainty—was I doing the right thing? Sadness—knowing that I would be separated from my own flesh and blood, the child I had held in my arms only weeks before. Anger—that Jeff hadn't helped me through any of this. Despair—failing to have found "another way" after searching very hard. And finally, resolve—deep in my heart I knew what had to be done, and by God, somewhere I was going to find the courage to do it. Each time I go through the pictures I have of my son I get a rush of all these emotions, as well as a sense of loss. But there is also a sense of hope that when he reaches the age of 18, and I contact the agency, he will be willing to meet with me. The hope is what keeps me from breaking down on the eleventh day of every month, even now, two years and nine months after his birth.

Marie's account of her crisis at 17 illustrates the complex tapestry of emotions involved in a critical life event. It is partly because of our biological makeup, partly because of the complexity of our perceptual and thought processes, and partly because of the complexity of the environment and the stimulation received from it that human beings rarely respond to events with a single pure emotion. More likely, our thoughts and the events in our lives evoke a complex pattern of emotions. You experience interest and joy in strengthening family ties and realizing the power of shared love, as well as in play or recreation and at work, if you like your job. Situations that make you angry often elicit disgust as well, and sometimes even contempt. In some threatening situations you may feel fear, then anger, then fear again. You may get angry at yourself when you feel guilt. If you are depressed for a long time, sadness is not the only emotion you feel. Anger, including self-directed hostility, may surface, as well as shame and fear.

One of the advantages in becoming well acquainted with the characteristics of each emotion is being able to understand when we are experiencing two or more emotions at once or, as is more likely, in rapid succession. This is particularly important in trying to improve our understanding of ourselves and our motivations, for life's most important situations elicit more than one emotion.

To understand emotions and their values in critical life events, we must look at emotion on the stage of human affairs as well as in the laboratory. We need to utilize both what we can learn from our own and others' experiences and what scientists have learned through research and objective analysis. Yet, it is difficult to try to start defining and analyzing an emotion after reading Marie's moving story of her crisis at 17, and it becomes apparent that a simple or brief definition of emotion will fail to do the concept justice.

What Is a Basic Emotion?

There is no way of classifying emotion that will be acceptable to all behavioral scientists. Some allow the notion that there are fundamental emotions.

Psychologists who do not distinguish between emotion or emotion feeling on one hand and perception/cognition on the other are more likely to argue against the notion of basic emotions (Mandler, 1975). Such psychologists usually believe that we *construct* emotions from our life experiences. They argue that emotions are products of culture, social experience, and learning. In their view, we can learn or construct as many emotions as are needed or as we are capable of. A better way of understanding the role of cognition and experience in emotion is to view what we construct through our own experiences as affective–cognitive structures, as defined in Chapter 1.

Here are some criteria that have been used to determine which emotions are fundamental:

1. Fundamental emotions have distinct and specific neural substrates.
2. Fundamental emotions have a distinct and specific configuration of facial movements or facial expression.
3. Fundamental emotions possess a distinct and specific feeling that achieves awareness.
4. Fundamental emotions were derived through evolutionary–biological processes.
5. Fundamental emotions have organizing and motivational properties that serve adaptive functions.

The emotions that meet these criteria are interest, enjoyment, surprise, sadness, anger, disgust, contempt, and fear. If we allow gaze aversion and head movement as a substitute for a specific facial expression, we can add shame to that list. If we consider face, eyes, and body in describing the expressive component, we can add shyness.

Guilt is considered a basic emotion, though it apparently has no distinct facial expression or bodily movements. There are special problems in distinguishing among shame, shyness, and guilt and in deciding whether or not they are truly fundamental emotions. We shall describe the distinctive features of these emotions when they are discussed in detail in later chapters. For now, suffice it to say that a complete definition of humanness requires that we include shame, shyness, and guilt as basic elements of human nature.

There are a number of other characteristics of emotions to be considered in deciding whether or not they are universal (Ekman, 1984). These characteristics supplement the previous criteria, though they do not necessarily replace or restrict them.

Emotion expressions are more likely to be indicative of a basic emotion if the facial expression of the emotion can be traced phylogenetically (Chevalier-Skolnikoff, 1973). That is, if you look carefully, you can see similarities between the facial expression of human beings and of nonhuman primates.

Expressions are more likely to be indicative of basic emotions if they involve distinct changes in tone of voice (fundamental frequency) or possess other individual acoustic characteristics. Some psychologists believe that all of the emotions have distinct vocal expressions.

The facial expressions of the fundamental emotion last for a limited amount of time. Most adult facial expressions last from approximately ½ second to 4 seconds. Facial expressions of less than ⅓ second or more than 10 seconds are rare, and emotion expressions outside this range are more likely to be false. Facial expressions maintained for many minutes would probably result in muscle spasms (Ekman, 1984).

The timing of fundamental emotion expressions has certain characteristics. Each expression has a latency (from the time of stimulation to the time the expression begins), an onset (the period from latency to maximal level of expression), an apex (the period during which the expression is maintained at maximal strength), and an offset (from the apex until the expression disappears). Research suggests that genuine emotion expressions can be distinguished from false emotion expressions on the basis of one or more of those temporal characteristics, which also vary with a number of other conditions—the strength of the stimulus or the stressfulness of the situation, the strength of ongoing drive states such as level of hunger, fatigue, or the like, and the person's biological predisposition. Some people have lower thresholds for emotion than others, and a person who is hungry or fatigued probably has a lower threshold for anger than one who is comfortable and relaxed.

There are also causes of the basic emotions that are common across all cultures. Threat of a real danger causes fear in all peoples. However, while raw fish on the dinner plate is a source of pride in Japan, it is the source of quite a different set of feelings in Western homes unacquainted with Japanese customs and cuisine.

Emotion expressions have several other characteristics, though they are not necessarily to be depended upon for sorting basic and complex emotions. Emotion expressions are graded in intensity, and the intensity of the expression may reflect the intensity of the felt experience. In adulthood, probably even by late childhood, an emotion expression can be completely inhibited. Of course, under some conditions such as extreme and sudden threat, it is exceedingly difficult to inhibit emotion expressions. Regardless of the circumstances, some emotion expressions are more difficult to control or inhibit than others.

How to Understand Emotions

In the subsequent chapters of this volume, we shall deal with each of the basic emotions of human experience, as well as with some of the more complex motivational phenomena—patterns of emotions, emotional blends, affective–cognitive structures—and it will be worthwhile to know the kinds of questions to ask in order to comprehend the various aspects of an emotion.

What are the neural substrates of the emotion?. Although it is not within the scope and purpose of this text to discuss what is known about the neuroanatomy, neurophysiology, and neurochemistry of emotions, it is appropriate to discuss in general terms what is known about bodily changes that accompany emotion, the effects of body activity on emotion processes, and the effects of emotion on the body. As noted earlier, bodily changes in intense emotion can dominate consciousness. You might be concerned that your very rapid breathing and pounding heart are going to get the best of you. Note that there are even some bodily changes in mild or moderate emotion, though these underlying physiological events may not achieve awareness.

How is the emotion expressed? We are able to answer this question with considerable precision because scientific knowledge of this component of emotion far exceeds that of the other components. In particular, we can detail the neuromuscular changes in the face that give rise to the patterned movements or configurations that signal emotion. We can also determine the time of emergence for these expressions in early development and track the developmental changes that occur in expressive behavior as a result of maturation and socialization. We can also tell something about how we come to manage or control emotion expressions.

What are the causes of the emotion? At the biological level the cause of a sad or angry *feeling* is the direct result of underlying neural and neuromuscular processes. If we are considering the cause of emotion at the cognitive level, then we examine the appraisal, attributional, and other perceptual–cognitive processes that activate the emotion process. It is important to remember that emotions are activated by neurochemical, neuromuscular, affective, and cognitive processes.

What is the phenomenology of the emotion? In particular, precisely what is it like to feel joy or sadness? What can be said to help us get a clearer and more precise picture of the subjective experience of the emotion?

What are the functions of the emotion? We have stated that each of the emotions has unique motivational and adaptive functions. Each emotion does something to us and for us, and usually what it does is helpful. The exception to this rule occurs when the emotions become more intense than is required by the situation, for intense emotion may become disruptive and disorganizing. Normally, however, emotions are constructive forces in our lives.

The functions of a given emotion can be considered at three levels. Sometimes an emotion has a specific biological function, such as redirecting the blood supply and energy resources of the body from the smooth muscles of our internal vital organs to the exterior muscles of action, as in the case of anger. Emotions also have motivational functions for the individual. This element of the emotion is involved with organizing, guiding, and driving perception, thought, and action. Finally, each emotion has a social function. The expressive behavior associated with emotions constitutes the signal-sending aspect of a vitally important social communication system.

As we discuss the development of a given emotion, we shall consider how the expression of that emotion in early infancy influences social bonding—the vital attachment between mother and infant—long before the infant has the capacity to communicate verbally. In human development, emotion expressions of one individual serve as motivational cues for another. We shall also consider the cue-producing functions of emotions, for these are extremely important not only in social communication between the prelinguistic infant and its caregivers but also in the development of relations between emotion and cognition.

How does the emotion develop from infancy through maturity and adulthood? Which component or components of emotion change with age, and which do not? What changes occur in the power of events and situations to elicit emotion? What are the effects of socialization? Do cultures shape different emotion expression styles, and do these cultural changes make a difference in the individual's type of personality as well as the whole society that emerges?

How do we come to be able to manage or regulate the emotion feelings and emotion expressions? This is a major topic in the study of emotional development. During the formative years, we accomplish a great deal in this domain; however, the business of managing or regulating emotion is with us throughout life. Sometimes when stress is high or negative life events come thick and fast, the ability to manage our emotions is called into question. We need to examine as carefully as possible techniques whereby emotions are managed or regulated effectively.

How does the emotion interact with physiological drives and other emotions? It seems as though there are some more or less natural relationships between certain drive states and certain emotions, such as the one between fatigue and anger. Further, some emotions seem more likely to be associated with certain other emotions, particularly in some psychological disturbances or disorders. For example, it has been well established that in depression, sadness and anger frequently go together (Izard, 1972).

How does the emotion relate to perception, thought, and action? The relationship between emotion and cognition is currently a hot topic in the behavioral sciences. Some psychologists debate whether emotion can be activated independently of cognition, while others are concerned with the role of emotion in unconscious cognitive processes (see Singer, 1990). Perhaps most importantly, many scientists are investigating the reciprocal effects of emotion and cognition.

How to children understand emotions? Harris (1989) has presented an interesting account of children's understanding of emotions. He described a number of experiments demonstrating that young children's beliefs and desires play a role in determining what emotions they experience. Further, he showed that young children can anticipate what emotion will ensue when a particular desire is satisfied or frustrated. Children's achievement of the capacity to anticipate an emotional outcome gives them an additional way of regulating their emotions. By anticipating an emotional outcome, they can, for example, attempt to change the outcome or, at least, plan for it. Harris's analysis of children's understanding of emotions provides insights for understanding our own emotions.

Summary

As a general rule, theories of personality and behavior have failed to deal explicitly with the discrete emotions of human experience. Similarly, many popular theories of emotion have had little to say about the role of the emotions in the development of personality and in influencing thought and action. Most emotion investigators have been concerned with only one of the components of the emotion process. Some theories have attempted to work out some aspects of the relations among emotion, cognition, action, and the personality as a whole, but much remains to be done both at the theoretical and empirical levels.

Although classical psychoanalytic theory does not deal systematically with discrete emotion concepts, it emphasizes the importance of noncognitive phenomena, or affects, in human behavior. Freud's early emphasis on the importance of affects as motivational variables launched the psychodynamic tradition in psychology and psychiatry. Although Freud's conception of instinctual drives as the wellspring of motivation has been severely criticized or rejected by some contemporary psychoanalytic thinkers (Rapaport, 1960), his seminal notion that motivational phenomena (including wish impulses) are represented by bonds between ideas and affects still thrives in various forms and contents. It can be seen in Klein's and Holt's concepts of the wish, and it probably influenced Dahl's conception of emotions as fundamental human motives, Singer's views that draw from both psychoanalysis and differential emotions theory, as well as Helen Lewis's work on the role of shame and guilt in personality that reinterprets Freud and draws from the work of Witkin.

The dimensional approach links emotion and personality functioning less convincingly than does psychoanalytic theory, particularly the work of contemporary psychoanalysts. This approach began with Spencer's conceptualization of emotions or feelings as dimensions or states of consciousness and became established as a tradition in psychology when Wundt proposed that the sphere of consciousness described by emotion or feeling could be accounted for by the dimensions of pleasantness–unpleasantness, relaxation–tension, and calm–excitement. Building on the conceptions of Spencer and Wundt, Duffy proposed that all behavior can be explained in terms of organismic arousal (level of tension or energy). Emotion was seen as a point or range of points on the high end of the arousal dimension. That is, according to Duffy, emotion represents high levels of tension or energy in the tissues of the organism. This system, like that of Lindsley, allows emotion to vary quantitatively but not qualitatively.

Woodworth and Schlosberg, who directed attention to the observable aspect of emotion, showed that the facial expressions of emotions could be reliably categorized and that these categories could be rather accurately predicted on the basis of ratings of the dimensions of pleasantness–unpleasantness, attention–rejection, and sleep–tension. Later research showed that attention–rejection and sleep–tension may not be independent dimensions, but several investigators found other reliable dimensions. The research in this tradition has yielded rather substantial evidence that qualitatively distinct emotions may be represented as points or clusters of points in multidimensional space. As shown by a study of Bartlett and Izard (1972), dimensional concepts such as pleasantness, tension, self-assurance, and impulsiveness can be useful in describing the subjective experience associated with various discrete emotions.

A number of theorists have explained emotion as a consequence of perceptual-cognitive processes. Some cognitive theories are rooted in rationalism and tend to view emotions as undesirable entities that disrupt or disorganize thought and action. Arnold's version of this approach defines emotion as a felt-action tendency and distinguishes emotion from biological drive on the one hand and motive (action impulse plus cognition) on the other. Schachter's version of cognitive theory defines emotion as undifferentiated arousal plus cognition. In his view the underlying physiological state is the same for all emotions, and qualitative distinctions result from cognitive appraisal of the situation that elicited the arousal.

Plutchik defines emotion as a patterned bodily reaction corresponding to an underlying adaptive biological process. For example, the adaptive pattern of rejection gave rise to disgust, and that of destruction to anger. Plutchik defined eight primary emotions and indicated that these eight primaries mix to form secondary emotions in much the same way as primary colors mix to form new colors. The mixing of the primary emotions, taking two or three at a time, results in hundreds of mixtures or new emotions; for example, pride = anger + joy, and modesty = fear + acceptance. Plutchik suggests that personality traits can be analyzed in terms of mixed (or secondary) emotions. For example, social regulators (superego phenomena) can be understood as mixtures of fear and other emotions.

Glossary of Terms

As a partial summary and glossary for differential emotions theory, the definitions of some key terms are presented below.

Emotion (fundamental, discrete). An emotion is a complex phenomenon having neural, motor-expressive, and experiential components. The intraindividual process whereby these components interact to produce the emotion has resulted from evolutionary biological processes. For example, in the human being, the expression of anger and the experiential phenomenon of anger are innate, pancultural, universal phenomena.

Patterns of emotions. A pattern of emotion is a combination of two or more fundamental emotions that under particular conditions tend to occur together (either simultaneously or in a repeating sequence) and to interact in such a way that all of the emotions in the pattern have some motivational impact on the organism and its behavior.

Drives. A drive is a motivational state brought about by tissue change or tissue deficit. Drives are exemplified by the common phenomena of hunger, thirst, fatigue, and the like. The motivational intensity of all the drives except pain avoidance is cyclical in nature. Two of the drives, pain avoidance and sex, have some of the characteristics of emotions.

Affect. Affect is a general nonspecific term that includes all the foregoing motivational states and processes. Thus, the affective domain includes the fundamental emotions, patterns of emotions, drives, and their interactions. The affective domain also embraces states or processes in which one of the affects (emotions, drives) is linked with or interacting with perception or cognition.

Emotion–emotion interaction. An emotion–emotion interaction is the amplification, attenuation, or inhibition of one emotion by another.

Emotion–drive interaction. These are motivational states characterized by the amplification, attenuation, or inhibition of drive by emotion or vice versa.

Affective–cognitive structure and emotion traits. We have identified the discrete emotions and discussed the criteria by which we can judge whether or not an emotion is basic or fundamental. We also noted that emotions often occur in patterns, two or more in a given situation. Discussion of these fundamental emotions will constitute the bulk of the pages of this volume, but it is important to note that we shall also give attention to the complex motivational phenomena that are really affective–cognitive structures. In these mental structures, the affective component is an emotion or a complex combination or pattern of emotions, while the cognitive component is made up of a network of images, symbols, and ideas associated with these emotions. Affective–cognitive structures can become organized as emotion traits. The complex, multifaceted phenomena of anxiety, depression, hostility, jealousy, pride, and love all belong in this category, and they will be considered in later chapters.

Affect expressions. Affect expression occupies a middle ground between an experiential/motivational state and behavior. For example, the patterning of the striate muscles of the face in the form of anger expression can be described as facial responses or facial behavior. However, the essential feature of a facial, vocal, gestural, or postural expression that is integral to the emotion process is its motivational property, not its behavioral structure. These definitions distinguish between experiential/motivational phenomena and behavior and thus narrow the meaning of the latter. Behavior includes perceptual and cognitive processes (perception, imaging, thinking, remembering, planning) as well as manipulatory and locomotor activity.

Action or behavior. Behavior is a general term that cannot be defined precisely without going against long-standing tradition. Behaviorists use the term to refer to observable responses, but others use it to refer to any organismic function, whether affective, cognitive, or motor. The present author prefers to avoid the term behavior when a more precise or limited term (e.g., cardiovascular, perceptual, cognitive, motor) is applicable. Because of the surplus meanings and ambiguities surrounding the concept of behavior, the interchangeable term *action* is preferred (when the term behavior is used, it is meant to include cognition and action). Action refers to motor acts (including vocal activity or speech) other than those involved in the expressive component of emotion. Action is distinguished from affective states and processes. Thus emotions, emotion patterns, and drives are not considered as behavior or action, but as the motivational phenomena that produce action or action tendencies. Action or behavior will refer mainly to activity of the individual as a whole, activity that follows from the experiential/motivational phenomena of affective processes and which may include activities of all nonaffective subsystems.

The three components of emotion. There is increasing scientific evidence that each emotion has distinct neural (neurophysiological and neurochemical) underpinnings. Thompson (1988) provides a thorough discussion of how physiological systems participate in emotion and how emotions affect physiological functioning.

Each of the fundamental or basic emotions has an expressive component. Later we shall learn about the distinct facial configuration for each of the emotions. Vocal, gestural, and bodily expression are also important; but less is known about the distinctive features that enable us to match particular emotions with particular physical changes in vocal quality and in body movement. Nevertheless, much of the time, common sense equips us to tell the difference between voices that are happy, sad, angry, or fearful. In fact, at the present time, your judgment about the emotional quality of speech is as good or better than the results of computer-based complex analyses of the physical properties of speech—fundamental frequency (pitch), envelope, and the like.

Feeling is by definition a conscious experience; thus, feeling always operates at some level of awareness, though not necessarily at peak or focal awareness. Because the feeling component remains within conscious experience and because it is the most accessible aspect of emotion and can be most readily related to the organization and guidance of cognition and action, we have constructed the brief and incomplete description of emotion (Chapter 1) in terms of this third component.

Suggested Readings

Harris, P. L., Johnson, C. N., Hutton, D., Andrews, G., & Cooke, T. (1989b). Young children's theory of mind and emotion. *Cognition and emotion*, *3*, 379–400.

In three experiments, 3- to 7-year-old children watched while animal characters were offered various types of containers. The children demonstrated that they understood that the animal's emotion on opening the container would depend on the animal's beliefs and desires about its contents.

Lazarus, R. S., Coyne, J. C., & Folkman, S. (1984). Cognition, emotion and motivation: The doctoring of Humpty-Dumpty. In K. R. Scherer & P. Ekman (Eds.), *Approaches to emotion* (pp. 221–237). Hillsdale, NJ: Erlbaum.

A theoretical account of the relations among emotions, cognition, motivation, and person–environment interactions.

Lewis, H. B. (1979). Shame in depression and hysteria. In C. E. Izard (Ed.), *Emotions in personality and psychopathology* (pp. 371–396). New York: Plenum.

A psychoanalytic account of the role of shame in depression and hysteria.

Roseman, I. J. (1984). Cognitive determinants of emotion: A structural theory. In P. Shaver (Ed.), *Review of personality and social psychology* (Vol. 5, pp. 11–36). Beverly Hills, CA: Sage Publications.

A detailed theory of the cognitive antecedents of emotion. The basic principle is that appraisal processes that compare one's situation to one's motivations produce emotions.

Smith, C. A., & Ellsworth, P. C. (1987). Patterns of appraisal and emotion related to taking an exam. *Journal of Personality and Social Psychology*, *52*, 475–488.

A social-cognitive approach to the analysis of the appraisal processes that activate emotions. Emotions were differentiated and described in terms of six dimensions such as pleasantness, attentional activity, and self–other responsibility/control.

Weiner, B., & Handel, S. J. (1985). A cognition–emotion–action sequence: Anticipated emotional consequences of causal attributions and reported communication strategy. *Developmental Psychology*, *21*(1), 102–107.

An empirical study of the antecedents and consequences of emotions in the framework of social-cognitive or attribution theory.

3

Emotions, Consciousness, and Emotion–Cognition Relations

> No longer is it possible to throw the question out as meaningless, though it is stranger than science has ever met before: Has the universe had to adapt itself from its earliest days to the future requirements for life and mind? Until we understand which way truth lies in this domain, we can very well agree that we do not know the first thing about the universe.
>
> One view holds that as we keep on investigating matter, we will work down from crystals to molecules, from molecules to atoms, from atoms to particles, from particles to quarks—and mine to forever greater depths. A very different concept might be called the "Leibniz logic loop." According to this view the analysis of the physical world, pursued to sufficient depth, will lead back in some now-hidden way to man himself, to conscious mind, tied unexpectedly through the very acts of observation and participation to partnership in the foundation of the universe. To write off the power of observation and reason to make headway with this question would seem to fly against experience. (Wheeler, 1974, 688–691)

Although a number of scientists have always considered consciousness to be the primary subject matter of psychology, it has received a disproportionately small amount of attention from theorists and investigators. In some respects consciousness has been taken for granted. It has been considered as the background or the "given" underlying the more restricted discrete variables that are manipulated and measured in scientific psychology. There is no widely accepted definition of consciousness, and clear and concise definition is difficult. Scientists often talk about consciousness without attempting a definition and without delineating it from the related concepts of mind (mental structures) and subjective experience. This chapter cannot solve all of these problems, but it will attempt to bring some of them into clearer focus. It will present some definitional statements about consciousness and a tentative delineation of consciousness from related and overlapping concepts. This will be followed by a discussion of the emotions as organizing factors in active representational consciousness, modes of consciousness, and brain–emotion–consciousness relationships.

Conceptualizations of Consciousness

Everyday language distinguishes between consciousness and unconsciousness, wakefulness and sleep. Although we do not distinguish between consciousness and wakefulness, we customarily think of sleep and unconsciousness as different things. Sleep, or at least REM sleep, is an active process that can be considered as a state of consciousness in which the thresholds of sensory receptors are increased over wakefulness thresholds. We dream during sleep, and dreaming is an affective–cognitive process that serves a useful purpose in human life. Our own experience, as well as laboratory research, tells us that it can be very disturbing to be deprived of our dreaming.

Apparently, affective–cognitive processes such as dreams occur with little or no input from the environment and depend in large measure, if not entirely, upon imagery originally created by the individual during a waking state. Novel images or image sequences occur in dreams by virtue of some kind of recombination of past images.

No one can seriously question the occurrence of emotion during sleep; the proof is in the dream process. Who at one time or another has not been awakened in terror by the events in a dream? Apparently such waking occurs when the emotion reaches such an intensity that it changes the threshold of receptors; in other words, the emotion by its own intensity created wakeful consciousness.

In a state of unconsciousness there are apparently no perceptual or cognitive processes, no emotions, no dreaming. We cannot make reports on what happened during moments of unconsciousness. We not only lose awareness of the world around us, we lose awareness of time and place. We are for the moment no different sensibly from a rose or a tree. We are alive but have no awareness of being alive. The Freudian unconscious is a different matter. In it, Freud assumed, cognitive processes operate outside the realm of awareness. It is now generally accepted that some kinds of "mind processes" operate at a preconscious or unconscious level (or at a low level of awareness, out of focal awareness) and influence consciousness and conscious processes. The latter, however, are the primary concern of this chapter.

Consciousness as Stream of Thought

Since a clear and succinct definition of consciousness has not been presented in the literature, it is necessary to begin with partial definitions, descriptive statements, or ideas about consciousness. Many of our current ideas about consciousness stem from the pioneering writings of William James, whose work remains a rich resource for the student of consciousness, although it does not provide a singular definition. In speaking of "personal consciousness," James said: "Its meaning we know so long as no one asks us how to define it, but to give an accurate account of it is the most difficult of philosophic tasks. . ." (1890, p. 225). Here, at least, James indicated his belief in the personal nature of consciousness. In his view, consciousness is identified with a single individual. Beyond this point James failed to distinguish between consciousness and the contents of consciousness, and, in fact, most of his writing on the topic focused on the cognitive processes of consciousness. In his famous description of the continuity of consciousness, he equated stream of consciousness with stream of thought. It is not unusual to find contemporary scientists who do not draw any clear distinctions between stream of thought and consciousness, thus de-emphasizing the role of affects.

James's failure to distinguish between thought and consciousness created one of the problems in devising a definition or even a set of characteristic statements about consciousness. It is clear that James did not actually exclude emotions, since he used the term *thought* in a very general sense, meaning everything that goes on in the mind. He spoke of recognizably different classes of conscious states: seeing, hearing, reasoning, willing, recollecting, expecting, loving, hating, "and the hundred ways we know our mind to be alternately engaged" (1890, p. 230). Nevertheless, neither in James's work nor in that of many contemporary scientists can we find clear distinctions between consciousness (as sensibility/awareness/attention) and the contents and operations of consciousness, although Cantril (1962), Deikman (1971), Mandler (1975), and Tart (1976) have given some attention to this problem.

Thus James's ideas seem to apply mainly to the content and operations of consciousness rather than to the sensibility/awareness that characterizes the mind. We have already noted that James characterized thought or mind-stuff as persona in nature. He noted that the breaches between the thoughts and feelings of individuals were the most absolute breaches in nature. He also felt that it is very important to recognize that the content of consciousness is in constant change. He held that even sensations change and that the same bodily sensation is never experienced twice by the individual. "Experience is remolding us every moment and our mental reaction on every given thing is really a resultant of our experience of the world up to that date" (1890, p. 234).

James noted that the contents of consciousness are "sensibly continuous." Even when there is some kind of time gap in consciousness, the consciousness before the time gap seems to belong to the consciousness that comes after it. In this respect consciousness feels unbroken. In addition to the continuity in the time sense (continuity over time), there is also continuity in the sense that the parts of consciousness seem inwardly connected, belonging together as parts of a common whole. According to James the natural name for this common whole is myself, I, or me. Toward the end of his writings on consciousness James said: "Looking back, then, over this review we see that mind is at every stage a theatre of simultaneous possibilities. Consciousness consists in the comparison of these with each other, the selection of some, and the suppression of the rest by the reinforcing and inhibiting agency of attention" (1890, p. 288). It is clear that here James is talking about the contents and operations of consciousness, and he provided useful insights about these. Other of James's observations on consciousness will be noted in later sections.

An Experimental Approach to the Stream of Consciousness

The stream of consciousness is never a random process. From birth the infant perceives the surrounding world selectively, showing, for example, a strong visual preference for the human face. Environmental factors also play an important part in the development of the infant's style of selectively perceiving and processing information. Parents who model make-believe activities and exert less control over their children's time and activities have children who engage in fantasy and make-believe more frequently and more fancifully (Sheaffer, Gold, & Henderson, 1987). Children whose stream of consciousness is nurtured by fantasy and imagery are also creative thinkers. In particular, in children with high IQs, there are significant correlations between measures of imagery and measures of creative thinking (Shaw & De Mers, 1987).

Singer and his colleagues (Antrobus, Singer, & Greenberg, 1966; Pope, 1977; Pope & Singer, 1976; Rodin & Singer, 1976; Singer, 1974, 1975; Singer & Antrobus, 1963) have conducted a series of important studies on problems of consciousness and inner experience. Theoretically, they are in the tradition of James and Tomkins, but they have added contemporary concepts and rigorous scientific method in an area often thought to be scientifically unmanageable.

Their studies have focused on separate aspects or functions of consciousness such as daydreaming, imagery, and fantasy. For example, Singer has proposed that such internal processes compete with external stimuli for focal attention or dominance of consciousness. A study by Antrobus *et al.* (1966) supported this idea. They showed that task complexity significantly reduced the frequency of stimulus- or task-independent thoughts. They measured the latter by interrupting subjects during task performance and asking them whether they were aware of task-unrelated thoughts just prior to the interruption. In another study, they showed that subjects who heard about a serious escalation of the Vietnam War just prior to participating in a signal-detection experiment showed a significant increase in stimulus-independent thought.

Personality characteristics, richness of environment, and a number of other factors apparently influence the balance in the processing of internal events and external stimulation. Singer and Antrobus (1963) and a number of other investigators have factor analyzed the contents of daydreams and found evidence for three fairly stable patterns, or styles, of daydreaming.

One is a guilty-dysphoric style involving self-recrimination, hostile wishes, and concern over achievement striving and failure. The second style is characterized by distractibility, mind-wandering, and underlying fear. The third is associated with positive affects and includes future-oriented, playful fantasies.

Rodin and Singer (1977) found that obese individuals were more sensitive to external cues than others. Thus sensory data from the environment, including food and food symbols, have a greater impact on the stream of thought in overweight people. Pope (1977) found that verbalization tended to slow down the stream of thought or otherwise to alter self-report of ongoing mental processes.

Singer and his colleagues (Pope & Singer, 1976) have discussed eleven determinants of the stream of consciousness: the mind as activity, sensory input, a continuum of awareness, attention, a bias favoring sensory input, predictability of the environment, the matching function (how input is assessed), affect, current concerns, the set toward internal processing, and structural characteristics of the stimuli. Schachtel (1959) and Tomkins (1962) influenced Pope and Singer's treatment of affect and led them to attribute considerable importance to affect as a determinant of consciousness and as a regulator of schema development.

Consciousness as a Paradigm

In Tart's (1973) view, an ordinary state of consciousness, like a paradigm in science, constitutes a set of rules and theories that facilitates person–environment interactions and interpretations of experiences. The rules are mainly implicit and operate automatically, and in following them people feel they are doing the natural thing. In keeping with his concept of consciousness Tart defined knowledge as an immediately given "feeling of congruence between two different kinds of experience, a matching. One set of experiences may be regarded as perceptions of the external world, of others, of oneself; the second set may be regarded as a theory, a scheme, a system of understanding" (p. 45). The scheme or system of understanding in Tart's framework would be the personal paradigm or consciousness.

Tart (1976) postulates a basic awareness, an awareness of being aware, or self-awareness, and attention/awareness, the focusing of which is partially volitional. He distinguishes between discrete states of consciousness (d-SOCs—unique, dynamic patterns of psychological structures) and discrete altered states of consciousness (d-ASCs—a departure from some baseline of d-SOC). A d-SOC is stabilized by volitional focusing of "attention/awareness energy" and by positive and negative feedback processes. A d-ASC is induced by disrupting forces that push various structure subsystems beyond their limits of stable functioning and by patterning forces that organize a new system of structure subsystems. The ten major subsystems that play varying roles in known d-ASCs are: exteroceptors, interoceptors, input processing, memory, the subconscious, emotions, evaluation and decision-making, time sense, sense of identity, and motor output. Thus, Tart recognizes emotions as one of the subsystems of consciousness (or d-ASCs), but he does not elaborate on the significant interactions that can occur between emotions and the other postulated subsystems.

Tart's analysis seems to allow for the possibility of studying consciousness as sensibility/awareness/attention apart from its contents and operations. The difficulties that most Western scientists and philosophers have in thinking of consciousness or any aspect of consciousness as distinct from its contents was well illustrated by Scher (1962), when he wrote:

> In the absence of "sensory flux," consciousness cannot be maintained (Hebb, 1961); but sensory flux alone is not consciousness. Novelty (Vernon, McGill, Gulick, & Candland, 1961), order and meaning (Freedman, Gruebaum, & Greenblath, 1961), differential responsiveness (Lindsley, 1951), amplitude and rate of change (Kubie, 1961) all help to shape the participating mind. (p. 356)

Consciousness as the Complement of Biological Organization

Deikman (1973), unlike most other Western theorists, has emphasized the importance of the distinction between consciousness and contents of consciousness. As evidence of the validity of this distinction, he pointed out that in disciplined meditation one heightens consciousness, or awareness, by subduing the conventional operations of the mind (perceptions, thought, memory). Thus, to expand consciousness is to expand its sensitivities, not its contents. In Deikman's view thoughts, images, and memories are chief examples of the contents of consciousness. He believes that it is possible for thoughts, sensations, images, or other mental phenomena to disappear, while consciousness, or awareness, remains. The contents of consciousness are functions of neurological systems consisting of receptor organs and brain mechanisms. Deikman believes that this is not the case for awareness, or consciousness. Awareness is viewed as the organization of the biosystem, not the product of a particular neural circuit. More particularly, "awareness is the complementary aspect of that organization, its psychological equivalent" (1973, p. 319). Deikman sees consciousness and neural mechanisms as complementary aspects of the biological system that constitutes an individual. On the biological side, the organization of certain chemical entities constitute life, while on the psychological side, this organization constitutes awareness. He likens the electrochemical and psychological aspects of the biological system to the apparent duality that obtains when physicists observe the wavelike characteristics of light under one set of conditions and the particlelike characteristics under another. Deikman does not mean that there is a separate system that senses consciousness in the way that the eye senses light or the ear senses sound. Rather, he means that "awareness is the complementary aspect of organization—it is organization, itself, in its mental dimension." He maintains that the contents of consciousness (e.g., sensations, thoughts) are individual-bound or persona, while awareness itself is universal.

It may prove useful both for science and for the student's understanding of the area to distinguish between consciousness on the one hand and the operations and structures of consciousness on the other. Without making these distinctions the concept of consciousness might be so broad that it would be meaningless. If consciousness is defined as the total array of sensations, perceptions, cognitions, and affects that characterize the individual, then the study of consciousness becomes the study of everything mental or psychological, and the organization of these things may be equated with personality. The structure and operations of the mind may give consciousness its "character," but it is not at all clear that they adequately define it. If we do assume that consciousness is distinct from, or more than, its contents, then perhaps it is more accurate to think of special states as changes in structures and operations of consciousness (e.g., emotion, perception, cognition) rather than as altered consciousness.

While Deikman's treatment has intuitive appeal, it may be subject to the criticisms that apply to any philosophic dualism. In one sense it is nothing more than a contemporary resolution of the ancient mind–body problem. There are several ways of responding to this criticism. First, the fact that there is a dualistic conception of life may simply indicate the current limits of mind attempting to understand itself. Second, such limitations do not apply only to the chemical organization–consciousness duality, but a dualistic conception also yields the most workable characterization of a number of phenomena of nature, such as light. Third, instead of considering Deikman's concept a duality, it may be described as two levels of conceptualization. Finally, we simply may be epistemologically unwilling to accept as fact that a certain complex organization of a particular origin is a singular whole that can be conceptualized equally well as an electrochemical complex or as consciousness. In any case, Deikman's views do not readily lend themselves to empirical test, and they have generated little or no systematic experimentation.

Consciousness Derived from Experiencing Biological Processes as Emotions

Sinnott (1966), approaching the problem from the standpoint of a geneticist, claims that his conception of physical life and consciousness avoids the pitfalls of philosophic dualism. He argues that the steps from physical materials to life to mind were a natural progression in evolution and that consciousness was a logical outcome of biological processes. In short, he maintains that consciousness is simply the "felt" or "experienced" electrochemical activities of the body, mainly the brain. This position is similar to that of Feigl (1962), who proposed an identity theory to resolve the mind–body problem. In this theory, the mental and physical are the same in the sense that certain phenomenal terms refer to the same events as those referred to by certain neurophysiological terms. Thus neurophysiological and phenomenal terms have identical referents, and these referents are "the immediately experienced qualities, or their configurations, in the various phenomenal fields" (Feigl, 1962, p. 577). Perhaps Bertrand Russell came as close to a succinct resolution of the mind–body problem as anyone when he said that the difference between matter and mind is merely one of arrangement.

Sinnott interprets consciousness and mind in terms of biological organization and biological processes. Fundamental to his argument is the proposition that there is a genuine similarity between the processes of bodily development and the functions of mind. He pointed out that bodily development is a controlled progression, regulated at every step so as to produce a precise end, and this same regulation to ends is evident in behavior. Biological development toward a precise end is similar to the more complex goal seeking evident in behavior. Biological development conforms to norms (or innate neural programs) that are imbedded in the organism in such a way that growth is "set" for a particular course toward a precise end. According to Sinnott, behavioral norms, like biological-developmental ones, are represented by protoplasmic patterns, chiefly in brain cells. In making his point, Sinnott (1966) raised the provocative question as to when embryological development ends and behavior begins.

> Where, in the hatching egg, does embryology end and behavior begin? When the chick, with a peck of its beak, breaks the shell, we call this behavior, an instinctive act; but how does it differ, in essence, from earlier movements of the growing embryo that lead up to it? (p. 148)

Sinnott further illustrated the morphogenetic nature of behavior by pointing out that an ornithologist can identify a species of bird by the nest it builds, and an arachnologist the species of spider by its web alone.

A vital link in Sinnott's argument is that the biological directedness toward ends that characterizes living things is experienced as desire and purpose and that "physical life is the sense of being consciously oriented towards ends" (p. 153). (Sinnott does not use the word "purpose" in a teleological sense but simply to recognize "the presence in a system of something that guides the activity of that system in conformity to a particular norm set up in it as in a feedback mechanism" [p. 154]). Sinnott does not attempt to explain how the all-important phenomenon of experiencing comes about; he simply states that in any living system where there is a brain pattern or norm that directs behavior toward specific ends it is logical to expect such directiveness to be felt. The feeling of being oriented or drawn toward a particular end produces desire or want. "Desire, at bottom, is that same sort of biological orientation evident in the far simpler directiveness of bodily development, but it is subjectively experienced. Wanting, desiring, craving (and their opposites) are emotions" (Sinnott, 1966, p. 153).

Sinnott maintained that consciousness as such is more than a general awareness of the environment, and that it includes an element of directiveness and an involvement of the organism with the environment. He maintained that human consciousness is always accompanied by at least some degree of wanting or desiring (emotion), and thus consciousness is an active condition of a clearly biological nature. It is awareness of being alive and actively involved with the surround, and in Sinnott's conception this means experiencing desire or emotion. Whether or not emotion-experiencing is consciousness or a structure/operation of consciousness that tends always to be present, the position of the present author is congruent with that of Sinnott's in seeing the emotions as the chief determinants of the quality of life and as the main provider of blueprints for cognition and action.

The Emotions as Organizing Factors in Consciousness

Although it is considered useful to distinguish between consciousness as sensibility/awareness and the contents of consciousness, it is recognized that consciousness is typically conceived as a set of structures and operations. The conscious mind has a strong tendency to be active, and its activity typically involves images, thoughts, emotions, and affective–cognitive orientations—the latter being the most common structures in consciousness. While disciplined meditations deriving mainly from the philosophies and religions of the Orient have taught us that consciousness can exist seemingly without content and apparently with a minimum of activity, this absence of content is a special state of consciousness. In contrast, ordinary states of consciousness and most other special states are characterized by contents. The position taken here is that the most fundamental contents of consciousness and the ones that provide it with its essential organization and directiveness are the emotions and affective–cognitive orientations.

Anshen (1966), editor of *Credo Perspectives*, a series of intellectual autobiographies by some of the outstanding minds of our times, wrote:

> Personality itself is an emotional, not an intellectual, experience: and the greatest achievement of knowledge is to combine the personal within a larger unity, just as in the higher states of development the parts that make up the whole require greater and greater independence and individuality within the context of the whole. (p. 9)

She went on to point out the critical role of emotion in life and in creative endeavor: "Refusing to divorce work from life or love from knowledge, it is action, it is passion that enhances our being" (p. 17).

Many scientists, philosophers, and artists have recognized the ultimate importance of the emotions in human consciousness and behavior. Himwich (1962) coined a new term, "thymencephalon," to designate the parts of the brain especially involved in feeling and emotion. The prefix of his term is from the Greek word *thymos*, which has as one of its meanings "strong feeling and passion." Himwich considered emotion a chief aspect of consciousness and maintained that the thymencephalon contributed to consciousness a crude awareness of emotion. John (1962) defined consciousness as the totality of endogenous and exogenous sensations and maintained that consciousness is "ordered and colored by the affect and evaluation unique to, and a characteristic of, the experiencing organism" (p. 81). Shagass (1962) defined emotion as the aspect of behavior that is subjectively felt and indicated that emotion may be an aspect of all behavior.

As already indicated, Sinnott (1966) believes that the sensing or experiencing of biological directiveness forms the wants and desires that constitute the emotions and bridge the gap from matter to life (consciousness).

> Human beings are material systems, to be sure, and subject to the laws of nature, but they are alive. With them comes into the material world a breath of uncertainty and of excitement. They are not automata, but creatures who think and feel; whose problems center around mind, soul, and spirit—the emotions, purposes, values, and ideals of men. (p. 88)

Sinnott remarked that the biologist studying life objectively from an external standpoint may never understand it as well as the poet who can feel what it is like. Here Sinnott was emphasizing the importance of affective experience even in the business of achieving understanding and knowledge.

In the following sections, various structures and operations of consciousness will be considered in their relationship to the emotions. In the framework of differential emotions theory the affects, especially the fundamental emotions, constitute the basic structures of consciousness. Affect is so constant and pervasive in consciousness that it is difficult to separate emotion as structure from consciousness itself, and whether this (or any) aspect of the distinction between consciousness and its contents proves valid or fruitful is a crucial problem for future research.

Sensation, Emotion, and Consciousness

In our present state of knowledge, sensation has to be considered as the most elementary aspect of consciousness. At the neurophysiological level sensation is the electrochemical response of the organism to any stimulation whether external or internal. In consciousness, sensation is the experiencing of this electrochemical response. When we ask the question How is sensation experienced? we are back to the basic problem of the transition from matter to mind.

The tendency among Western thinkers is to rule out the possibility of experiencing "pure" sensation (James, 1890; Nathan, 1969). According to this line of thought, when sensation achieves consciousness, we have perception. In other words, perception is defined as sensation plus meaning, and sensation typically acquires meaning immediately. "We hear music not sound; we see objects, not light reflected from edges and angles" (Nathan, 1969, p. 260). However, Nathan did allow for the possibility that sensation was separable from perception and suggested that sensation without meaning was a spur to further investigation.

Sensation, Meaning, and Emotion

The position taken here is that while sensation is a separable phenomenon, consciousness has a strong tendency to transform sensation or sensory data into affect, perception, and cognition. Sensory data are transformed first into affect, which in turn organizes ongoing sensory messages into perception and cognition.

The sensory data of day-to-day life are most frequently transformed first into the emotion of interest, the topic of Chapter 8. The postulate that some degree of emotion characterizes ordinary states of consciousness and precedes perception and cognition is also affirmed by Spitz (1965). Based on his analysis of the continual workings of emotion in consciousness, Leeper (1965) made a strong case for considering emotion as an actual part of the perceptual process.

When Western scientists and philosophers indicate that perception is sensation that has acquired meaning, they may be interpreted as being in agreement with the position of differential emotions theory if it is conceded that meaning involves some emotion (e.g., interest, joy, sadness, anger) at some level of intensity. The intensity of emotion in consciousness may be minimal and its effects very subtle. But it is emotion and its effects upon cognition and action that cause the meaning of things to change with time and season. When feeling fatigued and annoyed by the sounds and labor of operating a lawn mower, grass may be perceived as vexatious or noxious, but while experiencing sexual attraction and affection, grass may be perceived as a beautiful carpet on which to make love.

Affects and Levels of Consciousness

Differential emotions theory and psychoanalytic theory agree that emotion is by its very nature a phenomenon of consciousness, and the former theory postulates the subjective experiencing of emotions as the principal organizing factor in consciousness and the basis of the selectivity and directiveness that characterize the human mind. While emotion is always conscious, it is not always cognized or symbolized. Low levels of undifferentiated arousal may be neither conscious nor cognized. The relatively greater specificity of cues or information from emotions makes them of greater value for adaptation and effective behavior than is the case for undifferentiated arousal states. The emotion of interest provides much of the selectivity and focusing of attention that characterizes ordinary states of consciousness.

There seems to be no useful distinction between the concepts of subjective experience, consciousness, and awareness, and all these terms seem to imply an existential dichotomy—experiencing–not experiencing, conscious–unconscious, aware–unaware. However, such dichotomizing may not be the most accurate way of describing the processes of the mind. A wide array of things can exist in consciousness at different levels of awareness (Snygg & Combs, 1949). At present I am most keenly aware of my interest and sustained effort to write clearly and make a valid point. I know that I am sometimes saddened by the difficulty of the work or the thought of failing to do a good job; I am less aware of the pressure on my bottom from the pull of gravity, and even less (only sporadically) aware of the sounds in my office or on the campus outside. These things affect my thought and action (interest or annoy me) in relation to their status in my consciousness. As a rule the level of awareness of a phenomenon is an index of its motivational value for ongoing behavior.

Emotion and Perception

Classical studies of perception (e.g., Ittelson & Kilpatrick, 1951) show that the perceptual process as we know it in adulthood is almost never a simple transformation of sensory input. The observer tends to add something to the sensations resulting from the stimulus pattern. The "something" added has typically been explained as a function of the observer's past experience. After reviewing a number of studies that show how misperceptions can be caused by unusual and unexpected arrangements of stimulus configurations, Ittleson and Kilpatrick (1951) concluded:

> All these experiments, and many more that have been made, suggest strongly that perception is never a sure thing, never an absolute revelation of "what is." Rather, what we see is a prediction—our own personal construction designed to give us the best possible bet for carrying out our purposes in action. We make these bets on the basis of our past experience. (p. 184)

It seems quite reasonable to restate their conclusion: We perceive in terms of our wants, desires, and purposes, and our wants, desires, and purposes are our emotions or functions of them.

We perceive and attend to the stimulus patterns surrounding us in a highly selective fashion. This selectivity can best be explained as a function of affect. The affect that operates most frequently in guiding perception and attention in ordinary consciousness is the emotion of interest. It should be noted, however, that interest can operate at low levels of intensity as well as at the high levels that we sense as excitement.

Since some degree of emotion characterizes ordinary states of consciousness at all times; emotion may be said to precede the perception of objects, events, and people that parade through our field of awareness. The emotions or combination of emotions present in consciousness influence the perceptual process and, in effect, filter or otherwise modify the raw sensory data transmitted by the receptors. It is the interaction of emotion with sensory input that usually prevents pure sensation from registering in ordinary states of consciousness. Visual, auditory, somesthetic, and even gustatory and olfactory sensations can be altered by emotion. Rafe, joyous over a good test grade he just received, will see the instructor and hear the lecture and discussion that day in a quite different way than a dejected or disgusted student who just received a disappointing grade on the test. Ambiguous or highly difficult items might be seen by the former student as an unfortunate error on the part of the instructor but as unfair or even unethical by the latter student.

Each of the affects, and each of an almost endless variety of affect combinations, influences perception in a different way. In a state of joy we perceive the world through rose-colored glasses, and we see beauty and harmony everywhere. In sadness we perceive the world as if through dark glasses, and life appears to be dull and gloomy. In anger we have a greater tendency to perceive obstacles and barriers, and when disgust mixes with incoming sensations, what we perceive tends to be distasteful and ugly. In contempt we perceive others as in some way inferior or defective. In fear our perceptual field narrows and more things seem to be threatening. At the height of shame we seem to perceive only the self in error, and consciousness of self is sharply heightened. In guilt we perceive others in a different light as a result of the breakdown in interpersonal relations. To paraphrase Sinsheimer (1971), so much of what we perceive is in truth what we conceive, and what we conceive is born of an affair with our emotions.

The influence of emotion on the perceptual process has been demonstrated experimentally by Izard, Wehmer, Livsey, and Jennings (1965). Their experiment began with the selection of an equal number of photographs of positive and negative facial expressions of emotion. Also, an equal number of photographs depicting positive and negative interpersonal scenes were selected. Positive scenes portrayed friendly, cooperative interactions. Negative scenes portrayed what appeared to be angry or hostile interactions. Volunteer subjects were asked to view these facial photographs and interpersonal scenes through a stereoscope.

When the subjects arrived at the laboratory, half were treated in a warm and friendly way, while half were treated in a cold, formal, and unfriendly fashion as to annoy them or make them a little angry. The photograph and scenes were presented stereoscopically in a completely random and balanced fashion. Thus, the subjects, whether they were right-eye dominant or left-eye dominant, saw either type of photograph an equal number of times with each eye. Subjects who were made to feel comfortable and happy saw significantly more of the happy facial expressions and friendly interpersonal scenes. Subjects who were treated in a cool and unfriendly fashion and experienced some annoyance or mild anger, saw significantly more of the negative facial expressions and hostile interpersonal scenes. This experiment demonstrated clearly and convincingly that the emotion one is experiencing can actually determine what one sees.

Moods also have been shown to affect the way we learn about, judge, and remember the characteristics of other people. For example, subjects in a happy mood formed more favorable impressions of people than did subjects in a sad mood (Forgas & Bower, 1987).

Emotion–Cognition Interactions and Consciousness

Most operations of consciousness involve some kind of representational process. To be conscious of an object is to represent that object in the mind. The representation formed by the receptors is transmitted by the sensory nerves as a message to the brain (e.g., subjective experience of emotion). Thus the usual contents of consciousness result from a unique type of representation by which one represents (duplicates, imitates) to one's self some other aspect of the world.

Conditioning Emotion Activators

Emotion can exist in consciousness as a result of a conditioned stimulus (CS), via classical conditioning. In "traumatic conditioning" in animals, the response is most often described as "emotional excitement . . . manifested by behavioral signs of physiological arousal. . ." (Janis, Kagan, Mahl, & Holt, 1969, p. 42). Some studies of animal learning have inferred that traumatic conditioning also works in the case of the discrete emotion of fear (e.g., Liddell, 1962; Miller, 1948) and hence that fear can be learned as a conditioned response (CR).

Classical conditioning can also be viewed as a source of information randomly acquired (Fair, 1969). The conditioned stimulus (1) may be unattended or at low level of awareness or (2) it may be a random sight or sound or other stimulus having no logical relationship to the unconditioned stimulus (US) or the unconditioned response (UR). Thus the CS–UR connection may be inaccessible (unavailable) in a logical sense. When the UR is an emotion or undifferentiated arousal there may be important consequences following from a "random" or "unattended" stimulus.

Liddell's (1962) studies of classical conditioning in the sheep provide an excellent illustration of an association between a CS and UR (emotion) and demonstrates the potential hazards of this type of learning. Liddell observed that a brief electric current that would hardly be noticed by a human being would produce vehement struggling in the laboratory-accommodated sheep, suggesting fear at the level of panic. After about 20 repetitions of the shock, the sheep appeared to regain composure and to react with a brisk energetic flexation of the stimulated forelimb followed by nose licking, teeth grinding, and yawning. After associating a metronome clicking once per second (CS) with the electric shock (US) on 10 occasions, a CR was formed. Now simply the sound of the metronome clicks would produce the fear and panicky behavior. After 100 simultaneous presentations of the metronome beats and the electric shock, the conditioned fear response was established for the life of the animal. "Over thirty-five years of experimental work in our laboratory confirmed this seemingly dogmatic statement. The animal can never again listen to the metronome with equanimity. Indeed, the clicking of a typewriter visibly disturbs her" (Liddell, 1962, p. 204). According to Liddell, many of our emotion experiences arise from such "seemingly innocuous coincidences." In the case of most conditioned emotional responses, the individual "is compelled to behave ineffectually in response to the inevitable" (p. 204). Liddell argued, further, that, as such, conditioned reflexes are ineffectual in adjusting to actual situations. Because these conditioned emotions and emotion-related responses result from a misperception or misconception of stimulus situation and are ineffectual in adapting or coping, they may be considered as neurotic traits (Liddell, 1962).

Liddell's ominous conclusion was in the tradition of the founder of behaviorism, John B. Watson (1919). After his study with Raynor (Watson & Raynor, 1920) demonstrated a conditioned fear response in a human infant, Watson concluded that emotional development consisted of the acquisition of conditioned emotional responses (CERs). This suggests that getting rid of an unwanted CER would be simply a matter of identifying the original US and extinguishing (deconditioning) it.

Later research has shown that conditioning explains far fewer significant emotion responses than once thought. In particular, conditioning apparently does not explain the kinds of fears and phobias ("neurotic traits") alluded to by Liddell (Jacobs & Nadel, 1985).

Jacobs and Nadel (1985) have presented evidence that indicates that negative emotion states or stress can render the locale or context learning system dysfunctional. In this condition, emotion–cognition–action sequences lack the goal orientedness or directionality they ordinarily possess. Further, the individual is more vulnerable to the reemergence in consciousness of fears learned in infancy, before the hippocampus (the brain mechanism that mediates context learning) has matured enough to be functional. The implications of Jacob and Nadel's work for learning of fears and phobias will be discussed in Chapter 12.

Another line of research that demonstrates effects of emotion on consciousness is concerned with the mood-congruity effect. The idea is that a particular emotion or mood has a particular selective effect on learning, such that material congruent with the mood is learned more efficiently than material incongruent with the mood. Gordon Bower and his associates have repeatedly shown that when people in a sad mood are required to learn sad and happy material, they selectively learn more sad than happy material. Similarly, people in an angry mood selectively learn more anger material than sad or happy material, and other emotions have a similar effect on learning (Bower, Gilligan, & Monteiro, 1981).

Emotions are organizing forces in consciousness, and they continually organize sensory input and reorganize information in creative ways. And the human being has the greatest array of differential affects of any animal.

Emotions, Consciousness, Cognition, and Action

Because emotion can exist in consciousness independent of cognition, it is not unusual for a person to respond in terms of an emotion without cognizing it—without labeling it as such. To experience anger and to cognize anger are two different phenomena, although they can and frequently do influence each other via emotion–cognition interactions. Experiencing anger tends to elicit anger-related ("angry") thoughts and actions, and cognizing or reflecting on one's anger tends to alter the anger experience.

Thus, cognition can exercise a certain amount of control over the emotion process, as in the case when an individual deliberately decides to inhibit the facial expression of an emotion. This decision and the lack (or minimizing) of expression may serve to decrease the intensity of the subjective experience of a discrete emotion. A person can initiate and sustain cognitive and motor activities that inhibit the facial expression component of emotion; it is also possible for such inhibitory processes to influence the feedback from a facial expression in such a way that the subjective experience of the discrete emotion does not occur. When the energy generated by an emotion activator is not channeled into facial expression and subjective experiencing of emotion, unexpended energy exists in the nervous system. This energy may be directed to the brain stem reticular formation, resulting in an increase in nonspecific activation or undifferentiated arousal. In this case the internal (arousal) cues for thought and action are vague. Action may become ineffective or maladaptive; inaction may lead to psychosomatic symptoms.

After much debate on the question of whether emotion causes cognition or cognition causes emotion, the issue remains controversial (Lazarus, 1982, 1984; Zajonc, 1980, 1984). A reasonable answer to this question is that both are true. Emotion can activate and influence cognitive processes and vice versa; that is, the dynamic relations between emotion and cognition (perception, imagery, memory, thought) are reciprocal.

One can make a good case for the primacy of emotion in evolution and development. It is certainly obvious to all students of infant development that emotion expressions (some of which are present at birth) precede representational processes and the appraisal or evaluative processes that are dependent on mental representation. Unlabeled and semantically unidentifiable emotion feelings, whether in infant or adult, occur in consciousness without prior conscious appraisal processes.

Hemispheric Functions and Emotions

Most of the evidence relating to the role of the two brain hemispheres in emotion has come from observations and investigations of clinical cases of brain-damaged individuals. The most widely held opinion is that emotion processes are primarily nondominant (right) hemisphere functions, while cognitive processes are primarily dominant (left) hemisphere functions. For example, Galin (1976) believes that verbal and nonverbal (e.g., facial) types of information are processed by the left and right hemispheres, respectively, and that difficulties in coping with messages containing conflicting verbal and nonverbal cues can be understood at the neurological level in terms of conflict between hemispheres. The scant evidence on emotions and hemispheric functions is divided.

Schwartz, Davidson, Maer, and Bromfield (1973) studied patterns of hemispheric dominance in musical, emotional, verbal, and spatial tasks while recording EEG activity from both left and right hemispheres. From their review of the literature, they had concluded that for right-handed subjects, cognitive processes such as verbal activity and sequential logic occurred in the left hemisphere, while musical and visual–spatial activities were processed in the right hemisphere. Mainly on the basis of the clinical studies of various investigators, they hypothesized that emotion, like visual and spatial matters, was primarily a right-hemispheric function. In their experiment, Schwartz *et al.* had subjects whistle melodies (right-hemisphere task), recite lyrics (left-hemisphere task), and sing a familiar song (a dual-hemisphere task). They used degree of alpha (brain-wave) blocking as a index of hemispheric dominance (alpha blocking is the highest in the hemisphere that is dominant at any given time). They found that whistling produced relative right dominance, talking, relative left dominance, and singing resulted in comparable alpha blocking in both hemispheres. In a second experiment, they used right or left lateral eye movement as an index of hemispheric dominance, while subjects answered questions of a verbal, spatial, or emotional nature or some combination of these. Spatial questions resulted in significantly more frequent left lateral eye movements (indicating right-hemispheric dominance), and emotional questions had a similar effect. The data suggested that while important cognitive processes are primarily left-hemisphere functions, emotion processes are primarily right-hemisphere functions. This conclusion was also supported by Safer and Leventhal (1977), who showed that for most subjects emotionally toned monaural vocal cues were more salient for those who listened with the left ear (indicating right-hemisphere processing).

A series of studies conducted at the Institute of Evolutionary Physiology and Biochemistry in Leningrad (e.g., Deglin, 1973) yielded data inconsistent with the conclusion of Schwartz *et al.* (1973) and Safer and Leventhal (1975). These studies compared the effects on depressed patients of electroconvulsive seizures in either the right or left hemispheres of the brain. Instead of administering shock in the traditional manner (bilaterally to both hemispheres), they administered shock either to the right or left hemisphere, the shock being sufficient to block or impair functions in the shocked hemisphere for a brief period of time. They found that certain basic sensory functions were about equally impaired, regardless of which brain hemisphere had been paralyzed by electric shock. After finding that the shock to the right hemisphere not only failed to produce aphasia but made the patient more talkative, they concluded that the right hemisphere had a suppressive effect on verbalization. They inferred the possibility that the mutism sometimes observed in depression may be a result of right hemisphere suppression of the left hemisphere.

A number of findings led them to a different conclusion than Schwartz *et al.*

regarding hemispheric dominance and emotion. After administration of shock to the right hemisphere, patients showed a significant decrease in their ability to recognize vocal intonations indicative of discrete emotions such as joy, sadness, and anger. More importantly, they found that after administering shock to the right side, the patient showed very definite changes in facial expression and emotion as he recovered from shock. The patient's face gradually changed from a silly smile to what appeared to be a real smile of joy. In keeping with the apparent joyful facial expression, the patient's vocal intonations, verbalizations, gestures, and posture appeared commensurate with that of a happy person. In contrast, after the left hemisphere had been paralyzed by electric shock the patient displayed distressful and fearful facial expressions and consonant verbalizations, intonations, gestures, and posture.

Recent research has generally supported Deglin's position. Indeed, studies of brain lateralization in infants show that some specialization of hemispheric function in affective reactions is present in the newborn. Fox and Davidson (1986) administered sucrose and citric acid solutions to 2- or 3-day-old infants. They measured facial behavior with Max (a facial movement coding system; Izard, 1979) and hemispheric involvement by electroencephalography (EEG). Facial behavior and EEG discriminated among responses to the two tastes. They found that sucrose was associated with more interest expressions and relatively greater EEG activity in the left hemisphere, while citric acid was associated with more disgust expressions and relatively greater EEG activity in the right hemisphere. These investigators (Fox & Davidson, 1982) have also shown that in 10-month-old infants, there is greater right-hemisphere activity when the child is viewing negative emotion expressions, and vice versa for positive emotion expressions.

Emotions and the Organization of Consciousness

Differential emotions theory proposes that the affects, particularly the emotions, are the principal organizing and controlling forces in consciousness, self-awareness, and the ego or self-concept. The affects exert their control or influence by means of an intraindividual communication system consisting of feedback loops and interactive systems. According to this theory, the organization of consciousness is as follows. Sensations from both interocepters and exterocepters provide the basis for consciousness. Consciousness at its most basic level is awareness of sensation. Emotion is the most fundamental organization of sensation that has significance or meaning (and that has specific experiential, motivational properties). The very basic sensory-cortical process that produces affect lays the groundwork for perception, cognition, and all other operations of consciousness. Consciousness that consists of awareness of "pure sensation" or of sensation that is only loosely organized by the usual perceptual-cognitive processes is attained by adults only under unusual conditions. Ordinary states of consciousness are cha... affect and, most importantly, in human beings, by emotion; and the emotions in consciousness influence all perception, cognition, and behavior.

A number of social psychologists have reported evidence for affect and cognition as separable but interacting variables in attitudes. For example, Kilty (1969) correlated scores on a cognitive measure of attitude with an independent measure of affect. He interpreted the relatively low correlations as support for a conceptualization of attitude that distinguishes affect and cognition as relatively independent components. In a later study Kilty showed that the relationship of attitudinal affect and cognition was a complex one. He found that the strength of the affect–cognition relationship depended on such variables as type of concept and source of beliefs involved in the attitude. Attitude as studied by Kilty is quite similar to the concept of affective–cognitive orientation, which allows for a great variety of affect–cognition relationships, not only in terms of the concept, but also in terms of the quality and intensity of the affect.

In his analysis of natural cognitions, Scott (1969) gave a significant role to affect, although he dealt with affect only in terms of the broad classes of like–dislike or desirable–undesirable. He maintained that objects as conceived by persons have an affective attribute that is closely related to evaluative attributes but orthogonal to purely descriptive attributes. This suggests that his concept of natural cognition has some similarity to the notion of affective–cognitive orientation. He defined *affective balance* as a mode of integrating attributes so that objects (concepts, images) are grouped cognitively in a fashion consistent with their affective relevance to the individual. He concluded that affective balance is incompatible with the ambivalence toward objects that is found in schizophrenia and other types of maladjustment.

A study of the effects of positive and negative feedback on cognitive and affective responses provided further evidence for the notion that the emotion system and the cognitive system can function relatively independently (Swann, Griffin, Predmore, & Gaines, 1987). The investigators used a self-report measure to select subjects with a positive or negative self-concept. Each subject delivered a speech, with the understanding they would be observed through a one-way mirror and rated on the basis of their nonverbal communication. Five minutes after the speech the subject was shown either a positive or negative handwritten evaluation, prepared in advance. The evaluation focused on self-confidence and social competence.

After reading the evaluation, the subjects completed inventories that measured their cognitive reactions (e.g., perceived competence of the evaluator) and their emotional reactions (e.g., feelings of depression) to the feedback. With regard to cognitive reactions, subjects with positive self-concepts who received favorable feedback regarded it as accurate and the evaluator as competent. Subjects with negative self-concepts tended to react in the opposite way. They viewed unfavorable feedback as accurate. With regard to emotional reactions to the feedback, individuals with positive self-concepts as well as those with negative self-concepts were anxious and hostile after negative feedback.

A factor analysis of the measures of cognitive and affective reactions showed that the cognitive measures were closely related to one another but were relatively independent of the affective measures. Similarly, the affective measures were closely related to one another but were relatively independent of the cognitive measures.

The results of the Swann *et al.* study support the hypothesis that the emotions system and cognitive system perform different functions and can operate relatively independently (Epstein, 1983; Gazzaniga, 1989; Izard, 1984; Tomkins, 1962). For example, the emotions system enables the individual to react quickly on the basis of the raw data from the senses or after only gross, automatic perceptual processes have occurred. The cognitive system is then motivated to perform analytical, logical, and planning functions.

Stable Characteristics of Emotions That Have Implications for Consciousness

Several emotion theorists hold that emotion feeling states are invariant over time, meaning, for example, that the feeling of sadness is the same in the infant and the aged (Campos & Barrett, 1984; Emde, 1980; Izard & Malatesta, 1987). Some of these theorists also believe that some emotion is being experienced all the time. Because the principles of invariance and constancy of emotion feelings have significant implications for understanding consciousness, the arguments and evidence relating to them are presented below.

The Quality of an Emotion Feeling Never Changes

It is important to understand what is meant by the constancy of an emotion feeling. The idea that the quality of a particular emotion feeling does not change from infancy to old age may seem strange, but there are good reasons to believe it is so. When you observe that your feelings toward a certain person have changed, what you probably mean is that you now have different emotions in relation to that person. Perhaps an individual who once made you anxious now merely amuses you. This does not mean that the feeling associated with fear or enjoyment has changed; rather, you now have different emotions in relation to that person.

What evidence is there that the feeling of sadness in an infant is the same as the feeling of sadness in the infant's grandparent? First, it is important to remember that we speak here of the phenomenological component of the emotion, the feeling itself. The baby's sad feeling does not have the complex set of images and memories associated with it that the grandfather's feeling of sadness does. Associations between feelings and thoughts do change. They change remarkably with development and throughout life and for a variety of reasons, but the feeling of joy or sadness or anger remains the same. For example, one reason for believing an emotion feeling remains the same throughout life is that the full-blown prototypical expression of sadness in the infant is the same as it is for the adult (see Figure 9-1). The same muscles contract, causing the same basic configuration or pattern on the face. The only differences in the expressions of infants and adults are those associated with the greater plasticity of the infant's skin and the relatively larger amount of fatty deposits underneath it. The baby's face may bulge where the adult's will wrinkle, but the expression is the same. It must also be remembered that the adult may by choice or by force of circumstance inhibit the facial display of an emotion, whereas an infant has not yet acquired the skills to do so.

When babies express anger, they are behaving quite differently than when they show joy or sadness; when they show joy, they are behaving differently than when they show fear. There are specific action tendencies associated with particular emotions, and these action tendencies are also consistent over age. Thus the feeling of disgust, whether in a baby or an adult, leads to rejection of the undesirable object. The feeling of enjoyment leads to receptiveness and to approach, while the feeling of fear serves a protective function by motivating avoidance or escape from the threatening source. If the feelings associated with disgust, joy, and fear were fickle or inconsistent, you might make such drastic mistakes as consuming a poisonous substance or running in the direction of danger.

Other evidence that supports the notion of emotion feeling remaining constant throughout the life span relates to those characteristics of human beings that seem to have their roots in the emotions. People are capable of affiliative responses and social bonding. They are also capable of empathy and altruism. These characteristics, prized as part of the human heritage, are apparently mediated by emotion experiences that are not only invariant across the life span but have remained constant through evolution since the emergence of the species (Hoffman, 1981). When you see someone showing the unmistakable signs of distress or sadness, you are capable of sharing their experience vicariously, which in turn can give rise to altruistic behavior. Research has demonstrated that when children's attention is focused on the sadness of others, altruistic behavior is likely to follow. Therefore, it appears that the very important human qualities of empathy and altruism are mediated or sustained by emotion feelings that are constant over time.

Social bonding is an important human characteristic that seems to be a function of the emotions. There can no longer be any serious doubt that human beings are social by nature, and that without social relationships and some form of social organization we would become something other than human or cease to exist altogether. Drawing on the work of a number of behavioral scientists, such as John Bowlby, Mary Ainsworth, and Jerry Kagan, the anthropologist Melvin Konner argued that inborn social fears play a significant role in the development of attachment between mother and infant (Konner, 1982).

There are at least two other characteristics of human beings that are hard to account for without the principle of constancy of emotion feeling. One of these is the sense of self-continuity—the feeling that you are the same person yesterday, today, and tomorrow. As we grow up, our life is subject to constant change and flux. Human development itself is characterized by a series of dramatic changes: from baby to toddler, from toddler to child, from child to adolescent, from adolescent to adult, and from young adult to middle-aged and old adult. Yet through all of these changes, there remains a central core of your self that is constant. This core is emotional in nature. You know that the familiar face of a loved one gave you joy yesterday and in years past, that it gives you joy today, and that it will give you joy in the future. Likewise, the loss of a loved one will bring with it great sadness, and you know that the same feelings will occur whenever such a loss is suffered. The constancy of emotion feeling under the varying conditions that you must experience as you pass through life lends a sense of continuity to it all and helps you to develop a concept of self that is stable.

Always Emotion: We Are Never without Feeling

Three ideas have kept many people from accepting the notion of emotion being always present in consciousness, always influencing perception and behavior. One of these ideas is that emotions are episodic. This idea came from the early physiologists who focused their studies on episodes of strong negative emotion. Walter B. Cannon and his students studied rage and fear and spoke of emotions as emergency responses to extreme stress or challenge (Cannon, 1927), but emotions serve many functions other than organizing and guiding our behavior in emergencies. Interest sustains our efforts to learn and to develop new skills and competencies. Mild enjoyment provides reward for the little accomplishments we experience in daily life. Mild fear or even the anticipation of fear may help us avoid stressful or dangerous situations before an emergency arises.

The second idea that has kept people from accepting emotion as always present in consciousness is that if an emotion exists it must be possible, at least upon reflection, to label it as well as to talk about it. We can look to our own experience to decide whether this is true. Most people can probably remember occasions when they were aware of a feeling, an emotion, but were unable to label or describe it. Since Freud's early work, many clinical psychologists and psychiatrists as well as many personality theorists have agreed that much of the motivation for human behavior is unconscious. It may be that unconscious motivation can be explained as emotion feeling that we cannot label or as emotion feeling that is at a low level of intensity or outside the focus of our attention.

The third idea that has kept people from believing the mind is continually influenced by emotion is the notion that emotion is necessarily brief and intense. The focus on emotion responses to stress both in science and in popular writing contributes to the idea that emotions are brief and intense experiences. The fact that expressions of emotions are brief (lasting on the average approximately ½ to 4 or 5 seconds) also contributes to the perception of emotions themselves as being brief. However, emotion feelings far outlast emotion expressions. For example, a person may be depressed for a long period of time without exhibiting overt emotion expressions. Further, both positive and negative emotions vary in intensity from very mild to very strong. Your everyday experiences tell you that a minor affront when you are otherwise comfortable and content may only annoy you, but the same affront when you are tired and irritable may enrage you. Both the annoyance and the rage can be considered as points on a continuum—the anger continuum. Emotions vary along a continuum of intensity.

Feeling, Perceiving, and Knowing

So, emotion feelings are always with you, and those feelings play a very significant role in the way you perceive and interpret the world around you. It takes only a moment's reflection to realize that your perceptual system—the system that tells you what is going on within you and in the external world—does not operate by chance or in a random fashion. Whether you are sitting at home, in the garden, by a brook, in the park, or in a great metropolis, you do not see everything around you with equal clarity, nor do you look an equal amount of time at each of the objects or events in your surroundings. Any two people sitting in the same place for any length of time will attend to various things happening around them; if the two were asked to relate their experiences, their accounts might be sufficiently different as to raise a doubt that they were really in the same place at all.

An important reason why two people will see different things in the same situation is because they have different feelings, different interests. In the next chapter, we will take a careful look at the subtle and pervasive influence that the emotion of interest has on our lives. For the moment, let us emphasize that interest is a motivational condition and that it has a powerful influence in selecting what we perceive in the world and in focusing our attention, as well as in maintaining our attention during efforts to explore, learn, and understand.

Developmental Changes in Emotion Processes and the Operation of Consciousness

Even though the quality of a given emotion feeling is constant over the life span, its causes and consequences change as the individual develops and matures. For example, the activation of certain emotions is dependent on cognitive development. In the early months of life the infant does not clearly differentiate self from other. This is beautifully expressed in Tennyson's *In Memoriam* and Figure 3.1.

FIGURE 3-1. This 3-week-old girl has not yet developed a concept of self and perceives no boundary between herself and her mother.

The baby new to earth and sky
What time his tender palm is pressed
Against the circle of the breast,
Has never thought that "this is I?"
But as he grows he gathers much,
and learns the use of "I and me,"
And finds I am not what I see,
And other than the things I touch.

Emotions that are triggered by or dependent on self-consciousness or awareness of a separate self cannot be experienced in this stage of development. After the child can recognize and refer to her self, she can experience such emotions as shame (heightened self-consciousness, self-as-overexposed, -inept, -inadequate), contempt (self-as-superior), and guilt (self-as-blameworthy, in violation of internalized standards). As the self-concept becomes more extensive and complex, there is a concomitant increase in the variety of situations that can instigate the emotions related to self-awareness and the self-concept.

Causes and consequences of other emotions also vary with situation and circumstance. They vary with the time of day and with the individual's drive states. That is, causes and consequences of emotion depend to some extent on how hungry or tired or uncomfortable or sexy a person feels. They also vary dramatically from one culture to another and to some extent within a single culture. There is even variation from family to family and from individual to individual. There can be all of this variability in emotions and their activation because of the developmental changes in the individual and the pool of possible elicitors and responses for an emotion. In contrast, drive states are associated with a smaller and more fixed range of stimuli. For example, only a limited set of stimuli can elicit hunger or amplify the sex urge, and an even more limited range of objects can satisfy these needs.

Developmental Changes in Response to Emotion Feelings

Fear will probably send the young child running to the protective arms of a parent or older sibling. In the older child or adolescent, such behavior could bring about shame, which might be as difficult to live with as the fear. Consequently, he or she would seek other ways of dealing with the fear—trying harder to assess the extent of the danger, negotiating or maneuvering into a more advantageous position, or if all else fails, ignoring the threat or becoming emotionally removed from it. As a rule, younger children are more likely to try to escape from a situation by using their legs, while older children are more likely to talk their way out of it. During development an individual will learn many ways of responding to feelings of fear, yet they ultimately add up to the same type of response—reducing, avoiding, or escaping the perceived threat.

Another example of change in emotion-related responses can be seen in the behavior of children at play. Interest in toys will lead the 10-month-old to explore and manipulate them. At this age, experiencing the sensations that accompany the banging and throwing of toys is a great deal of fun. On the other hand, the 14-month-old might demonstrate what is called relational play—relating one toy to another, as when placing a toy spoon in a toy cup or putting a toy telephone on its receiver. The 3-year-old exposed to the same toys and responding to the same feelings of interest may make an imaginary phone call to father or mother, a playmate, or even an imaginary friend. Interest in toys can lead to banging or make-believe play, yet the underlying motivational feeling is the same. What is different is the individual's capacity to harness the interest at ever-increasing levels of organization and complexity. With increasing age, your responses to emotion feeling tend to become softer and more subtle. You are more likely to use words and subtle facial expression rather than hands and feet to express emotion. As you grow up, you are less likely to cry when you feel sad, less likely to turn your head and try to hide when you feel shy, and less likely to blush when you feel shame.

Developmental Changes in the Causes of Emotion

As with the changes that occur with development in response to emotion feeling, the elicitors of different emotions also change as the infant grows older. At 3 weeks of age, a high-pitched human voice will summon a smile, while in later life, an unchanging high-pitched voice might irritate or even make an infant angry. Mother's departing face may cause no particular response in a 3-month-old, but it may evoke angry protest in a 13-month-old. Depending upon the circumstances, the departure of both mother and father may bring joy to the teenager who wants to have her friends over. Thus the same event elicits different emotions depending upon the individual's age and maturity and the circumstances.

When Feelings Dominate Consciousness: A Critical Event in Adolescence

For many people, adolescence is a time in life when the influence of emotions on their mental life is most apparent. This was especially true for Michele, whose early teens were troubled by the departure of her father for the war in Vietnam. While a junior in college, she wrote the following account of that difficult time. Note how her feelings dominated her awareness and guided her behavior at critical moments in her life.

> I remember the day my father received his orders saying he had to go to Vietnam. I remember that day like it was yesterday.
>
> At first I was confused. I didn't understand exactly what was going to happen. My parents both tried to cover things up so I wouldn't worry. It worked for awhile but, as the time got closer for him to leave, I saw right through their "fronts."
>
> I can remember the day he left, waking up that morning and hearing my mother crying, not just ordinary crying but weeping that sounded like it could never stop. I remember taking my father to the airport. It was horrible. I felt like my whole world was falling apart around me. I wanted everything to be happy, to go back to the way it had been before he got his orders.

It is difficult to be certain from reading a summary of a complex and enduring emotional episode, but we are probably justified in assuming that in this passage Michele is describing her fear of the loss of her father. In view of her father's imminent departure for aerial combat duty in Vietnam, Michele's stating that she felt like her "whole world was falling apart" was equivalent to stating that she was terrified.

> I remember seeing the huge metallic B-66 airplane that was to take him away. It looked like I felt inside—cold, grey, empty, and alone. But I knew I had to be strong. My father and I had an agreement. He asked me if I would take care of my mother and sister while he was gone. He said I had to be happy for them. I had to be his "little ray of sunshine."
>
> I fought back the tears so bad that it hurt as we walked closer to the plane. I couldn't cry, no matter what. Everyone cried but me. Even my father had big tears in his eyes as he said his goodbyes.

Fear was certainly not the only emotion Michele experienced on her father's departure. Sadness was also strongly felt, though she consciously suppressed the expression of it.

> My sadness never completely went away. Instead it turned to anger and at times even to jealousy, like on Father's Day at school when I saw all the other children with their fathers.

Feelings changing from fear to sadness to anger might seem strange at first glance. We can understand the changes if we consider two aspects of the problem. First, none of the three emotions were really new to Michele. Quite understandably, she felt all three the day her father left for Vietnam—afraid that she and her mother and sister would not be able to cope and feel secure in her father's absence, an absence she knew might be permanent; sad at the separation and possible loss of her dearly loved father; and now, resentful and angry that her father had "abandoned" her.

After being unresponsive to her father when he telephoned from Vietnam, yet another emotion arose.

> When I got off the phone I felt incredibly guilty. How could I have been so selfish and cold? How could I even think of hating someone who was doing something so wonderful for his country? I wanted to pick up the phone and call him to apologize, but I knew that it wasn't possible. I wanted to make up for my behavior and for my hateful thoughts.

Michele felt guilt for resenting her father and for treating him coldly when he departed for Vietnam and when he called long distance. However, guilt, like all emotions, has adaptive functions. In this case, it helped heal the emotional wounds caused by separation and the angry resentment that followed. The feeling of guilt helped Michele realize that she really loved her father and cared for him deeply. Notice also that Michele's immediate impulse following her feelings of guilt was to right the wrong she felt she had committed. Eventually, the love rekindled and the guilt was resolved. The anger was redirected, and the sadness resurfaced from time to time. The fear remained.

> Sadness would come and go and there were even a few happy times, but the fear would never disappear completely. I was scared that he would die and never come back. Then what would I do?

Multiple emotions are common in complex life situations. This period of sadness and fear ended for Michele when her father returned safely from Vietnam.

> I was feeling very excited inside, and when I did eventually see him walking off the plane I froze. It was as if every bone and muscle in my body was paralyzed. The closer he came the more my heart began to race. I was oblivious to everything around except for the image of him. He hugged us all. I held on so tight I thought I'd never be able to let go. He was back! He was home! I could see him and hear him and touch him! I was overwhelmed with so many emotions at once that I thought I would burst. I couldn't fight back the tears any longer, and for the first time in 2 years I cried. I cried for myself, for my family, and especially for my father and the hell he had been through. It was finally over.

Michele was fortunate. Though severely troubled by strong negative emotions during the 2 years of her father's wartime absence, she had the personal resources and family support to aid her in resolving her difficult problem and to grow stronger in the process. Her story is a vivid demonstration of principles discussed earlier in this chapter—emotions are always present, influencing how you see the world and shaping what you think and do.

Summary

There is renewed and vigorous interest in the study of consciousness, a concept largely neglected in the first half of this century. Theoretical developments, changes in the current of belief, and advances in the methodologies and the technology of the behavioral sciences have brought the study of consciousness back into psychology. Although it is widely accepted that some "mind processes" operate in the preconscious, in the unconscious, or out of focal awareness, the concern here is with consciousness, its structures and operations. Modern concepts of consciousness began with James, who emphasized that consciousness is personal in nature, sensibly continuous, the source of self-identity, and highly selective with respect to what is processed.

Although it appears heuristically profitable to distinguish between consciousness as sensibility/awareness and the structures and operations of consciousness, few theorists and investigators have given this division much attention. Tart is at least a partial exception, since he postulates a basic awareness, a kind of self-awareness, and attention/awareness as phenomena that are distinguishable from structures or structure subsystems such as input processing, memory, and emotions.

Deikman also argues for a distinction between consciousness and its contents. He defines consciousness or awareness as the complementary aspect of the organized biosystem. Deikman notes that the great challenge for the investigators in this realm is to elucidate the processes whereby neurochemical events are transformed into perceptions, cognitions, and affects.

Singer and his colleagues, unlike Tart and Deikman, have extended the theorizing of James and Tomkins and developed rigorous empirical tests for their ideas. Their studies support the notion that consciousness can be considered an alternative stimulus field to externally derived sensory information and that it is possible to change the balance between internal (imagery, fantasy) and external sources of stimulation (information) by manipulating environmental input.

Sinnott argued for continuity between embryological development on the one hand and the development of consciousness, feeling, thought, and action on the other. He believes that all living organisms are characterized by a biological directedness that is experienced as desire and purpose. Thus basic consciousness is simply the felt or experienced electrochemical activities of the brain and body. In Sinnott's view consciousness includes not only directedness but the kind of involvement of the organism with the environment that comes from wants and desires, which Sinnott equates with emotions.

In differential emotions theory, the affects, primarily the fundamental emotions, constitute the basic structures of consciousness. The interactions of emotions with perception and cognition make possible an infinite variety of affective–cognitive structures and orientations that influence perception, thought, and action (input and output processing). It is argued that emotion can exist in consciousness independent of cognition and that this helps explain why a person may respond in terms of an emotion without cognizing it or labeling it as such. Experiencing anger and cognizing anger are different phenomena, although such emotion experiencing and related cognition are typically intertwined in affective–cognitive interactions. Although emotions are the most fundamental of the motivational phenomena, cognition can play a significant role in the activation and regulation of emotion processes.

The emotions play a critical role in the self-awareness and self-identity aspects of consciousness. For example, shame plays a role in the development of self-awareness and self-identity.

Differential emotions theory proposes that emotion is the most fundamental organization of sensation that has meaning or experiential/motivational significance. The basic sensory-cortical process that produces affect lays the groundwork for all other operations of consciousness. The affect that is most typically present in consciousness and active in perceptual selectivity and cognitive processes is the emotion of interest. Special states of consciousness characterized by certain combinations of interest and joy facilitate intuition, tacit knowing, and the receptive mode. Analytical-critical processes may involve interest in interaction with a negative emotion such as sadness. Altered states of consciousness result from a radical shift of interest and a breakdown of strong and early-learned affective–cognitive processing patterns. The theory holds that the basic quality of an emotion feeling is invariant and that some emotion is always present in consciousness, influencing perception, cognition, and action.

Suggested Readings

Bower, G. H., Gilligan, S. G., & Monteiro, K. P. (1981). Selectivity of learning caused by affective states. *The Journal of Experimental Psychology: General.*

Studies demonstrating the effects of emotions on memory.

Davidson, R. J., & Fox, N. A. (1982). Asymmetrical brain activity discriminates between positive and negative affective stimuli in human infants. *Science*, *218*, 1235–1237.

A study of the different contributions of the two brain hemispheres to emotion, particularly emotion information processing.

Ekman, P., Davidson, R. J., & Friesen, W. V. (1990). The Duchenne smile: Emotional expression and brain physiology II. *Journal of Personality and Social Psychology*, *58*(2), 342–353.

A study showing the relations of the morphology of the smile to subjective experience and differential activity of the two brain hemispheres.

Isen, A. M., & Means, B. (1983). The influence of positive affect on decision-making strategy. *Social Cognition*, *2*, 18–31.

An experimental demonstration of the influence of positive emotion on decision-making.

Pope, K. S., & Singer, J. L. (1978). Introduction: The flow of human experience. In K. S. Pope & J. L. Singer (Eds.), *The stream of consciousness: Scientific investigations into the flow of human experience* (pp. 1–6). New York: Plenum.

A contemporary description of the Jamesian concept of the stream of consciousness and an overview of relevant theory and research.

Singer, J. L. (1978). Experimental studies of daydreaming and the stream of thought. In K. S. Pope & J. L. Singer (Eds.), *The stream of consciousness: Scientific investigations into the flow of human experience* (pp. 187–223). New York: Plenum.

Techniques for studying daydreaming and imaginal processes and their relations to stimulus-independent thought and personality.

4

Interest–Excitement: Activation, Expression, and Experience

William James called attention to the fact that some kind of selection process constantly guides perception and attention and thus keeps the brain from treating with equal importance the multitude of stimuli that impinge upon our sensory receptors at all times (see Figure 4-1). "Accentuation and emphasis are present in every perception we have. We find it quite impossible to disperse our attention impartially over a number of impressions" (James, 1890, p. 163). James actually used the term *interest*, but not systematically and not, strictly speaking, as an explanatory concept. For example, he stated that "thought is always interested" and in explaining the different impressions that four individuals would bring home from a tour of Europe, he said: "Each has selected, out of the same mass of presented objects, those which suited his private *interest*. . ." (James, 1890, p. 165, italics added). It seems quite compatible with James's theorizing to recognize something like an innate emotion of interest that provides the motivational support for the mechanism that executes perceptual and attentional selectivity and brings order as well as excitement to the individual's world.

For example, Fantz concluded that the infant's "visual interest in those configurations which accompany social objects or in those which will later aid in object recognition and spacial orientation, is seen as a type of primitive knowledge of the environment which provides a foundation for the vast accumulation of knowledge through 'experience' " (Fantz, 1973, p. 628, italics added). Gibson (1969, 1970) reached a similar conclusion.

Charlesworth (1968) suggested that more attention to emotions and their facial expressions might facilitate the study of perceptual and cognitive development. He leaned toward acceptance of the notion that innate mechanisms such as those underlying surprise and interest may help explain adaptive functioning in early infancy. He proposed that further study of these mechanisms and the

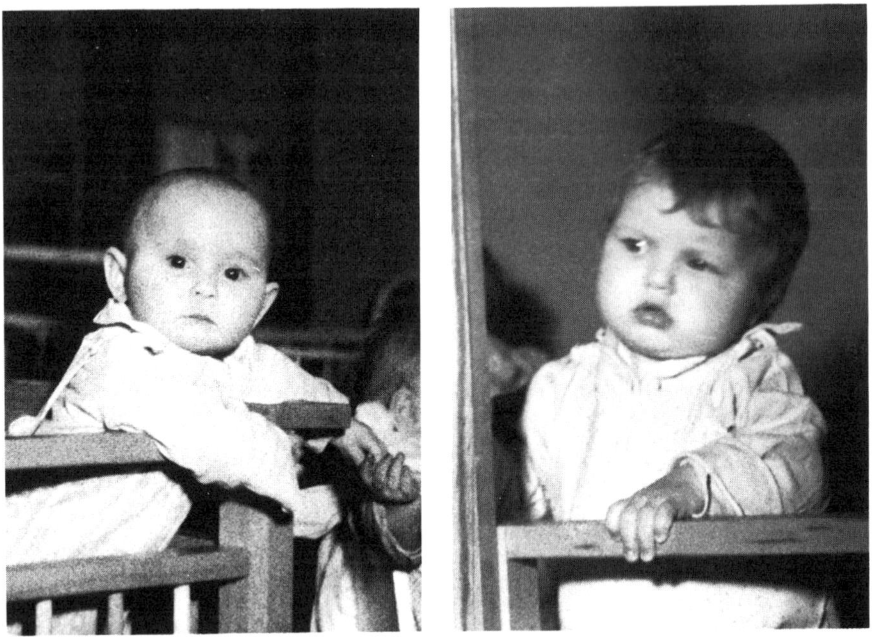

FIGURE 4-1. a. Russian infants attending selectively to the variety of sights and sounds in the environment.

preprogrammed behavior related to them should balance our study of the role of learning in the ontogenesis of cognition and action.

G. W. Allport (1955, 1961) maintained that human activities that lead to personal growth and creativity are accompanied by tension or excitement. "It is only through risk taking and variation that growth can occur. But risk taking and variation are fraught with new and often avoidable tensions which, however, we scorn to avoid" (1955, p. 6). Allport was describing human beings' penchant for investigatory and exploratory activity and his well-chosen illustrative material helped document his point that growth motives are characterized by a tension that sustains behavior directed toward distant and sometimes unattainable goals. His description of the key motivational condition involved in personal growth, exploration, and creative endeavor seems quite similar to the present conception of the emotion of interest–excitement.

In addition to the theoretical arguments for the continual presence of affect in ordinary states of consciousness, studies with affect and mood scales lend empirical support (Nowlis, 1965; Wessman & Ricks, 1966). In administering the Differential Emotions Scale to several large samples of high school and college students under instructions simply to rate their emotions and feelings at the present time, no individual ever failed to indicate the presence of one or more emotions, and interest was typically elevated (Izard, Dougherty, Bloxom, & Kotsch, 1974).

FIGURE 4-1. (cont.) b. Slightly knit brow and softly rounded mouth are also signals of interest.

Differential emotions theory assumes that interest is the most prevalent motivational condition for the day-to-day functioning of normal human beings. It is often in combination, and sometimes in conflict, with one or more of the other affects, and it continually interacts with perceptual-cognitive processes. Interest–cognition interactions that frequently recur form the affective–cognitive orientations or structures that characterize the constructive and creative activities of the healthy individual. To the extent that one is free of survival needs and negative emotions, one is free to act in relation to the positive motivational thrust of interest–excitement and interest-dominated affective–cognitive structures. Joy, the other positive emotion, plays only a secondary role in supporting constructive, creative endeavor (see Chapter 6).

Characteristics of the Emotion of Interest

Interest is the most frequently experienced positive emotion. It is an extremely important motivator in the development of skills, competencies, and intelligence. Interest is the only motivation that can sustain day-to-day work in a healthy fashion. It is essential for creativity.

The emotion of interest should not be confused with the orientation reflex. If a hungry infant's cheek is touched by the nipple it will reflexively orient the mouth toward the nipple. Auditory stimulation will activate orienting reactions in 1- to 5-day-old infants (Sameroff, 1971). In the visual system a bright object will usually cause an infant or adult to orient toward it. There are also involuntary orienting reflexes that operate for the senses of hearing and touch. These motor reflexes may subserve and support interest. Interest combined with these orienting reflexes "enables the individual to sustain attention to complex objects" (Tomkins, 1962, p. 338).

In the early weeks and months of life, the infant seems to have a built-in interest in the human face and voice. Infants as young as 2 months of age will gaze far longer at a human face, even that of a stranger, than they will at the artificial face of a store mannequin. That 2-month-olds look significantly longer at a mannequin than they do at an inanimate object with scrambled facial features further demonstrates the rudimentary interest value of the human face (Langsdorf, Izard, Rayias, & Hembree, 1983). So interest is something other than or more than attention.

In some cases the emotion of interest may initiate the orientation reflex, and the role of the orientation reflex, then, is to direct the head and eyes toward the object of interest. Interest is distinguishable from the orientation reflex since it can be activated by imagery and memory, both of which can occur without external stimulation. Further, shifting of the eyes away from the external object may be indicative of a high degree of interest in the object, since shifting away gives time for rehearsal and reflection on information about the object (Meskin & Singer, 1974). Finally, interest in ideas requires no particular orientation of the head in space.

Interest should not be confused with surprise or startle, although surprise also tends to give the individual the appearance of being grossly absorbed by the object and of rapid orientation toward the object for increased input from it.

The emotion of interest, like all of the fundamental emotions, is receptive to nonspecific amplification by the brain stem reticular activating system. It is very important in the understanding of interest (or any fundamental emotion) to see the emotion as separate and distinct from its amplification, and thus distinct from what is usually termed activation or arousal.

When the emotion of interest is using the visual system, the eyes tend to fixate on the object and quickly explore it. While the eyes are fixated the interested person is caught and fascinated. When the eyes are exploring, the individual is actively working to increase his or her knowledge of and experience with the object (Tomkins, 1962, p. 340). In principle, interest uses the other sensory systems in a similar fashion.

This selectiveness of perception and attention is by no means confined to infancy. It would be difficult to overestimate the pervasiveness of the effect of the emotion of interest. Consider the differences in what is seen and heard by two people sitting in the same spot in the park or following the same path through town and country. Interest literally determines the content of our minds and memories, for it plays such a large part in determining what it is we actually perceive, attend to, and remember.

One basic difference between the emotion of interest and the cognitive processes of attention and information processing can be understood in terms of our definition of an emotion. You may recall that every emotion involves physiological processes, expressive behavior, and a feeling. When you are intensely engaged in reading a book, conversing with someone you find attractive, or attending to an important meeting that affects your future, you may become aware of the feeling of interest–excitement. Perceptual and attentional processes related to objects or events that have no special meaning or emotional significance have a minimal feeling component. Indeed, when cognitive scientists attempt to study various aspects of perception in the laboratory, they often deliberately choose as stimuli geometric forms or isolated letters of the alphabet in order to minimize or preferably eliminate emotional feeling. The subject in such an experiment probably has to have some interest in what is going on to perform the task intelligently. But, in these cases, it is the experimenter and the experimental task as a whole that elicit the subject's interest in cooperating, not the stimuli as such.

The Activation of Interest

Although in one sense the causes of interest are virtually infinite in number, there are certain broad classes of activators or causes that can help us to understand how interest is activated or increased.

Change

When life gets a little dull or tedious as we follow our routines day after day, we often desire a change of scene. The change may not bring us to a new place. It may in fact be a return to an old and familiar place; but the net effect is that we change our surroundings, thereby changing the stimulation received by our sense organs. We may even get a new appreciation of a very familiar scene by visiting it at a different time than we normally do or when we have no responsibilities to perform. This kind of change allows for new levels and types of stimulation that activate interest. Change as an elicitor of interest carries over to two other causes of interest, animation and novelty, both of which are closely related to—if not a variation of—the concept of change.

Animation

As a cause of interest, animation helps account for why the infant of only a few weeks of age will show more interest in and attend longer to the human face than to the artificial face of a store mannequin (Langsdorf *et al.*, 1983). In the

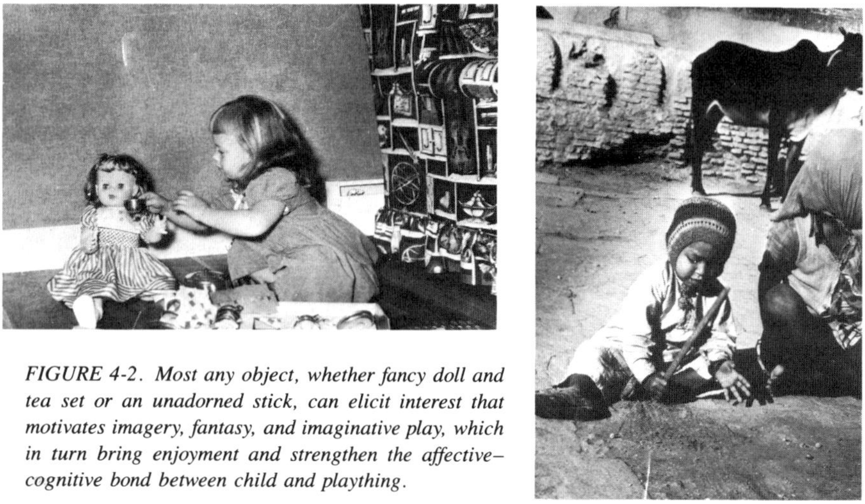

FIGURE 4-2. Most any object, whether fancy doll and tea set or an unadorned stick, can elicit interest that motivates imagery, fantasy, and imaginative play, which in turn bring enjoyment and strengthen the affective–cognitive bond between child and plaything.

Langsdorf *et al.* interest experiment, instructions were given to the person who exposed her face to the infant to remain as still as possible. Yet, despite her best efforts, there was slight animation—she moved her head slightly and, of course, blinked her eyes. There may be other less obvious aspects of the live human face that help account for its attractiveness to the infant, but the slight animation must be figured as part of the reason.

Some portion of the infant's interest in the human face and in the animated human form is undoubtedly determined in the genes. Some "social interest" is built into us; it is a part of human nature. It helps guarantee that we will form social bonds and that we will be social creatures. Sociobiologists (Wilson, 1979) have presented convincing evidence that human sociability and human social groups are essential parts of human nature. Social bonds and social interactions have been essential to our survival and to our evolution as human beings. They continue to be essential for normal human development and for the maintenance of health and psychological well-being (Harlow, 1971).

A very clever experiment showed that young infants preferred to watch biological movement (i.e., movement made by a human walking) over other types of movement (Fox & McDaniel, 1982). The investigators attached lights to the arms, legs, and body of a human being and then photographed the person's movements in a dark room. Thus, the film showed only the lights moving in the normal rhythm created by human movements. The investigators constructed a similar arrangement of lights that were moved by electromechanical forces rather than by biological ones. Although the amount and general direction of the movements were similar, infants of 4 to 6 months of age showed a very definite preference for the pattern of moving lights that was generated by human movement. Not only do we have built-in interest for the contours and animated activities of the human face, we are additionally "prewired" so that our interest is sparked by signs of human body movement. This is another indicator of our built-in social interest, the motivating force that guarantees our sociability.

Novelty

Novelty is also a very dependable cause of interest. Novelty is such a reliable elicitor of interest and such a powerful attraction to our senses that psychologists pair a familiar object with a novel one as a way of measuring the infant's ability to discriminate one object from another (Fagan, 1980). If we want to know if a baby can tell the difference between two faces, we begin by familiarizing the infant with one of the faces. We would do that by repeatedly presenting the face to the infant as a specified distance (about 45 centimeters) and for a specified period of time (about 10 to 20 seconds). We would present the face to the infant until the amount of time that the infant looked at the face for any given presentation was only half as long as on the initial presentation. Finally, we would present the infant with the familiar face alongside a novel face. If the infant looks longer at the novel face than at the familiar one, we can conclude that the infant has discriminated (detected a difference between) the faces.

The power of novelty to elicit interest can be illustrated by many examples from daily life. If you visit a part of the country to which you have never been, you are much more likely to experience a higher level of interest or excitement due to the stimulation of the surroundings. This is particularly true if the new region has a very different climate and topography. If the countryside near your home consists largely of plains or rolling hills, the Rocky Mountains would be a source of amazement and excitement. If the terrain around you is dry or desertlike and the vegetation meager, the Mississippi Delta and Louisiana Bayou country would excite you with many fascinating sights and sounds. If you are lucky enough to visit a foreign country that has a different language and a distinct culture, excitement and interest in the almost continuous bombardment of novel stimuli will keep interest high for a very long time. We can see this clearly in Jessica's account of her first trip abroad when she was a high school senior.

> My trip to France was full of unforgettable memories, especially from the first day, and I would not trade these memories for anything.

All emotions energize and help organize behavior. We can see in Jessica's account how intense interest or excitement provides energy and what appears to be patience for a task that might prove to be tedious were she in another mood.

> Upon arriving at JFK airport, a long and tiresome line awaited us at the baggage check counter. This situation might have exasperated other travelers, but not us.
>
> While waiting for our flight to be called, we posed for pictures and chatted excitedly about the adventures which lay before us. It was hard to believe that we would soon be boarding an airplane to France and leaving the United States. . .

High excitement can cause you to perceive the world around you in a qualitatively different way. It can lend an almost magical effect, as it did for Jessica.

> Landing at Charles de Gaulle and stepping off of the plane seemed like an unreal moment. I never thought I would ever really set foot in France. It was as if I was in a dream. We were hustled onto the bus that would transport us to our hotel in Paris. The bus was sparked with electric excitement as we waited to leave.

Interest enhances your ability to receive and process information from your environment. It is essential in facilitating exploring and learning. It put Jessica in a very receptive frame of mind.

> The hotel was located on one of Paris's side streets. Almost as soon as we were checked in, we were out the door and on our way to the Metro, the Parisian subway.
>
> We emerged from the underground passage onto a sunlit street full of people and peddlers. At the top of the hill sat the Sacre Coeur Cathedral in all its immaculate white glory. It was a truly breathtaking sight. Fascination filled me as we ran up the grand marble stairs, eager to see the interior.

On occasion, we wonder where we got the courage to try something new and perhaps risky. The answer in some cases is the emotion of interest–excitement. Sometimes a really exciting adventure calls for taking a chance in situations where failure would be frightening or embarrassing. Jessica's next episode in French culture and language shows interest winning out in an interest–fear interaction.

> Our next destination was the Latin Quarter located on the Left Bank of the Seine. We were set loose to do as we pleased. I was excited to try out my speaking ability in a store. I wanted to see if I could successfully handle a sales transaction in French. My friends and I browsed in few stores and tried on some clothing. I was afraid of saying the wrong thing, being embarrassed, insulting someone accidentally, and being laughed at. I built up my courage and asked to try on a pair of shoes. It was exhilarating yet frightening to speak the French language with its fluent natives; and, to my own surprise, I was able to pull it off rather well. To say the least, I was quite proud of myself.

In work or at play, in creative endeavors or in recreation, no one can stand indefinitely the rapid pace motivated by high excitement. The feeling of having experienced or learned a great deal, or the feeling of having accomplished something especially worthwhile often leads to relief, contentment, or joy. This was the case at the end of Jessica's first long day in Paris.

> Before we knew it, the time had arrived to meet the rest of our travelling buddies and head back to the hotel. It had been a very long and exciting day for us all. I could not believe that this was only the first of eleven days in France; and although I was exhausted, I was anxiously anticipating the adventures in the days ahead.

What a wonderful and inspiring day for Jessica! Although exhausting, it left her happy and eagerly anticipating tomorrow. She said she was "anxiously anticipating" the coming adventures, but she was very probably experiencing excitement rather than fear. In this case, it is most likely explained as a matter of syntax—many people use the word "anxious" when they really mean "eager."

However, if she did feel anxiety, it was presumably only to the extent that she felt a combination of excitement for adventure and a little apprehension or fear of the unknown.

Before leaving the topic of novelty, we should note that under some circumstances extreme novelty may elicit fear or some other negative emotion, as in Jessica's first experience speaking French in Paris. For now, let us say that we are not exactly certain what it is about extreme novelty that elicits fear. Perhaps using another term—"strangeness"—would be a better way to consider these cases.

Imagery and Thought

The newborn infant is so responsive to the human face and voice that it is easy to believe that she comes into the world with mental images of maternal sounds and sights. This might not be true, but it is certainly true that the child is born with a brain finely tuned for the reception of communicative signals from her mother. By the time the infant is 4 months of age, she shows signs of distinguishing mother's face (assuming mother is the primary caregiver) from that of others and may show some negative emotion if play with mother is interrupted by her departure. At some point between 4 and approximately 8 months of age, the infant develops an ability to form and keep in mind an image of mother's face. By 7 to 9 months of age, departure of the mother often elicits negative emotions in her (Ainsworth *et al.*, 1978; Shiller *et al.*, 1986). At 12 to 14 months of age, 75% or more of infants display strong negative emotion when mother leaves them alone. One way of explaining this strong negative response to separation is in terms of the toddler's cognitive ability to recognize the absence of the mother and to miss her. Although mother is gone, the infant can still evoke a mental image of her. While mother is absent, the child cannot look around and find a match for the image that she now holds in mind. She can remember mother and is disturbed that she cannot find her.

Although the infant may have no mental images at birth and relatively few in the first half-year of life, by approximately 8 months of age the infant can demonstrate her ability to form an image of an object and to remember it for at least a short time. From this point onward, the development of mental images proceeds at a rapid rate.

If, as an adult, you close your eyes, you can evoke innumerable mental images. If you recall the image of a loved one who is far away, you are very likely to feel some emotion; perhaps joy that you are having a mental meeting of sorts with someone you love. Then perhaps you will feel sad as you realize he or she is still a great distance from you. If you continue to play with the image for a long period of time, it is possible to run the gamut of emotions that you have felt in your relations with this person. Thus, the images you can recall are an almost limitless source of emotions; interest will invariably be one of them, as it is so vital to the thought process and imagination.

Words and ideas are another vast source of emotion. Words and ideas associated with mental or physical adventure, with novelty, and with change are those that excite our interest.

The Expression of Interest

In the experiment in which we placed babies in a comfortable seat and then pulled a curtain to expose either a live human face, a mannequin, or an inanimate object with scrambled facial features, we measured the infants' facial expressions of interest.

Izard (1979) developed an objective system for coding facial movements that signal the basic emotions. He began by studying the anatomy of the face and determining precisely what facial muscles move in order to make a particular expression or component of an expression. He then determined what expression changes, called "appearance changes," were involved in each of the universal expressions of emotion. He assigned each of these appearance changes a code number. To analyze expressions, trained coders watch one region of the face (brow, eye/nose/cheek, and mouth) at a time to determine onset and offset of each appearance change. Once all of the appearance changes of the face in response to a particular stimulus or interaction have been recorded, it is then possible to examine them, determining by means of established formulas exactly what emotions have been expressed facially. For most of the fundamental emotions, the full expression will involve one or more appearance changes in each of the three regions of the face. For a number of reasons, adults are more guarded in displaying facial expressions of emotion and often minimize them. In later life, a single change in only one region of the face may indicate the presence of a particular emotion.

The interest expression is a bit different from the expressions of some of the other emotions. From the very beginning of life, interest may be signalled by a movement in one region of the face—lifted brows, brows drawn medially (together but neither raised nor sharply lowered), visual tracking, softly opened mouth, or pursed lips. Any of these movements either on their own or in any combination may signal interest.

It is important to note that the expressions are generally brief. They may last from ½ a second to 4 or 5 seconds or longer. The neural activity and the feeling of the emotion may last much longer. Thus a person may continue to maintain interest without showing any of the facial expressive signals of interest; however, if the person does not display any of these signals for an extended period of time, it is reasonable to infer that interest has decreased.

When judging facial expressions of interest, it is also important to attend to the tone of the facial muscles. It has been hypothesized that even when an expressive movement is not visible to the naked eye, some tension or muscle tone would be detectable through physiological measurement. Studies in which electrodes are placed on certain expressive facial muscles suggest that there is such a thing as covert expression. This type of physiological measurement is known as electromyography or EMG. We shall discuss later and in more detail what is to be learned about the emotions from EMG and other physiological measures.

Physiological Changes Accompanying Interest

In the experiment in which baby's face was videotaped while viewing a human face or facelike objects, we recorded its heart rate using electrodes attached to the infant's body and connected to a polygraph. Our studies indicated that when the curtain was pulled and the infant saw the stimulus, the polygraph showed that the infant was experiencing bradycardia, a slowing of the heart beat. Bradycardia, or heart rate deceleration, was greatest when the infant saw a live human face and least when it saw an inanimate object with scrambled facial features. You may recall that the results for facial indicators of interest were just the reverse. There was greatest interest expression in response to the human face and least to the inanimate object. Thus when a person or object comes into the visual field and activates interest, there is one definite bodily change—slowing of the heart.

In psychophysiological research, heart rate deceleration has also been associated with the orienting reflex—turning toward a new stimulus. It may be that the orienting response and bradycardia comprise only the initial phase of interest activation. In any case, a few seconds following interest activation, the infant's heart rate returns to normal and may even accelerate. Prolonged and intense interest–excitement may be accompanied by some heart rate acceleration.

A study of cardiac activity during expression of emotion replicated the finding of heart rate deceleration in interest (Cohen, Izard, & Simons, 1986). Facial expressions were videotaped and later identified by an objective coding system (Izard, 1979), and heart rate was recorded by polygraph interfaced to a computer. The contrasting cardiac activity for interest and anger in 4½ month-old infants is shown in Figure 4-3. The results show heart rate deceleration following the onset of interest expression and heart rate acceleration following the onset of anger.

There is evidence that the left and right hemispheres of the brain respond differently to positive and negative emotion. Studies measuring brain waves (EEG) of 10-month-old infants in response to positive and negative facial expressions show that activity in the right hemisphere is more likely to be involved in mediating negative emotion and the right hemisphere positive emotion. These investigations have led to the hypothesis that the left hemisphere, associated with verbal and logical reasoning, is more involved during the emotion of interest than is the right hemisphere (Fox & Davidson, 1984).

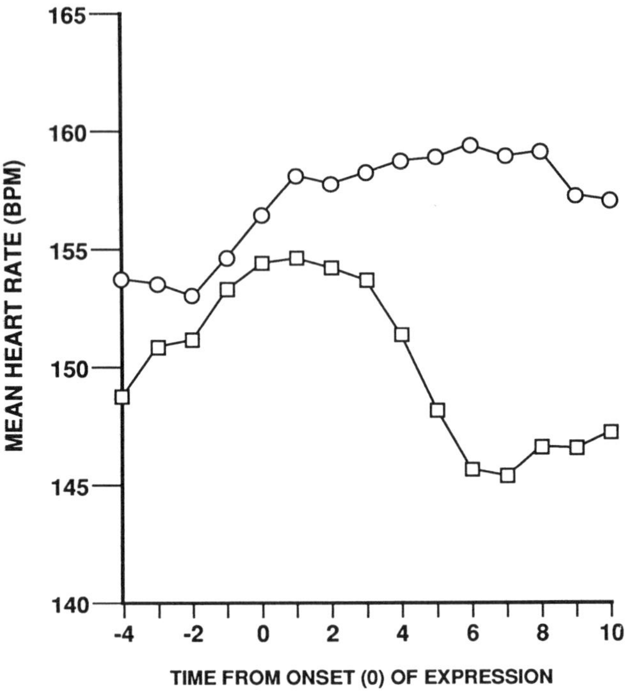

FIGURE 4-3. Cardiac activity during expressions of interest (□) and anger (○) in 4½-month-old infants.

The Subjective Experience of Interest–Excitement

At the experiential level, interest–excitement is the feeling of being engaged, caught up, fascinated, or curious. There is a feeling of wanting to investigate, become involved, or expand the self by incorporating new information and having new experiences with the person or object that has stimulated the interest. In intense interest or excitement the person feels animated and enlivened. It is this enlivenment that guarantees the association between interest and cognitive or motor activity. Even when relatively immobile the interested or excited person has the feeling of being "alive and active."

Two Approaches to the Study of Subjective Experience

The dimensional approach to the study of subjective experience requires the individual to rate his or her feelings on a number of general scales on which affective states vary quantitatively. Affective states are differentiated by analysis of the pattern of scores on the relevant dimensions. The discrete emotions approach relies on emotion-specific self-report. The theory and research underlying these two approaches has been detailed elsewhere (Bartlett & Izard, 1972; Izard, 1971), so a brief summary will suffice here.

The Dimensional Approach and a Dimensional Rating Scale. The dimensional approach to the description of feelings has roots in Spencer's concept of a pleasantness–unpleasantness (P–U) continuum and in his early enunciation of the concepts of activation and adaptation level (Spencer, 1890). In an extension of this line of thinking, Wundt (1896) proposed that emotion experience varied along the dimensions of pleasantness–unpleasantness, excitement–quiet, tension–relaxation. Woodworth (1938) modified the meaning of these dimensions when he concluded that "pleasantness and unpleasantness correspond to the attitudes of acceptance and rejection, excitement and depression to the momentary level of muscular activity or readiness for activity, tension and relaxation to the degree of muscular tension" (p. 241). Woodworth's concept of emotion experience as a function of attitudinal and neuromuscular processes anticipated elements of both cognitive theory and differential emotions theory. The Spencer–Wundt–Woodworth tradition has a number of other contemporary offshoots. Duffy (1941, 1957, 1962) and Lindsley (1951, 1957) used a concept of neurophysiological activation in an attempt to explain emotion and behavior in general (Schlosberg, 1941, 1952, 1954). Triandis and Lambert (1958), Frijda (1970), Frijda and Phillipszoon (1963), and Abelson and Sermat (1962) delineated dimensions of facial expression and considered these as dimensions of emotion. Osgood (1966, 1969), Block (1957), Davitz (1970), and Nowlis (1970) developed dimensions of verbal expression and treated them as indexes of emotion or emotion expression.

In the Bartlett–Izard study of the subjective experience of fundamental emotion, the investigators assumed that the assessment of subjective experience in terms of dimensions was a complex process in which the essential measurement technique, self-report, reflects aspects of feeling, cognition, and behavior. For this reason, each general scale on their Dimensional Rating Scale (DRS) was represented by three subscales, one for each of these three levels of functioning. The instructions defined the feeling level as bodily cues, such as breathing, heart rate, respiration, and muscle tension. The behavior level was defined as primarily facial–postural expression. The thought-level subscale permitted a subject to evaluate the way in which he or she was cognitively appraising (Arnold, 1960a, 1968) the emotion situation. The intention was to give additional specificity to the dimension as well as flexibility to the communicator. The DRS is presented in Table 4-1.

Dimensions were selected on the basis of their apparent salience for assessing subjective experience in a specifically defined emotion situation. Since the results of the study showed that most of the information from the DRS was represented by four of the eight dimensions, only these will be considered here. The rationale for selecting these dimensions for the DRS was as follows.

Pleasantness was unequivocally the first dimension to be chosen because of

TABLE 4-1
Dimensional Rating Scale (DRS)

Directions: A number of questions are given below that ask people to describe themselves. As you recall and visualize the emotion situation, please try to answer each question by taking a moment to evaluate thought patterns, behavior (e.g., facial expressions) and inner bodily feelings (e.g., breathing, heart rate, perspiration, muscle tone, etc.). Give your answer by circling the appropriate number to the right of each question.

There are no right or wrong answers. Do not spend too much time on any one question.

	Not at all		Moderately		Extremely		
1.							
a. How active do you feel?	0	1	2	3	4	5	6
b. How active are your thoughts?	0	1	2	3	4	5	6
c. How active is your behavior?	0	1	2	3	4	5	6
2.							
a. How deliberate do you feel?	0	1	2	3	4	5	6
b. How deliberate are your thoughts?	0	1	2	3	4	5	6
c. How deliberate is your behavior?	0	1	2	3	4	5	6
3.							
a. How tense do you feel?	0	1	2	3	4	5	6
b. How tense are your thoughts?	0	1	2	3	4	5	6
c. How tense is your behavior?	0	1	2	3	4	5	6
4.							
a. How impulsive do you feel?	0	1	2	3	4	5	6
b. How impulsive are your thoughts?	0	1	2	3	4	5	6
c. How impulsive is your behavior?	0	1	2	3	4	5	6
5.							
a. How controlled do you feel?	0	1	2	3	4	5	6
b. How controlled are your thoughts?	0	1	2	3	4	5	6
c. How controlled is your behavior?	0	1	2	3	4	5	6
6.							
a. How self-assured do you feel?	0	1	2	3	4	5	6
b. How self-assured are your thoughts?	0	1	2	3	4	5	6
c. How self-assured is your behavior?	0	1	2	3	4	5	6
7.							
a. How extraverted do you feel?	0	1	2	3	4	5	6
b. How extraverted are your thoughts?	0	1	2	3	4	5	6
c. How extraverted is your behavior?	0	1	2	3	4	5	6
8.							
a. How pleasant do you feel?	0	1	2	3	4	5	6
b. How pleasant are your thoughts?	0	1	2	3	4	5	6
c. How pleasant is your behavior?	0	1	2	3	4	5	6

its wide empirical support and obvious salience for assessing the hedonic tone of subjective experience. Tension was chosen as a dimension to represent neurophysiological activation, which has both theoretical and empirical support as an amplifier of emotion. The tension dimension was thought to relate to activation and to reflect phenomena such as increased muscle tone and inhibition in the expression of emotion semantically and behaviorally. The hedonic and activation dimensions were expected to be the necessary but not sufficient dimensions for distinguishing between discrete emotion experiences.

Following Osgood's (1966) suggestion, the dimension of impulsiveness was selected. The degree of reported impulsiveness communicated a lack of anticipation or preparedness for the given emotion situation. The impulsiveness scale also carries the connotation of spontaneity, which characterizes the suddenness with which an emotion is experienced. Spontaneity also implies a personal mode of expression.

The final dimension was the positive pole of Frijda's (1970) self-assured–insecure dimension. The self-assurance dimension enables a person to communicate feelings of competence and adequacy. On the cognitive level one can report the degree to which one understands the dynamics of the emotion-eliciting situation. At the behavioral level one can report the degree to which one thinks one's actions are appropriate for the emotion situation.

The Discrete Emotions Approach and the Differential Emotions Scale. Differential emotions theory provides the rationale for the measurement of subjective experience in terms of discrete emotions, affects, and affective– cognitive structures. In particular, this position maintains that the fundamental emotions and certain other affective states are qualitatively distinct and differentiable by self-report in terms of affect-specific descriptors. An earlier work (Izard, 1972) presented a number of studies with early versions of the Differential Emotions Scale (DES), and the DES Manual (Izard *et al.*, 1974) reported studies of its reliability, validity, and standardization. In brief, each of ten fundamental emotions and eight other affects or affective–cognitive structures are represented by three substantive items on 5-point scales. The item content and psychometric data for the emotion scales are presented in Table 4.2 The state form of the DES asks the subjects how they feel at the present time. The trait form asks how often they experience the emotions in daily life.

The Bartlett–Izard DES–DRS Study

The 229 subjects who participated in this study were volunteers from the Vanderbilt University classes in general psychology. This population of subjects had an approximately uniform socioeconomic status, intelligence, and level of academic achievement.

Each subject received a packet containing a statement of purpose, formal instructions, and eight sets of the DES and DRS (stapled together), one for each of eight discrete emotion situations. The procedures was as follows:

1. The subjects were given the name of a fundamental emotion and were asked to recall a situation or event in their lives in which that emotion was strongly experienced.
2. They were asked to give a brief description of the event.

TABLE 4-2
Differential Emotions Scale

	Factor	Item	Item–factor[a] correlation
I.	Interest	Attentive	.88
	(.76)	Concentrating	.79
		Alert	.87
II.	Enjoyment	Delighted	.81
	(.87)	Happy	.87
		Joyful	.86
III.	Surprise	Surprise	.83
	(.75)	Amazed	.85
		Astonished	,87
IV.	Sadness	Downhearted	.86
	(.85)	Sad	.79
		Discouraged	.82
V.	Anger	Enraged	.74
	(.68)	Angry	.84
		Mad	.86
VI.	Disgust	Feeling of distaste	.86
	(.73)	Disgusted	.85
		Feeling of revulsion	.78
VII.	Contempt	Contemptuous	.89
	(.78)	Scornful	.90
		Disdainful	.84
VIII.	Fear	Scared	.88
	(.68)	Fearful	.90
		Afraid	.89
IX.	Shame/	Sheepish	.73
	shyness	Bashful	.87
	(.83)	Shy	.88
X.	Guilt	Repentant	.78
	(.77)	Guilty	.83
		Blameworthy	.80

[a]Item–factor correlations for "state" instructions, $N = 259$; test–retest reliabilities for "trait" instructions given in parentheses, $N = 63$.

3. They were asked to recall and visualize or imagine the event as vividly as possible while filling out the DES and DRS. The order of presenting the DES and DRS was randomized for each emotion situation.

The order in which the emotion situations were visualized was left to each subject's preference. However, since the completion of two or more situations at one sitting might attenuate the intensity with which the latter situations were recalled or experienced, subjects were asked to visualize and rate only one situation per day. They were requested to average at least three a week.

As analysis of variance of the DES and DRS showed that both instruments discriminated among the emotion situations. The DES and DRS profiles for interest will be considered here (the data on the other emotions will be discussed in subsequent chapters).

When a person visualizes a particular emotion situation, a pattern of emotions emerges, with the target emotion showing the highest mean and the means of other dynamically related emotions also elevated. The profile of emotions in the imagined interest situation, as measured by a modified DES, is presented in Figure 4-4. (The Bartlett–Izard study used a modified DES representing eight emotions on 6-point scales, score range 0–18, while the standard DES represents ten emotions by three 5-point scales, score range 3–15.) The profile of substantially elevated emotions consists of interest, joy, and surprise. No other emotion means were remarkably elevated. It is reasonable that, on the average, the positive

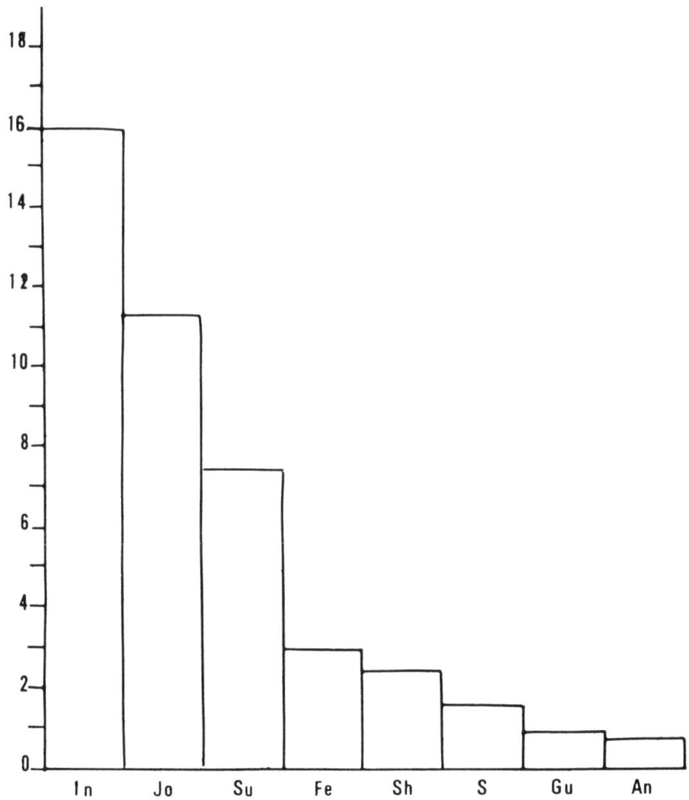

FIGURE 4-4. The profile of emotions in the interest situation, as measured by the modified Differential Emotions Scale (DES). N = 229; 113 females, 116 males. In, interest; Jo, joy; Su, surprise; Fe, fear; Sh, shyness; S, sadness; Gu, guilt; An, anger.

emotion of joy would be the second most prominent emotion in an interest-eliciting situation. If the second highest mean had been on the emotion of disgust, one would have grounds for suspecting the validity of the DES.

Results very similar to those shown in Figure 4-4 have been obtained in other studies using the standard DES. The profile for interest using the standard DES is presented in Figure 4-5. In this study (Izard, 1972), the positive emotions were elevated as in the Bartlett–Izard study, and none of the means for negative emotions were above 5.30, the level arbitrarily adopted as the intensity necessary for inclusion in the discussion of the emotion dynamics of a situation.

The results shown in Figure 4-6 describe subjective experience in an interest situation in terms of the general affective dimensions of the DRS. On the average, the individual in the interest situation experiences a positive hedonic tone, the pleasantness scale mean being the highest of the four dimensions. The individual experiences greater pleasantness in only two other emotion situations—those for joy and surprise. The fact that the interest situation is characterized by less pleasantness and more tension than the joy situation suggests that in the interest situation the individual is relatively more alert and prone to person–environment interactions. It was also found that self-assurance is lower in the interest situation than in the joy situation.

Summary

With his idea that perception and attention operate selectively, William James paved the way for the conception of interest as an emotion. It is easy to infer from James's writing that it is one's interest that guides perception and thought and focuses one's attention. Allport (1955, 1961) described the particular condition related to the human penchant for investigation and discovery that accompanies behavior directed toward distant or even unattainable goals. He came very close to the current conception of the emotion interest–excitement. In the past two decades, numerous studies have shown that selective attention operates in infants from the very beginning of life. One of these investigators (Charlesworth, 1968) suggested that more attention to emotions and their facial expressions might facilitate the study of perceptual and cognitive development.

Interest is assumed to be one of the innate fundamental emotions and the most prevalent of all emotions in normal, healthy human beings. It is assumed that some emotion is present in ordinary consciousness at all times, and that is the emotion of interest, together with interest–cognition structures and orientations that guide perception, cognition, and action much of the time. The only exceptions occur when high drive states (survival needs) or negative emotions dominate consciousness.

Tomkins suggested that at the neurological level interest is activated by an increase in the gradient of neural stimulation. At the conscious level, change and

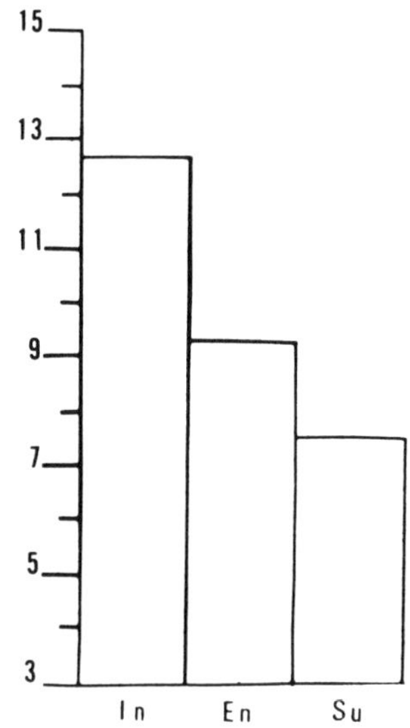

FIGURE 4-5. The profile of emotions in the interest situation, as measured by the standard DES. N = 44. In, interest; En, enjoyment; Su, surprise.

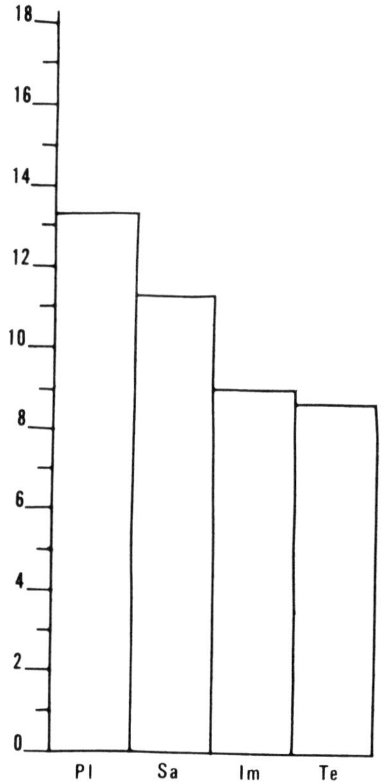

FIGURE 4-6. The Dimensional Rating Scale (DRS) profile of dimensions in the interest situation. Pl, pleasantness; Sa, self-assurance; Im, impulsiveness; Te, tension. (Adapted from Bartlett & Izard, 1972.)

novelty are the key determinants of interest. As activators of interest, change or novelty may relate to something outside the self, or they may emerge from imagery, memory, or thinking. When one is interested, one takes on the countenance of a person who is alert, of one who is looking and listening or attending intensely. One feels engaged, caught up, fascinated, curious; the phenomenology of interest is also characterized by a relatively high degree of pleasantness, self-assurance, and a moderate degree of impulsiveness and tension. Joy is often part of the pattern of emotions in an interest-eliciting situation.

Physiologically, the emotion of interest has been linked to bradycardia, or heart rate deceleration (Cohen *et al.*, 1986; Langsdorf *et al.*, 1983). There is also evidence that interest is mediated by the left hemisphere of the brain (Fox & Davidson, 1984).

Suggested Readings

Field, T. (1979). Visual and cardiac responses to animate and inanimate faces by young term and preterm infants. *Child Development*, *50*, 188–194.

Effects of prematurity on attentional and cardiac responses to human faces and facelike stimuli.

Langsdorf, P., Izard, C. E., Rayias, M., & Hembree, E. A. (1983). Interest expression, visual fixation, and heart rate changes in 2- to 8-month-old infants. *Developmental Psychology*, *19*(3), 375–386.

The effects of the human face and facelike stimuli on interest expression, attention, and heart rate in 2- to 8-month-old infants.

Renninger, K. A., & Wozniak, R. H. (1985). Effect of interest on attentional shift, recognition, and recall in young children. *Developmental Psychology*, *21*(4), 624–632.

A quasi-naturalistic study of children's interest in toys and the effects of interest on learning and memory.

Sigman, M., Cohen, S. E., Beckwich, L., & Parmalee, A. H. (1986). Infant attention in relation to intellectual abilities in childhood. *Developmental Psychology*, *22*(6), 788–792.

Effects of attentional responses in early infancy to measures of intelligence in later childhood.

5

Interest–Excitement: Development, Social Relations, and Personality

The significance of the emotion of interest–excitement in individual development, personality, and human relations can hardly be overestimated. This chapter will consider its significance in the evolutionary-biological and psychological realms.

Evolutionary Significance of the Emotion of Interest

Interest played an important role in the evolution of human beings. Although it is difficult to present hard data for this conclusion, the arguments seem quite convincing, especially if we accept the definition of interest that we have discussed. Hass (1970) argued:

> Among primitive men, this simple procedure [widening of eyes and head turning in appropriate direction] no doubt possessed importance as a signal to the young and to other members of the clan, who could deduce from it where the center of interest lay—a potentially important piece of information to those out hunting or in danger. If the clan leader, normally the most experienced individual, had noticed something, the ability to indicate its position silently might well be crucial in the next few moments. (p. 113)

Interest and the Evolution of Social Life

People obtain and remain in relationships with each other in large part because the human being holds greater interest for people than any other being, object, or situation. People are the most complex units in our world, and the emotion of interest thrives on complexity. People are the most changing and unpredictable aspects of our world, and as we discussed in Chapter 4, interest is activated and sustained by change and novelty. In nonhuman and human primates the activities described as play are initiated and sustained in large measure by interest, and play provides a vehicle for the formation and maintenance of social units (Jolly, 1966). It also keeps the young together and engaged in play and exploratory, venturesome activities while keeping the parents together maintaining watchful eyes.

Interest in the Support of Sustained Sexual Relationships and the Family Unit

Emotions and sex were discussed in Chapter 1, but in considering the evolutionary significance of interest, it should be noted again that interest plays an important part not only in heightening sexual pleasure but in the maintenance of a long-term sexual relationship. Sexual partners or the married couple who continue to interest each other as human beings are the ones who stay happily married and who still enjoy each other's presence after many years.

Interest and the Development of Competencies and Intelligence

This topic will be developed further when we consider emotions and creativity, but within the evolutionary perspective it is necessary to note that the emotion of interest keeps the individual engaged in an activity or skill until he or she becomes competent with it (see Figure 5-1). Competencies add up to funda mental intelligence. It is also interest that sustains a person's effort to differentiate

FIGURE 5-1. Interest sustains this young Nepalese boy's efforts to master the ancient wheel-and-stick game with only a crude circle of stiff wire and a twig for props.

and delineate the aspects of his or her world and that gives him or her the feeling of wanting to know and to experience.

The Functions of Interest

The Biological Functions of Interest

By all appearances, emotions seem to energize behavior. However, emotions do not create energy, for it is created in the body through the processes of ingestion, digestion, and metabolism. Because emotions organize and guide our energies, and because they create specific and recognizable action tendencies, we tend to think of them as energizing behavior.

An emotion's capacity to organize and direct energy is primarily a biological process. For example, some emotions direct more of our energy-bearing blood supply to the muscles of instrumental action than do others. In the study where we exposed faces to young infants, we learned that upon their first orienting response to the face or object, there was a significant decrease in heart rate. Even in adults, a shift of attention associated with gathering information from the environment is marked by bradycardia (Lacey & Lacey, 1970). The deceleration of the heart rate seems to create optimal conditions for reception of information through the external sensory organs. Thus, the heart rate decrease during activation of interest appears in infants to be part of a kind of quieting response. This physiological calming enables the infant to receive and to process information optimally, and then, to respond appropriately. Interest maintained at low to moderate levels organizes sufficient energy to sustain behavior over long periods of time. Long-term tasks or projects must maintain our interest if we are to pursue them effectively and without arousing negative emotions.

The Motivational Functions of Interest

Each emotion has two types of motivational functions. The first type relates to internal processes that motivate an individual in a given direction or toward a specific goal. The second type is social motivation, the process whereby an individual's emotion expression motivates behavior in the observing or interacting person. We shall examine the first type of motivation here and the second in our discussion of the social functions of interest.

The baby's gazing at the mother's face, his looking and listening to the sights and sounds in the environment, the toddler's movements toward parents or objects, the child's transactions with all aspects of the environment are all motivated in large part by the emotion of interest. The young child's seemingly ceaseless efforts to explore the environment, manipulate objects, and master increasingly complex transactions with objects is convincing testimony to the power of interest. Favorite toys or games often sustain interest at such a high level that it masks underlying sensations of hunger or fatigue. When this occurs at mealtime, parental interruption of play for routine feeding may cause frustration and outbursts of negative emotion. Helping the child to wind down and beginning the meal with a playful interchange may help. When excitement over toys and games occurs at bedtime, we say that the child is "fighting sleep." In this case, too, if we can help the child relax by singing "rock-a-bye baby" or by turning going to bed into a quiet game, we might have more success.

Young children are not the only ones whose interest and excitement propels them through activities despite hunger and fatigue. Any one of us might get so caught up in our work that we go right through lunch without thinking of food. Excitement can even mask pain. Athletes might play for a long time, even until the end of the game, before realizing that they have sustained an injury. Mountain climbers become oblivious to all sorts of strong physiological needs or drive states in the last stretch to the peak. Great explorers become so captivated by the excitement of adventure and discovery as well as interest in the ultimate goal that they continue their quest despite weeks, months, even years of great hardship.

Exploration and Learning. Providing the child with the opportunity to pursue his or her interests in an environment rich in possibilities for exploration, manipulation, and learning presumably facilitates cognitive development and the development of important skills. Evidence from animal research suggests that the development of the brain itself may be influenced by the richness of the environment provided for the young of the species. Although infants are born with almost 90% of their brain cells in place, a great deal of brain growth and development remains to be completed. Indeed, most of the connections among the trillion or so brain cells are made *after* birth. Some researchers contend that the environment influences the formation of these connections. They hypothesize that some of these neural pathways develop as a function of learning, and that changes in these connections do not occur once they have been established. It is probable, then, that in motivating sustained sensory transactions with the environment, interest also functions to promote brain development.

Psychologists at Swarthmore and Bryn Mawr (Renninger & Wozniak, 1985) conducted a controlled experiment demonstrating the powerful role of interest in attention, learning, and memory. They began by determining, through naturalistic observation during play sessions, which two toys were of greatest interest to each child in a group of nursery school children. Interest was measured in terms of the amount of attention given to the various toys available to them. These "target objects" were then utilized in various tasks. In the first task, photographs of the target objects and other toys were arranged and presented to the child in such a way that the experimenters could measure the child's shifting attention among them. Results showed that the children shifted visual fixation to the given target object in the photographs more frequently than to the others. Thus, the shifts in attention were not determined solely by the physical characteristics of the toy, but also by the interest value of the object for the child.

The second experiment dealt with recognition memory. The investigators devised a game that required the child to remember which of a group of toys another child, Steve, had taken to a friend's house. The child was shown pictures of all of Steve's toys (one dozen) prior to the memory test. After the experimenter showed the twelve toys, she indicated to the child which six toys (this set always included one of the original target objects) Steve was taking on his visit to his friend's house. Later, the experimenter showed the photographs of the same six toys along with photographs of other toys the child had not seen. Results indicated that the child was more likely to recognize one of the toys if it was an item of high interest to him or her.

In the third experiment, the investigators examined the influence of interest upon the child's ability to recall what toys he or she had just seen. A task involving recall memory is more demanding than one requiring recognition memory, and makes for a more stringent test. It is easier to recognize what we have seen before than it is to recall it in its absence. For this experiment, the child watched the experimenter place several toys through the slot of a brightly colored box where they were hidden from view once inside. At the end of each trial, the experimenter would ask the child to recall what toys had been placed in the box. Although there was only one of the target objects in each set, the child demonstrated significantly better recall for the target object than for any of the other toys. The target object was always placed in the box fifth in a series of nine. Learning research has indicated that the best remembered item should be the last one, in this case, the ninth toy placed in the box. However, children remembered the target object equally well or better than the last item they saw. Considering all three of their experiments, the investigators concluded that a child's interest is strong and directed, and that an individual's interests are a reflection of the person's knowledge and value systems that he or she utilizes in organizing experience, memory, and action.

The Social Functions of Interest

We have said that each of the fundamental emotions has social functions. Interest is no exception. Adler (1964) believed that social interest was one of the principal driving forces of human behavior. Because we are essentially social beings and a degree of social organization and order is necessary for human welfare and civilization, some level of social interest is a characteristic of every human being. The social functions of the emotion of interest can be demonstrated when considering the role of interest in play and social communication.

Play. Virtually all higher forms of life engage in play. This is particularly true of the young. Play involving objects or toys may range from banging and dropping to rich fantasy and make-believe. Each type of play at the appropriate stage of development may be of critical importance. Psychologists Jerry and Dorothy Singer and their colleagues (Singer, 1979) have shown that fantasy or make-believe play can provide a very good index of the child's emotional and cognitive development.

It is believed that children who learn to deal with their negative emotions through fantasy or make-believe play are acquiring a useful and adaptive skill for later in life. Klinger (1971) concluded that people who have more experience with aggressive fantasy are less likely to engage in active aggressive behavior, while children and adults who have not dealt as much with anger and aggressiveness through fantasy and make-believe are more likely to express this through overt aggressive behavior.

Interest is the driving force in all types of play. Children play with the toys that peak their curiosity or fascinate them, and they play with other children who tend to make the game interesting. It is also true that children are not equally active in play. Some are born with higher activity levels and engage in as much exploration and manipulation of the environment as their motor development permits, while others are born with a lower activity level and require more external stimulation. Caregivers will need to spend more time with these children, engaging and interesting them. Failure to do so could seriously limit the child's ability to explore and learn about the physical world.

Interest Expression and Social Communication. The spontaneous expression of an emotion is a clear and poignant signal of one's internal state. Such expressions are never neutral and rarely go unnoticed. You will react in some way to the emotion signals of others with whom you are interacting, just as they will respond to your expressions. Emotion expressions play a large role in our communication with others.

Nowhere is the impact of emotion expression more clearly observed and its importance more clearly understood than in early infancy. It is especially evident in the social interactions between infant and mother, where an expression of interest indicates the infant is engaged with and attentive to the other. The ability of mother or caregiver to attract and hold the baby's attention is a sure sign of an alert infant. As the infant develops, it learns a great deal by watching the expressions of its parents and siblings. Thus, when faced with an ambiguous situation, the child can look to the facial signals of mother or father, whose interest expression will serve as a positive stimulus encouraging the child to become involved.

Researchers who have devoted a great deal of time to the study of gaze behavior have found that direct eye contact is almost always an indication of involvement, and under certain circumstances, it can indicate an intimate relationship (Argyle, 1972). Gaze behavior is often a function of the emotion of interest, although other emotions (e.g., anger accompanied by a stare) and drive states (e.g., sexual excitement) may be involved. In young infants and children, gaze behavior, and in particular, direct eye contact, is a pretty good indication of interest.

The Development and Socialization of Interest

Interest characterizes the infant's functioning from the beginning of life. Except when the infant is experiencing the discomfort of a strong drive state or a negative emotion, its looking, listening, vocalizing, and motor movements are motivated and guided by the emotion of interest. Interest also facilitates intersensory and sensorimotor coordination and skill development (B. White, 1975). Interest-motivated activities and interactions build the foundations for growth and development in all spheres, and their absence can result in gross developmental retardation (Dennis, 1960). Hunt (1965) has cited evidence to support the contention that lack of interactions that result in positive involvement of the infant produces apathy. He wrote, "Although hunger and thirst are of the essence for survival, opportunities for such informational interaction are very likely of the essence for *interest* in objects, persons, and places" (p. 234, italics added).

The infant's interest in the human face is connected to his ability to discriminate his mother from other people. Interest in mother's face also leads the infant to track it through space and to begin to learn something about distance and spatial relations between objects. Interest in space and movement is necessary for the infant to learn to walk. For the infant to learn to deal with objects, his interest must support his efforts to learn about forms and spatial relations among objects. To judge distance he must be interested in the size and brightness of objects. What seems in adulthood to be an automatic perceptual process is actually the product of perceptual learning originally motivated and sustained by an interest in adapting

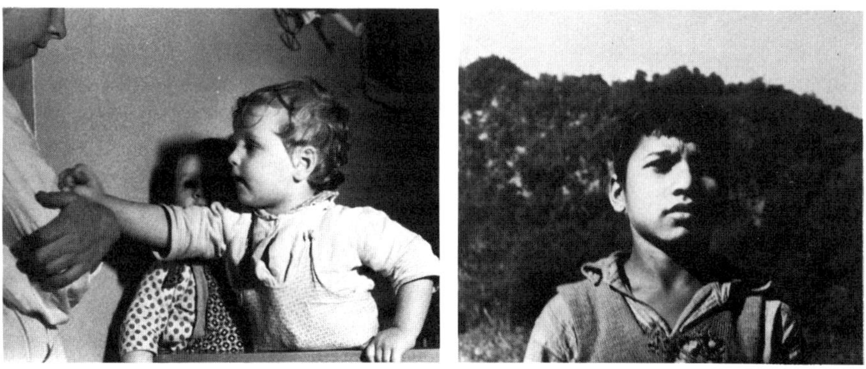

FIGURE 5-2. A partially hidden object elicits heightened interest (and action) from Russian toddlers (left), and movement in the brush captivates a teenager in the hill country of northern India (right).

and exploring. As Huxley (1954) suggested, sense data are only gradually "subordinated to the concept" (p. 25).

The Development of Interest and Interest Interactions

Some of Piaget's notions about intellectual development and Hunt's ideas on the development of intrinsic motivation have some implications for the emotion–cognition interaction model, a model concerned with the development of the emotion of interest and the interactions of interest with perceptual, cognitive, and motor activity. Hunt (1965) gave a detailed description of the development of intrinsic motivation and compared some of his ideas with some of Piaget's observations.

Hunt divided the development of intrinsic motivation (motivation inherent in processing information) into three stages. Stage 1 is characterized by an innate responsiveness to change (incongruities) in ongoing input. At this stage the standard or norm by which new inputs become incongruous (and hence instigate processes that have motivational properties) is the ongoing input and, thus, exist outside the organism. Hunt agreed with Piaget's observation that the motivational basis for the responsiveness in stage 1 is comparable to the Russian concept of orienting reflexes. However, an orienting reflex can account only for the initial sensory contact with the object, and the concept of an innate interest affect can better account for the infant's continuing responsiveness. Further, the affective–cognitive model maintains that the infant is never merely responsive, as Hunt suggests, but is also an active participant in person–environment interactions. Even in the first 3 or 4 months of life, which Hunt claimed to be the period of responsiveness (stage 1), the innate emotion of interest generates perceptual and sensorimotor activities.

According to Hunt, the second stage (age 4 to 9 months) in the development of intrinsic motivation emerges when the infant begins acting to regain perceptual contact with various kinds of receptor input. As Piaget (1932/1952) observed, the infant now carries on activities "to make interesting spectacles last." Hunt deduced from this that in stage 2, spectacles are interesting because they have been encountered repeatedly. He developed the hypothesis that the effects of such "emerging recognitive familiarity is a basis for cathexis or emotional attachment" (p. 237). Hunt believes that during this stage of development, objects acquire their attractiveness through repeated encounters and become interesting because of their recognitive familiarity.

In terms of differential emotions theory what is being observed in this stage is the emergence of joy responses to one's own activity, and it is this interaction of interest and joy that sustains repetitive activity. Familiar persons, places, and objects are more a stimulus for joy than for interest–excitement. It is the interaction of interest with the joy derived from recognitive familiarity that supports efforts to obtain or regain perceptual contact with the familiar.

It is only in stage 3 (at about age 9 months), according to Hunt, that the infant becomes interested in things that are novel. This is not consistent with the affective–cognitive model, which sees novelty as an interest activator from the beginning of life; nor does it seem consistent with the previously reviewed studies that demonstrated the effects of novelty and complexity on infant perception and attention. Despite some differences between Hunt's formulation and the emotion–cognition interaction model, both agree on the importance of interest in novelty. Its impact on development in the last quarter of the first year of life and throughout the second was convincingly demonstrated by Hunt. He pointed out three developmental consequences of interest in novelty during this period. First, interest in novelty provides the motivation for "the shift of attention from spectacles and action schemas *per se* to objects and what objects do as the infant drops them, throws them, and manipulates them" (Hunt, 1965, pp. 248–249). An interest in the action schema of "letting go" (for the joy of it) changes from a seemingly passive dropping to an action schema that consists of intentional throwing and attention to the trajectory of the object and other subsequent events. Second, interest in the novel motivates "what Piaget calls 'discovery of new means through active experimentation' " (p. 250). Action schemas are no longer merely repetitive but are now modified to influence the environment in some new or different way. Third, the infant's interest in novelty motivates imitations of the actions, gestures, and vocalization that are so important in development and in socialization.

These ideas of Hunt are essentially congruent with the affective–cognitive model, except for the following differences. First, differential emotions theory postulates that the emotion of interest is innate and that novelty is an innate activator of interest. Second, developments like those summarized by Hunt have their beginnings in the neonate rather than in the 9-month-old infant.

The Socialization of Interest

Some of the important factors that influence the socialization of interest are very general and pervasive. Among these are socioeconomic conditions, the amount and variety of stimulation provided in the neighborhood, and the complexity of the family in terms of the occupations, hobbies, and other activities of its members. Poverty tends to restrict the variety of constructive activities available to individuals and thus to limit the possibilities for the development of strong and varied investments of interest. Poverty also leaves less time to pursue intellectual and artistic endeavors and other activities that are relatively free of drives.

Regardless of socioeconomic conditions, however, the happy infant, toddler, and growing child has a low threshold for interest–excitement, and a healthy interest affect can develop if parents permit and encourage play, exploration, and investigation. If the parents' preoccupation with their own needs or frustrations make them intolerant of the child's interest–motivated ventures, the child's curiosity and exploratory urges will be punished and hence inhibited.

Curious adventuresome parents are much more likely to nourish strong interest–cognition orientations in their children than are parents who are disturbed by change and novelty and prefer to live by established opinions and dogmas. Parents, by their actions and words, can either encourage or discourage the curiosity and exploratory activity of their children. Parents who are themselves open and receptive to new experiences are much more likely to transmit to children similar attitudes and to foster the development of a low threshold for interest-motivated constructive activities.

Giving a child freedom to play, to enjoy make-believe and fantasy, and to move freely from the real to the imaginary world has a strong and lasting influence (Singer, 1966). Such activities have a decisive effect upon the development of the child's capacity for excitement and interest. Even when socioeconomic or other cultural–familiar conditions restrict the variety of stimulation and the possibilities for novelty and change, the child with proper encouragement and help can find a never-ending variety of people, places, objects, and events in the make-believe worlds created by his or her own imagination. The work of Singer and his colleagues (Singer, 1973) and Klinger (1971) testifies to the importance of imaginative play and fantasy in the life of the growing child. The research of Smilansky (1968) suggests that certain types of deprived children may be deficient in imaginative play and make-believe and that such children may require special help in developing these important aspects of childhood.

The Development of Interest–Cognition Interactions

The discussion of the interactions of interest with perception and cognition should be considered as an extension of the preceding ideas on the early development and socialization of interest. Whether interest interacts with perceptual-cognitive processes and the action system to produce constructive, intellectual, artistic, or creative activities on the one hand or nonconstructive or psychopathological behavior on the other is in part a matter of how interest is experienced and socialized in the early years.

In discussing the psychological significance of interest, it was pointed out that interest is the primary motivational accompaniment and underpinning of perception, attention, and the cognitive processes. Even the very fundamental process of perceptual learning in the infant requires the sustaining motivation of interest.

Interest and Perceptual–Cognitive Development

Interest plays a significant role in the development of competencies and skills and in the development of intelligence. The relationship between interest and the development of cognitive functions has been aptly described by Tomkins (1962):

> Interest is not only a necessary support of perception but of the state of wakefulness. Indeed insomnia may be produced not only by disturbing negative affect but also by sustained intense excitement. Again, without interest the development of thinking and the conceptual apparatus would be seriously impaired, . . . The interrelationships between the affect of interest and the functions of thought and memory are so extensive that absence of the affective support of interest would jeopardize intellectual development no less than destruction of brain tissue. To think, as to engage in any other human activity, one must care, one must be excited, must be continually rewarded. There is no human competence which can be achieved in the absence of a sustaining interest. (p. 343)

In order for the infant to perceive any object, she must attend to it over a period of time. Almost any object is too complex for her to perceive instantaneously. It is necessary for her to attend to the various features of the object, yet she must perceive it as a whole; she must perceive its diversity as well as its unity. Her interest must hold her attention on a given feature until it has been grasped and then move her attention to another aspect of the object. Only sufficient interest can keep attention moving from one feature of the object to another long enough to see its diversity and unity, without destruction of attention by the multiplicity of other stimuli in the environment. Without this kind of focusing of interest on particular objects in the environment, the infant's attention might bounce around randomly to the great detriment of perceptual development. Tomkins (1962) has summarized the role of interest in perceptual development as follows:

> In order to shift from one perceptual perspective to another, from the perceptual to the motor orientation and back again, from both the perceptual and the motor to the conceptual level and back again, and from one memory to another, one must at the very least maintain a continuing interest in all of these varying transactions with what is the same object. Without such an underlying continuity of motivational support there could indeed be no creation of a single object with complex perspectives and with some unity in its variety. (p. 348)

In the discussion of the psychological significance of interest, it was pointed out that interest plays a highly significant role in an individual's cognitive development and intellectual functioning. A person's intellectual activity is guided and sustained by his interest. He cannot become immersed in a subject in which he has no interest. He can memorize facts out of fear of failure or to avoid the shame of defeat, but such learning will have limited life and limited value. For him to be imaginative and creative in a given field, he must have the kind of investment and involvement that only strong interest can sustain. If adventure into the depths of a subject becomes a way of life, sustained effort to go beyond existing knowledge will become an exciting adventure. The work of Singer (1966, 1973) suggests that it is the interaction of interest and joy that forms the motivational basis for the very origins of imaginative, creative endeavor.

Interest, Art, and Intellectual–Creative Activity

Interest also plays a significant part in the development of artistic and aesthetic activities. To become an artist, the individual from early childhood must develop strong interest in the requisite skills of artistry. For example, to be a ballerina, one must not simply have sufficient interest to learn the necessary skills and techniques, although this in itself requires a great deal of motivation and energy, but one must also have a keen appreciation of the human body and its capacities. One must have an intuitive appreciation for the role of the emotions and other affects in body movements. One's interest in the body and its capacity for rhythmical and patterned movements must lead to a continuing appreciation of kinesthesia and proprioception. Similar processes are involved in the development of a skilled secretary or a devoted scholar or scientist. Expanding on the pioneering ideas of Perry (1926, 1954), Schachtel (1959), and Tomkins (1962), Wessman and Ricks (1966) gave the following insightful description of the role of interest in aesthetic and intellectual activity.

> This is a feeling or experiential quality that is seldom violent, dramatic, or disruptive, but it attends every event or proceeding of any significance to the individual. It is an affective accompaniment of any degree of conscious awareness and attention. It is an affect that would seem a necessary part of any object-cathexis made by the individual—some "object" (thing, person, symbol, idea) has become affectively important to him or

FIGURE 5-3. Interest–excitement expressed gracefully and beautifully, with the entire body.

FIGURE 5-4. Interest facilitates work and creativity.

> sufficiently salient to occupy his attention and mental process. Interest will often appear prior to the arousal of other affects, and seems to be a constituent of any experience or thought important enough to be registered in conscious awareness. Its "purest" and most vivid state is found in completely absorbing and sustained intellectual or esthetic activity. When this affect is fully developed, experience becomes immediate and real, competing distractions and disruptions are suspended in the pursuit of some goal of complete understanding or participation. (p. 5)

In his discussion of the creative attitude, Maslow (1971) has given the emotion of interest a central role without conceptualizing it as such. He said

> . . . the creative person, in the inspirational phase of the creative furor, loses his past and his future and lives only in the moment. He is all there, totally immersed, fascinated and absorbed in the present, in the current situation, in the here and now, with the matter in hand. (p. 61)

This kind of total immersion, fascination, and absorption is precisely what follows from intense interest or excitement.

Maslow speaks of two phases of creativeness, primary and secondary. The primary phase is characterized by improvisation and high inspiration. In this phase the individual is undoubtedly motivated by intense interest or excitement. Secondary creativeness is the working out or the development of the original inspirations spawned in a moment of high excitement. The secondary phase requires a continued creative attitude but also a lot of discipline and plain hard work. Many

FIGURE 5-4. (cont.)

more people are capable of primary creativeness (the inspiration) than of primary plus secondary creativeness.

> Inspirations are a dime-a-dozen. The difference between the inspiration and the final product, for example, Tolstoy's *War and Peace*, is an awful lot of hard work, an awful lot of discipline, an awful lot of training, an awful lot of finger exercises and practices and rehearsals . . . and so on. (Maslow, 1971, p. 59)

If primary creativeness—the improvisational phase—is characterized by excitement, the secondary creativeness or the working out and development of the creation has to be characterized by a moderately high level of interest. The interest may fluctuate, but it must be strong and continuous enough to counteract fatigue and negative emotions. The plain hard work of developing the final product of creative endeavor inevitably results in periods of distress and fear—discouragement, dejection, loneliness, isolation—and in the weariness of fatigue and negative emotion states, the motivational power of sustained interest is essential to overcoming the hurdles to creativity.

Kierkegaard's (1844/1944) provocative and insightful analysis of anxiety is a precursor of the Tomkins–Izard idea of the relationship between interest–excitement, fear, and creative endeavor. Kierkegaard maintained that anxiety was the possibility of freedom, the result of man confronting choice of possibilities. Such possibilities involve unknowns, uncertainties, and, hence, anxiety. According to Kierkegaard, the more "possibility" one has, the more creativity one is capable of and the more likely one will experience fear or anxiety. In linking anxiety with freedom and creativity, Kierkegaard was laying the groundwork for differentiating the positive emotion of interest–excitement and the pattern of emotions called anxiety (Izard, 1972). He came very close to making the differentiation when he distinguished between fear, as the emotion that supports avoidance or retreat from the object, and anxiety, as the basis of an ambivalent relation to the object. This ambivalence is what Tomkins (1962) and Izard and Tomkins (1966) have described as an oscillation between fear and excitement. The fear may result from the unknown, uncertain qualities or possibilities in the object or choice; the excitement from the novelty and possibility as such and from investigatory activity that reduces the uncertainty and fear and permits interest to operate. Fear places limits on a person's thrust into the unknown; interest–excitement sustains the exploration.

Interest–Cognition Orientations

The interaction of innate individual differences in emotion thresholds and life circumstances leads to a great variety of interest–cognition structures and orientations. A person may become primarily interested in (oriented toward) objects (object oriented), ideas (intellectually oriented), or people (socially oriented), and within each of these broad orientations a person's interest and activities can take on many different forms. Further, on any of the possible interest–cognition orientations relating to objects or people, a person may superimpose one that makes him or her primarily a thinker or a "doer," or one that places more emphasis on affective experiencing than on thought and action.

Adler's (1964) concept of "social interest" or "social feeling" may be considered a type of interest–cognition orientation—one characterized by interest in human beings and their welfare. He wrote:

> The surface of the earth on which we live makes labour and the division of labour a necessity for humanity. Social feeling takes the imprint here of cooperative work for the benefit of others. The socially minded man can never doubt that every one is entitled to the reward of his labour, and that the exploitation of the lives and the toil of others cannot in any way further the welfare of humanity. (p. 58)

Adler thought that only people with an adequate endowment of social feelings could be expected to solve the great problems confronting human beings.

Spranger's (1928) types of value orientation and Jung's (1933) psychological functions or types of personality organization may be understood in terms of the differential investment of interest in different objects and types of activities. For example, a person in whom the thinking function is dominant is one who is excited by thinking; one in whom the feeling function is superior is a person who is interested mainly in affective experiences; a "doer" is one who is interested in action and excited by the results of her or her activities. The myriad individual variations in human personalities are created by the innate differences in emotion thresholds and capacities and the differential investment of all the affects, but the investment of interest–excitement is the crucial one for attracting and holding the individual to a particular way of life. In the poetic language of Tomkins (1962), "I am, above all, what excites me" (p. 347).

The Interaction of Interest with Other Emotions and Drives

Interest interacts with other emotions and drives. The interaction of interest with another emotion can create conflict, or it can bring about constructive results.

Interest and Pain

Consider the athlete who has injured himself but does not yet know it. If the sensations from the wound do not achieve awareness, no pain can be felt. Anyone so wholly immersed in a task or thought can achieve the same effect. In this way, one can even exercise some control over the intensity of pain (such control is not, however, a recommended substitute for medical intervention). Research has indicated that focusing attention away from the sensation of pain can dull the experience of it, though individuals will vary in their abilities to successfully channel and amplify their interest away from a source of aversive stimulation (Leventhal, 1982).

Interest and Joy

The interaction of interest and joy is most apparent in the play of young children. Indeed, these two emotions and their interaction account for much of the motivation in the play life of infants and children. Interest keeps a child at a game or at the task of mastering some skill associated with the game. Success at the game or mastery of the task leads to joy. Joy provides a relief, a period of rest from the vigorous activity motivated by interest. After the brief recovery period provided by the experience of joy, interest again rises and play reconvenes.

Even in later life, interest keeps us working at some task or toward some goal. Completing the task or attaining the goal is a source of enjoyment. The enjoyment slows us down for a moment, allowing some time in which to recover full energy and enabling us to gain a new perspective. Then, interest mounts and we are at it again.

Interest and Fear

As we have already mentioned, Kierkegaard (1944) described a conflict involving anxiety that can be interpreted as the interaction between interest and fear. Interest motivates us to surge ahead, to explore. But sometimes adventure and exploration bring us face to face with the strange and unknown. Strangeness can be frightening, and fear tends to motivate us to get away or escape. If, however, the adventure is sufficiently exciting, we will want to return, moving further toward our unknown destination. But again, the closer we get, the more we may feel overwhelmed, that we are getting in over our heads; this may drive us away once more. This oscillation between interest and fear, whether it characterizes the thought processes or physical adventures, probably occurs more often than is realized. It is also true that an ability to tolerate some fear is essential for life and growth.

The Regulation of Interest–Excitement

The question arises as to why anyone would need to regulate a positive emotion such as interest. Normally, the regulation of interest is not a concern, though there are times when interest may lead an individual down too many pathways at once. In such a case, there is a need to regulate interest, to focus it more sharply. Choices will present themselves, and they are best made when the individual considers how well his or her interests match his or her achievement values, abilities, and skills.

There are other occasions when interest may need to be regulated. These are times when what an individual is involved in is so consuming that it may become mentally and physically detrimental. In this case, emotion regulation is necessary and may be achieved through a variety of means, including relaxation, meditation, and temporary shift to a less challenging environment.

Interest–Excitement and Psychopathology

There is very little research dealing with the possible role of the emotion of interest in mental health problems. However, descriptions of certain disorders suggest that it may play a role in their affective symptomatology. Clinicians regularly describe depressed people as having lost interest—sexual interest, social interest, interest in life. Studies of depressed children and adults regularly reveal that the emotion of interest is seriously deficient during the periods of depression (Blumberg & Izard, 1985; Izard, 1972; Izard & Blumberg, 1985). This certainly corresponds to the fact that depressed individuals are often described as apathetic and listless, seemingly lacking in energy.

Clinical descriptions of people suffering from a manic disorder often indicate that their interest–excitement level is chronically high, to the point of being intense and overpowering. The idea that manics are euphoric and happy may be misleading. Manics are characteristically highly excited; their minds race out of control. They are sometimes highly creative during manic episodes; though usually, the excitement drives the mind and sometimes the body at uncontrollable and potentially dangerous speeds. They may not be experiencing euphoria or genuine enjoyment.

As noted in an earlier chapter, Zuckerman's (1979) definition of the sensation-seeking motive overlaps substantially with the concept of interest–excitement as an emotion. Zuckerman's treatment of the sensation-seeking motive differs from differential emotions theory in isolating the cortex as the sole site of the sensation-seeking motive and optimal level of arousal as its source. Despite this difference in definition at the neural level, much of Zuckerman's work continues to suggest similarities between the two concepts at the experiential level.

It is conceivable that extremely low or high levels of sensation seeking may represent pathological states (or thresholds) of interest–excitement. Zuckerman reviewed theory and evidence suggesting that high or low levels of sensation seeking are associated with various problems of adjustment. Brownfield (1966) and Kish (1970) used Zuckerman's sensation-seeking scale and showed that chronic schizophrenics tended to score lower than normals and certain other psychiatric groups. This was considered to be consistent with several theoretical formulations of schizophrenia that suggest that schizophrenics have difficulty screening out irrelevant stimuli and focusing attention. Thus, since they already suffer from a sensory overload, they would tend to avoid rather than seek stimulation. Differential emotions theory postulates that a properly functioning emotion of interest provides the screening of stimuli and focusing of attention that is lacking in schizophrenia.

Zuckerman also reviewed studies that suggest a relationship between sensation seeking and sociopathy. In one study, female delinquents and felons scored significantly higher on sensation-seeking scales than did a sample of psychiatric patients. Marshall and Izard (1972a) found that interest as measured on the Differential Emotions Scale was extremely low in both normal and psychotic depressives.

Interest and Personality Development

Although few systematic studies of relations between emotions and personality have been completed, existing research and theory demonstrate links between patterns of interest experience and the personality characteristics of sociability, shyness, and achievement motivation.

Interest and Achievement

Just as every teacher knows that the interested student learns more, the observant colleague, supervisor, or manager knows that people who are "ego involved" (interested) in their work are more productive. You don't have to be an artist or a scientist to experience the uplift of work that is engaging. In fact, any task, no matter how menial, can be seen in a larger context and thus be made more meaningful. If it is impossible to find anything interesting in a particular job, and the worker cannot find another, he may be able to invest interest in fellow workers or even to the larger purpose to which his job contributes.

Researchers in human motivation and personality point out that how we perform on a particular task is determined by the strength of our motivation for success, our values with respect to achievement, and the relevant skills and competency we bring to the job (McClelland, 1985). Examination of these factors in successful performance will demonstrate how each relates to the emotion of interest.

Motivation to Succeed. Emotion plays a vital role in motivation. A motive can be described as a thought–feeling bond or affective–cognitive structure, and there are as many kinds of motives as there are possible combinations of feelings and thoughts. The motivation for success or achievement must be measured in terms of the emotion of interest. The more a task interests you, the greater your motive for success in performing it.

Consider the components of your job, or what it takes to be a full-time student. What things interest you the most? The least? Do you regard the application of your personal skills and the meeting of demands imposed upon you as important, or do you care more about establishing relationships with your classmates or colleagues? You may or may not hold achievement and the struggle for success as a personal value.

Achievement Values. Emotions also play a significant role in the development of your value system. It is difficult to conceive of a value that does not relate to the holder's feelings. We value things about which we have feelings, and the stronger these feelings, the stronger the values.

How do we acquire achievement values? No one really knows in detail exactly how this occurs. We know that success and achievement values generally vary between cultures, though perhaps what really varies are the cultural concepts of what constitutes success or achievement. We know too that these standards of achievement vary greatly from community to community and even from family to family.

High-achievement-oriented parents do not necessarily pass on this value to their children, though they often do. If the child perceives the achievement and success of the parent(s) to be associated with excitement and enjoyment, then the ambition for high achievement is more likely to be passed along. However, if the child views success as achieved only through continual and aggravated struggling, overwhelmingly stressful conditions, or sacrifice of recreation and social life, he or she will less likely adopt the goals and lifestyle of the parents. A child may even rebel, seeking a radically different style of life, one not marked by the pursuit of "success." Thus, for a healthy regard for achievement to be passed along, the parents or role model must have a genuine interest in their endeavors, yet be able to keep their successes and failures in perspective so that this particular value does not overshadow all others.

Skills. There are many different kinds of skills. Manual laborers and craftsmen possess certain types, as do athletes, ministers, and politicians. So how does the emotion of interest relate to skills? It plays a large role in the acquisition and maintenance of skills.

The acquisition of a skill is determined by a complex combination of things:

talent, or ability, and interest. A high degree of skill in certain areas requires inborn aptitude; but no matter how much talent a person possesses, it must be honed through practice or fail to reach its maximum. Practice also serves to maintain a high level of performance.

Usually it is easy, at least in hindsight, to recognize a match between your abilities and interests. Listen to John Henry describe two of his hobbies.

> At one time I was interested in learning how to play the guitar. I knew I was not especially gifted musically, but I admired guitar playing very much and thought that practice would make my playing okay if not perfect. After buying a guitar and working at it for awhile, I felt that I was so inept that I lost interest in practicing, and that was the end of that avocation!
>
> In contrast, there was a time in the development of my tennis game when I thought that it had reached a plateau. I thought I would never get any better because I couldn't hit a successful approach shot, follow it to net, and volley effectively. But the excitement I experienced playing tennis kept me at the game; and with the help of some good coaching and quite a bit of practice, approach and volley became my favorite parts of the game.

It is good to recognize our limitations and even to change our goals, as John Henry did, when abilities and desires to not match. On the other hand, it pays not to give up too soon. One may only need a little coaching and a great deal of practice.

In summary, then, all the determinants of performance—motivation to succeed, achievement values, and skill—are all related in some way or another to the emotion of interest. People who work day after day at tasks that do not truly interest them are probably having to look beyond the task for ways of investing this vital human emotion. Those who find their daily duties or job interesting, even exciting from time to time, have a much greater chance of performing well and achieving related personal goals.

Summary

The emotion of interest has played a large role in the evolution of the human being, serving adaptive functions developed over the course of humankind's existence. The nature and development of human relationships has been shaped largely by the fascination the human race holds for itself—people are more interesting to people than anything else. Interest also plays a significant part in the attainment of sexual pleasure as well as in the maintenance of long-term sexual relationships. Interest also assists in the development of competencies and, thus, intelligence.

The emotion of interest can be invested in possibility and thus supports investigation, exploration, and constructive activity. It is a necessary support for perceptual and cognitive development, and it plays a powerful role in the processes of attention, learning, and memory.

Interest characterizes the infant's functioning from the beginning of life. It is the power of interest to focus and sustain attention that makes possible perceptual learning and cognitive development. Differential emotions theory postulates that novelty is an innate activator of interest and that interest-sustained development of perceptual-cognitive and motor activities begins in the neonate.

Although interest is innate, its socialization plays a great role in its development and hence in the shaping of the human personality. Socioeconomic conditions can effect the development of interest adversely, while tolerant and encouraging parents can nourish the development of this all-important emotion.

The interaction of an innate capacity for interest with forces of socialization determines the types of interest–cognition interactions and orientations that develop. Interest may be focused on anything, but of most importance for human welfare, it can be invested in intellectual, artistic, and other creative and constructive activities. A person may become primarily interested in objects, ideas, or people. An interest–cognition–action relationship may determine whether a person is primarily a thinker, a doer, or one who places more emphasis on affective experiencing.

Emotions regulate drives as well as other emotions, and the emotion of interest is perhaps the most important of all the emotions as a source of drive amplification.

Interest may be used either consciously or automatically to dull the sensation of pain by focusing attention elsewhere. Interest and joy working in tandem motivate all kinds of play and work. Interest and fear often interact, creating anxiety.

Interest–excitement gone awry can result in psychological problems and even psychopathology. During manic episodes, the level of interest the individual is experiencing typically skyrockets. Abnormally high or low levels of sensation seeking may represent pathological thresholds for interest–excitement that are associated with various problems of adjustment.

Interest is vitally involved in achievement. Motivation for success can be measured by the amount of interest involved. It also plays a vital role in the acquisition of skills, as interest motivates the necessary practice to hone inborn talents.

Suggested Readings

Miller, P. H., & Zalenski, R. (1982). Preschoolers' knowledge about attention. *Developmental Psychology*, *18*(6), 871–875.

A demonstration of children's understanding of the concept of distraction and the motivational impact of interest on attention and learning.

Tomkins, S. S. (1962). Interest–excitement. In *Affect imagery consciousness; Vol. 1, The positive affects* (pp. 336–368). New York: Springer.

A highly original, landmark essay on the dynamics of interest and its influence on learning, creativity, and personality.

Watson, D., & Clark, L. A. (in press). On traits and temperament: General and specific factors of emotional experience and their relation to the five-factor model. *Journal of Personality*.

Empirical studies of the relations of emotions and personality. Their attentiveness scale probably measures aspects of the emotion of interest, and their positive affect scale includes interest and enjoyment. Both these scales were significantly related to personality characteristics.

6

Enjoyment–Joy: A Force for Psychological Well-Being and Social Bonds

Smiling and laughing, the signs of enjoyment and joy, appear early in life and remain rather constant over the life span. We learn to smile on many different occasions and to vary our smile to some extent in order to suit the occasion. However, the genuine smile of joy is very much the same in infancy and old age.

The Characteristics of Joy

Like each of the fundamental emotions, joy has unique characteristics. We can gain a new appreciation of this positive emotion if we look carefully at each of these characteristics and examine closely its various functions.

Joy Is Not the Same as Sensory Pleasure

To fully understand the emotion of joy, it is first important to distinguish it from the pleasures we obtain through the senses, such as taste and touch. Eating when we are hungry can be pleasurable without being a cause of joy. If what you eat is your favorite meal prepared at your favorite restaurant, then the pleasure might run quite high. If you have company that you like, your partner or any number of other events may readily elicit joy during the course of the meal. But the sensory pleasure of eating fine food is quite different from the joy you feel on hearing of your companion's good fortune or on hearing him or her say "I love you."

Sex is another phenomenon where we can make a distinction between the emotional feeling of joy and sensory pleasure. Sexual pleasure is based primarily upon the sense of touch, and it can be quite independent of the experience of joy. Sexual experience is often related to the emotion of interest–excitement and is often accompanied by or followed by feelings of enjoyment, but these emotion feelings are in addition to sexual pleasure. It is quite possible for people to experience the sensory pleasure of sex even when they are sad. When this happens, it is clearly evident that sexual pleasure is distinct from the feeling of joy.

I have made these distinctions between sensory pleasure and the feeling of joy because it is important to the understanding of the emotion, its causes, and its consequences. In a very real sense, the emotion of joy is more elusive than sensory pleasure. We can get a little sensory pleasure every time we eat a candy bar or an ice cream cone. It is not so easy to locate or schedule joy experiences. Some students of joy think that it is more of a by-product of our efforts than a direct result of anything we do. In other words, you can go out looking for sensory pleasure and probably find one sort or another. You cannot with equal confidence go chasing after the experience of joy and expect to find it at the nearest ice cream parlor.

The Causes of Joy

Although as adults we cannot schedule and plan pursuits that are certain to lead to joy, there are certain types of stimulation or events that regularly produce joy in the infant and young child. Interestingly, the first sure sign of joy in the human infant is the *social* smile. The high-pitched human voice can elicit the smile of enjoyment in the infant of 3 weeks of age. Beginning at about 4 or 5 weeks of age, the human face becomes a very effective stimulus in eliciting joy. Although joy is not purely social in nature, the effectiveness of these early activators suggests that enjoyment has a basically social aspect and that social interaction or social relations may be one of the best sources of joyful experiences.

The baby's behavior in response to a smiling, nodding face may tell us something more about the joy experience and about human nature. From about the

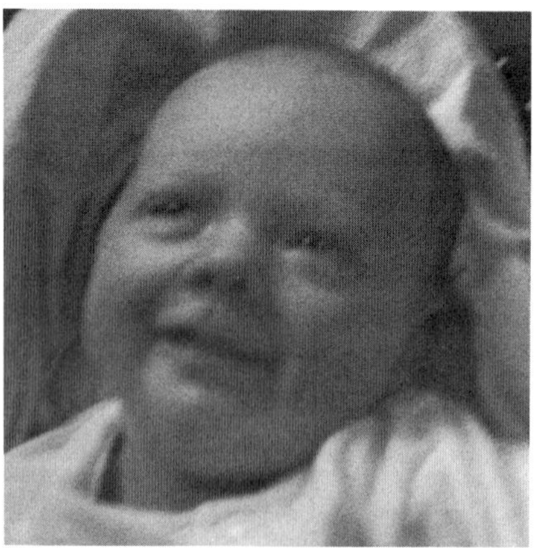

FIGURE 6-1. This 3-week-old girl's first social smile was elicited by a high-pitched human voice and smiling face.

age of 4 or 5 weeks to the age of about 4 to 5 months the infant will smile at any human face that nods gently toward it from about 2 feet away. It is as though the infant has an endless supply of smiles, a virtually limitless quantity of joyful feelings to be shared with any other human being who will take the time or provide the right stimulation.

In the everyday world of mother and infant, the young infant's ability to smile prolifically has a profound effect upon its developing relationship with its mother and other caregivers. As the mother bends over the baby to minister to its needs, the baby smiles. The baby's smile tends to elicit a smile and positive vocalizations from the mother. The increased social stimulation that is purchased by the infant's easy smile is a very positive force for the baby's health and well-being. Babies who are deprived of this kind of social interaction may experience depression, withdrawal, and even a physical debilitation (Spitz, 1945).

We have already shown that play is a source of joy. From early infancy, parents find little games that elicit smiling in the very young infant and laughter in the infant of about 4 months or older. When the child is old enough to play on its own, interest changes to joy when the child realizes a particular accomplishment or goal that was derived through the play. The sense of accomplishment or the achievement of mastery in a game, task, or intellectual pursuit can be a stimulus for joy. The joy can be even greater if it emerges despite setbacks and episodes of depression. The problems that Martha resolved would not be judged objectively as very severe, but they loomed during her adolescent years, and her determination, persistence, and accomplishments led to joy and lasting self-confidence.

> Before I entered junior high, I had expected so many wonderful things to happen to me. I would meet new people and befriend them, make important decisions, and become just a little more grown up. As it turned out, the 3 years I spent in junior high school were to be among some of the most difficult I would ever know.
>
> I wanted to become popular; this was something that was very important to me. I wanted to have the boys flirt with me and ask me out on dates and be envied by the other girls who, like me, were too shy and awkward to even be noticed in the crowd, except possibly to be picked on. But just to be acknowledged by that crowd, to be accepted, would make my dreams come true, and then I could be happy.

The next episode in Martha's story illustrates one of the surest sources of joy—overcoming obstacles or triumphing over a handicap, whether real or imaginary. Martha's successful struggle to make the basketball team gave her pride and joy. Even though this joy did not last long, it very likely did a lot for her self-confidence. Joy tends to elicit good feelings about the self and to strengthen positive self-regard.

> I saw my opportunity for popularity come when the tryouts for the ninth-grade girls' basketball team was announced. I believed I would train myself (although I had never touched a basketball before this), and so I went with all this blind ambition and bought a basketball of my own. When the other girls who were trying out for the team found out that I was attempting to tryout, they laughed at me, saying that I was too much of a "spaz" to compete at their level. Consequently, my ambition turned into determination. My conscien-

> tious hours of practice eventually paid off, as I made the team that fall. My triumph over these girls made me feel so proud, even though I played the third string.

Martha suffered another setback and became depressed. Confidence in her self and her self-esteem were not yet high and firm. She remained determined, however, and went on to other achievements that were very important to her during her teens, and they propelled her to a new level of self-esteem and enjoyment of life. She was selected for the color squad of her high school marching band.

> My new esteem carried me to great heights, particularly in my senior year of high school. I was even popular (not that I really was popular, I was just a lot more popular than I have ever been). After serving a year on the Colorguard squad of my high school marching band, I was chosen as the squad captain. I finally became a member of that elite crowd I had envied for so many years! I went to all the football games, but more than that, I got to choreograph our routines and teach them to my squad. Talk about being in your glory! Each Saturday for 9 weeks I was front and center for a few hundred counts of "Malaguena," and for the beginning of "New York, New York." Saying I enjoyed the experience is like saying that the Empire State Building is "kind of tall."

Martha's story makes it clear that one important source of self-confidence, self-esteem, and enjoyment of life is persistence toward your goals. There is just no substitute for dogged determination and plain hard work. Work (or practice or try, try again) usually pays off in achievements, and joy is a pretty certain by-product of goal attainment. Martha also showed the ability to realize her limitations and shift her goals accordingly. She didn't have the talent to become a star athlete so she set and achieved other goals.

The Expression of Joy

The facial expression of joy is one of the easiest to make and one of the easiest to decode. The simplest smile involves the action of only one pair of muscles: the zygomatic major on each side of the face pulls the corners of the mouth back and slightly upward.

Joy is expressed through smiling and laughter, easily recognized signs of enjoyment. However, the meaning of the very first smile, that of the newborn, remains something of a mystery. It is apparently mediated entirely by internal (brain stem) activity, for it occurs during drowsy states and sleep (the rapid-eye-movement, or REM, stage of sleep).

The genuine social smile often involves action of the orbicularis oculi muscle, which surrounds the eye. In the adult, the contraction of the orbicularis oculi creates little wrinkles (crow's-feet) that radiate out from the outer corners of the eye. The action of the zygomatic major and orbicularis oculi together result in raising of the cheeks and a slight narrowing of the eye fissure (the space between the upper and lower lid). There are many variations on this expression. Whether all these variations should be called smiles or not is an open question in behavioral science. But in the popular language all these variations are referred to as smiles.

These various smiles have different meanings, and one can begin to see variations in the smile even in infancy.

Ekman and Friesen (1982) identified felt, false, and miserable smiles. They described the felt, or genuine, smile as we have described it above. Most of the smiles that they have measured in adults were between ⅔ of a second and 4 seconds in duration.

They described two kinds of false smiles. In the phony smile there is not much feeling but a strong effort to appear as if one is enjoying oneself. A masking smile is one that is used to attempt to conceal negative emotion. Ekman and Friesen note that there are several differences between genuine and false smiles. First, the orbicularis oculi muscle around the eye is usually inactive in the false smile and thus there is often no sign of raised cheeks or the little wrinkles radiating from the outer corners of the eye. If a false smile is an extremely intense one, the action of the zygomatic muscle may result in enough raising of the cheeks so as to make it difficult to distinguish it from a genuine smile. Smiles of mild to moderate intensity are more easily distinguished by the absence of raised cheeks and "twinkling eyes."

False smiles are also more likely to be asymmetrical, with movement stronger on the left side if the person is right handed. They also note that false smiles appear earlier or later than would be called for by the situation. False smiles also differ from genuine ones in their timing. The apex of the false smile is usually longer than that of a genuine smile. The onset is too short, making it appear abrupt. The offset is either abrupt or irregular in some way such that it does not fade away smoothly.

Finally, Ekman and Friesen (1982) described miserable smiles as smiles that are superimposed on a negative emotion expression. These occur when the person really does feel miserable but tries to smile despite their misery and despite outward appearance. The careful observer will not have too much difficulty identifying the miserable smile. Such a smile will not seem at all convincing, and there will probably be clear signs of negative emotion on the face.

Laughter. Laughter is considered by many people to be an expression of intense joy. I think this is true sometimes, but not always. Laughter that results from intimate exchanges, from reunions with a loved one, from finding the solution to a difficult problem, may well be expressions of intense enjoyment. Laughter that results from hearing a good joke, understanding a good cartoon, or from seeing two things in a very unusual and unexpected relationship is laughter at the incongruous. We sometimes laugh at incongruity, that is, when we see or hear things together that don't really belong together. This kind of laughter presumes mental work. You have to figure out a relationship or understand that it is ridiculous or absurd. When a toddler laughs at you when you toddle in his or her direction, the toddler has to perceive the incongruity or the ridiculousness of your behavior. Some laughter does not require such complex cognitive processes. When an infant laughs in response to tickling, the laughter requires no mental work.

Playing and Cavorting. While the smile is the facial sign of joy, playing and cavorting are probably a pretty good indication that the underlying subjective experience consists at least in part of the emotion of joy. As we have already noted, one way to understand the motivations behind play is to see them as the interacting forces of the emotions of interest and enjoyment.

Bodily Changes in Joy

The physiological changes that accompany the feeling of joy have not been extensively studied. Several laboratory experiments have shown that heart rate increases during periods of joy. One study that demonstrated this very clearly was conducted with very talented professional actors and actresses from the theaters and theater schools in Moscow (Rusalova *et al.*, 1975). We asked these highly

FIGURE 6-2. A 4-year-old boy playing and cavorting in the soft mud and sand of a creek bank.

talented people, who were gracious enough to participate in a study that we conducted in the Laboratory of Emotions of the Soviet Academy of Sciences, to imagine a time when they were joyful. While they imagined themselves in a situation in which they were enjoying themselves immensely, we videotaped their faces and recorded their heart rate. Even though they were instructed to sit still and not move their arms and legs, their heart rates increased significantly, sometimes as much as 20 or 30 beats per minute.

The substantial changes in heart rate during strong feelings of enjoyment do not really tell us how bodily changes in joy differ from that of other emotions. The heart rate increases in a number of other emotions as well. Ekman, Levenson, and Friesen (1983) have shown that by taking measures of heart rate and skin temperature, the emotion of joy can be distinguished from several other emotions. Cohen *et al.* (1986) have shown that the spontaneous smiles of 4½-month-old infants can be distinguished from other emotions on the basis of patterns of heart rate and skin temperature changes. These data suggest that several of the fundamental emotions are accompanied by distinctly different patterns of activity in the autonomic nervous system, but more data are needed for a firm conclusion.

The Subjective Experience and Functions of Enjoyment–Joy

As in the case of all the emotions, the core feeling of enjoyment is the same for babies as for adults. Trying to imagine what joy is like for the baby may help us get a better appreciation of what the true feeling of joy is for the adult. For the infant the experience of joy can be described as pleasant even though it is different from sensory pleasure. Joy is not dependent on stimulation of erogenous zones or the taste buds. Nor is it dependent on beautiful sounds or lovely colors. All of these types of stimulation may lead to joy indirectly, but they are not necessarily a direct stimulus for joy. Nevertheless, joy is sensed as a pleasant, desirable, positive, rewarding feeling. It includes a sense of psychological comfort and well-being. Mind and body are in a ready state to relax or play. There is an absence of mental or physical stress. The feeling is of lightheartedness, which extends to the entire physical and mental self. Movements seem easier, even enjoyable in themselves.

These core feelings that constitute the subjective experience of joy in the infant have counterparts in the adult. When we are enjoying life we have a sense of confidence. We feel that our life is meaningful and significant. We feel that we are lovable. We feel contented with ourselves and with the world. There is a real sense of vigor and a feeling that we can deal with the challenges that face us.

Joy increases the individual's capacity to savor and appreciate the world. This means that the joyful person is more likely to see beauty and goodness in nature and in fellow human beings. While experiencing joy, people are more inclined to savor an object than to dissect it or analyze it. They appreciate the object as it is rather than wanting to change it. They feel closeness with the object rather than wanting to objectify it and put it at a distance. The object is seen as enhancing the self of the perceiver. Perhaps one reason why some mystical experiences bring great joy to us is because we stand before a mystery in awe, and realizing that we cannot fully understand it or exhaust its meaning by objective analysis, we savor it and appreciate it (Meadows, 1968).

Joy makes us feel that we have a distinctive bond between ourselves and the world. Joy is more than a positive attitude toward self and the world. It is a special kind of link or bond. This has been described as a keen sense of belonging, or of oneness with the object of joy and with the world.

Although it may not be an integral part of the joy experience, joy is often accompanied by feelings of strength and vigor. Both personal experiences and empirical research have produced evidence of this feature of joy. Studies with the Differential Emotions Scale have shown a significant and positive correlation between scores on the joy experience scale and on the scale measuring vigor. The combination of joy and the feelings of strength and vigor is also associated with the feelings of confidence and competence.

Perhaps as a corollary of the tendency for joy to be associated with feelings of strength and competence, joy also tends to be accompanied by a feeling of transcendence or freedom (Meadows, 1968), the feeling that we are more than or different from our usual selves and that for a moment we exist in the realm of the extraordinary. In ecstatic joy we may feel light and bouncy, or that we could soar, or that we are soaring and that everything has a different perspective because of our unusual vantage point.

Joy is often accompanied by a sense of harmony and unity with the object of joy and, to some extent, with the world. Some people have reported that in ecstatic joy they tend to lose individual identity, as in the case of some mystical experiences associated with meditation.

Before leaving the phenomenology of joy, it should be noted that some of the foregoing characteristics of the joy experience may involve the products of joy or the interaction of joy with perceptual and cognitive processes. There are great individual differences in the way that joy interacts with perception, memory, thought, and imagery, and consequently there may be great individual differences in the way people describe the joy experience and those phenomena that are typically associated with it.

There is an unsolved problem with respect to the role of activeness in the phenomenology of joy. Many people, including such theorists as Dumas (1948), make a distinction between active and passive (or receptive) joy. This may not be a theoretically useful distinction. One might argue that the joy experience is a distinct subjective or phenomenological process. Although it varies in intensity, it is qualitatively a unitary phenomenon. The variation in intensity may in part explain the origin of the concepts of active and receptive joy. A high intensity of the joy experience is more congruent with the notion of activity. In the direction of passivity or receptiveness there is another quite distinct state of consciousness that may be conceptually confused with low-intensity joy. This is the feeling state that has been termed calmness-tranquility. This concept has emerged as a relatively independent empirical scale in various factor-analytic investigations (Izard, Dougherty, *et al.* 1974). Joy plus tranquility may yield what some people call receptive joy.

We have already noted that joy tends to be associated with a sense of vigor and with feelings of strength, confidence, and competency. While these later events are more correctly described as affective–cognitive orientations, there is a strong tendency for them to be associated with intense joy. The concept of active joy, therefore, may derive from the tendency for intense joy to be associated with feelings of confidence and vigor. Other variations in the phenomenology of joy may also result from variations in joy–cognition interactions.

Other Functions of Joy

Social Functions of Joy

The feeling of joy also has social significance. Repeated joy expressions between mother and infant and between father and infant increase the parent–child social bond or affectionate attachment. During infancy and toddlerhood, this attachment is a very important part of the child's healthy development. If the child feels secure in the attachment, then knowledge of the mother's presence or knowledge of the availability of the mother gives the child the feeling of confidence necessary for the exploration of its world.

The results of experience and expression of mutual joy between the child and its parents are not unlike the effects of the enjoyment of social relations in later childhood and adulthood. If you enjoy and continue to enjoy the company of a particular person, chances are very good that you will come to rely upon and trust that person. The development of an affection for another person and the building of mutual trust are extremely important functions of the feeling of joy.

The Biological Functions of Joy

Joy is a rewarding experience. During the experience of joy all of our internal systems function easily and smoothly, and both our mind and our body have time for recuperation or recovery from periods of stress and strain. There are informal reports of people recovering from illness more quickly when they can experience joy often. Clinical investigations show that the absence of social stimulation that usually accompanies the positive emotions of interest and joy can result in serious psychological and physical ailments (Spitz, 1946).

The Development and Socialization of Joy

We have already indicated that we probably cannot achieve joy by deliberately pursuing it. Joy often comes after we have accomplished something or

FIGURE 6-3. Father and expectant mother dance a "pas de trois" to celebrate pregnancy.

achieved a goal. All joy experiences are not a result of direct effort. This is not to say that we cannot set up plans and take directions that might more readily lead us to joy experiences. Practice or hard work in the acquisition of a skill is more likely to lead to a sense of mastery, and mastery is truly a source of joy. Hard work is also likely to bring about achievement, and the sense of achievement can be a source of joy. But as a rule we don't work hard in order to feel joy. We work hard in order to get the job done, improve our performance on the task, finish the course, complete the project. We work because we are interested in what we do. Joy follows as a by-product of the successful doing.

So if joy cannot be directly pursued, how do we nurture the development of our children such that they can experience their fair share of joy? The very first thing we can do is try to help our infant develop a sense of security in his or her relationship with us. A secure attachment to a parent is not only a comfortable base from which the child can explore the world, but it is also a source of joy both directly and indirectly. The parent's smiles of joy are reciprocated by the child. Explorations from the secure base of the attachment lead to discoveries, achievements, and masteries that result in joy.

FIGURE 6-4. Imitating father was this 3-year-old boy's goal. Joy followed success in getting into and walking in father's shoes.

It is a mistake to expect all children, even all children in the same family, to experience joy with the same frequency and intensity. Psychologists who observe and study infants note differences in infant smiling and laughing from the early weeks of life. These differences are probably due to heredity, information that is built in to the particular individual's genes. One of the earliest systematic studies of children's emotion expression found wide differences among the children's emotion responsiveness, including their smiling and laughing (Washburn, 1929). Four children in the group being observed laughed as early as 12 weeks. One child did not laugh until 1 year of age. Kagan (1971) found that 4-month-old infants who smiled more at human masks showed longer epochs of sustained play at 27 months. This kind of evidence suggests that our thresholds for emotions, including the emotion of joy, is to some extent determined by our genetic makeup.

Further evidence along this line was obtained from observations of infants and toddlers in a communal nursery in the Soviet Union. Although these children shared common quarters in the Institute of Pediatric Sciences, and although they "shared equally" the care and affection of the same pediatricians, nurses, and caregivers, they differed widely in the ease with which they would return a smile and in the amount of smiling and laughter they showed in their play with one another. Some were veritable bundles of joy, smiling and laughing readily and frequently at seemingly the slightest provocation. Others, though apparently interested in what was going on around them, smiled infrequently and laughed only rarely.

The foregoing evidence that the joy threshold is determined to some extent by genetic factors certainly does not mean that cultural, social, and familial forces are not important in the development of positive emotion. A culture, or any group within a culture, that lives in poverty is likely to have fewer opportunities to experience the emotion of joy. Even in an affluent society, frequent bickering or open conflicts between parents can endanger the development of joy in the child.

The Interactions of Joy with Other Emotions

Any emotion can influence another emotion, and joy is no exception. There are some emotions that are more likely to be influenced by experiences of joy. We have already noted that joy and interest frequently interact in play or in work that we find challenging yet within our capabilities. Further, these two emotions interact in the development and maintenance of positive relationships. A person who continues to be interesting to you day after day, year after year, is likely to be a person who is also a stimulus for joy. The combination of interest and joy is an important part of the basis of a good romance and a successful marriage.

Joy and shame sometimes seem to be complexly related in certain situations. An example may occur when a doting parent asks a child to perform for guests. The child enjoys performing but feels shy in the presence of strangers or people outside the family. Applause or praise at the end of a successful performance in this situation may bring a combination of shame and joy—the joy from a good performance, the shame at the overexposure of the self.

Joy may also interact with the negative emotion of contempt. This interaction can have implications for psychological well-being or mental health, and it will be discussed in a later section.

The Regulation of Joy

Is there any need to talk about the regulation of joy? Is it possible to experience too much joy? If joy is a good feeling and a rewarding experience, if it gives us a sense of vigor and confidence, and if it allows us to have time to recuperate from periods of stress and strain, how can there be too much joy?

If laughter is the expression of extreme joy, then we will all agree that we can have too much intense joy. Most of us have probably had one or more occasions in our lives when we remember laughing till it hurt, literally hurt. Laughing is a fairly vigorous activity for the lungs and muscles of the chest and for the throat and vocal chords. Laughter for a long period of time can create some pain. This may be one of nature's ways of telling us that life is not just a series of laughs, that it is not possible to find one's way through life while experiencing only joy. If indeed we did find people who experienced only joy, then we would wonder about their accomplishments, for they would not have had the motive force of interest–excitement to keep their shoulder to the wheel long enough to accomplish anything. We would also question whether they were very socially sensitive human beings. How could they empathize with another's distress or show sympathy for another's sadness? Would it be possible for them to show compassion?

There is also a question as to whether experiencing joy too frequently might keep us out of the swing of things. We have talked about active joy, but there is the question as to whether active joy may not often be some combination of the experience of joy and the experience of interest. Excitement certainly increases our proneness to activity, whether mental or physical. But on a lot of occasions joy may simply lead to a warm comfortable feeling and relaxation.

One more important point may be made in relation to the experience of joy and the possible need for its regulation. Joy, like interest and all of the other emotions, typically occurs in situations that also elicit other emotions. The experience of pure joy over very long periods of time may be rare indeed. Perhaps joy is best when it occurs in the context of other emotions. How can we fully appreciate the feeling of joy if we have not experienced the hard work that it takes to pursue our interest, or if we have not ever experienced sadness or shared someone's despair?

The Pursuit of Happiness: How Do You Find Joy

We may not be able to obtain genuine joy experiences by direct effort when joy itself is the goal, but we can become aware of things that will increase the likelihood of experiencing joy. We can begin by removing the obstacles to joy. Then we can work toward worthwhile goals and undertake creative endeavors. Success, or even a good effort to succeed, may bring joy.

Obstacles to the Experience of Joy

William Schutz (1967), in his book *Joy: Expanding Human Awareness*, discusses what he views as some of the obstacles to joy. He defined joy almost completely in terms of self-fulfillment: "Joy is the feeling that comes from the fulfillment of one's potential" (Schutz, 1967, p. 15).

Although self-fulfillment often leads to the joy experience, it is very likely that self-fulfilling acts include other emotions besides joy, particularly excitement. In any case, if self-fulfillment is a prerequisite of joy, then it would follow that self-fulfillment cannot be pursued and captured any more than joy itself.

In Schutz's theory, obstacles to the fulfillment of one's potential are obstacles to realizing joy. He points out that such obstacles come from everywhere. Several specific obstacles were discussed:

1. One pervasive obstacle to self-fulfillment and the realization of joy is the method sometimes used to organize social institutions. Sometimes rules and regulations squelch creativity, lead to overcontrol, and impose mediocrity.
2. Society is often characterized by relationships that are superficial and hypercritical.
3. Dogma relating to child rearing, sex, and some religious organizations makes it difficult for individuals to know themselves and to like and trust themselves.
4. Confusion about maleness and femaleness and uncertainty about one's sex role tends to block self-knowledge and self-fulfillment.
5. In addition to the foregoing obstacles relating to personal and social functioning, poor physical condition of the body can also inhibit self-fulfillment and the realization of joy. A male or female that is not physically fit is less capable of realizing the sensations and experiences that lead to fulfillment and joy.

It appears that one cannot achieve joy in the same way that one achieves a skill or "success" (Frankl, 1962). But this conclusion is based more on observations and reports of a personal nature than on rigorous experimentation. Many people undoubtedly have found that goal-directed activities and goal attainment often lead to joy, but in these cases the goal itself was not joy. When a person's efforts become pursuits for joy itself, they tend to change in nature and joy eludes the pursuer.

For the most part, people pursue goals because the goal-oriented activity and the possibility of goal attainment excites them. Often people do things because they are both exciting and enjoyable, but when joy comes into the picture, the activity or pursuit may slow down and change in other ways as well.

Schutz, like Maslow (1971) and Rogers (1961), maintains that openness and honesty are essential ingredients in the process of realizing one's full potential and in experiencing joy.

> A man must be willing to let himself be known to himself and to others, he must express and explore his feelings, and open up areas long dormant and possibly painful, with the faith that in the long run the pain will give way to a release of vast potential for creativity and joy. This is an exhilarating and frightening prospect, one which is often accompanied by agony, but which usually leads to ecstasy. (Schutz, 1967, pp. 16–17)

To realize one's potential one has to attend to the biological, psychological, and social aspects of one's nature. It has already been noted that a body in poor physical condition can be an obstacle to self-fulfillment and joy. Self-fulfillment and joy come more readily when the body functions smoothly with a measure of grace and without undue strain. Good posture, good muscle tone, and a nervous system that is neither too sensitive nor too insensitive facilitate self-fulfilling activity and the experiencing of joy. This is an area in which anyone can make progress if he or she is willing to extend the effort. Strength, stamina, and physical skills that lead to a sense of fulfillment can be obtained through exercise and practice. Such achievements often lead to an increased sensory awareness and to a new appreciation and sensitivity to bodily feelings and inner experiences.

A second area that can be developed is what Schutz called personal functioning. In addition to the biological aspects already noted, Schutz maintained that logical thinking and creative potential could be nurtured. He also advocated the development of bodily functions that control the emotions. "Awareness of emotions, appropriate expression of feelings [and their relations to other functions such as thinking and action] can be trained" (p. 18). Thus observation is very similar to some of the notions about emotion control discussed in differential emotions theory.

The third area that can be developed in such a way as to facilitate self-fulfillment and joy is what Schutz called social functioning. Schutz's theory of interpersonal needs and interpersonal functioning is summarized in Schutz's own words:

> This theory asserts that our needs from and toward other people are three: inclusion, control, and affection. We achieve interpersonal joy when we find a satisfying, flexible balance in each of these areas between ourselves and other people. Inclusion refers to the need to be with people and to be alone. The effort in inclusion is to have enough contact to avoid loneliness and enjoy people; enough aloneness to avoid enmeshment and enjoy solitude. The fully realized man can feel comfortable and joyful both with and without people, and knows with how much of each—and when—he functions best. In the area of control the effort is to achieve enough influence so that a man can determine his future to the degree that he finds most comfortable, and to relinquish enough control so that he is able to lean on others to teach, guide, support, and at times to take some responsibility for him. The fully realized man is capable of either leading or following as appropriate, and of knowing where he personally feels most comfortable. In affection the effort is to avoid being engulfed in emotional entanglements (not being free to relate without a deep involvement), but also to avoid having too little affection and a bleak, sterile life without love, warmth, tenderness, and someone to confide in. The fully realized man is aware of his needs, and functions, effectively not only in close, emotionally involving situations, but also in those of lesser intensity. As in the other two areas, he is able to both give and take, comfortably and joyfully. (pp. 18–19)

According to Schutz, even if all the other requirements of body (physical) conditioning, personal functioning, and social functioning are met, self-fulfillment remains dependent in part upon the support of society. A repressive society with dehumanizing institutions and humiliating laws and practices or one that is characterized by bigotry and prejudice will place considerable restriction on self-fulfillment and the realization of joy. Thus a society characterized by optimal openness, honesty, and freedom is necessary for optimal self-fulfillment and joy experiencing.

Finally, it cannot be overlooked that one of the most important aspects of the effort toward self-fulfillment and joy consists of unlearning or undoing some of the events brought about by society and our present lifestyle. Perhaps most people will have to overcome some degree of shame, shyness, guilt, or fear before undertaking the more positive activities that facilitate self-fulfillment and joy. We may be afraid to be open and honest and to express our emotions, even when expression is very much in order. We may be afraid that we will express the wrong feelings at the wrong time. Some may feel guilty over failure or over failing to try. Some may feel shame as they engage in the process of self-expression. Learning to control fear, shame, shyness, and guilt is one of the most difficult aspects in the effort toward self-fulfillment and the joy experience.

Consider Leslie's story of her triumph over scoliosis and the accompanying social stigma. She overcame physical pain, fear, sadness, shame, and shyness in a battle for her health and well-being. Her triumph led to a deep and meaningful experience of joy that lasted because it was accompanied by a strengthening of character and self-esteem.

> When I was 11 years old I was diagnosed as having scoliosis—curvature of the spine. I saw several doctors—orthopedists, chiropractors, specialists—but was never afraid; that is, not until I was finally shown an X ray of my spine. Then I began to get scared. Before seeing the X rays I had thought of the whole experience as rather interesting; it was something to tell the kids at school about and I got a lot of days out of school to see doctors. The attention I was receiving from my parents and teachers was also nice, but the instant I saw those X rays, I realized the seriousness of my disease. I was told by my doctors that I was going to have to wear what is called a Milwaukee brace—a steel and plastic contraption designed to push the spine into proper alignment.
>
> The brace was heavy, cumbersome, painful, and most of all, ugly and disfiguring. It showed no matter what I wore to hide it. I got the brace over Christmas vacation in sixth grade. My parents were understanding and supportive, and I bore the brace as best I could. I hated wearing it—it hurt and gave me bruises all over; I was never comfortable, yet I wore it without too much complaint—I wanted to get better.
>
> It was painful, but the brace itself was not as painful as the reactions I got at school. By the time I entered seventh grade, I had learned to hate school because I was always stared at and got nasty comments every single day. But I never let myself get outwardly angry. Instead, I tried to ignore them. I did a pretty good job of it, but I wasn't very happy. I had a few friends but stuck mostly to academics; I was better in this field than in the social one. Though I was extremely interested in boys, they were just as uninterested in me. I was very jealous of the 12- and 13-year-old girls who were pretty and popular and always had a new boyfriend. I wanted too much to be like them, to be friends with and to be one of them. I never really was, but since I was always quiet and nice, they liked me, but never accepted me totally. I learned to laugh at the jokes made at my expense and to ignore the pain.

Learning ways to manage and control pain is an important avenue to enjoyment in life. Leslie undoubtedly brought a strong and resilient personality into her battle with scoliosis and the brace, but through determination she additionally developed an ability to endure physical pain and emotional hurt and to prevent negative emotions from getting in the way of life. She told herself in effect that suffering the pain of the brace was the only way to a normal physical life.

Leslie was also able to manage the negative emotions that resulted from the reactions of her unsympathetic peers. Their response caused her much sadness and shame. She was even able to try to laugh at the teasing and the cruel jokes, and she showed a remarkable strength of character in doing so at such a delicate time in her life and without at some point breaking down.

> So I went through the seventh grade, did well in all my subjects, and made a few friends. I didn't lead a very happy or exciting life, but I was surviving and doing what I had to do in order to help my back. In the middle of the eighth grade, I went to see my orthopedist. He showed me my X rays; I wasn't getting any better. As a matter of fact I was getting worse. The curvature had deepened; the brace wasn't working. I remember sitting there and letting the tears stream down my face. I was scared of the operation, and I was angry that I had spent 2 years wearing the brace, going through a lot of hell, and I was going to have to have the operation anyway. But pretty soon I realized that with the operation I would be finished with all the treatment in 9 months, and with the brace I would need another 4 or 5 years of treatment.
>
> I grew very confident that the operation would be successful. I also didn't mind missing 2 months of school. The operation went well, but I don't remember very much about the month I was in the hospital—most of the time they kept me pretty doped up.
>
> When I returned to school a month later, I was sporting a huge body cast from my neck to my hips. It was very uncomfortable and heavy, but I didn't get teased about it as much as I did about the brace. I still basically stuck to studying, but was much happier now that the end was in sight.
>
> That summer really changed my life. I had always been interested in acting, and despite the cast I joined a drama club and took acting lessons. I really enjoyed it and got to meet a lot of great people.
>
> One girl in the class became a good friend. I practically spent the whole summer at her house, where she lived with her older brother. Her lifestyle seemed much more exciting and wild than mine, and I loved being with her, her brother, and all of their friends. They made me feel really good about myself because they were older and fun and "cool," and most of all they really liked me. For the first time in years I did not feel self-conscious; I could really be myself around these people.
>
> Between the acting lessons and this group of friends, that summer I completely and irrevocably overcame my shyness. I had for the past 2 and a half years been putting myself inside a protective shell to avoid the pain of being laughed at. It had been very difficult for me to relax around people and I considered myself a social failure. But during that summer I was accepted by a bunch of people I really liked and admired. I had more fun than I had ever had before, and I really started to like myself and to gain self-confidence.

As Leslie began the home stretch toward triumph in her struggle with scoliosis, she again showed determination to find a niche for herself and to develop a satisfying social life. She was able to venture into a new domain—a drama club—and find friends, a place for herself, and renewed joy in living.

Leslie's story is a wonderful example of the way a girl in her late childhood and early adolescence overcame a major obstacle and experienced well-deserved joy in her accomplishments. She demonstrated persistence and resilience at an age of extreme sensitivity about body image and appearance. Her story also illustrates the complex interplay of a variety of emotions that occurs during significant episodes within the course of living, for these events rarely if ever result in the experience of a single emotion. Sometimes a particular pair or group of emotions occurs with regularity, forming what is called an emotion pattern. In Leslie's case, shame, anger, and disgust constituted a recurring pattern of emotions until she overcame her difficulties. She demonstrated a remarkable ability to control or manage these negative emotions and physical pain.

Joy and Mental Health

Joy has not been implicated in any serious psychological disorder. In youth, one might be prone to do foolish or unwise things for a laugh, and contagious laughter that leads to group hilarity may result in some disturbance or embarrassment in the classroom or community. However, these are usually transient phenomena and are not really a cause for alarm.

Masochists are sometimes described as people who enjoy pain, inflicted by self or others, but there have not been careful scientific studies to demonstrate that what the masochist experiences is really joy. The anomalies involved in masochism guarantee a thorough mixture of emotions related to the experience of pain, but there is no clear evidence that joy is one of them. Masochists may be satisfying a need for punishment created by guilt. Their "enjoyment" of pain might actually be a diminishing of feelings of guilt. Very possibly, it is because of this guilt that a masochist may feel the need to endure pain before sexual pleasure.

Sometimes children or even adults will laugh at the misfortune of another person. This laughter may turn to derision, which consists of a mixture of joy and contempt. Derision can have very negative consequences for the person to whom it is targeted, for the person who is habitually derisive may be capable of hostile and destructive behavior. When an individual has come to chronically thrive on and enjoy the ill fortune or afflictions of others, a serious psychological disorder may very well be forming.

We have already discussed joy as a result of mastery or triumph. However, when the occasion for joy is mastery of other people or triumph over them and when this becomes the primary source of joy, there is, again, a strong likelihood of a serious psychological problem involved. The joy of triumph is often a perfectly valid and wonderful experience so long as the triumph is a personal victory, the result of achieving a worthwhile goal attained through constructive effort. It is unhealthy, however, to count on triumph over others as the only source of joy. Such a strategy may be costly in terms of the cost of one's physical and mental well-being.

Summary

A smile of sorts may appear on an infant's face in the first hours of life, but the social smile does not appear until several weeks later. The smile seems to be preprogrammed, and the effectiveness of activating stimuli change with increasing age. The indiscriminate smiling of the 3- to 5-month-old infant in response to the human face probably testifies to the importance of smile-elicited affectionate behavior in the infant's welfare and healthy development. The effect of mutual smiling on the mother–infant relationship and infant development underscores the importance of emotion and emotion expression as motivational variables in human affairs.

Laughing develops a little later than smiling and progresses through certain developmental states of its own. Theory and research have linked laughing to certain aspects of cognitive development, but the emotion dynamics in laughing have been little investigated. Laughter, like smiling, can foster interpersonal affective ties and social development. It can also foster opportunities for new experiences and learning.

In differential emotions theory the joy experience is distinguished from drive satisfaction or sensory pleasure, although the latter may reduce the threshold for joy. Phenomenologically, joy is characterized by a sense of confidence, contentment, and often by a feeling of being loved or being lovable. Joy experiences vary along an active–receptive or active–passive dimension. The expression of joy is readily recognized, but the social smile may function more as a greeting than as an indicator of joy experience.

The discussion of the causes of joy at the phenomenological level must be tempered by the fact that joy seems to be more a by-product than a direct result of deliberate thought or action. Joy may follow from the reduction of stimulation from undifferentiated stress or negative emotion states, from the recognition of the familiar, or from creative endeavor.

In evolutionary perspective, joy complements the emotion of interest in guaranteeing that human beings will be social creatures. The effects of reciprocal smiling on facilitating mother–infant interactions and attachment probably increase the infant's chances of survival and help provide the social framework within which the infant can learn and grow. At the psychological level joy can increase frustration tolerance and promote confidence and courage. Joy's slowing-down effect makes it an antidote for the rat race or "success-or-death" syndrome. The joy experience facilitates recuperation from stress or illness.

Although joy cannot be taught directly, parents can share their joy and serve as models demonstrating the kinds of lifestyles that facilitate joy experiences. Biogenetic, socioeconomic, and cultural factors play a role in the development of the joy threshold. Given a reasonable degree of biological well-being and a relatively unrestrictive environment, children will show an amazing capacity to create their own fun and games.

Joy interacts with other emotions and with perception, cognition, and action. Joy can slow down performance, but it can also create a kind of openness and receptivity associated with intuition and creativity.

Different thresholds for joy tend to create different styles of life. Some people experience a conflict between excitement and joy as they ponder the relative importance of tranquility and the vigorous pursuit of goals.

Empirical studies of joy in adults have increased our understanding of the antecedents and consequences of joy and of joy phenomenology. Other studies have shown sex-linked changes in frequency of joy experiences or happiness during college years. One in-depth study of happiness has shown significant relationships among personality characteristics, joy thresholds, and types of joy experiences. Psychophysiological studies suggest the possibility of differentiating joy from other emotions on the basis of neurophysiological functions.

Although it is probably not possible to pursue joy for its own sake, it is feasible to reach a better understanding of certain obstacles to joy, such as overcontrol and restrictive dogma relating to child rearing, sex, and moral-ethical development. Learning to control negative emotions and unlearning unduly restrictive inhibitions can develop the kind of openness to experience that facilitates self-fulfillment and joy in living.

Bradburn (1969) showed that people who participate more in their environment (become involved socially) and have more new or varied experiences report more positive affect. High socioeconomic status, which helps reduce the amount of drabness and monotony in life, was found to be positively correlated with positive affective experiences. Bradburn's data suggested, however, that money and status "may enable one to increase his joys, but it cannot decrease his sorrow" (p. 226), a point consistent with the finding that positive and negative emotionality are relatively independent.

Suggested Readings

Bainum, C. K., Lounsbury, K. R., & Pollio, H. R. (1984). The development of laughing and smiling in nursery school children. *Child Development*, *55*, 1946–1957.

A study of young children's smiling is differentially affected by attention from mother, a strange adult, and attractive toys. The role of joy in social interactions and play.

Harris, P. L., Johnson, C. N., Hutton, D., Andrews, G., & Cooke, T. (1989). Young children's theory of mind and emotion [Special issue]. *Cognition & Emotion*, *3*, 379–400.

Studies of the influence of children's beliefs and desires on their understanding of the emotion reactions of others. Anticipation of the consequences of an event and the regulation of emotions.

Isen, A. M., Daubman, K. A., & Nowicki, G. P. (1987). Positive affect facilitates creative problem solving. *Journal of Personality and Social Psychology*, *52*(6), 1122–1131.

An ingenious study showing the effects of the induction of positive affect on creative behavior. Isen's concept of positive affect includes aspects of the discrete emotion concepts of interest and joy.

Jones, S. S., & Raag, T. (1989). Smile production in older infants: The importance of a social recipient for the facial signal. *Child Development*, *60*, 811–818.

Rosenhan, D. L., Underwood, B., & Moore, B. (1974). Affect moderates self-gratification and altruism. *Journal of Personality and Social Psychology*, *30*(4), 546–552.

The effect of induced joy and sadness on children's self-gratification and helping behavior.

Sroufe, L. A., & Wunsch, J. P. (1972). The development of laughter in the first year of life. *Child Development*, *43*, 1326–1344.

Studies of the development of laughter and the kinds of stimuli that elicit laughter at various stages of cognitive development during the first year of life.

7

Joy

EMPIRICAL STUDIES

In recent years several studies have addressed the question of positive emotionality as a personality trait. The evidence indicates that people do vary in the amount of positive emotion they experience, and the amount for a given individual tends to remain constant over time. Further, this research shows that the trait of positive emotionality is relatively independent of negative emotionality. A person can be high or low on either or both (Diener & Emmons, 1984; Tellegen, 1982). For example, it has been shown that positive emotionality, but not negative emotionality, is useful in distinguishing between anxiety and depression, two syndromes that have a number of common features (Blumberg & Izard, 1986; Watson, Clark, & Carey, 1988). The concept of positive emotionality undoubtedly includes interest as well as joy. There are few empirical studies that focus primarily on the discrete emotion of joy.

Recent developments may facilitate research on the emotion of enjoyment–joy. At least one temperament scale for infants includes a dimension of smiling and laughing (Rothbart, 1973), and there are methods for the objective measurement of smiling in infants and young children (e.g., Izard, 1978). A few studies with these instruments suggest that there is some consistency in an infant's joy expression over time. However, it is too early to say that the data support the notion of a trait of enjoyment–joy in early development.

The Development of Joy in the Child

Because joy is not a direct product of human effort or a goal that can be pursued for its own sake, the development of joy in the child may proceed in a somewhat different fashion than is the case for interest–excitement. Parents cannot teach or train the child to be happy, nor can they model ways of pursuing joy that are certain to be effective through the life span. It is possible to entertain and engage the child in fun and games, and though joy so derived is important for healthy development, it is short lived and dependent on the generosity of others. Parents can and should share their joy with the child, and the child may experience joy vicariously, but in the long run each individual must find joy as a part of his or her own lifestyle.

Biogenetic Factors

As is the case with interest, intelligence, motor agility, and musical aptitude, the capacity for joy varies from individual to individual depending upon genetic makeup. Some people are born with a high threshold for joy, and this affects them directly—their happiness, sense of well-being, and confidence. The frequency with which people express joy plays a significant role in others' responses to them and in the development of what Fitts (1971) has called the social self-concept—one's ideas about others' perceptions of one's self. Some people are born with greater capacities for sustaining joy, and this may be negatively related to their threshold for excitement. Studies of emotion expression in infants (Izard *et al.*, 1980) and toddlers (Washburn, 1929) lend support to the hypothesis of biogenetic determinants of joy (and other fundamental emotions). Frequency of smiling and laughing varied significantly among Soviet toddlers institutionalized since birth, despite a communal living and care system in which infants are supposed to share equally the attention and affection of the caregivers (Izard, 1977).

In her early study of laughter, Washburn (1929) observed wide individual differences among her subjects, noting that in response to her stimuli, four children laughed as early as 12 weeks, and one child did not laugh at any stimulus until 52 weeks of age. McGrade (1968) found that "stress reactions" to removal of a nipple between 3 and 4 days of life were associated with stress reactions during developmental testing at 8 months of age. She also found that infants at 3 and 4 days of age who showed relatively little activity after nipple withdrawal were rated as happier, more active, and less tense at 8 months of age.

Socioeconomic and Cultural Factors

Cultures and subcultures vary immensely in the opportunities they afford for experiencing joy. Some of the specific obstacles to joy will be discussed later. For the moment let us note that economic, social, and cultural conditions that create fatigue and boredom, and in which people literally must struggle for survival, produce frequent negative emotion experience and militate against the experiencing of joy (Coles, 1971; Davis & Dollard, 1940). Despite these limitations one might argue that an impoverished environment affects the development of interest more than it influences the development of joy; at least this would be true for restricting conditions that are not painful or that do not create high drive states. Children have an amazing capacity to create their own fun and games out of whatever resources are available to them, but if the material at hand offers little challenge to the growing mind, the expansion of interest, skills, and competencies will be deficient.

The Socialization of Joy

Just as joy as an experience is more a by-product of the pursuit of some other goal, so very probably is the socialization of joy. You can facilitate the development of interest, at least within limits, by exposing the child to a variety of objects, places, and people, and by pointing out new facets of a thing or how to see it in different perspectives. Everyone will agree that a child may readily learn what to be afraid of and what to be angry or disgusted or contemptuous about, but it is unlikely that you can teach a person what to be joyful about.

In all cases it may be necessary to elicit some of the emotion in question to teach a person something about one of the activators of that emotion. This seems to hold especially true for joy. Creating or eliciting joy in the infant and child is probably the best way to see that joy develops in the child's life and that his or her life has an appropriate quantity and quality of joyful experiences. If parents can elicit joy in a wide variety of situations and in relation to a wide variety of persons, events, and situations, then through social learning the infant and child may enjoy a broader spectrum of people, activities, and objects.

The Development of Smiling and Laughing

Charlesworth and Kruetzer (1973) and Vine (1973) have presented extensive reviews of the literature on the development of smiling in the infant. Sroufe and Wunsch (1972) and Rothbart (1973) have reviewed the literature on the development of laughter in infants and children. These reviews make it clear that there is still much to be learned about the development of the expressions of joy in infancy and childhood, but the major hypotheses and findings regarding these developmental processes are well worth summarizing here.

The Development of Smiling in Infants

It is now generally accepted that the smiling response is innate and universal (Darwin, 1877; Eibl-Eibesfeldt, 1972; Goodenough, 1932; Thompson, 1941; Tomkins, 1962; Wolff, 1963). Wolff (1963) made a detailed study of smiling in newborn infants. He observed them for 4 hours a day for 5 days and for 10 hours on the sixth day. He reported faical movements that morphologically resembled smiling 2–12 hours after delivery. This occurred during irregular sleep or drowsiness and was considered as a spontaneous unlearned discharge of a reflex nature. He found a recognizable smile to be elicited in the first week of life by a variety of sounds including a high-pitched human voice. The broad, clear-cut smile appears about the third week in response to the high-pitched human voice. By the fifth week the voice alone loses its efficiency in evoking a smile, and the infant begins to respond to vocalization with a vocal reply. By the fifth week of age a number of visual stimuli, including variations on the human face, elicit the smiling response. In the second and third month the baby smiles spontaneously without seeing or hearing anyone. Wolff concluded that the most effective single stimulus for eliciting the smile is the normal human face.

In a series of studies at the Academy of Medical Sciences in Moscow, Kistiakovskaia (1965) reported that healthy infants began to exhibit the animation complex (positive emotional reaction including smiling) toward the end of the first and beginning of the second month of life. In addition to smiling, the animation complex includes quick and generalized animated movements with repeated straightening and bending of hands and feet, rapid breathing, vocal reactions, and eye blink. Several of Kistiakovskaia's conclusions have important implications for parents or caregivers: (1) an adult may become a source of positive emotions in an infant simply by supplying the infant with auditory and visual sensations for a sufficiently extended period of time to enable the infant to practice and master the actions of visual concentration; (2) the satisfaction of an infant's organic needs may best be conceived as a method of eliminating the causes of negative emotions, thereby creating the condition for positive emotion experiences; (3) positive emotions tend to sustain the duration and enhance the stability of visual concentration.

The classic study by Spitz and Wolf (1946) suggested that between the ages of about 2 and 5 months, the social smile is elicited more or less indiscriminately by any human face. At about 4 to 5 months of age the infant begins to discriminate mother from others, and after this age the infant is less likely to smile at strangers than at mother or at other familiar faces. After their intensive study of the smiling response, Spitz and Wolf concluded that the emotions play a pioneering role in the general development of the infant and in "every human activity, be it perception, physical proficiency, memory, inventiveness, or understanding" (p. 94).

Observations of the effect of infant smiling on the mother tend to support the hypothesis that emotion and emotion expression is motivating. Smiles produce smiles and facilitate attachment, interpersonal bonds, and the exchange of warmth and affection.

Emde and Koenig (1969) investigated the relationship of neonatal smiling and the organismic states characterized by crying, fussiness, alert activity, and the various stages of drowsiness and sleep. Their 30 infant subjects met several criteria for normality and were observed during the days while the mother and infant were still in the hospital following the delivery. During 45 different observation sessions they observed 194 smiles, all but 4 of which occurred in the state of sleep characterized by rapid eye movement (REM). So little smiling was observed in other organismic states that the authors concluded that smiling during the first days of life occurs predominantly, if not exclusively, during the state of REM drowsiness and REM sleep. The newborn smile is not an intentional social response, but it usually delights parents and fosters affection.

Emde and Koenig (1969) found that the infants of the 16 mothers who received depressant medication within 8 hours of delivery smiled significantly less than infants of mothers who did not receive such medication. They considered this finding consistent with those of earlier researchers who had shown that medication given during the mother's labor decreased sucking efficiency (Kron, Stein, & Goddard, 1966) and had an adverse affect on visual fixation (Stechler, 1964) during the first days of postuterine life.

In the course of their investigations, Emde and Koenig obtained substantial evidence that neonatal smiling is unrelated to gas in the gastrointestinal system. They designated burps, regurgitation, and flatus as indicators of gas and then showed that of the observed 138 "gas behaviors," only 1% occurred within one minute of a smile; 76% of the gas behaviors occurred during feeding, but only 13% of the smiles occurred during this time.

Emde and Koenig suggested that it is not appropriate to assume that neonatal smiling has the same "meaning" as social smiling. For one thing, neonatal smiling is essentially spontaneous and linked to an internal state, while social smiling is typically elicited by another person. However, the authors thought that neonatal smiling and social smiling might well be similar at the neurophysiological level. The authors concluded that the smiling and frowning seen during the

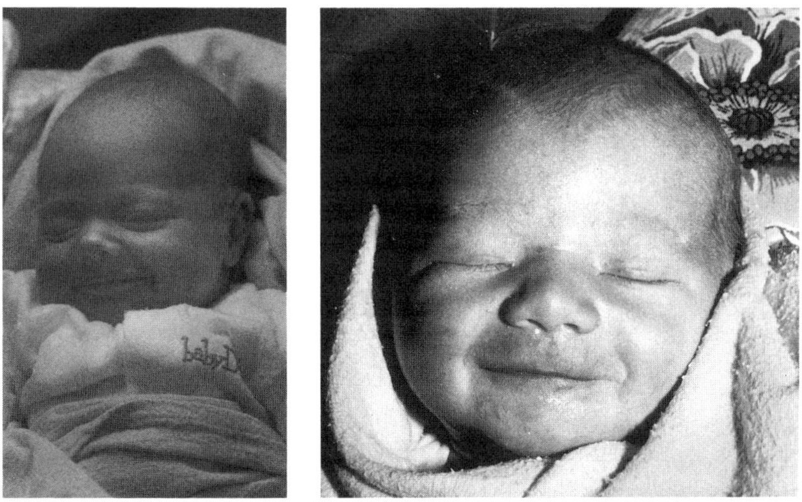

FIGURE 7-1. The big newborn smile in a 3-week-old girl happened to follow vigorous nursing at mother's breast, but evidence shows no connection between neonatal smiling and alimentary functions. The baby boy's smile in the second photograph occurred 48 hours after birth.

neonate's REM sleep are associated with activity of the limbic system, an area of the brain that has generally been accepted as involved in human emotions.

In summary, the smile is an innate expression, preprogrammed in the human infant to elicit and assure a strong bond with the mother and to facilitate positive social interactions with other human beings. A morphological facsimile of the smile appears in the first hours of life, and a readily recognizable smile enlivens the face by the end of the third week postpartum. The fact that the infant smiles indiscriminately at all human faces from approximately 3 to 5 months of age probably testifies to the importance of smile-elicited affectionate behavior for the infant's welfare and healthy development. The effect of mutual smiling on the mother–infant relationship and infant development probably shows more clearly than any other situation the importance of emotion and emotion expression as motivational variables in human affairs.

The Development of Laughing

A number of observers have reported laughter in infants as early as 5 to 9 weeks of age (Church, 1966; Darwin, 1877; Major, 1906). Wolff (1966) recorded vocal responses of 5-week-old infants to a patty-cake game, and these responses were later judged by adults to be laughter. Laughter is typically associated with joyful experiences as distinct from simple sensory events, for as Rothbart (1973) observed, the sensory pleasure of sucking does not produce laughter.

Washburn (1929) conducted the first empirical study of laughing in infancy. She used several different stimulus situations in an effort to elicit laughter, but most of the stimuli involved both intense auditory and tactile stimulation (e.g., "rhythmic hand clapping"). Using this restricted range of stimuli, she found no developmental changes in amounts of laughter for the different stimulations and no relationship between frequency of laughter and developmental status.

Sroufe and Wunsch (1972) have conducted much more extensive research on the ontogenesis of laughing. Building on the work of Washburn, and following suggestions of Bergson (1911), Darwin (1872), Koestler (1964), and Hebb (1949), they developed a much more heterogeneous set of stimuli than that used by Washburn and proceeded to conduct a number of systematic studies with large samples of infants. In their first study they tested 70 healthy white babies (29 males and 41 females), ages 4 months through 12 months. They used 24 test items grouped into four categories: auditory (e.g., speaking to the infant in a high-pitched, squeaky voice), tactile (e.g., kissing stomach), social (e.g., peekaboo), and visual (e.g., mother crawling on floor). In all instances the mother administered the test items in the home. The investigators hypothesized that items making the greatest cognitive demands on the baby (visual and social items) would tend to elicit laughter later in development than cognitively less demanding items (tactile and auditory stimuli). Mother's judgement and independent raters determined whether the baby laughed or not.

With their more heterogeneous test items, these investigators, in contrast to Washburn, found a substantial increase in the amount of laughter with age. They also found a developmental trend in the type of items eliciting laughter, especially in the comparisons of 7- to 9-month-olds and 10- to 12-month-olds. The older group laughed significantly more in response to the visual and social items, while the younger group laughed significantly more at the auditory and tactile items. For the 4- to 6-month-olds, 9 of the 11 items that produced laughter involved auditory or tactile stimulation. The most effective social item for the 4- to 6-month-olds ("gonna get you") included both auditory and tactile stimulation.

Another study using a more standardized and less animated procedure for presentation of test items resulted in considerably less laughter than was the case in study 1, but the overall pattern of results was the same for both experiments. The modal ages for the four categories of stimuli were as follows: tactile 6.5 months; auditory, 7.0 months; social, 8.0 months; visual, 10.5 months. The median modal age at which the most "cognitively sophisticated" items elicited laughter was 11.5 months, tending to support the investigators' hypothesis that items making the greatest cognitive demand on the infants would elicit laughter only in the older infants. The investigators also found some evidence for the relationship between the development of laughter and motor development. They found a statistically significant relationship ($r = .69$, $p < .05$) between the age of crawling and the age of first laughter to mother crawling on floor.

Sroufe and Wunsch thought their data were generally consistent with Zigler, Levine, and Gould's (1967) cognitive congruency principle or cognitive challenge hypothesis—children are more likely to laugh at jokes (incongruities) that are neither too obvious nor beyond their comprehension, things that lie at the growing edge of their capacities. McGhee (1971a, 1971b) refined this idea and verified the role of cognitive challenge in relation to cognitive mastery by measuring the specific developmental cognitive acquisitions of his subjects. In a later study, however, McGhee (1974) suggested that with increasing age cognitive challenge plays a lesser role, and emotional factors such as the type of affect involved in the incongruity and affective state (or mood) of the subject play an increasingly important role.

Sroufe and Wunsch's (1972) extensive studies of the development of laughter also offered further support for the hypothesis that emotion is motivational and plays a role in guiding behavior. They concluded: "We have observed repeatedly that when an infant cries he pulls back in the high chair and turns from the stimulus, whereas when laughter occurs the baby maintains an orientation towards the agent, reaches for the object, and seeks to reproduce the situation" (p. 1341). The emotion appeared to be related to the direction and intensity of the behavior of the infant.

In discussing the functions of laughter, Rothbart (1973) made a cogent argument for a function of laughter other than that of dissipating tension in the individual. She maintained that if arousal due to discrepant or strange stimuli always elicited negative responses (distress, fear), the infant would very likely be comforted by the caretaker and removed from the disturbing stimulus. However, when the infant responds to such stimuli with laughter the mother or caretaker is inclined to reproduce the stimuus, giving the infant the opportunity to experience and explore the situation. She also suggested that early laughter games may foster two kinds of learning: (1) the development of general expectations and (2) the social experience of learning that one's actions (in this case expressive behavior) inflence the activities of other people. The observations of other theorists and investigators, together with those of Rothbart, make a good case for the adaptive value of infant laughter.

Rothbart correctly pointed out that it is the infant who initiates the behavior sequence involved in mother–infant interactions surrounding distress and laughter. The child's crying in distress initiates the mother's efforts to comfort and care for the child; and in the laughter game, although the mother may present the initial stimulus for arousal, if the child does not laugh, the sequence is terminated and the game does not continue.

Humor Appreciation

Humor at its best involves the positive affect of joy, but when humor occurs at other people's expense it may be associated with anger, contempt (as in derisive laughter), and subsequent guilt. Humor appreciation is a function of both affect and cognition, and in differential emotions theory it is considered a special kind of affective–cognitive interaction. Laughter games in infancy set the stage for the development of humor appreciation, and one's ultimate sense of humor depends on one's freedom during developmental years to express vocally the sudden bursts of joy that accompany certain cognitive–affective processes.

Zillmann and his colleagues (Cantor, Bryant, & Zillmann, 1974) studied the effects of prior arousal or "excitation transfer" (Zillmann, 1971) on humor appreciation. They found that residual excitation from both positive (sexual) and negative (distressing, fearsome) stimuli enhanced subsequent appreciation of cartoons and jokes. Their position is that residual excitation enhances emotion responses only when it is not attributed to its actual source (Cantor, Zillmann, & Bryant, 1975). They found that both positive and negative arousal subsequently enhanced humor appreciation and presumably an accompanying positive affective state.

Leventhal and his colleagues describe an information-processing model of humor appreciation. The steps in the process consist of perception, interpretation, information integration, and overt judgment. They assume that each step represents different processes and that sex differences may occur at any one of them.

Leventhal and Mace (1970) showed children a humorous film under an inhibition condition ("restrain from laughter") and a facilitation condition ("laugh as much as you like"). They confirmed their hypothesis that expressive behavior (laughter) would increase the strength of subjective feeling, a finding consistent with theories linking facial expression and experiential emotion.

Cupchik and Leventhal (1974) showed that audience (canned) laughter and self-observation of one's own expressiveness affected males and females differently. Audience laughter caused females to be more expressive and to give higher funniness ratings to cartoons, but self-observation of their expressiveness produced significantly lower funniness ratings. When males heard audience laughter and observed (rated) their own expressiveness, they did not show the same pattern of responses as females but differentiated more sharply between good and poor cartoons. The authors inferred that women are more susceptible to expressive reactions as such, while males are more susceptible to informational influence. They found support for this inference in a later study that showed that females were more influenced by "canned laughter from a party," while males were more influenced by "canned laughter from a classroom" (Leventhal & Cupchik, 1975).

Leventhal & Cupchik, (1977) further confirmed the foregoing assumptions and empirical findings. They concluded that, as compared to males, females base their humor judgments more on feelings and that feelings vary as a function of level of expressive behavior.

Interactions of Joy with Perception, Cognition, and Action

The interaction of joy with the perceptual system has marked and readily observable effects. All sensory input seems relatively more pelasant than when you are distressed or experiencing some other negative emotion. Roses are redder, violets are bluer, and the sunshine is brighter; even rain that might be a pesky nuisance on other occasions may be refreshing or soothing. It is while experiencing joy that one "sees the world through rose-colored glasses." The apparent change that joy effects on the perceptual system (thus increasing thresholds for negative emotions) makes the person experiencing joy seem imbued with patience, tolerance, and generosity. Joy tends to have the same kind of salubrious effect on cognition that it has on perception. Problems melt and float away—they either are solved or become of less concern.

Depending upon the cognitive tasks at hand, joy may bring about a decrease in productive thinking. If the kind of problem at hand requires a great deal of persistence and hard work, joy may cause the problem to be put aside before it is solved. In some situations, then, the interaction of joy and cognition may be paradoxical. If your intellectual performance, whatever it may be, leads to joy, the joy will have the effect of slowing down performance and removing some of the concern for problem solving. This change in pace and concern may postpone or in some cases eliminate the possibility of an intellectual or creative achievement. In some cases the paradox can be effectively resolved. If excitement causes the "rushing" or "forcing" of intellectual activity, a joy-elicited slowing down may be exactly what is needed to improve intellectual performance and creative endeavor.

Maladaptive Interactions of Joy, Cognition, and Action

The possible maladaptive effects of certain joy–cognition interactions can be illustrated by a description of the role of joy in the formation of addiction (Tomkins, 1962). In addiction, a particular object becomes the only or primary means by which an individual obtains positive and/or prevents negative emotion. An addiction is somewhat similar to the bond that exists between a person and the familiar objects in the environment. Such familiar objects as one's room, a favorite chair, a pet, a tennis racquet, school books, blue jeans, or a picture represent a variety of commitments. An addiction represents an extreme and virtually irreversible commitment.

The emotions of joy and interest play a part in the development of psychological addictions. According to Tomkins, addiction to an object results when it elicits two kinds of emotion responses. First, the object by its presence physically, or by its place in our imagery or reverie, evokes intense joy or excitement. Second, the absence of the object, or an awareness of the possibility of its absence in the future, creates intense negative emotion. When this complex of emotion–cognition responses characterize our relationship to an object, the relationship may be described as a psychological addiction.

All addictions are by no means totally negative. We can become addicted to learning or creating. Many people become addicted to achievement and success, and for them the presence or absence of the currently desired sign of success (status symbol) is a powerful stimulus for positive or negative emotion.

Antecedents and Consequences of Joy

In thc study of the patterns of emotions in the joy situation (Izard, 1972), the participants in the study listed a wide variety of phenomena that were imaged or visualized as joy situations. A large proportion of these situations related to loved ones. Three types of situations involving loved ones led to joy: (1) making someone you love happy, (2) someone who loves you going out of his or her way to please you, and (3) simply sharing experiences with someone you love. The category of "making others happy" included doing something out of the ordinary with someone you love, seeing gratitude in the face of a loved one for something you did, and feeling that you are making someone joyful simply by being with him or her.

Companionship with friends was also a frequently mentioned joy situation. Such situations included things such as meeting a friend after a long absence and being with friends in a "nature setting."

A number of individuals indicated that joy resulted from various activities ranging from "creative nonrational thinking" to completing a difficult project after much personal involvement. However, they did not say that they undertook these tasks in order to experience joy.

It has also been suggested that joy is distinguished from drive pleasure, though it has been recognized that drive pleasure may lower the threshold for joy experience. Perhaps because of the latter phenomenon, a number of individuals described joy situations associated with drive pleasures. Such situations included an intimate dinner with a member of the opposite sex and sexual intercourse.

The study of the antecedents and consequences of the fundamental emotions was described in Chapter 4. The results of the study of the emotion of joy are presented in Table 7-1. This effort to summarize the antecedents and consequences of joy is intended only to give the reader an appreciation of the variety of phenomena that lead to joy and that follow from it. As is the case with every emotion, the specific experiences that lead to joy and that follow from it are in some measure idiosyncratic.

The Pattern of Emotions and Experiential Dimensions in the Joy Situation

The Bartlett–Izard study, described in Chapter 4, showed that the profile of emotions and dimensions in the imaged joy situation are more like those in the interest situation than in any other emotion situation. The DES profile of emotions

TABLE 7-1
Antecedents and Consequences of Joy[a]

Responses	Percentage of subjects giving response
Antecedents of joy	
Feelings	
1. Enjoyment	31.5
2. Relieved, problemless, relaxed, comfortable	26.9
3. Self-confident, successful	25.4
4. Accepted and needed, have something of offer	11.5
5. Other	4.6
Thoughts	
1. Of pleasant, happy times	26.9
2. Of a particular person, or activity	23.8
3. Of people, special activities	21.5
4. About own capability, success	12.3
5. About goodness of life and future	6.2
6. Of being accepted and needed, having something to offer	3.8
7. Other	5.4

[a]N = approximately 130 college students.

TABLE 7-1 (continued)

Responses	Percentage of subjects giving response
Actions	
1. Doing one's favorite thing	32.3
2. Doing well, one's best	28.5
3. Helping others	14.6
4. Doing something with a particular person	11.5
5. One's duty	6.9
6. Being involved in something stimulating	4.6
7. Other	1.5
Consequences of joy	
Feelings	
1. Enjoyment–joy	51.1
2. Feel relieved, relaxed, good, carefree	27.7
3. Self-confident, successful	5.8
4. Interest–excitement	5.1
5. Desire to share joy with others	2.9
6. Healthy, active, energetic	2.9
7. About specific person, activity	1.4
8. Other	2.9
Thoughts	
1. Pleasant, happy thoughts	40.9
2. How great life is	16.8
3. About one's favorite things, good times	13.9
4. About event that caused joy	9.5
5. Of self-confidence, success	4.4
6. About sharing joy with others	4.4
7. Gratitude for joy	3.6
8. About one's achievments	2.9
9. Names specific person, activity	1.4
10. Other	2.2
Actions	
1. Favorite things	27.7
2. Expresses joy, verbally or physically	19.0
3. Shares joy with others, friendly acts	13.1
4. Does something to continue joy	9.5
5. Becomes carefree and happy	6.6
6. Does well, one's best	4.4
7. Contemplates joy inwardly	2.9
8. Other	11.6

[a]N = approximately 130 college students.

in the joy situation is presented in Figure 7-2. As expected, the joy situation was characterized by a very high level of joy and a moderately high level of interest. The interaction of joy and interest probably characterizes the subjective experience of most individuals in a joy situation. The mean of surprise is also moderately

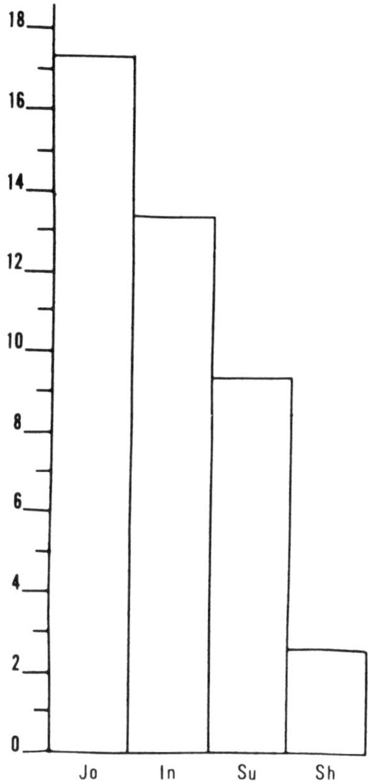

FIGURE 7-2. The DES profile of emotions in the joy situation. Jo, joy; In, interest; Su, surprise; Sh, shyness.

high in the joy situation. This is consistent with data from other studies suggesting that in the American culture a surprise is more often associated with positive emotion situations than with negative emotion situations. No negative emotion registers to any appreciable degree in the joy situation, and only shyness showed a mean exceeding the arbitrary cutoff point of 2.5. A joy–shyness interaction is observed whenever one is seen laughing in joy and at the same time lowering the face and averting the gaze in shame or shyness.

The profile of experiential dimensions, as measured by the Dimensional Rating Scale (DRS), is presented in Figure 7-3 (Bartlett & Izard, 1972). The gaps between all the means in the joy situation were highly significant ($p < .01$). As expected, pleasantness had by far the highest mean of any of the dimensions, and self-assurance had the next highest mean. Students' descriptions of the phenomenology of joy led to the expectation of high scores on the dimension of self-assurance, and the self-assurance mean in the joy situation was substantially higher than in any other emotion situation. The self-assurance means closest to that in the joy situation were those in the surprise and interest situations. The high mean on impulsiveness is also consistent with the phenomenological description

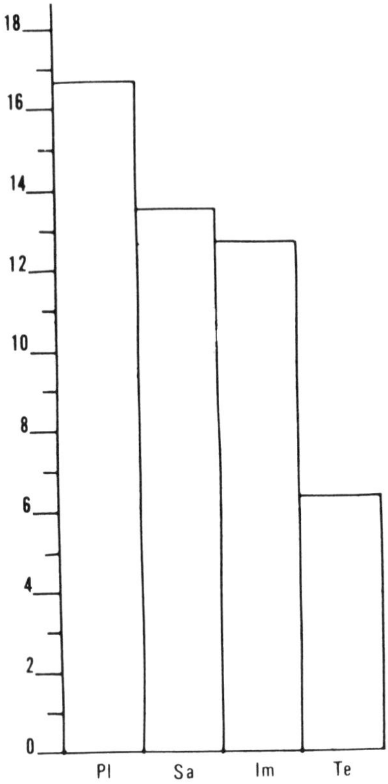

FIGURE 7-3. The DRS profile of dimensions in the joy situation. Pl, pleasantness; Sa, self-assurance; Im, impulsiveness; Te, tension.

of joy. The tension in joy is low and undoubtedly hedonically positive. The amount of tension is expected to vary with the degree to which the joy is active or passive. The pleasant, self-assured, and carefree nature of the joy experience undoubtedly plays a role in lowering the threshold for impulsiveness. The mean for impulsiveness was higher in the joy situation than in any other emotion situation except for anger. Judging from the data from the study of antecedents and consequences, it is reasonable to assume that the nature of impulsive thoughts and actions in joy are quite different from those in anger.

Cognitively Induced Joy Facilitates Empathy, Altruism, and Creativity

Moore, Underwood, and Rosenhan (1973) studied the effects of happy thoughts and imagery on altruistic behavior in 7- and 8-year-old middle-class white children. The experimenter told the children that they were helping test some new hearing equipment by taking a brief hearing test. The experimenter administered the hearing test individually to the children, gave each 25 pennies for participating, explained that some money would be given to the students who did not get a chance to participate, and then told them that if they so desired they could contribute some of their pennies for the nonparticipants by putting them in a nearby container. The experimenter then left the room so the children could donate, or not, in privacy. Before the 25 pennies were given to the children they were asked either to think about things that made them happy or things that made them sad, or they were assigned to a neutral condition. As the experimenters predicted, the children who thought about happy occasions contributed significantly more of their pennies than those in the neutral condition, and those who thought about sad occasions contributed significantly less than those in the neutral condition. The experiment demonstrated very clearly that the type of affective–cognitive interaction is a significant determinant of action, and that, specifically, on the average a cognitively induced joy experience increases altruism while sadness decreases it. As we shall see in Chapter 8, however, sadness can facilitate altruism if attention is focused on a friend in need and not on one's self.

Isen (1984) and her colleagues have conducted an extensive series of studies that show that relatively small favors or bits of good luck (like finding money in a coin telephone or getting an unexpected gift) induce positive emotion in people. This positive emotion state, which undoubtedly includes enjoyment, regularly causes the subjects' subsequent behavior to be more empathic or altruistic (Isen, Daubman, & Norwicki, 1987).

These investigators have also demonstrated that positive emotion facilitates cognitive processes such as thinking, remembering, categorization, and creative problem solving (Isen & Daubman, 1984; Izard, Nagler *et al.*, 1965). One of these studies showed that positive emotion enhanced cognitive performance. It increased the likelihood of seeing relations among objects, resulting in better performance on a categorization task. Another study showed that positive emotion enhanced creative problem solving by enabling subjects to see relations among objects that would otherwise go unnoticed.

In an early study of the induction of emotion states (Izard, Nagler, *et al.* 1965), positive and negative emotions were induced by having subjects interact with an actress who was either happy and encouraging or hostile and critical. Following the emotion-induction episode, subjects who interacted with the actress who role-played a friendly, encouraging person perceived the experimenter more favorably and performed better on measures of intellectual functioning and creativity. For example, as compared to subjects in the negative emotion condition, those in the positive emotion condition were able to name more uses for common objects, an ability associated with creative problem solving. In another series of studies (Isen *et al.*, 1987), positive emotion induced with a few minutes of an amusing film or a gift of a small bag of candy caused subjects to perform more effectively on intellectual and creative problem-solving tasks. For example, given a box of tacks, a candle, and a book of matches, subjects in the positive emotion condition were more likely to figure out how to attach the candle to the wall (corkboard) in such a way that it would not drip on the floor.

A number of studies have shown that these effects of positive emotion on thinking, memory, and action can be demonstrated in preschool and older children. In one study (Bartlett, Burleson, & Santrock, 1982), children were asked to think of happy or sad experiences and to continue remembering these events while learning a list of words. Two types of tests (free recall, cued recall) showed that the induction of happiness significantly increased learning and memory. In another study (Nasby & Yando, 1982), fifth-grade children were asked to recall and visualize an experience that made them happy, sad, or angry. Following the emotion induction, they were asked to learn a list of words that had either positive or negative connotation. After the learning task, the emotion induction task was repeated and memory tests administered. The results showed that a happy mood during learning or during the memory test facilitated the recall of positive words. Sad and angry moods decreased memory for positive words, and the angry mood increased memory for negative words.

Explaining the Functions of Emotion Experiences

There are two kinds of factors that contribute to the salubrious effects of positive emotion on perception, learning, creative problem solving, and prosocial behavior. The first set of factors, emphasized by cognitive-social theories, relates to cognitive processes. Positive emotion cues and positive material in memory (Isen, Shalker, Clark, & Karp, 1978) is more extensive than neutral and negative material (Boucher & Osgood, 1969). The second set of factors, emphasized by biosocial theorists, relates to the intrinsic motivational and organizational influences of emotion and to the particular characteristics of the subjective experience of positive emotion. For example, theorists maintain that the experience of joy is characterized by heightened self-esteem and self-confidence. These qualities of consciousness increase openness to information and flexibility of mental processes. Biosocial theorists see the positive emotion that is induced by experimental manipulations and by experimental tasks as including the emotion of interest as well as enjoyment. The subjecive experience of interest is characterized by curiosity and the desire to explore and learn. Even in young infants, stimuli that elicit greater amounts of interest expression also elicit the most attention (Langsdorf *et al.*, 1983).

In summary, biosocial theories hold that the motivational and organizational functions of the positive emotions of interest and enjoyment account for their facilitative effects on perception, cognition, and action. However, the explanatory concepts emphasized by biosocial and cognitive-social theories are not contradictory or mutually exclusive.

An Empirical Analysis of the Phenomenology of Joy

Following his exhaustive review of the literature on joy, Meadows (1975) developed a 61-item joy inventory with items representing each of six aspects of joy phenomenology. He reasoned that joy could be adequately described by the dimensions of activeness–passiveness, individuation–affiliation, and excitement–serenity. Activeness was seen as an aspect of joy that is felt when one plays an active role in the events that brought about the joy or when one feels active during the joy experience. Passiveness is similar to what has been discussed as receptiveness. Individuation was defined as a feeling of "centeredness" of self, a feeling that the self is distinct and separate from the surrounding world. Affiliation was described as that aspect of joy that arises from communal participation, a sense of oneness with the persons, objects, or events in the surrounding world. The excitement aspect of joy was characterized as a feeling of vigor (associated with alertness). Serenity was defined as a relaxed peacefulness, an absence of muscular tension, and a tendency to savor the world and experience a sense of harmony.

Five of these six aspects of joy emerged as distinct factors in a factor-analytic investigation of the data from the administration of Meadow's Joy Scale to 333 college students. The sixth factor, activeness, emerged as one end of a bipolar factor with passiveness at the other end. The alpha coefficients (internal reliability indexes) for individuation, excitement, serenity, and activeness ranged from .70 to .62, and these are sufficiently high to suggest that Meadow's ideas about joy phenomenology are worthy of further investigation. One important question is whether all these factors represent aspects of joy or a combination of joy and other affects.

An Empirical Study of Happiness and Personality Development

Although happiness is not necessarily synonymous with joy, the two concepts are certainly related, and most would readily agree that a happy person experiences more joy or experiences joy more frequently than does an unhappy person. Constantinople (1970) did a relatively large-scale cross-sectional study of four college classes (freshman through senior year) to test the relationships among level of happiness, personality development, and attitudes toward goal attainment in the college environment. She found that males began college life at a lower average level of happiness than did females. However, college males increased in average level of happiness significantly from freshman to senior year, while college females decreased in level of happiness. The decrease for females was not statistically significant, but it should be noted that the direction of change was opposite for men and women. Means for males and females decreased significantly on shame and guilt and increased significantly on autonomy and identity from freshman to senior year. For all participants, level of happiness was positively correlated with basic trust, initiative, and identity and negatively correlated with basic mistrust, guilt, and isolation.

An important question raised by Constantinople's study was why the women showed a decrease in relative level of happiness as they progressed through college despite the fact that men showed an increase. Constantinople suggested a possible answer. She pointed out that although the development of social competence may be an indirect goal of some residential colleges, it is rarely deliberately fostered. This may be the crux of the problem, at least for those women who judge their social competence in terms of their romantic relationships and place high priority on life goals of marriage and motherhood. Pressures to attain such goals become greater as the senior year passes. Social competence judged by the senior woman in terms of progress toward the goal of marriage may be as important an ingredient of her identity as vocational competence for men. However, contrary to her needs, her sphere of social influence seems to decrease through the college years, as indicated by the significant increase in the women's average score on isolation.

Constantinople's study was conducted in the late 1960s. It would be interesting to see the extent to which changes in women's attitudes and values relative to sex, marriage, and family on the one hand and autonomy, competence, and career on the other would result in different findings if this study were repeated today.

An In-Depth Study of Elation–Happiness and Personality

Wessman and Ricks (1966) conducted an extensive longitudinal study of affective states and personality. Working in the tradition of Gordon Allport and Henry Murray, Wessman and Ricks developed a set of 16 ten-item affective scales (Personal Feelings Scales) and applied them in the study of a small sample of college men and women who were given an intensive personality assessment. Although most of Wessman and Ricks's scales do not correspond to discrete emotions or single affects, the one scale (elation–depression) that proved most important in terms of personality criteria appears to involve the fundamental emotions of joy and sadness. In particular, the items at the positive pole appear to be rather straightforward joy items.

Their studies led them to conclude that for both men and women the most frequent and reliable element of happiness was the feeling that life was full and abundant. Wessman and Ricks also found that elated states were often characterized by high levels of energy and self-confidence, tranquility, love, sociability, companionship, and receptivity. This characterization of elation is quite similar to Meadow's findings on the phenomenology of joy.

Wessman and Ricks administered their Personal Feelings Scales to 25 Radcliffe women and to 18 Harvard men. The group of Harvard men were intensively studied by means of a number of projective and objective personality tests, as well as through interview. They found that happy men and women exhibited zestfulness, high energy, and relatedness to others during their zest phase.

Wessman and Ricks considered their Personal Feelings Scales as a means of measuring moods. In a fashion similar to that of Nowlis (1965), they defined mood as a basic expression of the individual's continuing total life condition, as a characteristic of the individual that is intimately related to feelings and behavior. Mood as defined by Nowlis, as well as by Wessman and Ricks, seems rather similar to the concept of emotion trait in differential emotions theory.

On the basis of their Personal Feelings Scales they delineated four types of people: happy, unhappy, variable (in mood), and stable. They concluded that these four types experienced elation or their "highest mood" in somewhat different fashion. Happy people experience elation as zest, a feeling characterized by intense energetic, open, and receptive interest in a full and abundant world, a world in which they actively engage themselves. Unhappy men and women tend to experience their highest mood as a sense of relief, a kind of temporary or transient peace in an otherwise turbulent world. Stable men and women experience their peaks of elation as contentment, feelings of harmony with others, tranquility, love, and sexual tenderness. People who are variable in mood tend to experience their peaks of elation as joy, as intense inner feeling of satisfaction in a full and abundant world. This state is distinguished from zest by less active engagement in the world and greater involvement with inner feelings such as self-assurance and freedom from care.

Wessman and Ricks used a number of self-description inventories (Q-sorts), projective techniques (including the Thematic Apperception Test and the Rorschach), and interviews in their intensive study of the personalities of their subjects. They found that happy men were more self-confident, more optimistic, and actually more genuinely successful. They enjoyed intimate and mutually rewarding relationships. Their work showed continuity, purpose, and meaningfulness. They had a rewarding sense of identity and the necessary skills and mastery to achieve their goals and receive a great deal of satisfaction in the process of doing so. The less happy men were more unsure and more pessimistic. Fear, anger, and guilt tended to characterize their interpersonal relationships, and they showed a certain tendency to withdraw and isolate themselves from others. Their work proved more burdensome, less satisfying, and a sense of failure led them to be self-critical and less effective. Their lower sense of ego identity and poor ego integration left them less well equipped to meet the challenges of day-to-day life and to experience personal growth.

Wessman and Ricks's studies led them to some inferences about the sources of happiness and unhappiness. Happy men apparently enjoy frequent success experiences during childhood, enabling them to develop a strong sense of competence. The nature of their relationships enables them to achieve trust and intimacy and to enjoy initiative and industry. Happy men typically appear to be well-adjusted social extroverts who obtain a great deal of satisfaction from their work and their personal relationships. Unhappy men on the other hand show little zestful commitment to their studies and do not achieve regular satisfaction from their academic work. Happy men are apparently more capable of achieving what Freud thought the normal personal should be able to do well: to love and to work.

Psychophysiological Studies of Joy in Adults

Most psychophysiological studies of affective phenomena have investigated various physiological responses to laboratory-induced arousal, activation, or complex affective states such as anxiety. A few psychophysiological studies have focused on discrete emotions, including the emotion of joy.

One of the problems in conducting psychophysiological studies of discrete emotions is that of inducing the emotion in the laboratory. Two techniques for eliciting joy, as well as other emotions, are self-induction through imagery and the use of films especially selected for their ability to elicit a particular emotion. In the imaging technique participants are requested to recall, visualize, and/or imagine a situation in which they experienced the desired emotion. They are asked to take time to get into the scene as completely as possible and to picture the situation as vividly and clearly as they can. This is the technique used in obtaining the emotion profiles and the profiles of dimensions in emotion experiences discussed in Chapter 4 and the preceding sections of this chapter. In those studies, however, the only evidence for the presence of emotion was the participants' self-report (e.g., on the Differential Emotions Scale). The effectiveness of the imaging technique has now been substantiated by means of other (objective) indexes of emotion or arousal. Rusalova *et al.* (1975) had each subject image a joy situation while the experimenters measured heart rate and changes in muscle potential in the expressive musculature of the face (EMG) and took self-report. In the condition in which the subjects imagined a joy situation and consequently reported a joy experience, they showed a substantial increase in heart rate and in facial muscle activity. Changes in the facial muscles took place in those muscles that were predicted to be the ones involved in the expression of joy.

Schwartz *et al.* (1974) compared the EMG profiles of subjects who were instructed to self-generate happy, sad, and angry imagery so as to feel the target emotion. They also recorded EMG activity while the subjects thought about a "typical day." They recorded from the frontalis, corrugator, depressor, and masseter muscles and showed that the changes in muscle potential in these selected muscles varied significantly from one emotion to another. They also showed that the profiles of muscle activity from happy imagery and from thinking about a typical day were more similiar for normals that for depressives.

Figure 7-4 shows the profile of EMG activity for self-generated happiness and for subjects who were told to make an exaggerated smile and hold it for 30 seconds. Although the muscle activity in the smile condition is greater, the profiles

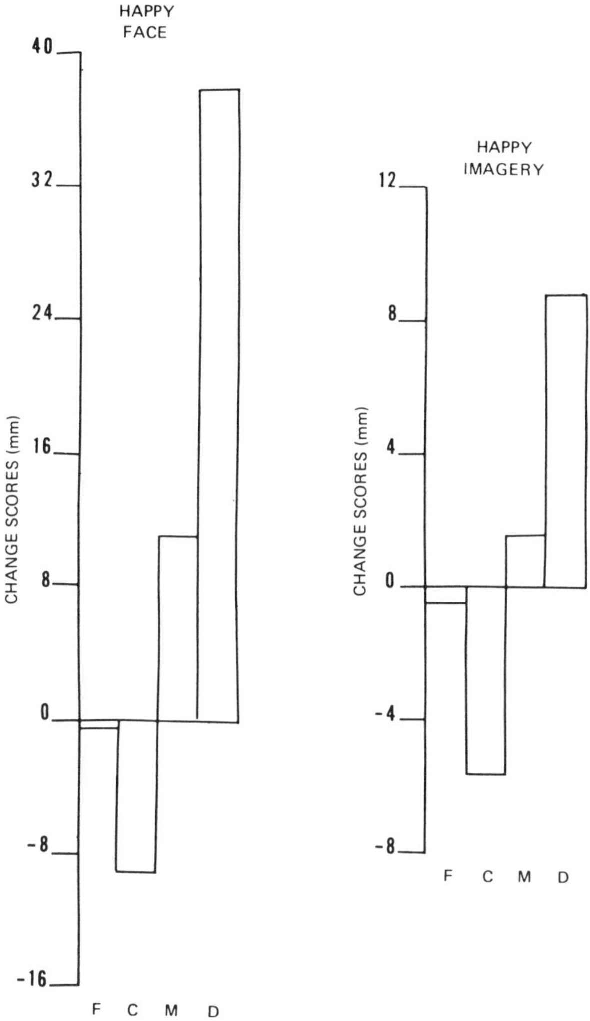

FIGURE 7-4. Average change from baseline in muscle activity for the frontalis (F), corrugator (C), masseter (M), and depressor (D) in a voluntary smile and imagery-induced joy (N = 12). (Data from Schwartz et al., *1974.)*

for the happy imagery and smile conditions are quire similar. Averill (1969) studied autonomic response patterns during joy (mirth) and sadness. He used movies as stimuli to induce the desired emotions. For the mirth condition he used an adaptation of Mack Sennett's silent film "Good Old Corn" (Warner Brothers) with music and commentary added. For the sadness condition he used the film "John F. Kennedy 1917–1963" (Twentieth Century Fox), edited to give prominence to the assassination, funeral, and burial of the president. He found four physiological measures that distinguished sadness from mirth, but only one of these—respiration irregularity—distinguished mirth from the control condition, and this was seen largely as a function of the laughter that occurred in the mirth condition. In summary, he considered changes in respiration as more characteristic of mirth, while changes in the cardiovascular system were more characteristic of sadness. However, this study was not successful in providing a number of clearly distinguishing physiological reactions for sadness and mirth as induced by these particular stimuli.

Summary

Laughing develops a little later than smiling and progresses through certain developmental stages of its own. Theory and research have linked laughing to certain aspects of cognitive development, but the emotion dynamics in laughing have been little investigated. Laughter, like smiling, can foster interpersonal affective ties and social development. It can also foster opportunities for new experiences and learning.

Joy interacts with other emotions and with perception, cognition, and action. Joy can slow down performance, but it can also create a kind of openness and receptivity associated with keen intuition and creativity.

Different thresholds for joy tend to create different styles of life. Some people experience a conflict between excitement and joy as they ponder the relative importance of tranquility and the vigorous pursuit of goals.

Empirical studies of joy in adults have increased our understanding of the antecedents and consequences of joy and of joy phenomenology. Other studies have shown sex-linked changes in frequency of joy experiences or happiness during college years. One in-depth study of happiness has shown significant relationships between personality characteristics, joy thresholds, and types of joy experiences. Psychophysiological studies suggest the possibility of differentiating joy from other emotions on the basis of neurophysiological functions, especially in terms of facial electromyography.

Recent studies have revealed a trait of positive emotionality, but this concept is broader than joy. A few studies suggest individual stability of frequency of smiling and laughing in infancy, but there is insufficient data to say that a trait of enjoyment–joy or positive emotionality exists in early development.

Suggested Readings

Diener, E., & Emmons, R. A. (1984). The independence of positive and negative affect. *Journal of Personality and Social Psychology, 47*(5), 1105–1117.

A demonstration of the traitlike nature of positive emotionality and its independence of negative emotionality.

Malatesta, C. Z. (1990). The role of emotions in the development and organization of personality. In R. Thompson (Ed.), *Socioemotional development* (pp. 1–56). Nebraska Symposium on Motivation.

Theory and data on the role of emotions on the development of personality.

Watson, D., & Clark, L. A. (in press). On traits and temperament: General and specific factors of emotional experience and their relation to the five-factor model. *Journal of Personality.*

Joy or happiness is represented in Watson and Clark's joviality scale and in their positive affect scale.

Wessman, A. E., & Ricks, D. F. (1966). *Mood and Personality.* New York: Holt, Rinehart and Winston.

A pioneering, longitudinal study of the relations between joy (happiness) and unhappiness and personality characteristics.

8

Surprise–Astonishment

Surprise is not an emotion in the same sense as joy or sadness. It does not have all the characteristics of the other emotions.

The Activation, Expression, and Experience of Surprise

Surprise is activated by a sharp increase in stimulation. The external condition for surprise is any sudden and unexpected event. The event may be a clap of thunder, the boom of fireworks, or the unexpected appearance of a friend.

The look of surprise, as shown in Figure 8-1, is easy to recognize. The brow is lifted, creating wrinkles across the forehead and giving the eyes a large, rounded appearance. The mouth is opened in an oval shape.

Everyone is familiar with the feeling of surprise, but it is difficult to describe. One reason for this is the fact that the feeling does not last very long. However, the most important reason is because the mind seems to be blank in the moment of surprise. It is as though ordinary thought processes are momentarily stopped. Thus there is very little thought content associated with surprise. It is a little like receiving mild electric shock; your muscles contract rapidly and you can almost feel the tingle of the electrical activity that occurs in the nerves and makes you jump. In the moment of surprise, you do not know exactly how to react. There is a feeling of uncertainty created by the sudden unexpected event.

Figure 8-2 shows the profile of dimensions in the surprise situation. The graph, adapted from the Bartlett–Izard study, shows that a surprise situation is characterized by a high degree of pleasantness. This is consonant with the commonsense observation that most people think of surprise in a positive way. If young people are asked to recall a time when they were surprised, they usually recall a situation that turned out to be happy and pleasant. Situations that evoke surprise are usually experienced as being about as pleasant as situations that elicit a high degree of interest. Situations that cause surprise are generally remembered

FIGURE 8-1. The expression of surprise.

as less pleasant than situations that cause joy but as much more pleasant than situations causing any negative emotion—sadness, anger, disgust, contempt, fear, and shame.

In the surprise situation, the mean for pleasantness was significantly higher than the means for self-assurance and impulsiveness, and the latter means were significantly higher than the mean for tension. Impulsiveness was significantly higher in surprise than all the emotions studied except for anger and joy. Self-assurance was significantly higher in surprise than for any of the negative emotions. The mean for tension in the surprise situation was significantly lower than for any of the negative emotions, approximately equal to the mean for the interest situation, and significantly higher than was the case for the joy situation. The data for the dimension of tension furnish some support for Tomkin's (1962) notion that surprise occupies a place in between the positive and negative emotions. Even though middle-class American students typically image a surprise situation that is characterized by pleasantness and self-assurance, the amount of tension felt is as near to that felt in sadness as to that felt in joy. Since the means for tension are significantly higher in all of the negative emotions than in surprise and the two positive emotions of interest and joy, it is reasonable to conclude that the subjective experience of tension is experienced as negative once it reaches a

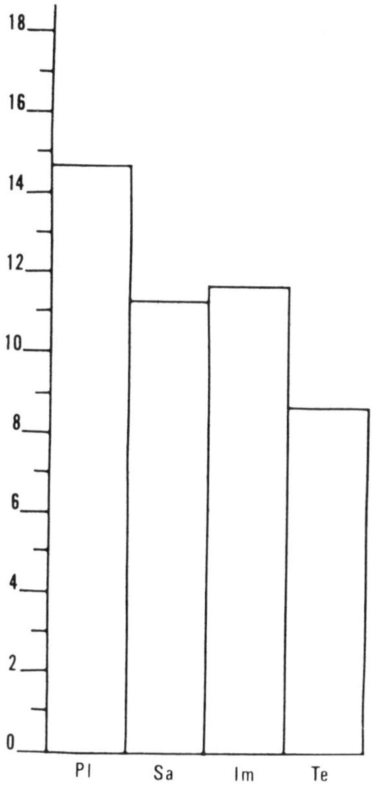

FIGURE 8-2. The DRS profile of dimensions in the surprise situation. Pl, pleasantness; Sa, self-assurance; Im, impulsiveness; Te, tension.

certain level. However, a level of tension significantly higher than that experienced in joy can still be experienced in relation to the positive affect of interest–excitement.

Figure 8-3 shows the profile of emotions in the surprise situation. The differences between each successive pair of means shown on the graph are significantly different. The surprise–joy–interest pattern is the most typical combination of emotions for the type of subjects sampled in the Bartlett–Izard study. The data show that the negative emotions most likely to be involved in a surprise situation in this class of subjects are shame/shyness and fear. Sometimes an individual is ashamed of the fact that he or she was "caught by surprise." Such a situation may be characterized by the feeling that the individual is overexposed. The appearance of fear in the larger pattern has a sufficiently low mean to suggest that in the population sampled, fear is not frequently associated with a surprise situation. The fact that it occurs at all may lend some support to the notion that surprise and fear have similar or overlapping components at the neurophysiological level (Tomkins, 1962).

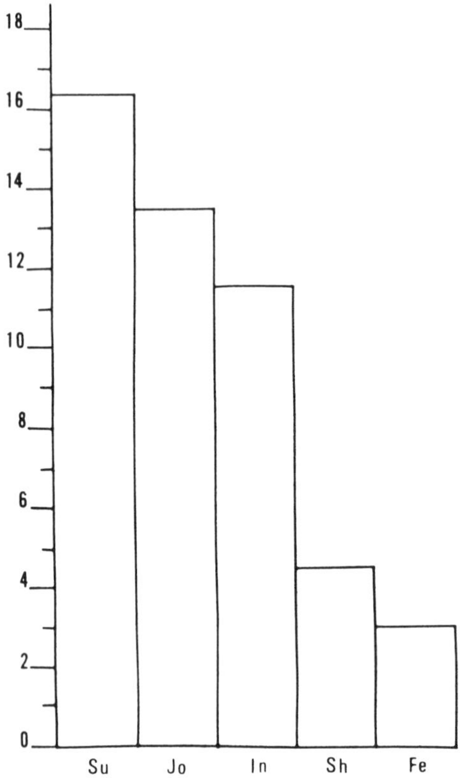

FIGURE 8-3. The DES profile of emotions in the surprise situation. Su, surprise; Jo, joy; In, interest; Sh, shyness; Fe, fear.

The Significance of Surprise

From the foregoing description of the experience of surprise, it is clear that it is a highly transient feeling; it comes and goes quickly. Unlike other emotions, surprise does not motivate behavior for long periods of time. In some respects surprise is not a real emotion like the other fundamental emotions considered in this book.

If surprise is so fleeting and motivates very little thought or action, what is its function? Its primary function is to help prepare the individual to deal effectively with the new or sudden event and with the consequences of this event. It is important for the person to be able to deal with sudden changes. From an evolutionary standpoint, failure to change one's motivational set after the sudden appearance of some predatory animal or threatening situation could result in serious harm or death.

A person is always experiencing one emotion or another and often more than one. Some emotions, once they are activated, have great psychological inertia—

TABLE 8-1
Antecedents and Consequences of Surprise[a]

Responses	Percentage of subjects giving responses
Antecedents of surprise	
Feelings	
1. Surprise synonyms: startled, shocked	31.4
2. Unexpectedly aware of something	22.3
3. Lost, bewildered, confused	12.4
4. Physically/mentally stimulated	8.3
5. Misled, hurt, used by others	7.4
6. Distress synonyms: depressed, sad	4.6
7. Shame synonyms: embarressed, shy	.7
8. Other	12.4
Thoughts	
1. Something wrong, stupid	27.3
2. Of some specific person, activity	23.9
3. Unexpected awareness	19.8
4. Something original, creative	16.5
5. Other	12.4
Actions	
1. Something original, creative	33.9
2. Unexpected success or failure	33.1
3. Something stupid, makes mistake	15.7
4. React to stimulus	7.4
5. Other	9.9
Consequences of surprise	
Feelings	
1. Surprise synonyms	37.6
2. Bewildered, confused	14.3
3. Fear synonyms	10.5
4. Interest synonyms	10.0
5. Happy or sad, depending on the context	6.8
6. Enjoyment synonyms	4.5
7. Shame synonyms	2.3
8. Other	14.3
Thoughts	
1. About what caused surprise	39.9
2. Shouldn't have been surprised	33.9
3. Anticipate consequences, response	11.2
4. Of possible reward	.7
5. How to regain control of self and situation	.7
6. Other	13.5
Actions	
1. Try to understand cause	28.5
2. Regain control of self or situation	21.8
3. Express surprise, verbally or physically	18.8
4. Depends on situation, whatever is appropriate	9.2
5. Anticipate consequences, reaction	7.5
6. Something panicky, irrational	3.0
7. Express enjoyment	2.3
8. Other	9.2

[a]*N* = approximately 130 college students

they tend to continue. Sadness is a good example of an emotion that is difficult to stop quickly. Mental health professionals know how difficult it is to break up a depression, a complex of emotions and feelings in which sadness dominates. The sudden appearance of a poisonous snake or speeding automobile in the path of a depressed person could mean certain death if surprise did not facilitate a change in his or her emotion state.

Thus the function of surprise is to clear the nervous system of ongoing activity that would interfere with adjustment to a sudden change in our environment. Tomkins (1962) has aptly called it the "channel-clearing emotion." It clears the neural pathways for new and different activity.

If Rafe is given pleasant surprises relatively often he will come to view the overall effect of surprise as positive, though strictly speaking is it neither positive nor negative. If Rebecca has relatively frequent unpleasant surprises, she may come to view the effect of surprise as negative and become less capable of dealing with situations of surprise. If the socialization of surprise is very severe, the individual may become fearful or ineffective in the presence of anything novel or different whether or not it appears suddenly.

The study of antecedents and consequences of surprise in college students is presented in Table 8-1.

Charlesworth (1969) presents an extensive review of the literature on surprise, defining it specifically as a function of misexpected (as distinguished from unexpected) events. Surprise so defined cannot occur until 5 to 7 months of age, when cognitive development enables the infant to form expectations or assumptions. Working within this conceptual framework, Charlesworth makes a good case for assigning an important role to surprise in cognitive development. He sees it as instigating, "illuminating," and reinforcing a variety of responses that contribute to changes in cognitive structures. He attributes to surprise some of the characteristics that differential emotions theory assigns to interest.

In contrast to Charlesworth's position, Bower (1974) reports evidence of startle or surprise (terms he uses interchangeably) a few hours after birth. The two investigators agree, however, on the value of surprise as a measure of certain cognitive processes and possibly as an index of stages of cognitive development.

Suggested Readings

Charlesworth, W. R. (1964). Instigation and maintenance of curiosity behavior as a function of surprise versus novel and familiar stimuli. *Child Development*, *35*, 1169–1186.

A study demonstrating the facilitating effects of surprise on activating and maintaining exploratory behavior.

Charlesworth, W. R. (1969). The role of surprise in cognitive development. In D. Elkind & J. H. Flavell (Eds.), *Studies in cognitive development* (pp. 257–314). New York and London: Oxford University Press.

A discussion of the dynamics of surprise and its relation to cognitive processes.

Ekman, P., Friesen, W. V., & Simons, R. C. (1985). Is the startle reaction an emotion? *Journal of Personality and Social Psychology*, *49*(5), 1416–1433.

An experiment that specifies precisely the pattern of movements in genuine startle and a discussion of its status as a reflex and its differences from the emotion of surprise.

9

Sadness

Though sadness is generally considered to be a negative emotion, it is somehow very special. The classification "positive" or "negative" is one of convenience, and it does not adequately characterize the discrete emotions. As we have already discussed, excitement can sometimes cause insomnia and is sometimes associated with manic disorders.

The Expression, Experience, and Functions of Sadness

Sadness may have positive effects on our lives. Imagine living in a world without this vital human emotion. Would there be any strength in a social bond? Indeed, what would keep an individual from breaking the ties that bind one person to another if there were no sorrow felt on parting? And how "human" would you consider a species that could not mourn the death of a loved one or respond empathically to the sorrow of another?

Causes of Sadness

As we have seen, there are some natural causes for each of the emotions. By natural, we mean a cause that is common to all people everywhere regardless of culture, ethnic origin, education, or socioeconomic background. Novelty and change are universal elicitors of interest. Under certain circumstances, recognition of a familiar face is a cause of joy that transcends ethnic and cultural barriers. So, too, there are universal elicitors of sadness.

Separation, whether physical or psychological, remains throughout life one of the basic and most common causes of sadness. When we have to leave our family or dear friends we feel sad, but we may be separated or alone psychologically even in a crowd of people. Psychological separation takes many forms—inability to communicate with others, express true feelings, or obtain sympathy. Or, we may feel left out, that we do not belong.

Death of a close friend or member of the family is perhaps the cause of the most profound sadness. To lose a loved one means you have lost a person with whom you have established an enduring and endearing relationship. It often means that you have invested many hours of your life in this other person and have shared good times and bad. Losing a loved one means the rupturing of strong bonds of friendship, companionship, and love, and often results in the experience of grief.

Disappointment may also be a basic cause of sadness, particularly when it comes as the result of shattered hopes. Disappointment, too, may share something in common with separation, loss, and loneliness. This is especially true in circumstances where the elicitor is the failure of a friend or loved one to call, to show up when expected, to remember your birthday, or to talk to you about an important decision he or she has made. Though other emotions will be undoubtedly stirred in different combinations, sadness will almost always be present under these circumstances.

Sadness is also a frequent response to failure in achieving an important goal. Different people care about different things and set very different goals. For example, one student may be very happy to receive a B or a C in a course, while another may be crushed to received anything less than an A.

A leading psychiatrist (Beck, 1967) has made a very strong case for the role of cognition as an important source of depression. It is important to look at the way an individual sees or thinks about himself or herself, the world, and the future when examining the influence of emotions, in this case sadness. Sometimes children who experience uncontrollable misfortunes may come to blame themselves for these events and come to think of themselves as failures. A daughter's perception of her own role in a misfortune that befalls her and her family will depend in large measure on the reaction of her parents or older siblings. If a father berates himself for losing a job, even though the real cause was an economic recession, the son may adopt a similar attitude toward an injury or an illness that befalls him.

Individual Differences in Proneness to Becoming Sad

As with each of the emotions, there are two sources of differences in the proneness with which individuals experience sadness—biological makeup and experience. Neuroscientists have shown that several neuronal, chemical, and physiological mechanisms are involved in the regulation of emotion (Puig-Antich, 1986). There is evidence of a genetic predisposition to depression (Nurnberger & Gershon, 1984), a disorder in which sadness is the key emotion. In addition to biological makeup, an individual's unique experiences through life can determine a tendency toward sadness. There are many life events that cause sadness but over which the individual has no control. You may be performing very well on a job that you enjoy, but economic forces may force you to be laid off. Injuries to yourself or your loved ones may also be real sources of sadness over which you have little or no control. As we have already discussed, children may experience enough uncontrollable misfortunes during their formative years that they become more vulnerable to sadness and even depression.

The Expression of Sadness

The photographs of a sad infant and adult (Figure 9-1) provide the basis for a good description of the facial expressions of these emotions. The inner corners of the brows are drawn obliquely upward and together, while the eyes are slightly narrowed and the corners of the mouth are pulled downward. Sometimes the chin is pushed upward and quivers. Depending upon the age of the person and intensity of the sadness, crying or sobbing may add a vocal element to the expression.

Note, however, that a sad person will not always look like the faces in the photographs. There are many reasons for this. First, the expression of sadness is more fleeting than the feeling of sadness. Although the full expression of sadness may last only a few seconds, the feeling may continue for a long time. While the feeling of sadness is present, often there is some indication of it, though the signs may be very subtle. The face may appear droopy and lacking in muscular tone. The person's eyes may not seem as bright as usual. Speech may be slower and less frequent.

It is also true that some people will attempt to smile and maintain a pleasant countenance despite feelings of sadness. In fact, in older children and adults it is quite possible to completely inhibit the expression of sadness and even to entirely mask it through the forced expression of another emotion. Recall Ekman's "false smile" discussed in Chapter 6. Nevertheless, the keen observer will usually be able to detect one or more of the subtler signs of sadness.

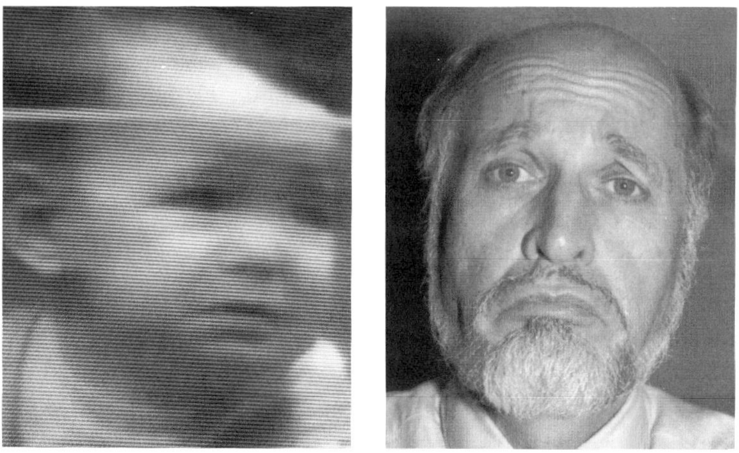

FIGURE 9-1. The sadness expression in an infant and in an adult.

The Subjective Experience of Sadness

When you are sad, you feel blue, downhearted, and discouraged. It is often said that in sadness the heart is heavy. In fact, the face, chest, arms, legs, and the whole body may feel heavy, as if the weight of the world were on its shoulders. It can feel as though a dark and heavy cloud surrounds you. There is no brightness, no color, no warmth in life. You may feel as if there is no person in the whole world to whom you can reach out, or that no one could possibly understand your present feeling of emptiness.

The total subjective experience of sadness often carries with it more than just the feelings discussed, for often these feelings will be associated with and accompanied by certain individual images, thoughts, and memories. A feeling of sadness will often touch off memories of other sad events—it often influences the way you perceive the world, as it seems you are looking at it through smoked glass or as reflected in a dingy mirror.

Intense sadness hurts. It can feel as though there were real pain in the face and chest. Some students of emotion believe that it is possible to distinguish between the physically manifested feelings of distress and the emotional suffering of sadness. Indeed, there are similarities between some forms of distress and sadness, yet the physical distress that is felt from the acute pain of banging a finger with a hammer is not at all like the feeling of sadness. Thus there are clearly different types of distress. However, the hurt that is felt in the face and chest in intense sadness may be the mental equivalent of physical distress. Sadness may produce a kind of mental pain, and in some ways this kind of hurt can be deeper and more profound than any physical suffering.

The DRS profile of experiential dimensions in the sadness situation is presented in Figure 9-2. In sadness, the dimension with the highest mean is tension, but, in keeping with differential emotions theory, tension is lower in sadness than in any other negative emotion. Thus, as already indicated, and as pointedly emphasized by Tomkins (1963), sadness is much more tolerable than fear or the other negative emotions. Interestingly, impulsiveness, the second highest experiential dimension in sadness, is lower for this emotion than any other emotion studied in the Bartlett–Izard experiment. The experiment showed that self-assurance in sadness is not significantly different from that in shyness and guilt but is significantly higher than in fear. As to be expected, the dimension of pleasantness is as low in sadness as it is in fear, anger, and guilt, and significantly lower than it is in shyness.

The profile of emotions (modified DES) in the sadness situation is presented in Figure 9-3. To indicate the reliability of emotion profiles obtained in imaged sadness situations, the profile obtained using the standard DES is shown in Figure 9-4. The profiles in the two samples are essentially quite similar. Sadness is extremely high. After the key emotion of sadness, the next highest emotion, fear in one sample and interest in the other, is only about 50% the magnitude of the key

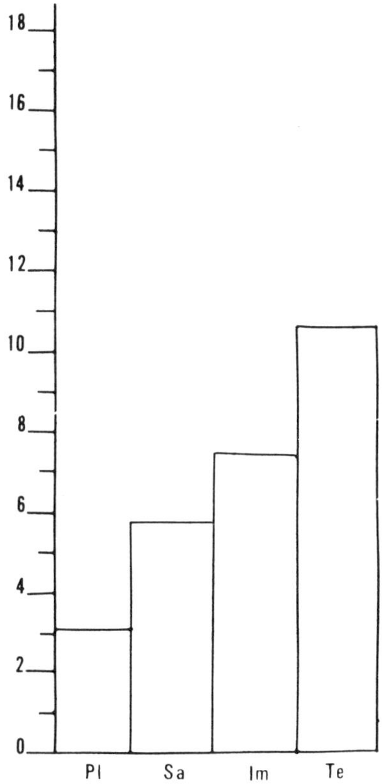

FIGURE 9-2. The DRS profile of dimensions in the sadness situation. Pl, pleasantness; Sa, self-assurance; Im, impulsiveness; Te, tension.

emotion. The slight difference in the fear and interest means were not significant in either study. As can be seen in the two profiles, many emotions are elicited in a situation that people visualize as primarily sad.

Of all the emotion situations examined in several different studies, the emotion profile in the sadness situation is one of the most complicated. Only the guilt and shyness situations have an equal number of elevated emotions. It is worth noting that in the profile of emotions in the sadness situation, fear and interest are significantly higher than anger. Anger and other indexes of hostility are not as prominent in sadness situations as in depression.

Functions of Sadness

We have said that no emotion is always completely positive or completely negative, good or bad, desirable or undesirable. This is true of sadness. There are times and occasions when sadness is an appropriate response.

The most obvious set of circumstances in which it is appropriate to feel sad is

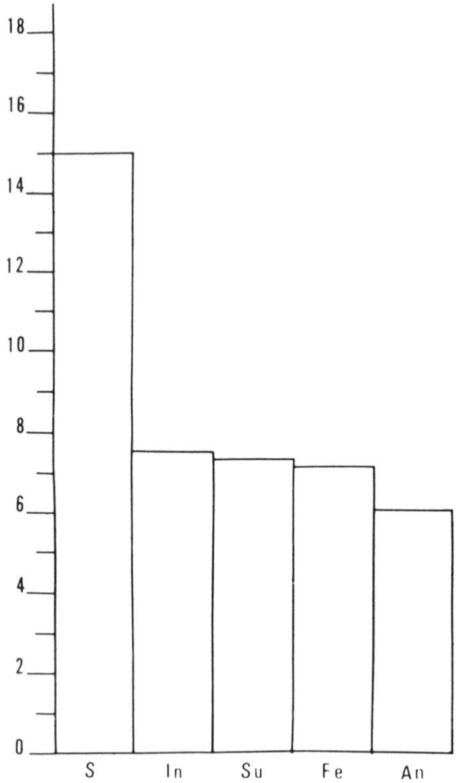

FIGURE 9-3. The profile of emotions in an imagined sadness situation, as measured with the modified DES. S, sadness; In, interest; Su, surprise; Fe, fear; An, anger.

at the death of someone you love. At a time of death, a family comes together to mourn, and although it is death that brings about this closeness, there is nevertheless a keen sense of the deep and affectionate ties with other members of the family. This sense of togetherness, or belonging, is an extremely important part of a person's psychological roots. Shared sadness over the loss of a loved one can thus reunite a family and strengthen the sources of social support that every individual needs for a happy and healthy life.

A time of sadness is also an occasion for slowing down the pace of one's life and for taking stock. Because sadness is accompanied by a slowing of both mental and bodily functioning, it means that the sad person is going to see the world differently. This new perspective can lead to further sadness, or it may shed some light onto some tough issues. Perhaps you will see that you have rushed too quickly past some of life's most precious offerings. Or perhaps in the case of the loss of a loved one, you may be reminded and regain an appreciation of the importance of affectionate ties with others. Sadness can remind you of the value of doing little things for others that make a difference, and it can even remind you of the value of life itself.

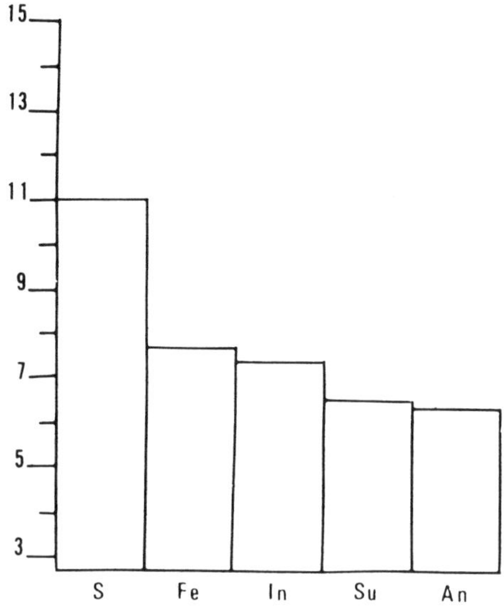

FIGURE 9-4. The profile of emotions in an imagined sadness situation, as measured by the standard DES, N = 68. S, sadness; Fe, fear; In, interest; Su, surprise; An, anger.

In addition, sadness communicates to the self and to others that all is not well (Tomkins, 1963). This is accomplished, in one primary instance, by the cry of the infant (but as has been noted, the infant, like the adult, may cry for reasons other than sadness). The expression of sadness tells you you're troubled, and it tells others you need some kind of help. Under some conditions the help can come only from yourself, motivated by your own sadness. Help may also come from others. Your everyday experiences tell you that a sad face, particularly the sad face of a child, tends to elicit empathy and sympathetic responses from the observer. This effect of the sadness expression was demonstrated in a study by Savitsky and Sim (1974). They showed judges a series of standardized one-minute videotaped segments of individuals playing the role of juvenile offenders and expressing either sadness, anger, joy, or no emotion in an interview with a person in the role of a social worker. The supposed offenders had all committed offenses that were prejudged to be equal in seriousness. The subjects' task was to decide what punishment they would recommend for the offenders. Savitsky and Sim found that significantly less punishment was recommended for the interviewees who expressed sadness at what they had done than for those who expressed either anger or joy.

Sadness, like all other emotions, is motivating. It can motivate an individual to renew and strengthen bonds with others. If the sadness is due to some disappointment or failure that could have been prevented, sadness could motivate you to solve the problem. To some degree "negative motivation" is necessary to make us responsive to our own problems and to the problems of the world. But if a problem frightens us, we are more likely to flee from it than to try to cope with it. Fear is too toxic and intolerable to provide continuing motivation for sustained work toward the solution of a problem. Indeed, it would not be desirable or adaptive to learn techniques for fully inhibiting or eliminating sadness, for its motivational powers play important roles in individual growth.

Sadness may play an important role in empathy. Mothers respond to children's sadness expressions with like feeling, and they are motivated to comfort and minister to the child (Huebner & Izard, 1988). Interestingly, the feeling of sadness may motivate either self-gratification or empathic and altruistic behavior. When sadness is induced through cognitive processes (recalling and visualizing sad events), the subjects will be more prone to indulge in self-gratifying behaviors if the sad experience they recall is autobiographical. However, if the subjects recall a sad event in the life of a friend or loved one and attention is focused not on the self but on the plight of another, they are much more likely to experience empathy and behave altruistically (Moore, Underwood, & Rosenhan, 1984).

Sadness and Physiological Drives

Emotions can become linked to or bonded with other emotions through learning and experience. As discussed, certain circumstances can lead to a link between sadness and guilt such that when the child feels sad, guilt is also evoked in response to the feeling of wanting to cry. In the same manner, learning and experience can contribute to bonds between an emotion and a physiological need. Under certain circumstances, sadness and sexual needs may become associated. Recall that in sadness there is a tendency to feel isolated and alone. Such sadness is often brought about through loss or separation from a loved one or friend. Breaking up with someone you have loved not only leaves you short on intimacy, affection, and sexual satisfaction, it is also likely to leave you feeling socially isolated and alone. The need for affection and sexual intimacy may interact with feelings of sadness, resulting in a desire to seek out another intimate relationship before the necessary period of recovery from the initial loss is undergone. A repeating pattern of breaking up and falling in love again can result in a strong relationship between sadness and sexual feelings.

Then again, this kind of association between sadness and sexual desires may develop purely on the basis of romantic fantasy. If a person exerts a great deal of emotional energy in a relationship that is purely one-sided and exists only in the person's mind, the loss of this fantasy may yield a similar effect as if the relationship were actual. Again, there may develop the bond between sexual urges and sadness. Such a combination is made easier by the fact that both sadness and sexual needs respond to sympathetic and affiliative responses from another person. That is, there is a natural similarity between sad feelings and sexual feelings in that both are satisfied through the deepening or strengthening of a social bond.

Sadness can interact with other physiological conditions. To feel sad is to feel downhearted and discouraged. If the response to such feelings is that of immediate physical gratification through eating, particularly chocolate or junk food containing high amounts of sugar and caffeine, the result may be that of an immediate though temporary pick up. The quick energy attained is the desired effect and may slightly overshadow feelings of sadness associated with lack of muscle tone, droopiness, and weakness. For the time being, you feel a little more alive, a little less crippled by the weight of sadness or depression. However, the habitual consumption of fast foods or sweets in order to gain temporary relief from feelings of sadness can lead to an association between sad feelings and consummatory behavior, an antecedent condition for eating disorders and weight control problems.

If a person is upset about being overweight or by the threat of being overweight, then the sad–mad pattern may combine with the hunger drive. Thus the individual becomes sad and discouraged, eating to overcome the sadness and alternately becoming angry at his or her self-indulgence. If in the process the individual becomes overweight and the resulting self-directed hostility becomes sufficiently chronic, the individual may be well on the road to serious depression.

Feelings of fatigue may also contribute to sadness, and a fatigue–sadness association can develop under certain circumstances. If you are tired from working hard and are not satisfied with your progress, you may quite naturally experience both fatigue and discouragement or sadness simultaneously. Fatigue can also have physical, mental, and social components. You can become tired from incessant repetition of almost anything, even tasks that you enjoy on occasion. If repetition is a part of your job, and you become skeptical as to the ultimate worth of your work, a tired–discouraged–sad complex of feelings can result in burnout.

The Development and Socialization of Sadness

There is very little empirical research on the socialization of specific emotions, but Tomkins has presented a provocative theory of the socialization of distress. His definition of distress includes bodily and mental suffering. However, his description of the facial expression of distress is more like that of sadness than of physical distress or pain (Izard, Hembree, Dougherty, & Spizirri, 1983), and he hypothesizes a direct relation between a specific expression and corresponding specific experience. Because his description of the distress expression is similar to that of sadness, and because he includes sadness in his description of the phenomenology of distress, his theory of the socialization of distress is presented here, with the term *sadness* used where he would use *distress*. The model is presented in some detail, because in some respects it may be generalized to the socialization of other emotions.

In the opinion of Tomkins (1963), there are four main types of socialization of sadness: (1) punitive or right wing, (2) rewarding or left wing, (3) incomplete rewarding, and (4) mixed. He wrote:

> We consider socialization of distress—anguish [i.e., sadness]—punitive whenever the distress cry itself is punished or rejected or whenever there is a failure of help in remedial action to reduce the source of distress, or both. This punitive socialization may or may not be consistent or general. (p. 88)

The Punitive Socialization of Sadness

The punitive type of socialization of sadness occurs when the parent or guardian habitually chooses to show a negative or punitive response to the distress cry of the child, regardless of the stimulus that has caused the sadness in the child. A good example of this is demonstrated by the parent who on one occasion scolds a young child for refusing to go to bed and on another occasion scolds him the same way for crying after he has lost his favorite toy. Repeated indiscriminate punishment of sadness produces even more sadness in the child, and his reactions to sadness compounded will bring on more punitive measures from the parent. Tomkins calls this a multiple-suffering bind, in which there is "no way out" and no way to express sadness or sadness-induced anger without experiencing more punishment. In the end, according to Tomkins, this will cause compulsive behavior, isolationism, low frustration tolerance, poor individuation, excessive avoidance of sadness, externalization of all types of sadness, habitual apathy, and fatigue in a sadness-laden individual. If the parent does follow up the punishment with a form of remedial help, then with time and patient the child may be able to gain a respectable degree of self-confidence and self-assurance.

> One of the further consequences of the punitive socialization of distress [sadness] through the evocation of fear is the complication of the problem of physical courage. The human being responds innately to pain from his body with the cry of distress. If this innate response is inhibited by fear, the individual's fear of pain will be greatly increased. . . . Although pain is not easy for the human being to tolerate, it can produce panic the more distress itself has been linked with fear. . . . It seems likely that the greater tolerance of pain, in our culture by women and in Oriental cultures by both men and women, is due to the less punitive early socialization of the distress cry. (Tomkins, 1963, p. 93)

When father punishes son repeatedly in order to control the child's crying, there is a very good chance that the boy will form a connection between sadness and fear. In this case, the child has learned through repeated experience that the sound of his crying often brings about the pain of punishment. Anticipation of pain is a reliable source of fear in children. In this way, a child's sadness may compound with fear. He may not fully understand how this connection was learned, for in later years the processes by which the association was made may be completely forgotten. In this case, occasions involving sadness are made even more complicated for the individual. He may at these times begin to feel apprehensive or afraid. Despite his best efforts to understand his mixed feelings, he may not be able to recognize the connection between the sadness and fear that he now experiences and the crying that was punished in childhood.

Rewarding the Sadness Response during Socialization

In employing the rewarding type of socialization of sadness, the parents attempt to comfort the child and make evident their attempts actively to reduce the severity of the stimulus for sadness. It is more important that the parents act on the stimulus of sadness, for if they only offer kind words and sympathy the child will be plagued with a severe case of chronic infantilism throughout adolescence and adulthood. If the parents do come to the rescue and offer not only comforting words but also some action upon the negative stimulus, then the child's freedom to express and cope with sadness will be much more broad and natural. With such treatment, according to Tomkins's theory, the child will tend more to trust other people; she will be more likely to be honest, helpful, understanding and sympathetic with herself and others. She will have more physical courage and a much higher tolerance of frustration. She will successfully and rightfully experience sadness in a context of love and joy, and she will have a much more optimistic attitude toward herself and life in general. This style of socialization of sadness appears to have more desirable effects than the punitive approach. The style adopted depends largely on the past experiences and the deeply rooted affective–cognitive orientations of the parents, but the biologically based characteristics of the child (e.g., positive and negative emotion thresholds) also play a role. The infant with a low sadness threshold will cry more often and perhaps more intensely than one with a high threshold, and frequent bouts of crying are more difficult to live with than frequent states of calmness or joy. The infant who smiles easily affects parents differently than the infant who cries easily.

The Incomplete Rewarding of Sadness

According to Tomkins, when the parents employ the method of sadness socialization known as incomplete rewarding, they are nurturing what may eventually develop into alcoholism and drug addiction. This type of socialization is displayed by the parents who simply kiss, hug, and pat their crying children without any effort to act upon the elicitor of sadness or to make the object of it obvious to their children so that they may be able to cope with it in the future. Tomkins proposes that if the parents continue to act in this manner, the children will, as adults, be forced to find sedation, whether it be physical, mental, emotional, or social, when they are faced with a sadness-eliciting situation.

Mixed Methods of Socializing Sadness

All forms of sadness socialization are not as patterned and concise as the foregoing categories; there is a special class that includes all those mixtures of socialization methods that are so often employed by so many parents. These mixtures can be in numerous combinations, such as parents who reward the crying infant, but punish the toddler. There may be a split in the punitive and rewarding socialization methods between the father and the mother. Tomkins maintains that results of a mixed socialization of sadness are retardation in personality integration, social restlessness, and an interest in promoting interpersonal communication and resolving social conflict. Also, individuals who experience such socialization will show varying reactions to different aspects of their environment, based on the type of sadness socialization they were given in these varying situations. An example of this is seen when there is rewarding socialization of sadness done in private and punitive socialization of sadness done publicly.

A more effective means of dealing with the child's sadness would call for a different approach. Initially, the parent might respond with empathy, demonstrating to the child that mom or dad also feels something of the child's plight. Secondly, the parent may then move toward comforting the child and, insofar as is possible, change whatever is causing the sadness. Ideally, this is a joint effort for parent and child. Finally, the parent should if possible provide encouragement and support, doing whatever is necessary to facilitate the child's own actions to remedy the situation. In this way, the child learns effective coping strategies for changing situations that bring about sadness.

The Interaction of Sadness with Other Emotions, Cognition, and Action

Sadness–Anger Interactions

One of the most common interactions among the emotions of human experience is that of sadness and anger. Infants as young as 4 months of age have been observed showing components of both anger and sadness expressions in response to the acute pain of inoculation (Izard, Hembree, & Huebner, 1987).

Tomkins (1963) hypothesized that sadness is an innate activator of anger. Most people have had the experience of feeling discouraged and downhearted, followed by the experience of feeling angry with themselves or with someone else for their misery. The sadness–anger interaction can cause a father to react to his child's sadness with a display of anger. The father may not be angry with the child, but with the source of sadness. The anger may also be a counteraction to fear, suggesting the possible existence of a sadness–anger–fear bind. Such a complex affective orientation could have its origin in an experience like this: a young boy is left alone in an automobile while his father goes shopping. It is a strange area of town and it is almost dark. The boy begins to feel lonesome and begins to cry in sadness. As time passes the boy may feel some anger toward the father for abandoning him for so long. A feeling of abandonment in a strange place with darkness falling elicits fear in the child. The fear exacerbates the sad crying and is very difficult to tolerate. If the boy manages to get angry with his father, the anger counteracts and attenuates the fear as well as the sadness. Repetition of such situations may teach the boy to become angry at disappointments and setbacks, lest he suffer the sadness–fear bind. The way in which a sadness–anger interaction can contribute to normal and psychological depression will be discussed in the section on depression.

The Sadness–Fear Bind

The toxic debilitating effects of fear make the linkage of sadness and fear a factor important for adjustment. Such a linkage can occur under a variety of conditions. For example, if a young child cries when left alone and the parent punishes the child for crying, sadness may become a learned activator of fear. If this sadness–fear bind generalizes so that whenever this person faces sadness he or she becomes afraid, the relative frequency of the sadness experience will make the toxic effects of fear so common that the problems of coping with life become overwhelming. Such a person will likely stop trying to solve difficult problems, live in dread of the new situations and uncertainties each day may bring, and become very cautious about trusting and liking one's self and other people. This individual will spend more energy in attempting to avoid the experience of sadness and the circumstances that provoked it than in attempting to control its sources. When an early and strong linkage of sadness and fear snowballs, the result is likely to be severe maladjustment.

The sadness–fear bind may produce a lack of physical courage. Pain may elicit sadness. If there is a strong sadness–fear linkage, then the sequence is likely to be pain → sadness → fear, with subsequent panicky behavior rather than courageous action. The role of a sadness–fear bind in impending individuation and in the development of anxiety neurosis will be discussed later.

The Sadness–Shame Interaction

Sadness can also become associated with shame. If a child's crying leads to rejection or indifference on the part of the parent, the child may sense reproach and respond with shame. If this pattern is consistently repeated through development, the child's sadness will ultimately evolve into a trigger for shame. This pattern of response may lead to the development of a painfully shy person.

If the child's father shames him when he cries, and at the same time emphasizes that he should do something about his problem rather than crying about it, the child may come to feel shame in difficult situations for two reasons. First, he may feel shame because he feels like crying, and second, he may feel shame because he feels passive and unable to do anything constructive about the situation. According to Tomkins (1963), such a sadness–shame bind can result in the externalization of sadness. What this would mean for the child is that his chief concern in life would become the troubles and complaints of himself and others, but his focus would be on external objects and situations, not on his own sadness experience. Not being tuned to his own sadness experience, he would become unable to recognize sadness in others and thus be incapable of showing sympathy.

Similarly, the child may be made to feel that it is wrong to show sadness. If the child is led to sense that crying or feeling sad is a kind of wrong-doing, then any feeling of sadness can evoke guilt.

Sadness, Cognition, and Action

There can be no doubt that sadness influences perception and thinking. The feeling of sadness tends to cause a person to perceive the world as bleak and gloomy. It leads to withdrawal and isolation. Yet sadness is not all bad. There are occasions when sadness is an appropriate emotion and one that needs to be expressed, such as occasions of loss or separation. At such times, people are brought together, they renew social bonds and strengthen affective ties to family and friends.

Sadness also alerts the individual to the fact that there is something wrong within the self or within one's world. Yet sadness is usually not so debilitating that the person cannot attend to the problem or trouble. Sadness may in fact motivate a person to do something about the situation that is causing the sadness.

In fact, the expression of sadness tends to draw assistance from others. Experience should tell you that the sad expression, especially shown on the face of a friend or loved one, causes a desire to help. The sadness expression is an automatic appeal for empathy and sympathetic concern.

The frequency and intensity with which you experience a given emotion influences your self-image or self-concept. If it happens that you are frequently discouraged and frequently sad, it is only natural that you will come to think of yourself as a person who is easily saddened. We have already discussed how imagery, thoughts, and memories can trigger emotions. The network of images, thoughts, and feelings that you have in regard to yourself is very influential in the way you perceive, think, and act in the world. If you have a picture of yourself as a sad person, it will influence your approach to just about everything. Such a self-concept is associated with chronic discouragement, low self-esteem, and feelings of inability to cope effectively with the normal problems of everyday life.

In describing the experience and effects of the feeling of sadness, we noted that it slows down our movements as well as our mental activities. These effects were demonstrated in a study of the influence of mothers' sadness expressions on infants' gaze behavior, emotion expressions, and play behavior (Termine & Izard, 1988).

On separate visits to the laboratory, 36 nine-month-old infants (18 male, 18 female) watched their mothers express joy or sadness, facially and vocally, during a 2-minute emotion induction period. After the induction period, mothers continued to express joy or sadness while their infants played with four sets of attractive toys. Infant emotion expressions were analyzed with anatomically based objective coding systems (Izard, 1979; Izard, Dougherty, & Hembree, 1983), and infant play behavior was coded with an independent system (Belsky & Most, 1981). The amount of time the infants looked at their mothers was also measured. Findings were generally consistent with differential emotions theory. The infants expressed more joy and looked longer at their mothers during the joy condition, and they showed more sadness, anger, and gaze aversion during the sadness condition. The infants engaged in more play behavior in the joy condition than in the sadness condition (see Figure 9-5). The infants' gaze behavior, emotion expression, and slowed play behavior suggested that they experienced mothers' sadness vicariously.

The effects of sadness on infant's play is rather profound. The young of all mammalian species engage in play during most of their waking hours. The play of children is very easily stimulated and very difficult to inhibit. That mothers' brief expressions of sadness had a significant (slowing down) effect on young infants' play with attractive toys is remarkable testimony to the communicative function of the expression of sadness and the power of sadness experience to change mental and motor activities.

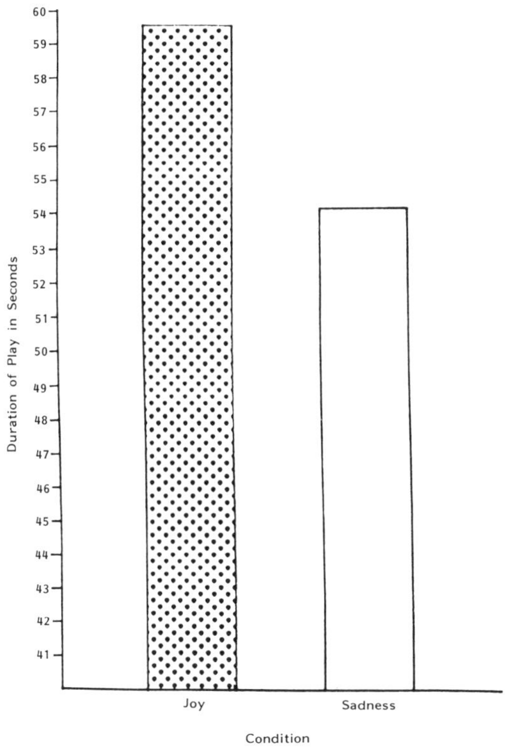

FIGURE 9-5. The effect of mothers' sadness expressions on the exploratory play of their 9-month-old infants.

The Regulation and Control of Sadness

As in the case of all emotions, there are, aside from drugs, three avenues for regulation and control—another emotion; cognition, or thought; and action. Regulation by means of another emotion consists of a deliberate effort to activate or experience an emotion that is counteractive to the one you wish to regulate or inhibit. Cognitive control is the use of attentional and thought processes to regulate or change the emotion. Action control is the actual use of the voluntarily controlled muscles of the body to engage in activities that counteract the undesired emotion. Effective emotion control often calls for the interplay of feeling, thought, and action. For example, in sadness, it is very difficult to simply direct attentional and thought processes in such a way as to decrease or inhibit the sadness. However, if you can direct your attention to conditions or events that will elicit interest or joy, you have greatly increased your chances of reducing the sadness. If at the same time you can also engage yourself actively with the object, or if you can somehow get your body and your mind active and engaged in something of interest, you have even more greatly improved your chances of experiencing some enjoyment and of decreasing or inhibiting the feelings of sadness.

Summary

Psychological causes of sadness include many problem situations that occur in everyday life, high drive states, other emotions, imagery, memory, and other cognitive processes. The prototypical sadness situation is the separation of the infant from the mother. The innate expression of sadness includes inner corners of eyebrows drawn together and raised, transverse forehead wrinkles, and a mouth downturned at the corners. A primary cause of sadness is loss of a loved one through death or separation.

The experience of sadness is typically described as downheartedness, discouragement, loneliness, isolation. While sadness can become quite noxious, it is characterized by less tension than most other negative emotions. Consistent with the differential emotions theory of the dynamics of sadness in grief and depression, normal subjects imaging a sadness situation report fear as the second strongest emotion in sadness-eliciting situations.

Sadness can serve several psychological functions. At a time of grief sadness can strengthen the bonds of an individual's or family's support network; it brings a slowing down of both mind and body allowing time for reflection; it communicates to the self and to others that all is not well; and it motivates the strengthening and renewal of bonds with others.

The punitive socialization of sadness can cause compulsive behavior, low frustration tolerance, poor individuation, and loss of physical courage. The incomplete rewarding of sadness and mixed methods of socializing it can produce problems in personality development.

The ubiquity of sadness means that it frequently interacts with other emotions in day-to-day life. A sadness–anger interaction can cause a father to respond to a child's sadness with a display of anger. A sadness–fear bind can impede individuation and lead to "anxiety neurosis.' When a child is repeatedly blamed for crying, a sadness–shame bind can develop and produce a painfully shy person. Sadness–cognition interactions are common in consciousness. The work of a number of investigators has shown that experimentally manipulated cognitive processes can induce sadness experience and alter subsequent thought and activity.

There are three avenues for the regulation and control of sadness—activating another emotion that counteracts sadness, cognition (using attentional or thought processes to regulate or change the emotion), and physical action (counteracting the physical expression of sadness through voluntary expressions and actions).

Suggested Readings

Barnett, M., King, L. M., & Howard, J. A. (1979). Inducing affect about self and other: Effects on generosity in children. *Developmental Psychology*, *15*, 164–167.

An experiment showing how the focus of attention or the object of sadness (self or other) affects the prosocial or altruistic behavior of children.

Cialdini, R. B., & Kenrick, D. T. (1976). Altruism as hedonism: A social development perspective on the relationship of negative mood state and helping. *Journal of Personality and Social Psychology*, *34*, 907–914.

Shows how the effects of induced sadness and happiness on self-gratification and prosocial behavior changes with age.

Moore, B. S., Underwood, B., & Rosenhan, D. L. (1973). Affect and altruism. *Developmental Psychology*, *8*, 99–104.

An experiment showing that induced sadness or happiness influences a child's self-gratification behaviors and orientation toward the needs of others.

Termine, N. T., & Izard, C. E. (1988). Infants' responses to their mothers' expressions of joy and sadness. *Developmental Psychology*, *24*(2), 223–229.

Demonstrates the effects of mothers' sadness expressions on the gaze behavior, emotion regression, and exploratory play of 9-month-old infants.

Tomkins, S. S. (1963). *Affect, imagery, consciousness: Vol. 2. The negative affects*. New York: Springer.

Chapter 14, "Distress–anguish and the crying response," offers an eloquent description of the functions and dynamics of distress–anguish, which includes the concept of sadness.

10

Sadness in Grief and Depression

Grief and Sadness

Theorists and investigators generally agree that sadness is the predominant emotion in grief and that the prime cause of grief is loss. The loss may be temporary (separation) or permanent (death), real or imagined, physical or psychological.

The determinants of grief may be sorted into biological, cultural, and psychological classes, although each of these classes tends to be interrelated and interactive. Some of the determinants of grief may also play a role in the grief-cognition-behavioral interactions that characterize the individual and the social matrix within which grief occurs.

Biological Determinants

Since grief is conceived as an interaction of sadness and other fundamental emotions, it is reasonable to infer that grief has genetic determinants and biologically adaptive values. In an insightful and scholarly analysis of the nature and significance of grief, Averill (1968) made an excellent case for the assumption of a biological basis for grief. His argument rests on the well-supported assumption that human beings and higher primates in general are group-living forms whose survival and well-being are enhanced by social relationships (Hamburg, 1963; Jolly, 1966). In evolutionary perspective and to some extent in contemporary life, the social group affords protection from aggressors (or predators) and efficiency in locating and maintaining food. In turn, separation from the group diminishes chances for survival. In sum, Averill holds that "grief is a biological reaction, the evolutionary function of which is to insure group survival. This is accomplished by making separation from the group, or from specific members of the group, an extremely stressful event both psychologically and physiologically" (p. 729). Averill argues that grief is a more powerful force for social cohesion than positive incentives alone, since the latter would offer little help during periods of satiation and satisfaction. In a later section we shall see how each of several fundamental emotions involved in grief may serve biological as well as social and psychological functions.

Cultural Determinants

In his analysis of the bereavement behavior complex, Averill (1968) delineated two components, grief and mourning. He defined mourning as conventional bereavement behavior, determined and prescribed in large measure by sociocultural influences. Mourning practices vary extensively from culture to culture. The Japanese may smile at acquaintances and strangers during bereavement in order not to burden the other with their sorrow. The bereavement behavior of individuals in some societies appears to the Western eye as celebration, but on more careful examination, such behavior follows well-defined cultural rules and customs.

The experiential-motivational phenomena associated with grief may also vary to some extent from culture to culture, depending upon the extent to which the different cultures inhibit or facilitate the interactions of sadness with various fundamental emotions. For example, Block (1957) showed that grief and guilt were highly correlated in members of his American sample but orthogonal in his sample of Norwegians. Sociocultural practices also influence the intensity and duration of grief. An example is the child-rearing system of the Ifaluk, a Micronesian culture (Spiro, 1949, cited in Averill, 1968). Since the rearing of an Ifaluk child involves parents, siblings, and many persons outside the family, the grief displayed upon loss of a family member may be intense, but it is exceedingly brief in comparison with that shown in other cultures. A similar phenomenon has been observed among nonhuman primates, though in this case species characteristics play a role. Pigtail macaque monkeys, who form close one-to-one mother-infant attachments, show more profound separation grief than do bonnett macaque monkeys, among whom mothering is widely shared among the adult females of a clan.

Perhaps the most significant cultural determinant of grief is that of role loss. Roles of father, mother, child, husband, and the like are prescribed by culture, and loss of a loved one often means the loss of a role (e.g., loss of wife means loss of role as husband). As Averill and others have pointed out, role loss is essentially a disruption of a functional relationship through the loss of a significant other person. Role loss or changes in roles are significant determinants of grief when they entail loss of self-esteem (Bibring, 1968). Role changes or any other phenomena that deprive the individual of meaningful relationships or meaningful relations with the environment can produce grief (Becker, 1962; Das, 1971).

Psychological Determinants of Grief

Psychological causes of grief derive from an affectional attachment with the person, object, idea, or other symbol. Separation or loss from the object of attachment thus means loss of a source of joy and excitement and, depending upon the age of the person and the nature of the object, loss of affection, security, and sense of well-being. The factor common to all psychological causes of grief is a perceived loss of something valued and beloved and to which there was a strong affectional attachment.

Expressive and Experiential Characteristics of Grief

The predominant expression on the face of the grieving person is that of sadness. The expression of grief may sometimes consist of blends, however, since other fundamental emotions are often involved.

The predominant experiential quality of grief is consonant with that of the predominant emotion of sadness. As other emotions interact, the experiential phenomena of grief become more complex. As already noted, Block's (1957) study of the phenomenology of grief by means of semantic differential scales showed a strong tendency for guilt feelings to be associated with grief. Block's study also showed that grief was highly correlated with the concepts of worry and envy and highly negatively correlated with the concept of contentment. Anecdotal evidence connects anger and fear with grief. A widow may feel anger on being deserted by a lifelong companion, and a child may fear for her safety without her father.

The aspects of grief associated with emotion-emotion interactions and emotion-cognition interactions may vary from culture to culture. As already pointed out, Block found a substantial difference in the association of grief in American and Norwegian cultures. He also found substantial differences between samples of these two cultures in the association of grief with worry, envy, and contentment. The general trend of Block's findings are consistent with Izard's (1971) finding that cultures differ in their attitudes toward the fundamental emotions and hence in the frequency with which certain emotions interact with others.

The Functions of Grief

It has already been pointed out that grief serves a biological and social function in facilitating social affection and group cohesiveness. As are all emotions or patterns of emotions, grief is contagious—particularly so—and this contagion facilitates empathy and strengthens bonds among all those who are bereaved. These effects tend to generalize to the wider community, since mourning rituals are typically highly visible to the public.

The foregoing function of grief is biological and social, but grief also has inherently adaptive functions for the individual. Normal grief is psychologically adaptive for the individual since it enables him or her to "work through" and adjust to the loss. In a sense, grief is a way of paying homage to the loved one that was lost. The stressful experience of grief motivates the individual to reestablish an adequate level of personal autonomy. According to Bowlby (1960, 1961, 1963), grief is adaptive for the individual because it functions as motivation to recover the lost object. Further, some expressions of grief can serve a communicative function, eliciting empathy and succor. Finally, grief and its expression communicate to significant others and to the wider community the fact that the bereaved individual is a loving and caring individual. Other functions of grief will be touched on in the following sections.

Grief in the Context of Attachment and Separation

In a monumental, two-volume work, Bowlby (1969, 1973) presents a theory of attachment and separation and the psychological problems related to these phenomena. We have already considered Bowlby's theory of the prototypical interpersonal attachment, the mother-infant bond. It is in the context of the breaking of this bond—the separation response syndrome—that Bowlby discussed grief. Bowlby maintains that whenever a young child has normal opportunities for social development and forms attachment to a mother figure, its unwilling separation from the mother produces distress. Following separation, the infant or young child's behavior follows a typical sequence: protest, which consists of vigorous efforts to recover the mother or caregiver; despair, which is characterized by grief and mourning; and detachment, which consists of the development of various defenses to compensate for the loss. Responses to separation are, in part, a function of age. Since attachment does not become fixed and strong until about the age of 6 months, the separation response syndrome does not occur until sometime in the second half of the first year of life. From this period through early childhood even brief separations may elicit sadness and the various phases of the separation response syndrome. Older children may be able to comprehend the relative insignificance of brief separations and are distressed only by longer ones. Adults are upset when separations are prolonged or permanent, as in the case of the death of a loved one.

According to Bowlby, the protest phase of the separation response syndrome is characterized, first and foremost, by the emotion of fear. Separation connotes being left alone, and Bowlby has marshaled considerable evidence supporting his notion that being alone is one of several natural clues to increased danger and hence a condition that often elicits fear. The fear serves as motivation to escape the danger, primarily through efforts to gain proximity to the absent mother. As fear abates, the infant may show anger, "a reproach for what has happened and a deterrent against its happening again" (Bowlby, 1973, p. 253). Bowlby's postulate that fear and anger interact in the wake of separation is consistent with the differential emotions theory of grief (explicated in more detail in a later section).

In the despair phase of the separation response syndrome, the infant shows signs of grief and mourning. In Bowlby's system grief is defined largely in terms of despair or sadness since other participating emotions are treated separately in the other phases of the syndrome.

In the detachment phase of the separation response syndrome, the child develops various defenses. The infant and young child's chief means of recovery from the trauma of separation is the development of another healthy affectional attachment. Older children, adolescents, and adults may use any of a variety of defenses against distress or separation. Perhaps the chief defense is that of suppression or repression. The individual may attempt to repress all ideation associated with the sadness experience. As Peretz (1970) has pointed out, the individual may also use the defense of isolation of affect, displacement (especially of the anger component), substitution, and denial.

Grief and Sadness

> In high school, you could find Luke outside of the school in the smoking court, puffing away. Whenever I had a problem with my boyfriend, he would always have the time to lend an ear. He was also always willing to do just about anything new and different. A real friend, something I have not had in a while. Ones like him are hard to find.
>
> One night in the middle of my freshman year of college, I was awakened by a phone call. It was my old boyfriend, Chris. I thought it was just another everyday phone call. Unfortunately, I was mistaken.
>
> Chris told me that around 3:00 in the afternoon, Luke shot himself through the chin and died immediately. Apparently the principal caught him with some marijuana and promised him that if he admitted to having it he would not be turned over to the authorities. But he was anyway, and Luke's father had to come to the station to pick him up. They apparently got into a fight and Luke, upon returning home, went into the garage and shot himself.
>
> After I was told this, I hung up. The next thing that crossed my mind was "what next?" I cried most of the night and woke up with tears down my cheeks and in my hair. The next day was very hard. I did not go to classes and spent most of the day asking myself, if it was that bad, why didn't he just call me? We could have worked it out just as we always did. The following days seemed to get easier, until the funeral. I had never been to a funeral and it was a terrible experience. The feeling of wanting to cry out loud but knowing that you cannot is the worst possible feeling I have experienced. I just wanted to run over to the casket and throw it open, hoping he would sit up and hug me, and everything would be back to normal. But I soon realized that this was not the case and that it would never happen. The only time I will ever see his face is in pictures.

As is evident from K. B.'s reaction to the untimely death of a high school friend, sadness is a major component of grief, the experience that follows the loss of a loved one. However, grief and the process of mourning is complex, involving more than one emotion as well as innumerable images, memories, and thoughts. The experience of grief results from the interaction of sadness with other affects and from affect-cognition interactions. The stronger and deeper the ties, the more numerous the shared experiences both positive and negative, the more likely it is that the sadness will be the largest component of grief.

Since sadness is the primary emotion in grief, the eventual occurrence of anger and aggression is not surprising. If Tomkins's (1963) assumption is correct, extended sadness is an innate activator of anger, and the sadness experience is usually prolonged in grief. Anger may also occur as a result of the individual blaming the absent or lost loved one for desertion or as a result of blaming someone else for the separation. Further, as Averill has pointed out, the loss of a significant individual can be a highly frustrating experience. A relationship is lost, plans involving the other person cannot be carried out, and desires and fulfillment depending upon the other person cannot be gratified. Such disruption of behavior and such unfulfilled expectations can easily elicit anger.

Grief can often be even more complex, and emotions more difficult to understand and to deal with than anger may come into play. In cases where there have been emotional conflicts in a relationship, often that have gone unreconciled, the survivor can experience large measures of guilt and shame. There may also be a certain amount of inner-directed anger. In essence, this person is blaming himself or herself for the loss, even though he or she had no control over the fact that the relationship ended when and as it did. Shame may occur when the individual feels that others are condemning him or her for not being closer to the deceased or more helpful during the period of illness. Feeling large amounts of sadness, guilt, shame, and anger, particularly anger directed inward toward the self, characterizes severe depression, which can accompany and linger after the experience of profound grief.

Indeed, the cause of the most profound and extended grief is the loss of the person one loves the most dearly, but Peretz (1970) has pointed out three other forms of loss. One of these is the loss of some aspect of self-attractiveness or vigor, loss of some sensory or motor capacity, loss of intellectual power, or loss of positive self-attitudes such as self-esteem. Another form of loss is that of material objects such as money, treasures, homeland. A final form of loss is developmental loss, or the type of loss that occurs in the process of growth and development (e.g., loss of the nurturing breast, baby teeth, status as center of parental attention). Peretz points out that loss is simultaneously a real event and a perceptual or psychological one by which the individual bestows personal or symbolic meaning upon the loss. Thus a real loss may constitute symbolically a loss of honor or loss of face. He also noted that serious losses also carry with them the threat of additional, future losses.

Grief and Psychopathology

In a volume edited by Schoenberg, Carr, Peretz, and Kutscher (1970), a number of contributors present theory and evidence that support the notion that illness and death become more likely following the loss of a loved one. For example, Carr and Schoenberg, while noting that the evidence relating object loss to somatic symptom formation is mainly correlational, suggest that object loss and grief may contribute to such diverse somatic reactions as cancer and glossodynia. They presented evidence for significant increases in medical office consultation rate and in death rate of widowed people. Other contributors to the volume consider psychological and somatic reactions to other types of loss and possible therapeutic procedures for the management of these phenomena.

Sadness and Depression

It is important to draw a distinction between sadness and depression. Sadness is a single emotion that has its own particular expression as well as its unique subjective experience. Depression involves a complex combination of emotions, images, memories, and thoughts. It also involves bodily states. Sadness can be experienced at appropriate occasions throughout one's lifetime without being a part of serious depression, but most people do experience at least mild depression at some time during their lives. During these periods of mild to moderate depression, sadness becomes mixed with other emotions—most frequently self-directed hostility and shame.

Like sadness, depression is often associated with loss. The important difference is that the depressed individual feels, and often actually is, incapable of dealing with the loss. Further, in depression, loss may not necessarily involve the death of a loved one. It can instead follow the loss of self-esteem, the loss of a job, the loss of a companion, the loss of friends or a love relationship. In each of these cases, the depression must be resolved before the individual can attempt to deal with the loss, whereas in simple sadness, the individual is capable of taking another look at the source of trouble and doing something about it. Listen to Sheryl's description of a time in her life when she was sad and depressed and notice the emotions involved, their effects, and her strategies for coping with them.

> Episodes of severe depression began for me in my freshman year of high school. I was a new girl in a strange school and suddenly became a loner. This time was also the beginning of a long struggle with eating disorders. I was anorexic for almost 2 years and then bulimic for the remainder of high school and into college. My eating problems went hand in hand with my states of depression. It was in fact my binge-purge pattern of eating that drove me to hurt myself for the first time.
>
> It was March of 1983, my senior year in high school. I had just come back from spring vacation in Florida with my family. My abuse of diuretics and laxatives had drained me mentally and physically during the trip. But this did not stop the intense drive to binge. I decided a batch of fudge would suit my craving. I made the fudge and ate almost all of it and would not let myself throw up as punishment for being such a glutton. I went to bed that night and got up the next morning feeling guilty, disgusting, fat, and hating myself intensely. I felt that I had reached the ultimate low. I knew I needed help. I really felt the intense wish to die. I remember resolving to starve myself to death and soon ruling that out as too slow.
>
> After pacing around my room like a desperate caged animal for hours, I gradually built up so much physical tenseness and fury that I do not believe that I was in any way rational. I

> wanted to teach myself a lesson, to punish myself for being so out of control. I grabbed an empty pewter flower vase off my dresser and proceeded to hit myself in the face with it until my right eye was swollen shut. I had targeted my right cheekbone and counted to 100 hard hits before I felt my dirty and disgusting binge had been repented for.

A fairly common set of related phenomena, especially in teenage females, is that of depression, anorexia, and bulimia. There is no scientific evidence to say for certain which of these ailments comes first or whether one causes another. Differential emotions theory holds that emotions are fundamental motivators and that some emotion is always present and influencing behavior. This suggests that depressive emotions play a causal role in anorexia and bulimia, but it does not mean that we can stop here in our analysis. In thinking about the causes of complex human behavior, causation must be considered at several different levels. An emotion, for example sadness, is causal, though it usually has an antecedent, or cause, also. The cause may be a thought, perhaps a negative thought about one's self, as in Sheryl's case. This kind of thought suggests that some sadness may have already been present, but it could have been stimulated by inner-directed interest or self-concern, which in turn involves other factors and antecedents—the causal chain goes on and on. There are also physiological causes of behavior, like genuine hunger, as well as psychological causes, as in using food as a means of solace. Despite the great complexity of processes that motivate and guide behavior, sometimes an immediate cause can be determined and dealt with as the search for understanding of distal causes and causes at other levels continues. In Sheryl's case, an immediate cause of her eating disorder seems to have been depressive feelings brought about by social isolation and loneliness.

Sheryl also experienced a pattern of emotions that is often seen in depression—sadness and anger. Even psychotherapists who are not discrete emotion theorists often describe depressed children and adolescents as sad-mad patients. As she perceived herself as fat, Sheryl may also have felt shame—shame being another common cause of depression (Blumberg & Izard, 1985; Izard & Schwartz, 1986; Lewis, 1971).

> While striking my face with the vase I experienced a large range of emotions. One was a feeling of retribution. I really had convinced myself that I deserved this punishment for being such a low and worthless person. Another feeling was of anger toward myself and the rest of the world. I was angry at myself for losing control and to some extent angry at myself for being unable to commit suicide. I felt angry at the world in general because I felt it was partly responsible for my inner torment. After all, wasn't I always obsessed with being thin because it was fashionable? I remember thinking of girls in my high school who never seemed to have any problem with their eating, yet were still very thin. I hated them for being able to look the way I wanted to, and I hated myself for not being able to look like that. My feelings that I deserved to be punished included a drive to put some visible scar or bruise on my face so that I would look into the mirror and be reminded never to binge again. In effect, the bruise would serve as a warning. I would also notify the world that I had done wrong. I didn't know it at the time, but attention seeking and a cry for help were also involved unconsciously. Another element of feeling present during the self-abusing was an element of hope. Perhaps this was the new way I could control my eating!

In the final episode of Sheryl's story, guilt again played an important part in helping her toward a resolution of her problem. At this stage she began to feel guilty for making her parents so very upset. To feel guilt, one must have a meaningful loving relationship with those toward whom the emotion is felt. Her guilt in relation to her parents reminded her that she loved them and that they loved and cared for her. This was very therapeutic, and after 3 years of counseling, she has managed to gain control of her behavior.

> I must admit that I am ashamed of having hurt myself. I do not tell anyone of this part of my life's past. I always have feared that it would convince people that I am not totally sane.
>
> I feel I am just beginning to show some love for this person I am. After so much incredible hatred I must say it feels wonderful. I am convinced that to survive not only must one be surrounded by people who love you, but you must also love the person you are.

Sheryl managed the ultimate resolution of a depressive episode. She made herself likeable in her own eyes.

Being alone when you do not want to be is another universal cause of sadness. Under these circumstances, being alone is somewhat like the loss of a loved one, for you feel separated and isolated for those you care about. Other emotions may contribute to the feeling of being alone and isolated, but loneliness will undoubtedly include feelings of sadness.

Neurophysiological and Biochemical Approaches

Research on the biochemistry of depression has focused on the biogenic amines and on water and electrolyte balance. To date, the biogenic amine hypothesis has received the greatest attention (Davis, 1970; Whybrow, Akiskal, & McKinney, 1984). This hypothesis states that the synthesis and metabolism of the biogenic amines are importantly related to depression and mania. More specifically, depression is associated with a low level of amines in the brain, mania with a high level (Kety, 1970). The amines receiving most attention are norepinephrine, dopamine, and serotonin. Some studies have shown complex interrelationships among these amines, with levels differing with type or severity of depression (e.g., Asberg, Thoren, & Traskman, 1976). At present, most of the evidence indicates that norepinephrine deficiency in the brain and sympathetic nervous system is the single most critical factor in the biochemistry of depression. One study suggested that the mechanism for the influence of steroids on depression may be one that mediates an increase in norepinephrine in the nervous system (Maas & Mednieks, 1971).

Research on the biochemistry and neurophysiology of depression has led to the clinical use of a number of antidepressant drugs. One class of such drugs is the monoamine oxidase inhibitors (MAOI), which block the catabolism of naturally occurring amines and thereby provide an increase in the level of norepinephrine in the brain and the sympathetic nervous system. Unfortunately, MAOI drugs have not only proved ineffective with many depressives but may also lead to a number of side effects, especially when taken in conjunction with certain foods and beverages (Goodman & Gilman, 1970). A second class of antidepressant drugs is the tricyclic type, of which the most frequently used are imipramine and amitriptyline. Though the biological mechanism for the action of tricyclic drugs is different from that of the MAOI drugs, the net effect is the same—increasing the amount of free functional norepinephrine in the nervous system. The tricyclic drugs also have been found limited in effectiveness and also may lead to serious complications and adverse side effects (Davis, 1970; Puig-Antich, 1986).

The problems with antidepressant drugs do not rule out their use with some patients. Authorities in biochemistry and psychopharmacology caution, however, that the use of antidepressant drugs requires an extensive knowledge of their effects, of the patient's history, and of the particular type of depression being treated.

Differential emotions theory has some implications for neurophysiological and biochemical investigations of depression. If we assume that sadness is the key emotion in depression, then depression involves increased activity of the trophotropic system. In the case of dominance by the trophotropic system, there would also be parasympathetic dominance, cortical synchronization, and a tendency toward sleeplike EEG potentials.

If we assume that depression involves a combination or pattern of emotions, including both inner- and outer-directed anger, then it is necessary to allow for the possibility that the ergotropic system is also involved. With ergotropic dominance, there would be increased sympathetic activity, cortical desynchronization, and indexes of behavioral EEG arousal.

Differential emotions theory holds that depression represents a particular interactive balance between the trophotropic and ergotropic systems. Such a balance implies either a certain level of simultaneous functioning in these two systems or an alternation of dominance by the two systems. The balance may shift with type or severity of depression, as different emotions increase or decrease in intensity. In any case, the assumption that both systems are involved highly complicates the neurophysiology and biochemistry of depression. (For a more complete review of neurohormonal factors in depression, see Thompson, 1988, Ch. 12.)

Biogenetic, Sociocultural, and Cognitive Views

The picture of depression is not complete without a consideration of biogenetic, sociocultural, and cognitive factors. Theory or research in each of these areas has contributed something to our understanding of the subject.

Kraines (1957) presented a rather detailed biogenetic theory of depression. He considered the etiology of depression to be essentially physiological (hereditary and hormonal influences). Kraines defines the mechanism of depression as dysfunction in three areas of the brain: the diencephalon, rhinencephalon, and the reticular formation. He maintains that biogenetic theory explains the cyclic nature of depression and the efficacy of radical therapies, phenomena not so readily explained in terms of psychoanalytic or cognitive theory.

Kraines summarizes the evidence for the role of heredity in depression. He points out, for example, that among monozygotic twins, when one member of a pair has a psychotic depression, chances are between 70 and 96 in 100 that the remaining twin will also suffer from manic-depressive psychosis.

Kraines points out a relationship between biological factors and a number of depressive symptoms. He attributes visual paresthesias to disturbance in the optic thalamus and emotional isolation to inappropriate transmission or ineffective integration of the sensory processes involved in emotion. The research on the biochemistry of depression and on body types and depression are generally compatible with Kraines' biogenetic theory.

A number of studies have found apparent relationships between sociocultural factors and the occurrence of depression. Depression has been reported less frequently in Africa and Ireland than in England (Silverman, 1968). Some studies have suggested that blacks suffer less frequently and less severely from depression (Prange & Vitols, 1962; Tonks, Paykel & Klerman, 1970). However, some sociocultural factors such as family background and ethnic membership may be confounded with hereditary factors.

Beck (1967, 1976) has presented a comprehensive cognitive theory of depression. His central theses are very similar to those of the cognitive theorists reviewed earlier. Essentially he maintains that cognition is the primary determinant of emotions, moods, and behavior. He describes as the primary triad of cognitive determinants one's way of viewing oneself, one's world, and one's future. A negative view of self causes depressives to see themselves as inadequate and unworthy and to attribute their misery to personal defects. Their negative view of the world leads them to interpret their interactions as failures, steps toward defeat and disparagement. Their negative view of the future causes them to anticipate an indefinite continuation of their suffering. Beck explains most of the typical depressive symptoms such as paralysis of will, suicidal wishes, and self-devaluation as the result of one or the other of these cognitive determinants.

Instead of seeing a pattern of emotions as defining and determining depression, Beck sees a cognitive organization or schema that determines how an object or idea will be perceived and conceptualized. The schemata of depression involve such themes as personal deficiency and negative expectations. Beck does not address himself to the problem of the determinants of the necessary selectivity of perception and cognition that go into the making of a schema. Differential emotions theory holds that such schemata develop from emotion-cognition interactions, with fundamental emotions or patterns of emotions serving as the primary determinants. Beck does, however, recognize the importance of emotions, but he believes that they are a *result* of cognition rather than a cause.

Beck presents a comprehensive and very useful analysis of the symptomatology and phenomenology of depression. He summarizes the attributes of the depressive in four major groupings. He suggests that emotional manifestations are exemplified by the frequently observed sadness or dejected mood and that cognitive manifestations are exemplified by the depressive's tendency to see himself or herself as deficient in attributes that are particularly important to him or her. Beck holds that motivational manifestations include passivity, dependence, withdrawal wishes, and paralysis of will and that vegetative and physical manifestations are exemplified by loss of appetite and sleep disturbance.

Behavioral Learning Theories of Depression

As Wright and McDonald (1974) observed, behaviorists who have addressed the problem of depression have been more concerned with therapeutic procedures than with theoretical models. Learning-theory approaches to the analysis of depression received impetus, however, when Seligman and his associates (Seligman & Maier, 1967; Seligman, Maier, & Geer, 1968) began the experimental work that laid the foundation for the concept of depression as learned helplessness. Seligman and his associates showed that dogs that received a large number of inescapable electric shocks ultimately learned to become passive and accept the electric shock in apparent helplessness. According to Seligman, the dog learned that there was no adaptive response, and since there was nothing he could do to escape the shock, he learned passivity and helplessness. By using yoked controls who received the same amount of shock, but who were able to control or escape it, the experimenters were able to conclude that it was not the amount of shock or physical trauma that produced the passivity or learned helplessness in the experimental animals. Further, Maier (1970) showed that training dogs to stand still in order to escape shock did not result in a passivity that generalized to other situations where the animal could escape shock by jumping over a barrier. Rather, helplessness results when the animals learn that environmental outcomes are independent of instrumental responding. The motivation to act on the environment in order to control outcomes is thereby reduced. The resulting behavioral apathy becomes pathological when it interferes with the general process of learning that responses alter or control environmental events.

Seligman and his colleagues have maintained that the "learned helplessness" phenomenon resulting from an extended series of inescapable electric shocks is analogous to reactive depression in human beings. They suggest that what depressing situations have in common is that they are situations in which one thinks one has no control over events, particularly over those aspects that are perceived as most important. In generalizing his work to human beings, Seligman was influenced by the work of Beck (1967) and Kelly (1955). Kelly's theory of personality as a function of personal constructs emphasized the need of human beings to predict and control their environment.

Seligman (1975) has suggested that the opponent-process theory of emotion (Solomon & Corbit, 1974) is compatible with his own theory of the development of depression. A noxious event (electric shock in Seligman's animal paradigm) produces fear and panicky, dysadaptive responses. With repetition of the frenetic activity sequence, the organism learns that the fear-motivated responses are dysadaptive. As the experience is repeated, helplessness and the feelings accompanying depression increase. Ultimately, depression serves as an inhibitor of fear and keeps the latter within tolerable limits (fear and depression operated as opponent processes). After termination of the noxious event, fear may be relieved, while the opponent process of depression remains. As already noted, some psychanalytic theory (e.g., Rado, 1928/1968) and differential emotions theory recognize emotion-emotion interactions inherent in the profile of emotions in depression, and one of these is that between distress and fear. In some respects fear is incidental rather than causal in Seligman's theory of depression; nevertheless, his experimental paradigm begins with shock-induced fear, and the question as to what other affective states might leave the organism susceptible to the development of learned helplessness and depression is left unclear.

The provocative experimental findings and the consequent model developed by Seligman and his associates have evoked considerable interest among those concerned with the understanding and treatment of depression. The most serious problem with the theory may be its limited scope. Seligman himself acknowledges that it applies only to reactive depressions, and he implies that it does not account for all of these. If we assume antecedent situations that elicit fear plus only dysadaptive responses, then Seligman's model may be useful in conceptualizing one type of affect-cognition-action sequence that leads to what a number of theorists (e.g., Beck, 1967; Bibring, 1968) have recognized as symptoms of depression—feelings of hopelessness or helplessness.

Klerman's (1974) insightful review raises some questions for learning theory approaches. He concluded that rather than being a set of learned dysadaptive responses, depression serves several adaptive functions in animals and infants: (1) social communication, (2) psychological arousal, (3) subjective responses, and (4) psychodynamic defenses. He maintains that depression in infants acts as a signal of distress and helplessness and elicits helping responses from parents or caregivers. Although Klerman was not confident about the adaptive function of depression in adults, he concluded that it was an inherently adaptive process at any age. In support of his point he noted that reactive depression is generally self-limiting in duration (a factor that he thought indicated its benign quality).

In his behavioral analysis, Forster (1972) suggests that depressed persons are characterized by the loss of certain adaptive behaviors and by an increase in escape and avoidance behaviors such as complaints, requests, crying, and irritability. Complaints and requests are the depressive's efforts to remove aversive conditions. More important than the ineffective avoidance efforts is the decrease in frequency of types of behavior that were originally positively reinforced. The reduction of adaptive behavior that was positively reinforced is a function of three different factors. First, there are things that limit the repertory of available responses in particular situations. The process of limiting the available responses can be exemplified by Forster's treatment of the role of anger in depression. Since anger is typically directed toward another person, it may reduce the possibility that the object of anger will provide positive reinforcement for the expressor. Further, the expression of anger is often punished, and to avoid punishment a person may suppress the punished behavior. In the process, potentially adaptive responses may also be repressed, resulting in unnecessary constriction of the individual's repertory of activities that could lead to positive reinforcement. A second factor that constricts adaptive behavior that was once positively reinforced develops as a result of inconsistent rewards and punishments. The individual becomes unable to understand and predict the contingencies of reinforcement. If parents or caregivers administer rewards or punishments arbitrarily to adaptive and maladaptive types of behavior, the child may develop inaccurate perceptions of actual contingencies, become confused, and develop the feelings of hopelessness and helplessness pictured in many theories of depression. The third factor discussed by Forster consists of changes in environment. If the environment, particularly the social environment, is altered in such a way that previously reinforced responses are no longer positively reinforced, these responses will tend to drop out of the individual's repertory. Following clinical tradition, Forster gives as a prime example of this problem the loss of a loved one or significant other who has been a source of positive reinforcement.

Lewinsohn's (1974) position is similar to that of Forster. He maintains that the dysphoria of depression is a result of a low rate of positive reinforcement. Lewinsohn's treatment of affects and affective-cognitive interactions in depression (feelings of guilt, pessimism, and loss of self-esteem) is rather cursory. He suggests that these more discrete phenomena derive from one's effort to label one's vague and general feelings of dysphoria. Liberman and Raskin (1971) propose a behavioral theory similar to the preceding ones, adding the proposition that the depressed person's problem is exacerbated by reinforcement of maladaptive behavior.

By virtue of their orientation, the behaviorists in general do not deal extensively with the discrete affects and affective-cognitive interactions in depression. The usefulness of these theories may be in providing ways of conceptualizing the origin of particular responses or activities of depressives. Costello (1972) has argued that a strict learning theory approach and the concept of loss of reinforcement cannot adequately explain many of the clinical cases of depression. He gives as an example the man who loses his wife and refuses to eat; Eating has, at least temporarily, lost its effectiveness as a reinforcer. Costello remains in a learning theory tradition by maintaining that it is not loss of reinforcement of adaptive behavior but loss of reinforcer effectiveness that better explains the phenomenon of depression. Costello attempts to supplement his learning theory by incorporating the idea that biochemical and neurophysiological changes can contribute to loss of reinforcer effectiveness. In his view, Seligman's animal-laboratory model of depression does not generalize to depression in humans (Costello, 1978).

Psychoanalytic Theory of Depression

First, consider the origin and role of the various discrete emotions in depression, as presented by the psychoanalysts. All agree that sadness is part of the picture of depression (see, for example, the fine collection of papers in Bibring, 1968). According to psychoanalysts, the sadness results from real or imagined loss that may threaten the individual's self-esteem, self-confidence, and emotional security. They hold that the predisposition to sadness is acquired in the oral (early) stages of infancy at the height of the individual's helplessness and dependency.

Second, almost all the psychoanalytic theorists agree with Abraham's (1911/1968) early observation that anger is part of the picture of depression. All the psychoanalysts agree that the anger and hostility of depression stem from the early frustrations and the tendency toward fixation at the oral and sadistic stages of psychosexual development. Fromm-Reichmann (1953) and Bibring (1968), however, relegated anger and hostility to a lesser role.

Guilt figures prominently as an emotion involved in depression, and for Rado the mood of gloomy repentance is the predominant one. The phrase "gloomy repentance" implies some combination of sadness and guilt. Guilt arises, according to the psychoanalytic system, as a result of the depressed individual's relatively uncontrollable anger and rage and the behavior that the latter determines.

Fear or anxiety is mentioned by a number of psychoanalytic theorists, some viewing it as due primarily to the fear of losing sexual potency. By inference one could see fear resulting from the individual's feeling of inadequacy, and incapacity in the face of threat or danger. Janet (1928) spoke of fear of action as a key determinant of depression, and Bowlby (1969, 1973) sees fear as part of the separation syndrome in young children.

The emotion of shame figures in the dynamics of depression in some psychoanalytic views and not in others. Freud (1968) felt that the depressed person lacked shame, whereas Fromm-Reichmann (1953) and Helen Lewis (1971) emphasized that shame was present and important. Most of the psychoanalysts agree that loss of self-esteem, self-confidence, and self-respect figures as a prominent dimension of depression. One could consider this loss of self-esteem and the accompanying feelings of inferiority as indexes of the emotion of shame.

Psychoanalysts use discrete emotions in the description of depression much more than they do in analyzing anxiety. One or another of the psychoanalytic investigators has touched on most of the components of depression that are hypothesized by differential emotions theory.

Differential Emotions Theory and an Empirical Analysis of the Phenomenology of Depression

Differential emotions theory holds that the subjective experience, or phenomenology, of depression is a variable combination or pattern of affects and affective-cognitive interactions. Depression phenomenology is an even more complex pattern than that for anxiety: more emotions are activated and there are more possibilities for conflicts in the emotion-emotion dynamics. The fundamental emotions involved in the phenomenology of depression are sadness—the key emotion—and anger, disgust, contempt, fear, guilt, and shyness. It is hypothesized that anger, disgust, and contempt (hostility) is expressed toward both the self and others.

Although the fundamental emotions are considered the primary and most important elements of the phenomenology of depression, there are other factors that are frequently present—decreased sexuality, decreased physical well-being, and increased fatigue. These elements may be most properly considered as immediate effects or by-products of depression. Nevertheless, they have motivational properties and, consequently, influence the other components of the depression and its course.

Differential emotions theory suggests that the lack of sexual interest and concern over sexual adequacy is determined in part by the combined effects of inner-directed hostility on the one hand and the fear and guilt components of depression on the other. The concern over physical well-being results in part from the elevated nonemotion factor of fatigue as well as from the feeling of debilitation and motor retardation that results from emotion-emotion conflicts. The increased fatigue is determined in part by the expenditure of energy in the emotion conflicts inherent in the depression pattern.

Analysis of the Phenomenology of Depression with the DES. The application of differential emotions theory to the analysis of the phenomenology of depression was accomplished by means of the Differential Emotions Scale (DES). In modifying the DES for the study of the phenomenology of depression (Izard, 1972), the items relating to anger, disgust, and contempt were included once for measurement of feelings toward self and again for measurement of feelings toward others (inner- and outer-directed hostility components). Subscales were added for sexuality, vigor or physical well-being, and fatigue. Finally, the items for the depression scale of Zuckerman's (1960) Multiple Affect Adjective Checklist (MAACL) were added. The Zuckerman items scored positively for depression were designated Z, and those scored negatively as Z−. The DES items, the new subscale items, and the Zuckerman items were placed in random order, and the total scale was designated the DES+D.

In the study of normal depression, all subjects in the sample visualized the depression situation and completed the DES+D. Table 10-1 presents the profile of emotions for normal persons recalling and imaging a depression situation. The

TABLE 10-1
Rank Order of Scale Means of a Priori *and Empirical Factors in a Recalled or Imagined Depression Situation*[a]

A priori scales (from DES items)		Empirical factors (from DES+D items)		
Factor	Scale ($\bar{x}$)		Scale ($\bar{x}$)	Alpha
Sadness	4.24	Sadness + Z[c]	3.8	.89
Disgust	3.14	A/D/C: hostility, inner directed[b]	3.1	.86
Contempt	2.86	Fear	2.8	.90
Anger	2.85	Fatigue	2.6	.77
Fear	2.80	Sociality/sexuality	2.5	.61
Fatigue	2.64	Guilt	2.4	.83
Guilt	2.41	A/D/C: hostility, outer directed[b]	2.3	.93
Suprise	2.23	Surprise	2.2	.92
Interest	2.20	Physical well-being (vigor)	2.0	.85
Shyness	2.05	Joy + Z −[c]	1.2	.78
Enjoyment	1.14	Shyness	2.0	.80

[a]From Izard, 1972 (N = 332 college students).
[b]A/D/C = anger/disgust/contempt.
[c]Z items are those scored positively, and Z− items are those scored negatively on the Zuckerman MAACL depression scale.

profile for the emotions represented by the *a priori* scales of the DES are shown in column 1. The DES *a priori* scales describe the subjects' feelings toward or within themselves. The obtained profile is quite similar to that predicted by differential emotions theory. Sadness is the key emotion and is elevated substantially above all other emotions in the pattern.

The second-, third-, and fourth-ranking emotions in the *a priori* depression profile are disgust, contempt, and anger, the three emotions designated as the hostility triad. These elevated means represent hostility directed toward the self. The rank of this component in the pattern is indicative of its relative importance in the depression situation. The fifth- and sixth-ranking emotions are fear and guilt, which are related in complex ways to each other as well as to the other emotion components of depression (the nonemotion factor of fatigue is actually the sixth-ranking mean in the profile; the reasons for its presence in the pattern have already been discussed).

The more complex picture of the phenomenology of depression is presented in column 2 of Table 10-1, which shows the empirical factors derived from the factor analysis of the DES+D. In the factor analysis, most of the Z items merged with the DES sadness scale and the Z− items with the DES joy scale.

Looking at the empirical factors that correspond to or represent fundamental emotions, it can be seen that the rank order of the emotions as represented in the empirical factors is virtually identical with the rank order of the emotions in the pattern based on *a priori* scales. The differences are due largely to the presence of the new affective factors (sexuality, vigor, fatigue) that hold positions among the emotion factors.

Between the emotions of fear and guilt in the empirical profile is the fifth-ranking factor, sociality/sexuality, which consists of items from the Zuckerman depression scale. The decreased sociability and loss of interest in sexual activity undoubtedly relate to the inhibiting emotions of fear and guilt and also to the feelings of incompetence and inadequacy brought about by inner-directed hostility. The decreased sexual involvement may also be related to the individual's lowered sense of vigor or physical well-being. The decrease in physical well-being is undoubtedly a function of both the factor of fatigue and emotion-emotion conflicts, which make heavy demands on the energy of the depressed individual.

The seventh-ranking component in the empirical factor pattern for depression is outer-directed hostility. The outer-directed hostility may serve an adaptive function by keeping inner-directed hostility from mounting higher and higher. Outer-directed hostility may also serve to allay some of the guilt and fear in the pattern.

The presence of fear in the depression pattern may be adaptive in two ways. First, it may continue to function as motivation for the depressed individual to remove himself or herself from the situation or otherwise to change the scene. Second, the fear may also serve as a check against excessive inner-directed hostility and thus decrease the chances of suicidal behavior.

The study of depression in college students was replicated in a sample of 330 high school students from middle and upper-middle socioeconomic groups. The DES+D affect profiles from the two studies were remarkably similar, attesting to the construct validity of the DES+D factors and the meaningfulness of the differential emotions theory analysis of depression. In both samples, sadness and inner-directed hostility were first and second respectively, and guilt sixth. Fatigue was fourth in the college group, third in the high school sample. Among the first six factors, the biggest difference between the college and high school profiles was a reversal of the ranks for fear and outer-directed hostility, third and seventh in the college group and sixth and fourth in the high school sample. This higher outer-directed hostility in the younger subjects suggests that on the average they are closer to the peak of the rebellious period that frequently characterizes adolescence. The higher outer-directed hostility in this group may suppress the fear component and account for its relatively lower rank.

Patterns of Emotions of Depressive Clients in Psychotherapy. The Differential Emotions Scale has been used as a tool to facilitate psychotherapy with depressive persons. Table 10-2 presents a DES profile for two psychotherapy clients. Both of the profiles are somewhat similar to the profile of depression obtained for normal subjects recalling or imagining a depression situation, but the fact that they differ from each other and from the average profiles in imaged depression is quite as expected in terms of differential emotions theory. The depressive pattern may vary from individual to individual or from time to time

TABLE 10-2
DES Profiles of Two Depressed Psychotherapy Clients[a]

Woman suffering from marital upheaval (age 29)		College male suffering from loss of father and feelings of personal inadequency (age 20)	
Sadness	15	Sadness	15
Surprise	7	Fear	14
Anger	7	Disgust	13
Guilt	7	Guilt	13
Fear	7	Shyness	11
Fatigue	5	Contempt	10
Interest	5	Fatigue	9
		Anger	8

[a]Adapted from Izard, 1972. DES scores range from a maximum possible of 15 to a minimum possible of 3.

within the same individual. The particular pattern as it exists at the time can be used to guide the therapist in his or her treatment of the client.

In the case of the first profile in Table 10-2, the woman and her husband were having extramarital affairs with the knowledge and consent of each other. Actually, the woman could not fully consent and could never adapt happily to the quadrangle affair. Sadness was the most prominent emotion in her pattern, but surprise was also high. She was continually astonished to find herself in this situation. Anger, guilt, and fear were also elevated.

The client represented in column 2 was considerably more debilitated and retarded in his functioning than was the wife. This could be inferred from the fact that fear, the most toxic and debilitating emotion, was second only to sadness in the profile. For this client, disgust and contempt were largely inner directed. Guilt and shyness also played an important role in this young man's reactive depression.

Patterns of Emotions and Feelings in Hospitalized Depressive Patients. Marshall and Izard (1972b) administered a modified form of the DES+D to 30 female and 10 male hospitalized depressives. Table 10-3 compares the rank order of the DES+D factor scores for the depressed patients with the high school sample described earlier. Considerable similarity obtained between the profile of emotions and feelings for the depressed patients and that for the high school students describing a recalled and visualized period of depression. Differences of two or more ranks were found between three of the factors. One of these was not predicted, but the other two were quite as expected in a comparison of depression in hospitalized patients and normals. The patients reported relatively less fatigue than the high school students. This was somewhat surprising, until we considered the differences in environmental conditions and treatment. The patients may not experience as much fatigue because of their confinement, freedom from usual responsibilities, relative inactivity, and the use of antidepressant drugs. As

TABLE 10-3
Rank Order of DES+D Factors for High School Students Recalling and Visualizing a Depression Situation and for Depressive Patients

Factor	High school (N = 313)	Depressive patients (N = 40)
Sadness	1	1
Inner-directed hostility	2	3
Fear	3	2
Fatigue	4	7
Guilt	5	4.5
Outer-directed hostility	6	8
Physical well-being	7	6
Shyness	8	4.5

expected, the depressed patients reported relatively less outer-directed hostility. This is consistent with the developmental phenomenon already mentioned, with clinical observation, and with differential emotions theory, which suggests that outer-directed hostility could be adaptive in allaying inner-directed hostility and militating against the fear and guilt components of depression.

The largest difference between the depressed patients and the high school students was on shyness, where the depressed patients had a considerably higher rank. This tends to favor differential emotions theory and Fromm-Reichmann's position that shame is important in depression. It disconfirms the Freudian notion that the depressive is one who lacks shame and shyness and makes defensive use of exhibiting his or her miseries and woes. The differences in shyness and outer-directed hostility could result in part from differences in severity of depression and overall psychological adjustment. Despite these minor differences in relative rank order of affects, the profile of normals recalling and imagining a depression situation is essentially similar to hospitalized depressive patients.

Schultz (1976) showed that therapist-directed imagery and fantasy relating to anger, pleasure, and relaxation resulted in a lessening of depression in hospitalized depressives. His finding is compatible with the principle of emotion interaction (e.g., anger inhibiting or attenuating sadness) and with the positions of Beck (1967) and Lazarus (1968).

An EMG Analysis of Discrete Emotions in Normal and Depressed Persons. Schwartz, Fair, Salt, Mandel, and Klerman (1976) asked normal and depressed individuals to self-generate happy, sad, or angry thoughts or feelings, and the thoughts and feelings associated with a typical day of their life. Using surface electrodes, they recorded the EMG activity of the frontalis, corrugator, depressor anguli oris, and masseter muscles of the face. As in their earlier study, the experiment showed clearly different profiles of facial muscle activity in the happy, sad, and angry conditions (see Figure 10-1).

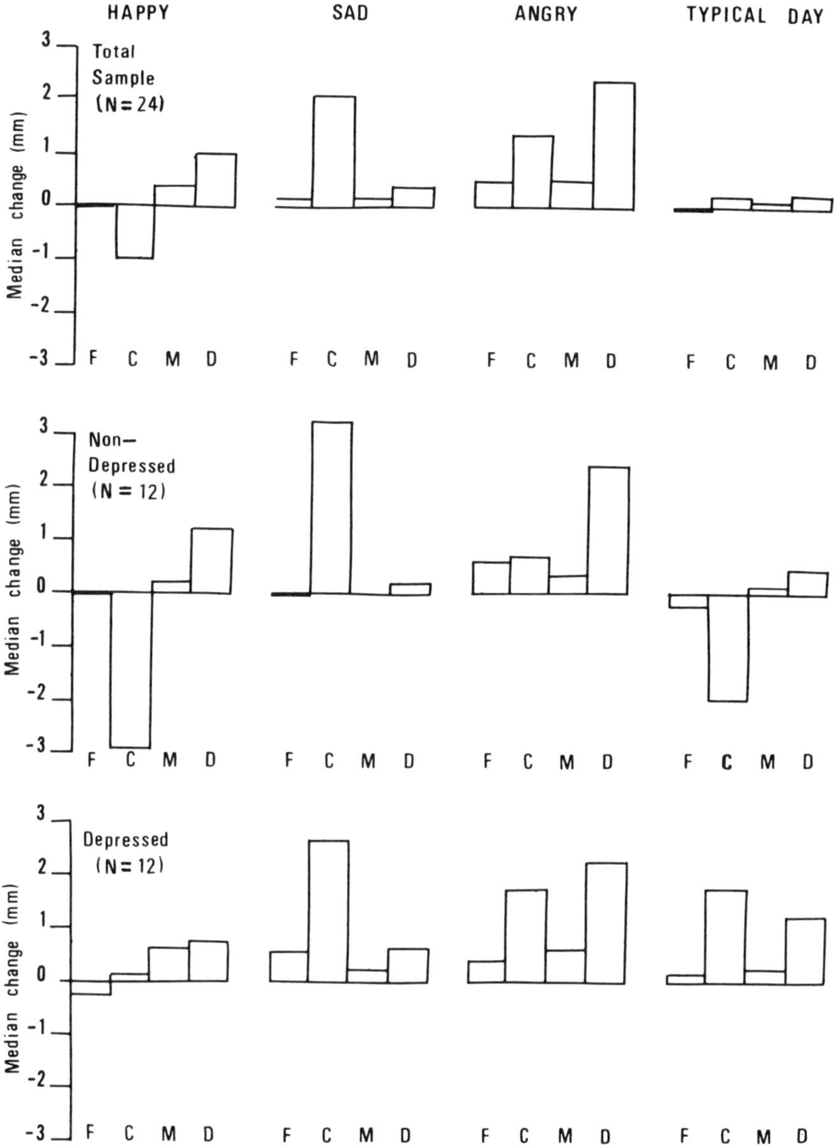

FIGURE 10-1. Changes in EMG profiles of depressed and nondepressed individuals imaging a happy, sad, and angry situation and a typical day. F, frontalis; C, corrugator; M, masseter; D, depressor anguli oris. (Adapted from Schwartz et al., 1976.)

In the experimental (happy, sad, angry) conditions the profiles of the nondepressed persons and the depressed patients were somewhat similar in form, but there were differences in the magnitude of response in some muscles. In the happy condition the depressed subjects showed considerably less change in the corrugator muscle and somewhat greater change in this muscle in the angry condition than did nondepressed subjects. The EMG profiles as a group distinguished between the nondepressed and depressed individuals. The depressives showed an attenuated pattern in the happy condition. Further, the profiles for the two groups while imaging a typical day were strikingly different. The profile for the typical day in normals is rather similar to that of the profile for the happy condition, while the profile for the depressed patients visualizing a typical day looks like a mix of their sadness and anger profiles. The finding of a sadness-anger pattern in the life of depressed individuals is consistent with both psychoanalytic theory (Abraham, 1911/1968; Freud, 1968) and differential emotions theory (Izard, 1972).

The Phenomenology of Depression in 10- and 11-Year-Old Children. Figure 10-2 shows the profile of emotions in depressed and nondepressed children, as determined by the Children's Depression Inventory (CDI; Kovacs & Beck, 1977). The children's form of the DES (DES IV) was used to assess the affective symptomatology of depression.

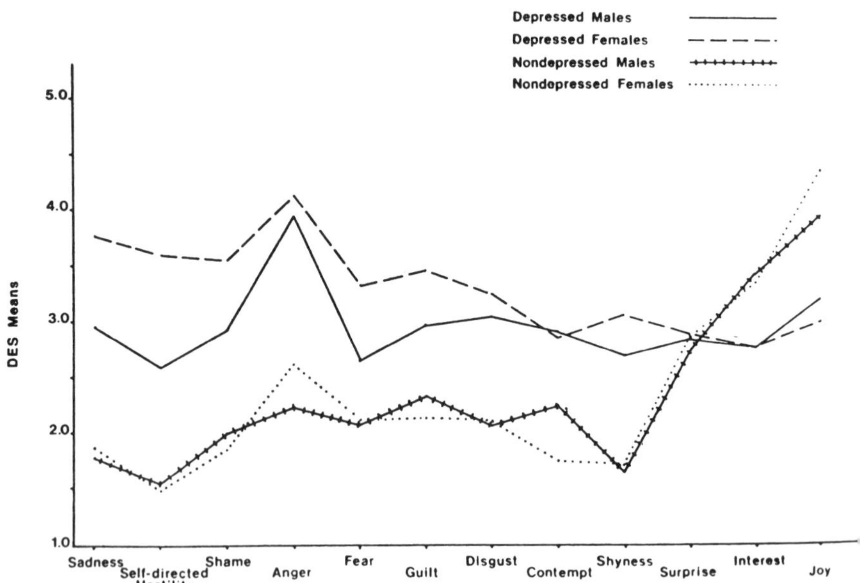

FIGURE 10-2. Mean emotion scores for high and low scorers on the Children's Depression Inventory (depressed boys, N = 19; depressed girls, N = 14; nondepressed boys, N = 23; nondepressed girls, N = 28).

For girls, the profile of emotions in depression is quite similar to that in adult depression. The DES-IV sadness, inner-directed hostility, shame, anger, contempt, guilt, and fear scales were positively correlated with depression as indexed by the CDI, and the joy scale was negatively correlated with the CDI. For the boys, the DES-IV sadness, inner-directed hostility, anger, shame, and shyness scales were positively correlated with the CDI, but these correlations were not as high as for girls. Although sex differences were significant with the first sample and with a combination of the first and second samples, they were not significant with the second sample alone. Thus, the question of developmental continuity and change in these sex differences remains for future research.

The importance of inner-directed hostility for girls indicated that girls who score high on the CDI are phenomenologically similar to depressed adults. The feeling of inner-directed hostility is likely to be associated with self-blame and low self-esteem, which are generally considered symptoms of depression (e.g., Beck, 1967; Seligman & Peterson, 1986). Also, like adults, girls who scored high on a measure of depression performed more poorly than others on a problem-solving test but no worse than others on a measure of verbal intelligence. The reports of frequent anger from girls who scored high on the CDI appeared to be the major phenomenological difference between them and depressed adults. Consistent with this finding, Jacobsen, Lahey, and Strauss (1983) and Kazdin, Esveldt-Dawson, Unis, and Rancurello (1983) found that depression in boys and girls was significantly related to measures of conduct disorder and aggression.

The importance of anger and the unimportance of self-directed hostility as predictors of boys' CDI scores suggested that the phenomenology of boys who scored high on the CDI was different from that of high-scoring girls and depressed adults. Although anger is often a component of adult depression, the distinguishing features of depression are generally considered to be sadness, self-contempt, shame, guilt, and low self-esteem (e.g., Beck 1967; Lewis, 1971). Izard, Blumberg, and Oyster (1985) found no sex differences in a study parallel to this one with college students as subjects, so the sex differences for emotion correlates of depression, if they are genuine, seem to be unique to children. More research is needed to understand the sex differences and developmental changes in depression.

Summary

Grief over the loss of a beloved person or a highly valued object is a virtually universal human experience. The most profound grief comes from the loss of a loved one. While sadness is the dominant emotion in grief, the conditions eliciting grief frequently evoke other interacting emotions. The extent to which fear, anger, guilt, and shame interact with sadness during the period of grieving depends upon the particular individual's life experiences and the prevailing conditions at the time of loss. It has been argued that grief is biologically based and biologically adaptive, serving as a cohesive force in maintaining social organization in species that are essentially group-living forms.

Bowlby extensively outlined the course of grief in response to separation. Following separation from caregiver, the infant or child's behavior follows a typical sequence: protest consisting of vigorous efforts to recover mother or caregiver, despair characterized by grief and mourning, and finally emotional detachment. Intense grief such as that suffered over the loss of a lifelong mate can render the grieving adult more susceptible to disease and death. A number of clinical investigators have concluded that grief can take on pathological characteristics.

Consistent with the notion that sadness is the most ubiquitous negative emotion, depression is considered the most common psychological or psychopathological problem. There are a number of viable theories of depression. Most of them agree that it is a complex phenomenon involving neurophysiological and biochemical factors, a number of affects, and various affective-cognitive interactions.

Studies of monozygotic twins have indicated genetic determinants of depression. Biochemical studies have shown relationships between depression and the synthesis and metabolism of biogenic amines. Biochemical research has led to the development of antidepressant drugs, and although they provide relief to many depressives their therapeutic value has not been completely determined. Beck's (1967, 1976) cognitive theory of depression holds that one's view of one's self, one's world, and one's future constitutes the principal determinant in depression. This theory presents a highly useful analysis of the symptomatology and the phenomenology of depression.

There are a number of behavioral or learning theory approaches to the study of depression. Though some of them recognize biological factors, most of them emphasize only the role of learning. One holds that repeated exposure to inescapable pain or threat leads to fear, distress, and learned helplessness and hopelessness (depression). Another behavioral theory holds that depressives have lost certain adaptive behaviors and have increased escape and avoidance behaviors as a result of inappropriate or absent reinforcing conditions. Another holds that depression results from the loss of reinforcer effectiveness as it applies to certain types of adaptive behavior.

Psychoanalytic theory has recognized the role of a number of discrete emotions in depression. Neoanalytic theories have extended the causal concept of loss to include loss of self-esteem, loss of confidence, and loss of self-respect.

Differential emotions theory holds that depression is a pattern of fundamental emotions including the key emotion of sadness and variable combinations of anger, disgust, and contempt (inner- and outer-directed hostility), fear, guilt, and shyness. It also recognizes the role of other affective factors such as decreased sexuality, increased fatigue, and loss of the sense of physical well-being. Empirical studies of normal subjects and hospitalized depressives using the DES support the differential emotions theory conception of depression. Further, the DES profile of emotions and affective-cognitive structures in normal and pathological depression are quite similar. The differences are readily explained in terms of varieties of depression or overall psychological status of the normal subjects and depressives.

DES profiles of depressed individuals in psychotherapy show the main features of the depressive profile, but they also illustrate variations in the importance of different emotions depending upon the individual client and the life situation.

EMG studies of facial muscle activity in normal and depressed persons yielded results quite consistent with differential emotions theory. Facial muscles involved in the expression of joy and sadness distinguished between the two groups.

Profiles of depression for 10- and 11-year-old children indicate that for girls the emotion patterns are similar to those in adults. The depressed girls were also similar to depressed adults in that they performed more poorly than others on problem-solving tasks but no worse than others on a measure of verbal intelligence. The phenomenology of depression for boys was different, with the role of the emotion of anger being more prominent.

Suggested Readings

Averill, J. R. (1968). Grief: Its nature and significance. *Psychological Bulletin*, *70*, 721–748.

A description of the functions of grief from an evolutionary perspective.

Blumberg, S.H., & Izard, C. E. (1985). Discriminating patterns of emotions in 10- and 11-year-old children's anxiety and depression. *Journal of Personality and Social Psychology*, *49*(1), 194–202.

An empirical analysis of depression in children in terms of discrete emotions. Depicts the characteristic profile of emotions in 10- to 11-year-old children.

Gaensbauer, T. J., Harman, R. J., Cytryn, L., & McKnew, D. H. (1984). Social and affective development of infants with a manic-depressive parent. *American Journal of Psychiatry*, *141*, 223–229.

Characteristics of children with manic-depressive parents. A longitudinal study of their responses to mother, stranger, and a frustrating task.

Zahn-Waxler, C., Cummings, E. M., McKnew, D. H., & Radke-Yarrow, M. (1984). Altruism, aggression, and social interactions in young children with a manic-depressive parent. *Child Development*, *55*(1), 112–122.

An exploratory study of the emotional and social functioning of young children of manic-depressive parents. Discusses the problems of the deviant behaviors of these children and the implication of these behaviors for the development of psychopathology.

Zahn-Waxler, C., Kochanska, G., Krupnick, J., & McKnew, D. (1990). Patterns of guilt in children of depressed and well mothers. *Developmental Psychology*, *26*(1), 51–59.

A psychiatric interview and a semiprojective procedure revealed that children of depressed mothers have aberrant guilt feelings that are not well linked to empathy and prosocial behavior, a linkage that was found in normal children.

11

Anger

Anger is an important emotion. It is often undesirable and typically avoided in so far as possible. Sometimes when you look back on your anger you are embarrassed. This is especially so if you expressed your anger openly, and someone you respect saw that display. You are embarrassed because you "lost control." An untimely display or a volley of angry words can temporarily shake up a relationship. As we have seen, anger can become connected to sadness, and inner-directed anger in combination with sadness and other emotions can lead to depression. Anger can also become associated with guilt and fear.

If anger expression is restrained, you may feel tormented at your inability to free yourself of the shackles that restrain you or the barriers that frustrate your efforts to reach a goal. Under certain conditions suppression of an outward show of anger may be associated with abnormally high activity of the autonomic nervous system, resulting in increased diastolic blood pressure, increased heart rate, and other physiological changes. Repeated exposure to situations that create such disturbances in cardiovascular and other physiological functions can lead to psychosomatic disorders.

If anger can be the source of so much misery, why then is it such an important emotion? A more complete understanding of the characteristics and functions of anger, its relation to other emotions, drives, thought, and action can help us appreciate its overall significance for the individual and society.

In frustrating situations that trigger anger, the emotions of disgust and contempt are frequently activated. Anger, disgust, and contempt frequently form what we shall call the hostility triad. They are a triad of negative emotions that characterize many situations in which daily hassles become too numerous or too entangling. This hostility can be directed either inwardly toward the self or outwardly toward others or vaguely toward the situation or the "system." Although anger, disgust, and contempt often operate in combination, it is important to understand the distinguishing features of each. One way to help yourself get a handle on them is to be able to identify each of them clearly, to label them for what they are. In a later section we'll look at the distinguishing features of the three members of the hostility triad. First, let us examine anger.

Some Common Causes of Anger

Restraint

The feeling of physical or psychological restraint is a pretty certain activator of the emotion of anger. Campos and Stenberg (1981) have shown that infants as young as 4 months of age respond to arm restraint with expressions of anger. The experimenters had the mother gently hold the infant's arm so as to prevent movement. The infant's facial responses were objectively coded as anger. By 7 months of age, the same treatment not only elicited expressions of anger but gaze behavior directed at the mother.

Although it has not been tested systematically in different cultures, physical restraint is probably a universal cause of anger. One reason for believing in the universality of physical restraint as a cause of anger is that eventually virtually any kind of restraint can trigger anger. To the older child or teenager a verbal restraint or prohibition can provoke anger just as quickly or evenly more quickly than physical restraint. As adults, rules and regulations sometimes make us angry because they have the effect of putting us in a straightjacket. The significant thing in physical or verbal restraint is the blocking of the person from a desired course of action or from obtaining a goal.

Blocking or Interrupting Goal-Oriented Behavior

So another way of understanding causes of anger is to view them in relation to the person's desired direction or goal. Anything that deflects a person from his or her path to the goal can trigger anger. Interruption may be sensed as a restraint or as a deflection from the goal path. Thus, interrupting a person who is concentrat-

FIGURE 11-1. Uninhibited anger in a toddler frustrated by her sister's playful effort to restrain her from sucking her thumb.

ing on some complex task or who is rushing frantically to get something finished on time may well cause anger. There are, of course, occasions when people welcome interruptions, but these are times when they do not feel pressure to make progress toward the goal every moment or at least they do not feel such pressure as much as they desire the diversion offered by the interruption.

Aversive Stimulation

After years of extensive study of anger and aggression, Berkowitz (1990) concluded that aversive stimulation is sufficient cause of angry feelings and aggressive inclinations. He reasoned that unpleasant events, such as immersion in cold water, extended exposures to high temperature, foul odors, and morally repugnant scenes, generate negative affect or unpleasant feelings. This negative affect activates anger directly. Contrary to cognitive theories of emotion activation, Berkowitz argued that available evidence indicates that anger can arise from the negative event without antecedent appraisal processes (e.g., Frijda, 1986; Lazarus, 1984) or attribution processes (Weiner, 1985).

Berkowitz maintains that once anger is activated directly by aversive stimulation and negative affect, it may then be amplified and sustained or attenuated and inhibited by cognitive processes. For example, telling oneself that the pain will soon subside or that the exposure to high temperature will soon be alleviated by a trip to the beach should attenuate the anger feelings. Berkowitz's model and differential emotions theory have several features in common.

Although Berkowitz recognizes noncognitive causes of anger feelings and aggressive inclinations, he calls his theory a cognitive-neoassociationistic model. The model assumes that specific types of feelings (e.g., anger) are linked to particular thoughts and memories (e.g., aggressive plans or fantasies) and to motor-expressive and physiological reactions by a network of associations. Activation of any one component of the associative network of negative affect, anger feelings, ideas, and memories tends to activate the other parts as well. As already noted, even noncognitive (e.g., pain) activated anger feeling may be modulated by subsequent cognitive appraisals or attributions.

Living with Anger: A Personal Account

Another common cause of anger is the thought of being misled and unjustly hurt by others. A traumatic experience in the life of a high school athlete illustrates the point. Jonelle was seriously injured during a high school field hockey game. In her account of what followed, it is clear that her posttrauma headaches and blurred vision were misdiagnosed and mistreated. The constant, severe pain and the ever-present thought that she was consistently mistreated during a long period of suffering led to chronic anger. Before she settled into an angry attitude toward those who misdiagnosed and mistreated her, she experienced several emotions, including terror at the thought of losing her sight. This is her account of the accident and the events that led to her anger.

> I'm simply angry now, at everyone who was involved and about what they did to me and how they did it. But the emotional swings that brought me to this point were all but simple.
>
> My life changed drastically on October 11, 1977. During field hockey practice after school, I collided head-on into another player, knocking myself unconscious. Upon regaining consciousness several moments later, fear and confusion crept through me. As if I had only closed my eyes and opened them in the same instant, I remembered nothing of the accident nor the ensuing minutes, but instead it seemed to me that I had relocated myself from practice field to side lines in the blink of an eye.
>
> My disorientation was brief, for when I recognized the pain, it seared with a vengeance through my head and down my neck. A large bump swelled on my forehead and directly below it, the vision in my left eye blurred. The pain redoubled my panicked state as my heart raced and I rolled onto my side into a fetal position to ease my gasping lungs. When I was able to sit up, and later stand and walk, I stumbled into my coach's car and was driven speedily home.

Jonelle's account of her trauma and the subsequent sequence of pain and emotions moves very rapidly. Her opening statement, "I'm simply angry now," is retrospective, but had she not been knocked unconscious, she might have experienced anger immediately after the collision. Our extensive studies of young children's emotion responses to the acute pain of inoculation has shown convincingly that anger is a natural response to unanticipated pain. Infants express anger following painful injections *before* they have the ability to anticipate that the procedure will hurt them. Of course, Jonelle had the ability to anticipate, and although she did not anticipate the collision, she could anticipate possible future consequences of such severe pain. Such anticipation led to fear. The continuing pain, however, continued to trigger anger, which became the dominant emotion.

Chronic pain does not always lead to chronic anger. It did not in Michelle's struggle with scoliosis. There were, of course, situational as well as individual differences in the two cases.

As we shall see, Jonelle was not simply angry. She had bouts of strong fear and anxiety, and sadness and depression.

> I fell, my head spinning, into the back seat of my parent's car and was rushed off to the emergency center in the city's hospital.
>
> Pokings, proddings, X rays, tests—for days, this was my sterile, painful world. But for all the examinations and experimentation, nothing was found other than the obvious signs; headache and blurred vision due to concussion. The treatment: aspirin and sleep. I was assured it would get better.
>
> But it didn't.
>
> For 2 years, I was plagued with horrible, incapacitating headaches and a stiff neck. I fell behind in school. My friends disassociated themselves from me. I was continually exhausted and frustrated, and therefore, outwardly biting, sarcastic, selfish, and intolerant. I was terribly depressed. At that time, as in no other time in my life, I cannot recall ever feeling any excitement or joy about anything. I was unable to hold my interest on any

project. Even 30-minute sitcoms on television were intolerably long. I was terribly anxious, continuously nervous with "butterflies" and bitten nails.

The fall of 1979 brought a change . . . for the worse.

I probably shouldn't have been in school anyway. I was disruptive *in* class and delinquent *out* of class. But on the morning of September 14, I was in biology when the blurred vision in my left eye turned to *no* vision in either eye. It happened so quickly, with no accompanying symptoms other than my nearly 2-year-old headache. Perhaps because my body had been so wired up for 23 months, I was unable to shriek or gasp at the sudden, startling turnabout in my homeostasis. Or perhaps through my depression I had gained a self-destructive attitude, which contented itself with the worsening of my condition. Whichever, I calmly reported to my lab partner that I needed the teacher to escort me to the school nurse's office. No one else in the room suspected anything out of the ordinary.

In reflection, I'm not sure how well any individual can put off or ignore *terror*, but I know that I walked, hand-in-hand, with my biology teacher down two flights of stairs and into the nurse's office without a thought about falling or, more importantly, being blind for the rest of my life. I suppose it was mechanical behavior, or a will to do what must be done, and survive, a fighting spirit I thought I had lost in a blow on a hockey field so long ago.

But upon lying down in wait of assistance, I abandoned myself to the display of deepest anguish. I sobbed and cried out, drawing my extremities up to my body and rocking. I remember little of what went through my mind at that time except perhaps the idea that if this is what life is, I don't want it.

I was admitted almost an hour later to the hospital. My vision was gradually returning; I could see shadows and bright light but little else. A resident doctor saw me, quickly, and left. He referred me to a neurosurgeon. Dr. Patterson, a renowned neurologist and surgeon, visited me early the next morning. He ordered a CAT scan, skull X rays and an EEG (electroencephalogram), but before he was able to carry out his tests, my body convulsed, I saw spatterings of black and white, and half-consciously I experienced the first seizure of my life. Later, exhausted, I fell asleep.

In the following episode, note that Jonelle had the ability to experience and express anger even in the midst of the intense fear that we call terror. Anger, like all emotions, has adaptive functions. Here it was probably doing at least two things for Jonelle. It helped counteract the fear, and it gave her the energy and determination ("will") to keep trying.

That evening I awoke with halting, slurred speech. Beyond being frustrated with my inability to communicate, I was petrified that I had experienced brain damage. I wanted to roll back the 2 years since my accident and absolutely mutilate the girl who walked away from our collision with little more than stars before her eyes. I had a vengeance that was reflected in my every action and every slurred word. I was angry, outraged, and bitter toward the whole world and even toward God for allowing this to happen to me. But never let it be said that I was only raging and wrathful. I was also very scared. I cried a lot the first few days after I was admitted. My family held me and consoled me and placated me, but what was inside of me was tearing me to shreds. I wanted so badly for this to be over with and gone . . . it was unbearable. Yet I had realized that I *did* have a will to come back from the living dead.

I attempted to cooperate with the bungling nurses and interns who ran test after tiring test on me, but I became so frustrated with their lack of results and my inability to communicate with them that, at times, I fought their help. After almost 2 weeks of inconclusive tests, during which I experienced more seizures, total losses of vision, slurred speech and, of course, the incessant headache, Dr. Patterson came to me and my parents with a final suggestion—to prepare me for surgery and perform a dangerous exploratory. My parents refused, wanting another opinion. Put off, and at wit's end, Dr. Patterson insisted that any other doctor would come to the same conclusion. I was released the next morning.

My parents travelled up and down the East Coast with me for the next 2 months, seeking out specialists. They tested but could not diagnose my symptoms. I began to believe what each successive doctor implied but few were bold enough to say outright. There was no physical problem. I *was* doing all of this to myself. I was destroying myself. I feared being alone, terrified of what I might do to myself other than mental self-mutilation.

Some specialists suggested that I see a psychiatrist. If my problem *was* mental, *not* physical, then I needed one . . . badly. But I came to realize that whether my problem was physical or psychological in origin, I needed help to deal with the trauma of the past 2 years. (This was probably the most important decision of my life to date. It was definitely the best decision of my life. Through my psychiatrist, I was able to separate the physical hurt from the emotional hurt and in that way, work with the problems I was capable of overcoming.)

In the final stages of Jonelle's ordeal, she felt some guilt for what her problems had done to her family. The guilt may have softened her negative emotion expressions within the family, but she felt no guilt in relation to the medical personnel who misdiagnosed and mistreated her, and her anger toward them is still unabated.

Regretfully, I found that my problems were affecting the other members of my family as well. My mother developed stomach pains that we all feared were ulcers. My father's temper flared frequently. My brother's school work slackened. None of us were happy. *Guilt* crept upon me because I could remember how different things had been before my accident and ensuing travels. I felt that I was destroying myself *and* my family.

Strangely, after 2½ years, it was my brother who discovered and diagnosed my ailment. An article in *Sports Illustrated* caught David's eye. A young athlete, it seems, had experienced a similar accident to mine, but had been treated (successfully!) by a dentist for Temporomandibular Joint Dysfunction Syndrome, referred to as TMJ. David came squealing to my bedside late one night to share his discovery with me. We cried together, and even prayed together before we wakened our parents to diffidently discuss my brother's findings.

My mother called our family dentist in the morning to discuss dental specialists in the area who might have some knowledge about the little-known syndrome. Our dentist knew of a colleague who had trained in the treatment of TMJ and similar syndromes. I believe my entire family was heart sick when we were told that he had had a stroke and was not accepting new patients.

Perhaps it was our prayers, or perhaps it was the doctor's heartstrings that were pulled, but no feeling of elation will ever compare to that which I felt when George Charles, D.D.S., called me himself only days later to tell me that he had heard of my case through several colleagues and was willing to take me on for treatment, even in his semiretirement.

A treatment schedule was set up, the first appointment being an intake evaluation which lasted for hours. But at the end of that day, when Dr. Charles positively diagnosed my *physical* affliction as Temporomandibular Joint Dysfunction Syndrome, and assured me that he could have me virtually pain free within 6 months, the tears I cried were of the most intense joy and relief.

Three months later, my vision cleared. In another 2 months, my constant, 3½-year-old headache subsided. Dr. Charles had lived up to his promise.

I can recall, clearly, the first morning in more than 3 years upon which I was able to awaken from a deep, restful sleep and actually crack a broad smile. I *had* returned from the living dead! And like the weight of the world off my shoulders, I felt a warm, glowing confidence that I had made it through the worst.

Now, 7 years after the original accident and 3½ years after my diagnosis, I can say that I am simply angry (and maybe a bit contemptuous) at the bumbling, unfeeling doctors who were involved in my maltreatment and about what they made me do to myself.

Jonelle has learned to live with the anger she experiences. Her anger may have counteracted the terror that struck more than once and given her will power to go on. Because the anger was outer directed, but never associated with acting-out or aggression, it may have warded off the depression that sometimes accompanies intractable pain. She is doing very well in college and expects to graduate in June.

Several years ago I did a survey of college students in an effort to sort out what people saw as the antecedents and the consequences of anger (See Table 11-1).

TABLE 11-1
Antecedents and Consequences of Anger[a]

Responses	Percentage of subjects giving responses
Antecedents of anger	
Feelings	
1. Of being misled, betrayed, used, disappointed, hurt by others, treated unjustly	40.8
2. Anger–rage	17.6
3. Hatred, dislike, disapproval of others, detrimental thoughts	12.0
4. Aggressive, revengeful, like attacking others	8.0
5. Of failure, disappointed in self, self-blame, inadequacy	5.6
6. Sense of injustice in world	3.2
7. Sadness	.8
8. Other	12.0
Thoughts	
1. Of hatred, dislike, disapproval of others, detrimental thoughts	31.2
2. Of being mislead, betrayed, used, disapproved, hurt by others	19.2
3. Of having failed, disappointing self, blaming self, inadequacy	10.4
4. Injustice, world problems	10.4
5. Of destruction, revenge	14.4
6. Irritating, things go wrong	8.0
7. Other	6.4
Actions	
1. Something wrong, stupid	34.4
2. Something violent, rash, let off stream	16.8
3. Something unappreciated by others	12.0
4. Something that you don't want to do, others impose their will	8.8
5. Aggression, revenge	8.0
6. Something legally or morally wrong or harmful	7.2
7. Other	12.8

[a]N = approximately 130 college students

TABLE 11-1 (continued)

Responses	Percentage of subjects giving responses
Consequences of anger	
Feelings	
1. Anger	28.8
2. Hot, tense, etc.	24.2
3. Revengeful, like attacking others, destructive	24.2
4. Hatred, dislike, disapproval of others	6.8
5. Sadness	2.3
6. Justified	1.5
7. Other	10.6
Thoughts	
1. Of revenge, attacking others, destruction	43.9
2. Of ways to regain, maintain control of self, situation, or change situation	13.6
3. Hatred, dislike, disapproval of others	12.1
4. Of expressing anger, verbally or physically	7.6
5. Negative, hostile thoughts (unspecific)	7.6
6. About event which caused anger	4.5
7. Angry, detrimental thoughts toward self	4.5
8. Other	6.1
Actions	
1. Tries to regain or maintain control of self or situation	35.6
2. Verbal attack or physical action against object of anger	24.2
3. Takes action, aggresses against object or situation causing anger	18.9
4. Does something impulsive or irrational	11.4
5. Other	9.8

[a]*N* = approximately 130 college students

We can analyze the antecedents of anger or any emotion in terms of the (1) actions, (2) thoughts, and (3) feelings that lead to the emotion of anger. Some common actions seen as causes of anger are doing something wrong or stupid, doing something that is not appreciated by others, having to do something you don't want to do, having others impose their will on you, someone doing harm to others. Note that some of these events seem to cause anger toward self (such as doing something stupid), while others relate to the actions of others.

Several kinds of thoughts precede anger. The most frequent listed by the college students is thinking you have been misled, cheated, treated unfairly or unjustly. This was the cause of Jonelle's anger.

Another cognitive cause of anger is thinking that others are disapproving of you. For a few people (10%), thoughts of having failed or disappointed oneself led to anger. About an equal number indicated that thoughts of the injustices and the problems in the world lead to anger.

A few of the students indicated that certain emotion feelings sometimes led to anger. Among those listed were sadness and shame, described by the students in terms of failure and disappointment.

Moral Indignation

As Berkowitz (1990) noted, there are occasions when we get angry because someone offends us morally. Some people call it righteous indignation, and for the incident described below that's not a bad name. The following is an entry in Jackie's diary when she was 17.

> April, 1981.
> Dear Diary,
> It's been almost 5 years since I last saw Mr. K. Five years since I let myself even feel hatred for that man. I didn't think I could ever feel such coldness again. I'll never forget that day when he came to visit my parents; everyone thought that he was an upstanding member of our church. He sure had us fooled! It took me almost 2 years to face that man after his suggestive offenses toward me. I was 13 and he was 60. I thought I had learned to control the animosity I felt toward him, but he did it again. Mr. K., now at the age of 65, has once again attempted to assault another 13-year-old girl, except this time he succeeded. This man must be mentally ill. How could he do things like this? The thoughts running through my head are so malicious. He should be locked up in jail, or at least in a mental institution. I thought I had forgiven him, but not now! It's an evil thought, but I wish he'd die. I wish he'd fall off the face of the earth. Maybe, then, he would stop hurting innocent young girls.

Summary of Common Causes of Anger

First, pain is a direct and immediate cause of anger. Even in very young infants, we see anger expression to inoculation long before they can appraise or understand what has happened to them. Thus the sensations from pain are sufficient cause of anger. Thought, memory, or interpretation are not necessary for the anger to emerge. Of course, as in Jonelle's case, if you believe that particular people cause the pain or keep the pain from being relieved, your anger will be directed toward them. In such cases it is good to remember that pain alone can lead to anger, regardless of the source of pain. You can prove this to yourself by recalling the last time you stubbed your toe or banged your shin in the dark. It is wise to remember that discomfort from any source—hunger, fatigue, mental stress—can make us angry while we remain oblivious of the real culprit. Even mild discomfort when prolonged can make us more irritable, or in the language of psychology, lower our anger threshold.

Physical restraint may cause anger because it leads to discomfort or pain. It appears to be another event that is an effective stimulus for pain without thought or interpretation, for as already noted, research has shown that arm restraint produces anger expression in 4-month-old babies.

Psychological restraint as a cause of anger is like physical restraint in that both thwart us and block our freedom of action. Psychological restraint, however, assumes thought and memory—an ability to understand the rule or prohibition and a memory of the consequences for violating it. Probably the first psychological restraint is the parental "No No," said to the infant who has achieved the ability to throw food on the floor, climb on tables, and move into other precarious or dangerous places. "No No" is heard much more often as the toddler becomes even more efficient in rearranging things around the house and toddling outdoors mindless of the neighbor's tulip bulbs and newly planted garden. This era is well known as the "terrible twos."

Others' actions that we see as unfair to us will cause anger. Our interpretation of the action is important here. Before we become angry, we place blame. In Jonelle's case, she blamed the first group of health care professionals who tried and failed to diagnose and treat her. She thought it was their responsibility to treat her appropriately or refer her elsewhere. What made her angry with them was the thought that they could control what was happening to her. If she had assumed that their lack of knowledge of her true condition and their belief that they were treating her appropriately made them unable to control or change her painful condition, she would not have blamed them and become angry with them.

Just as the sensation of pain can lead to anger, without intervening thought or memory, so can an emotion feeling. Prolonged sadness may be a cause of anger. Anger is certainly frequently associated with sadness in depression. The feeling of disgust with yourself (as when you see yourself as "overweight and ugly") or disgust with others can lead to anger.

The Facial Expression of Anger

The photos in Figure 11-2 show the expression of anger in an infant and an adult. Note that the two expressions involve exactly the same muscle movements and the overall configuration is the same. Any differences in appearance changes can be accounted for by the greater elasticity of the infant's skin and the thicker deposits of fatty tissue underneath the skin. The latter may cause bulges in infants, where wrinkles or furrows are seen in the adult. The forehead and brow component of the anger expression is easy to detect. The skin of the forehead is pulled tight by action of the muscles that lower the brows. The brows are drawn sharply downward and inward creating a bulge on or slightly above the nasal root. Vertical furrows or ridges appear between the inner corners of the brows of adults.

The forehead-brow component of the anger expression is displayed automatically and essentially uncontrollably by young infants when anger is activated. In intense spontaneous anger this component may be seen in its full strength at any time of life. However, the full strength of the full-face expressive behavior is rarely seen in adults. Somewhere around the end of the first year of life, children begin gaining a measure of voluntary control over expressive movements. Part of this control is a result of the maturing of the brain, in particular the development of the

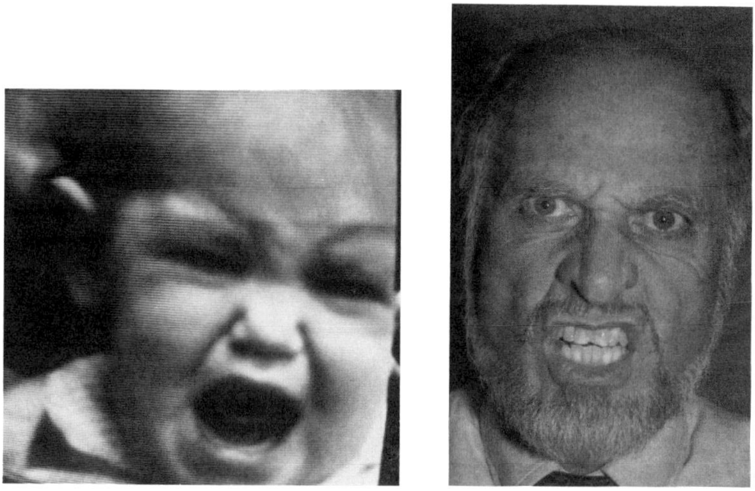

FIGURE 11-2. The expression of anger in an infant and an adult.

brain mechanisms that enable the child to inhibit or dampen the motor activity that makes the expression. In part, voluntary control over emotion expressions is learned as a function of parental intervention and socialization. Thus through maturation and learning, the automatic anger brow gradually comes under control, and a severe frown can be modulated into a mild one.

Indeed, one has to be careful in interpreting frowns once facial behavior comes under control. Some people regularly frown a little or knit their brows when focusing their attention or concentrating. This is one of the movements we discussed as a signal of interest. I have a colleague who knits her brows very frequently when she lectures or listens intently during a conversation. When she knits her brows they appear to be drawn downward and inward as in the anger frown. She says that she is often asked if she is annoyed or angry when in fact she is only interested and concentrating very hard on what is going on. She has to make a special effort to regulate this brow movement and compensate for it in other ways. Fortunately, she smiles easily and frequently.

If you are a brow knitter, you may want to take a close look and see if it approximates the anger frown. If it does, you can actually correct this by practicing the contraction of muscles that prevent the brows from pulling downward and inward. You can do this by slightly lifting your brows when you knit them. Be careful not to lift them too much or you will take on the appearance of sadness.

In anger, the eye region changes in several ways. The lowered brows tend to make the eyes appear narrow, a bit angular and hard. They lose the softness associated with a rounded appearance. The eyes stare at the source of annoyance or anger. This can be a very important aspect of the anger expression. It may be a clue as to the direction any hostile behavior will take.

In the innate expression of anger as seen on the faces of infants or young children, the mouth takes on a squarish or rectangular shape. The upper and lower lips become thin parallel lines, and they may protrude a bit. The corners of the mouth give up their normally soft curve for a hard angular appearance. In the older child and adult, a tightly closed mouth, clenched jaws, and compressed lips may be seen. Although this may be a learned modification of the square mouth, bared teeth component of the anger expression, cross-cultural research suggests that it is universal. This cross-cultural research showed that the compressed lips, tightly closed mouth, and clenched jaws convey anger in a wide assortment of literate cultures and in preliterate cultures as well. It can be explained as a learned alteration of the innate expression, a modification that conceals the bared teeth and probably weakens the intensity of the emotion signal.

Over the course of development, the anger expression is typically modified in a number of ways. As we have indicated, the forehead and brow component may become softened by controlling the intensity of the expressions. Staring can be avoided or made much less intense by shifting the gaze from time to time. The bared teeth may be covered with compressed lips, or the whole set of movements in the mouth region may be abandoned except for tightly clenched jaws and perhaps some teeth grinding.

In interpreting expressions that are modified through learning, one must be very careful. People frown a little, stare a little, and clench their jaws for other reasons than the feeling of anger. Consequently, the more the full-face expression

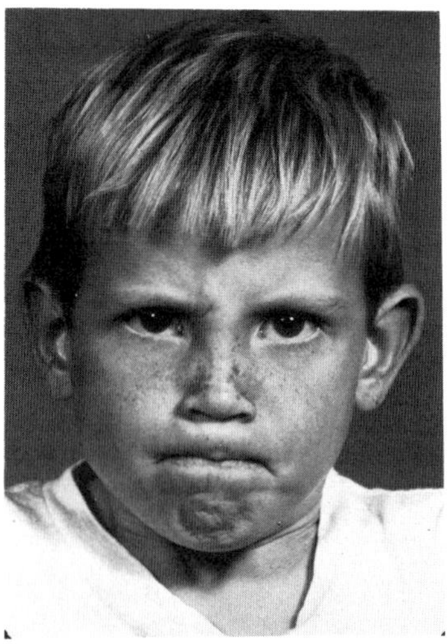

FIGURE 11-3. The anger expression modified by compressed lips, from Tomkins Affect Pictures.

of anger or any emotion is modified, the more you have to know about the individual and the situation to make a correct guess as to what emotion is felt.

The Subjective Experience of Anger

In anger the blood "boils," the face becomes hot, the muscles tense. There is a feeling of power and an impulse to strike out, to attack the source of anger. The stronger the anger the stronger and more energetic the person feels and the greater the need for physical action. In rage the mobilization of energy is so great that one feels one will explode if one does not bite, hit, or kick something, or "act out the anger" in some way.

Figure 11-4 shows the DES profile of emotions in the imagined anger situation. As seen from the graph, the pattern is dominated by what has been termed the hostility triad—anger-disgust-contempt (Izard, 1972).

The mean for the key emotion of anger is higher than that of any other key emotion in the situations for negative emotions. Further, the dynamically related emotions of disgust and contempt, which occupy the second and third places in the anger situation, are considerably elevated.

For the most part, the emotions with the highest means in the anger pattern interact and sustain a high level of activity that is clearly focused and directed. Sadness (not shown on graph) is moderately elevated and is the most difficult

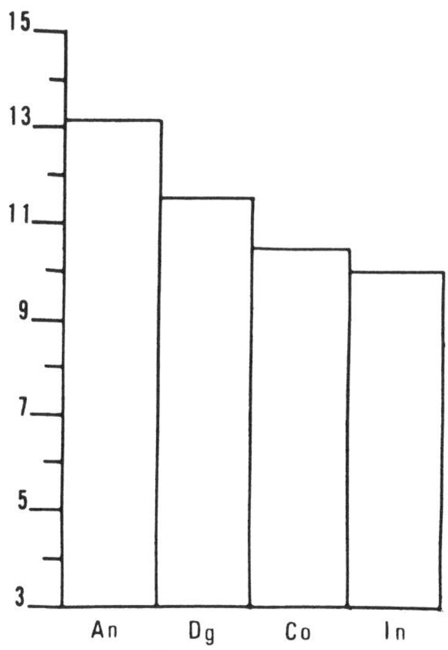

FIGURE 11-4. The DES profile of emotions in an imagined anger situation. An, anger; Dg, disgust; Co, contempt; In, interest.

emotion to analyze as a part of the dynamics of the anger pattern. As already noted, anger and sadness, according to Tomkins (1963), are activated by similar gradients of neural firing. This may help explain the presence of sadness in the pattern, but not its role. The role of sadness might be to moderate the intensity of anger and the related emotions of disgust and contempt. Should anger lead to aggression, sadness could serve as a basis for empathy with the victim and thus serve as a sort of safety valve. It is also quite possible that as a result of social experience and learning, individuals may feel some sadness in anger situations because anger is so seldom expressed in openly satisfying and rewarding ways in our society and because it often arises in the face of disappointment resulting from thwarting or postponement of goals. It should be noted that in the anger situation, fear is lower both in absolute value and in relative rank than in any other negative emotion situation. This follows from the fact that anger inhibits fear. The probable role of fear in the anger situation, like that of sadness, is to exercise a moderating effect on the potentially dangerous hostility triad.

The DRS of the Bartlett-Izard study (see Figure 11-5) showed that anger

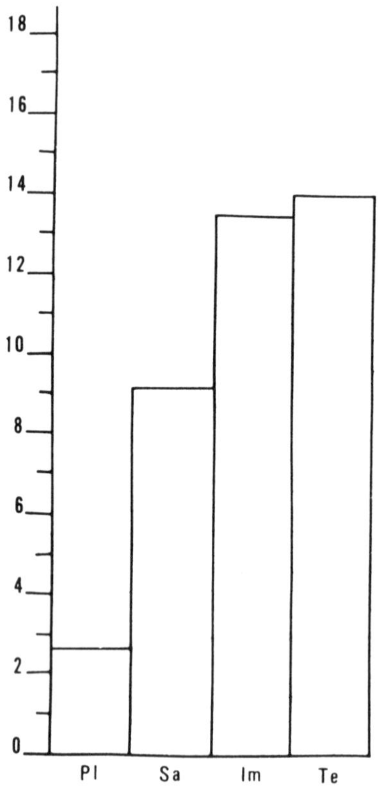

FIGURE 11-5. The DRS profile of dimensions in an imagined anger situation. Pl, pleasantness; Sa, self-assurance; Im, impulsiveness; Te, tension.

causes the person to feel great tension, second only to that in fear, and far more self-assurance than in any other negative emotion. The sense of physical strength and self-assurance tends to make the person feel brave and courageous. We do not always associate anger with courage because in many cases the anger is quickly reduced by feelings of fear or guilt over the possible consequences of the anger.

Figure 11-5 also shows that the experience of anger is accompanied by a strong feeling of impulsiveness. The mean for the dimension of control, not shown on the graph, was lower in anger than in any other emotion. Although the control mean in anger did not differ significantly from that of several other emotions, the combination of high impulsiveness and low control helps explain why the rules for anger expression and "acting out anger" are carefully laid down during socialization. The combination of muscle tension (strength), self-assurance, and impulsiveness help explain the individual's readiness to strike out or engage in some kind of motor activity. Anger is a relatively unpleasant feeling, though the mean on the pleasantness dimension was not significantly lower in anger than in fear, sadness, or guilt. The study also showed that, on the average, individuals feel significantly more extraverted in anger than in any other negative emotion.

After an anger episode, you may be very proud of what you were able to do when angry or feel very foolish and regretful. How you feel will depend upon circumstances and whether or not your anger is justifiable.

The Significance of Anger

As human beings evolved and progressed toward the establishment of cultures and civilizations, the road took many turns that led past challenges and dangers. Undoubtedly, anger played a critical role in coping with some of these challenges and dangers and was essential to the survival of the species. One reason why this is believable is that anger mobilizes energy for action, induces a sense of vigor and self-confidence, and thereby makes individuals more capable of defending themselves. With the rise of civilization, occasions when people needed to use anger-mobilized energy for physical defense and survival tactics became less and less common. Many people, including behavioral scientists, came to view anger as more a liability than an asset.

That we are still subject to anger and even rage is what some ethologists have cited as an example of cultural evolution out running biological evolution. This kind of thinking implies that it would be better if we somehow could eliminate anger from the repertoire of human capacities. Except in the case of self-defense or defense of loved ones, an attack made in anger is almost always viewed as a violation of legal and ethical codes. Hostile attacks not only bring harm to the victim but often get the aggressor in serious trouble.

Perhaps we should not try to wish away the emotion of anger. It is a part of human nature. We should of course learn to control it. At the same time, we should remain open to the use of anger in a controlled fashion on occasions when it is necessary for the well-being of ourselves and our loved ones. We may rarely need anger-mobilized energy for physical defense, but we may have legitimate occasions to use the motivational impact of mild to moderate anger for the psychological defense of the self. People who attack your integrity may have to be dealt with firmly and with determination. Such firmness and determination can be supported by a little anger. People who break laws and rules and in so doing endanger your life or the life of others may benefit from an expression of indignation.

This is not to suggest that you let your anger become habitually associated with hostile behavior. Taking a hostile stance and behaving aggressively is a pretty sure way to bring misery on yourself and others. The point is that you can also bring misery on yourself by letting hostile people or individuals who behave in an overly aggressive fashion push you around without justification. There is no need for you to get angry at every expression of hostility or aggressiveness that comes your way, but you put your self-image and your integrity in jeopardy if you allow yourself to be continually hassled, harassed, insulted, or bested by inconsiderate acts of careless or insensitive people.

Sometimes you feel there is nothing you can do but swallow your anger, even though you will later wish you had defended yourself. Remember Leslie, who overcame scoliosis and the many embarrassing and frustrating situations associated with it? She tells of a time when she was teased, verbally abused, and angered and could not fight back.

> I was riding home on the bus and I could hear two of the older girls whispering and laughing at me. I could feel my face get red and I tried to read my book and ignore them. The next thing I knew they were throwing spitballs and everyone was laughing. I was never till then, nor since then, more humiliated in my life. I was fighting several different emotions, and I didn't know how to handle them. I was angry with the girls, and with everyone else, for laughing and being so mean when I didn't deserve it. I think that I was also angry with myself for not having the courage to stand up to them. But I was very afraid of them also, they were bigger and older, and not known for docile behavior. I was totally embarrassed because it was obvious that I was not going to stand up to these girls. I was also actually surprised at the depth of their cruelty. So I just sat there immobile, frozen. I think I must have blocked out what was going on because I don't remember getting off the bus and walking home. I was too embarrassed to tell my parents, and from that day on I found other ways of getting home from school. I was really afraid of these girls and my reaction was to avoid them rather than to confront the situation. This was my normal pattern. I did not ever let on that I was upset, I avoided confrontation, and actually I rarely felt any hostility or aggression. But the bus ride incident has always stuck with me. Those girls made me feel terrible about myself, and shook up my self-confidence quite a bit. I felt awful because I knew I looked awful, and because I was too much of a coward to fight. So while I loathed these girls, I was also not too fond of myself at the time. I felt like a real failure.

Years later Leslie wrote: "I regret not exploding at the two girls on the bus, and at others at various times." Leslie may have done the right thing by trying to ignore the teasing. She was outnumbered by larger street-wise girls, and she was not stuck with them for the rest of her life. However, we should defend our integrity when we can—often the odds against us will change when we speak out.

You can overlook minor and occasional insults or aggravations from insensitive or careless people and be better off for ignoring it. On the other hand, if you have to live with, work with, or regularly socialize with such a person and you are continually buffeted by their remarks and actions, you may need a little anger to give you the strength, the courage, and the confidence to protect yourself. Should this be the case, you might want some practice or even training in self-assertion so that your anger is well controlled and matched by the appropriate social skills.

The Development and Socialization of Anger

Izard *et al.* (1987) did a longitudinal study of emotion responses to the acute pain of diphtheria-pertussis-tetanus (DPT) inoculations. We know from our own experience and from the reports of children when they are old enough to describe their feelings that such injections are acutely painful. The DPT immunization series requires inoculations at approximately 2, 4, 6, and 18 months of age. The experimenters, who followed 25 babies through this entire immunization series, videotaped their facial expressions from the moment of injection until the time they soothed (stopped crying and showed only positive emotion expressions on the face).

This study revealed a great deal about the development of emotions. At 2 months of age and throughout early infancy (2 through 7 months), the infants' automatic instinctlike response to this painful medical procedure was a physical distress or pain expression accompanied by loud crying. In the facial expression of pain, the infant's brows are drawn downward and inward and the eyes are closed, the eyelids tightly shut together. These brow and eye muscle actions cause the tissue to bunch up or lump together over the root of the nose. The mouth takes on a squarish or rectangular form, and this action, together with the action of the muscles surrounding the eyes, raises the cheeks and causes some bulging across the bridge of the nose.

The rather awesome pain expression and the accompanying strident cry dominates the baby's whole being for several seconds after the inoculation. It is an all out emergency response, a cry for help. This emergency expressive behavior seems to consume all of the infant's energies and preempts all of its physiological and behavioral systems. However, most (90%) of the infants we observed had a second expression during the inoculation episode. In this 90%, a clear cut, full-faced anger expression followed the physical distress expression. In early infancy this anger expression was secondary to the physical distress expression and appeared on the face for a relatively short period of time.

When these children came for their fourth DPT, they were toddlers, with an average age of 19 months. They showed no sign of remembering the clinic setting or the nurse who administered the DPTs, and therefore they showed no sign of dread or anticipation of a painful event. All the evidence pointed to the fact that the pain of this fourth DPT inoculation was completely unanticipated. These toddlers responded to this unanticipated pain with anger. Every one of them showed clear, full-faced expressions of anger, and the anger expression was dominant on the face for a relatively long period of time. Of the babies, 72% did show the physical distress expression, but this all-out emergency response that is so consuming of the infant's energies was expressed for a relatively short period of time. Of these infants, 28% did not show the physical distress expression at all. For most of the time that the children were upset, they expressed anger, as though mad at the physical insult over which they had no control.

Now what does the developmental change and the children's responses to unanticipated pain tell us about emotional development? First, it tells us that in early infancy the children are capable of responding automatically and with instinctlike precision to aversive stimulation, in this case unexpected pain. The young infant is incapable of defending himself against such stimulation, so the baby channels all of his energy into the physical distress expression, an all-out plea for help. This is the most natural and adaptive thing for the relatively helpless and defenseless young infant to do. However, as the child becomes capable of warding off painful stimulation or participating in his own defense, channeling all of his energies into a plea for help would not be maximally adaptive. Our study showed that as the baby matures, his expressive behavior changes. The all-consuming physical distress expression gives way to the anger expression. The anger expression is more adaptive in the face of unanticipated painful stimulation because anger mobilizes energy that can be used for protection and defense. With the help of parents and caring others, the young child can learn appropriate behaviors for warding off or avoiding painful stimulation. Of major importance in this aspect of socialization is the teaching of discriminations between situations in which instrumental action against the agent of harm is appropriate and when it is not. That is, eventually the child has to learn not only how to regulate or inhibit anger but how to harness anger-mobilized energy in instrumental acts of self-defense when situations call for it.

That observed parental anger sometimes leads to aggression in human infants has been demonstrated. Cummings, Zahn-Waxler, and Radke-Yarrow (1981) studied the responses of 1 to 2½-year-old children as bystanders to naturally occurring and simulated expressions of anger between family members. Of these children, 24% responded to observed anger with anger expressions of their own. Over a third of these children subsequently engaged in physical aggression toward one or both of the antagonists, and most of the remainder were verbally aggressive.

The tendency of anger and aggression to beget further anger and aggression was demonstrated in a study by Main and George (1985). They observed responses to age-mates' distress (crying or signs of fear or panic) in 10 abused toddlers and 10 matched controls from families experiencing stress. The nonabused toddlers responded to the distress of age-mates with interest, concern, empathy, or sadness.

The abused toddlers often responded to their age-mates' distress with anger and physical attacks. These data are consistent with reports from investigators working with abusing parents. It appears that parental anger and aggression make child anger and aggression more likely. Eron (1987) found that this was true for 8-year-old boys who identified with their punitive father. Eron also found that watching violent shows on TV at age 8 was significantly correlated with the seriousness of the subjects' criminal acts at age 30.

Anger and Aggression

Because we have just talked about the possibility of anger mobilizing energy for instrumental action and self-defense, it is important to understand the relationship between anger and aggression. At the outset let me emphasize that there is no evidence for any direct connection (in either the nervous system or at the behavioral level) between anger and aggressive behavior. What I said in the foregoing section was that *anger mobilizes energy* for instrumental actions that with appropriate regulation and training can be effective in defense of the self. This does not mean that anger necessarily leads to aggression.

Pain, Anger, and Aggression

If an animal is put in a cage and subjected to aversive stimulation (heat, noise, electric shock), often it will attack any available target. If two animals are placed in a cage and given painful stimulation, frequently they will fight (Azrin, Hutchinson, & McLaughlin, 1965). Sometimes, however, they will simply flee or try to escape (Potegal, 1979). Whether they fight or flee is dependent on the social history and drive state of the animals and a number of contextual variables such as the possibility of escape and the status (sex, size, dominance position) of the other animal.

If human infants experience acute pain (e.g., DPT inoculation), they regularly encode facial expressions of anger (Izard *et al.*, 1987). The data suggest an innate connection between pain and anger. These data together with that from animal research on aversive stimulation (Berkowitz, 1983) are consistent with the notion that pain is an innate activator of anger and aggressive tendencies. Whether the action tendencies become aggressive actions depend on a number of intra-individual and contextual variables.

Anger Leads to Physical Aggression Relatively Infrequently

Indeed, the relationship between anger and aggression is often misunderstood. Anger is maligned by many people and given a bad name in situations where it really might not be the culprit. Anger never necessarily leads to aggressive action.

It is only fair to say that under certain circumstances anger can increase the likelihood of aggression. It is also true that anger does create an impulse or urge to strike out. Most emotions are associated with an *action tendency*. It is important to note that this is only a tendency to act, however, and not a command. The anger expressions we observed in young infants were not accompanied by banging and kicking things; however, some of the latter behavior was seen in toddlers. At this age, however, some of this "acting-out" behavior may have been learned. Such behavior is probably a joint function of the action tendency created by the emotion of anger on the one hand and social learning on the other. In any case, we know that most people in most situations can and do inhibit or greatly dampen the tendency to strike out, either verbally or physically, when angry.

In short, anger *prepares* us for action. It bolsters physical strength and courage to match the impulse to act. We may never feel stronger or more invigorated than when we are really angry. Yet anger, like any other emotion, consists of neural activity, expressive behavior, and a feeling state. An emotion proper does not include thought or action. Thus, anger prepares us well for action, but it does not command or compel us to act.

The action that follows anger is a joint function of the anger feeling and a cognitive appraisal of the situation. For most people the appraisal of the situation leads to inhibiting or modulating the tendency to act out. Averill's (1983) study of the causes and consequences of anger confirms this principle. He obtained descriptions of anger experiences from 80 college students and 80 randomly selected community residents. A third group of 80 students described their experiences as targets of another person's anger.

The great majority of subjects attributed their anger experiences to (1) a voluntary and unjustified act (59%) or (2) to a potentially avoidable accident or event (28%). A majority of the subjects described anger episodes involving a loved one or someone well known and liked.

The subjects described a wide variety of responses to their anger experiences. Only 10% of the 160 anger experiences led to physical aggression or punishment, and 49% to verbal aggression. Nonaggressive responses (talking over the incident) occurred in 60% of the episodes. (The percentages do not add to 100 because more than one type of response was described in some episodes.) Interestingly, the ratio of beneficial to harmful consequences described by the subjects was 3 to 1. The kinds of benefits described included "realizing your own faults" (76%), "realizing your own strengths" (50%), and "your relationship with the angry person was strengthened" (48%). The latter benefit has been observed by therapists, and the therapist's advice for angry encounters is "keep channels of communication open" (Izard, 1965). If you can express your anger and your perception of its causes and freely allow the other person to respond, you have a good chance of getting to know each other at a deeper level and thereby strengthening the relationship.

Anger Experience, Anger Expression, and Aggression

From the large body of research on aggression we shall consider only a few studies that focus on the role of anger, expressive behavior, and emotion communication. A study by Zimbardo (1969) showed that the physical presence of the victim influenced the behavior of the aggressor. This suggests that face-to-face emotion communication may play an important role in regulating aggressive behavior. It has been disappointing that so few investigators of aggression have followed the implication of Zimbardo's finding and examined the effects of the victim's communication on the aggressor. A number of studies have shown that eye contact influences behavior in agonistic encounters. This research has been summarized by Ellsworth (1975) and Exline, Ellyson, and Long (1975).

Aside from the work on eye contact, the bulk of the work on the effect of the victim's communication on subsequent aggression has come from ethology. Ethological studies have shown that expressive behavior often eliminates or reduces overt aggression in coral reef fish (Rasa, 1969), elephant seals (Le Boeuf & Peterson, 1969), and baboons (Kummer, 1968).

Both expressions of threat and expressions of submission, or appeasement, have been judged as effective in influencing agonistic behavior among nonhuman primates. In rhesus macaque monkeys, submissive expressions range from the fear grimace to presenting the rump as in sexual invitations. These expressive communications have been judged as effective in inhibiting aggressive behavior (Hinde & Rowell, 1962). The effect of a threat expression may vary considerably with the status of the animal and the situation. A high-status animal in its own territory will frequently succeed in avoiding fights by means of threat displays. But a territorial intruder or low-status animal may provoke fighting with a threat expression. Morris (1968) suggested that people can avoid an attack by a potential aggressor by displaying fear and humility and by avoiding threatening expressions. Morris's inference is based primarily on observations of nonhuman animals.

The equations for predicting the effect of expression on subsequent aggression are always multivariate, and both organismic and environmental variables are involved. A couple of examples will illustrate the complexity of the problem of prediction. If an aggressor is not particularly angry or ego involved in the encounter, the anger expression of the potential victim may signal a counterattack that the aggressor would choose to avoid. In this case the threat expression would decrease or avoid further aggression. On the other hand, if the potential aggressor sees himself as a winner, the anger expression of the potential victim may elicit greater aggressive behavior. In summary, hostile communication (via affect expression) tends to change the threshold of aggression, but the direction of the change may vary with social status, territorial prerogatives, and other ecological factors.

The ethically controversial studies of Milgram (1963, 1964, 1965) showed that the aggressive responses made by subjects in response to the request of an "authority" were significantly influenced by the victim's presence and proximity, conditions that facilitate emotion communication. Proximity varied from a condition in which there was no visual or vocal contact between subject and victim (remote condition) to a condition in which the subject forced the victim's hand onto the shock plate (touch-proximity condition). Proximity or immediacy, which undoubtedly altered affective-cognitive interactions in the subject, proved to be a potent deterrent of aggression. The percentage of subjects who obeyed the experimenter and continued to give shocks to the maximum (labeled "danger: severe shock"), in spite of screams of pain and urgent protests from the victims, varied from 66% in the remote condition to 30% in the touch-proximity condition. Thus, while proximity made a large difference in the subject's willingness to agress on command, 30% of subjects recruited from the community represents a rather sizable segment who were apparently willing to risk executing a subject because an authority (experimenter) told them to do so. The reduction in aggressive responses as a result of the proximity of the victim is consonant with Zimbardo's (1969) concept of individuation as a deterrent of aggression and with the arguments of ethologists (e.g., Ardrey, 1966; Lorenz, 1966) that wars are more likely because our vast weapons technology makes it possible to kill from great distances. Certainly, there is little opportunity for the victim's emotion expressions to influence aggression in high-tech wars.

Other studies have attempted to assess the effect of the victim's nonverbal communication, but the results of these studies are not consistent. Wheeler and Caggiula (1966), Feshbach, Stiles, and Bitner (1967), and Hartman (1969) found that a victim's display of pain was followed by an increase in shock aggression. In the latter two studies, the subject had previously been insulted. On the other hand, Buss (1966) and Baron (1971a, b) have found that pain cues from the victim reduced the subject's aggressive responses. One of the reasons for the inconsistency in the results of these studies may have been the failure to specify the emotion state of the subject, the relative status of experimenters and subjects, and the precise nature of the nonverbal cues emitted by the victim. In many cases, the nonverbal cues were simply described as grunts and groans, without any indication as to the specificity of such communications. Baron's study, which showed a sharp reduction in aggressive responses as a result of pain cues, represents an exception. Subjects observed a "pain meter" to see the effect their shock was having on the victim. While Baron's feedback was specific, it had the disadvantage of removing the victim from the possibility of face-to-face encounter with the aggressor.

In a study by Savitsky and Izard (1970), the experimenter's confederate communicated well-defined facial expressions of specific emotions to the subjects. Half the subjects (aggressors) were insulted by a confederate victim, and the other half were treated neutrally and not insulted. Then subjects were assigned to a victim who expressed facially either fear, anger, joy, or a neutral countenance following the delivery of shock by the subjects. Shock was purportedly related to performance on a learning task.

Two of the confederate's emotion-specific facial expressions did significantly influence the aggression of the subjects. Subjects who were exposed to a smiling victim gave a consistently higher level of shocks. Apparently subjects in this group perceived their victim as not being harmed and as enjoying the task. The victim (confederate) appeared to enjoy the penalties (shock), and the subject apparently enjoyed delivering them. It is possible that some subjects were also motivated to increase shock in order to get the subject to be more serious about the task.

Subjects exposed to the anger expression decreased their aggressive responses. The decrease in shock aggression on the part of the subject may have been motivated by anticipation of subsequent retaliation or an embarrassing confrontation with the victim. The victim's anger expression may also have threatened the subject and acted directly as an inhibitor of aggression.

The Stability of Aggressive Behavior

Although the relation of anger to aggressive behavior is not fully understood, two things are clear. In most people, anger does not characteristically result in aggressive action. However, on occasion, and perhaps with some regularity in certain individuals, anger does lead to verbal or physical aggression. Both anger expression and aggressive behavior show stability over time, suggesting that they may reflect a trait of personality. Infants aged 2–7 months who express a lot of anger in response to the pain of diphtheria-pertussis-tetanus inoculation tend to be high on anger expression to the same procedure at 19 months (Izard *et al.*, 1987). Similarly, infants who express a lot of anger to brief separation from mother at 13 months of age tend to do the same at 18 months (Hyson & Izard, 1985).

Extensive reviews of the longitudinal research on aggressive behavior have shown that Time 1-Time 2 correlations range from about .70–.90 when the interval is 3 years or less and .40–.50 for intervals up to 21 years (Olweus, 1980, 1982; Parke & Slaby, 1983). These data show that aggressive infants tend to become aggressive children and that aggressive children are rather likely to become aggressive adults. Of the many factors that contribute to the continuity of aggressive behavior, one of them may be anger threshold. People with a lower anger threshold would likely experience anger (aggression-motivation) more frequently. Although anger does not necessarily lead to aggression, frequent anger experiences would increase the probability of some form of aggressive behavior.

The Effects of Not Expressing Anger

Holt (1970) reasons that failure to express anger can be maladaptive. He uses the term *expression* here to include both emotion expression (facial, vocal changes) and aggressive actions, primarily verbal aggression. Anger expression and appropriate anger-related behavior can be constructive when the angry person wishes to

> establish, restore, or maintain a positive relationship with the other. He acts and speaks in such a way as to give direct and genuine expression to his own feelings, while maintaining enough control so that the intensity is no greater than what is necessary to convey their true quality. (Holt, 1970, pp. 8–9)

For Rafe to use anger constructively, his anger expression and verbal aggression must communicate fully and clearly how he perceives the anger-instigating situation and how it affects him, and he must make it clear why he feels the way he does. Holt implies that this kind of behavior leaves communication lines open to both parties, and no one has to be seen as "losing." On the contrary, destructive anger expression and verbal aggression come from the person who wants to win at any cost to the other person or to the relationship.

Holt presented clinical evidence suggesting that anyone who repeatedly fails to express anger and appropriate anger-related behavior tends to develop one or more of a variety of psychosomatic symptoms. Though not necessarily the sole cause, unexpressed anger has been "implicated by psychoanalysts in the etiology of rheumatoid arthritis, hives, acne vulgaris, psoriasis, peptic ulcer, epilepsy, migraine, Raynaud's disease, and essential hypertension" (Holt, 1970, p. 9). Recent evidence shows that people who habitually repress all negative emotions are at risk for psychological and medical disorders (Bonanno & Singer, 1990; Schwartz, 1990; Weinberger, 1990).

In considering the problem of expressing or not expressing anger and aggressive tendencies, it is appropriate to consider briefly the relationship between aggression and sex. A number of experimental studies with animals showed that the male hormone testosterone apparently has some association with aggressive behavior. Experiments have shown that injections of testosterone will make young female rats and monkeys more aggressive. Perhaps from both biological and cultural factors, aggressiveness and sexual potency are often associated with one another. Fathers who fear that their sons will grow up to be cowards or homosexuals may be particularly concerned that their sons be appropriately aggressive. Many people have a tendency to associate masculinity and aggression.

Aggression and the Need to Understand Ourselves

In his book *Statistics of Deadly Quarrels*, Richardson (1960) pointed out that in the 126 years between 1820 and 1945, man killed his fellow man at the rate of one every 69 seconds in wars, skirmishes, quarrels, or murders. The killings during this period totalled 59,000,000 people.

Tinbergen (1968) concluded that human beings' propensity to kill their fellow beings characterizes them as unhinged killers. He said:

> There is a frightening, and ironical paradox in this conclusion: that the human brain, the finest life preserving device created by evolution, has made our species so successful in mastering the outside world that it suddenly finds itself taken off guard. One could say that our cortex and our brainstem (our "reason" and our "instincts") are at loggerheads. Together they have created a new social environment in which, rather than ensuring our survival, they are about to do the opposite. The brain finds itself seriously threatened by an enemy of its own making. It is its own enemy. We simply have to understand this enemy. (p. 1416)

Some literary and scientific thinkers have considered human beings to be creatures that thrive on conflict and crisis. In *The Skin of Our Teeth*, Thornton Wilder, the brilliant American playwright, sketched humans' progress from the dawn of history to modern day by depicting them in a series of crises that range from the avalanche of ice that covered much of the earth in the ice age to the atom bomb that destroyed most of humankind in the "last great war." The great historian Toynbee maintains that human beings raise themselves to new levels of creativeness by meeting the challenges that they face. Gardner Murphy (1958) put it this way:

> Man, if he is to be man at all, must somehow create and somehow escape his engines of destruction. He is the kind of animal who lives from one crisis to another, and it is his nature to surmount them. He will surmount those of the present century because he continues to be man. (p. 3)

Human beings may indeed reach some new understanding of themselves through facing and overcoming crises, but today people are capable of confronting themselves with crises that cannot be overcome—for example, total nuclear war. Thus, human beings are faced with the crisis of surmounting their dependency on crisis. We must accept as a crisis of our times the need to understand basic human nature, to understand ourselves as living beings with capacities for a virtually limitless range of aggressive acts, including the destruction of the human species.

Human beings are not only capable of hostility and aggression that lead to crime, murder, massacre, and even global conflicts and crises, they are capable of hiding their crimes and escaping punishment. Take an example from a black college campus on May 14, 1970, when uniformed policemen (highway patrolmen), accompanied by city police and hundreds of national guardsmen, fired into a crowd of black students and into a women's dormitory, killing two students and injuring more than a dozen others. A psychologist, a team of lawyers, and a presidential commission independently studied the incident and concluded that the killing of the students was totally unjustified. Yet, a local grand jury impaneled to investigate the case cleared all lawmen involved, indicting no one. The presidential commission said that the policemen not only killed the black students needlessly but later lied to their superiors and to the FBI to help cover up the crime. Judging from the history of such incidents, it is not likely that anyone will suffer much for the killing and wounding of these black students. Indeed, past experience suggests that little will be done to find and punish the guilty.

The Hostility Triad

Many studies of the emotion of anger lead to the conclusion that situations that elicit anger often elicit disgust and contempt as well. When people are asked to imagine a situation that makes them angry and then to describe their feelings, the three emotions of anger, disgust, and contempt are frequently listed. As we have already noted, this triad of emotions when directed inward toward the self is a significant aspect of the symptomatology of depression. The hostility triad probably also figures into certain types of aggression.

It is important to recognize that situations most frequently thought of as anger provoking may also elicit emotions of disgust and contempt. It is also worth noting that this pattern of emotions can be directed either inward toward the self or outward toward others. Although these three emotions frequently occur together, each has distinct characteristics, and each influences behavior in a different way. When they occur together, each one is contributing something special to the effects on one's thought and actions. For these reasons, the following chapter is devoted to the distinguishing characteristics of the emotions of disgust and contempt.

Summary

Anger, disgust, and contempt are discrete emotions, but they frequently interact in human experience. Situations that elicit anger often elicit some degree of disgust or contempt. Any combination of these three emotions may constitute the main affective component of hostility.

Many of the causes of anger can be subsumed under the rubric of frustration or restraint. Pain and prolonged, unrelieved sadness may be natural (unlearned) activators of anger.

The anger expression includes the brows drawn down and together and either bared teeth or compressed lips. The experience of anger is characterized by a high degree of tension and impulsiveness. The feeling of self-assurance is far greater in anger than in any other negative emotion.

Some of the adaptive functions of anger are more readily understood in evolutionary perspective than in day-to-day life. Anger mobilizes energy for physical defense of self and imbues the individual with a feeling of vigor and strength. However, these feelings can also inspire verbal or psychological defense and lead to appropriate assertiveness. Thus, anger may be justified in contemporary human affairs. Further, controlled anger may be used therapeutically to inhibit fear.

For heuristic purposes, differential emotions theory differentiates between hostility (affective-cognitive processes), affect expression (including anger expression, hostility expression), and aggressive acts. Aggression is limited by definition to verbal or physical actions intended to insult or harm.

The profiles of emotions in imaged hostility and anger situations are very similar. The pattern is fairly similar between hostility, disgust, and contempt, though in the imaged situations for the latter two emotions there are some potentially important changes in the magnitude and relative rank of emotion means.

Anger, disgust, and contempt have important interactions with other affects and with cognition. Stable interactions among any of these emotions and cognitive structures can be considered as a personality trait of hostility. The management of anger, disgust, and contempt presents some problems. The unregulated influence of these emotions on thought and action would create a serious adjustment problem, while the suppression of thought and action related to these emotions can produce psychosomatic symptoms.

There is some evidence that emotion communication plays a significant role in interpersonal aggression. There are a number of other important variables, including proximity of the parties and eye contact, but much more research is needed before we achieve full understanding and control of destructive aggression.

Although anger does not necessarily lead to aggression, it is sometimes part of the motivation for aggressive behavior. It must be emphasized that there are typically many other causes for aggressive behavior: culture, family life, and the particular experiences of the individual can contribute to aggressiveness. Aggressive behavior may be observed in childhood, and evidence has shown that children who are high on aggressive behavior (or low on prosocial behavior) are more likely to show aggressive behavior and criminal behavior in adulthood. These data suggest that aggressiveness can take on traitlike characteristics and become a stable part of the personality.

In contrast to aggressive action, the experience and expression of anger can have positive consequences. This is especially so if the anger episode is sufficiently controlled so that communication is maintained between the parties concerned. Appropriate expression of justified anger may even strengthen the relationship between the angry person and the person who is the target of the anger. Nevertheless, there is always some risk in expressing one's anger, and these risks have to be weighed against the negative consequences of anger expression and the effects of not expressing one's anger.

Suggested Readings

Averill, J. (1983). Studies on anger and aggression: Implications for theories of emotion. *American Psychologist, 38*, 1145–1162.

Summarizes evidence on the antecedents and consequences of anger. Findings interpreted in terms of a social-cognitive or constructivist theory of emotions.

Berkowitz, L. (1990). On the formation and regulation of anger and aggression: A cognitive-neoassociationistic analysis. *American Psychologist, 45*(4), 494–503.

An integrative article discussing the relations among negative affect, negative thoughts, anger, and aggression. Presents a cognitive-neoassociationistic model of emotions.

Cummings, E. M., Zahn-Waxler, C., Radke-Yarrow, M. (1981). Young children's responses to expressions of anger and affection by others in the family. *Child Development, 52*, 1274–1282.

Presents evidence indicating that 1- to 1½-year-old children are aware of and affected by others' expressions of anger and affection.

Lewis, M., Alessandri, S. M., & Sullivan, M. W. (1990). Violation of expectancy, loss of control, and anger expressions in young infants. *Developmental Psychology, 26*(5), 745–751.

Violation of an expectation established by instrumental learning or frustration elicited during the extinction of a gamelike response pattern apparently leads to anger expression in 2- to 8-month-old infants.

Weiner, B., Graham, S., & Chandler, C. (1982). Pity, anger and guilt: An attributional analysis. *Personality and Social Psychology Bulletin, 8*(2), 226–232.

Anger and other emotions as a function of the perception of the provocation, an analysis based on attribution theory.

12

Disgust and Contempt

We do not know exactly how or at what point in the evolutionary process the various emotions emerged. It is very likely, however, that disgust was among the first. Biological systems for the motivation of approach and avoidance had to come into play very early in even the simplest of life forms because approach and avoidance behaviors are so fundamental to survival.

In the complex interactions between a modern human being and the social and physical environment, there are many kinds of approach and avoidance reactions. Similarly, there are many motivations for approaching another person, object, or event and an equal or greater number of motivations for avoiding stimuli. Early in the evolution of life forms, approach and avoidance processes were much simpler and the motivations fewer. Approach was probably largely in terms of consumatory and mating behaviors and avoidance behaviors served to escape pain or reject distasteful and potentially dangerous substances. The primitive system that motivated the rejection of distasteful and potentially dangerous substances evolved as the emotion of disgust.

Disgust

The study of disgust and its expression provides information on some of the essential characteristics of human emotions. Emotions are fundamental to our existence as human beings. It is not possible to conceive of a being that is truly human without seeing that being as capable of emotion experience.

Evolutionary Origins of Disgust

The origins of the emotions in the evolutionary process cannot always be traced with precision and certainty. An exception may be found in the origins of disgust as a differentiated aspect of the primitive avoidance mechanism. Disgust has its evolutionary roots in the very old parts of the brain that serve the chemical sense of taste and eating behavior. A clear and specific expression of disgust can be obtained by putting a little bit of bitter substance on the tongue of the newborn infant. This is true even for infants in which the more recently evolved layers of the brain (the cerebral hemispheres) are dysfunctional due to disease or birth defect. Such disgust expressions obviously have little or no psychological component; that is, they are not based upon a cognitive evaluation or appraisal of the bitter substance. Thus, the disgust expression we see in young infants is primarily a function of neurochemical processes, which are independent of learning or memory.

Although the disgust expression can be mediated by the brainstem in infants without functional cerebral hemispheres, there is reason to believe that even such expressions are accompanied by a hedonic state or feeling, a subjective experience that matches the emotion expression. Steiner (1979), a neuroscientist who has worked extensively on the neurochemical bases of disgust, has concluded that the brainstem-mediated disgust expression is accompanied by a hedonic or feeling state and that it is the feeling that actually motivates the expressive behavior that results in the rejection of the distasteful substance.

This kind of evidence and argument support the premise that expressions and feelings are innate and innately connected. If this assumption is true, then any time an expression appears on the face of the young infant there is a feeling that matches the expression. The emotion feeling is crucial to the organizing and motivational functions of the emotion.

Because we can sketch a plausible course for the evolutionary origin of the emotion of disgust and specify its roots in the very old parts of the brain, it may serve as a model that teaches us something about all emotions. Here are some of the implications that follow from our knowledge of disgust and the disgust expression.

1. Emotion expressions are a very basic part of human nature.
2. There is a natural connection between expression and feeling. Thus, at least in early life, each expression is accompanied with matching feeling.
3. The feeling that occurs naturally with an emotion expression is motivational.
4. The demands of society and culture require that we learn to disconnect the inborn connection between expression and feeling.
5. It is through learning and experience that we gradually become able to cover up our sadness with a smile and our fear with the frown of anger.
6. Emotions can occur as the result of basic neurochemical processes independent of our experiences, independent of what we learn and what we remember.
7. Eventually, cognitive evaluation or appraisal, learning, and

memories play a very large part in our emotional life. For example, we learn to feel disgust toward a wide variety of stimuli.

8. Although emotions can be activated in early life either spontaneously or as a function of neurochemical and sensory processes, initially, emotions activated in this way may relate very little if at all to psychological processes involved in thought, memory, and anticipation. Nevertheless, all emotions eventually become connected to a vast network of symbols—words, images, thoughts, values, goals, and plans.

The Development of Disgust

In early infancy the effective stimuli for disgust are chemical in nature—a bitter taste or spoiled food. The human being eventually learns to feel disgusted with a wide variety of events and objects even including one's own self. Even the word *distasteful* eventually takes on different levels of meaning. It can mean that something tastes spoiled, or it can refer to a person, social behavior, or most any event. It can mean that someone's manners or etiquette are quite different from our own (such as someone seeming unconcerned about wearing smelly clothes or having food in his mustache).

We use the term *taste* to refer to people's manners or behavior, as when we say something is done in good taste. The dual meaning of the word *taste* is a clear indication that disgust that begins as a basic neurochemical process takes on psychological significance. Although spoiled food will always retain its capacity to be disgusting, we are pretty certain to acquire standards and values that might make even the most delicious food disgusting because of the way it is prepared or served.

Very simple changes in the way things are done can make the difference as to whether they seem perfectly normal and acceptable or whether they seem disgusting. For example, you swallow saliva all the time, but how do you feel about the thought of collecting it in a glass for later consumption? Disgusted, no doubt.

As we have seen, we learned something very basic about human emotions from our study of disgust. The disgust expression is served by the very oldest part of the brain, the brainstem, and the emotion of disgust serves a very basic function in human experience. Both the expression of disgust and the motivational condition that accompanies it serves significant adaptive functions, such as rejection of physically or psychologically harmful objects.

The Causes of Disgust

Rozin and Fallon (1987) have a theory of disgust in which disgust is defined strictly as a food-related emotion. They consider disgust as revulsion at the prospect of eating offensive objects. They restrict the range of offensive objects to animal and animal products.

Rozin and Fallon describe four types of food rejection—distaste (a food one does not like), danger (a food that is known to be poisonous), inappropriate (objects like wood and sand), and disgust (food objects thought to be contaminated). They see disgust as rejection based on cognition, particularly the idea that the object is contaminated. They mean psychological contamination. As an illustration, they relate a case where hospital nurses were drinking juices meant for children. When the juices were served in new urine-collection bottles, the nurses no longer drank the juice. Because the bottles were new, and the nurses knew it, there was no possibility of physical contamination. There was only the *idea* of past contact with urine and thus psychological contamination.

According to Rozin and Fallon, an offensive object might be rejected because of distaste, but to be rejected because of disgust one has to believe that the object has been in contact with the offensive object. Thus the development of the emotion of disgust, according to Rozin and Fallon, is dependent on cognitive development. In particular, it is dependent on the capacity to understand how a substance becomes contaminated and how contaminated foods affect the body. In their view, then, the emotion of disgust does not emerge until after 7 years of age. After this age, neutral objects can become disgusting through conditioning and learning. For example, any type of edible food or drink may become capable of eliciting disgust by its association with a contaminating substance. The contamination need not be physical. Psychological contamination can be very effective. Orange juice served from a new and perfectly sterile bedpan would be disgusting to most people. Younger children reject food because of distaste, danger, and inappropriateness.

Rozin and Fallon presented a very narrow definition of disgust. They imply that the disgust expression in infants and children under age 7 does not signal an internal emotional state. However, such young children express disgust and behave as though motivated by the feeling of disgust.

Rozin and Fallon's idea that disgust is only a food-related emotion was challenged by psychoanalysts who reported numerous cases of disgust with different forms of sexual activity (e.g., oral-genital and genital-anal intercourse) (David & Fahy, 1987). David and Fahy argue for a dynamic relation between erotic impulses and disgust. Their idea is supported largely by clinical cases (e.g., a man who was erotically stimulated by drinking female urine, a woman who got sexual pleasure from having a man urinate on her).

David and Fahy also think that sexually related disgust may serve adaptive functions. For example, disgust may result from contemplation of certain sexual practices and in this way play a role in setting the acceptable norms of sexual acts. Disgust with potentially harmful sexual acts may serve a protective function.

Most theorists agree that the original cause of disgust is anything that "tastes bad." Eventually, anything that even looks like it might taste bad or smell bad or anything that is objectionable by virtue of its appearance may, through learning and experience, come to be a cause of disgust. Either spoiled beef or a spoiled brat, either dirty smelly food or a dirty smelly street can make us feel disgusted. Certain sexual acts or the process of contemplating them may also lead to disgust.

Perhaps most serious from the standpoint of psychological well-being is the possibility that one's own self can become a source of disgust. Some personal characteristics that never bothered us in childhood may become disgusting to us in adolescence. For example, being plump may be seen as just a sign of strong appetite and good health in childhood but as a part of a body image that may prove to be disgusting in adolescence.

Disgust may join with sadness and other emotions in playing a role in the eating disorders that plague so many people. Widespread disgust with food may contribute to learned food aversions and anorexia. In the teenage years, some eating disorders show the twin symptoms of binging and purging. Causes of binging are complex, some perhaps related to biological factors and many to various sorts of emotional needs. Disgust however may in some cases be a central emotion in the purging process. After an overeating binge, many young people purge themselves by inducing vomiting. Seeing their binging behavior as disgusting or seeing a real or imagined "fat and ugly" body image may be disgusting. The psychologically created disgust might literally make it easier to vomit.

The responses from the study of antecedents and consequences of disgust are presented in Table 12-1.

The Expression of Disgust

In the infant and young child the expression of disgust is unmistakable (see Figure 12-1). In addition to the brows being drawn down and together in a frown and the wrinkled nose, the upper lip is pulled up, and the lower lip is pulled

TABLE 12-1
Antecedents and Consequences of Disgust[a]

Responses	Percentage of subjects giving responses
Antecedents	
Feelings	
1. "Sick of something," repelled, tired	27.7
2. Of failure, disappointment in self, anger toward self, incompetency	26.8
3. Of dislike, disapproval of actions of others	17.7
4. Disgust synonyms	11.5
5. Distress synonyms	6.9
6. Anger synonyms	3.8
7. Contempt synonyms	3.1
8. Other	4.6

[a]N = approximately 130 college students.

TABLE 12-1 (continued)

Responses	Percentage of subjects giving responses
Thoughts	
1. Hatred, dislike, disapproval of actions of others	24.6
2. Of failure, disappointment in self, anger toward self, incompetency	22.3
3. War, politics, racism	20.8
4. Smelly, unpleasant things	14.6
5. Unclear thoughts	4.6
6. Lonely, isolated, rejected	3.8
7. Other	5.4
Actions	
1. Blames self	30.8
2. Something wrong, stupid, a mistake	25.4
3. Has to do something unpleasant, others impose their will	15.4
4. Does something unappreciated by others	12.3
5. Does something legally or morally wrong or harmful	10.8
6. Other	5.4
Consequences	
Feelings	
1. Physical disgust: nausea, fatigue, sick, etc.	25.5
2. Disgust synonyms	18,8
3. Anger synonyms	15.0
4. Contempt synonyms	14.3
5. Like giving up, apathetic	7.5
6. Feels misled, betrayed, used, or hurt by others	3.8
7. Has failed, blames self, etc.	3.8
8. Feels bad, lousy, terrible	3.0
9. Other	8.3
Thoughts	
1. How bad the situation is	30.8
2. Thinks about event which caused the disgust	15.0
3. Of others, trying to forget, escape situation	15.0
4. Has failed, blames self, etc.	11.5
5. Hatred, dislike, disapproval of others	10.5
6. About a solution to the problem	9.8
7. Contempt synonym	3.0
8. Other	11.3
Actions	
1. Gets away from situation	39.8
2. Finds a solution to problem	21.1
3. Verbally or physically hostile	12.8
4. Evaluates attitude, tries to do better	4.5
5. Covers up feelings, puts up a front	3.0
6. Gets mad	3.0
7. Acts superior	2.3
8. Talks to someone, gets with friend	2.3
9. Other	11.3

[a]*N* = approximately 130 college students.

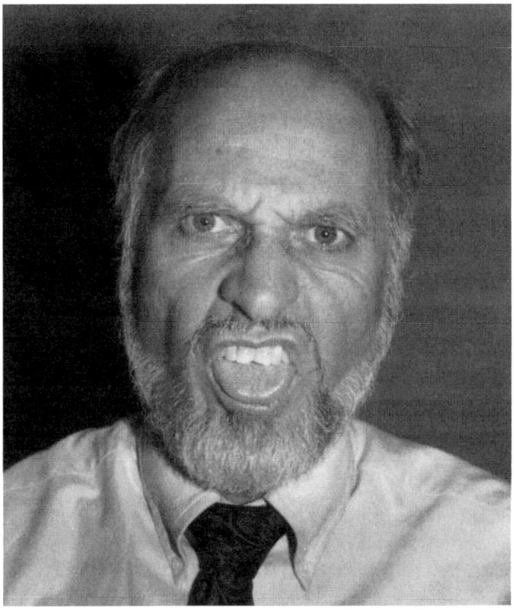

FIGURE 12-1. The full-face expression of disgust.

downward, sometimes giving the mouth a rectangular-like shape, and the tongue pushes forward to eject the distasteful substance (see Figure 12-1).

As with all emotion expressions the disgust expression eventually comes under voluntary control. We learn to mask and disguise it, and we learn to make it when we don't really feel disgusted. We also learn to make just one small component of the disgust expression and to use this single component to let someone know that what they are doing is disgusting to you. Children learn to stick their tongues out or simply to say "yucky" to let their peers know that something is disgusting. Adults may simply raise their upper lip or wrinkle their nose. The upper lip movement and nose wrinkling can become very subtle movements, so subtle that they may escape notice unless one is very observant. As with all expressive movements, the subtle nose wrinkling or upper-lip raising may be done more or less unconsciously, and the person making the movements may not be keenly aware that they are signalling their feelings of disgust.

The Feeling of Disgust

I have defined emotions as phenomena that include neurophysiological processes, expressive behaviors, and a particular subjective experience. There is clear evidence that disgust is a distinct emotion in terms of at least two of these components. We are particularly concerned about distinguishing disgust from anger on the one hand and contempt on the other because these three emotions are often experienced in the same situation. The expression of disgust as we have described it is unique and has components that are distinctly different from either the anger expression or the contempt expression.

Studies of the subjective experience of disgust indicate that it is also quite distinct from the other two emotions in the hostility triad. Whereas in anger you feel as though your blood is going to boil and you are in danger of exploding unless you can do something about your frustration, in disgust the most prominent feeling is one of rejection or avoidance of the stimulus. If the stimulus is a taste or odor, you may literally feel sick at the stomach—"yucky." If the stimulus is strictly cognitive or psychological in nature, you may feel strong revulsion or desire to avoid the object without actual nausea. This does not mean that it takes an actual taste or odor to elicit nausea and disgust, because sights and sounds can also make you truly sick at your stomach. When visual and auditory stimuli create sensations of nausea and the feeling of disgust, it is probably through conditioning and learning that we have a strong association between the sight and sound we see, on the one hand, and foul tastes and odors, on the other.

The feeling of disgust is like feeling "sick at the stomach," with a bad taste in the mouth. One wants to remove or get away from the object of disgust. If disgust is very intense it may actually make one sick at the stomach by creating nausea.

As can be seen by a comparison of Figures 11-4 and 12-2 the profiles for anger

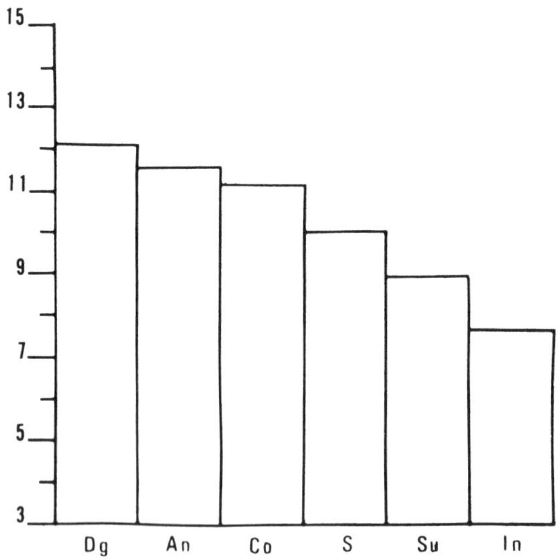

FIGURE 12-2. The DES profile of emotions in the imagined disgust situation. Dg, disgust; An, anger; Co, contempt; S, sadness; Su, surprise; In, interest.

and disgust are quite similar, but there are some noteworthy differences. In the anger situation, interest is considerably higher and sadness somewhat lower than in the disgust situation. This suggests that the object of anger captures the alert attention of the person more than does the object of disgust, which is more likely to motivate the turning of attention elsewhere.

The Biological and Social Functions of Disgust

A highly obvious biological function of disgust is the rejection of distasteful and potentially dangerous substances. Disgust can motivate the learning of a wide variety of associations between particular objects and events and rejection-avoidance behavior. Whereas taste is a chemical sense and reacts only to actual substances, the emotion of disgust can motivate rejection or avoidance even when sensations of taste and odor are totally absent. In this way disgust can actually keep us at a distance from potentially obnoxious substances or "foul situations" without our actually having to experience them. The disgust expression or any component of the expression that successfully signals disgust can serve as a warning that the target persons must either change their appearance or manners or some aspect of their behavior or risk rejection.

When something disgusts us we want to remove it or change it in such a way that it is no longer disgusting. In evolution, disgust probably helped motivate animals to maintain an environment sufficiently sanitary for their health and to prevent them from eating spoiled food and drinking polluted water. Disgust is not a perfect detector of dangerous contamination, but it helps. Also disgust probably plays a role in the maintenance of body hygiene. Foul body odors or a grossly dirty appearance may be disgusting to the self and others. Failure to clean up the environment may prove disastrous for the group, and failure to maintain body cleanliness that meets the group's standards may lead to rejection and isolation for the individual. As already noted, disgust may also help set the standards of sexual practices.

Disgust, like anger, can be directed toward the self, and self-disgust can lower self-esteem and cause self-rejection. As seen in Chapter 10, research with normal people and hospitalized patients has shown that inner-directed anger and disgust are usually characteristic of depression.

The Interaction of Disgust and Anger

Disgust alone may not be considered a serious cause of aggressive behavior. Usually rejection or avoidance of the stimulus is adequate. The emotion of disgust may become dangerous, however, when it interacts or combines with anger. Instead of motivation to simply reject or avoid the object, combined anger and disgust may create motivation to get rid of the object through attack and destruction.

Disgust and Psychological Disorders

We have already noted that disgust may play a role in eating disorders. What starts out as an eating binge may develop into bulimia or anorexia—psychological disorders that can have serious effects on physical and mental health. Disgust in combination with anger may result in an overly aggressive personality or in pathologically hostile behavior.

Disgust (as well as contempt) toward the self can figure in an eating disorder and the bouts of depression that are so often associated with it. Recall the episode in Sheryl's life when inner-directed hostility led to serious self-abuse. Part of the problem was an eating disorder, which involved a cycle of emotions and behaviors. At the point in the cycle when she went on an eating binge, inner-directed disgust and contempt were salient forces. Here is the description of this period in her life in her own words.

> During the time before I first gave myself my first black eye, I experienced chronic depression (with a capital *C*). This was due to many factors in my life; *hating* high school, feeling alone and lonely, feeling insecure and socially ineffective (shy), etc., etc. This depression was the first part of a complex cyclical/repetitive pattern involving my patterns of eating as well. My lowest points emotionally often coincided with the most erratic and maladaptive (but perhaps actually somewhat adaptive) eating binges and purges. It is hard to say which preceded the other—the depressive feelings or the eating binges. I would guess that it was 50-50. Sometimes my eating would cause me to feel guilt, shame, contempt, disgust, and depression first. Other times the deep depression would drive me to eat (which of course simply furthered my feelings of self-hatred and loss of control).

In Figure 12-3, constructed entirely by Sheryl, we have a clear view of the sequence of emotions and behaviors that characterized her eating disorder. Although there will be variations in particular details, this chart, complemented by her narrative account (story), undoubtedly will ring true for many who suffer from an eating disorder such as compulsive eating, anorexia, or bulimia. Her list of emotions in her story and chart is extensive. Her "self-hate" is what I have termed inner-directed anger or inner-directed hostility; her "sorrow" is equivalent to the emotion of sadness. Note that she lists both disgust and contempt and that they are primarily inner-directed. They probably helped motivate her physical self-abuse and are part of the "total rage towards oneself" that she mentions later. People with eating disorders may not ordinarily think of disgust and contempt as contributing to their misery and maladaptive actions, but they are sometimes very real and important factors.

> In understanding my depression, I find it is helpful to map out my cycle of eating, since the two are inextricably tied (no matter which came first).
>
> Through analyzing this cycle it is easy to see how depression could so easily play a role in the life of a bulimic or compulsive eater. It is also plain to see how such feelings of total rage towards oneself could build and gain momentum in such a circular fashion. It so happens that the numerous times that I blackened my eyes and cut my wrists were all eating related, and all took place during the guilt/rage/contempt stage of my eating cycle, after binging. The depression that would follow (or in some cases *lead up to*) is straight out of any

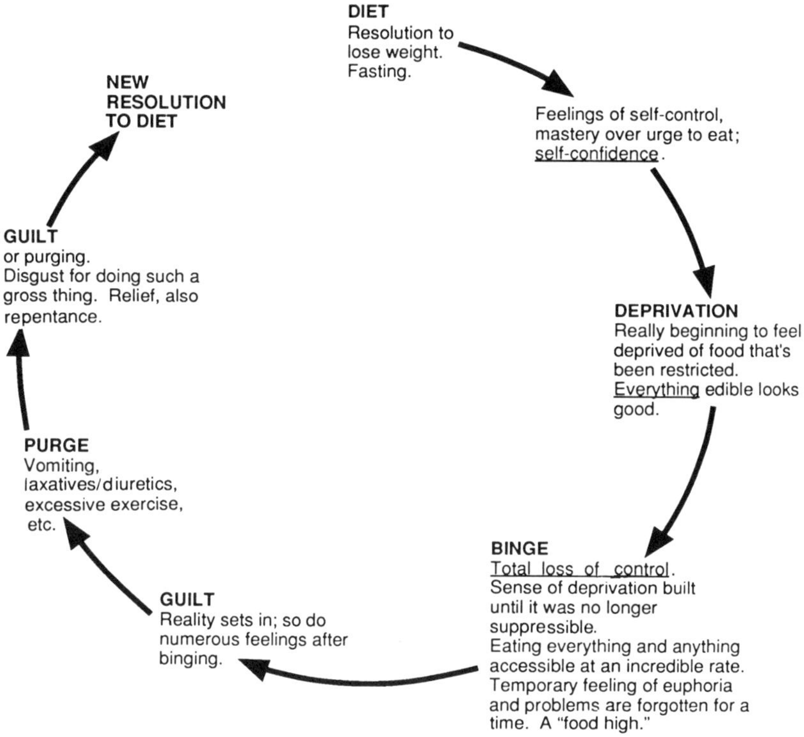

FIGURE 12-3. Sequence of emotions and behaviors that characterized Sheryl's eating disorder.

textbook—extreme fatigue, sometimes to the point of not having the energy or desire to get out of bed all day (I spent quite a few days in just this way); inner-directed hostility for being such a basket case and not being able to solve my problems. Also added is the hostility from binging, and of course, feelings of disgust and contempt were also very prevalent.

We probably have to feel contempt for anyone that we deliberately abuse or treat with prejudice. Similarly, you probably have to have contempt for self in order to be self-abusive. It is not until you learn to control or turn the hostility (including contempt) outward that the self is safe from some form of abuse.

Also true to my experience were the emotions of disgust, anger, and contempt, the hostility triad. Unfortunately, all of my hostility was directed inward. I am still learning to direct anger/hostility outward when it is necessary. This is something that previously was impossible for me to do. Whatever emotional negativity I felt, whether it was at a family member, a school institution, or a poor score on a test, I still directed the anger inwards—even when it probably would've seemed ludicrous to others to do so. This was my way of controlling my world (and unfortunately, often still is). When things go wrong or unpredictably on the outside world, there is always the insecurity or shyness or low self-esteem to blame. In fact, that was the function of dieting and fasting, to ensure some sort of control over some part of my life. I recently read an article that was titled "Stop Blaming Your Body for What's Wrong with Your Life." This really sums up the inner-directedness of my negative emotions. It just so happens that I picked the numbers on the scale (weight) as my area of concentration. Later, when this even felt out of control I chose self-abuse as a means of punishment and outlet.

The emotions of guilt and fear also played a part in my behaviors. After giving myself a black eye for the first time I really scared myself. The emotion of fear did play a part at that time in helping me to realize that my problems were more serious than I had thought. I was really afraid that I was truly going crazy. Such fear is a way of possibly decreasing suicidal behavior. I would agree that this was true in my case. I was sufficiently scared enough by my first eye-blackening *not* to hurt myself again for about a year. Also, when I cut my wrists for the first time I was afraid I would die (even though the cuts were superficial). This helped me to realize that I didn't really want to die after all.

When I think back to those experiences I still feel *very* emotional. Perhaps I always will feel that way. I feel I have come so far from the desperate person I was, I can now look back and really marvel at the change. I feel the difference most profoundly when I read poetry that I wrote during High School or journal entries. I'll share a poem with you here that is quite fitting for the eating-disordered person:

Bulimia

Good, Better, Best
You'll never pass the test.
When feelings seldom change
and goals are rearranged.
You'll clap the thin thin air
which holds sweet castles fair
and watch while all your dreams
are crumbling at the seams.
The purifying rite
will not renew your sight.
It just hands you the spade
with which you'll dig your grave.

Sheryl's "emotion autobiography," like the others in this book, were written by students in my course on human emotions. Although I had obtained written permission to include her story, I asked her again if she was sure she wanted to share such intimate, emotion-laden material. Her reply, below, speaks well of her present ability to control her emotions and to use her experiences constructively.

As a separate note, I would really like you to use this autobiographical sketch if you want to do so. If I could possibly help other young women suffering from depression or eating disorders or self-abusive tendencies, I would feel very happy. It doesn't seem frightening. In fact, I have given several talks this year to interested groups about my past experiences. So, if you did want to use any of my paper, I have no qualms.

Contempt

We have already learned something about the emotion of contempt from Sheryl's story of her eating disorder and self-abuse. Yet, contempt is a difficult emotion to understand, especially when we ask why it ever came to be a part of human nature.

The expression of contempt is clear enough, and the motivational experience that accompanies the contempt expression serves communicative functions. However, determining the constructive adaptive functions of contempt is difficult. Most of the behaviors that we associate with contempt are not very admirable. Indeed, we would often consider such actions as "contemptible!"

The Causes of Contempt

A triumph over a competitor may lead to contempt. If we interpret triumph very broadly to include all kinds of wins (physical, verbal, imagined), and we interpret the notion of competition or competitor equally broadly, then our triumph over a competitor may be a general and basic source of contempt. One part of the self (conscience, or superego) feeling superior to another part (body image) may lead to self-contempt.

Another way of viewing "triumph over competitor" is to take the vantage point of the winner. Any time you win or see yourself as triumphant in any way, it is easy to see yourself as superior, at least for the moment and at least in the particular situation you find yourself. These appraisals of yourself as triumphant and superior can lead you to view the loser with contempt. This experience is not confined to the individual or to contests between two persons. These appraisals can characterize the team that wins and all the supporters of the team. They can also characterize a family, a particular community, a socioeconomic class, an ethnic group, or race. The responses from the study of antecedents and consequences are presented in Table 12-2.

TABLE 12-2

Antecedents and Consequences of Contempt[a]

Responses	Percentage of subjects giving responses
Antecedents	
Feelings	
1. Of superiority	59.3
2. Feels misled, betrayed, used, disappointed, hurt by others	10.6
3. Disapproval, disturbed by actions of others	8.9
4. Disgust synonyms (revulsion, aversion)	3.2
5. Shame synonyms (embarrassed, shy)	2.4
6. Anger synonyms (irritated, annoyed, mad)	1.6
7. Other	13.8

[a]N = approximately 130 college students.

TABLE 12-2 (continued)

Responses	Percentage of subjects giving responses
Thoughts	
1. Disapproving of actions of others	40.6
2. Contempt synonyms	33.3
3. Of being misled, betrayed, used, hurt by others	7.3
4. Shame synonyms	4.9
5. Of being embarrassed	3.2
6. Other	10.6
Actions	
1. Acts superior, condescending	19.5
2. Succeed when others thought you could not, do superior work	15.4
3. Act sarcastic, hateful, hurt others	13.0
4. Something wrong, stupid, mistake	11.5
5. Disapprove, dislike actions of others	10.6
6. Act selfishly	5.7
7. Other	5.7
Consequences	
Feelings	
1. Of superiority	60.6
2. Confident, good, elevated	7.6
3. Anger synonyms	5.3
4. Shame synonyms	5.3
5. Hatred, dislike, disapproval of others	3.0
6. Disgust	3.0
7. Envy, jealousy, of others	3.8
8. Other	11.4
Thoughts	
1. Of being and feeling superior	37.9
2. Of hatred, dislike, disapproval of others	19.7
3. How to ignore, avoid object or situation	15.1
4. Questions reasons for behavior, thinks of what was done and why	6.8
5. Try not to feel contempt	5.3
6. Anger synonyms	1.5
7. Other	12.9
Actions	
1. Expresses contempt, either verbally or physically	38.6
2. Ignores, avoids object of contempt or situation	20.5
3. Tries not to show emotion, or feeling	9.1
4. Tries to regain control of self or situation	7.6
5. Tries to understand the other point of view	4.5
6. Other	19.7

[a]*N* = approximately 130 college students.

The Expression of Contempt

Cross-cultural studies of the expression of fundamental emotions have shown that it was possible to depict contempt in a way that is distinct from disgust and anger. The facial expressions depicted in Figure 12-4 were recognized by a vast majority of subjects in a wide variety of literate cultures as expressions of contempt, as distinct from disgust and anger. The expression is in part postural. When standing, the person expressing contempt tends to stand tall and tilt or cock the head upward at an angle, as though to look down on the object or person of contempt. The full face of contempt may also include a lifted brow, a lifted corner of the upper lip, or tightened mouth corners. Any one of these body or facial signals may convey contempt.

Ekman and Friesen (1986) presented evidence that the tightening of one mouth corner is universally recognized as an expression of contempt. This expression is made by contracting a single muscle, the buccinator. Buccinator contraction compresses the lips at the corner of the mouth, which is slightly lifted in the process. This muscle action tends to cause a dimple in the cheek area adjacent to the mouth corner. In a follow-up study, Ekman and Heider (1988) showed that this expression was recognized as contempt by 75% of subjects in 10 different cultures around the world.

Although the evidence that the tightened mouth corner signals contempt is quite good, the evidence from a number of researchers indicates that other facial or head movement may also signal contempt (e.g., one lifted brow and head tilted back). A sneer may also express contempt (Izard & Haynes, 1988). Indeed, there is the possibility that the tightened mouth corner is a learned modification of the

FIGURE 12-4. Expressions of contempt.

"sneer of contempt" described by Darwin (1872/1965). In the sneer, the animal raises the corner of the upper lip and bares the canine tooth. Humans can and do make the same expression. The compressed lip corners could be a controlled and socially and esthetically more acceptable version for the vulgar sneer.

Bodily Changes in Contempt

We know very little about the physiology of contempt. Observations of the three emotions of anger, disgust, and contempt suggest that contempt is accompanied by the least amount of physiological arousal. Whereas anger is a relatively high-arousal emotion (the blood boils, the body stiffens), contempt is a relatively cool emotion. This means that there is probably relatively little change in heart rate and respiration and other bodily functions that change rather dramatically in moderate or intense levels of anger. Thus, unless anger is combined or interacting with contempt, the latter is not likely to become an overwhelming emotional experience as in the case of rage or terror.

The Subjective Experience of Contempt

As we just noted, the emotion of contempt is not experienced as a body-shaking, heart-rending feeling. It is the "cool" emotion of the hostility triad. One feels superior in some important way to the person held in contempt. It is more than a feeling of indifference or of not caring, because with the feeling of contempt goes the evaluation of self as somehow better than other.

It is difficult to describe the feeling of contempt without reference to the associated images and thoughts. If you hold someone in contempt, then you consciously or unconsciously adopt a holier-than-thou attitude toward the person or group, and you experience feelings of superiority. Thus contempt tends to inflate one's sense of self-worth and devalue the object of contempt. The pattern of emotions in the contempt situation is presented in Figure 12-5.

The Functions of Contempt

Of all the emotions that we shall discuss, contempt is the most difficult one to explain in an evolutionary perspective. Evolutionary perspective suggests that all our biologically based characteristics serve some adaptive function or did so in the past. What adaptive function could contempt possibly have served in our evolution as human beings?

In evolutionary perspective, contempt may have emerged as a vehicle for preparing the individual or group to face a dangerous adversary. For example, a young man might prepare for defense of himself or of his group with such thoughts as: "I am stronger than he, I am better." Eventually this message might become a

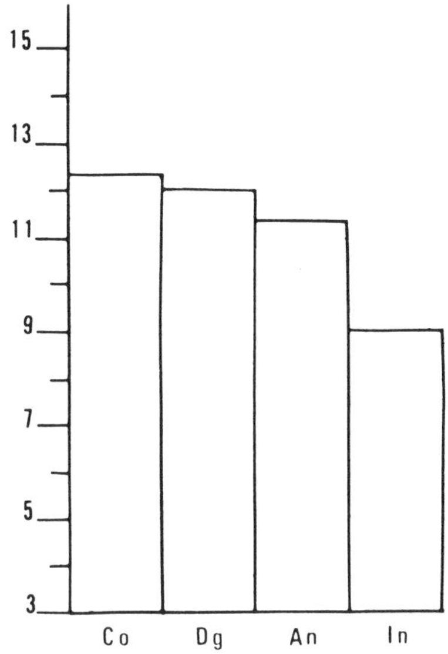

FIGURE 12-5. The DES profile of emotions in the imagined contempt situation. Co, contempt; Dg, disgust; An, anger; In, interest.

rallying signal for all the men in preparation for defense or attack. Perhaps those who were quite persuaded marshaled more courage (and felt less empathy for the enemy) and were more successful in surviving the hazards of hunting and fighting. Still today the occasions that elicit contempt are situations in which one needs to feel stronger, more intelligent, more civilized, or in some way better than the person one is contending with. Situations that elicit jealousy, greed, and rivalry are breeding grounds for contempt.

Once the contempt is turned against other human beings (or the self) it seems difficult to find anything positive or adaptive in this emotion. Perhaps it serves a socially constructive purpose when it is directed against those objectively deserving it; those who foster waste, pollution, immorality, oppression, crime, or war. There is the possibility that contempt may serve as a force for maintaining social norms or group conformity. If a person's behavior is considered to be highly deviant, particularly if the cause of the behavior is carelessness or neglect, he or she may be looked upon with contempt. If enough people share this contempt, it can become a strong pressure on the deviant individual to clean up his or her act or get out of the community. If the contempt is justified because the deviant behavior is illegal, immoral, or unhealthy, some good may come from the group's expression of contempt. Contempt may also elicit shame in the target person. As we shall see in Chapter 15, shame can be a strong motive for self-improvement.

It is easy to analyze the negative functions of this emotion. Contempt is the principal emotion in all kinds of prejudice, including racial prejudice. Of the three emotions in the hostility triad—anger, disgust, contempt—contempt is the most subtle, the most cold. Anger is a "hot" emotion, sometimes impelling forthright action. Contempt is cold and distant, more likely to foster aggression characterized by trickery and deceit. The feeling of contempt toward a human being tends to depersonalize the target individual, to cause the person to be perceived as something less than human. It is because of these characteristics that contempt can motivate murder and mass destruction of people.

Unfortunately, we know that contempt is still encouraged during the combat training of military personnel. Soldiers are taught to devalue and depersonalize the enemy on the grounds that such depersonalization will make him easier to kill. It would seem that a great deal of devaluing and depersonalizing would have to occur before soldiers could bring themselves to kill civilian women and children. Yet such killing has occurred repeatedly in war time. Only contempt could motivate the senseless slaughter of innocent and defenseless human beings.

Contempt appears in a much more widespread and sometimes subtle form in our society and in most every society under the sun. Since contempt for another is associated with devaluing and depersonalization, it is the emotion that lies at the heart of prejudice against fellow human beings—race prejudice, economic-class prejudice, social-class prejudice, ethnic-group prejudice, religious-group prejudice, gender prejudice.

History clearly tells us that prejudice against race or ethnic groups can oppress that ethnic group and deny it many of the rights and privileges enjoyed by others in the same society. The prejudice of whites against blacks cost black people enormously in personal, social, and economic domains. In the United States, the emancipation of blacks from slavery in 1864 was only the beginning of a long and difficult struggle for equality of human rights and privileges.

African blacks were not the first people to be enslaved. The Egyptians enslaved the people of Israel; Greeks enslaved Egyptians; the Romans enslaved Greeks; and so on through history, conquerors have enslaved the conquered. Victory means superiority. Defeat means being depersonalized and treated as chattel. The victor holds the vanquished in contempt, and with defeat comes shame and humiliation.

We cannot live with chronic contempt without paying a price. Contempt and the accompanying prejudice is a mind-shrinking process. A narrowed view of the world can decrease the richness of life. Similarly, to be held in contempt chronically is to be shamed or to anticipate shame and risk the possibility of low self-esteem, a characteristic feeling of self as inferior. A person pays a dear price for holding a prejudice. The cost is often paid slowly, and the effects may not always be clearly evident. The victims of prejudice are even less fortunate, and they are constantly aware of the burden of being labeled and treated as inferior.

Distinctions between Hostility and Aggression

The first task of this section is to distinguish between hostility and aggression and to give aggression a relatively more specific definition than it is sometimes accorded. The major distinction proposed here is that hostility consists of affective experience (emotions, feelings) and affective-cognitive orientations, while aggression consists of actions intended to harm.

Hostility is a complex affective-cognitive trait or orientation. It consists of a variable set of interacting emotions, drives, and affective-cognitive structures. The emotions most prominent in the pattern of hostility are anger, disgust, and contempt. Hostility also involves drive states, affect-affect interactions, and, usually, imagery or wishful thinking about harm, embarrassment, or defeat of the object of hostility. Such imaging and wishing does not necessarily include an intent actually to harm the object. Hostility has both experiential and expressive components, but it does not include verbal or physical activity. Anger, disgust, and contempt influence perceptual processes and tend to foster cognitive processes consonant with the underlying affect, the result being hostility. Since hostility communicates negative emotion (e.g., by way of anger expression), it can harm or embarrass the target, but the harm is primarily psychological.

Within the theoretical framework of differential emotions theory, aggression is defined as hostile action or behavior. Aggression is a physical act that may or may not be instigated and maintained in part by one or more of the emotions in the hostility pattern. It is intended to harm, embarrass, or defeat the object. "Physical act" includes speech as well as all other physical actions. The harm may be psychological or physical—a blow to the body or to the self-concept. Thus, the hurt caused by aggression may be from genuine pain, negative emotions, or both. Aggression may follow from hostility and the imagery and ideas that hostility produces. However, aggressive action can influence the ongoing hostility. Thus, hostility is considered as the complex motivational condition, and aggression the subsequent behavior. Although this section will have more to say about aggression, its central concern is with hostility and with the affects and patterns of affects that constitute it.

The conceptual framework outlined by these definitions indicates that emotion expression (e.g., facial, vocal, postural expression) may be agonistic but is not itself aggression, since the latter is defined as physical action apart from the emotion process. Affect expression does communicate anger, disgust, contempt, or hostility, and in doing so it can cause emotional hurt and do psychological damage. Thus, there is a need for regulation and control of hostility (affect expression), as well as aggression. The distinction between hostility (affects, hostile cognition, affect expression) and aggression (actions intended to harm) may help establish more refined principles of control for all types of agonistic phenomena.

Verbalizations (e.g., "angry words") directed toward another person occupy a middle ground between expression and physical action. They are a kind of motor act, but their harm is typically only psychological (like that of hostility). Verbal attack is something more than emotion expression (considering expression as a component of emotion); it is a consequence of emotion rather than a part of it. Thus it is more properly considered a form of aggression.

Patterns of Affects in Situations that Elicit Anger, Disgust, Contempt, and Hostility

Studies paralleling those for the fundamental emotion of sadness and the complex phenomenon of depression have also been completed for the fundamental emotions of anger, disgust, contempt, and the phenomenon of hostility. The standard DES profiles of emotions in visualized hostility, anger, disgust, and contempt situations are presented in Table 12-3. These results differ in some ways from those obtained in the studies of the sadness and depression situations. While the sadness and depression situations had emotion profiles that were quite distinct from each other and those of any of the other fundamental emotions, this was not the case for hostility. The profiles of emotions for the imaged hostility and anger situations were virtually identical. Further, except for the expected difference for the key emotion (the one named in a given imaging instruction), the profiles for disgust and contempt were very similar in shape to those for hostility and anger.

Of the four profiles, that for contempt is the most deviant. If we take the sum of the mean scores for anger, disgust, and contempt as a general index of the

TABLE 12-3

Profiles of Emotions in Visualized Hostility, Anger, Disgust and Contempt Situations[a]

	Situation			
Emotion	Hostility (N = 213)	Anger (N = 30)	Disgust (N = 33)	Contempt (N = 37)
Anger	12.46	12.53	10.39	9.86
Contempt	10.28	10.60	9.88	10.49
Disgust	10.05	10.97	10.70	9.19
Sadness	8.99	9.33	8.97	7.78
Interest	8.58	8.93	7.79	8.68
Surprise	7.66	7.87	7.09	6.62
Fear	5.62	5.97	5.27	4.89
Guilt	5.42	6.33	5.33	5.00
Shyness	4.64	4.57	4.61	4.08
Joy	3.43	3.80	3.70	5.16

[a]Scores derived from the Differential Emotions Scale; maximum score, 15; minimum score, 3.

intensity of hostility, then the contempt situation elicited the lowest amount of hostility. The largest part of the difference is accounted for by the fact that the contempt situation elicited substantially less anger than the hostility or anger situations and slightly less than the disgust situation. The contempt profile differs in some other ways. First, the amount of distress and fear elicited in the contempt situation is substantially lower than in the other three. There is also slightly less guilt and shyness in the contempt situation than in the others. The direction of the difference is reversed in the case of joy, which is highest in the contempt situation. Virtually no joy is reported in the hostility, anger, or disgust situations, but the mean in contempt is well above the absolute minimum of 3.00.

One might conclude from this that the situations that elicit contempt are less likely to result in aggression than those that elicit anger and disgust. If this conclusion is correct, contempt is the most benign of the three emotions in the hostility triad. However, if we look again at the profile of emotions in contempt, there are some factors that militate against this conclusion. The contempt situation elicited the least amount of sadness, guilt, and fear, three emotions that might serve to inhibit aggression. Further, the contempt situation is somehow more enjoyable, and presumably the concomitant experience and subsequent behavior are more tolerable.

It is no accident that we speak of the "heat of anger," for the flushed face of the angry individual feels and looks hot. Aggression that occurs in anger is more likely to be a direct result of relatively intense emotion in an individual whose energy has been highly mobilized. On the contrary, since contempt can be considered the "cool" emotion in the hostility triad, it seems reasonable that it is the contempt situation in which the "cold-blooded" aggressor operates, since contempt is a distancing and devaluing emotion.

Table 12-4 shows that drives and affective-cognitive orientations are part of the hostility pattern. As expected, vigor, egotism, and skepticism were substantially elevated, and tranquility and sex were depressed. (In a few individual profiles sex was elevated. These subjects described hostility situations involving a person of the opposite sex.) The data of Table 12-4 show that hostility is a complex pattern of emotions, drives, and affective-cognitive orientations.

The foregoing analysis supports the notion that there are a variety of emotion profiles that involve enough hostility to increase the likelihood of aggression. Awareness of the similarities and differences among these situations and their emotion profiles may increase our understanding of the motivations underlying or accompanying aggressive acts.

The rank ordering of emotion means in the hostility situation was identical for males and females. Females reported slightly higher scores in anger, disgust, and contempt, but they exceed the males even more in sadness and surprise. The greater mean in distress suggests that the hostility situation elicits in the female an emotion that could tend to inhibit aggressive acts.

TABLE 12-4
Profile of Affects in an Imaged Hostilty Situation[a]

Scale	Mean
Anger	13.34
Contempt	12.73
Disgust	11.48
Sadness	8.57
Vigor	9.48
Skepticism	8.27
Egotism	7.16
Fear	6.05
Sociality	5.14
Guilt	5.09
Sex	3.64
Tranquility	3.66

[a]Scores derived from a modified DES (scales added for vigor, skepticism, egotism, sociality, sex, and tranquility): maximum score, 15; minimum score, 3.

Summary

Research on disgust has provided information on some of the essential characteristics of human emotions. The basic function of disgust is to motivate rejection of distasteful or contaminated substances. Even the facial expression of disgust, in its prototypical form, functions as an instrumental rejection response in that it results in the ejection of unwanted substances from the buccal cavity.

The disgust expression is mediated by a phylogenetically old part of the central nervous system, the brain stem. The expression can be elicited in decerebrate animals and humans. The evidence on the neural basis of the disgust expression strongly supports the hypothesis that basic emotion expressions are innate and universal. It also supports the hypothesis that emotions can occur as a result of neurochemical processes, independent of cognition. Of course, through experience, we can learn to become disgusted with a wide variety of objects, including ideas and even ourselves.

One theory of disgust holds that it is entirely a food-related emotion and that it is elicited only by the idea that the food about to be consumed has been contaminated directly or indirectly by a noxious or poisonous substance. In this framework, the experience of disgust is dependent on a higher-order cognitive capacity (ability to understand the idea of contamination) that does not emerge until about 7 years of age. This is a narrow view of disgust, but it provides a basis for understanding the development of emotion-cognition relations and learned emotion responses.

Contempt is associated with feelings of superiority. There is little to admire in the emotion of contempt. In evolutionary perspective, we can speculate that arousing contempt for rivals or threatening enemies may have inspired defensive behavior in behalf of the social unit. Even today, soldiers being prepared for combat are encouraged to feel contempt for the enemy. Presumably it bolsters the soldier's feelings of courage by making him feel superior and makes killing easier by dehumanizing the enemy. Perhaps it is possible to rationalize contempt for such phenomena as waste, pollution, oppression, and crime.

The negative aspects of contempt are easier to observe. Contempt is the principal emotion in all forms of prejudice and in "cold-blooded" killing.

Situations that elicit anger tend to elicit disgust and contempt. These three emotions can be considered as the hostility triad. However, it is important to distinguish between feelings of hostility and aggressive behavior. Hostility feelings may increase the likelihood of aggression, but there is no necessary relation between them. A person can experience feelings of hostility indefinitely without acting aggressively. Contrariwise, one can behave aggressively without feeling hostile.

Suggested Readings

Ekman, P., & Friesen, W. V. (1986). A new pan-cultural facial expression of emotion. *Motivation and Emotion, 10*, 159–168.

Cross-cultural evidence for a universal facial expression of contempt.

Fallon, A. E., Rozin, P., & Pliner, P. (1984). The child's conception of food: The development of food rejections with special reference to disgust and contamination sensitivity. *Child Development, 55*, 566–575.

A study of the development of disgust as it related to food rejection and the idea of contamination.

Izard, C. E., & Haynes, O. M. (1988). On the form and universality of the contempt expression: A challenge to Ekman and Friesen's claim of discovery. *Motivation and Emotion, 12*(1), 1–16.

Cross-cultural evidence for multiple facial signals of contempt.

Rosenstein, D., & Oster, H. (1988). Differential facial responses to four basic tastes in newborns. *Child Development, 59*(6), 1555–1568.

An objective analysis of the facial responses (including disgust expressions) of newborn infants to the four basic tastes.

Rozin, P., & Fallon, A. E. (1987). A perspective on disgust. *Psychological Review, 94*(1), 23–41.

A theory of the development of disgust (defined as a food-related emotion). Reviews evidence on the role of perceived contamination in disgust and food rejection. A model for explaining learned emotion responses and the development of affective-cognitive structures (emotion-cognition relations).

Steiner, J.E. (1973). The human gustofacial response. In J. F. Bosma (Ed.), *Fourth symposium on oral sensation and perception*. Rockville, MD: U.S. Department of Health, Education, and Welfare.

Demonstrates that the neural substrates of the disgust expression are in very old subcortical areas of the brain. Observations of human infants born without a functional cerebral cortex.

13

Fear and Anxiety

Fear is the emotion many people dread the most. A number of years ago, Izard (1971) did a survey of attitudes toward emotions in seven different cultures: American, English, German, Swedish, French, Greek, and Japanese. Responses were analyzed for males and females separately in each of the seven cultures. More of the subjects named fear than any other emotion when asked, "which emotion do you dread most?" Perhaps its dreadfulness helps account for the fact that fear is relatively infrequently experienced. The subjects in the various cultures reported experiencing sadness, anger, disgust, and contempt, and even shame much more frequently than they experienced fear.

Characteristics of Fear

Yet, fear is a very real part of our world. Fear is experienced in a wide variety of situations, though all of them have one thing in common. They are sensed or perceived as a threat to our security or safety. Jane experienced fear, along with anger and other emotions, when at age 16 her parents separated.

> I think the biggest resentment I felt was the fact that I was seldom asked how I was doing, particularly by my father. He somehow seemed to lose sight of the fact that, yes, I had ears and often overheard conversations that may not have been meant for me to hear, and yes, I also was hurting and afraid. I was fearful of what the future would hold. Divorce? Tears filled my eyes whenever I thought of it. It seemed like my family was in constant flux. I felt that while my parents were separated, I also was separated from them.

In the next paragraph, Jane's description of her experience will depict one of the common causes of fear—insecurity. Because her home was breaking up, she was literally losing her base of security. She felt like she was being cut loose from her anchor, her roots, and this leads to a feeling of loss of control, part of the experience of fear.

> As I left my home in New Jersey to come to the University of Delaware, I knew there was a strong possibility that I might never be returning to it again in the same context. My mother mentioned the fact that she thought that around September 20, she and my sister would be moving into Beall Garden Apartments. I tried to push that thought away, for it was inconceivable to me to no longer know the house I grew up in would ever exist in the same way again. I think the most prominent emotion felt at this time was fear. There was again that feeling of instability and now even insecurity. It seemed that life was tough enough with my own personal changes and my own questions of what the next 4 years had in store for me, without the added confusion of not knowing where home really would be.

Jane's sense of insecurity left her feeling as though important aspects of her life were out of her control. The resulting feeling of insecurity is one of the basic causes of fear. Such insecurity is sensed as a threat to our safety.

An intense experience of fear is remembered for a long time. You can probably remember a time during childhood when you were very scared. You can remember the situation as vividly as though it were yesterday. The scene associated with the fear experience seems to be stuck more or less permanently in your mind. People who suffer from phobias know perhaps better then anyone else how difficult it is to get rid of a fear of some special object, event, or situation, even though it doesn't make any sense anymore to have such fear. Managing fear, particularly in the case of phobias, continues to be a challenge in behavioral science.

Conquering a phobia often requires the help of a highly trained professional, a psychologist or psychiatrist. All of us, however, can learn something about managing fear, and I shall return to this topic later in the chapter.

Defining Fear

Fear is not the same as anxiety. It is a separate and distinct emotion, worthy of its own separate category. Seeing it as a separate, distinct, and single emotion clearly sets it apart from anxiety. Anxiety is a combination or pattern of emotions that includes fear but that also includes other emotions.

Seeing fear as a separate emotion and as distinct from anxiety will enable us to consider the specific effects of fear on cognition and action as well as the way it interacts with other emotions to influence behavior. For a brief working definition, we can say that fear consists of certain specific bodily changes, expressive behaviors, and the feeling that results from the apprehension of threat or danger. In infants and young children, as well as in all nonhuman animals, the threat or danger is most likely perceived as relating to the comfort and well-being of the physical self. The dread is of physical harm or injury. By giving fear this seemingly simple definition, we do not mean to underestimate its power. The subjective experience of fear is awesome. Paradoxically, it can freeze you in seemingly helpless immobility or send you fleeing with all your might, totally abandoning all thought and action not relevant to escape.

As we grow older, the nature of the objects of fear change. For most of us fear of harm or injury to the physical self may become relatively unimportant, at least in terms of the frequency with which it occurs. More common fears are those relating to self-esteem and pride, to the failures in achieving treasured goals, or losses of a psychological sort that cause earthquakes in our minds.

The Causes of Fear

Tomkins (1963) discussed the drives, other emotions, and cognitive processes as causes of fear. Bowlby (1973) and others have discussed the development of fear as a function of the quality of the child's attachment to the primary caregiver. Others have studied specific events or situations as causes of fear.

Drives and Homeostatic Processes as Causes of Fear

In comparison with emotions and cognition, drive and homeostatic processes constitute the least significant class of fear causes. A drive becomes psychologically important when it increases to a point where it signals a critical deficit and activates emotion. In some of these cases the emotion activated is fear. Tomkins (1962) gave the following example:

> When the need for air becomes critical enough to require drive activation it also activates affect, ordinarily a massive fear reaction, which quickly reaches panic proportions if the obstruction to drive satisfaction is not immediately removed. The need is so vital that the massive affect in addition to the awareness of suffocation represents an important safety factor in guaranteeing immediate attention to drive satisfaction. (p. 46)

Other Emotions as Causes of Fear

Potentially, another emotion may activate fear by the principle of contagion, discussed in Chapter 5. According to Tomkins, similarities at the neurophysiological level make startle and excitement activators of fear. He thinks a basic interest–surprise–fear relationship derives from similarities in the neurophysiological mechanisms underlying these emotions. Tomkins (1962) holds that "the sudden reduction of intense, enduring fear, if complete, releases joy, but if incomplete releases excitement" (p. 290). The reverse would be interest–excitement escalating to fear. Indirect support for the close relationship of fear and excitement can be found in Bull's (1951) study of hypnotically induced fear. She reported that her frightened subjects were caught in a conflict between the wish to investigate and the wish to escape. She considered this as evidence of the dual nature of fear. Differential emotions theory interprets the conflictful behavior as a result of the oscillation between fear (motivating escape behavior) and interest (motivating investigatory activities).

Specific excitement–fear or surprise–fear connections may be learned. Any of the other emotions may also become learned activators of fear. Fear itself may be an innate amplifier of fear. For example, becoming aware of the sensory feedback from the expressive behavior of fear may increase the feeling of fear. In this sense, the experience of fear is frightening.

Cognitive Processes

Fear (or any emotion) may be activated by appraisal of a situation as dangerous or by what Tomkins called a cognitively constructed cause. Indeed, cognitive processes constitute the most general and pervasive fear instigators. For example, fear of a specific object may be activated by a cognitive construction in memory or anticipation. Unfortunately, such a cognition may not be accurate or precise. So one may learn to fear the wrong situation, too many situations, or all situations and life in general. Further, the memory or anticipation of fear itself is sufficient to activate fear. Thus if an individual mistakenly identifies a person as a source of fear, he or she may nonetheless experience fear in thinking about this person, then in anticipating meeting him, and for the third time in actually seeing him again. In this way a person, object, or situation may become a source of fear first (1) through hypothesis formation (imagining possible causes of harm), then (2) through anticipation of harm, and finally (3) through confrontation of the constructed (or imagined) dreaded object (Tomkins, 1963, p. 66).

Natural Clues to Fear

As with all other emotions, it is probably not very fruitful to try to classify the causes of fear into sharply dichotomous categories of inborn versus learned. However, there probably are a few causes for each of the fundamental emotions that are deeply rooted in our evolutionary-biological heritage, but this is not a basis for alarm or pessimism. Even the effects of events we are biologically prepared to fear can be modified through learning and experience.

Rather than trying to dichotomize the causes of fear as innate versus learned, it is better to think in terms of the relative contribution of biology and experience to fear activation. The psychiatrist John Bowlby (1969) considers those objects, events, or situations that elicit dispositional tendencies to respond with fear as "natural clues" to danger. His terminology and thinking is influenced by ethologists—biologists who study animals in their natural habitat. Bowlby lists only four natural clues to danger: pain, being left alone, sudden change in stimulation, and rapid approach. These are not necessarily innate releasers of fear, but we are apparently biologically prepared to learn to fear the situations that give rise to them. Although there are only a few natural clues to danger, these natural clues give rise to many learned derivatives or cultural clues.

Pain and Pain Anticipation

Pain, the first natural clue to fear, is a powerful teacher. More specifically, the fear associated with *pain anticipation* greatly enhances learning. Any object, event, or situation associated with a pain experience may become a conditioned stimulus that when encountered again brings the situation and experience to mind. Exactly what the conditioned stimulus triggers internally is still a matter of debate. For a long time psychologists assumed that when an animal avoided a previously painful situation, it did so because the situation acted as a conditioned stimulus that actually reinstated the fear experience, which in turn caused the animal to avoid the situation. However, once animals have learned to avoid the dangerous situation, their ability to avoid it seems also to eliminate or greatly reduce any signs of fear. In many cases, animals perform avoidance actions time after time without any obvious signs of the emotion of fear.

This of course is very adaptive for animals and humans. It means that pain has done its job as a powerful teacher. That is, we can learn to avoid situations where pain is likely and not suffer any of the consequences, not even the fear that might be aroused if the pain were unavoidable. It is only when individuals are uncertain of their ability to avoid danger that pain anticipation triggers fear. With this in mind we can ask the question: What is really going on inside us, or what precisely is the motivation that guides the avoidance actions that we perform every day?

Consider the example of crossing a wide busy street where there is no traffic light. The danger of being injured or even killed is present, although unlikely. Yet despite the potential danger, most people would say that they are not afraid when they approach and find their way across the street. Although most of us have never been injured while crossing the street, for most people an on-rushing automobile is a learned clue to danger.

We do not have to experience the pain of a particular event to acquire learned fear or learned avoidance behavior. Indeed, many people who suffer from phobias cannot relate a single incidence of harm or injury due to the feared object. There is the possibility that there was an actual incidence of pain in relation to the object of fear and that the entire experience is forgotten, and we shall discuss a theory of this process in a later section. In any case, there are many fears or phobias for which there is no known basis in actual life experience. People have a phobia of snakes who have never been threatened, much less bitten, by a snake, and people have phobias of flying who have never suffered in an airplane crash. So fears and phobias may have a real basis in actually experienced pain or injury, or they may be constructed from our own fantasy and imagery.

Consider, again, crossing a wide busy street. In most instances you probably cross the street without experiencing fear. There is the possibility that as a toddler or young child learning to cross the street, you did experience some fear, instigated by the dire warnings of parent or caregiver. As an older child, adolescent, or adult, you may cross the street with no fear whatsoever. Indeed, your successful avoidance behavior has become a way of managing your fear and or protecting you from danger. There is a slight possibility that you do experience a mild degree of fear on some crossings, and it is well to remember that fear, like all of the other emotions, is not an all or none experience. You can experience such mild fear that it is sensed only as apprehension, or you can experience intense fear that is felt as terror. During the days when you were learning to cross a crowded busy street, your behavior may have been guided more by fear anticipation than by pain anticipation. Fear anticipation therefore remains as one possible motive that might still operate in the person who successfully avoids danger while crossing the street. Most people, however, probably come to a point in life where they no longer even anticipate fear as they approach the curb, and they cross the street simply because they are interested in something on the other side.

The foregoing analysis actually gives us a hierarchy of motivations that can operate as we develop the necessary skills for avoiding danger while crossing a busy street: pain anticipation, fear anticipation, interest. Under certain conditions, such as failure to anticipate the speed of an oncoming car, our interest can change to fear anticipation and our fear anticipation to pain anticipation and fear, and our hurried walk across the street may change to a fast run. That this hierarchy of motivations is always there is important to the maintenance of the vigilance necessary for successful avoidance behavior. The possibility that the interest that takes us across the street can readily and instantaneously change to fear keeps the visual and motor skills involved keenly honed.

Being Alone

The second natural clue to fear is being alone. Being alone in certain situations usually alerts us to potential dangers that might not exist if we were in the company of other persons. Remember the old adage, there is safety in numbers. Like all generalizations, this one has its exceptions, yet it remains a bit of folk wisdom that is often applicable.

The child left on its own to cross a busy street is at a much greater risk of injury than when crossing with an adult. Bowlby (1969) analyzed the data on traffic injuries to children in one of the boroughs of London. In 44% of the cases, the children were alone when they were injured, and in another 34%, the child was with an age-mate rather then an adult.

Adults, too, in many circumstances are in greater risk when they are alone. Obvious examples are when swimming, sailing, mountain climbing, running rapids in a canoe or raft, and exploring caves. A considerably more common example is walking alone in certain urban areas, especially after dark.

Sudden Change of Stimulation

There is not much systematic evidence for the potency of a sudden change of stimulation as a stimulus for fear, but one type of this condition was considered as a source of fear by the early behaviorist John B. Watson. Watson and Raynor (1920) conducted some studies with young infants in an effort to determine the innate emotions. His observations led him to conclude that sudden loss of support was a stimulus for fear. What Watson may have observed was a startle response.

Young infants will often show signs of negative emotions just from being removed from their comfortable position in their mothers' arms to the arms of an experimenter. Even this kind of change of stimulation can result in negative emotions or physical distress, but what is seen is not necessarily fear. Perhaps to make a sudden change of stimulation a valid natural clue to danger, we would have to qualify it something like this: a sudden change of stimulation to which an individual cannot readily accommodate may be perceived as a clue to danger and fear.

Rapid Approach

Bowlby also mentions rapid approach as a natural clue to fear. In this case, too, the evidence is not strong. Bower (1971) interpreted the newborn infant's avoidance of an apparent looming object as fear. However, he did not have the advantage of contemporary objective systems for coding expressions of fear. Consequently, his criteria for judging fear would not meet present-day standards. When the baby turned its head and cried. Bower assumed that fear was present. Although this is not an unreasonable assumption, the baby might also turn its head and cry as a basic defensive maneuver or in physical distress.

There is one type of evidence that suggests that under certain conditions rapid approach is indeed a clue to anger. Many years ago the psychiatrist René Spitz observed that babies around 8 months of age sometimes responded to strangers with fear or anxiety. For many years the notion that stranger anxiety suddenly appeared in all infants at around this age was widely reported in textbooks and journals. After years of systematic research, investigators finally determined that infants do not regularly show fear to the approach of a stranger. They may show interest, joy, or anger. It is only under certain conditions that they may express fear when a stranger approaches. The qualities of the stranger and the rapidity with which the stranger approaches the infant are important factors in determining whether or not the infant expresses fear. A tall, male stranger who approaches the infant rapidly is much more likely to elicit fear than an approaching child. At least in infants, rapid approach becomes a natural clue to danger under certain conditions (Lewis and Rosenblum, 1978).

Strangeness

Strangeness should be considered as an addition to Bowlby's list of natural clues to danger. Strangeness can be seen as part of a category of stimuli that some psychologists have discussed in terms of a discrepancy hypothesis (Bronson, 1972; Kagan, Kearsley, & Zelazo, 1978). In its general form this hypothesis states that any stimulus that is sufficiently discrepant is potentially emotionally arousing. Some believe that the degree of discrepancy may influence the type and intensity of emotion that is instigated. While this hypothesis cannot explain why a particular discrete emotion is aroused by a certain discrepant stimulus, the hypothesis does have some explanatory value. A mildly discrepant stimulus may elicit interest, whereas a highly discrepant stimulus may elicit fear.

When the stimulus is both discrepant and strange, that is, different in degree and in kind from anything previously experienced, the likelihood of fear is increased. So how does strangeness differ from discrepancy? The term *strangeness* in this context implies a difference that is not only novel but weird. The weirdness is somehow perceived as strange and threatening. For example, a chimpanzee with a normal-sized head but a very small, yet otherwise functional body would probably strike a fellow chimpanzee as highly strange. As Hebb has shown, seeing a chimpanzee head with no body at all frightens other chimpanzees.

Evidence from research with human infants tends to verify Hebb's observation (Schwartz, Izard, & Ansul, 1985). Young infants of 7 and 14 months of age were shown three-dimensional masks of human faces with distorted or disarranged features. The masks were replicas of those used by Kagan *et al.* (1978). The experimenters arranged a little "theater" within the lab. The infant was seated approximately 4 feet in front of an opening in a partition that surrounded the baby on three sides. As the curtain opened, either a mask of a normal face or a mask of an eyeless (distorted) face was brought up in front of the baby either slowly or rapidly.

Not all of the infants showed the same emotion. Some merely showed intense interest. Some protested and showed anger. Others showed a full-face genuine fear expression. About 20% of the infants showed fear at 7 months of age, and about 35% of the infants showed fear at 14 months of age. The analysis of the data showed that it really did not matter whether the mask was brought up slowly or rapidly or whether it was a normal face or distorted eyeless face. Emotion responses across the different conditions and different types of masks were essentially the same. The experimenters concluded that the mask, which was of normal head size and mounted on a 12-by-12-inch white board, was discrepant and strange to infants in the same way that Hebb's disembodied heads were to chimpanzees. So even though it is difficult to define precisely what constitutes strangeness or weirdness, it appears to qualify as one of the natural clues to danger.

Heights

One other stimulus may serve as a natural clue to fear in human beings. At least under certain conditions and after certain developmental milestones have been passed, height elicits fear in human infants. Studies of infants responses to heights are conducted with an apparatus called a visual cliff. A visual cliff is a glass-topped table. Under one half of the table there is a checkered cover very near the glass top. In the middle there is a solid starting board on which the infant can be placed. On the other half of the table the glass top is separated from the same checkered cover by about 2 feet. Thus, if the infant sits on the starting board and looks in one direction, she sees what appears to be a solid surface. If she looks in the other direction, she sees what appears to be a cliff, or drop off.

Campos and his colleagues (1978) used two techniques in studying infants' responses to the visual cliff. One was to place the infant on the starting board and attempt to use various means of coaxing her to cross the deep side. In the other technique—direct placement—the baby was gently lowered to either the shallow or the deep side of the visual cliff.

Campos discovered that very young infants (6 months or less in age) did not show signs of fear on the visual cliff when tested by the direct placement technique. Some scientists thought that infants at these younger ages did not show fear because they had no depth perception and thus were incapable of perceiving the danger. However, Campos, using the direct placement technique, showed that infants did apparently perceive a difference between the shallow and the deep sides. These data were derived by measuring the infants' heart rates during the experiment. When infants were placed on the shallow side, their heart rate showed a deceleration. Heart rate deceleration had been shown by Lacey (1967) to be characteristic of orienting and with the intake and processing of new information. As noted in an earlier chapter, the emotion of interest in accompanied by an initial decrease in heart rate. Consequently, it is reasonable to assume that young infants placed on the shallow side of the visual cliff experienced interest, and processed the information available to their visual system.

When infants were placed on the deep side of the visual cliff, their heart rates accelerated sharply. Several studies have shown that negative emotions, including fear, are characterized by heart rate acceleration. Campos's data suggested that infants did indeed detect a difference between the two sides of the visual cliff, and the only difference that is obvious, even to the adult, is the difference in the apparent distance between the checkered cover and the glass-top table. Campos's data were indirect evidence that infants of 6 or 7 months of age were capable of detecting the drop off.

A few years later, experimenters designed a study to test directly whether young infants had depth perception (Fox, Aslin, Shea, & Dumais, 1980). The infant was exposed to two-dimensional and three-dimensional patterns that were identical except for the extra dimension that corresponded to depth. Fox and his colleagues showed that infants as early as 4 months of age had at least the rudiments of depth perception. Thus, Campos's indirect evidence based on heart rate and Fox's more direct evidence based on perceptual discrimination of two- versus three-dimensional stimuli make a strong case for the infant's ability to perceive the drop off by about 4 months of age.

Some factor other than lack of depth perception was accounting for the absence of fear in infants placed on the visual cliff between 4 and 7 months of age. In a series of ingenuous experiments, Campos and his colleagues showed that the factor that apparently accounts for the emergence of fear on the visual cliff is not the development of depth perception but the ability to perceive depth plus about 3 weeks of self-locomotion or crawling experience. There remains the possibility that some other factors may be involved, but Campos and his colleagues have not been able to detect them. At present it appears that although infants learn to crawl at varying ages from about 7 to 11 months, they demonstrate fear on the visual cliff only after they have had about 3 weeks of crawling experience.

Cultural Clues to Danger: The Role of Learning and Experience

We have already considered one of the ways that fear is learned—simple conditioning, or associative learning. In this case, a fear experience is associated with some neutral stimulus, and the neutral stimulus becomes capable of eliciting the fear in the absence of the original (unconditional) stimulus. The stimuli that are associated with pain, for example, become conditional stimuli, and they are capable of signalling danger and eliciting fear. Strictly speaking such conditioning requires that the individual experience the unconditioned stimulus (e.g., pain) in the presence of stimuli that are to become conditioned. Following this strict interpretation, it is uncertain as to how many of our fear experiences can really be accounted for in this way. Many people who suffer from fears and phobias cannot trace their problem to a traumatic experience or some unconditioned stimulus that caused pain or distress. More about this later.

Observational learning is responsible for many human fears, and it has been shown to be very efficient under certain circumstances. When a young child observes a fear response in a parent there is a very good possibility the child will immediately learn to fear the same object.

Mineka, Davidson, Cook, and Keir (1984) have studied the role of observational learning in the development of fears in rhesus monkeys. Some of the monkeys were reared in the wild and not brought to the laboratory until they were between 4 and 6 years of age. These monkeys showed a strong fear of snakes and objects resembling snakes. Monkeys born and reared in the laboratory with no experience in the wild did not show fear of snakes.

Although the wild-reared monkeys had been imported from India at least 24 years prior to the studies, their fear of snakes still persisted! As we have noted before, fear is a powerful teacher, and the fear experience has a way of making permanent impressions on our minds.

In Mineka's observational learning studies, a wild-reared monkey, who showed fear of snakes, served as a model for laboratory-reared monkeys, who quickly learned to show fear of snakes. The objects used to test the animal's reactions were a live boa constrictor, a lifelike model of a snake, a rubber toy snake, a black electrical cord, and four neutral objects such as a square wood block. In the test situation, the animals would see a Plexiglas box moving toward them. On the back of the box was a ledge on which food was placed. The animals could simply reach through the cage and obtain the food reward from the ledge on the back of the approaching Plexiglas box. On test trials the approaching Plexiglas box contained one of the test objects—the snake, snakelike objects, or neutral objects. When the Plexiglas box contained the snake, the wild-reared monkeys exhibited a number of behaviors that Mineka interpreted as signs of fear. When tested in the absence of a wild-reared monkey, the laboratory-reared monkeys did not show signs of fear and showed no differences in their reactions to the snakes, snakelike objects, and neutral objects. However, when the laboratory-reared monkeys were able to observe the reactions of the wild-reared monkey, they quickly learned to fear the snake and snakelike objects. Mineka's tests showed that this fear persisted for a long time. She also showed that the observers did not have to be offspring of the model to learn the fear. Interestingly, however, she found that when the model was a parent the learning was a little more efficient and the fear behaviors a little more intense.

Many lessons can be learned from Mineka's fascinating studies of observational learning. The studies show quite clearly that one does not have to have direct experience with the dangerous stimulus to learn to fear it. Her studies also demonstrate the power of expressive behavior as a teacher. The observers were not in direct contact with the model. They were never touched by the model during the study. All of their information came from the signals of fear that were transmitted by another monkey. It was as though the model's fear signals were the first stimulus for fear in the observers, and the snake was actually the conditioned stimulus. Mineka's studies suggest that many of our fears can be explained on the basis of observational learning. When a young child observes fear in a parent, a sibling, or even a stranger, the object, event, or surrounding situation may become a source of fear.

That the fear expressions of Mineka's models may have actually served as prepotent or biologically prepared stimuli in observer monkeys is supported by a number of experimental studies of fear expressions in conditioning studies. Ohman and Dimberg (1978) and Orr and Lanzetta (1980) showed that conditioning is facilitated significantly more when fear faces are paired with shock (as the UCS) than when happy faces are paired with shock. Even in the absence of reinforcement, the display of a fear face intensifies a subject's emotional reaction to a previously conditioned stimulus. Similarly, the display of a fear face during the extinction of a conditioned stimulus lengthens the extinction process. Lanzetta and Orr (1986) had subjects look at expressions of joy or fear during fear conditioning with electric shock as the UCS. They found that even after electrodes were disconnected and there was no rational basis for expecting shock, subjects who were looking at a fearful facial expression showed a higher level of ANS activation (higher levels of skin conductance activity) than did the subjects who were looking at joy expressions. Taken together, these studies suggest that the fear expression is a prepotent or biologically prepared stimulus for fear. This may explain why modeling an expression in a fear situation (as in Mineka's studies) facilitates learning of conditioned fear by the observer.

The Attachment Figure as the Primary Model for Learned Fear

Interestingly, Mineka found that not all laboratory-reared monkeys learned to be afraid of snakes when they observed the wild-reared monkey's behavior. In each study, something like 10–30% of the observer monkeys did not show fear. This raises the interesting question as to the reason for this difference. Is it a function of an inborn or unlearned trait of the individual or to differences in various aspects of the life history including rearing experience? One potentially important source of individual differences in tendencies to learn fear or to become fearful relates to the very first social relationship, the attachment that the infant develops with its primary caregiver or attachment figure.

An Insecure Attachment as a Source of Fear

John Bowlby (1969) pioneered in emphasizing the importance of the primary caregiver, or attachment figure, as an important source of security on the one hand, and insecurity and fear on the other. It has been said that misery loves company. Fear loves company too, but the ameliorating effect of company is better if it is someone who is unafraid or capable of controlling his or her fear. We have all had the experience of having our fears abated by the presence of someone we trust. This is the flip side of the condition in which we find our fears escalating when we are isolated or alone in a situation we perceive as dangerous. The presence of a trusted companion can be a strong deterrent to fear, and most people would agree with Bowlby that for the child the most trusted companion is the attachment figure.

Bowlby maintains that during our formative years, mother and father (or primary caregivers) are our most trusted companions and our primary attachment figures. If during these formative years, a child finds the caregiver both accessible and responsive, the child develops a secure attachment. The child can then use the attachment figure as a secure base from which to explore and expand its horizons.

Bowlby holds that individuals who develop a secure attachment are less susceptible to fear, as long as confidence in the attachment figure remains. Bowlby notes that confidence in the attachment figure continues to develop through infancy, childhood, and adolescence and then tends to remain stable throughout the rest of life.

Bowlby concluded that a child or adolescent's fearfulness is rarely if ever based on purely imaginary events or mere projections from within the individual. Children and adolescents who are prone to fear probably actually experienced a great deal of insecurity in the attachment relationship, the attachment figure proving to be inaccessible or unresponsive at critical times. Major events that lead to insecure attachment and proneness to fear, according to Bowlby, are threats of being abandoned and risks of losing a parent (often perceived when parents are quarreling).

Bowlby argued that anxious or insecure attachments give rise to some of the phobias of childhood. His clinical investigations convinced him that school phobia stemmed from one of four patterns of family interaction, all of which pointed to types of insecure or anxious attachment. In many cases, the child's fear or anxiety was a reflection of fear in one or more of the parents. Bowlby also noted that anxious attachment may lead to agoraphobia (fear of open spaces or of leaving home) and that the patterns of family interaction are very similar for school phobia and agoraphobia. Indeed, many agoraphobics report having experienced school phobia in earlier years.

Phobias

It is generally agreed that phobias, intense and often irrational fears of specific objects or events, are learned, but there is disagreement as to how they are learned. Some think a phobia is a simple conditioned emotional response. Others think the conditioning is added to a biological predisposition (or preparedness) to fear certain stimuli.

Jacobs and Nadel (1985) have argued that adults' fears and phobias have characteristics that do not fit a conditioning model:

1. Phobic clients cannot remember when the feared object was paired with a noxious event. Phobias seem just to happen, without apparent cause.
2. People with phobias are able to report many noxious events that did not lead to a fear or phobia.
3. Sometimes a mild fear is exacerbated following a period of stress that is not characterized by any specific traumatic event.
4. Once a fear or phobia develops, its manifestations occur without apparent relation to context or specific event.

5. Some fears (e.g., agoraphobias) generalize so broadly that the individual cannot specify what is frightening.
6. The fears of many phobic clients do not extinguish after years of exposure to the fear stimulus, even in the absence of aversive consequences. This is true despite the client's realization that the fear is irrational.

Jacobs and Nadel's work suggests that two conditions can set the stage for a learned fear that may later emerge as a phobia. Both of these conditions, immaturity of the nervous system and severe stress, can render the context learning system dysfunctional. Jacobs and Nadel hold that during infancy, learning is mediated by the taxon system. This system can mediate the learning of the fear response, but it does not help in learning contextual information.

During the first 2 years of life, the hippocampus, the brain mechanism that mediates contextual learning, is thought to be too immature to be functional. During this period, the infant may experience fear in response to a natural elicitor (e.g., height, being left alone, strangeness), and the fear may be associated with various objects that become conditioned fear stimuli. Because infants are incapable of contextual or locale learning, they store no contextual information. Thus, should the conditioned fear occur in later life, the individual has no way of understanding when, where, or under what circumstances the fear response is unnecessary and inappropriate. These context-free fears that are learned in infancy are particularly apt to reemerge in later life under conditions of severe stress, because stress renders the hippocampal–locale system dysfunctional, as it was in infancy. When this happens, behavioral control devolves on the stress-sensitized taxon system. In this state, the reemergence or relearning of an infantile fear experience is possible. In addition to this reemergence or relearning of fears that were stored in infancy and later forgotten (for lack of contextual data), the stage can be set for the establishing of a phobia anytime severe stress renders the locale learning system (hippocampus) dysfunctional.

McNally (1989) criticized some of the premises of Jacobs and Nadel. He cited evidence that suggests that only animal-phobic people commonly fail to recall the onset of their phobias, probably because they were learned very early. He also argued that agoraphobias do not manifest themselves without regard to contexts. He suggested that the various fear-inducing environments have a common denominator—they elicit the feeling of being trapped and helpless. Thus, elevators, business meetings, shopping malls, and theaters may all have the same psychological effect on the agoraphobic, although the environments appear to be quite different to the normal person. Finally, McNally observed that phobics are highly skilled at avoiding their feared stimuli. They avoid the object before they can experience any diminution of fear that might result from an uneventful exposure. Therefore, the long-term persistence of untreated phobias may be a result of lack of exposure rather than a failure of extinction.

"In-Born" versus Learned Fears

Some emotions, or at least some emotion expressions, apparently have innate releasers, or, at least, biologically prepared stimuli. That is, if the neonate is given the appropriate or effective stimulus the emotion expression is very likely to appear. For example, a bitter taste tends to elicit the disgust expression in the newborn infant. As we learned in Chapter 11, pain and certain types of stress regularly elicit anger expression in very young infants. Movement, especially of human faces, elicits interest in the newborn, and a high-pitched human voice will elicit the social smile at 3 or 4 weeks of age.

The evidence for biologically prepared stimuli for fear is neither clear nor strong, but there does seem to be a limited set of stimuli or conditions that may be considered as prepotent because we apparently learn to be afraid of them very easily. In Mineka's studies, for example, the monkeys showed the greatest number of fear behaviors to the real snake, and the number of fear behaviors toward the other objects diminished as they became less snakelike in appearance. Apparently, monkeys are biologically prepared to learn to fear snakes.

Some objects and situations more readily alert us to danger than do others. These are the ones we have called natural clues to fear: pain, being alone, strangeness, rapid approach, sudden changes in stimulation, and possibly heights. Obviously, it would not be adaptive for all of these stimuli to be perceived as dangerous under all conditions. If we were not able to cope with being alone, we would never achieve independence and self-reliance. If we could not tolerate the strange, we would never be able to leave our familiar surroundings. Nevertheless, it is useful to have an understanding of the natural clues to fear. Many of the other objects and events that tend to arouse fear in us can be understood as derivatives or relatives of the natural clues. It is adaptive to be alerted to the possible dangers than can exist under certain conditions. We do not actually have to experience fear in order to avoid danger, if our perception of the situation alerts us in time to maneuver through or around it.

Some Antecedents and Consequences of Fear

College subjects' free-response descriptions of the antecedents and consequences of fear are quite consistent with the psychology of fear presented in the foregoing sections. The data are presented in Table 13-1.

It appears that there is a very wide variety of sources of learned fears. Under certain circumstances even success can be a source of fear. Horner (1972) introduced the idea of fear of success to explain sex differences in achievement behavior. Early studies of this phenomenon suggested that women, as compared to men, show a weaker relation between desire to succeed and actual success. Later studies found no sex differences in fear of failure (Zuckerman & Wheeler, 1975).

TABLE 13-1
Antecedents and Consequences of Fear[a]

Responses	Percentage of subjects giving responses
Antecedents	
Feelings	
1. Threatened, in danger, in trouble, overpowered	31.2
2. Fear synonyms	26.4
3. Alone, lost, isolated, rejected	16.0
4. Threat to self-esteem, impending failure, feels inadequate	15.2
5. Other	11.2
Thoughts	
1. Of threatening, danger, or trouble	36.8
2. Of death, loneliness, sadness	28.0
3. Of loss of self-esteem, failure, of being inadequate	19.2
4. Of things not understsood (supernatural, etc.)	4.0
5. Other	12.0
Actions	
1. Something legally or morally wrong, harmful	32.0
2. Something dangerous	22.4
3. SOmething that threatens self-esteem	20.0
4. Panicky, irrational things	8.0
5. Trying to escape. run away, withdraw, protect self	7.2
6. External force (caught using drugs, drafted, ect.)	5.6
7. Other	4.8
Consequences	
Feelings	
1. Fear synonyms	31.5
2. Nervous tension	17.7
3. Inadequate, insecure	14.6
4. Need to escape, run away, withdraw, protect self	10.0
5. Lost, lonely, isolated, rejected	6.2
6. Surprise synonyms	3.8
7. In danger, physically threatened	3.1
8. Shame synonyms	3.1
9. Other	10.0
Thoughts	
1. How to escape, withdraw, protect self	43.1
2. Anticipating possible consequences or reaction to event	29.2
3. How to regain control of self or situation	8.5
4. Trying to understand causes or reasons for emotion	5.4
5. Other	13.8
Actions	
1. Run away, withdraw, protect self	45.4
2. Face situation, cope, try to act courageously	33.1
3. Something panicky, impractical	9.2
4. Talk to someone, get with trusted friend	2.8
5. Takes action or aggresses against object or situation	2.3
6. Other	9.2

[a]*N* = approximately 130 college students.

Hyland, Curtis, and Mason (1985) tried to resolve this controversy with the use of separate measures of fear of failure as a motive and as a cultural stereotype. They concluded that fear of failure is both a motive and a cultural stereotype. They found that there were sex differences in fear of success when the measure taps a motive to avoid behavior that is "inappropriate" for women—inappropriate in terms of the prevailing cultural stereotype. These findings appear to be sound, but it should be noted that cultural stereotypes change, and today's women are challenging the stereotype in choice of profession, behavior in heterosocial relationships, and in many other ways.

The Expression of Fear: Distinguishing Fear from Other Emotions

The older literature is notably deficient in validated lists of responses that characterize fear as distinguished from physical distress or even from anger and sadness. One of the more careful analyses of the problem is that of Bowlby (1973).

Bowlby listed a number of observable expressive and motor activities that he considers as indexes of fear: "They include wary watching combined with inhibition of action, a frightened facial expression accompanied perhaps by trembling or crying, cowering, hiding, running away, and also seeking contact with someone and perhaps clinging to him or her" (p. 88). Bowlby did not suggest that this was an exhaustive list, and his language was tentative when he described four reasons why these diverse forms of behavior could be grouped together: (1) many, though not all of them, tend to occur simultaneously or sequentially; (2) events that elicit one of them tend to elicit others (though not necessarily all others); (3) most, though not all of them, serve a single biological function, that of protection; (4) after the acquisition of language the persons exhibiting these responses say, when asked, that they are "feeling afraid or anxious or alarmed" (p. 88).

Crying cannot be considered an unequivocal index of fear. Crying is the prototypical response in sadness, and it may accompany anger or joy. Furthermore, a self report of "feeling anxious" is by no means a clear and unequivocal indication of fear and fear alone (Izard, 1972).

The list of fear indicators proposed by Charlesworth (1974) includes: "Momentary arresting or slowing of ongoing behaviors or prolonged freezing, heightened vigilance or awareness, stimulus-distance maintaining or expanding behavior, serious or fearful facial expressions . . ." p. 263). Charlesworth complicated the picture, however, with the observation that fear can be accompanied or followed by withdrawal, flight, wary exploration, and even smiling or laughing. Obviously this list of fear indicators, as well as those of Bowlby (1969) and Gray (1971), is in need of refinement and revision.

In some ways, the work of Kagan *et al.* (1978) on the development of negative affect in infants supports a more differentiated analysis of affects; they suggest that there are at least four "distress states" that have been called fear. The problem with their analysis is that they have used the term *distress* in a rather general fashion, considering it as virtually equivalent to a state manifested by crying. According to Kagan *et al.*, the causes of distress states are (1) unassimilated discrepancy, (2) anticipation of an undesirable event, (3) unpredictability, (4) recognition of inconsistency between belief and behavior, and (5) recognition of dissonance among beliefs. Only the last one of these is identified by Kagan *et al.* as a source of the distress state "typically called anxiety." Ultimately, their use of the term distress is vague and ambiguous. It may refer to fear or other negative emotions.

Two other investigators have raised problems with the taxonomy of fear causes and fear indicators. The work of Sroufe and his collaborators (e.g., Sroufe, Waters, & Matas, 1974; Sroufe & Wunsch, 1972) has shown that a number of the frequently used stimuli for fear actually produce laughter, interest, and approach behavior. Rheingold (1974) noted that many investigators have reported expressions of surprise in response to experimental manipulations designed to elicit fear. She also pointed out that infants often responded positively and in an affiliative fashion to strangers.

Some emotion researchers believe that the most reliable and unambiguous signs of fear are in facial expressions. In the full-face expressions of fear, the brows are lifted and slightly pulled together creating deeper wrinkles in the middle of the forehead than on the lateral portions. Eyes are opened wide, and sometimes the upper lids are raised, showing the white of the eyes between the eyelid and the pupil. The corners of the mouth are retracted straight back and the mouth is usually slightly open. The photographs in Figure 13-1 illustrate most of the characteristics of the fear expression. The first two have clear signals of fear only in the eye and mouth regions of the face. The third photograph is a full-face expression, with fear signals in all three regions of the face.

The first two photographs in Figure 13-1 were among those used in cross-cultural research on the universality of emotion expressions. These photos have clear fear signals only in the eyes yet in all the cultures sampled, they were recognized as expressions of fear.

FIGURE 13-1. Expressions of fear varying in intensity and completeness.

The protypical fear expression is modified through learning and experience and, hence, we see it rarely. We learn to mask and disguise our feelings of fear, and only under the most intense stimulation or in unguarded moments are we likely to make the full-face expression of fear.

The Subjective Experience of Fear

A highly potent emotion, fear has very marked effects on perception, thought, and action. In fear, attention tends to be sharply and narrowly focused on the object or situation that signals danger. Intense fear causes "tunnel vision." That is, it greatly reduces the range of perceptions, thoughts, and choices that one can make. In the same fashion it reduces the number of options for action. We feel compelled to respond only in those ways that will reduce the threat or danger that we perceive.

As we shall see, the effects of fear may serve adaptive functions. If fear is justified, and if we are able to marshal our energies and quickly reduce the threat to our safety, then the focused attention and behavior will have served its purpose.

The mildest form of fear is experienced as a feeling of apprehension or uneasiness. As fear becomes stronger, we feel uncertain about our well-being. Intense fear is experienced as complete insecurity or uncertainty about safety. There is the feeling that everything is running out of control. There is a sense of impending damage to the physical or psychological self and, in the extreme, a sense of threat to life itself.

Tomkins (1963) has called fear the most toxic of the emotions. It is potentially toxic in the sense that one can be literally frightened to death, as, for example, in the case of voodoo death. In extreme fear or terror the autonomic nervous system, which innervates the heart and other vital organs, is highly activated. Terror can create such a level of overactivity in the autonomic nervous system that vital organs are overloaded to the point of failure, and death. That extreme fear is a potentially dangerous experience may explain why we sometimes postpone fear the way Julie did the night she was robbed at gun point.

> It was Christmas Eve and I was walking from my house to meet my boyfriend about one-half mile away. I knew that there was going to be a ton of my friends meeting at another friend's apartment, so I packed my purse full of gifts for my friends. I had $90.00 that I had collected to help buy a camera for a friend, as well as jewelry and other gifts. I left my house around 7:30 p.m., full of excitement, anticipating how much fun the night and next day were going to be. I was about three blocks away from my friend's apartment when a man jumped out from the bushes and tried to grab my purse.

Julie's first reaction to the robber was probably startle. She called it "shock" and "surprise," both of which are fleeting in nature. Once the startle and surprise was over, probably only a matter of a second or so, Julie responded with anger, suggesting that she sensed the robber's intention as an insult. The anger may have served to keep matters from getting worse than they did. She found the strength to go on to the party and "let off steam." The anger precluded the onset of fear and prevented it from destroying her evening.

> I was shocked but still I held onto the purse; then the man yanked my head back by my hair and stuck a gun to my bare neck. Then he told me to "give him the purse or he'd blow my fucking head off." I was in such a state of surprise and shock that time was frozen—I couldn't think or believe this was happening. Then a million thoughts rushed into my head; should I hit him over the head with a bottle I had in my left hand, should I say something, what should I do? Then I felt the gun on my neck and heard his voice and my hand relinquished its hold on the purse. He grabbed it and ran.
>
> I stood there stunned and dumbfounded. Then all of a sudden, and for no apparent reason, the powerful emotion of anger came over me. I was so mad that I was in a daze. I just know I started screaming and with clinched fists ran in a blind rage after the man. I remember thinking "how dare he, this must be a dream," then remembering all the important things in my purse and wondering why my legs wouldn't move faster.
>
> He got away and I'm glad because I have no idea what I would have done if I caught him! All night I was filled with red hot anger. I just wanted to slam my fists into anything, to hurt and destroy things. I felt powerful, and strong. I wanted to find him and strangle him. A friend was nice enough to let me smash empty bottles in his bathtub and I'll never forget how satisfying the sound of breaking glass was. I doubt if I'll ever be able to let my anger out in that fashion again, but I'll always remember flinging with full force a bottle into the tub.

In the next paragraph, Julie describes a phenomenon that we know exists but cannot fully explain—the experience of delayed or postponed fear. The fear did not come for quite some time—it might have been more than a day. (She is not specific about the length of the interval, but we know it was not until she reflected on this event and appraised its potential danger.) Why did she not see the danger immediately? Several factors may have contributed to the late awareness of danger. She was excited and happy, on her way to meet her boyfriend and join a party. The unexpectedness of the intruder startled and greatly surprised her. There were three stimuli for anger—the pain from his pulling her hair and jerking her head back, the frustration of losing her purse with her valuables and ID, and the insult of being treated so crudely. Nevertheless, the assault could have immediately precipitated terror, and we cannot say precisely why it did not.

> Later, after time to think about that night, I experienced a strong emotion change from anger to fear. He could have done anything to me and I would have been completely powerless, because you can't argue with a man with a gun unless you are willing to die, and I'm not. I got this sick, nauseous feeling and a pounding heart when I recreated the scene. I felt very vulnerable and alone. I became afraid to walk outside alone at night. If I had to do so, my nerves were on edge. I would watch all around me, turning around often, and walking with a shaky fast walk, on the verge of breaking into a run. I continued to have these jittery, jumpy feelings for a while until I finally got over the worst fear. Still, 2 years later I'm more alert and suspicious of a stranger, and on Christmas Eve I have a strong fear of even walking to my car alone.

Perhaps another reason why Julie experienced her fear long after the threat to her safety was that she saw no means of escape. As we shall see, the primary function of fear is to organize and motivate escape from danger. When there is no escape, the experience of fear, with its powerful effect on our nervous system and vital organs, may simply add to the danger. Even though Julie's fear was postponed, it had a strong and lasting effect on her. It increased her vigilance in potentially dangerous situations, and this may well prove adaptive and beneficial in the long run.

Experiential Dimensions and Patterns of Emotions in the Fear Situation

The DRS experiential dimensions in the fear situation (Bartlett–Izard study) are presented in Figure 13-2. As expected, the dimension of tension showed a higher mean in the fear situation than in the other emotion situations. The mean for tension was almost 50% higher than the next highest mean shown in Figure 13-2, that for impulsiveness. The mean for impulsiveness was substantially lower than in the anger situation, about equal to that in the sadness situation, and somewhat higher than in any of the other negative emotion situations.

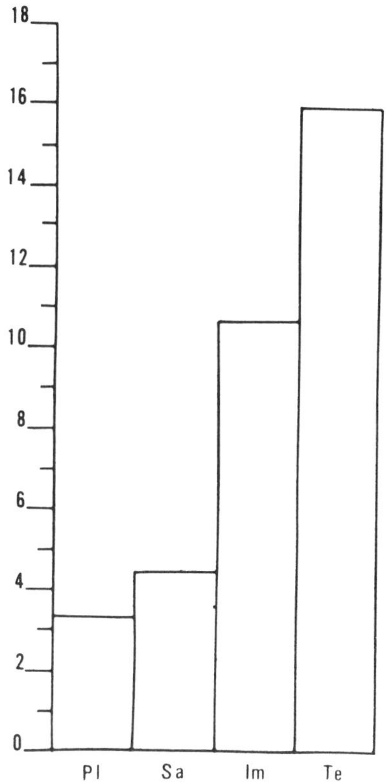

FIGURE 13-2. The DRS profile of dimensions in the fear situation. Pl, pleasantness; Sa, self-assurance; Im, impulsiveness; Te, tension.

The moderately high impulsiveness that characterizes the fear situation could be considered as adaptive, in view of the fact that the individual needs to experience a readiness to respond. On the other hand, the impulsiveness could lead to maladaptive behavior in the form of panicky responses that are not effective in dealing with the situation. The subjects had a higher mean on the dimension of activeness (not shown in Figure 13-2) in the fear situation than in any other negative emotion situation except anger. The combination of feelings suggested by this pattern—highly tense, active, impulsive—supports the idea that strong fear effectively supports only one type of behavior, that of avoidance or escape, which may take the form of "flight to one another" for protection. Other types of fear-related behaviors are a function of the interaction of fear with other emotions.

The mean for self-assurance was lower in the fear situation than in any other negative emotion situation. The differences in self-assurance between the fear situation and sadness situation, and between the fear situation and the anger situation, were statistically significant.

The DES profile of emotions in the fear situation is presented in Figure 13-3.

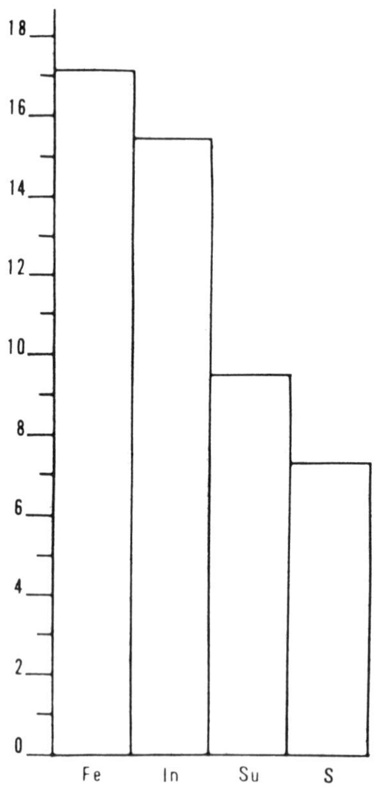

FIGURE 13-3. The DES profile of emotions in an imagined fear situation. Fe, fear; In, interest; Su, surprise; S, sadness.

The differences among the four emotions shown in the profile (fear, interest, surprise, and sadness) are all statistically significant. Not shown in the profile, the emotions of anger, guilt, and shyness are significantly lower than any of the preceding four emotions and are not significantly different from one another. The relatively low means of these three emotions suggest that ordinarily none of them plays a highly significant role in a fear situation, but for some individuals any of these emotions may be a part of the emotion dynamics.

Perhaps the most important aspect of the emotion profile in the fear situation is the fact that the three emotions with the highest means (fear, interest, and surprise) are the three that, according to Tomkins, are stimulation-increase emotions. The profile furnishes indirect support for the interrelatedness of these emotions at the neurophysiological level.

The high fear and interest in the fear-situation profile supports the differential emotions theory hypothesis that the duality of fear, discussed by Bull (1951) and Kierkegaard (1944), actually consists of fear-motivated avoidance and interest-motivated approach and exploration. How the individual eventually responds to the fear situation will depend on the relative intensity of fear and interest and the interactions of other emotions in the profile.

The Functions of Fear

Nina Bull's (1951) study of hypnotically induced fear provides interesting information on the experience of this emotion and on its seemingly paradoxical effects—causing the individual to freeze or flee. During hypnotically induced fear, Bull's subject made statements like this: "I wanted to turn away . . . I couldn't . . . I was too afraid to move." Another subject reported: "My whole body stiffened . . . I wanted to run away . . . I was petrified and couldn't move."

We don't really know for sure why fear sometimes leads to freezing—the total inability to move. Perhaps it is something inherited from animal ancestors who had to cope with predators who liked moving targets! This is really not so far fetched. There are carnivorous predators in the wild today that seem to require a moving target for successful predation. Thus it appears safe to conclude that both fleeing and freezing serve a protective function (cf. Plutchik, 1980).

There is no doubt about the other direct effect of fear—its power to motivate flight to safety. As we have already noted, fear is a powerful teacher. It is also a powerful and efficient protector: there is no more powerful motivation to take care of the self and seek secure and safe environments. In contemporary life, fear is not simply of physical objects and physical injury. We may also be afraid of losing someone we love or losing our job. Even more frightening can be the threat of loss of esteem and love, including self-esteem and inner-directed affection. Mild fear helps us avoid these threats to our psychological and physical self. No matter how successful we are in coping with daily stress and challenges and no matter how great our accomplishments, there is always the potential for danger and threats of either a physical or psychological nature.

As long as fear is kept within bounds, it need not be a highly dreaded emotion nor a maladaptive one. Its efficiency and power in protecting us from danger by causing us to think carefully about the risks that we have to take is not only adaptive but essential to well-being and happiness.

As we have already noted, fear even serves a social function. As the ethologist Eibl-Eibesfeldt observed, fear causes us to flee to one another. When there is a burglary in the community, good neighbors may get together to plan for prevention of a future occurrence. On any occasion that a family is threatened, they tend to draw closer together and reunite. The same is true of a community or even of a nation.

In summary, we have seen that fear has essential adaptive functions as do other human emotions. Fear should not be considered as something terrible and dreadful, at least as long as it can be kept within bounds and as long as it is appropriate to the reality of the situation. When Franklin Roosevelt said, "The worst thing we have to fear is fear itself," he may not have spoken an absolute or universal truth, but he did convey a measure of wisdom.

The Development and Socialization of Fear

When American men and women were asked which emotion they dreaded the most, 51% of women indicated fear but only 33% of men named fear as the most dreaded emotion. This difference between men and women was not consistent across the various cultures. For example, in Sweden, 60% of men indicated that fear was the most dreaded emotion, whereas only 35% of females indicated fear. These cultural and gender differences are undoubtedly due in part to differences in cultural practices in the socialization of fear.

We know that in the USA, boys are much more likely to incur disapproval for showing fear. Like the other fundamental emotions, fear is sometimes controlled or thought to be controlled by invoking another emotion. On the average, boys are much more likely to be scolded and shamed for "acting like a scaredy cat." In adolescence or adulthood, being branded a coward is humiliating.

As Tomkins (1963) observed, parents take many approaches to the socialization of fear. Some parents minimize the effects of the experience of fear. Even though the parents themselves may be afraid in a particular situation, they will try to protect the child without communicating their own fear. This approach may have the disadvantage of making the child see fear as only an emergency response, and the child may come to avoid any situation where any degree of fear is anticipated.

Some parents exaggerate the negative effects of fear. This may prove to be self-defeating and cause the child to be more afraid of fear than is necessary.

Some parents make special efforts to atone for fear experiences that they think they have brought upon the child. They are very careful to reassure the child and make sure that their relationship with the child is reestablished.

Some parents attempt to teach tolerance for fear, encouraging the child not be overwhelmed by fear but to accept it as an inevitable part of life. Parents who do this are generally people who can accept the fact that they experience fear from time to time and are not themselves debilitated by it. They have enough tolerance for fear to be able to teach tolerance to their children.

Finally, Tomkins (1963) reasoned that some parents are very careful to teach their children techniques for confronting and managing fear. In this case a parent is able to share his or her own fear experience with the child and describe his or her own coping strategies. The parent is also willing and able to confront the source of fear with the child and provide encouragement in developing whatever skill or technique is useful in reducing or avoiding the fear associated with the situation. Sometimes, of course, the parent may correctly teach the child simply to avoid the situation itself.

Although there is not any systematic evidence on the issue, it seems reasonable to assume that a number of practices in the socialization of fear have negative effects. Among these are the following: relying excessively upon fear as a technique of controlling the child; excessive effort to minimize the effects of fear; failure to make any effort to atone for needlessly exposing the child to a fear situation; failure to teach the child some tolerance for fear and relying too much on a "sink or swim" or "sweat it out" philosophy; failure to teach techniques for managing and coping with fear; and finally, failure to show concern about signs of fear in the child.

A sound approach to socializing fear will include several of the following techniques: A parent should be able and willing to make amends for needlessly exposing a child to fear. The parent should make a special effort to teach the child some degree of tolerance for the fear experience. The parent should be especially careful to take every possible opportunity to teach the child how to confront the source of fear, where this is appropriate, and how to develop strategies for dealing with the fear. Finally, a parent should be a source of comfort and security for the child and should be "emotionally available" to show concern when the child is afraid or when the child is trying to develop coping techniques for dealing with fear.

Some Interactions of Fear with Other Emotions

Some of the techniques for socializing the child with regard to fear can lead to patterns of emotion response that may become a characteristic of the individual. As we shall see later, some patterns of emotions involving fear are appropriately termed anxiety. First, let us consider the interaction of fear with a few of the other fundamental emotions.

Fear–Sadness

If for any reason a child is periodically punished for crying and the real reason for the child's crying is sadness, the child may develop what Tomkins (1963) has called a fear–sadness bind. Tomkins suggests that such a pattern of emotions can make it more difficult for the child to face and deal with the situation that caused the sadness. A parental threat of withdrawal of love may be a legitimate source of sadness for the child. If the child has been punished for sadness (crying), crying may become associated in the child's mind with anticipation of the pain of punishment and hence the experience of fear. Then anytime the parent threatens to withdraw love, the child may feel the sadness of loneliness and the fear of punishment. This may limit the child's ability to appeal for sympathy during times of sadness when sympathy is needed and appropriate.

One does not have to have a particular set of early childhood experiences that included punishment for crying to experience fear and sadness together. Some occasions call forth both these emotions, as, for example, when there is a life threat to a person one loves and counts on. This is exactly what happened to Jackie when she was 15, and she described it in her diary.

> There are some days in my life which I can recall so vividly. One in particular that stands out in my mind occurred in May of 1978. I remember walking home from school and finding no one home that afternoon. I checked around the house to see if anyone was there, and finding nothing unusual, I sat down to watch TV. The phone rang a little while later; it was my Mom. At first I was excited and surprised to hear her voice, but as I continued to listen, I realized that she was crying. I had never seen or heard my Mom cry before. I felt kind of scared, but I kept listening anyway. She told me that Daddy was in the Intensive Care Unit of the hospital because he had a heart attack. I didn't know what to say to her. I wanted to go and comfort her, for after all, she had taken care of me for over 14 years at the time. I didn't have a car and even if I did I didn't know how to drive anyway, so I had to stay home. I wanted so bad to say the "right" thing, but I could hardly think straight myself. Tears were streaming down my face. I guess Mom said more to me, I really can't remember now. I was so busy crying for fear of losing my father, and I was trying to decide what to do next.

Fear–Shame

If parents shame their children for showing fear, then children may eventually feel shame at any time that they feel threatened and afraid. A combination of fear and shame can be extremely debilitating and can, according to Tomkins (1963), eventually produce paranoid schizophrenia. Tomkins suggests that the paranoid schizophrenic experiences a fear of being caught and found guilty of some wrongdoing or being made to feel more and more inferior. Eventually the paranoid schizophrenic feels both the fear of being found out and the humiliation of incapability.

Techniques for Controlling Fear

There are several effective techniques for controlling fear. None is perfect or sure to work for everyone or all types of fear. In the hands of experienced therapists, however, they constitute useful approaches to relief from fear and phobias.

Desensitization. A technique developed by Wolpe (1969) works toward decreasing an individual's sensitivity to the objects or situations that cause fear. The technique combines relaxation procedures with repetitive presentation of a graded series of stimuli. First the client is taught how to relax the muscles of the face, neck, and body. Any or all of the muscles may be chronically tense in a chronically fearful person, and they are very likely to be tense in the fear situation. Once the individual has achieved the ability to become thoroughly relaxed, the therapist determines through clinical interviews a list of the situations that elicit fear. With the help of the patient the fears are graded from the most to the least fearful. While thoroughly relaxed, the individual is required to image the least fearful of the situations. This is repeated until the individual can visualize the fearful situation and still remain relaxed. The patient is carefully and gradually brought up through the various grades of fear until he or she if finally able to visualize the most frightening of the situations while still remaining relaxed, in the safety of the therapeutic situation. Modifications of this technique include cognitive instruction and graded practice with confrontation of fear outside the therapists's office.

Implosive Therapy. This method requires a client to imagine highly traumatic events. The event that is brought to mind has been selected on the basis of special diagnostic interviews by the therapist. Case reports based on this technique suggest that patients experience extreme fear or anxiety during the therapy situation, hence the term *implosive* therapy. The case reports also suggest that the technique does work for some people. The explanation as to exactly how it works is not yet known.

Modeling. This technique is based on vicarious learning or social imitation. The therapist, a loved one, or a friend models courageous behavior in approaching and handling objects or situations that frighten the phobic individual. Parents use this technique when they show a child how to confront and cope with a perceived danger.

Emotion Regulating Emotion. As in the case of any other emotion, fear can be reduced or sometimes eliminated by invoking another emotion. If it is possible to muster a little anger at the object or situation, fear subsides. Assuming the expression and posture of anger should help with this (Izard, 1990). When Julie was robbed, her anger apparently completely eliminated fear, at least temporarily. Fear control should result from practice in engaging in the expressive behavior and thought–imagery associated with an emotion that counteracts fear. Such practice should be most effective if done in situations that simulate the one that is feared (Gellhorn, 1970; Izard, 1971).

All the foregoing techniques for managing and controlling fear are applicable to anxiety as well. Because the key emotion in anxiety is fear.

Anxiety

A decade or so after the explosion of the first atomic bomb on Hiroshima, the poet W. H. Auden said that our era is the age of anxiety. It would be interesting to know how often some insightful observer of the human scene has made such a statement. Perhaps the first person to make such an observation lived tens of thousands of years ago when survival and well-being may have been even more precarious in some environments than it is now. In any case, we know that we use the term anxiety fairly often to describe our emotional state.

We probably often use the term anxiety without really stopping to consider precisely what it means. Most people who reflect on their feelings will say that when they feel anxious they feel uneasy, apprehensive, perhaps even shaky and jittery if the state is extreme. These adjectives suggest that the feeling state common to all anxiety is that of fear. Because fear, like any fundamental emotion, can vary in intensity, it may be at a low, moderate, or high level of strength when it is involved in anxiety.

The nineteenth-century philosopher Soren Kierkegaard noted that interest and fear tend to be in competition for our attention and action. This is well illustrated by the observations of the ethologist Korrad Lorenz (1966). The following is a paraphrase of Lorenz's observation. A raven spotted an object on the ground and flew to a branch at the top of a tall tree to view it more closely. The raven flew part way down, took a closer look, and quickly flew back to the top of the tree. It flew down again, but this time retreated to a limb only halfway up the tree. The raven repeated this approach–withdrawal cycle until finally it appraised the object as more delectable than dangerous; it then flew down and landed on the ground to explore it in detail.

We can probably think of incidents in our own lives when we behaved like the raven. Such behavior is particularly likely to occur in situations involving what we perceive as important, unknown factors. Successful explorers and people who participate in high-mountain climbing, parachuting, and white-water canoeing have long since learned to manage the conflict between excitement and fear. Because interest–excitement is a positive emotion that sets up approach tendencies and facilitates positive and constructive action, it is an all-important emotion in sustaining behavior in the face of fear.

Perhaps because the feeling of fear sometimes leads to a sense of isolation and aloneness, some people report sadness as a part of the pattern of emotions in anxiety. Sadness probably had some effect on its own, but its primary effect in the anxiety pattern is through its interaction with fear. A combination of fear and sadness calls for quite a different strategy than one of fear and excitement.

In describing their anxiety, some people report feelings of shame or guilt. In our society, children, particularly boys, are taught not to show their fear. Feeling fear and thus risking its display to others can cause one to feel ashamed or guilty. A fear–shame pattern in anxiety can be particularly debilitating because neither emotion is conducive to social interactions.

It is important to realize that when we say we are anxious we are probably experiencing some combination or pattern of various emotions. Each of these emotions affects social relationships, bodily states, perceptions, thoughts, and actions.

The Experience of Anxiety as a Combination of Emotions

A series of studies using the Differential Emotions Scale (DES) showed that anxiety, as conceived by psychologists and as defined or imaged by college students, could be broken down into a number of relatively independent affective factors (Izard, 1972). These studies will be summarized briefly.

The first study was a factor-analytic investigation of the DES, combined with the items of the Spielberger–Gorsuch–Lushene (1970) State–Trait Anxiety Inventory (STAI). The combined instrument (DES + A) was administered to 339 college students, who were instructed to complete the scale while recalling or visualizing situations in which they felt anxious. The factor analysis of the data from this study showed that anxiety, as defined by the STAI, was indeed a complex of affective factors. Most of the anxiety-related terms of the STAI loaded on a fear factor that included all of the fear items of the DES. A few of the STAI items loaded on a factor that combined the sadness and guilt items of the DES, and most of the nonanxiety items of the STAI (e.g., content, secure, confident) loaded on a joy factor that included all of the joy items of the DES. Thus, the factor analysis of the STAI in a context with items representing several of the discrete emotions confirms the hypothesis of differential emotions theory that anxiety is a complex pattern of emotion feelings, not a unitary phenomenon.

The DES was administered to a large group of black college students immediately after their campus had been invaded by armed national guardsmen and local police. During the occasion, police fired into a crowd of students and into a dormitory, killing two students and injuring several. The students were asked to recall the scene and its aftermath and to describe their feelings about it by completing the DES. As predicted, they showed significantly elevated means on fear, sadness, shame, anger, and interest, most of the hypothesized affective components of anxiety.

In another study (Bartlett & Izard, 1972), 160 college students were divided into high- and low-anxiety groups on the basis of their STAI scores. These students then took the DES under two conditions. First, in the quiet of their own dormitory rooms, they were requested to imagine a situation that made them anxious and then to keep the situation vividly in mind while completing the DES. On a second occasion, just prior to a midterm examination (real anxiety condition), the subjects were requested to complete the DES. Figure 13-4 shows the profiles of DES means for the high- and low-anxiety subjects in the real and imagined anxiety conditions.

The profiles for the high-anxiety subjects are quite consistent with predictions on the basis of differential emotions theory. The highest means are fear, interest, sadness, guilt, anger, and shame/shyness. The marked similarity in the profiles for the real and imagined anxiety conditions lend support to the imagining technique in the study of emotions.

Similar studies of the phenomenology of anxiety in children were conducted by Blumberg and Izard (1985). They used the State–Trait Anxiety Inventory for Children (STAIC; Spielberger, Edwards, Lushene, Montuori, & Platzek, 1973) as the measure of anxiety. They also measured depression with the Children's Depression Inventory (CDI: Kovacs & Beck, 1977). Emotion experiences were measured with the Differential Emotions Scale. The investigators found that fear, guilt, sadness, and shame were significantly related to anxiety. Using regression analysis, the investigators determined the amount of variance in anxiety that was accounted for by each of these emotions. The anxiety measure was analyzed in three ways: in its original form, with the variance due to depression (CDI) partialed out, and with all items on the STAIC with obvious affective content removed. The results of these analyses are presented in Table 13-2.

As can be seen from Table 13-2, fear is by far the most significant emotion in accounting for anxiety. In this particular study, sadness, guilt, and shame, and

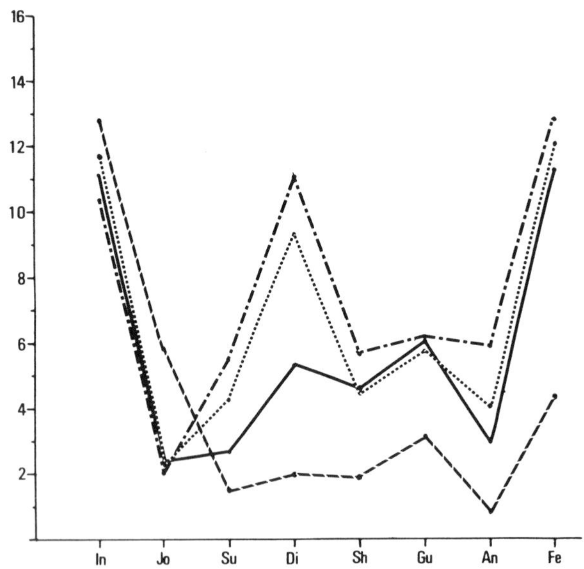

FIGURE 13-4. Profiles of DES means for high-anxiety subjects under real (—) and imagined (–·–) conditions and low-anxiety subjects under real (–––) and imagined (· · ·) conditions.

TABLE 13-2
Results of Regression of the Differential Emotion Scales (DES) on the State-Trait Anxiety Inventory for Children (STAIC), with Children's Depression Inventory (CDI) Partialed Out, and on Nonaffect STAIC

		Variance accounted for in:	
DES hierarchy	STAIC	STAIC with CDI partialed out	Nonaffect STAIC
Fear	42.1%*	22.78%*	38.05%*
Interest	—	1.09[a]	—
Guilt	6.9*	1.75*	5.6*
Sadness	13.9*	6.02*	8.89*
Shame	3.3*	2.33*	4.81*
Anger	—	—	—
Disgust	—	—	—
Contempt	—	—	—
Shyness	—	—	—
Self-directed hostility	—	—	—
Joy	—	—	—
Surprise	—	—	—

[a]The variance accounted for by these variables is a statistical artifact resulting from a suppression effect, so caution should be used in interpretations.

guilt were the second, third, and fourth most important emotions, respectively.

These data suggest that it is not fruitful to attempt to treat anxiety as a unitary phenomenon. Understanding and treating anxiety in adults and children requires an understanding of the various discrete emotions involved in the subjective experience. Individuals may differ in the relative importance of the various emotions in anxiety. A clear picture of the profile of emotions in a given individual's anxiety should facilitate understanding and treatment.

Summary

Although fear, especially extreme fear, is experienced relatively infrequently by comparison with some other emotions, it is highly dreaded. Fear is sensed or perceived as a threat to our security or safety, and it regularly motivates efforts to alleviate the threat and escape from harm. Fear may result from either psychological or physical threat.

There are a number of events or conditions for which we are biologically prepared to respond with fear. These "natural clues" to danger include such things as pain, being left alone, and sudden changes in stimulation. There are innumerable things that we may learn to fear. Many of them are related in one way or another to the natural clues to danger. A parent who shows his fear of an event in the presence of his child greatly facilitates the child's learning to be afraid of the same event.

The full-face expression of fear has been clearly identified in cross-cultural research, but it is rarely seen in everyday life. People learn to inhibit or minimize expressions of fear.

Fear is experienced as a sense of insecurity, uncertainty, and lack of control. The primary function of fear is to motivate cognition and actions that lead to safety and security. Fear tends to create tunnel vision, and it greatly narrows the range of behavioral alternatives. Fear may be seen as adaptive, however, in protecting us from harm. The anticipation of fear may motivate the strengthening of the self or the reduction of vulnerabilities.

The processes of the socialization of fear vary with parents, but a sound approach should include teaching some tolerance of fear, teaching techniques for confronting the source of fear, and developing skills and techniques that are useful in reducing or avoiding the fear stimulus. Modeling is an effective way to provide the child with an opportunity to learn to cope with fear.

A number of studies have shown that it is appropriate to distinguish between fear and anxiety. At the level of subjective experience, anxiety is best understood as a combination of several discrete emotions. Although fear is the key emotion, emotions such as sadness, shame, and guilt may be a part of the anxiety experience.

Suggested Readings

Bauer, D. H. (1976). An exploratory study of developmental changes in children's fears. *Journal of Child Psychology and Psychiatry*, *17*, 69–74.

A discussion of the types of fear characteristic of children at different stages of development.

Lanzetta, J. T., & Orr, S. P. (1986). Excitatory strength of expressive faces: Effects of happy and fear expressions and context on the extinction of a conditioned fear response. *Journal of Personality and Social Psychology*, *50*(1), 190–194.

The effect of fear expression as a stimulus in the acquisition and extinction of fear.

Mineka, S., Davidson, M., Cook, M., & Keir, R. (1984). Observational conditioning of snake fear in rhesus monkeys. *Journal of Abnormal Psychology*, *93*(4), 355–372.

A demonstration of the powerful effects of adult, particularly maternal, modeling of fear behavior in the acquisition of juveniles' fears.

Sorce, J. F., Emde, R. N., Campos, J., & Klinnert, M. D. (1981). Maternal emotional signaling: Its effect on the visual cliff behavior of 1-year-olds. *Developmental Psychology*, *21*(1), 195–200.

Infants' development of fear on the visual cliff.

14

Shyness

A man was holding his 4-month-old daughter comfortably in his arms. She was alert and very attentive to what was going on about her. A friend walked up to greet the father and admire the baby. When he got within normal conversation distance and began talking directly to the baby, she gave him a little smile as she quickly turned her head away from him and snuggled it closely against her father's chest. The friend remarked, "Oh, the pretty girl is a little shy." Like most people he saw the baby's facial expression, turning away, and gaze aversion as signs of shyness. Many, if not all babies, show this behavior beginning sometime around 4 months of age, and it continues to be seen in virtually the same form throughout infancy, usually peaking in the second year of life. At this age the shy toddler will hide her face in mother's skirt as the stranger approaches.

This particular set of shy behaviors has not been systematically tracked by scientists, and although the common inference that they signal real shyness seems valid, there is much that we still do not know about shyness and its development. Babies differ widely in their tendency to show shy behavior and in the frequency and intensity with which they manifest it. When it is only a mild and momentary response from which the child quickly recovers, it is usually considered as cute, and most parents show little or no concern about it at all. Such children recover quickly and soon turn their face and their gaze back to the person who stimulated the shy behavior, and normal social exchange resumes.

Some babies, perhaps a relatively small percentage, not only turn their face and gaze away from the approaching person but do it with great intensity and also cling to the parent. They do not recover so quickly, and it is much more difficult to engage the child in social interaction. For example, a mother brought her twin daughters to the university to participate in a project on emotional development. They were pretty girls who had just turned 2 years of age. They were look-alike twins, though not identical, and their behavior toward the experimenter was far from identical. The experimenter walked up to one of them, stooping as he approached to bring his face closer to the level of hers. The toddler quickly turned, took the step and a half to reach her mother, quickly turned her gaze from the experimenter, and buried her face in her mother's skirts as her arms tightly encircled her mother's legs. Her twin, who was about 5 or 6 feet away from the experimenter and playing with a doll, turned just as quickly toward him, walked boldly up to him and said, "My sister is shy. You want to play with my doll?"

This contrasting behavior seems altogether amazing, particularly since it was seen in look-alike twins. The mother explained that they had always shown this remarkable difference in personality despite her every effort to treat them exactly alike in regard to their social interactions. How could this happen? One possibility is that the difference is determined in part by heredity. Heterozygotic (or nonidentical) twins do not have identical genes; therefore, they can inherit different behavioral tendencies. The possibility that there is a shyness gene or an inherited tendency toward shyness is suggested by research that will be discussed in a later section.

Bodily Changes in Shyness

Buss (1979) has attempted to distinguish between shyness and shame at the behavioral and physiological levels. His data suggest that the two emotions reflect different types of autonomic nervous system reactivity, with shyness involving relatively greater sympathetic arousal and shame relatively greater parasympathetic arousal. This work has not yet been replicated in other labs.

Kagan, Reznick and Snidman (1986) have summarized evidence relating to cardiac functioning in children showing extreme behavioral inhibition, a trait they believe to be characteristic of extremely shy children. Children who show extreme behavioral inhibition to the unfamiliar respond to novel stimuli with a higher and more stable heart rate than do uninhibited children. This finding has been replicated with children several times by Kagan and his colleagues, but it is still not known precisely how extreme behavioral inhibition relates to the normal range of shyness or to other discrete emotions such as fear.

The Expression of Shyness

There is no single behavior that consistently and uniquely describes shyness, and no particular facial configuration is uniformly associated with it. Gaze aversion and head turning or lowering is associated with shyness, but they also may be associated with shame. Some data suggest that the act of smiling before gaze aversion and head turning may distinguish shame or embarrassment from shyness. Head turning is often followed by a glance back at the stimulus person, as in Figure 14-1.

Although facial cues are minimal, and other expressive movements difficult

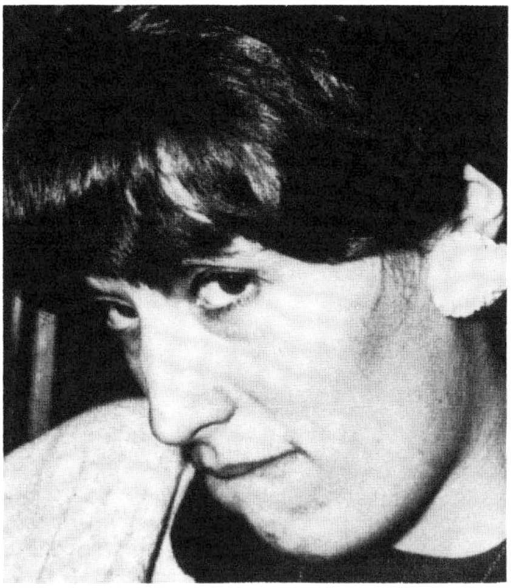

FIGURE 14-1. Shyness, shame, or both?

to measure objectively, just about everyone feels confident in identifying signs of shyness. The toddler who responds to an approaching stranger by turning her head, hiding her face, and clinging to mother or father is recognized as shy. Similar types of behavior can be observed in infants as young as 3 or 4 months.

The Experience of Shyness

Those who experience the emotion of shyness know that it can be a very significant factor in shaping personality and social relations. It is only recently, however, that it has begun to be studied systematically (Jones, Cheek, & Briggs, 1986). Although considerable research is being done on the experience of shyness, there is still not complete agreement on its definition. Definitions vary, but there tends to be a factor common to all of them, and the differences often provide additional insight into the meaning of this complex phenomenon.

The common core of the shyness experience is the feeling of vulnerability in social situations. It is the vulnerability of the self, the self-image, or ego that is involved. This may make the shy individual inclined to avoid certain types of social encounters, but it does not necessarily make them unsociable. Indeed, some studies have shown that there is little or no correlation between shyness and sociability (Crozier, 1986). The shy person may enjoy social life as much as the person who is not shy, but the conditions for social enjoyment may be different. Shy people enjoy interacting with family and close friends or people with whom they are familiar. Shyness becomes restricting when social occasions call for interaction with strangers or people perceived as threatening in some way. The shy person will see such people as potential sources of criticism and anticipate the subsequent uneasiness and discomfort associated with the feeling of shyness.

Zimbardo (1986) describes shyness as a "state of heightened individuation in which there is a perceived isomorphism between one's ego and one's performance" (p. 17). This means that criticism or rejection of any action of a shy person is perceived as equivalent to criticism or rejection of the shy person. Thus the shy person's ego is always on the firing line and highly vulnerable. Shy persons describe themselves as feeling clumsy, inadequate, apprehensive about talking, low in assertiveness, and subject to loneliness (Jones & Carpenter, 1986).

Zimbardo and his colleagues (see Pilkonis & Zimbardo, 1979) found that people who identified themselves as shy were indeed less extroverted, less capable of monitoring their own social behavior, and more socially anxious then their nonshy peers. They found that scores on their shyness inventory were correlated with a measure of neuroticism for men but not for women. They interpreted this as meaning that shyness is a more acceptable characteristic for women. However, women who were shy and who also were highly introspective tended to score high on the scale of neuroticism.

In a large sample of high school and college students, Zimbardo and his colleagues found that 42% described themselves as continually shy, indicating that their shyness was a significant part of their personalities. A large majority of these (79%) did not like their shyness, and many (63%) thought that it posed a real problem. Thus, the attractiveness of shyness may be more in the eyes of the beholder than in the eyes of the person who experiences it.

From the standpoint of the discrete emotions approach that emphasizes the distinct characteristics of each of the emotions, defining the experience of shyness is particularly difficult. This is true because shyness seems to share characteristics with other emotions, especially shame, guilt, fear, and interest. Both shame and shyness involve the self and the concept of self or self-esteem in a special way. Guilt, too, is certainly self-focused in that it is the self that has violated a standard. In shyness and shame there is heightened self-awareness, whereas in guilt, there is more concern with the relationship to the one who has been wronged. Shyness focuses more on what might happen in the future and on the possibility of being evaluated and found wanting. Shame is more often like a state, a momentary feeling of overexposure and ineptness in a particular situation.

Shyness seems to involve a mixture of, or a conflict between, positive and negative feelings toward social situations. Shy persons are attracted to people but concerned about how they will impress them. They are concerned whether they will communicate and relate to others in an effective and satisfying way. Thus shyness is often accompanied by interest, especially interest in people, and fear, especially fear of social encounters (Izard & Hyson, 1986).

The DES profile for students recalling or imaging a situation in which they experienced intense shyness is presented in Figure 14-2. It is noteworthy that the interest–excitement mean is the third highest in the profile, and the interest mean is

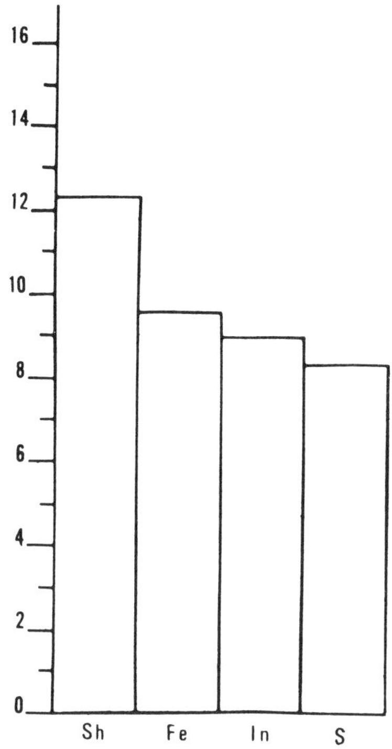

FIGURE 14-2. The DES profile of emotions in the shyness situation. N = 58. Sh, shyness; Fe, fear; In, interest; S, sadness.

not significantly lower than the second highest mean, that for fear. This is a higher mean on interest than obtained in any other negative emotion situation except for anger, where the interest score was 9.72. Even more remarkable is the fact that the mean score for enjoyment (6.36) is elevated in the shyness situation. Shyness was the only one of the six negative emotions in which the mean for enjoyment was substantially elevated. The amount of interest and enjoyment in the shyness profile strongly supports the notion that shyness is most likely to occur in situations where interest and enjoyment are also experienced.

The prominent position of fear in the DES profile is also consistent with our explanation of the dynamics of shame and shyness. Shame and shyness relate to the person's well-being, the self-concept, and self-integrity, It is quite reasonable that an emotion so closely related to the core of the personality should be dynamically related to the emotion of fear. In some situations shame and shyness may serve as front-runners, motivating the individual to cover or withdraw the extended or exposed self before more serious threat elicits the very toxic emotion of fear.

The DRS profile of dimensions in the shyness situation is presented in Figure

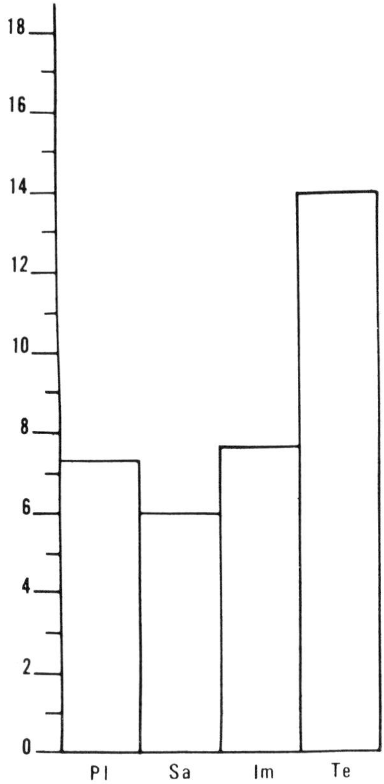

FIGURE 14-3. The DRS profile of dimensions in the shyness situation. Pl, pleasantness; Sa, self-assurance; Im, impulsiveness; Te, tension.

14-3. Of particular interest is the combination of high pleasantness (relative to the other negative emotions) and high tension. The tension in shyness, while lower than that in fear, is roughly equal to that in anger and guilt and significantly higher than that in sadness. The pleasantness reported in the shyness situation is lower than that in the positive emotions but significantly higher than in any of the other negative emotions.

Although, shyness may have a biological basis, it can be increased or decreased by family attitudes and practices and the overall process of socialization. Unrealistically high expectations of parents can cause a child to feel that his performance, and hence himself, will always appear inadequate or inept in some way. Such a relationship with parents, and its effects, was described as follows by Tomie.

> As a child I was very shy, especially between the ages of 9 and 16. During this time, people around me had great expectations for me. However, I could not possibly live up to some of

> the outrageous goals they set for me. I became withdrawn because I was afraid of failure. As a result of this, inner-directed hostility developed, because I was cheating myself out of things I enjoyed doing. So in my case, anyway, inner-directed hostility or self-blame seems to be a consequence of shyness rather than a cause; but it can also be cyclical in that the more inner-directed hostility you impose on yourself a feeling of ineptness occurs, and that translates into shyness.

In summary, to experience shyness is to feel unsure of yourself in a social situation. In shyness you feel you are not measuring up, and you feel very uncomfortable in the presence of others. You feel unable to communicate effectively. As long as you have to remain in the social situation, you are under a constant strain. You feel that any moment you may do or say something that will embarrass you. If the situation is prolonged, you may develop a tension headache from the stress. Shyness is a chronic feeling of inability to interact with people confidently and comfortably. It frequently reflects a true deficit in social interaction skills, and intensely shy people, who may be brilliant or highly talented, protect themselves from occupations and recreation that make high demands on social skills.

The Functions of Shyness

A basic premise of the discrete emotion theory is that all emotions have an inherently adaptive function. Mild or moderate shyness in the infant and young child may prevent the child from readily approaching and engaging in interactions with strangers. On some occasions and in some circumstances such interactions could prove dangerous. In general, then, shyness may function to maintain the child in familiar and safe surroundings, and closer to family and friends. Further, shy behaviors that increase the child's feeling of security may help regulate an overreacting autonomic nervous system.

Pilkonis and Zimbardo (1979) asked shy people to indicate the kinds of situations and people that elicited their feelings of shyness. The data are presented in Table 14-1. These responses are generally consistent with the data from the antecedents and consequences survey and with the theories that distinguish among shame, shyness, and guilt.

Shyness as a Trait

Daniels and Plomin (1985) showed that both heredity and socialization–environment play a role in determining individual differences in infant shyness. Their sample included 152 adopted infants, their biological and adoptive parents, and 120 matched nonadoptive families. The infants' shyness was assessed by parental ratings. Parents' shyness-related temperament and personality factors

TABLE 14-1
Inventory of Shyness Elicitors and Reactions[a]

Sources and symptoms of shyness	Percentage of students who label themselves shy
Situations	
Where I am focus of attention—large group (as when giving a speech)	72.6
Large groups	67.6
Of lower status	56.2
Social situations in general	55.3
New situations in general	55.0
Requiring assertiveness	54.1
Where I am being evaluated	53.2
Where I am focus of attention—small group	52.1
Small social groups	48.5
One-to-one opposite-sex interactions	48.5
Of vulnerability (need help)	48.2
Small task-oriented groups	28.2
One-to-one same-sex interactions	13.8
Other people	
Strangers	69.7
Opposite-sex group	62.9
Authorities by virtue of their knowledge	55.3
Authorities by virtue of their role	39.7
Same-sex groups	33.5
Relatives	19.7
Elderly people	12.4
Friends	10.9
Children	10.0
Parents	8.5

[a]Adapted from Zimbardo *et al.*, 1974. $N = 230$ college and high school students.

were assessed by standardized questionnaires. When heredity and family environment were shared by parents and infants (nonadoptive families), infant shyness at 12 and 24 months was related to mothers' shyness, low sociability, and introversion. These same relations emerged, though not quite as strong, in adoptive families, in which there was shared environment but not shared heredity, indicating that environment helped determine the infants' shyness. Finally, there were significant correlations between the adopted infants' shyness at 24 months and their biological mothers' introversion–extraversion scores, indicating that heredity was a significant determinant of the infants' shyness.

As seen in the study of Daniels and Plomin (1985), shyness has been associated with the personality trait of introversion. The introvert is a person who is not inclined to meet and to mingle with people and who has a tendency to be preoccupied with his or her self. Eysenck (1970), a leading researcher on introversion–extroversion, considers these characteristics to be basic aspects of personality structure. He has accumulated much evidence that these traits are rooted in a person's biological makeup.

Another leading personality psychologist, (Cattell, 1946) thinks of shyness as a biologically based trait that relates to the arousability of the nervous system. He believes that shy people have an especially sensitive and easily aroused nervous system that is particularly vulnerable to social stress. The idea that biological makeup and heredity play a part in determining shyness has now been tested in a number of empirical studies.

Suomi (1979) conducted some fascinating research on personality and temperament in rhesus monkeys. He developed both behavioral and physiological tests to help him identify infant and adult monkeys who were shy and withdrawn, and those who were aggressive and outgoing. After identifying a group of infants and adult females in each category, he placed shy infant monkeys with aggressive outgoing mothers, and aggressive and sociable infants with shy and withdrawn mothers. After 6 months, the infants had taken on the characteristics of their foster parents. Infant monkeys who earlier were shy and withdrawn became aggressive and sociable. The infants who were once aggressive and outgoing now appeared shy and withdrawn. These results are robust and remarkable evidence for the plasticity of intelligent, social animals. It testifies to their ability to learn to adapt to their social environment and to adopt the behavior of their primary model, the mother.

However, when Suomi took the juvenile monkeys and put them back in the original test situations to determine their temperament and personality characteristics, the young monkeys reverted to their original nature. Under the mildly stressful conditions of the test situations, the monkeys behaved in terms of their biologically based characteristics. Suomi's research suggests that shyness as well as social extraversion are characteristics that have an evolutionary-biological basis.

There is another kind of strong and direct evidence for the traitlike nature of shyness in children. Kagan and his colleagues (Coll, Kagan, & Reznick, 1984) have studied extreme shyness, or what they call *behavioral inhibition*, in toddlers and preschool children. They define inhibition on the basis of the following observable behavior: crying, fretting, distress vocalizations, withdrawal, and the absence of spontaneous interactions with the experimenter. These behaviors can reasonably be accepted as indications of shyness, though they may also be associated with fearfulness.

Kagan and his colleagues also measured the children's heart rates and heart rate variability during test situations that included novel and stressful events. They found that children who were extremely high on the behavioral indicators of inhibition or shyness tended to respond to the test situations with unusually high

FIGURE 14-4. The presence of a strange adult (photographer) completely inhibited this child's play, despite mother's effort at reassurance. The mother described the child as very shy.

and minimally variable or stable heart rates. Children who were uninhibited responded to the test situations with significantly lower heart rates and a more variable heart rate pattern.

Kagan and his colleagues have done two follow-up studies that confirm their earlier results. In the first follow-up, they tested the same children approximately 1 year after the original study. The experimenters ran a similar set of tests with the addition of a home visit by two adult female experimenters and an episode of peer play. In the peer play, an inhibited and an uninhibited child were matched on sex and age. The experimenters found a significant relationship between the degree of inhibition shown by the children at 21 months and the degree of inhibition shown at 31 to 32 months. Thus, they found a considerable degree of consistency in behavioral inhibition (or extreme shyness) over the 10-month interval. However, it should be noted that not all children were highly consistent in showing behavioral inhibition across all test situations and over the 10-month interval. About three-fourths of the children showed behavioral inhibition in some of the situations, and approximately one-third of the initially inhibited children remained extremely inhibited in all test situations. Kagan and his colleagues also found some consistency in the heart rate measures of inhibited and uninhibited children. Most of the consistently uninhibited children tended to have high heart rate variability, whereas the consistently inhibited children tended to have low heart rate variability and range at both 21 and 31 months of age.

The experimenters drew two tentative conclusions from their original and initial follow-up studies. First, extremely inhibited or shy children tend to show shyness in various situations and to exhibit this trait consistently over the period of childhood that was studied. Second, there is a moderate negative correlation between heart rate variability and behavioral inhibition at 21 and 31 months of age.

Kagan and his colleagues have done two additional follow-up studies, when the children were 4 and 5½ years of age. At these ages, they found similar results to those of the initial follow-up study. At 5½ years of age, the children initially identified as shy and inhibited at 21 months were more inhibited with their playmates at school and in the laboratory. They also showed more inhibition or shyness with an adult examiner in the test situation, and in situations of mild risk they exhibited more cautiousness. Again, at 5½ years, they found that the more inhibited children had a relatively high and stable heart rate. They also had larger pupil dilation during mild stress involved in cognitive tasks. Their mothers described them as shy with unfamiliar peers. A follow-up study of the children at age 7½ years has confirmed and extended the findings of the earlier follow-up studies (Kagan, Reznick, & Snidman, 1988).

In summary, the work of Kagan and his colleagues strongly suggests that at least for a small proportion of people, perhaps 10–15%, extreme shyness functions like a personality trait—a stable characteristic of the person. Their data suggest that this trait has a biological basis and that the autonomic nervous system and the vital organs that it innervates are differentially responsive in shy and nonshy individuals. However, Kagan *et al.* (1988) conclude that the actualization of extreme shyness requires chronic environmental stress acting upon the innate temperamental disposition.

Gough and Thorne (1986) have described the reactions of others to various aspects of a person's shyness. The work is based on a self-descriptive Adjective Check List (ACL), which assesses the characteristics of shyness perceived by others as positive or negative. For example, discrete, modest, tactful, and sensitive are positive attributes of shyness. Timid, meek, nervous, and withdrawn are seen as negative facets of shyness. All these facets of shyness usually correlate negatively with such personality traits as dominance, sociability, self-acceptance, and empathy, but the correlations are much higher for the negative aspects of shyness (shy-negative ACL index) than for the positive aspects of shyness.

In summary, Gough and Thorne emphasize the importance of assessing the various aspects of shyness. If shy persons' self-descriptions stress the positive aspects of shyness, they are more likely to be seen as possessing equanimity, modesty, and self-restraint. If their self-descriptions stress the negative aspects of shyness, they are more likely to be seen as awkward and inhibited.

If shyness is partly determined by heredity, as the evidence indicates, then either some people inherit a stronger tendency to shyness or their own learning and experience amplify the problem. Both biology and environment play a role in determining the strength of shyness and its developmental course. A shy child with a shy mother will grow up in quite different social circumstances than a shy child with a extraverted and highly sociable mother. Even in the case of identical twins separated at birth, we would not expect them to be equally shy.

Apparently, mild to moderate shyness is not sensed by the individual, or perceived by others, as being a social or mental health problem. Indeed, as we have noted, shy behavior in infants and toddlers is often seen as cute and coy. A certain degree of shyness proves to be an attractive personality characteristic in some individuals. This may be more true for females than males, but it is not entirely gender specific. In the Japanese culture, however, shyness in women is an especially preferred characteristic.

In a study of sexual standards, sexual experience, and emotion responses to imaging (visualizing) sexual intercourse (Izard, Spiegel, Alessio, & Kotsch, 1974), an analysis of DES trait scores showed that males experienced more shyness in their day-to-day lives than did females. This tends to disconfirm the hypothesis of Lewis (1971) that women are more prone to shame and shyness than are men. However, on the DES that measured state shyness immediately after visualizing sexual intercourse, women reported more shyness than men. Virgin women reported significantly more shyness than nonvirgins, and the difference here was quite substantial. With regard to sex standards, women who believed that coitus should occur only in an affectionate relationship reported substantially more shyness subsequent to imaging the sexual scene than did men who believed in coitus without affection.

Fear, shame, and shyness may play important roles in sexual adjustment. Homosexuality may be, at least in part, a result of one's susceptibility to fear and intense shame as one anticipates and approaches sexual relations with members of the opposite sex. The emotion dynamics of a homosexual in psychotherapy were discussed by Izard (1972). The DES emotion profile for this patient showed extremely high scores on both fear and shyness. He was described clinically as a "highly anxious" individual.

The clinical concept of anxiety often includes a component of shyness, in addition to fear, sadness, and guilt. Shyness is also an emotion component of some forms of depression. A study of depressive patients by Marshall and Izard (1972b) showed that shyness was one of the more important emotions in the emotion profile of depressive patients. Sadness, inner-directed anger (hostility), and fear were the three emotions receiving the highest scores, while shyness and guilt were next in order of magnitude.

Shyness and Problems in Social Adjustment

Intense and frequently experienced shyness can be a terrible burden for a person; it can become debilitating and lead to mental health problems. It is easy to see how extreme shyness could make adjustments to life's demands very difficult. Pilkonis and Zimbardo (1979) did an extensive study of shy people and summarized three negative consequences of extreme shyness. First, it encourages social isolation and thereby eliminates or reduces the availability of one of the greatest sources of rewards in the environment, other people. This is not simply a loss of the fun that comes with a good social life; it is also a loss of social support. Everyone throughout life needs a network of friends who are supportive in many ways. Social (emotional) support provided by a circle of friends is minimal or absent for the extremely shy person. Some experts believe that under some conditions this can lead to serious depression.

Second, the absence of social support makes the individual more vulnerable to the stresses of life that are ordinarily buffered by the encouragement and advice of friends and acquaintances. Jones and Carpenter (1986) found that shy people have a smaller social network and that it is usually made up of family members. As compared to the nonshy, shy persons report that they get less support from their social network and are less satisfied with their relationships. Jones and Carpenter's work also suggests that the shy person's ineffective interpersonal behaviors that contribute to unsatisfying relationships may be a result of their relatively poor appreciation for how they come across to others. There is evidence that shy people do not perform well in interpersonal encounters or in tasks such as soliciting the cooperation of others by telephone (DePaulo, Dull, Greenberg, and Swain, 1989).

Third, because shy people do not have open and candid conversations with other people, they often think they are worse off than they really are. Since they are often unaware of the plight of others or even of the knowledge that many other people experience at least some degree of shyness, they may tend to have an unrealistic view of their own social behavior.

Another way in which shyness can prove to be a problem for the individual is that shyness is not always interpreted as shyness by observers. People who identify themselves as shy are sometimes judged by their peers to be "reserved," "aloof," "condescending," and even "rejecting."

Researchers of shyness have found evidence that shyness takes quite different forms in different people. Two types have been fairly well identified—public shyness and private shyness. People who are publicly shy are concerned about whether their behavior will appear to be awkward to other people or whether or not they will be able to respond to others in a social situation. They are concerned about their performance in public. For the privately shy, subjective discomfort is the major problem. It is their private emotion experience that tortures them when they are in social interactions. They seem to be able to perform adequately, but they are terribly uncomfortable doing so and it is a great emotional drain. This type of shy person pays a great price for virtually every social encounter, particularly those involving groups. Privately shy persons suffer a great deal of subjective discomfort during social events. After a party they feel drained and exhausted rather than exhilarated or content.

Either because they are concerned with their performance or because of their subjective discomfort while performing, shy people are typically uncertain about what to do in social situations. This is particularly true in social situations like impromptu gatherings, parties, and affairs where the individual is pretty much left to his or her own initiative. A shy person does not like to be in social situations that are unstructured. This means they will have a tendency to avoid all novel and unfamiliar social situations. The more unstructured the situation, the more freedom there is to show initiative, make decisions, or take responsibility, and the more uncomfortable the shy person will be. Thus, in social affairs, the shy person is much more likely to "follow the leader" than to take charge. Eventually this can lead to negative self-evaluations and, perhaps, to depression.

Because shy people are sensitive to criticism and because they have trouble standing up for themselves in social situations, they may be especially vulnerable to peer pressure to drink or take drugs. They may be made to feel they are even more isolated if they don't "conform" and do like their friends or acquaintances.

Some experts also think that some shy people may on occasion be aggressive or even explosively violent. The reasoning goes like this: The shy person is continually under stress (experiences "abuse") in social situations and is never able to answer back or to respond effectively when he or she feels slighted. Shyness in such situations may be followed by anger. Either this anger builds up over a long period of time, or the person's ability to control the anger breaks down and there is a sudden outburst. The result may be bizarre and tragic violence. At present, the evidence for a link between shyness and outbursts of violence is anecdotal.

Extreme shyness is sometimes associated with sexual dysfunction. One of the basic reasons for this is quite obvious. A person who is terribly self-conscious is going to be even more self-conscious in a highly intimate sexual encounter. In this intimate relationship where the self is exposed physically and psychologically, the thought of not performing adequately or of criticism of any kind could be devastating. Finally, Gough and Thorne (1986) have shown that an index of the negative aspects of shyness is significantly correlated with depression and anxiety.

Summary

The emotion of shyness has attracted a number of researchers in recent years. The evidence from the research of these investigators has shown that shyness emerges very early in life. Anectodal evidence suggests that it appears in infants as early as 3 or 4 months of age, and there is solid empirical data to show that it is present in the second year of life. Longitudinal studies show that extreme shyness or extreme behavioral inhibition in the face of novel, social stimuli has traitlike stability. Children who are extremely shy as toddlers are also extremely shy at 7-1/2 years. The evidence suggests that extreme shyness is determined, in part, by genetic factors.

In addition to longitudinal studies, research on behavioral genetics show that shyness in the normal range also has a biological component. Adopted children are more likely to be shy if their biological mothers are shy.

Although there is convincing data that both shyness within the normal range and extreme shyness have genetic determinants, the evidence also shows that environment plays a part. The strongest relationships between shyness in children and shyness in parents comes from nonadoptive families where both genes and environment are shared.

No universal facial expression of shyness has been documented, but shy behaviors are readily recognized. Shy behaviors include turning away of the head, averting the gaze, and in other ways avoiding direct social stimulation. The experience or feeling of shyness seems to involve heightened self-awareness and perhaps a feeling of inferiority. Evidence suggests that shyness or situations that elicit shyness often involve a mix of positive and negative feelings. The profile of emotions in a shyness situation had a higher mean for enjoyment–joy than did any of the other negative emotions.

Shyness may serve some adaptive functions. It may protect the child from venturing too far into unfamiliar and unsafe surroundings. Shy behaviors may help regulate the more reactive autonomous nervous system that characterizes the shy child in social situations.

There can be no doubt, however, that extreme shyness can be maladaptive. It can greatly restrict the social network that provides the social support that buffers stress for nonshy people. Shyness can also restrict curiosity and exploration, particularly in social situations. Although the positive aspects of shyness may serve adaptive functions, the negative aspects of shyness were found to be significantly correlated with depression and anxiety.

Suggested Readings

Briggs, S. (1988). Shyness: Introversion or neuroticism? *Journal of Research in Personality*, *22*, 290–307.

A study of shyness in relation to sociability and psychological maladjustment.

Caspi, A., Elder, G. H., & Bem, D. J. (1988). Moving away from the world: Life-course patterns of shy children. *Developmental Psychology*, *24*, 824–831.

A 30-year follow-up of shy children. Effects of childhood shyness on careers, marriage, and lifestyle.

Daniels, D., & Plomin, R. (1985). Origins of individual differences in infant shyness. *Developmental Psychology 21*(1), 118–121.

Evidence from twins reared apart helps clarify the role of genes and environment on the development of shyness.

Jones, W. H., Cheeks, J. M., & Briggs, S. R. (Eds.). (1986). *Shyness: Perspectives on research and treatment*. New York: Plenum.

A source book of theory and research on the nature and treatment of shyness.

Kagan, J., Reznick, J. S., & Snidman, N. (1988). Biological bases of childhood shyness. *Science*, *240*, 167–171.

A longitudinal study of extremely shy children (2–7 years). Measures of behavioral inhibition and physiological responses that distinguish them from nonshy children. Discussion of the data in relation to the contribution of genes and environment.

15

Shame

Shame plays an important role in human affairs, but it has been much less studied than emotions such as anger and fear. The apparent relationships between anger and some forms of aggression and between fear and the complex concept of anxiety have resulted in extensive studies of certain aspects of these emotions. The social and clinical significance of normal and deviant anger- and fear-related behaviors have captured the attention of scientists for many decades. The effects of shame on the individual and on social relations, however, have been infrequently subjected to empirical investigation.

Definition of Shame: Biological and Psychological Characteristics

Shame, shyness, and guilt are sometimes considered as aspects of the same emotion, sometimes as quite distinct emotions, and sometimes as quite distinct emotions with some common characteristics.

Darwin (1872) used all three terms—shame, shyness, and guilt—but he apparently used shame and shyness as virtually synonymous terms. Occasionally he implied that there were some differences between shame and shyness, but he did not specify them. He did point out the difference between shame and guilt, and this will be considered in the next chapter. Darwin thought that shame belonged to a large group of related emotions—shame, shyness, guilt, jealousy, envy, avarice, revenge, suspicion, deceit, vanity, conceit, ambition, pride, and humility. Most contemporary emotion theorists would agree that all of these concepts definitely have an emotion component and an emotion connotation, but few would argue that each is a basic and distinct emotion with different neurochemical substrates.

The astuteness of Darwin's observational powers is again evident in the fact that almost all the concepts in the "shame group" are related in some important way to shame, shyness, or guilt. The shy woman who feels restricted in interacting socially may be more likely to feel jealous when her husband enjoys social encounters. The person who is shamed (disgraced) may seek revenge. Deceit may be used to hide guilt. Vanity and conceit may be defenses against shame or shyness. A person may become quite ambitious and develop great pride to avoid shame. Humility can be seen as a direct correlate of shame.

It has been generally assumed that Darwin considered each of the concepts in the shame group as representing a distinct emotion. Actually, though, he referred to these concepts consistently as representing mental states or states of mind. Although not a very precise phrase, "state of mind," considered as an equivalent of affective–cognitive structure, describes such concepts as revenge, conceit, pride, and humility better than does the term emotion.

The Expression of Shame and Its Physiological Aspects

The expressions of shame and shyness are similar. If Rafe feels shame, he typically averts his gaze and turns his face away, usually by turning his head to the side and downward. His head and body movements tend to have the effect of making him appear smaller (see Figure 15-1). Darwin thought that the eyes were the primary expressive device of shame. The "eyes are turned ascant" and "waver from side to side." The eyelids are lowered and held partly closed from time to time.

The tendency to curl up and make the body appear smaller was dramatically exemplified by a young woman who was participating in the making of a film on hypnotically induced emotions. When shame was induced, she averted her eyes, lowered her head, and then immediately curled up in the chair with her knees

FIGURE 15-1. Shame behaviors along with a smile in a 10-year-old boy of northern India.

against her breasts and her arms around her legs. In the posthypnotic inquiry she reported that she felt like a little rabbit all curled up in a furry ball, trying very hard not to be seen.

One of the physical attributes of shame is that rather mysterious phenomenon of blushing, which Darwin considered the most peculiar and most human of all the emotion expressions. Darwin was apparently correct in maintaining that blushing does not occur in nonhumans. (Darwin thought that animals did exhibit shame or shyness, and he gave examples of this behavior in dogs.)

It is generally believed that blushing cannot be controlled voluntarily. It is a result of certain activities of the autonomic nervous system. Darwin, as well as many contemporary emotion theorists, considers blushing a result of the emotion of shame. The fact that blushing is a function of the autonomic nervous system and an effect of shame experience places it in a different category from the facial expressions of emotions previously considered.

It is not certain that blushing is an inevitable accompaniment of shame. Some people reportedly feel shame without blushing. In any case, there are wide individual differences in the frequency of blushing, and the threshold for blushing apparently changes with age. In general, children and adolescents seem to have a lower threshold for blushing than do adults. It is not known whether this is a result of biological changes that occur as the person grows older or whether it is a result of psychological changes in the blushing threshold.

As already indicated, it is customary to consider blushing as a completely involuntary reaction. However, recent research on control of autonomic functions by means of biofeedback or by means of certain meditational practices makes it appear quite reasonable that blushing could be brought under voluntary control, from the standpoint of both production and inhibition, as one grows from childhood through adolescence and adulthood. It is also quite possible that at the same time the individual has learned other methods (or defenses) for the control of blushing by means of avoiding shame-eliciting situations.

Tomkins (1963) has suggested that blushing is an immediate effect of shame but is also a cause of further shame. By calling the attention of others to our embarrassment, blushing tends to make worse the shame we already feel. Thus, the inhibition of blushing may well attenuate the shame experience. The person who "never blushes" may indeed be one who feels little shame.

Blushing is apparently caused by an autonomic nervous system reaction that results in inhibition of the normal tonic and contracting activities of the capillaries of the face, allowing these vessels to fill with blood. The increased blood flow results in the flushed red appearance of the face. Darwin noted the possibility that the same kind of capillary action that causes blushing in the facial skin may occur in the part of the brain that controls blushing, thus resulting in the "confusion of mind" that occurs in shame.

Darwin thought that blushing was confined mainly to the face for two reasons. The first reason is the exposure of the face to the air, light, and temperature variations. He reported that people who go naked to the waist blush on their torsos as well as on their faces. Second, the attention of the self (and of others) is "directed much more frequently and earnestly to the face." The face, more than any other part of the body, is subjected to self-attention, by virtue of its being the "seat of beauty and ugliness" and the most "ornamented part of the body."

Although it is commonly accepted that visual stimulation is the most important type of input in the generation of shame and blushing, there is some evidence that it is not essential in shame activation. Darwin reported instances of blushing in a blind and deaf girl and cited instances of other blind children who were "great blushers." Darwin also reported instances of people who maintained that they blushed in complete solitude. Apparently, the memory of an embarrassing incident that occurred in the presence of another person or thoughts about the attitudes, remarks, or actions of other people can serve as sufficient stimulus to elicit the emotion of shame and the phenomenon of blushing.

As Tomkins (1963) has noted, adults modify the shame expression because it is not socially desirable for them to express shame too openly, too intensely, or too often. One modification of the shame response is for the individual to simply take a quick look downward. Sometimes an individual may hold the head high, in effect, substituting the look of contempt for the look of shame. A person may look chronically humble so that a shame expression will not be so noticeable. Finally, a person may hold the head back, the chin out, but still have a downward cast of the eyes.

The Experience of Shame

Darwin and all serious students of shame have pointed out that in shame a person feels a heightened degree of self-consciousness, self-awareness, or self-attention. In shame, our whole consciousness is suddenly and for a moment filled with the self. We are aware only of the self or some aspect of the self that we consider indecorous or inadequate. It is as though something we were hiding from everyone is suddenly under a burning light in public view. At the same time we feel totally ineffective and incompetent. We feel at a loss for words and actions. As Darwin put it, when one blushes in shame, one loses one's "presence of mind" and often utters "inappropriate remarks." The shamed person may also stammer and make awkward movements and strange grimaces.

Tomkins (1963) gave a very vivid description of shame. He considers shame, shyness, and guilt as one emotion served by the same neurophysiological mechanisms. He maintains however, that at least at the conscious, phenomonological level, shame and guilt are quite different phenomena. He describes shame as the emotion of indignity, defeat, transgression, and alienation:

> Though terror speaks to life and death and distress makes of the world a veil of tears, yet shame strikes deepest into the heart of man. While terror and distress hurt, they are wounds inflicted from outside which penetrate the smooth surface of the ego; but shame is felt as an

> inner torment, a sickness of the soul. It does not matter whether the humiliated one has been shamed by derisive laughter, or whether he mocks himself. In either event he feels himself naked, defeated, alienated, lacking in dignity and worth. (Tomkins, 1963, p. 185)

Tomkins described shame as the most reflexive of the emotions, an experience of the self by the self, in which the phenomenological distinction between the subject and the object of shame is lost and in which the increased consciousness, awareness, and visibility of the face generates the torment of self-consciousness.

Helen Lewis (1971) has also written a detailed description of the phenomenology of shame. In shame, the self is experienced as the object of contempt and scorn. The shamed person feels ridiculed, reduced, little. Feelings of helplessness, inadequacy and even paralysis flood consciousness. There are noxious body stimuli from blushing and sometimes from tears and rage when the shame elicits sadness and anger. The shamed adult feels childish, with all weaknesses exposed in full view of the self and others. The self feels as though it can function only poorly or not at all as a perceiver, thinker, and doer. The "ego boundaries" become permeable.

In shame the individual sees the "other" as the source of contempt, scorn and ridicule. The other appears as a powerful ridiculing being, intact and capable, sometimes expressing derisive laughter. The other may also appear as "going away" or abandoning. Lewis thought that the shame experience included feelings of shyness, bashfulness, modesty, embarrassment, chagrin, and mortification.

Lynd (1961) suggests that the feeling of shame includes an unexpectedness or

> astonishment at seeing different parts of ourselves, conscious and unconscious, acknowledged and unacknowledged, suddenly coming together, and coming together with aspects of the world we have not recognized. . . . The sudden sense of exposure, of being unable to deal with what is happening, characterizes shame. (p. 34)

Erickson (1950, 1956) expresses a similar view of shame phenomenology and adds the notion that shame also includes the feeling of a sudden loss of self-control.

Modigliana (1971) defined shame or embarrassment as a loss of situational self-esteem. He examined his concept of shame in a laboratory study of responses to "private" and "public" success and failure on an intellectual task. Experimental conditions (task failure) for inducing embarrassment occurred both in private and public and were either mitigated or not by cognitive input regarding the difficulty level of the task. The mean for self-reported embarrassment was highest for subjects who experienced public failure and lowest for those who experienced public success. The data showed that slight embarrassment occurred even in the private failure condition, and the author interpreted the cause as "anticipated presence of others." The results also showed a significant negative relationship between amount of embarrassment and eye contact.

The foregoing descriptions of the phenomenology of shame have a number of common themes. Shame involves the self in a very unusual and particular way. There is an extremely heightened consciousness of self and often of some particular aspect of self. The heightened self-awareness results in unusual and distinct self-perceptions. The self is seen as small, helpless, frozen, emotionally hurt, foolish, inept, out-of-place. The domination of consciousness by the self and by self-imaging results in a temporary inability to think logically and efficiently. In shame one feels a loss of words, especially of the right words—the appropriate ones for the occasion. Later one thinks of just the thing that he or she could have said in the speechless moment of embarrassment. Shame is usually accompanied by some measure of failure or defeat. At the very least we "lose our cool," and our customary style of expression is momentarily destroyed. In one respect we are anything but alienated. We are standing in flaming light before piercing eyes. However, we are quite alienated in the sense that we cannot easily reach out, touch, or communicate with the other person.

The complexity of the experience of shame and its relation to other emotions are illustrated in Nancy's description of a stressful event in her life. On this occasion she experienced anger, guilt, and shame, but shame seems to have been the most significant for her.

> At the age of 5, I started my kindergarten class, while at the same time my parents decided to separate. I can remember the day my father left—he had his suitcase in his hand and much to his surprise I was already awake, for it was early in the morning. When I asked where he was going the reply wasn't clear; it was something to the effect that he was going away for a little while. I remember his eyes filling up with tears, and the words seeming to get stuck in his throat. The following year was also different, in that my mother began working outside of our home 3 days a week. My sister and I seemed to spend most of our time with our neighbor.
>
> I would say it's quite possible that my perception of that time in my life may be somewhat less than accurate; nonetheless, it is the way I remember feeling. The contact with my father seemed seldom, and mostly what I remember is seeing him on Sundays when we would go to a place called Strattontown where we walked along a path, picking flowers and throwing stones into a stream. While I don't remember showing my feelings outwardly with regard to being sad, I do remember feeling confused. I don't think I was able to even have a fundamental understanding of what was taking place. Somehow I think I ended up feeling a sense of rejection; in some ways I felt as though my parents had so much to contend with, with regard to their own relationship, that it was difficult for them to give their all in parenting. I suppose that somehow the confusion of my environment at that time was more prevalent than my sadness. I can also remember being quiet by nature at that age; however, I believe I was somewhat more withdrawn than usual due to the situation. I would take this a step further, and say that in a way, I felt a sense of shame. This period of my life ended when my parents decided to get back together.

It is interesting that Nancy, even after 16 years, had difficulty recognizing or admitting that along with sadness was a sense of shame. Several things make it clear that shame was prominent: she felt rejected, she was withdrawn, and she felt confused.

In the moment of shame we feel that some awkward or defective aspect of self is exposed in a glaring light. This may just be another way of describing the heightened self-consciousness, but it emphasizes the negative or painful aspect of the experience.

The Causes of Shame

As in the case of the other fundamental emotions, the activation of shame at the neural level is considered separately from the conscious causes of shame. Although the precise mechanisms involved in the neural activation of shame have not been determined, there is fairly general agreement regarding a variety of causes of shame at the conscious level.

Tomkins (1963) considers shame as an emotion that is activated by a decrease in the density of neural firing. He thinks shame is activated by the partial reduction of the neural activity of the ongoing emotion of either interest–excitement or enjoyment–joy.

Tomkins's interesting hypothesis regarding the neural mechanism for the activation of shame has several implications for the psychology of this important emotion. First, if we assume the hypothesis is valid, then shame occurs only when the individual is experiencing one of the positive emotions, either interest or enjoyment. Thus, both neurologically and psychologically, shame is more closely associated with the positive emotions than any of the other negative emotions. Since the hypothesis states that shame is activated by only the partial reduction of the neural activity of a positive emotion, there is greater likelihood that the interrupted positive emotion will continue at some level or will alternate in consciousness with shame, particularly if the shame is not too intense.

All students of shame agree that it is characterized by a sharply heightened self-consciousness. It is consciousness of a self seen as awkward, unfit, or inadequate to the task or situation at hand and, thus, the accompanying feeling is distressing. If shame has as its core a particular kind of heightened self-consciousness, then it follows that some rudiment of the self-image or self-concept must be present before the infant can experience shame. This means that the child has developed the ability to distinguish self from others However, such a distinction can be made in an elementary way by about 4 months of age.

Because of the role of the self-image in the experience of shame, Lewis, Sullivan, Stanger, and Weiss (1989) have studied children's responses to a mirror to determine the age of onset of self-recognition and its role in the experience of shame. Essentially, the tests of self-recognition are based on the kind of behavior the young child exhibits on seeing his or her image in a mirror after red rouge has been placed on the child's nose. If the child gazes at the mirror and touches the mirror image, the experimenter assumes that the child sees its image only as an object. If the child first looks at the mirror image and then touches her own nose, then the experimenter assumes that the child recognizes the mirror image as an image of herself. That is, the assumption is made that the child knows that something is "wrong" with her face.

In the experiment of Lewis and colleagues, shyness was defined on the basis of the following behaviors: a staring, attentive look characterized by a neutral or sober facial expression, accompanied by sudden inhibition of ongoing vocal or other behavior and followed by gaze aversion. Their behavioral criteria for shame (they used the term *embarrassment*) were smiling followed by averting the gaze and moving the hands to touch hair, clothing, or face. They were able to obtain very high reliability between the coders who observed these behaviors.

No infants showed self-recognition by the mirror test until 15 to 18 months of age, when 30% of them exhibited self-recognition. At age 21–24 months, 88% of the infants showed self-recognition behavior when placed in front of the mirror with rouge on their noses. In one condition, infants seated in a high chair beside their mother were approached by a stranger. The stranger moved to different positions, each closer to the infant, finally touching the infants hand before walking away. The stranger never spoke. The experimenter's coding scheme indicated that 23 of the 27 subjects tested showed wariness or shyness behaviors toward the stranger, whereas only 2 showed shame or embarrassment. A second study of 44 22-month-olds showed that the mirror condition elicited embarrassment or shame behaviors more frequently. Eleven of the 44 infants showed signs of embarrassment or shame when they saw the rouge on their noses.

The authors reason that the mirror–rouge experiment is a reasonably effective one for eliciting shame or embarrassment because it directs the child's attention to herself. This is consistent with the common observation that a sharp increase in self-awareness is part of the experience of shame. The Lewis *et al*. data suggest that shame is indeed based on a kind of self-knowledge. Before shame is experienced, it appears that the child must have a *referential self*. That is, the child must have a sufficiently clear and stable image of herself to be able to refer to it. Thus when the child has the cognitive capacity to make references to herself, she is subject to shame.

There is a strong possibility that changes in the cardiovascular system—particularly the blushing phenomenon—play a role in the neurochemical processes of shame. Since they are probably subsequent to the initial subjective experience of shame, the cardiovascular changes such as that involved in blushing probably serve more of a regulatory function in the shame process. As Tomkins observed, the effect of blushing on the experience of shame is at least partly psychological: it increases the already heightened consciousness of the face, calls the observer's attention to the face, and thus amplifies the shame experience.

One possible source of shame can be traced to early shame experiences with strangers. In the young infant, the human face is typically a stimulus for excitement and joy. On seeing the human face, the infant usually desires social contact and attempts to increase communication with the other person. As a child is learning to differentiate the face of the mother from the face of a stranger, the first glimpse of the stranger will elicit the infant's desire to communicate. Recognition of the face as strange inhibits the infant's interest and enjoyment and reduces the desire to communicate. Shame or shyness results from the infant's mistake in recognition that led to the "familiar responses" to an unfamiliar person. If in childhood there is a series of negative experiences with strangers, one eventually learns that one is always subject to shame when one meets a stranger. As Tomkins (1963) put it:

> The expectation of an impediment to communication somewhat attenuates the excitement he experiences the next time he sees a stranger. Shame is then evoked again, and the child has taken the crucial steps in constructing in his imagination the class of people in whose presence one feels shy. (p. 142)

Many people have had the experience of seeing someone in a crowd and eagerly trying to greet and communicate with the individual only to find suddenly that the person whose attention has been claimed is a total stranger. The shame experienced in such a situation may be mild or intense, depending upon the circumstances. Since an unanticipated friend–stranger differential can elicit shame, Tomkins hypothesizes that as soon as the infant learns to differentiate the face of the mother from the face of the stranger (around the fourth month of life), the infant is vulnerable to shame. Henceforth, according to Tomkins, "shame is inevitable for any human being insofar as desire outruns fulfillment sufficiently to attenuate interest without destroying it" (Tomkins, 1963, p. 185).

Much of a healthy childhood and a great deal of the creative life of an adult is spent in some form of exploration that is accompanied by interest and enjoyment. Tomkins believes that in this condition any barrier to further exploration that reduces positive emotion will produce shame. However, it seems that certain barriers may not heighten self-consciousness or call undue attention to the self, and hence may not evoke shame. If Rafe is happily and excitedly exploring a mountain forest and he comes to a gorge across his path, his positive emotion may be partly reduced, but the cause (barrier) is completely impersonal and reflects in no way upon the self. In such a situation the individual may momentarily feel less excitement and enjoyment and perhaps even mild sadness or anger, but it would be no occasion for shame. On the other hand, if Rafe the explorer was escorting his girlfriend Rebecca to some point of interest beyond the gorge, he might, depending on his sensitivity to Rebecca's expectations of him, experience some embarrassment over his temporary inability to fulfill his promise on schedule.

Helen Lewis's (1971) position, influenced by both the psychoanalytic tradition and experimental psychology, is that failure to live up to one's ego ideal constitutes a pervasive source of shame. The gap between a self-concept and an ideal self-concept is a good example of Tomkins's principle of desire outrunning achievement. Rafe never quite becomes his ideal self. The more nearly he approaches the ideal self the more likely he is to revise his concept of the ideal, thus keeping it ever beyond attainment. Failure to live up to the ego ideal can certainly be seen as a condition that would weaken interest, at least from time to time, but not destroy it.

According to Helen Lewis, shame can occur only in the context of an emotional relationship with another person, and only in relation to a person whose opinions and feelings are valued (Lewis, 1971). The threshold of shame is correlated with sensitivity to the feelings and opinions of others about the self.

Contempt from self or others can activate shame. The feeling that the self or any aspect of self is inadequate, inept, or unbecoming is another precondition for the experience of shame. Fantasies about the inadequacy or unseemliness of the self may generalize to all aspects of the individual. If Rafe is dissatisfied with his physique, and attention is suddenly focused upon it, shame results. Similarly, Rafe as a teenager may be tortured with shame when attention is suddenly focused upon his "big ears" or "wide nose," or on his plumpness, frailty, clumsiness, complexion, and so on.

Rafe may think that his thought and speech are inadequate or inappropriate. What young man cannot remember vividly the frequent embarrassment created by his voice changing its pitch during adolescence? Later in life he may be embarrassed by his grammar, or by the quality of his thought as reflected in the substance of his speech.

Darwin alluded to the fact that although shame is most frequently elicited by blame, criticism, or derision, it can also occur in response to praise. Most young people can recall some embarrassment on an occasion when doting parents pointed out some virtue of their darling child. Darwin's observation appears sound, but the activation of shame by praise is a topic that has received very little attention. Why should such praise elicit shame? In such a situation at least one of the conditions for the activation of shame is evident—attention to the self is greatly increased. Tomkin's criteria of partial reduction of interest or enjoyment might be met also. It might well be that the child's interest or enjoyment in participation in an adult affair is partly reduced by the focusing of attention on the self and the feeling of inability to respond appropriately. On such occasions the feeling of shame could occur because children feel that they have suddenly been overexposed or described in terms they cannot live up to.

Lynd (1961) noted that under some conditions the perception of inappropriateness or incongruity elicits shame. She recognized that in other circumstances incongruity elicits interest or joy. Thus we have another basis for hypothesizing a dynamic relationship between the positive emotions and shame.

As is the case for all emotions, situations vary greatly in their potency for producing shame in different individuals. The situation that evokes shame in one person may evoke excitement and challenge in a second and anger and aggression in a third. Still others may respond to the same situation with sadness or fear. Even within the same individual, what produces shame in one situation or under one condition may produce an entirely different reaction on other occasions and under other conditions. A common theme across a great variety of situations that can prove to be sources of shame is the excitement or enjoyment that these situations typically elicit. Thus, in whatever situations we have invested interest and enjoyment we may find occasions for shame. The most common and ubiquitous objects involved in the activation of shame are the self (or self-concept), the body, love, work, friendship, close interpersonal relationships, or even brief encounters that have special meaning for the individual.

A summary of the free responses for shame on the antecedents and consequences test is presented in Table 15-1. These responses are generally consistent with the theoretical description of shame and shame–shyness dynamics, although some subjects apparently did not clearly distinguish shame and guilt.

A source of serious experiences of shame are the perceptions of self as having failed or been defeated. In one sense, defeat is just another way of exposing an aspect of the self with which you are not satisfied. You lose and you feel embarrassed. It does not much matter what the contest or confrontation; the psychological effect is usually the same. You can lose in an interpersonal encounter by feeling that you did not look as good, sound as intelligent, or act as sensitive and responsive as you thought you should. Your ineptness can be felt as a defeat that exposes some defect of the self. Even professional athletes in individual or team sports may feel ashamed after losing. Even a rich, famous, and obviously successful tennis player may feel so embarrassed after the match that he or she avoids everyone for awhile, especially people of the media who are eager to get a statement.

You don't have to be a professional or even a highly successful player to feel the shame of defeat in competition. All that is required is that you have the will and the desire to win. This is another paradoxical aspect of shame (Tomkins, 1963). You can reduce the likelihood of shame in any competition or encounter if you reduce the will and the wish to win. But consider for a moment the price of this insurance against shame. Sometimes the price is cheap because it may be in your best interest to reduce the desire to win when the odds against you are overwhelming and winning is not really important to your well-being. It may be that your interest or talent can be better directed somewhere else. On the other hand, the anticipation of shame in defeat may cause you to give up too quickly and too easily. Reduction of the will to win should not be a substitute for the thought, work, or practice that it takes to improve the skill or competency that is in question. Being able to make the proper judgment about when to reduce your will to win, when to redirect your interest somewhere else, and when to let shame anticipation drive you to self-improvement is a real test of emotional maturity.

The Evolutionary–Biological and Psychological Functions of Shame

It seems safe to assume that the various human emotions evolved over thousands and thousands of years, as our progenitors and their processes of adaptation became more and more complex. Because our emotions are a product of our evolutionary–biological heritage, we can infer that each emotion served an inherently adaptive function in the phylogenesis of human beings. It is fairly easy

TABLE 15-1

Antecedents and Consequences of Shame[a]

Responses	Percentage of subjects giving responses
Antecedents	
Feelings	
1. Of disappointment in self, inept	31.0
2. Self-conscious (shame synonyms, e.g., embarrassment, shy)	25.0
3. Has done something to hurt others	16.4
4. Of being legally or morally wrong	12.5
5. Isolation, rejection, loneliness, lost	4.7
6. Sadness synonyms	2.3
7. Other	7.8
Thoughts	
1. Of failure, disappointment, blameworthiness	32.0
2. Has done something to hurt others	21.8
3. Unclean, immortal thoughts	21.1
4. Something wrong, stupid	10.9
5. People are laughing at (rejecting) you	3.1
6. Other	10.9
Actions	
1. Has done something legally or morally wrong, harmful	35.9
2. Has done something wrong, stupid, made a mistake	28.9
3. Had done something to hurt others	21.9
4. Did nothing	2.3
5. Other	10.9
Consequences	
Feelings	
1. Shyness, embarrassment (other shame synonyms)	28.0
2. Feels inadequate, dissappointed, like a failure	25.8
3. Feels bad, terrible, lousy, discouraged, sad	24.3
4. Lonely, isolated, rejected, lost	6.1
5. Unclean, morally unfit	2.3
6. Other	13.6
Thoughts	
1. Has failed, is disappointed, blames self	30.3
2. Questions reasons for behavior, thinks about what was done and why	23.5
3. Rationalize, escape from feeling	18.2
4. How to atone, make amends, is sorry	10.6
5. Of being set apart (people are looking)	3.8
6. Other	13.6
Actions	
1. Repents, atones, makes amends, changes, improves, does not repeat offense	48.5
2. Is deliberately alone, retreats from others	22.0
3. Rationalize, forget it, escape from feeling	12.9
4. Questions, reasons for behavior, questions what was done and why	4.5
5. Punishes self	3.8
6. Other	8.3

[a]*N* = approximately 130 college students.

to deduce the role of certain emotions in adaptation, but the role of shame is not so obvious. On the surface, shame seems to have only negative consequences for the individual. A closer look may show that this superficial assessment of the value of shame is not altogether accurate.

Evolutionary–Biological Perspectives

Shame has some functions that may have survival value for the individual. First, shame sensitizes the individual to the opinions and feelings of others and thus acts as a force for social cohesion. It assures the group or society that the individual will be responsive to criticism, particularly criticism directed toward central aspects of the self. Thus, a man who did not fulfill his responsibility with regard to such things as group defense or risk taking involved in the essentials of life (exploring, food gathering, hunting) could be subjected to humiliation and isolation. Avoidance of shame can thus be seen as a powerful motive for social conformity and individual responsibility, as powerful as the value the person places on his dignity and honor.

> Men have exposed themselves repeatedly to death and terror and have even surrendered their lives in the defense of their dignity less they be forced to bow their heads and bend their knees. The heavy hand of terror itself has been flaunted and rejected in the name of pride (the shield against shame) . . . better to risk the uncertainties of death and terror than to suffer the deep and certain humiliation of cowardice. (Tomkins, 1963, p. 132–133)

Even in modern times the threat of shame has motivated many young men to risk pain and death in wars, even in a war that they did not understand and for which they had no sympathy.

It is also possible that the threat of shame served some kind of regulatory function in the sexual life of prehistoric human beings. It is quite possible that a sense of shame played an important role in pair bonding and in the reduction of conflicts and physical aggression over women. The emotion of shame is probably one of the motives that led people to seek privacy for sexual relations. The observation of rules regarding privacy in sexual relations will also serve the interest of social order and harmony. In many respects, shame continues to serve these functions in contemporary society.

A final reason for the evolution of shame was the role that it played in the development of skills and competencies necessary for the survival of the individual and the group. The self most subject to shame is the self without skills or competencies. To avoid the shame of ineptness, the individual is motivated to find his or her strength and develop it. Individuals with highly developed and varied skills and competencies make for a stronger and more defensible group.

The Psychosocial Functions of Shame

There is considerable overlap between the biological and psychosocial functions of shame. What is of significance for people biologically will certainly have significance for them psychologically, and what has significance for the psychological well-being of people may certainly affect their overall biological adaptation. Nevertheless, there are several functions of shame that are rather distinctly psychological in nature. These are summarized below. A more detailed discussion of various aspects of shame in personality development and adjustment can be found in Erickson (1956), H. Lewis (1971), Lynd (1961), and Tomkins (1963).

1. Shame focuses on the self or some aspect of the self, and makes it the focus of evaluation.

2. The heightened awareness of self and the exaggerated self-consciousness produced by shame tends to bring about more self-imaging. Cognition in the wake of shame works toward strengthening the self or decreasing vulnerability.

3. As H. Lewis (1971) has indicated, shame increases the permeability of the boundaries of the self. A person is more vulnerable in a state of shame. Sensitivity to shame makes it quite possible to experience shame for another person. A schoolboy may blush crimson for his pretty but inept young school teacher when the principal walks into her class and finds it in disorder.

4. The fact that shame generally is elicited by the words and actions of others guarantees a degree of sensitivity to the opinions and feelings of other people, particularly other people with whom we have emotional relationships and whose opinions we value.

5. Due to the fact that shame involves heightened self-awareness and blushing, it involves a greater awareness of the body than other emotions. This sensitivity to the self and body that obtains in shame may serve certain useful functions of both a biological and psychological nature; it may inspire the individual to practice good hygiene and hence, to guard his or her health. It may also motivate the individual to attend to his or her grooming and clothing and thus enhance his or her sociability.

6. Darwin, H. Lewis, and others maintain that shame has a highly adverse impact upon a person's rational intellectual processes. In comparing it with guilt, Lewis (1971) observed that shame is a less differentiated, more irrational, more primitive, more wordless reaction, with little cognitive content. However, reflection on the shame experience may inspire a great deal of thinking and imaging. Few people have suffered intense shame and not had fantasies of triumph over the one who evoked the shame.

7. Shame increases self-criticism and momentary feelings of impotence. Duval and Wicklund (1972) induced objective self-awareness by causing the subject to see himself or herself as in error, inept, or in some way discrepant from his or her standard of correctness. Their results suggest that such objective self-awareness is an aspect of the shame experience. Duval and Wicklund indicated that objective self-awareness typically results in an attempt either to reduce the discrepancy or to avoid the conditions that created the state. Further, the objectively self-aware person becomes more self-critical. They argued that the focus of

attention upon the self forces the individual to be aware of intraself discrepancies and to suffer a reduction of self-esteem, a reduction that results from falling short of one's personal standards of correctness. Another way in which Duval and Wicklund's concept of objective self-awareness coincides with a concept of shame is their belief that objective self-awareness tends to engender feelings of passivity and impotence. Further, Duval and Wicklund pointed out that one of the important determinants in the emergence of objective self-awareness is the individual's awareness of being observed by others. This is very much in keeping with the idea that shame focuses or gives direction to the operations of consciousness that bring about objective self-awareness.

8. Although efforts to avoid shame may subserve conformity, confronting and coping successfully with shame experiences can facilitate the development of autonomy, personal identity, and mutual love. In his discussion of the growth and crises of the healthy personality, Erickson (1956) sees shame and doubt pitted against the development of personal autonomy. He holds that in most Western societies, toilet training (the anal stage of psychosocial development) provides the original setting for the shame–autonomy conflict. In this period, the child struggles to learn self-control, when a loss of control means that one has exposed oneself "prematurely and foolishly" or shamefully.

> This stage, therefore, becomes decisive for the ration between love and hate, for that between cooperation and willfulness, and for that between the freedom of self-expression and its suppression. From a sense of self-control without loss of self-esteem comes a lasting sense of autonomy and pride; from a sense of muscular and anal impotence, of loss of self-control, and of parental over-control comes a lasting sense of doubt and shame. (Erickson, 1956, p. 199)

Lynd (1961) pursued Erickson's theme and developed the idea that confronting and transcending shame is essential to the sense of personal identity and freedom. She sees willingness to risk exposure and shame as a corrective for people's tendency to manipulate each other and for the tendency of long-term intimacy to diminish mutual love.

> Enlarging the possibilities of mutual love depends upon risking exposure. This risk of exposure can come about only with respect for oneself, respect for the other person, and recognition of nonpersonal values and loyalties that both persons respect. Through such love one comes to know the meaning of exposure without shame, and of shame transformed by being understood and shared. Aristotle distinguishes between feeling ashamed of things shameful "according to common opinion" and things shameful "in very truth." In love there can be the exploring together of the meaning of things shameful "in very truth." (Lynd, 1961, p. 239.)

Shame and the Defense of Self and Personal Integrity

Shame is responsive to criticism of the individual's most intimate possession, the integrity of the self. Shame protects self-integrity by increasing the individual's responsiveness to any indication that the self is overextended or overexposed. Shame and successful coping with shame experiences can play an important role in the development and maintenance of the self-concept and personal identity. The normal individual's desire to avoid shame or to develop a high threshold for shame serves as an important motive in the development of a set of intellectual, physical, and social skills that give the individual a sense of adequacy and competency. However, if individuals' early experiences, particularly their shame-socialization experiences, have given them concepts of themselves as dependent, inadequate, and inept people, they are likely to capitalize on certain types of ego defenses (H. Lewis, 1971).

Denial is one of the characteristic defenses against shame. Denial comes into play as a defense because shame is such a painful emotion, because it is difficult to tolerate, and because it is difficult to disguise or conceal. When Rafe feels shame, he wants to remove himself physically or psychologically from the source of shame. One way of accomplishing this, in the psychological realm at least, is to deny the existence or the importance of the source. Rafe also can try to deny that he feels shame. This is very difficult since he needs first of all to convince *himself*, and the self is typically acutely aware of the experience of shame. Nevertheless, if he is dependent on denial as a defense, he will stand with crimson face, lowered head or averted gaze, and staunchly affirm that he is not embarrassed.

A second way in which individuals defend themselves against shame is by the ego defense mechanism of repression. People try to repress their thoughts about embarrassing situations or situations in which they have experienced or may experience shame. Repression has more serious consequences for the psychological adjustment and well-being of the individual than does the defense mechanism of denial. When using denial, people merely disclaim their embarrassment at the moment they experience shame, but this does not preclude their thinking about or working through the situation at a later time. In using the mechanism of repression people deny themselves the possibility of thinking through the situation and making self-repair—"restitutions within the domain of the self, i.e., some narcissistic affirmation" (Lewis, 1971, p. 89).

The effort to repair and strengthen the self after experiencing intense shame often continues for several days or weeks. Even months or in some cases, years after an intensely embarrassing situation, an individual may recall it and rehearse techniques for coping with it. Through such rehearsal in fantasy and imagination the individual may develop many interpersonal techniques for coping with situations or conditions likely to elicit shame. When Rafe meets such a situation in the future he can practice the technique he has rehearsed in fantasy and then rehearse again and adjust the technique if necessary. These processes can lead to a sense of adequacy and enhance self-identity.

A third ego defense mechanism that the individual may use as a shame defense is affirmation of the self. If Rebecca uses this defense she will respond to shame by affirming some aspect of herself that may be totally unrelated to the shame situation. In other instances she may affirm the aspect of herself that has been criticized. Thus, if she is frequently embarrassed because of her short stature, she may respond to shame either by developing mental abilities that distract attention from her physique or by developing special motor skills that enhance her physical attractiveness and compensate for her short height.

According to H. Lewis, the most radical ego defense against shame is the affective disorder of depression. In Lewis's theory, the depression results from "undischarged shame." If a person frequently experiences shame, especially intense shame or humiliation, and is incapable of responding effectively or of using one of the more adaptive ego defense mechanisms (denial, self-affirmation), then the individual is likely to experience sadness, inner-directed hostility, fear, and guilt—the emotion components of depression (Izard, 1972). Phenomenologically, depression, like shame, is typically about the self—self-centered. The individual feels personally dejected, unworthy, incapable, and generally miserable. In depression, as in shame, the fault is generally considered to be personal and self-related and as a result there is typically self-blame. In depression, as in shame, the fault or the defect is not easily rationalized or justified.

Sociocultural Factors

The individual's social milieu and culture constitute important determinants of shame experiences. Each culture and subculture transmits certain norms or rules, the violation of which may lead to shame. Some aspects of the socialization of shame will be considered in the next section. This section will focus primarily on some findings from cross-cultural research on attitudes toward shame. These findings illustrate some differences between cultures that probably originate in child-rearing practices and the other aspects of the socialization process. The data were obtained by administration of the Emotion Attitude Questionnaire (EAQ; Izard, 1971) to groups of American, English, German, Swedish, French, Swiss, Greek, and Japanese college students. The seven cultural samples varied in size from 41 to 153 subjects. Prior to the administration of the EAQ, the students had completed an emotion recognition task and thus were familiar with photographs representing each of the fundamental emotions and with the names and definitions of the emotions.

EAQ question 1 asked: "Which emotion do you understand best?" Considering the average percentages of subjects from all cultures selecting each emotion, joy, as expected, was chosen more frequently than any other emotion, and not surprisingly shame was chosen less frequently than any other emotion. There are several reasons for the generally low frequency with which individuals indicated that shame was the best-understood emotion. The shame face tends to hide itself and the experience of shame elicits a tendency toward concealment and isolation. It is a threat to the self-concept (or ego) to be seen with a look of shame on the face, particularly during adolescent years when the self- and body image are relatively more vulnerable. In the socialization process, children are taught to hide their shame. These factors lead to a great reluctance to admit to the experience of shame, much less to reflect upon it and try to understand it. In addition to these forces, the experience of shame tends to hamper logical thought, and frequently there is little meaningful cognitive content accompanying the shame experience. This, too, makes it difficult for us to reflect upon and analyze and understand the shame experience.

In comparing the responses across cultures, it was found that a larger percentage of the Greeks than of any other cultural group indicated that they understood shame better than any other emotion. Of Greek men, 29% indicated that shame was the best-understood emotion, and this figure is two standard deviations larger that the mean frequency for all cultures. There is no specific evidence as to why the Greeks deviated in this way. It is generally agreed by psychological and anthropological observers that the Greeks are relatively high on sociability and emotion expressiveness, especially Greek males. Enjoyment and self-confidence in social situations reduce the sources of shame.

The second EAQ question was: "Which emotion do you understand the least?" In answering this question, far more Japanese than any other cultural group selected the emotion of shame. The percentage for Japanese males was 68%, two standard deviations higher than the average frequency for the eight cultures considered together. The next highest frequency, that of Swedish males, was 40%. Shame is apparently a highly important emotion in the Japanese culture (Benedict, 1946), especially prior to the influx of Western influence. An act bringing shame upon the self, or more importantly, upon one's family and the Japanese society was perhaps the greatest of indignities. In these earlier times, shame must have been considered a highly intolerable emotion.

The third question of the EAQ asked: "Which emotion do you dread the most?" Again the responses of the Japanese were quite distinct from the Western cultures, including the Greeks. Of the Japanese, 72% of the males and 69% of the females indicated that contempt was the most dreaded of all the emotions. Both these figures are more than two standard deviations greater than the average frequency for the eight cultural samples combined. The data from the previous EAQ questions, as well as the interpretation of the Japanese psychologist who collaborated in this research, indicated that the Japanese students interpreted this question to mean "What emotion expression from other people do you dread the most?" The use of the look of contempt to elicit shame is well known in Eastern and Western cultures, but apparently the look of concept is generally considered an adequate cause for shame by virtually all of the Japanese. According to Japanese folklore, when a samurai was looked upon with contempt, he had but two alternatives: to kill the person who held him in contempt, or to kill himself.

Marsella, Murray, and Golden (1974) used the semantic differential technique (Osgood, Suci, & Tannenbaum, 1957) to study ethnic variations among

Hawaiian students in their attitudes toward shame and other emotions. The subjects rated the emotions on semantic scales such as low–high and good–bad. Marsella *et al.* found that Caucasian Americans rated shame "more low, weak, and dull" than Chinese Americans and Japanese Americans. One of the authors' tentative conclusions was that shame was less clearly identifiable and understood by the Caucasian Americans.

There are many more cultural differences in the experiencing and expression of shame than we have touched upon here. It is reasonable to assume that the differences discussed in the foregoing paragraphs reflect real differences in shame thresholds and in the antecedents and consequences of the shame experience and shame expression. Although the data did not always support clear explanations of the observed cross-cultural and sex differences, they did clearly demonstrate that these differences exist.

The Socialization of Shame

The healthy child is curious and active. A wide variety of things interest her and prove to be possible sources of enjoyment. The young child's low threshold for excitement and for excitement-generated activity leads to a kind of natural self-expression or self-extension, often channeled into exploratory behavior. However, the child's excited response to a wide variety of stimuli will inevitably generate behavior that will be seen by parents, other adults, or children as inappropriate or wrong. From the child's vantage point, she is not really indecorous, she is merely indulging in natural self-expression; yet she is shamed. Children's great capacity for excitement and joy and the activity that these emotions generate greatly increases the range of possibilities for censurable behavior. The importance of a positive and nonpunitive socialization of shame is evident.

The socialization of shame is made difficult by the fact that shame is paradoxical. The experience of shame confronts the individual with puzzling contradictions; for example, it can facilitate both conformity and autonomy. The socialization of shame proceeds as the result of a series of confrontations of differences that range from trivial matters to serious conflicts.

If Tomkins is correct in assuming that the infant can experience shame as soon as he or she can differentiate the face of the mother from the face of a stranger, then the infant is vulnerable to shame by the age of 4 or 5 months. During the first half-year of life, it is the human face that has provided the infant the greatest source of excitement and joy. For about half of this time (about 2 to 5 months) the human face, any human face, is an innate releaser of the smile of joy on the face of the infant. Yet paradoxically, face-to-face encounters that once elicited only joy become the principal context for shame experiences. Our first experiences of shame occur in the parent–child relationship.

Another shame paradox is the nature of the association of excitement and joy with the activation and experience of shame. People experience shame in a way that focuses attention on the self. According to Tomkins, experiencing some level of interest or enjoyment is a necessary precondition for the activation of shame. Yet when the experience of shame is felt, it sharply inhibits the continuation of interest or enjoyment.

The potential for experiencing shame begins very early in life and continues until death. In childhood a continual source of excitement and joy comes from efforts to please parents and win their praise and approval. Often the effort to please is itself exciting and enjoyable for the child. But if the child's effort to please meets with disapproval and reprimand, interest in the activity decreases and shame is likely to result.

Over the years, through observation of her parents and other loved or admired people, the child, Rebecca, develops an image of an ideal self (self-ideal). There are numerous occasions where she is away from her parents, but her self-ideal is always present, and the self-ideal typically "incorporates," or is greatly influenced by her concept of her parents. The greater the distance between Rebecca's real self-concept and her self-ideal, the more likely she will experience shame as she fails to live up to her self-ideal. Similarly, the more intensely she desires to live up to her self-ideal, the more vulnerable she is to failure and resulting shame, and the more likely her shame will be intense.

Another of the shame paradoxes is the link between the shame experience (the phenomenon of experiencing shame) and the development of emotional ties. As already noted, shame is most likely to occur and is most likely to be intense when it happens in the context of an emotional or meaningful relationship. Yet when shame occurs, it temporarily destroys or greatly hampers social communication and interpersonal contact. We like to look at the person whom we love or admire, and in turn we like to have them look at us. But when shame occurs it is certain to reduce facial and social communication.

Shame and Sexual Development

Everyone is familiar with the association between the emotions of shame, shyness, and guilt, on the one hand, and sex characteristics and sexual behavior, on the other. This strong association holds to a greater or lesser degree in most cultures of both Western and Eastern civilizations. There are, of course, many cultural variations with regard to what sex-linked features or what sexual behavior elicits shame or pride. Despite these variations, the evidence from folklore, literature, and anthropology strongly supports the notion that those features that identify the individual as male or female are, under certain conditions, sources of shame or pride. Likewise, in virtually every society that has been studied by social scientists, there are some aspects of sexual behavior that elicit shame, shyness, or guilt, and similarly, certain types of sexual behavior that are sources of pride and self-confidence.

An even more fundamental problem than the shame–sex bond is the question of the origin of the relationship between shame and intimacy. The origin of the shame–intimacy bond may have its foundation in the mother–infant relationship. The relationship between mother and infant is close, intense, and intimate. It is replete with face-to-face contact and face-to-face communication. In these face-to-face communications, infants extend themselves, expose themselves, and give themselves openly and freely. It may well be that infants' first experiences of shame are activated on an occasion when they think they are beginning another intense and intimate encounter with the beloved face of the mother and the face turns out to be that of a stranger. In Tomkins's view, the interruption, interference, and partial attenuation of the infant's excitement and joy leads to shame (Tomkins, 1963).

Children's low threshold for interest–excitement and consequent exploratory activity almost inevitably lead them to visual and tactual exploration of their sex organs. It is also quite common for the young child to attempt to explore the sex organs of a member of the opposite sex. To the extent that such exploratory behavior is punished, the bond between shame and sexual activity is strengthened. In extreme cases, sexual activity or even the anticipation of sexual activity can evoke such intense shame as to inhibit and virtually destroy the individual's sexual life.

The older child and adolescent is faced with another shame–sex paradox. For a girl or boy to develop an appropriate sex identity, he or she needs to be proud of his or her sexual development and of those characteristics that are biologically or culturally associated with membership in his or her sex. Yet display of sex organs is forbidden, and the display rules governing secondary sexual characteristics are more or less strict in various cultures and subcultures. Most children at one time or another feel some shame about their sexual characteristics. Child-rearing practices and peer relationships can have very important influences on personality or self-development during those stages of life when the child and adolescent are highly sensitive about the status of their sexual characteristics.

The Interactions of Shame with Social Behavior and Other Affects

The interaction of shame with anger and guilt is illustrated in another incident in the life of Nancy.

> During this period of time my father experienced a dramatic drop in his income. This shook the family because we had traditionally expressed our feelings for each other in terms of material things. My father who is a very good man, although not very expressive, had always communicated his love for his family by being a good provider. Because of this, I had always associated security with money. When that security disappeared, I became frightened and disoriented.
>
> What I remember most about this period was a feeling of instability; it was as if the

bottom had suddenly dropped out from under us. I was also very ashamed of these feelings because they were caused by something as petty as money, yet I couldn't seem to be able to help it. Also I felt extreme guilt for being a financial burden to my parents. My sisters were coming to the age of financial independence, but I was only 15 and still very much dependent upon my parents for support.

I was also very concerned for my parents well-being, particularly my father. Because my father's self-concept was so much associated with being a "good provider," when that was damaged so was his self-esteem. The combination of guilt and concern for my parents acted as supreme motivations for me to try and cope with the situation. In general I tried to be as supportive as possible of my parents without letting them know of my feelings. And on a more practical level, I took on more hours at work.

I think I put a lot of my feelings on hold during this period. I really tried to be as strong as I possibly could be for my family and for myself. Unfortunately, my emotions demanded to be dealt with, if not sooner then later. During the next few years I certainly made up for the suppression of my emotions earlier on.

At the end of my sophomore year in high school I may have appeared to be strong and capable of coping on the outside, but on the inside I was beginning to feel the strain. What eventually set me off was simply my mother's suggestion that I see a doctor about weight and my skin and also that I get a haircut. That was about all it took to make me feel totally rejected for the person I was.

I guess my initial reaction to my mother's comments was intense shame. I was ashamed of my body and felt guilty for not being the perfect daughter for my parents. I can remember feeling like I just wanted to curl up in a dark corner somewhere and hide. What I actually did was go to my room and cry. When I finished crying I decided the only solution was to go on a severe diet.

I can hardly begin to tell you how I felt during this time. I was extremely angry at myself for being fat and at my mother for caring that I was fat. I wanted to punish myself for being so stupid as to actually believe that people really didn't care about what you looked like. Well, punish myself I did, 800 calories a day, a fast once a week plus eating laxatives in an effort to lose weight. I lost two pounds a week and dieted until I weighed 115 pounds. The awful part is that I still thought that I was fat, but my body refused to lose any more weight and became very unhealthy. I became frustrated.

It's hard to explain what I went through then. My world seemed very unstable. I had expected life to turn suddenly terrific when I lost the weight. I was working very hard in school and doing well, yet that still wasn't enough either. My self-image was distorted. I no longer was sure what was meaningful about a person; was it appearances or what was inside? My mental state can only be described as confused. My family and friends kept telling me how good they thought I looked and praised me for the responsibilities I had taken on, yet I was still terribly unhappy. And to top it off, I began to put the weight back on.

When I began gaining the weight back I started to avoid people because I was ashamed. I had almost nothing to fall back on emotionally because for the previous 6 months I had tried to conform so much to others' views of how I should be, that I forgot who I was. Finally, a close friend asked me how I was feeling. When I finished crying, we talked about my feelings and my confusion. After that I began to get my act together again. The tragic part of the whole thing is that I lost 18 months of my life going through all this nonsense.

There are several aspects of Nancy's story that tell us something important about shame. The disorientation she felt after her father's reduction in income may have been the mental confusion caused by shame, in this case vicarious shame. Nancy's own shame came when her mother scolded her for her appearance and seemed to reject her. Her urge to hide or disappear is a standard reaction to intense shame.

Shame, Sociability, and Conformity

Shame is used to develop and maintain conformity to the group's norms; shaming techniques are most readily observed when there is the need to inhibit or regulate deviations from the norm. Shame also promotes sociability by acting as a restraint on self-centeredness or egotism and thus fostering the investment of positive emotions in relationships with others. At the same time, conformity and the sense of belongingness increase people's self-confidence and security and render them less vulnerable to shame. Paradoxically, the greater their identification with the group and the stronger their sense of belongingness, the more vulnerable they are to the censure of the group and the more likely will their behavior be influenced by the anticipation of possible shame and by shame-avoidance strategies and techniques.

Shame and the Sex Drive

In the foregoing discussion of the socialization of shame, it was pointed out that there is usually a relationship between shame and intimacy and that often intimacy has a sensual or directly sexual connotation. It is not at all surprising then that there would be important interactions between the emotion of shame and the sex drive. Mild degrees of shyness are often perceived as attractive and even as sexually exciting. The maintenance of some degree of shyness or modesty may be quite important in maintaining and enhancing long-lasting sexual relationships.

Of course, sexual intercourse within the context of a love relationship should be free of shame. If shame is sufficiently intense, the sex drive will be inhibited.

Shame Interaction with Other Emotions

Everyday experience and theoretical considerations indicate that shame is often experienced at the same time as other affects. As with other emotions, the experiencing of shame concomitantly with drives and other emotions results in the development of associations or bonds between shame and other affects. In this way, shame may become an activator of other emotions, and other emotions may come to activate shame. Similarly, shame may serve in some way to defend the individual against other emotions, and other emotions may be used as anticipatory defenses or methods of coping with shame. The interactions of shame with interest, joy, sadness, anger, and fear were discussed in previous chapters.

Tomkins (1963) thinks that shame and contempt rarely exist separately. Contempt from another or from the self is an activator of the shame experience.

Under certain conditions shame can be reduced by self-contempt—by a rejection of that aspect of the self of which one is ashamed. However, at the same time, the more the individual is invested in that part of the self that caused shame, and the stronger the wish not to lose that part of one's self, the more likely, according to Tomkins, will the contempt that rejects that aspect of the self lead to shame.

Shame and Depression

Having just discussed the relationship between defeat and shame, we should consider briefly the relationship between shame and depression. More than one expert on human emotions has seen a relationship between proneness to shame and proneness to depression.

There are a number of ways in which shame can be seen as directly related to depression. Recall the earlier discussion of the symptomatology of depression. The pattern of emotions in depression includes sadness as the key emotion followed by inner-directed hostility, shame, and fear. Evidence from systematic research and clinical investigations shows that after being shamed we often feel angry. Sometimes the anger is directed in fantasy toward triumph over the person or group that caused the shame. Not uncommonly, however, the anger is directed inwardly. You get mad at yourself for being "stupid," "inept," "awkward," or "clumsy." If this becomes a chronic way of responding to situations that elicit shame, then we have a large part of the pattern of emotions in depression. If you begin to feel sorry for yourself, and thereby add sadness to the shame and inner-directed hostility, we have the emotion symptoms of depression. Depression becomes serious when loss and sadness, defeat and shame, and inner-directed anger begin to make you think of yourself as incapable or helpless. Beck (1976) has shown that the depressed person comes to think negatively of self, world, and future.

Summary

Shame is expressed by lowering or turning the head, averting the gaze, lowering of the eyelids, and blushing. Blushing may exacerbate the shame experience by calling further attention to the face. People also report physiological reactions that suggest sympathetic arousal in the shame experience.

The shame experience begins with a sudden and intense heightening of awareness of the self. Awareness of the self so dominates consciousness that cognitive processes are sharply inhibited, causing a loss of presence of mind and increasing the likelihood of stammering inappropriately and coping clumsily. Shame typically occurs in the presence of other people who play some role in activating the shame, but shame can occur in privacy. Self-consciousness, concern over the impression one makes, and concern over social evaluation are frequent responses to shame experiences. There is a tendency for shame to make the self seem small, helpless, and inept. Paradoxically, shame sometimes occurs after a complimentary evaluation by others.

According to Tomkins, at the neurological level, shame is activated by the partial reduction of the neural activity of the ongoing emotion of either interest or enjoyment. At the psychological level, shame may be activated by any situation that focuses attention on the self or some aspect of the self that is found wanting. Any experience that gives one the feeling of inappropriate self-disclosure can elicit shame. The prototypical shame experience probably occurs when the infant mistakenly makes "familiar" overtures to an unfamiliar face. In later life, failure to live up to one's self-ideal may constitute a pervasive source of shame.

Shame has two functions that suggest its role in evolution. It sensitizes the individual to the opinions and feelings of others and thus facilitates a degree of social conformity and social responsibility. Shame also motivates the learning of skills and the development of social competence.

Shame increases the permeability of the boundaries of the self. At the same time it may play a significant role in the development of self-control and autonomy. Confronting and transcending shame can increase the sense of personal identity and psychological freedom.

People use the defense mechanism of denial, repression, and affirmation of self in dealing with shame. Frequently, shame that is not dealt with effectively can lead to sadness and depression.

Attitudes toward shame vary widely across cultures, and these differences in attitude lead to various methods of socializing this emotion. Children's interest-instigated activities lead them into shame-eliciting situations. Parental handling of shame experiences in young children requires sensitive attention since shame tends to hamper social communication and interpersonal contact. It is difficult to deal effectively with an emotion that tends to reduce facial and social communication.

Properly dealt with, shame can play a positive role in self-development and self-improvement. Since it calls attention to the self or some aspect of the self, reflection on the shame experience can increase self-knowledge.

The highly intimate and emotional character of the sexual relationship makes it fertile ground for shame and shyness. Sexual intercourse leads to self-exposure, and self-exposure may be a precursor of shame.

An early source of the shame–sex interaction comes from children being caught unaware while exploring their sexual organs. Shame is readily elicited during periods when sexual organs and secondary sexual characteristics are developing.

The mother–infant relationship is probably the origin of the shame–intimacy relationship and of the relationship between eye contact and personal involvement or intimacy. The association between eye contact, intimacy and sensual pleasure is probably the source of the widespread taboo on extended eye contact between nonintimates.

Shame has important interactions with social behavior and other affects. It plays a role in the development of sociability. Under favorable circumstances, some degree of shyness or modesty may enhance sexual relationships, but under less favorable conditions it can inhibit or destroy them. Shame interactions with interest, joy, sadness, anger, and fear were discussed in previous chapter In this chapter, it was noted that contempt was often an activator of shame and that the contempt may be from one's self as well as from others.

Shame has unique motivational-experiential characteristics, and the shame experience can be of great significance to the individual and to society.

Suggested Readings

Eales, M. (1989). Shame among unemployed men. *Social Science and Medicine, 28*, 783–789.

Home interviews with unemployed British men revealed that a substantial percentage of them experience shame that interfered with social relations and led to modification of behavior patterns.

Lewis, H. B. (1979). Shame in depression and hysteria. In C. E. Izard (Ed.), *Emotions in personality and psychopathology* (pp. 371–396). New York: Plenum.

A psychoanalytically oriented psychologist examines the relations among styles of cognitive functioning, shame, and the disorders of depression and hysteria.

Lewis, M., Sullivan, M. W., Stanger, C., & Weiss, M. (1989). Self-development and self-conscious emotions. *Child Development, 60*, 146–156.

Studies of the development of self-recognition (with the mirror–rogue technique) and its relation to cognitive development and the emergence of behaviors indicative of shame (or embarrassment) and other emotions.

Parrott, W. G., Sabini, J., Silver, M., (1988). The roles of self-esteem and social interaction in embarrassment. *Personality and Social Psychology Bulletin, 14*, 191–202.

Examines the role of social interaction (self-presentation) and self esteem in the activation of shame (embarrassment).

Tangney, J. W. (1990). Assessing individual differences in proneness to shame and guilt: Development of the self-conscious affect and attribution inventory. *Journal of Personality and Social Psychology, 59*, 102–111.

A technique for measuring shame proneness and guilt proneness. Attempts to distinguish between shame and guilt.

Tomkins, S. S. (1963). Shame–humiliation versus contempt–disgust: The nature of the response. In *Affect, imagery, consciousness: Vol. 2. The negative affects* (pp. 118–183). New York: Springer.

A brilliant essay on the significance of shame, its relations to other emotions and to personality.

16

Guilt, Conscience, and Morality

> One important point with regard to morality should not be forgotten: unless it has a fervor of emotion, unless it is touched with spiritual warmth, it is nothing but formal rectitude. True morality, like beauty, needs more than intellect. It includes a feeling of good will for others that is warmed by an inner fire. (Sinnott, 1966, pp. 181–182)

Perhaps all of the emotions play some part, directly or indirectly, in the development of conscience and morality. Fear, anger, and shame are likely to emerge if harsh physical punishment is used in teaching right–wrong discriminations. Excitement and joy in caring for and helping others, especially when no reciprocation can be expected, may characterize the mature conscience and the highest form of moral behavior. Nevertheless, guilt is the emotion most essential to the development of the affective–cognitive structures of conscience and the affective–cognitive–action patterns of moral behavior.

In differential emotions theory, guilt is considered a fundamental emotion that emerged, like other fundamental emotions, through evolutionary-biological processes. The experience of guilt, like the experience of fear, is unlearned. As with fear, there are some innate activators or natural clues for guilt that operate under minimally favorable sociocultural conditions. In addition to the natural clues to guilt, each culture and each institution (e.g., family, religious organization) concerned with human ethics and morals prescribes certain standards of conduct and attempts to teach them to growing children. These prescriptions (moral and ethical principles) constitute the cognitive component of conscience. In the mature conscience they are linked with emotion to form affective–cognitive structures that guide the actions we call moral and ethical behavior. The compelling fact that makes guilt rather than fear the chief affect in conscience is this: The experience of guilt binds the person to the source of guilt and does not subside without reconciliation that tends to restore social harmony. Fear motivates escape from the source and subsides at a safe distance from threat of harm. The balance between fear-elicited conformity and guilt-induced responsible actions provides an index of the maturity of conscience and conduct. The feeling of responsibility, the central guilt–cognition orientation in conscience, facilitates behavior that minimizes intense experiential guilt.

Because shame and guilt are in some respects closely related, one of our concerns in this chapter will be to compare the two emotions and thus point up the distinct features of each. People usually find it easy to tell the difference between these two emotions in their personal experiences, but they may not be aware of all their different effects.

Characteristics of Guilt

There are good reasons why people confuse shame and guilt or fail to distinguish clearly between them. The two emotions are often experienced in the same or similar situations. Both emotions tend to make people want to conceal something or to set something right, but as we shall see, what one wants to conceal or set right is quite different in shame and guilt.

The Expression of Guilt

All of the other negative emotions have more distinct facial characteristics in their expression than does the emotion of guilt. This helps account for the well-known difficulty in detecting the culprit, even when the guilty one is too young to inhibit or disguise facial expression effectively.

Guilt may sometimes change our outward appearance, and it most certainly changes internal events, including the workings of our mind as well as neurophysiological and hormonal processes. However, as of now, no one has been able to identify absolutely reliable external or internal indicators of guilt. The popular notion that you can detect guilt with a lie detector (polygraph) is at best a partial truth. It is not a reliable method.

The Phenomenology of Guilt

In describing the phenomenology or subjective experience of guilt, our concern is with moral, ethical, or religious guilt, not with guilt in the legal sense. Legally, a person may be incorrectly convicted and thus guilty in the eyes of the law, but such a person may never experience any feelings of guilt. There may even be cases in which the individual is justly convicted of some misdemeanor but feels no guilt (e.g., if Rafe runs a stop sign that he did not see, he feels no guilt, despite the fact that his misdeed may cost him a day in court and a fine).

If Rafe does feel guilt, he has an intense, gnawing feeling that he is "not right" with the person or persons he has wronged. If he is religious he will have the additional burden of feeling that he is not right with God.

It is quite common for a person to feel guilty for wrongdoings against the self. One may feel that one's misconduct has affected only one's own character.

Guilt hangs heavy on one's mind. While shame befuddles one's thinking temporarily, guilt stimulates a great deal of thought, usually cognitive preoccupation with the wrongdoing and the development of schemes for setting things right again. People dread facing up to their misconduct. Before coming face to face with the one wronged in order to make amends, the scene is often rehearsed in memory and imagination, over and over again. People who can muster the courage to face up to their guilt and begin immediately working toward amelioration will not suffer as long from the agony of the cognitive rehearsal of the guilt situation as people who postpone facing up to their guilt.

The DES profile of emotions in the guilt situation is presented in Figure 16-1. The profile helps make certain important points about the dynamics of guilt and related emotions. The separateness of guilt and shyness is substantiated by the fact that shyness is only the fifth-highest emotion mean in the profile of the guilt

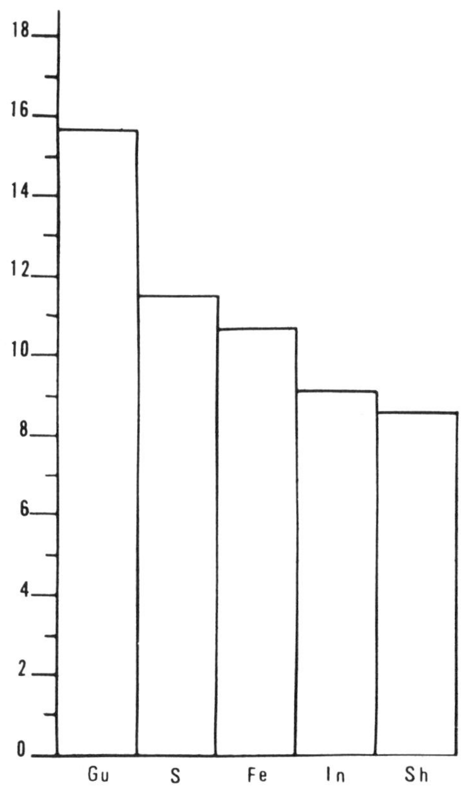

FIGURE 16-1. The DES profile of emotions in the guilt situation. Gu, guilt; S, sadness; Fe, fear; In, interest, Sh, shyness.

situation. As a number of theorists have suggested, fear is relatively prominent in the guilt situation. This suggests that for many people a guilt situation is often accompanied by a substantial amount of fear. However, the mean for fear is not quite as high as the mean for sadness. Judging from this profile, one would have to conclude that both sadness and fear are likely to be significant motivations in the guilt situation.

The DRS profile of dimensions in the guilt situation is presented in Figure 16-2. While the emotion profile for the guilt situation is quite distinct by comparison with the profile for other emotion situations, the profile of dimensions for guilt is not clearly distinguished from the profile of other negative emotions such as anger and fear. The dimension of pleasantness, however, is significantly lower in guilt than in shyness.

A Personal Account of a Guilt Experience. When Brad was 13 years old, he was walking through the woods with his 6-month-old dog, a thoroughbred collie. His best friend's dog, a 2-year-old German shepherd, saw them leave and

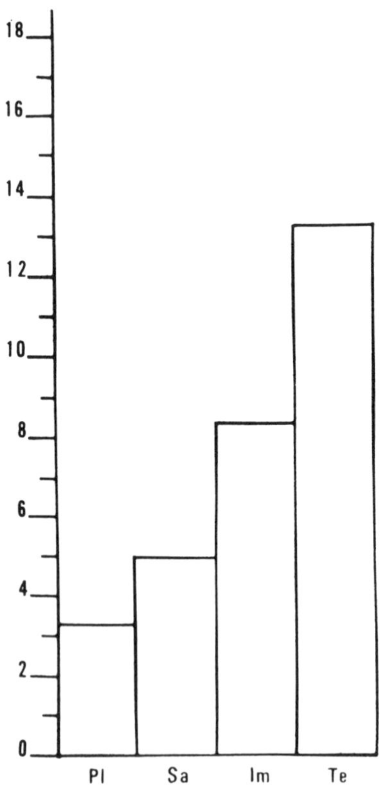

FIGURE 16-2. The DRS profile of dimensions in the guilt situation. Pl, pleasantness; Sa, self-assurance; Im, impulsiveness; Te, tension.

followed. Brad was a little miffed that the German shepherd was coming along. He really wanted to walk through the woods with only his collie pup for a companion. His resentment subsided as the dogs greeted each other playfully, then sniffed and moved along like trail dogs. From time to time the dogs would suddenly stop exploring and engage in rough-and-tumble play or chase.

When they reached the top of a tall bluff overlooking a beautiful stream below, Brad stopped to rest and enjoy the sights and sounds around him. The dogs were playing chase when suddenly the sharp teeth of the young collie penetrated a bit too deeply into the hind leg of his playmate, and the older and much stronger German shepherd attackhed the young collie viciously. The dogs had worked themselves onto a ledge over the cliff. To the right of the ledge was about a 4-foot drop. To the left there was a 50-foot drop to jagged stones and the white water of the mountain stream. The boy picked up a heavy stick and moved toward the dogs. The German shepherd reared on its hind legs and the boy was aware that he could push him either to the right or to the left. He saw his collie pup's bleeding ears and in a moment of fury he knocked the German shepherd over the precipice to a sudden death on the stones below. His body was quickly washed away in the rapidly flowing stream. The boy quickly tended to his dog and saw that he was not seriously wounded. He then looked down to see his friend's German shepherd being tossed by the currents of the mountain stream, soon to disappear forever in the deep still water that lay just ahead.

The boy suddenly overwhelmed with the thought that he had betrayed his friend. He could have easily pushed the German shepherd in the other direction and ended the scuffle because it would have taken the dog a long time to find his way out. In a moment of anger he had avenged the attack on his young collie, but at the same time he had willfully done something that he considered wrong. He could no longer see the beauty of the wildflowers and trees around him. The sparkling mountain stream did not seem enticing anymore. Everything had changed. Brad's misdeed ran through his mind, over and over again. He thought of all the ways he could have done things differently.

He began wondering how he could tell his friend. He even wondered for a while whether he would have the courage to do so. He could remain silent, if he wanted to, living with this dark secret for the rest of his life. No one else knew what he had done. No one was within a mile. No one could ever discover his secret, but he was not at all satisfied with the thought of not telling his friend. He felt he really could not face his friend again. He knew that it would not be fun playing with his friend as long as he kept his misdeed a secret. He knew how much the German shepherd had meant to his friend.

Brad started thinking of ways to tell his friend what had happened. He thought again and again of the events of the day. He imagined his friend's reaction. He worried whether or not what he had done would ruin his friendship forever. As he thought of such a consequence, he tried to tell himself that this terrible thing didn't really happen, that somehow the German shepherd landed in the water and would swim safely to the shore. He couldn't really believe that. He told himself that he only pushed the German shepherd away from his collie and that the German shepherd accidentally fell off the precipice. There was no way that he could convince himself that it had not happened or that it was an accident, but his mind kept trying.

Then he started thinking of things that might make his friend understand and forgive him. He remembered how much his friend trusted him. He remembered how he had only recently helped his friend when work piled up because of his father's illness. Then the sight of the German shepherd landing against the jagged rocks would flash in his mind, and all that he had ever done for his friend paled in significance.

When Brad got home, he remembered that his friend had left only the night before to spend the first month of summer with his grandparents. He breathed a sigh of relief knowing that he would not have to face his friend immediately.

He busied himself with his chores but really could not free his mind of the events of the afternoon. It grew late and he tried to sleep. Every trick he had ever learned to relax and get to sleep failed him completely. He knew what he had to do. In the middle of the night he picked up pen and paper and started to write his friend the full story of the day's tragedy. It was not until he had finished the letter and told everything exactly as it had happened that he was able to sleep. With the confession of his wrongdoing he began to think more realistically that in time his friend would come to accept his apology. He tried to believe his friend would understand that he had acted impulsively in a fit of anger. He hoped that all their years of friendship and good times together would not be washed away by a single deed.

Guilt as judged in the framework of rules, regulations, and the law may not involve the emotion experience of guilt, but we are not concerned with guilt in the legal sense. We are concerned with the kind of guilt that Brad suffered when he realized he had intentionally killed his best friend's German shepherd. Brad's story illustrates much of the subjective experience, or phenomenology, of guilt. Although Brad's primary concern was with his relationship with his friend, he also had feelings for the German shepherd. He had always liked and admired the dog. He had lots of fun playing with him before he got his Collie pup. His guilt in relation to the dog was mixed with compassion and sadness. It is the guilt he felt in relation to his friend Pete that will be considered in more detail.

Brad's experience, like that of anyone suffering the emotion of guilt, was dominated by a deep sense of betrayal, of having violated the trust his friend had for him. Brad felt that his relationship with his best friend was in danger. The losses he would suffer from a breakup with his best friend were many and significant.

The closer you are to the person whose trust you violate, the stronger the feelings of guilt and the greater the sense of danger from the loss of the relationship. Anticipation of this loss can trigger the additional emotion of sadness. Threat of losing the relationship can also lead to fear, because the loss may leave you feeling abandoned, insecure, and unsure about your future.

Among the many ruminations of the guilty mind are fantasies about the reaction of the wronged person. Will the person respond only with sadness or will he or she be sad for awhile and then angry? Will his or her anger lead to hostility and retaliation? What form will the retaliation take? In Brad's case he might wonder if Pete will become depressed, if he will ever speak to him again, if he will retaliate against the young collie. Fantasies about different reactions of the wronged person can cause the suffering person's guilt to be joined with sadness or with fear.

It is also important to know that during the experience of guilt one might also feel shame. In Brad's case we would call it moral shame (H. Lewis, 1971). Brad's shame is an example of moral shame because it resulted from wrongdoing. Shame from bad manners or inappropriate attire in a given situation would be nonmoral shame. Brad was truly ashamed of himself for having lost control in a moment of anger. It was a very difficult moment for Brad, because he was afraid for his puppy and at the same time angry with the attacking German shepherd. A combination of guilt and shame can become very burdensome, as can the combination of guilt and fear, when ruminations about retaliation by the wronged person go on and on.

To summarize, the experience or feeling of guilt is a tormenting sense of isolation—isolation from the one who has been wronged. For the religious person, it means a deeply felt need to seek forgiveness and get right with God. At the peak of the guilt experience you feel as though the isolation is absolute and that the barrier separating you from your loved one is insurmountable. In guilt, your mind is highly active. You cannot keep thoughts of your deed, the wronged person, efforts to make amends, your friend's reactions, and the future of your relationship from running through your mind time after time. As we saw in Chapter 15, shame has the opposite effect. In shame, the gears of the mind go into neutral and you suddenly become speechless. In guilt, images and thoughts force themselves upon your mind. Even if you try hard to think of something else, thoughts of the wrongdoing will intrude harshly and become dominant.

The Causes of Guilt

Eibl-Eibesfeldt (1971) argues that there is a biological basis for the development of ethical norms, and in agreement with differential emotions theory, he implies that there is a genetic basis for the subsequent development of a sense of personal responsibility and guilt. Ausubel (1955) does not directly endorse a biogenetic mechanism for guilt, but he believes that it is so basically human and so fundamental to the developmental and maintenance of social norms that it will develop in all cultures if conditions are even minimally favorable. He hypothesizes three psychological conditions that are essential for the development of guilt:

(1) acceptance of moral values, (2) internalization of a sense of moral obligation to abide by these values, and (3) a sufficiently self-critical ability to perceive discrepancies between actual behavior and internalized values.

Ausubel (1955) holds that there are some uniformities across cultures in the acquisition of guilt and guilt-related behavior. These uniformities stem from (1) basic aspects of parent–child relationships, (2) minimum cultural need for the socialization of children, and (3) certain trends or stages in cognitive and social growth. The single most important basis for the development of conscience and guilt, according to Ausubel, is the powerful need for parents and society to develop a sense of responsibility in growing children.

The phenomenological determinants of guilt are perhaps easier to explain than the determinants of any of the other negative emotions. Guilt results from wrongdoing. The behavior that evokes guilt violates a moral, ethical, or religious code. Usually people feel guilty when they become aware that they have broken a rule and violated their own standards or beliefs. They may also feel guilt for failing to accept or carry out their responsibility. Guilt, like all other emotions, has a great deal of generality. Since it is associated with behavior in the broad sphere of morality, ethics, and religion, the causes of guilt vary widely from individual to individual, from one ethnic group to another, and from culture to culture. Some people may feel guilty over eating meat on Friday, others over eating meat any time, and yet others may not have any concern over eating meat or any other edible substance at any time. Some people may feel guilt when they do not work hard enough to meet standards set by themselves, their parents, or their reference group (primary social group), while others may feel guilty for being so preoccupied with their work that they do not take sufficient time to enjoy their family and friends.

Misconduct can also cause shame, but in this case the deed need not be wrong except in the sense of being misfitting, inept, or inappropriate. If we should feel shame because of moral, ethical, or religious misconduct, it would probably be because others observed our deed and have knowledge of it. The shame would then be a result of the heightened self-consciousness brought about this time by others' observations of the misconduct.

In contrast to guilt, shame can result from actions that have no implications for moral, ethical, or religious codes. This is what Ausubel (1955) calls "nonmoral shame." In his view "moral shame" follows from the negative moral judgment of others about actions not necessarily immoral in the eyes of the offender. Moral shame also occurs in association with guilt when one violates a moral standard and then images the censure of others. Ausubel holds that shame always involves external sanctions, either overtly expressed by others or imaged by the individual. Guilt, on the other hand, includes self-reactions that are independent of the judgment of other people. These self-reactions include self-reproach, lowered self-esteem, remorse, and in Ausubel's view, a special type of moral shame.

It should be noted that the feeling of guilt is not dependent upon one's belief and adherence to written or explicit moral, ethical, or religious codes. The codes may be implicit and accepted intuitively. Almost everyone has an ethical framework that guides his or her interpersonal and social behavior, but very few people carry the structure and details of this framework in consciousness all the time.

Guilt occurs in situations in which one feels personally responsible. There is a strong relationship between one's sense of personal responsibility and one's threshold for guilt. Shame is more frequently evoked by the actions of other people. Guilt comes from one's own acts or one's failure to act. It should be emphasized that guilt may occur as readily and as frequently from omission as from commission—from failure to feel, think, or act in a certain way at a certain time as well as from actual feelings, thoughts, or acts that violate moral codes or beliefs.

While the feeling of guilt, like that of the other emotions, is the same the world over, the causes and consequences vary widely from individual to individual and from culture to culture. However, there are some spheres in which the misconduct–guilt relationship is virtually pancultural. There are few if any cultures in which violation of strictly held sexual taboos (e.g., incest) would fail to elicit guilt. The same is true for the act of murder, especially of a member of one's own family or group. In addition to these extreme types of misconduct, all cultures have some moral and ethical standards relating to other sexual and aggressive acts. For this reason, guilt is widely associated with these spheres of feeling, thought, and action.

Simply put, the principal cause of guilt is wrongdoing. We can describe the wrongdoing as moral transgression, the violation of an internal standard, or a betrayal of trust. Although each of these may add a slightly different nuance of meaning, each is clearly just another way of saying "wrongdoing."

What is wrong for one person may be a perfectly harmless delight for another. It is wrong for some people to eat a hamburger at McDonald's because their religion requires them to follow a special diet or to eat specially prepared foods. For some it is a sin to drink alcoholic beverages, for others a sin to dance, and so on. The main point here is that there are few universal wrongs, most of them involving the doing of mental or physical harm to another living being; wrongs are defined in large part by religion, family, and culture.

Although the basic cause of guilt is wrongdoing, sometimes you may judge yourself at fault when you really are not or when there is very little opportunity for you to act differently. In effect, the perception that you have done wrong can elicit guilt whether or not you have transgressed. Consider the following occasion when Jane felt guilt during her struggle to adjust to her parent's separation. When she came home from college one weekend, she found all her things missing.

> I couldn't believe it was real—that my parents were now actually living in two different places. When I arrived at the apartment where my mother had moved, everything that I had missed at the house could now be found. I immediately felt angry with my mother for leaving the house so bare, and sorry for my father, for he was now living alone. Somehow it seemed that they had neglected to make me a part of the move. I felt torn, so on vacations I

would sleep a few nights at one place, and a few nights at the other. This reinforced my own instability, for I did not know where I fit in. It was more natural for me to want to be where my mother was, but I ended up feeling guilty about my father not having anyone. Eventually I came to the decision that I would work my way into feeling at home in my mother's apartment.

Jane could not help feeling guilt, but most people would hardly hold her responsible for what she saw as her father's loneliness. For her to feel guilt, she had to have the feeling that she owed her father loyalty and companionship, a commendable attitude. She felt guilt because she thought she was abandoning her father. Yet, she could not be blamed for the separation of her parents, and in fact, she was the one who was abandoned. In a way she suffered vicarious guilt, the guilt that might have been experienced directly by one or both of her parents. Jane had to make a choice as to where she would try to feel at home. The choice, though a reasonable one, left her feeling guilt over abandoning her father, a guilt she did not deserve.

For the emotion of guilt to occur, the standards for your behavior have to be "internalized." What this means is that your own mind must become the source and keeper of rules and the monitor of your own behavior. You must be in charge and feel responsible for your actions for you to realize that you did the wrong and are therefore accountable.

Although Jane's guilt seemed unwarranted, she felt guilt because she was a good daughter. She had internalized the values relating to family life, and she had standards for her behavior toward her parents. Her parent's separation forced her to violate her own "child-behavior" standards toward one parent or the other. She couldn't live with both or feel at home in two different places, each with a missing parent.

Standards for many kinds of behavior vary between cultures and even between families in the same community. Standards also change from one generation to the next. Some of the events in Sylvia's adolescence show that her standards of sexual behavior were different from those of her parents and perhaps from yours. She had many sexual experiences that would have caused some to feel guilt because the behavior would have violated their ethical or religious standards. As we shall see, her sexual behavior ultimately got her in trouble with her conscience and she felt terribly guilty. The standard she violated, however, was not so much related to sexual behavior as to her concepts of friendship and loyalty.

In the seventh and eighth grades, I became friends with three fairly "wild" girls (as wild as girls get in Catholic schools, which is to say they were normal). One of them, Maria, showed me how to put makeup on, and how to kiss, and "what boys do to you." She would pretend that she was a boy, which confused me, because it was fine with me that she was a girl. I didn't then and don't now have any problems with being bisexual. A girl named Isabel became my best friend.

The summer before I went to high school, I was raped by a very minor acquaintance, who was 19 at the time. My only concern was pregnancy, and I told no one, never even considering it rape until I began participating in S.O.S. (a hotline for rape victims) on

> campus. After that and some mild sexual abuse by a trusted friend of the family (8 years older than I), I became fairly promiscuous. I rarely dated in high school but would sleep with men considerably older than myself, usually with my best friend present. I felt that because of my age I had no right to expect anything from these men, especially not love. I matured very quickly in my looks, and I seriously looked 20 when I was 14.
>
> In the spring of my sophomore year, my best friend Isabel was violently raped. I recall being far more upset about it than she was, although it was to affect her much more later. Isabel and I were so much alike that it was the source of some jealousy between us. She matched me in intellectual, artistic, and poetic ability and uniqueness.
>
> She became involved with a guy in her junior year, and, for reasons still not entirely clear to me, I began a secret affair with him. I felt unbelievably guilty and evil, and I still classify it as the only truly stupid and senseless thing that I've done in my lifetime. I finally confessed to her some 8 months later, and she literally did not say one word to me for an entire year, despite the fact that we had art class together 5 days a week for an hour, and there was only one other person in the class.
>
> I met my current boyfriend in the spring of my senior year, in a communication workshop. It was truly love at first sight. He was 25 at the time, and just out of prison for 2 weeks (he didn't look it). I was heart-thumpingly *in love* with him for an entire year. We went to my senior prom together. Isabel was taking sensitivity training the same time as he, and I was terrified she would somehow discover that he was my boyfriend and try to avenge herself. She called me one night at 3:00 a.m. to talk to me after a year. It was the happiest moment of my life. I was crying and shaking all over. I graduated high school with honors, my friend Nick, valedictorian, sitting beside Isabel, with my new love in the audience with my proud parents. It was wonderful. Isabel and I also attended our beloved teacher's funeral together. We slept together for the first time that summer, after years of false accusations. We had a good laugh over that. I remember being unable to decide whether I was more in love with her or John, my new boyfriend, but it passed.

Sylvia made very clear the cause of her guilt—betrayal. Betrayal, particularly betrayal of a friend or loved one, is probably a universal cause of guilt, because it violates standards common to all cultures. Sylvia loved Isabel, perhaps as friend and lover, and thus her betrayal led to intense guilt.

On another occasion Sylvia reveals the depth of her guilt over betraying Isabel.

> An area for consideration in my adolescence was also the terrible guilt I experienced, which was somewhat generalized, but largely arose from my relationship with my girlfriend's lover. I had had quite a few sexual encounters (in absence of love) before I graduated high school, and experienced very little, if any, guilt about this; but in the case of the relationship with Isabel's boyfriend, the guilt was crippling, probably due to the fact that there was "wrongdoing" involved. My self-esteem dropped, and the lowered self-esteem took the form of considering myself "evil," an odd label to arise from a person as nonreligious as myself. The feeling of evilness came from having fully comprehended all consequences and having continued nonetheless. I felt responsibility not only for participating in the affair, but also for the subsequent personality change in my girlfriend, which was pervasive (not limited to her reactions to me), and negative. I felt that my act separated me not only from my friend, but from all people of integrity and loyalty.

Sylvia's betrayal demonstrates once again the principle of emotion patterning. Significant life events almost always elicit a complex pattern of emotions.

> Although I have concentrated on guilt in the aforementioned situation, the experience was laden with a host of other strong emotions. I was extremely fearful and fraught with anxiety at the possibility of being discovered. I was sad and distressed at the inevitable dissolution of an old friendship. I was ashamed by my transgression, but at the same time excited by his charismatic personality, and the intellectual stimulation and dry wit Isabel's boyfriend provided. Ironically, having felt no guilt in those previous loveless encounters, I felt horrible guilt in this relationship in which I did feel love for the other person. Although this ordeal eventually ended with great joy and with reconciliation of my friend and myself, I do still occasionally experience guilt feelings about this incident.
>
> In view of all I've said, it is not surprising that my graduation day was exhilarating and joyful for me. That single hour or so symbolized the resolution of many conflicts, the excising of my self-doubts about my own worth, and the presence of a loving and accepting individual.

As we have noted many times before, even unpleasant and unwanted negative emotions serve adaptive functions. In Sylvia's case, guilt over betrayal of a friend was accompanied by feelings of responsibility for the victim's unhappiness. Successful reconciliation soon followed and with it came significant personal growth.

Origins, Functions, and Malfunctions of Guilt

Guilt, like all the other emotions, undoubtedly played a significant role in the evolution of human beings and human societies. Guilt served as a check on wanton waste and on sexual and aggressive exploitation. The anticipation of guilt or guilt avoidance heightens one's sense of personal responsibility. Guilt complements shame in fostering social responsibility and reparation for wrongdoing.

Another very special function of guilt is to motivate behavior that sets things right with the person who has been wronged. If you feel guilty, you are very strongly motivated to repair the damage, to make amends. Indeed, such behavior may be the only effective way to resolve genuine guilt.

In contemporary life, guilt and the anticipation and avoidance of guilt continue to serve these functions. Without guilt and shame people would lose their grip on morality and ethics. It seems quite likely that the absence or drastic reduction of guilt and shame was highly significant in the psychodynamics of Watergate and its aftermath.

Without guilt, the rules of fair play would have to be monitored by a special police force, but who would train and monitor the police? A society in which no one had a sense of guilt would indeed be a poor and dangerous place in which to live. Fostering compliance with the rules of fair play is one of the constructive functions of guilt (or guilt anticipation and guilt avoidance), and several empirical studies (reviewed in the next section) have shown that guilt does increase compliance.

The foregoing conclusion is not intended to suggest that blind compliance to any set of rules or to any system is necessarily good or adaptive. What is indicated is that the emotion of guilt plays a role in the development of personal and social responsibility and that without guilt or guilt anticipation there would be a significant loss in the need and desire to abide by the rules of fair play. The emotion of guilt helps us perceive the wronged individual as injured, suffering, hurt, and in need of the appropriate words and actions that will heal the wound. The effect of guilt in making us feel responsible fosters growth toward adulthood and a greater psychological maturity.

After showing how various cultures and child-rearing practices result in different guilt antecedents and consequences, Meade (1950) suggested that guilt served a basic function for the human species. She wrote:

> But we may also consider whether, in addition to the specific nurturing situation, there may not be a biological basis for guilt of another order, covered by the conception of the "metaphysical guilt of creatureliness" . . . guilt which arises inevitably from the nature of life and death itself, guilt over the domestication which men endure who become responsible fathers and the pain which women take on who become mothers, guilt over all who have suffered and died as the human race struggled to its present position in the world—a deep guilt which is reactivated by any failure in the individual organism to grow, to attain full sex membership, to use its particular gifts and capacities. Such guilt, such consciousness of a debt to life which can be paid by living, may be so inherent in the nature of human beings, who live in a culture, that it is ineradicable and will always be both the mainspring of man's spiritual strivings and the guarantee of his humanity. (p. 372)

The Development of Guilt and Its Relation to Empathy

Before children can experience guilt, they must reach an age where they are capable of understanding that they can do things that harm others. They must realize that they have control of their actions and that they are accountable for them. A complete understanding of responsibility and accountability of one's actions takes years to develop. This does not mean, however, that young children have no sense of right and wrong or that they have no appreciation of the consequences of their actions. Zahn-Waxler, Radke-Yarrow and King (1979) studied 1½- to 2½-year-old children's responses to others' distress (sorrow, discomfort, pain). The mothers of the children were trained in techniques of observation. They recorded their child's reactions and their own reactions to everyday occurrences of distress that were observed by the young child. On special occasions, the mother and the investigator also pretended to be in distress. In addition to the observations of the children's responses to others' distress, investigators made visits to the homes of the participants and rated the extent to which mothers showed empathy in caring for their children. The investigators also classified the explanations that mothers gave to children when the children were the cause of others' distress. Of central importance, they found that children as young as 1½ years showed clear signs of understanding the consequences of their actions. Children made this clear both through their verbalizations ("Did I make you sad?") and through their actions, which included efforts to make reparation.

This was especially true when children were the cause of mother's distress, but it occurred on some occasions when children were completely innocent bystanders, suggesting that young children may be especially vulnerable to guilt induction because of their inability to distinguish clearly their role in causing the other person's distress. The investigators also found that the way children respond to others' distress is significantly related to mother's socialization practices in relation to the children's involvement in the distress of others. For example, mothers who use physical restraint or physical punishment had children who were not likely to try to make reparations for the distress they caused or observed in others. Mothers who explained to their children the consequences of their actions and who gave explanations that had affective tone and content were more likely to have children who tried to make reparation for their transgressions. The children's efforts to make reparation were interpreted as evidence that the children experienced guilt and empathy and that the affective response motivated the prosocial behavior or reparation.

With normal development, children increased their capacity to appreciate fully the consequences of their actions and to select appropriate ways to make reparation. Although there may well be some few actions that universally lead to guilt, individuals generally adopt the standards set by their family, community, and culture. Because one's vulnerability to guilt may grow as one's social responsibility or power increases, an individual may continue to develop a keener and keener sense of guilt throughout the life span.

Guilt and Psychopathology

The role of guilt in psychopathology has not been the subject of very many empirical studies. A major reason for this is that theories of psychopathology frequently do not treat guilt as a separate and distinct motivational variable. Since Freud (1936) interpreted guilt as a moral or "conscience" anxiety, many theorists of various orientations have failed to recognize guilt as having distinct and important characteristics of its own. For example, Mandler (1975) suggests that the only difference between anxiety and guilt may be the situational variables that give rise to the labels that the person uses to describe inner feelings. Thus, in his view, a person experiencing guilt is simply one who feels anxious about some real or imagined misdeed. Mandler pointed out that this type of anxiety (labeled by the individual as guilt) often leads to the use of the defense mechanism of undoing. This defense mechanism, typically characterized as guilt motivated, consists of attempts by the individual to atone for or to neutralize damage done by misdeeds.

Rosenhan and London (1970) recognized guilt as a separate and distinct motivational phenomenon. They suggested that one of the functions of guilt was to reduce anxiety and militate against serious psychological disorder. London (1968) pointed out that the delusions of psychotic depressives are often concerned with feelings of guilt and worthlessness.

Lewis (1971), who draws important distinctions between guilt and shame, has argued that while shame often plays an important part in depression, guilt can lead to obsessive–compulsive neurosis and paranoia. She recognized the lack of empirical research on the role of guilt in psychopathology but indicated that careful effort differentiate the effects of shame and guilt should help in understanding the formation of neurotic symptoms. It should be noted that not all writers in the field agree with Lewis regarding guilt as a factor in obsessions and compulsions. The more traditional view (e.g., Henderson & Gillespie, 1956) maintains that fear, not guilt, supplies the motive for obsessive thinking.

Mowrer (1960) holds that conscience and real guilt (from acts one has committed but wishes one had not) are central in the development of neurosis. Mowrer believes that the neurotic gratifies wishes while hurting others and thus develops genuine grounds for realistic guilt. Peterson (1967) conducted a study of socialization, the results of which he interpreted as consistent with Mowrer's hypothesis. He found that children with neurotic characteristics (shy, anxious, withdrawn, and insecure) were poorly socialized and had failed to integrate socialization and behavior. Also supportive of Mowrer's view is a finding by Johnson, Ackerman, Frank and Fionda (1968) showing that conscience as measured by resistance to temptation correlates positively with good adjustment. Ogren and Dokecki's (1972) insightful analysis of moral development and behavior disorders in young children also presents some arguments consistent with Mowrer's position. They point to decentering (decrease in egocentrism) and social integration as common themes in Erickson's (1950) and Mowrer's theories of conscience development and note that moral immaturity may lead to breakdown in peer-group interactions, neurosis, and even paranoid schizophrenia.

Theoretical Conceptions of Guilt

Guilt has been a major topic in theology and philosophy since their beginnings. In the more orthodox Jewish and Christian theologies, a person is born in sin and finds salvation only through God's forgiveness. More or less liberal variations on this theme include sin against God and humanity as sources of guilt, and interaction with God (prayer and contrition) and with people (rectification) as means of absolving guilt. Many contemporary theologies and philosophies have psychological overtones in that they recognize a relationship between self-development and capacity for guilt. The "age of accountability" for one's conduct is considered a function of ability to discriminate between right and wrong, and the age of accountability for a given act may differ with the difficulty of the discrimination.

In this section, the focus is on psychological conceptions of guilt. As is so often the case, one of the earliest contributions came from psychoanalysis.

A Psychoanalytic Conception of Guilt

In classical psychoanalytic theory, the stage is set for the development of guilt only after the basic structure of the personality has emerged (the id, the ego, and the superego). First to develop is the *id*, conceived largely as an innate set of impulses, instincts, or drives. It is largely sexual and aggressive in nature. The *ego* emerges as the child develops the capacities to conceptually separate the self from others, to think and choose, and to cope with and act upon the environment (reality). The *superego*, popularly thought of as the conscience, develops as children internalize or accept as their own a sense of proper conduct (rules of right and wrong behavior), either identical with or sufficiently similar to their parents or that of their reference group to be acceptable by those concerned. Psychoanalytic theory maintains that the superego develops primarily as a function of mechanisms of incorporation, or introjection (taking the thought or feeling of someone else as one's own), and identification (the process whereby the child assumes the identity of the parent or says in effect, "I am like him" or "I am like her"). Using these two mechanisms, the superego incorporates the standards and values of the parents, with individual differences depending on the resolution of the Oedipus conflict.

Piers and Singer (1953) presented an interesting elaboration of basic psychoanalytic theory and discussed some distinctions between the dynamics of guilt and shame. They followed standard psychoanalytic theory in arguing that guilt arises from tension between the id and superego. Like Lewis (1971), they held that shame develops from tension between the ego and the ego-ideal. Shame occurs when people fail significantly in their efforts to obtain their goals and live up to the image of their ego-ideals. The "unconscious, irrational threat" that operates in shame is the threat of abandonment.

On the other hand, guilt is elicited by violation of a value or standard of conduct that characterizes the superego. Piers and Singer see a close relationship between guilt and fear, fear of the wrath of the parent figure. They hold that the "unconscious, irrational threat" that operates in guilt is the threat of mutilation or castration.

The Concept of Existential Guilt

Rollo May (1958) defined three forms of existential guilt. The first form is a result of a forfeiting of potentialities. Potentialities for development exist in the intellectual, social, emotional, and physical spheres. The individual's capacities for "being" are seemingly unlimited. However, people do not always choose to develop their potentialities. A person may neglect or completely abandon his or her potentiality in a given sphere of life. According to May, such a forfeiture of human potentiality results in the first form of guilt. A similar view has been presented by Boss (1963) and by Bugental (1965).

> Existential guilt is the recognition that we do, indeed, have responsibility. It matters how we employ our potential to take action. We are not hapless bits of fluff totally at the mercy of the winds of contingency. We have weight and substance. To be sure, we are still within the bounds of the finiteness of our awareness, and so we cannot perfectly exercise our potential for action. We never fully bring it into coordination with that of which we are aware. Thus there is existential guilt as an inevitable part of the human experience. (Bugental, 1965, pp. 37–38)

Khanna (1969) made some provocative criticisms of this concept of existential guilt. He noted that newborn children have a vast and virtually limitless number of potentialities and that they will inevitably give up some and develop others as a result of their unbringings, their social interactions, and their life situations. The existential implication that one must develop all of one's potentialities sets such an impossibly high standard that it becomes meaningless. As it is with any individual, Rafe must be free to develop those potentialities that he consciously chooses and to give up those that do not interest him, without feeling guilt in the usual sense. That is, such an exercise of choice should not cause him to feel guilt as he would experience it if he violated a code of conduct. Khanna pointed out that potentialities exist in anyone in a continually changing hierarchy so that at any given time he or she is preferring and responding to some to a greater extent than others. Rafe might rightly feel guilty for denying a potentiality that is important for his development and existence as a human being or for cultivating a potentiality that makes him an immoral person. However, to say that Rafe is guilty for actualizing his potential as an artist while denying his potential to become a scientist makes no more sense than to say that he is guilty because he is alive and makes choices.

The second type of existential guilt, according to May, develops as a result of one's separation from one's fellow beings. It is not possible for us to see our fellow beings exactly as they see themselves. It is not possible for us to have perfect empathy. It is not possible for us to be completely one with another individual. Thus, there is a basic separateness or aloneness that characterizes every human life. And, according to the existential view, the insulation set up by this separateness creates barriers and conflicts in interpersonal relations. Khanna maintains that this separateness of human beings needs to be recognized and accepted but not considered as a reason for guilt. Other human beings are essential for the realization of a major aspect of our potentiality. Other people are essential, but not for the purpose of complete identification with them. Inability to speak and feel in perfect harmony with another human being is a fact of human existence and human individuality that cannot be reasonably regarded as guilt.

The third form of existential guilt results from separation from nature. Khanna points out that this type of guilt is dependent upon the assumption of a value system where oneness with nature is right, good, and important, and that human beings somehow become separated from nature. Since by birth we are a real and genuine part of nature, a tricky problem arises in the definition as to what exactly constitutes union and what exactly constitutes separation.

Khanna's comparisons and criticisms of existential guilt were made with reference to the standard or conventional meaning of the term—an emotion elicited by deviation from a code of conduct and an emotion that motivates the individual to get back in line or suffer punishment. Khanna concludes his critique by pointing out that the concept of existential guilt describes some very important aspects of human life but falters when it makes the concept of guilt so general that it is equivalent to being human. Khanna observes that existential guilt can meaningfully refer to instances where people's actions deviate from the hierarchy of value and standards that they have accepted and developed.

Some Learning Theory Conceptions of the Developmental Origins and Consequences of Guilt

O. H. Mowrer (1960b, 1961) has presented some interesting and provocative ideas on the origin of guilt, its effects upon the individual, and ways to deal with it in psychotherapy. In his view, guilt develops essentially as a function of the learning process. As young children are repeatedly rewarded for doing things that are considered good and right and repeatedly punished for doing things that are considered bad and wrong, they gradually develop their own sense (or concepts) of proper and improper behavior. Mowrer agrees with one of the traditional distinctions between shame and guilt, noting that shame occurs in the presence of another person, while the mechanism of guilt can operate when the individual is entirely alone and in the absence of the source of punishment.

According to Mowrer, the sense of right and wrong is learned largely through the mechanism of identification and imitation. He criticized a strict behavioristic analysis and interpretation of guilt on the grounds that it is inadequate to deal with the highly generative and verbally abstract aspects of the phenomenon of human guilt. Mowrer thinks that the methods used in the study and analysis of the development of guilt would have to parallel those used in the study of the development of language.

A number of theories take the position that a close relationship exists between guilt and fear (e.g., Mandler, 1975). Mowrer goes a step further and defines guilt as a type of fear—the fear that arises after performing a previously punished act. Mowrer defines temptation as the fear and conflict that occur before such an act. He defines conscience as representing both the capacity to resist temptation and the capacity for remorse.

Following his learning theory orientation, Mowrer maintains that discipline and punishment are essential in the development of guilt, although he does recognize the possibility of constitutional or hereditary differences in susceptibility to guilt or guilt training. (Punishment can also elicit fear, sadness, and anger. For a detailed discussion of punishment, see Cheyne and Walters, 1970.)

Mowrer suggests that the development of guilt is facilitated when the learner feels dependent upon another person who is also the source of punishment or discipline. This is consonant with the theoretical material discussed in Chapter 15 wherein shame was considered as an emotion that occurs primarily, if not only, in the context of an emotional relationship.

Sarason (1966) presented a conception of guilt very similar to that of Mowrer. He, too, believed that the development of guilt was contingent on the use of punishment. He did not really carefully delineate his notion of guilt from his concept of fear and anxiety, except to note that guilt is related more closely to the individual's self-concept and attitudes.

In addition to the theories already reviewed, a number of other writers (e.g., Switzer, 1968) have drawn a close relationship between guilt and fear. Unger (1962) presented a rather detailed analysis of guilt in which fear or anxiety constitute an integral part, but unfortunately his definition of anxiety was highly ambiguous. He defined anxiety as "the conditionable 'residue' of noxious experience . . . a particular pattern of autonomic–visceral events and attendant feedback." For present purposes we shall consider his concept of anxiety as meaning fear (a term he used interchangeably with anxiety). He sees his position as an expansion of that of Mowrer.

Unger defines guilt as a two-stage mediating process. The first stage is a verbal evaluative response (e.g., "I shouldn't have done that!") The verbal evaluation process of the first stage triggers the second stage, the autonomic–visceral reaction of fear. Unger's analysis attempts to specify the contingencies and conditions of parent behavior and parent–child relations that result in the development of guilt. He found a number of studies in support of his assumption that emotion can be verbally mediated and that semantic conditioning (e.g., Luria & Vinogradova, 1959) can put autonomic responsiveness under the control of verbal mediating processes.

Unger notes that postulating a prototypical verbal component in guilt implies that it is a uniquely human phenomenon. On this point he is in disagreement with a number of scientists from Darwin to Mowrer. The latter pointed to differences in guilt reactions among various species of dogs as evidence of a hereditary component in guilt susceptibility. However, Unger agrees with Mowrer and others that guilt develops in the context of an emotional relationship.

According to Unger, it is the individual's dependency and emotional tie to the other person (typically the parent or parent figure) that sets the stage for the development of dependency and separation anxiety, which are fundamental in the development of guilt. Like Sarason and Mowrer and others who work within the framework of learning theory or general behavior theory, Unger defines guilt, or at least the affective component of guilt, as a type of fear.

In Unger's view, the nurturance of the infant and young child by a loving and caring parent develops a powerful dependency in the infant. The parent is closely associated with the infant day after day and week after week, and throughout the early months and years of life the parent is responsible for their termination and amelioration of hurtful and frustrating situations. Thus the presence and availability of the parent become matters of high importance for the young child, and conversely, the absence or nonavailability of the parent evokes "dependency anxiety"—the prelude to the development of guilt.

The nurturance of the child and the concomitant development of the capacity for dependency anxiety under conditions of parental absence or nonavailability set the stage for guilt training. According to Unger and the other learning theorists, this training begins, or at least beings to take effect, at around age 4 or 5. When the parent observes the child's transgression, the child is confronted by a stern-faced parent who says in a harsh voice, "How could you do that, that was a bad thing." The incident contains a verbal evaluation: "Never do that again; bad, shame on you." The parent's words and actions, according to Unger, are interpreted by the child as signs of withdrawal and separation, and hence they elicit dependency anxiety. After a number of such training episodes, the child learns to evaluate his or her behavior in the absence of the parent. "I did a bad thing; Mommy or Daddy says that's wrong, I must not do that again." Unger maintains that these evaluation-mediating responses interweave with reverberating anxiety over a more or less extended period of time. Eventually, the child learns to evaluate the situation in advance and avoid the transgression and hence the dependency anxiety that Unger sees as the affective component of guilt.

Unger cited the classical studies of Solomon and his associates (e.g., Solomon & Wynne, 1953; Wynne & Solomon, 1955) as evidence that extinction of guilt-mediated responses is difficult if not impossible. However, in the series of studies by Solomon and his associates, the stimulus was painful, and the affect very probably was fear; therefore, the strength of Unger's argument depends upon one's acceptance of his proposition that a form of fear constitutes the affective component of guilt.

Unger makes some cogent arguments for the proposition that psychological ("love-oriented") disciplinary techniques are more potent in guilt training than physical ("materialistic") techniques. He cited studies by McKennan (1938), Whiting and Child (1953), Faigan (1953), Miller and Swanson (1956), Funkenstein *et al.* (1957), and Unger (1962) in support of this argument. He emphasizes that psychological techniques of guilt training would work only if there was a background of parental nurturance and a continuing affectionate relationship between parent and child. Love cannot be withdrawn where none exists.

Unger also makes a case for the soundness of clear and immediate punishment or discipline in guilt-training episodes. Sometimes parents make unpredictable threats of unknown punishments (e.g., "God will punish you," "You can never make up for hurting your mother"). Under such threat, the child's evaluative response, "I did wrong," can reverberate over a highly protracted period of time and possibly mediate serious intrapunitive behavior aimed at relieving the guilt (dependency anxiety).

Sears, Maccoby, and Levin (1957) strongly support the thesis that identification with warm and accepting parents who use "love-oriented techniques of discipline" facilitates the development of a healthy conscience. They argue that withdrawal of love is particularly effective in morality training. They point out that the development of too strong a conscience may result in an inflexible, guilt-ridden individual, while too weak a conscience can produce an immoral bully. The antisocial impulses of the latter individual are controlled only by his fear of being caught and punished.

A study by Glueck and Glueck (1950) showed that psychological techniques of control were used more frequently by parents of nondelinquents and physical punishment more frequently by parents of delinquents. Affection, warmth, and feelings of attachment were much more characteristic of the nondelinquent population than of the delinquent one.

McKennan (1938) studied the relative effects of psychological and physical punishment by way of retrospective reports of Harvard students. The students were asked to report their reactions to each type of punishment. The memories they had of their reactions to physical punishment were "anger, stubbornness, resentment, antagonism, annoyance, obstinacy, hatred, cold dislike, and so forth" (p. 500). The reactions they recalled in relation to discipline that made them feel inferior, unworthy, and temporarily unloved, were "felt ashamed, sorrowful, conscience-stricken, repentant, desirous to apologize, anxious not to offend again, and so forth" (p. 498).

Maher (1966) defines guilt in a fashion very similar to Unger. He describes guilt as a particular instance of anxiety, the anxiety resulting from expectation of loss of love and similar punishments for one's own behavior. He also sees guilt and other criteria of conscience as dependent upon the use of punishment in moral training. Like Unger, he defines guilt as consisting of verbal evaluations plus emotional–visceral responses (essentially fear). Maher added the notion that the subjective experience of guilt tends to cause the individual to seek punishment. He supports Mosher's (1968) conclusion that sensitivity to situational cues regarding propriety of behavior is a function of strength of trait guilt—the higher the guilt the less sensitive to situational cues and the more sensitive to internal processes.

Maher applied the concept of guilt as developed by Unger, Mosher, and others to an analysis of the psychopath. He described the psychopath as an individual who is essentially deficient in guilt or conscience. There is the implication that the psychopath never experiences parental nurturance or at least does not have moral training in the context of a warm, affectionate relationship. Maher cited psychopaths' tendencies to antisocial acts and sexual promiscuity as evidence of their guilt deficiencies.

Maher suggested that as children, psychopaths learn to use suitable expressions of repentance and promises to avoid punishment. They learn to use charm and social skill to get what they want. They get no training in learning to work and wait for long-term rewards. They do not learn to tolerate frustration. They learn to get affection or approval by being "good looking," "charming," and "clever." Psychopaths are remarkably capable to getting people to help them and to avoid punishment. As the result of not being punished for wrongdoing, they do not learn that their actions distress and harm other people.

Maher maintains that conscience consists of resistance to temptation, self-instruction to obey, and capacity for feeling guilt. He sees resistance to temptation as a function of avoidance learning, and self-instruction to obey moral principles as a function primarily of imitation of the loved parent. Maher cited a number of studies in support of his analysis of the psychopath as a guilt-deficient individual. One of these studies showed that psychopaths perform more slowly on tasks where remote previous responses had been reinforced but performed in superior fashion on tasks when deficient performance was determined by immediate previous reinforcement.

In an incisive paper on the role of parental discipline in the development of conscience and guilt, Hoffman and Saltzstein (1967) differentiate between power-assertive disciplinary techniques and two types of non-power-assertive techniques: love withdrawal, in which parents give direct but nonphysical expression to their anger or disapproval, and induction of empathy, which involves the child being made aware of his or her own role in distressing or hurting others. Their experiment showed that simple love withdrawal was not as effective as the induction of empathic responses accompanied by communication to the child of his or her role in others' distress or pain.

Differential emotions theory allows for the possibility that withdrawal of love as a punishment technique for teaching morality can produce sadness, anger, fear, guilt, or some combination of these depending upon the individual, the relationship, and the situation. When love withdrawal is perceived as threat of separation, sadness might be the most likely result if such separation is seen as resulting in being left alone for a while without the joy, excitement, and comfort that are contingent on the presence and availability of the parent or loved one. Fear may be the result when the love withdrawal appears to leave the individual more vulnerable to hurt or harm. The individual sees loss of love as a loss of protection from danger. Guilt is more likely to obtain when the individual sees the withholding of love as a sign of disapproval of wrongdoing. Withdrawal of love may thus be seen as not being "right" with the loved one. In this case it is a kind of estrangement, a kind of inability to relate in the normal and affectionate way, an estrangement in which real or imagined wrongdoing stands as a barrier between the child and the parent or caregiver.

Hoffman and Saltzstein's (1967) empathy induction technique is seen in differential emotions theory as an application of the principles of emotion contagion and emotion communication. Techniques of conscience development based on these principles of interpersonal emotion processes may prove the most effective route to the development of a healthy conscience and a more uniformly ethical society.

Experimental Studies of Guilt

In the last few years, a number of empirical investigations have been undertaken to experimentally induce, manipulate, and evaluate guilt. Most of these studies were based on drive-reduction learning theory, social-learning theory, and psychoanalytic theory—positions that have not traditionally fostered careful delineation of discrete emotions. Although this body of research sometimes confounds or fails to differentiate emotion states, it is helpful in furthering our understanding of guilt and the interaction of guilt with other emotions, cognition, and action. An excellent selection of research and theoretical articles from the early literature on guilt is presented in Johnson, Dokecki, and Mowrer (1972).

The Interaction of Guilt and Anger

Gambaro (1967) conducted a study of the interaction of guilt and anger in a frustrating situation. Gambaro's experiment was rather sophisticated in that he did not simply assume that his frustrating condition would elicit anger. He used a self-report measure to check on the success of his manipulation in altering the subjective experience of anger.

He hypothesized that frustration-instigated anger would raise diastolic blood pressure and that expression of aggression under this condition would lower diastolic blood pressure. Further, he hypothesized that subjects scoring high on the Mosher Aggression– Guilt Scale (Mosher, 1967) would respond differently in the experimental conditions from subjects scoring low on this scale. There were four experimental conditions. In the first condition subjects were frustrated and then allowed to respond to their anger directly by administering electric shock to the frustrator (the experimental assistant). In the second condition the subjects were frustrated but were allowed only an indirect response to their anger—they could allow the experimenter to shock the frustrator. In the third condition the subjects went through the frustration sequence but were not allowed to respond overtly to their anger. In the fourth condition the subjects went through the experimental procedure but there was no frustration condition and no cause or opportunity for aggression. They completed "fill in" activities instead.

A self-report measure of anger, the check on the success of the frustration manipulation, showed that subjects under frustration rated themselves significantly angrier than did the control group. Further, the diastolic blood pressure of all subjects in the frustration conditions was significantly elevated above that of the control group. All subjects in the direct-response condition (those who were frustrated and allowed to shock the frustrators) showed a significantly greater decrease in diastolic blood pressure than did the subjects in the no-response group (those who were frustrated and allowed no overt response to their anger). The subjects in the indirect response condition (allowing the subject to shock the frustrator) showed no more change in diastolic blood pressure than did the no-response group. Although the high- and low-guilt subjects did not differ on the blood pressure measure in the frustration conditions (both groups showed significant increases), the high-guilt subjects showed significantly less decrease in diastolic blood pressure than did the low-guilt group during the postfrustration activities. The high-guilt group in the indirect-response condition actually showed a slight mean increase in diastolic blood pressure.

This interesting study has important implications for understanding the dynamics of guilt, particularly as it is associated with the experience of anger and subsequent aggression. The study shows very clearly that the extent to which people feel guilt after they aggress (even when the aggression may be objectively justifiable) is significantly related to the effects their feelings and actions will have on their physiological functioning. Subjects who experience strong guilt over their aggressive actions (whether or not they may be considered objectively justifiable) may increase their physiological disturbance (increased diastolic blood pressure) if they respond to their anger through physical aggression. On the other hand, subjects who can operate on the "eye-for-an-eye, tooth-for-a-tooth" principle of aggression tend to get their system back in equilibrium (decrease in diastolic blood pressure) by responding to their anger through physical aggression. Of course, these generalizations must be tempered by careful consideration of the experimental conditions and their generalizability to real-life situations.

Solomon, Turner, and Lessac (1968) conducted a study with dogs and concluded that their study had implications for guilt and guilt-related behavior in human beings. They taught dogs to "resist the temptation" of eating a more desirable canned dog food and to eat instead a less desirable dry meat. They taught them to discriminate between the taboo food and the acceptable food by means of punishment (a blow on the nose). They varied the length of delay between the dogs' yielding to temptation and eating the desirable canned dog food and the time of punishment. The variations in delays of punishment did not affect the ease with which the dogs learned to resist the temptation and avoid punishment. However, patterns of emotionality, reactions to absence of experimenter, and reactions to violation of the taboo varied greatly for different delays in the schedule of punishment. The authors concluded that their findings were relevant to child-rearing practices in that delays of punishment following a child's wrongdoing would be correlated with "the intensity of shame and guilt in children."

The authors' generalization from conditioning in dogs to the socialization of children should be weighed carefully but probably should not be ignored. If Rebecca is made to feel guilt, the timing and manner of her punishment will undoubtedly make some difference in what happens to her guilt feelings and to guilt-motivated thought and behavior. For example, if she is made to feel guilty and then has to wait a long time before she gets the expected punishment, she will have much longer to live with the guilt, rehearse the guilt situation, and ruminate over its seriousness and consequences. A mother should weigh carefully the possible effects of creating guilt in a child (caught in the midst of wrongdoing) and then telling her to "wait until your father gets home and you'll get the spanking of your life."

Guilt and Compliance

Freedman, Wallington, and Bless (1967) reviewed studies by Freedman and Fraser (1966), Wallace and Sadalla (1966), Brock and Becker (1962), and Carlsmith and Gross (1969) and concluded that their experimental results supported the conclusion that guilt increased compliance. However, Freedman *et al.* (1967) thought there were weaknesses in some of these studies, and they extended this line of research with a series of three additional experiments.

In the first experiment, subjects were put into a situation in which they either denied or admitted to the experimenter the fact that they had been given previous knowledge of the experiment in which they were about to participate. All subjects were then asked to volunteer for a future experiment of either an unpleasant or neutral type. A significantly greater number of the subjects who withheld information from the experimenter ("lie condition") volunteered for a future experiment than did subjects in the control condition. The pleasantness or neutrality of the future experiment had no effect on the number of individuals complying with the request to participate in it.

In a second experiment, subjects either sat at a wobbly table where they inevitably upset some supposedly carefully arranged index cards, or at a steady table where the cards remained in order. Following this treatment condition, the experimenter asked the subjects to volunteer for an experiment being run by a graduate student whose office and cards had been involved or for an experiment being conducted by a graduate student unrelated to the events of the day. Of the subjects in the group who upset the index cards, 75% complied with the request to participate in a future experiment, while only 39% of the control group volunteered. There was no difference in the frequency with which members of the guilt and no-guilt groups volunteered for the experiment with the graduate student who had nothing to do with the experimental situation, but there was a great difference in the number volunteering to help the graduate student whose index cards had been disarranged. In the guilt condition, 9 out of 10 of the subjects (who did not expect to be identified as the "culprit") volunteered to help by participating in the future experiment of the "victimized" graduated student, while only 5 out of 15 volunteered in the nonguilt condition. The questions to the effect of having to face the "wronged" individual when volunteering to help ("do recompense") was examined in a third experiment.

The setup for the third experiment was similar to that for the second, except that all subjects were requested to help the victimized graduate student. Half were asked to help in such a way that it was necessary to meet him and work side by side with him; the other half were asked to help in a way that did not require meeting him. Again, there was significantly greater compliance with the request by the group in the guilt condition. There was no difference between the guilt and nonguilt groups in response to the request to help by working with the victim, but in responding to the request that did not require meeting the victim, 11 out of 15 subjects in the guilt condition complied but only 3 out of 17 in the nonguilt condition complied.

Unfortunately, these studies did not measure the subjective experience of guilt and hence, made no direct check on the guilt manipulation. Guilt was operationally defined as a condition arising from actions contrary to normal standards of behavior (telling a lie, afflicting a hardship on another person). The results indicated that such a "guilt condition" had a fairly potent influence on the subjects' willingness to comply to a request that involved some of their time and effort at some point in the future. Interestingly, but not surprisingly, subjects in the guilt condition were much more reluctant to comply if compliance involved meeting and dealing directly with the person who had been wronged. This might mean that the subject did not want to add to his or her burden of guilt the possibility of an unpleasant confrontation with the wronged person, but generalization to real-life situations must be tempered by the fact that these were rather contrived situations in which the parties involved were strangers. However, the validity of the finding that experimental subjects suffering from experimentally induced guilt are reluctant to comply with a request requiring them to meet and deal with the victim was further supported by a study of Silverman (1967). This study involved 199 sixth-grade students. The students were presented with the temptation to falsify their answers on a test to win prize money. The experimenter (who was victimized by losing money to the cheaters) requested the students volunteer to work with him in a future experiment. There was no significant difference in the number of volunteers among noncheaters, low cheaters, and high cheaters. This finding is consistent with those of Freedman *et al.* (1967) and Wallace and Sadalla (1966) that transgression *per se* (guilt as operationally defined by these manipulations) is not sufficient to obtain compliance when compliance means having to meet and deal with the victim.

Development of Guilt as a Personality Trait

As in the case for other fundamental emotions, guilt and the interactions of guilt with other emotions, cognition, and action is considered as a trait or cluster of traits in the human personality. A number of other theoretical positions and numerous empirical investigations support the notion that guilt can be considered as a personality trait.

One of the earliest studies of the development of trait guilt was that of Whiting and Child (1953, pp. 218–262). They used the Yale Human Relations Research Files to do a cross-cultural study, focusing especially on the data from preliterate cultures. They analyzed the individual's attitude toward illness and used willingness to accept blame for the problem as a measure of guilt. Influenced by psychoanalytic theory and behavioristic learning theory, they looked through data on chid-rearing practices in the various cultures to find correlates of guilt. They found that early weaning, early independence training, training in modesty, and inhibition of heterosexual play tended to produce a higher level of guilt. They concluded that the mechanism of identification mediated the development of guilt in these cultures. Parents who adopted child-rearing practices that resulted in early weaning, early development of independence, modesty, and control of heterosexual play were relatively more powerful models with whom the children could identify. In monogamous societies, age of weaning correlated with the individual's willingness to take blame or responsibility for his or her illness (the index of guilt). The same was not true in polygamous societies. One of their interesting though speculative conclusions was that guilt was derived from identification with the male role. Their more generally accepted conclusion was that guilt plays an important role in social control (cf. Levine, 1973, p. 64).

The studies of Whiting and Child, as well as the work of Benedict (1934), Mead (1956), and Izard (1971), support the notion that shame and guilt are transcultural phenomena. Some cultures seem to be more shame oriented and others more guilt oriented. Benedict (1946) characterized certain cultures as shame cultures and others as guilt cultures. Johnson and Medinnus (1965), in their child psychology textbook, suggested that in American culture urbanites are moving from a guilt to a shame orientation. They pointed to several factors as determinants of this change—the influence of psychoanalysis and psychotherapy, which point to the dangers of severe guilt socialization, alterations in American culture that cause parents to be unsure of their own value judgments, and the apparent increased power of the influence of peers on the development of moral and ethical standards.

Although there is a possible tendency to reduce the guilt orientation in American culture, Johnson and Medinnus noted that shame is more likely to be effective in small societies than in a large heterogeneous one like that in the United States. Their notion makes some sense in relation to the psychology of shame and guilt. Since shame is most often elicited in the individual by other people, it might be a more effective control in relatively closed groups where "everybody knows everybody." However, in urban societies, where individuals enjoy a great deal of anonymity and multiple group membership, it would be more necessary for the individual to exercise the internal control that derives from the incorporation of parental and adult standards that form the basis for conscience and guilt.

Traditionally, people have thought of religion and religious training as one of the principal sources of conscience and guilt reactions. Most people with a strong religious upbringing recognize that religion played a role in the development of their consciences and in determining some of the causes and consequences of guilt. People who maintain strong religious affiliations continue to consider religious values and codes as guides to certain aspects of their conduct. However, even in the most devoutly religious, other factors such as morality, human ethics and local customs relating to right and wrong play a role in the development of conscience and guilt thresholds.

London, Schulman, and Black (undated) examined the relationship between subjective experience of guilt and religious affiliation. There were some problems with the sampling: there was a sex difference in responses to their questionnaire, and the different religious groups were not balanced by sex. Regardless of religious affiliation, the male subjects reported significantly fewer guilt feelings than females. There was a statistically significant ($p < .05$), though not very substantial, difference, indicating that Jewish subjects had somewhat higher levels of personal guilt than Protestant subjects. The authors concluded that guilt feelings did not differ strikingly among denominations, but they thought that sex differences were more substantial. The authors' analysis of other aspects of the data led them to conclude that guilt as a contributor to psychopathology was probably equally important in all religious groups.

Katz and Ziegler (1967) reasoned that the development of guilt in the individual was positively correlated with the development of ability to make finer cognitive judgments and with growth toward maturity. This is consistent with the previously presented theoretical concepts on the relationship between, and the development of, personal and social responsibility. The authors did a survey of 120 fifth-grade, eighty-grade, and eleventh-grade students. Their questionnaires were designed to measure differences between the individuals' concept of their "real selves," their "social selves," and their "ideal selves." Their results showed that discrepancy between the individual's real and ideal self-concepts was related to age and IQ. On the basis of their results, they argued that neither guilt nor anxiety functioned as a strictly negative agent in the "individual's total psychic economy." They saw the increasing disparity between individuals' concepts of their real and their ideal selves as accompanying higher levels of development. They thought that the increasing age of the individual resulted in greater capacity for cognitive differentiation and for self-derogation and, hence, for the experience of guilt. They suggested that the data supported their contention that the increasing disparity between real and ideal self-concept and increasing development of guilt or capacity for guilt was related to maturity. The more mature the children the greater their self-demands, thus the more likelihood of experiencing guilt.

A similar study by Nicholas (1966) supported the conclusion that there is a significant relationship between guilt and a person's self-concept. His study pointed up another interesting aspect of these complex emotion–personality dynamics. He found a significant negative relationship between guilt scores and self-acceptance scores. Nicholas concluded that within certain "normal" limits there is no significant relationship between guilt and personality adjustment. Earlier research by Rogers (1959) and his colleagues had shown that high discrepancies between real and ideal self-concepts and low scores on self-acceptance are indexes of maladjustment.

The work of Rogers and his colleagues, as well as the studies reviewed above, are not really inconsistent with the notion that a certain threshold for guilt is essential for personal responsibility and social-emotional maturity. It is severe and chronic guilt or an extremely low guilt threshold that leads to serious psychological problems and maladjustment. This conclusion is further supported by a study of Fenyes (1967), in which she illustrated a relationship between a high level of moral judgment and the relative absence of inappropriate self-blame. Using a projective measure she also found that a tendency to take other people's points of view into account was associated with a tendency to react with self-blame for another person's distress.

Guilt and Hostility

Mosher and his students and colleagues have made significant contributions to the psychology of guilt. Beginning his work in the framework of Rotter's social learning theory, Mosher reasoned that individuals who violated a religious, moral, or ethical code would be significantly influenced by actual or anticipated external punishment (fear-arousing condition) and by internal punishment (guilt). Mosher defined guilt as an expectancy of self-mediated punishment for violating or failing to attain internalized standards of proper behavior. (Internalized standards, which differential emotions theory interprets as the result of guilt–cognition interactions, have both an inhibiting [should not] component and a positively valued ideal-goal [ought to] component.) The "expectancy for guilt" was defined by Mosher as a function of the individual's social learning history (socialization), during which time the internalization of standards were reinforced by producing approval and avoiding punishment. Mosher maintained that the behavior that would materialize in a situation that was potentially fear arousing and guilt arousing would be the function of three variables: (1) the value of the goal (or reinforcement) to be obtained by the behavior, (2) the strength of the expectancy that the behavior will lead to externally mediated punishment (the fear-arousing condition), and (3) the strength of the expectancy that the behavior will lead to self-mediated punishment (guilt).

Mosher's first instrument for the measurement of guilt was a sentence-completion test. He conducted several studies with this instrument and confirmed and elaborated some of the previously discussed findings relating to guilt as a personality trait. These studies tended to confirm his notion of a fear–guilt interaction as a basic factor in determining people's behavior in situations where they are confronted with a possibility of violating religious, moral, or ethical codes. For example, he showed that low-guilt subjects were more influenced by expectancy of external punishment than high-guilt subjects. He also found that the level of guilt was positively related to verbal conditioning of guilt-related content.

Partly as a result of these initial studies, Mosher decided that guilt experience could be subdivided into three aspects: (1) hostility guilt—guilt elicited as a result of feelings of hostility and by acts of aggression; (2) sex guilt—guilt associated with thoughts, feelings, and actions in the sexual sphere; and (3) morality—conscience guilt. Several studies were conducted by Mosher and his colleagues relating to the first two types of guilt. He showed that sex guilt was significantly related to perceptual defense against sexual stimuli (the higher the guilt, the higher the threshold for the perception of sex-related words). Mosher suggested that subjects low on sex guilt were more sensitive to cues suggesting the possibility of external punishment, while subjects high on sex guilt tended to respond more in terms of internal standards. Although high sex guilt tended to facilitate verbal conditioning of self-related content, high hostility guilt seemed to inhibit the conditioning of material with hostile content. These and other experiments led Mosher to the interesting and quite reasonable conclusion that high guilt tends to override the force of situational cues in determining behavior. He obtained some empirical support for the notion that high-guilt subjects were actually less responsive to the probability of external punishment or disapproval. Conversely, subjects low on guilt were less responsive to the possibility of internal punishment (guilt feelings) and more sensitive to the possibility of external punishment or disapproval.

Guilt and Sexual Behavior

Mosher and his colleagues conducted a series of studies relating to sex guilt (e.g., Mosher & Galbraith, 1970). These studies led to the following conclusions: (1) there is a negative correlation between sex guilt and the ease with which a person free-associates to words with a sexual connotation; (2) subjects high on sex guilt show less awareness of the sexual and nonsexual connotations; (3) only low sex-guilt subjects show an increase in sexual associations on a word association task following sexual stimulation (e.g., looking at nude or scantily clad pinup girls by male subjects).

The Mosher and Galbraith (1970) study is a good example of the kind of experiment that contributed to the foregoing conclusions. The authors examined the recall ability of high- and low-guilt subjects for associations given under sexually stimulating and sexually nonstimulating conditions. The subjects were divided into low and high sex-guilt groups on the basis of the scores on the Mosher Forced-Choice Guilt Inventory. Half of the high sex-guilt subjects and half of the low sex-guilt subjects were in each of the two sex-stimulation conditions. The sexual stimulation procedure required the subjects to rate 27 photos of nude or seminude girls on sexual attractiveness. Following this task the subjects were given a double entendre word association test. The test included 30 double entendres and 20 neutral words. The subjects were required to respond as rapidly as possible with the word that the stimulus word suggested to them. Word association latencies were measured with an openly displayed stop watch. Immediately after the word association test the original words were repeated, and on this occasion the subjects were required to recall their original association. Again, the response latencies were recorded. Accuracy of recall was also scored.

The results showed that high sex-guilt subjects made the largest number of recall errors when in the sexual stimulation condition and fewest under the control condition. The high sex-guilt subjects even showed a slight impairment in recall ability for neutral words under the sex-stimulation condition. Low sex-guilt subjects showed no impairment for recall of either sexual or neutral words: they even showed a slight improvement under the sexual-stimulation condition. Mosher and Galbraith explained the poor recall of high sex-guilt subjects on the basis of negative emotions. Probably a combination of fear and guilt caused the subjects to give associations that were only weakly related or associated to the stimulus word. Thus recall was more difficult.

Mosher (1968) conducted a study of the effects of sex guilt (measured as a personality trait) on females' emotion responses to the reading of an erotic passage of literature. High and low sex-guilt subjects read either a neutral or erotic passage with a like-sex (female) experimenter either present or absent. Only the high-guilt subjects who read the erotic passage showed a significant increase in state guilt as measured by Nowlis's Mood Adjective Checklist.

Izard and Caplan (1974) did a follow-up of Mosher's study using both male and female subjects. Males who read the erotic passage reported significantly higher sexual arousal, interest, and enjoyment, and less disgust than did the females, but there were no differences between the males and females on fear. The liberalization of views on sex, together with the greatly increased openness and vividness with which sex is treated in literature and in the media (particularly the movies), was seen as a significant factor in the difference between Mosher's study and the Izard–Caplan study, conducted 5 years late.

The Izard–Caplan study was replicated (Izard, Caplan, Walker, & Kotsch, 1977) with the modification that the experimenter and subject were of opposite sex. As in Mosher's study and the 1974 Izard–Caplan study, the erotic passage was Chapter 72 of Calder Willingham's *Eternal Fire* (1963). The affects measured were sexual arousal, interest, joy, surprise, sadness, anger, disgust, fear, shyness, and guilt. Our concern here will be primarily with the state measure of guilt and the relationships between Mosher's sex-guilt scale (a trait measure of guilt) and the foregoing emotions measured as states by the DES.

There were 112 male subjects and 112 female subjects. One half of the subjects of each sex read either the neutral or erotic passage with the observer present, and the other subgroups read one of the two passages with the observer absent. As in the 1974 Izard–Caplan study, the subjects were contacted by telephone and later visited in their own rooms for the administration of the experiment. The DES was administered before and after the reading of the passages. An analysis of the pretreatment DES scores showed that simply as a result of the presence of an opposite-sex experimenter in their rooms, males reported significantly greater sexual arousal, surprise, anger, disgust, fear, shyness, and guilt than did the females.

Since the design of this study and the Izard–Caplan study was the same except for the opposite-sex condition, the pretest data of the two experiments were compared to examine further the effects of an opposite-sex experimenter. This analysis showed that the presence of an opposite-sex experimenter brought about a highly significant increase in sexual arousal in males and a slight, though not significant decrease, in females. On the guilt scale the males showed a significant increase, and the females showed a decrease of equal magnitude, though it was not statistically significant. The data do not tell exactly why males were generally more emotionally responsive to the presence of opposite-sex experimenters in their rooms. It is quite reasonable that the increase in sexual arousal in males was a significant determinant of other observed changes. A big increase in sexual arousal may have activated guilt as well as other emotion responses.

Analysis of the joint effects of opposite-sex experimenter and the "literary treatment" (neutral or erotic passage) showed that those who read a passage (whether neutral or erotic) with the opposite-sex observer present expressed more guilt than those who read their passage with the observer absent.

At the conclusion of the second DES, Mosher's sex-guilt scale was administered. Scores on the sex-guilt scale were correlated with scores from the DES. The trait sex-guilt scores showed modest, though statistically significant, negative correlations with sexual arousal ($r = -.19, p < .01$) and joy ($r = .21, p < .05$). Trait sex-guilt was significantly positively correlated with disgust ($r = .31, p < .01$) and with the DES state measure of guilt ($r = .24, p < .01$). These are logical findings that could be predicted from an understanding of the psychology of guilt and of guilt–sex interactions. The findings are consistent with those presented by Mosher (1965).

We have already suggested that one of the determinants of the higher emotion scores for men in the opposite-sex experimenter study was the substantially greater sexual arousal on the part of the males. In the American culture it is generally thought that males are more readily sexually aroused by the presence of a member of the opposite sex than are females. Because of the linkage of sex and guilt in socialization, the higher sexual arousal could help account for the males' higher guilt scores. But what of the males higher scores on anger, disgust, and fear? Perhaps part of the reason for the increase in these emotions was the male's frustration and uncertainty as to what to do about their increased sexual arousal. For the males, the experiment reversed the traditional (stereotyped) male and female roles. A young woman (fellow college student) had, in effect, invited herself into a young man's room; further, she was the experimenter ("authority figure") and in charge of the situation. This relatively unusual social situation may have interacted with the relatively high sexual arousal to recruit the emotions of anger, disgust, and fear.

Izard, Spiegel *et al.* (1974) conducted a study of the effects of moral-ethical standards relative to sexual behavior and sexual experience on emotion responses to imaging (visualizing) sexual intercourse. The study was conducted in the form of an anonymous survey handled entirely by student experimenters. From a booth that was placed at several points on the campus, 495 students accepted questionnaires as they passed by. To insure anonymity the participants were supplied with self-addressed envelopes and requested not to sign the experimental material. Of the 275 students who responded, 255 returned complete and usable research forms.

The major hypotheses were that sexual standards and sexual experience would be significantly related to emotion responses subsequent to imaging the sexual scene. It was also hypothesized that subjects with conservative sexual standards would respond with more negative emotions (particularly fear and guilt) than those with liberal standards.

The test materials that were passed out to the students contained four research forms: the DES II (the trait version of the DES), the Reiss Scale of Sexual Standards (Reiss, 1967), a modified Podell–Perkins Sexual Experience Scale (Podell & Perkins, 1957), and the DES (state measure of emotion). The items on the sexual standards scale measured the participants belief in (or agreement with) behavior ranging from "kissing with affection" to "sexual intercourse without affection." The sexual experience scale asked the participants to indicate the frequency with which they performed the various sex-related activities ranging from kissing to sexual intercourse. The data for each emotion trait and for each posttreatment emotion state (subsequent to visualization of the sexual scene) were analyzed in a 2 × 3 × 3 factorial design: 2 (male–female) × 3 (sexual virgin, relatively inexperienced, sexually more experienced) × 3 (standards that do not permit premarital coitus, standards that permit coitus with affection, and standards that permit coitus without affection). In this summary we shall be concerned primarily with responses related to shyness and guilt. Remember, the participants completed the DES II (trait measure of emotions) before seeing any of the rest of the test materials. They completed the DES (state measure of emotions) immediately after imaging and visualizing sexual intercourse.

The DES II revealed an interesting curvilinear relationship between amount of sexual experience and amount of trait guilt. The participants who had had sexual intercourse only one or a few times reported the highest amount of guilt, the more sexually experienced participants reported the least amount of guilt, and virgins occupied the middle position. Perhaps subjects who had had sexual experience only a few times were still working through their guilt feelings, and such affective–cognitive preoccupation resulted in higher scores on trait guilt. This finding is consistent with results cited by McCary (1973).

The individual's level of sexual experience also had a significant effect upon the amount of state guilt aroused by visualizing sexual intercourse. In the case of female participants, the more sexually experienced the individual, the less guilt was aroused. In the case of the male group, men who had a single experience or only a few sexual experiences reported more guilt subsequent to visualization of sexual intercourse than did the men who were virgins or the men who were sexually more experienced. Thus the males' scores on the state measure of emotion following visualization of intercourse follow the same pattern as that of all subjects on the trait measure of guilt. Again the data suggested that, at least for males, the period when a person is first obtaining sexual experience is likely to be relatively more guilt laden than periods of virginity or sexual sophistication.

The sexual standards of the individuals also affected the amount of guilt aroused by visualizing the sexual scene. Participants who indicated that they did not believe in premarital intercourse reported greater guilt as a result of visualizing sexual intercourse than did participants who accepted premarital coitus. In general, the more liberal the participants' sexual attitude, as measured by the sexual standards scale, the less guilt they felt when they visualized sexual intercourse. The data are not entirely consistent with Lewis's (1971) hypothesis that men tend to be more guilt prone whereas women are more prone to shame and shyness. As noted in Chapter 14, males report greater trait shyness than females. The same is true for trait guilt. Thus while men reported slightly more shyness and guilt in their day-to-day lives (irrespective of cause), women reported more shyness and guilt subsequent to visualization of sexual intercourse. Further, female virgins reported significantly more guilt in their day-to-day lives than did male virgins. This may help explain the fact that, at least until quite recently or perhaps still today, within a given age group, more women are virgins than are men. It should be noted that Lewis's hypothesis applied to behavior in general, while these data related only to sexual behavior.

Considerable research data support the conclusion that guilt as a personality trait (trait guilt) and guilt as a psychological state (state guilt) are reliable and valid psychological phenomena that have important consequences for personality and social behavior. Trait guilt may be defined in terms of an individual's guilt threshold or his or her generalized expectancy of self-mediated punishment for violating or anticipating the violation of internalized standards of proper behavior or codes of conduct. Thus, guilt as a personality trait or tendency serves as a regulator of behavioral propriety and as an inhibitor of improper thoughts, feelings, and actions.

Research support for the construct of trait guilt was provided by Mosher's (1965) finding that guilt over hostility (hostility guilt) prevents the expression of verbal hostility in a verbal-conditioning study. Also, Okle and Mosher (1968) found that subjects high on trait guilt showed significant increases in state guilt after engaging in hostile–aggressive behavior in a laboratory situation. The Mosher and Galbraith (1970) finding that subjects high on sex guilt were inhibited in making sexual responses to the double entendre word association test was also evidence of the validity of the concept of trait guilt.

In addition to the laboratory studies already discussed, several studies of prison inmates have also supported the notion that trait guilt has a real and important influence on certain aspects of human behavior. Oliver and Mosher (1968) and Persons and Marks (1969) showed that prisoners scores on the Mosher guilt scale were positively correlated with MMPI subscales associated with inhibition and negatively correlated with MMPI subscales indicative of acting-out behavior. Mosher and Mosher (1967) found that prisoners who commit offenses against property have higher guilt than prisoners who commit offenses against people. Persons (1970a) showed that there was a negative relationship between trait guilt and total number of crimes committed by an inmate. Further, he showed that there was a significant negative relationship between hostility guilt and crimes of violence and between sex guilt and sexual crimes. A more detailed study of the relationship of the various Mosher guilt subscales in the prison population showed that the guilt–crime relationship was highly complex (Persons, 1970b). For example, both trait and state guilt showed a significant interaction with race and type of crime. Further studies of trait and state guilt in real-life situations are needed.

Managing Guilt

The best way to manage guilt is to live by your standards of behavior. If you find that you are often experiencing guilt because of the violation of one of your standards, there is nothing wrong in reexamining the rule you have made for yourself. There are some basic rules of conduct that we all want to follow—those requiring respect for others and their rights and freedoms. It is entirely possible, however, that you have internalized or adopted a rule or standard that is unnecessarily restrictive and does nothing to facilitate your welfare or that of others.

When you have wronged someone and you experience guilt, there is typically the feeing that your relationship has been damaged or even temporarily lost. You manage this aspect of guilt by beginning to behave in such a way as to restore the other person's faith in you and to reestablish the trust that was once there. Healthy and happy relationships require mutual trust, and the more intimate the relationship, the greater the degree of trust that is required. Guilt is always an individual as well as a social burden. Until you can make amends and restore the relationship, both personal and interpersonal affairs will suffer.

Summary

In discrete emotions theory guilt is the key emotion in the development of personal and social responsibility and the phenomena of conscience. While there probably are some basic human conditions that universally elicit guilt, conscience consists mainly of affective–cognitive structures that include precepts inculcated by parents and societal institutions. These affective–cognitive structures motivate and guide moral and ethical behavior. Though guilt is predominant in the development of the feeling of responsibility, positive emotions may characterize altruism that is extended without expectation of reciprocation—the highest form of moral-ethical action.

Shame and guilt often occur together. Tomkins argues that they are essentially one emotion with two representations in consciousness. Ausubel holds that guilt involves a component of moral shame, but he recognizes that guilt includes other important self-reactions and that nonmoral shame is independent of guilt.

Most theorists agree that shame typically involves the real or imagined sanctions of other people and that guilt is mainly a function of internal sanctions, though external ones may also be involved. Guilt results from the violation of ethical, moral, or religious standards. While certain ethical standards may have a basis in evolutionary-biological history, the specifics of various codes are internalized through identification with parents and significant adults, imitation or modeling, induction of empathy, and other forms of social and experiential learning.

The expression of guilt is not as sharply defined as the expression of other negative emotions. Guilt may cause the person to hold the head lower and to avert his or her gaze.

The experience of guilt consists of a gnawing feeling that one is in the wrong—"not right" with others or with the self. The DES profile of emotion in guilt situations shows a relatively high mean for sadness and fear. The frequency with which fear is elicited in guilt situations probably accounts for the lack of a clear differentiation between these two emotions in a number of theories. The guilt experience is characterized by a high degree of tension, a moderate degree of impulsiveness, and relatively little self-assurance.

Guilt complements shame in fostering social responsibility, and it serves as a check on wanton waste and sexual and aggressive exploitation. The development of guilt and conscience fosters growth toward greater psychological maturity.

An overdeveloped conscience or too low a threshold for guilt may lead to serious adjustment problems or psychopathology. Several theorists hold that high guilt proneness can lead to obsessive–compulsive disorders and even to paranoid schizophrenia.

In Freudian theory, the development of conscience and guilt is dependent upon the way the Oedipus conflict is resolved in the child's developing superego. Existential theorists hold that one inevitably experiences guilt because of one's failure to live up to one's full human potentialities. In Khanna's critique of existential theorists, he points out their failure to differentiate between being guilty and being human.

Various learning theory conceptions of the developmental origins of guilt have contributed significantly to our understanding of conscience and morality. These theories have emphasized the role of various forms of social learning in the internalization of guilt. Most of them agree that a warm, accepting relationship with a parent figure forms the best background for the development of a healthy conscience and an appropriate guilt threshold. Both theoretical arguments and a number of empirical studies suggest that some combination of temporary withdrawal of approval, induction of empathic responses, and understanding of one's role in bringing harm to others provides the best framework for discipline that leads to an appropriate guilt threshold and a mature conscience.

Suggested Readings

Graham, S., Doubleday, C., & Guarino, P. A. (1984). The development of relations between perceived controllability and the emotions of pity, anger, and guilt. *Child Development*, *55*(2), 561–565.

Evidence relating to developmental changes in children's reasoning about the causes of emotions and the type of reasoning or attributions that lead to guilt and other emotions. Evidence linking guilt to particular types of cognitive processes suggest that it is a qualitatively distinct emotion.

Mosher, D. L., & Vonderheide, S. G. (1985). Contributions of sex guilt and masturbation guilt to women's contraceptive attitudes and use. *Journal of Sex Research*, *21*(1), 24–39.

The data suggest that high sex guilt may have an adverse effect on sex attitudes and use of contraceptives.

Nunner-Winkler, G., & Sodian, B. (1988). Children's understanding of moral emotions. *Child Development*, *59*, 1323–1338.

Examines 4- and 8-year-old children's attributions of emotions to a story figure who violated a moral rule. Shows clear differences between the two age groups' understanding of wrongdoing and its emotional consequences.

Zahn-Waxler, C., Kochanska, G., Krupnick, J., & McKnew, D. (1990). Patterns of guilt in children of depressed and well mothers. *Developmental Psychology*, *26*(1), 51–59.

A semiprojective assessment technique revealed that children of well mothers described adaptive themes about guilt, themes of responsibility and separation, whereas children of depressed mothers expressed aberrant themes about guilt. Discussion of the effects of depressed mothers on children's adaptation and moral development.

17

Love

Love seems so fundamental that you must wonder why it comes so late in this book on human emotions. In our hearts it is clearly first. Yet, it is shrouded in more mystery than any of the emotions so far discussed. Perhaps mystery is the wrong word, complexity might be better. No one will argue with the idea that love is complex.

What Is Love

Traditionally, psychologists have neglected studies of affection (Berschied, 1982). They have studied "interpersonal attraction" and typically formulated their hypotheses in terms of the concept of attitude.

Typically, assessment of the affective component of the interpersonal attraction consisted of a bipolar scale of liking (ranging from "like very much" to "dislike very much"), and the stimulus person was a photograph or video segment of a more or less attractive person unknown to the subject. Berschied suggested that making the stimulus person personally irrelevant to the subject was likely to result in data that underestimated the emotional component of interpersonal attraction or love. She concluded that interpersonal attraction and love could not be effectively investigated without more careful attention to the emotional roots of these phenomena. She suggested that students of interpersonal attraction and love could profit from more attention to emotion theory.

There are a number of ways in which love is different from the emotions we have considered in the previous chapters. The emotions we have already studied, like joy and sadness, anger and fear, are considered discrete fundamental emotions. Each is definable as a particular phenomenon, involving a single unique feeling. It is partly because an emotion like interest or fear has its own expression, its own specific feeling state, and its own particular pattern of activity in the nervous system that we think of the emotions that we have studied up to now as primary. Love is basic and fundamental, but in the case of love these descriptions take on a different and more complex meaning.

In one sense, love can be defined as a pattern of emotions, drives, and cognitions. Love includes *feelings and thoughts*, and in addition to basic emotion feelings, some types of love include sexual feeling and hence a biological drive is involved. Because love is all these things it is highly complex and perhaps a bit mystical.

Love as a Pattern of Emotions. It seems that love most assuredly involves both interest–excitement and enjoyment–joy. These basic emotions may be a very important part of the motivations that guide our behavior in love relationships. Further, when we think of love in terms of a relationship between two people, is it possible to rule out negative emotions?

There are certainly times when our love for someone puts us in situations in which we experience sadness. This may be due to a disappointment or separation, but it is because of our love relationship that we feel the sadness. We also know that the one we love can make us very angry. Some people think their greatest frustrations and their most intense anger is elicited by people they love. What I am suggesting is that the intense involvement between two people who love each other make possible the arousal of strong emotions of several varieties.

Types of Love. One reason why it is necessary to treat love as different from the emotions considered in the foregoing chapters is that there is no single definition of love. This is true because there are several types of love, but perhaps all types of love have something in common. Something makes each of them important and significant, something that cuts across all types of love—romantic love, love of parent and child, sibling love, love in friendship, love of country, of home, love of pets, love of values and ideals, and love of God. In addition to the several types of love, there is a distinction to be made between love as an experience of the moment or occasion and love as a relationship.

It might be possible to look at a moment of love or an act of love and describe the experience rather completely and accurately. To do this we would have to determine the type of love involved and the nature of the experience or act. Love as a relationship between two people extended over many occasions and across a long period of time may involve virtually all of the emotions at one time or another and it may include images, thoughts, and fantasies in almost as great a variety as that of which the human mind is capable.

Love is Excitement and Joy in Sharing and Caring. Excitement and joy in being with and doing for others is what all types of love have in common. Love is strong, perhaps the strongest of all the phenomena in the domain of emotions. But as already noted, love is truly a many-splendored thing, and each aspect of it is rooted in our biological as well as our social selves. Love has a long history, perhaps about as long as the history of our species, *Homo sapiens*. If for a moment we consider that love is a bond or attachment between two individuals, then we can

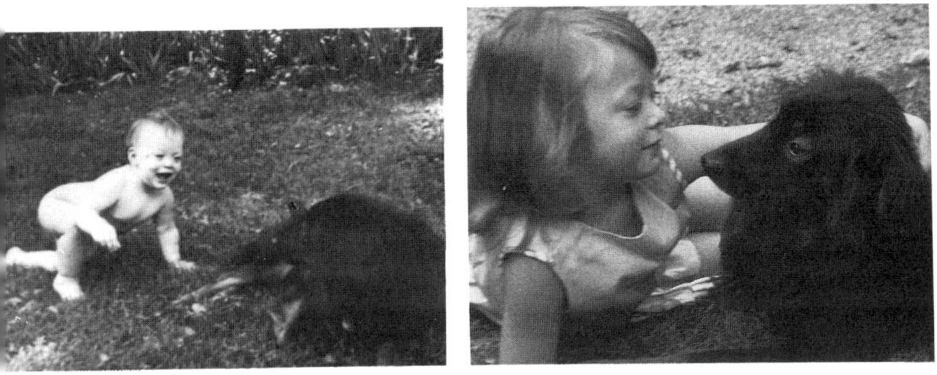

FIGURE 17-1. The same girl shows her love for her dog at ages 1 and 4 years.

say that nothing so strong or so universal could be a product of a whim or a recent invention. Love is part of our human nature.

The Origins of Human Love: The Biological–Evolutionary Heritage

For the first one or two billion years after the emergence of life, bacteria and blue-green algae were the only life forms. It took a few more billion years to reach the epoch that experts consider the beginning of events that led to human evolution (Mellen, 1981). Such events began to take place around 65 million years before the present (B.P.). Such events began to occur more rapidly about 35 million years B.P., and the first apelike form appeared on the earth approximately 15 million years B.P. About 12 million years were yet to intervene before the seeming miracles of evolution and nature were to produce the genus *Homo*. That happened about 3 million years B.P. The genus *Homo* includes several species, such as *Homo erectus*, *Homo habilis*, and our own species, *Homo sapiens*.

One of the great forces that facilitated evolutionary events leading to human beings was sexual reproduction—a factor that might also be seen as playing a role in the evolution of love. Nonsexual reproduction occurs in animals that simply duplicate themselves. Every offspring is a duplicate of the parent. If changes in the environment make adaptation for such an animal highly difficult, then all the difficulties experienced by the parent will be experienced in equal measure by the offspring. The offspring have no chance of having characteristics different from their parents that might enable them to adapt and survive.

In sexual reproduction, the male and the female each brings an equal number of genes to the reproductive process. To use an example given by Mellen (1981), a relatively simple animal with only 10 thousand genes could give rise through sexual reproduction to 210,000 unique genetic combinations of offspring. This is what biological scientists mean by genetic variation. In practical terms it means that a particular species of animal can give rise to a great variety of individuals, each with somewhat varying characteristics. Each one has a little different chance of adapting to changing conditions and of surviving to produce other offspring. Thus, variety is not only the spice of life for an individual, it may be the very stuff that enables his or her group or species to survive.

One other phenomenon in biological evolution was probably of special importance in the evolution of human beings and, in particular, in the evolution of certain emotions. It is what geneticists call *kin selection*. Kin selection is a process whereby certain special traits of individuals are passed on through their genes or the genes of their relatives to future generations. Before describing this phenomenon it is important to point out that genes and genetic traits that are advantageous to a species as a whole are not especially important in evolution. Traits that are important in evolution are those of particular and special value to the individuals possessing them.

A number of geneticists have presented evidence and arguments suggesting that kin selection may have accounted for the emergence and evolution of altruistic behavior in human beings. They argued that in the course of evolution there were many occasions when self-sacrifice on the part of an individual may have meant the difference in the survival of his family and close kin. To illustrate, let us imagine a father and three sons of early genus *Homo* going away from the home base and out into the savanna to hunt. After they have secured wild game and are on their way home with fresh meat for the rest of the family and kin folk, they see that they are being followed by a pack of large predators, hyenas. They know that if the hyenas attack them none will be able to survive. The oldest son, almost full grown, proposes that he remain behind hidden in the tall grass until the hyenas are almost upon him. Then he will leap out and distract them, giving the father and the younger brothers plenty of time to gain a safe distance toward the home base, not too far away now. Realizing the grave risk, the father and younger brothers object. But the father also realizes that it is his only chance to save the two younger brothers and to feed the rest of the family back home. So the older brother courageously and gallantly sacrifices his life and saves his father and brothers and contributes to the welfare of the rest of his family and kin. Now he has not only made possible the lives of his father and two brothers, he has increased the likelihood that the genetic trait that gave him the courage and desire to sacrifice himself will be safe in his father and younger brothers. Therefore, the genes that helped enable this noble act of altruism will be preserved and will spread to others through his father and brothers, eventually becoming a trait of the entire species.

Hoffman (1981) has argued that this altruistic behavior has at its core the response of empathy and that emotion feeling is an essential part of empathy. In our illustration, the older brother had the ability to feel for his father and younger brothers and for the family back home. It doesn't seem to be much of a stretch of the imagination to call the act of the courageous older brother an act of love.

Our Primate Heritage

With the increasing complexity of life and the appearance of apelike forms, various stages of growth and development from childhood to adolescence to adulthood became longer and longer. In monkeys and baboons, there are approximately 3 to 5 years between birth and the onset of adolescence; whereas in human beings, it is between 11 and 14 years. At the same time that we were evolving longer and longer stages of infancy and childhood, tendencies to protect and nurture the young were also evolving. In the case of many lower animals, parents have little or nothing to do with their offspring. In these species, offspring are strictly on their own even from the moment of birth. It seems that the more complex and intelligent the animal, the longer the period of relative dependency and the stronger the tendency in the adult (particularly the mother) to care for and nurture the young. Such protection and nurturance of the young is clear evidence of an all important type of love.

Evolutionists have made strong and persuasive arguments supporting the notion that progressive elongation of stages of growth, and particularly the extension of the relatively long period of helplessness in infancy and early childhood, were adaptive in the evolution of human beings. This certainly could not have been so if at the same time human beings had not also evolved a strong tendency to nurture and care for the young. The latter could not have been accomplished without the powerful bonding effect of emotion. The attachment between mother and child is an emotional attachment, and therefore it is easy to see that emotion played a significant role in the protection and care of the young and hence in our evolution as human beings.

Two other factors probably played a major role in our evolution and in the evolution of emotions. One was the establishing of home bases that served 10 to 50 people. The second was hunting, the set of skills that brought protein to our diet.

Virtually all students of human history agree that hunting was a great influence on evolution. (Authorities agree that hunting was done primarily by men and that women stayed closer to home base, caring for the young and gathering nearby vegetables and fruit.) According to Mellen's (1981) summary of the characteristics of a successful hunter, the development of hunting has also gone hand in hand with certain important aspects of the evolution of emotions. Perhaps our early human ancestors did not *have* to learn to hunt. After all, they could have survived on the fruits and vegetables that could be more safely obtained near the home base. So, initially, men did not hunt merely to satisfy hunger or a craving for protein. The successful hunter had to be curious about hunting and challenged by it. With this in mind, it is not difficult to see a role for the emotion of interest and excitement in the development of hunting skills.

Threat to life was commonplace on the savanna in the early years of human existence. A successful hunter had to be able to experience fear that would motivate escape behavior when appropriate, and he had to be able to control or manage the fear. He had to be able to keep it at a level that would not interfere with his mental and physical powers. As Mellen (1981) suggests, he had to have the capacity to suspend fear, and this happens to be largely a human capacity. It is possible that the suspension of fear could have been accomplished by a number of methods, including what we would now call cognitive control (refocusing attention). It may also have occurred by virtue of the individual's ability to use one emotion, such as interest or excitement, to regulate another, such as fear.

As Mellen (1981) has pointed out, in the early days of human existence the hunt was arduous work. It required great stamina and persistence, and men may have wandered 3 or 4 days or more from the home base before being ready to return with fresh meat for the women and children. Mellen raises the interesting question as to why the hunters would bother to return to a home base that, at best, was temporary. After exhausting themselves in the chase, why would they load themselves down with the animals they had taken and start the long trip home. They were made even more vulnerable by their heavy load. Mellen proposes that early human beings did it for the same reason we do similar things today. They did it because they wanted to, because of the attachment they had for a woman and children back at the home base. Images of the woman and children with whom they wanted to share the meat would stir feelings that gave them the desire and strength to return.

In these sketchy highlights of human evolution, we have seen a number of ways in which emotions play a vital role. It seems clear that we would not be what we are today had it not been for emotions that bonded us together and made us social creatures. It is easy to infer that the most important emotional ingredient in the bonding of parent and child and man and woman is what we call love. Let us now consider several types of love, each different and each vitally important in the grand scheme of nature and human affairs.

Mother Love

If we accept attachment, protectiveness, and nurturance as part of love, then love of a mother for her young is special. It is special in several ways, not the least of which is its vital role in the nurturance of lives. The evidence comes from many sources. We have seen how care and nurturance of the young was an absolutely essential part of our evolution as human beings. Later we shall see evidence from contemporary behavioral science that clearly shows the importance of mother love in the life of the individual.

What do behavioral scientists say about love? Most scientists agree that love for a infant can be shared by mother and father, and by siblings when they arrive. Many also agree that the adult female has very decided advantages over the male in her capacities to provide mothering and mother love. Some, though certainly not all of the functions of mothering, are fostered, if not compelled, by hormones that are special to women. This does not mean that all women make good mothers or

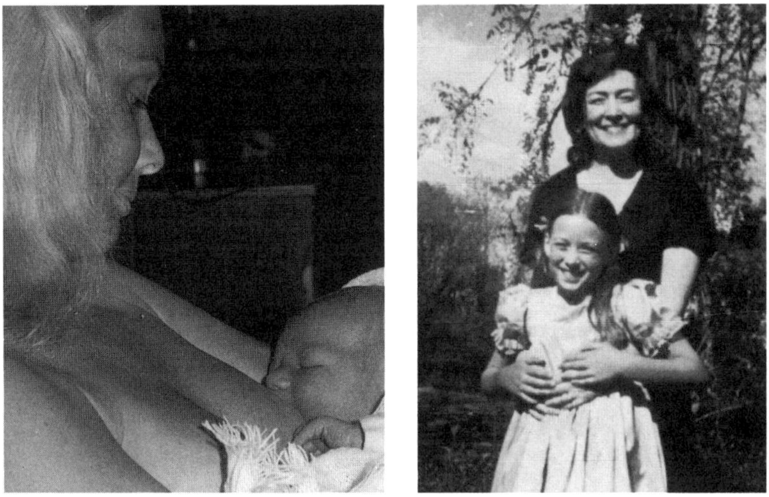

FIGURE 17-2. Mother love.

that mothering can be done only by women. Mothering defined as the affectionate nurturing of the young can be done by a man, adequately and effectively.

Also, fathering has come to mean far more than biological parenting. Father love and father care plays a significant role in the socialization and upbringing of children. Let me hasten to say however that we know of no reason why a single parent of either sex cannot accomplish the whole task of parenting adequately and effectively. When it is done in this fashion it probably means that the single parent manages to do rather well many of the things normally done by two parents of opposite sex. For this reason, the challenges of a single person, especially when parenting a child of the opposite sex, are many and great. With these qualifications in mind, let us return now to our consideration of the elements or characteristics of mothering and mother love.

First of all, mothering involves warm and gentle cuddling. The famous monkey experiments of Harry Harlow (1971) demonstrated very convincingly the power of this dimension of mothering. Harlow reared newborn monkeys with substitute mothers. One type of substitute mother was made entirely of wire, the other of cloth. Four of the young monkeys were raised in an area where both kinds of substitute mothers were available but could find the nipple that gave milk only on the wire mother. Another four monkeys were reared in a room where they were exposed to both wire and cloth substitute mothers but could nurse only on the cloth mother.

Almost from the beginning, all of these baby monkeys, regardless of whether they were reared with the dry-cloth mother or the nursing-cloth mother, spent far more time on the cloth mother than on the wire mother. So even the infants who always nursed on the wire mother would generally remain on the wire mother only long enough to feed. Harlow concluded that contact or contact–comfort was the essential ingredient in mother–infant attachment.

Similar observations have been made with institutionalized human infants. When one staff person only feeds, bathes, and changes the infants and a different person plays with them, the infants show a marked preference and a much stronger attachment to the latter. Thus, in the case of human infants, contact alone is not enough. It remains an important ingredient, but other factors, primarily of a psychological nature, play a part (Spitz, 1965).

These are marked and stable differences in the amount of close physical contact that infants desire to have with their mothers. A fairly wide range of differences should be understood and tolerated. However, when a baby turns out to be strictly a noncuddler and strongly resists any effort at cuddling, this should be brought to the attention of a professional. One way to determine whether the child is forming a normal attachment to the mother, despite the fact that he or she requires considerably less cuddling, is to observe his or her gaze behavior. If infants who are low on cuddliness frequently gaze toward their mothers and thereby maintain visual contact, then all may be well. In such a case the child may only be substituting close visual contact for a certain amount of physical contact.

As we already indicated, another characteristic of mothering and mother love is the attachment or strong emotional bond that develops between mother and infant. Following the work of John Bowlby (1969, 1973), Mary Ainsworth (Ainsworth, Blehar, Waters, & Wall, 1978) devised a scheme assessing the quality of the attachment between the mother and the infant. Based on the baby's reaction to a number of events in a strange room, the psychologist can assess the quality of the attachment.

The child is given toys to play with while the mother sits in the background. The various episodes of the procedure include the approach of a stranger, the mother leaving the child alone with the stranger, the baby being left all alone, the baby's response to the return of the stranger who attempts to comfort the child, and ultimately the response of the child to its reunion with the mother. Based on the child's behavior during these episodes, particularly the final reunion with the mother, the child may be judged to be either securely attached to its mother or insecurely attached. The insecurely attached child may either tend to avoid the mother on her final return (avoidant attachment) or show considerable resistance and ambivalence during the reunion with the mother (ambivalent–resistant attachment). Although this method of assessing the quality of attachment has met with some criticism and is not considered to be completely adequate from a scientific point of view, it has led to a great deal of research on mother–infant attachments, and this research has increased our knowledge of the attachment process and its significance for the well-being of the child.

The broad classifications of secure versus insecure attachment are reasonably reliable and stable over time so long as no major change occurs in family life.

Divorce, loss of a job by one or both parents, excessive friction and conflict in the family, or any other major crisis can change a secure mother–infant attachment into an insecure one. On the contrary, an insecure attachment may become a secure attachment if conditions in the home and the quality of mothering change for the better (Thompson, Lamb, & Estes, 1982).

One group of investigators has studied the relationship between attachment in toddlerhood and adjustment in preschool years (Matas, Arend, & Sroufe, 1978). Their data suggested that infants judged to be securely attached at one year of age were generally happier and better adjusted during their preschool years than were children who had an insecure attachment at one year. Although these studies have not been replicated in other laboratories, they are very suggestive of the potential power of early attachment to influence adjustment and competence in later years.

Another characteristic of mothering and mother love is emotional availability. This is not simply the physical presence or proximity of the mother, but the availability of the mother to provide cuddly contact, affection, and, when the child becomes capable of understanding it, verbal reassurance and encouragement.

Another characteristic of mother love is sensitivity to the needs of the child and a willingness to respond to those needs. A certain degree of sensitivity to a child's needs is probably absolutely essential to its health and welfare. However, mothers vary considerably in the degree to which they are sensitive to their children's needs, and children are capable of tolerating a range of sensitiveness and responsiveness.

Although we have no long-range studies to support the conclusion, it seems quite reasonable to infer that the degree of sensitiveness and responsiveness will play a role in shaping the personality characteristics of the child. For example, almost all of the foregoing characteristics of mothering and mother love make possible in the child the development of a deep and abiding sense of trust. Of course the child's trust is, first and foremost, extended to the mother or primary caregiver, but it is readily extended to a caring father and to affectionate siblings. The trust extends to other members of the family and then to friends and other people in the larger social community. Eventually, most people must learn that trust, like love, cannot be extended blindly to every fellow human being. In certain circumstances we learn that trust must be withheld or extended with great caution. Everyone needs someone who is trustworthy, and the wider we can extend the circle of trust into the social community in which we live, the better our mental health, well-being, and happiness.

Discrete Emotions in Mother Love

We have talked about mothering and mother love quite a bit without discussing specific emotions that are involved. Some of what we call mother love may very well have some of the characteristics of physiological drive. After all, we have said that mothering in many species, including human beings, is facilitated by hormones characteristic of females, especially after the onset of adolescence. Some mothers describe their love for their children as having a physical and sensual aspect. This certainly does not necessarily mean sexual feelings. All sensuality is not sexual. One can appreciate the warm, soft skin of the infant and young child without feeling sexual arousal. Indeed, Mellen (1981) has discussed a possible genetic basis for the taboo against sexual contact between parent and child and between siblings. Scientists have reported that even children who are not biologically related feel no sexual attraction for members of the opposite sex with whom they were reared. Children reared in an Israeli kibbutz provide an example.

In addition to a possible physiological drive aspect or biological basis of mother love, the positive emotion of joy is definitely prominent. Such joy is social joy, joy in being together, joy in seeing the growth and accomplishments of others, in seeing a child take his first steps, roll a ball, catch a ball, learn a new word, put on a coat, tie a shoe—all of these little things can bring sheer delight to the doting parent.

Another ingredient in mother love is the emotion of interest. A mother who loves her child is genuinely interested in the child and in all his activities. Interest in your child will express itself in many ways. Perhaps the most important way is in play. Mother finds the young baby and virtually everything he does interesting and exciting. When the newborn babe is calm and alert, his every little move, his every expression and sound engages mother's interest. This interest in all aspects and activities of the infant invites playful interaction by the mother. Almost from the beginning, the baby responds to mother's playful activity. Within a few weeks, it is very evident that the baby is engaging in the playful endeavor. If a mother sits opposite her baby, maintains a silent still face, and shows no interest or response to the baby, the baby may become upset (Tronick, 1990). Tronick has shown that the baby's behavior proceeds through certain stages if mother maintains this poker face for a 3-minute episode. The baby may wait for awhile, then seemingly try to engage the mother in interaction, and then ultimately withdraw, as though depressed.

Hembree (1986) objectively coded the changes in the infant's facial expressions while his mother sat with still and silent face. During the phase when the baby is seemingly making an effort to reengage the mother in play, he shows interest and joy. Many mothers find it impossible to resist their infant's smile even though they know that the experiment calls for them to remain still and silent. After 20 or 30 seconds, most infants protest their mother's poker face and show the anger expression. They also show the facial expression of sadness. The infants will show these varieties of facial expressions as early as 3 months of age. We doubt very seriously that these emotion responses have been learned by this age. We think the results are further evidence that the child comes into the world with the capability of perceiving changes in emotion expressions in his mother's face and of responding appropriately to these expressions. These capabilities increase with age, and children learn many different ways of responding to mothers with various degrees of expressiveness.

Sibling Love and Friendship

The love relationship between sisters and brothers is also a special phenomenon. A brother or sister is sometimes a child's first playmate. Almost always, a brother or sister is someone who provides some of the same kinds of care and social support that is provided by a parent. Ultimately, the affectionate social support provided by all members of the family is important to personal well-being and mental health.

Of course, siblings do not always live in perfect harmony. Everyone knows about the phenomenon of sibling rivalry. Almost always the birth of a sibling is a major event in the life of a child. A first child is no longer the sole recipient of the interest and joy that a mother and father exhibit toward their offspring. Attention of both a physical and psychological nature must now be shared with someone else. Some degree of sibling rivalry and jealousy is almost inevitable. How serious it becomes is partly a function of the success of the parents in making each child feel wanted, needed, and secure. The nature of the rivalry is also influenced by the ages, temperament, and interests of the siblings.

The various manifestations of sibling rivalry can be quite alarming to a parent. A quite charming and playful 3-year-old may become a problem child soon after the birth of a sibling. Such was the case of a 3-year-old-girl who had a baby brother. Because both parents worked, she had been in nursery from a very early age. She was a very well behaved child, and her behavior was of no concern to

FIGURE 17-3. Sibling love.

teachers or parents until after the birth of a sibling. A little more than 2 months after the birth of a baby brother, she began showing quite aggressive behavior toward her playmates at school. In the words of her father, "She is attacking other children for apparently no reason."

The child was reacting not simply to the birth of her baby brother but to the changed patterns of interaction within the family. The newborn required much more time for his basic needs than did the older sibling. He had been waking up frequently at night in the early weeks of life (a not unusual occurrence). The frequent waking, with all the other aspects of child care, had taken its toll on the parents. The parents had thus not only divided their attention between two children, they had divided their energies, and it is likely that they were not as fresh and free to play and interact with the older child as they had been previously. For all of these reasons, it is important that parents make a special effort to help the older sibling understand what is taking place. The understanding cannot possibly be all at the intellectual level. The child must be frequently and lovingly reassured of her unique place in the lives of her parents.

How much rivalry develops between siblings will depend not only on parental behavior but on the sex of the children, their age difference, and the individual temperament or personality of each child. Same-sex children close in age (less than 3 years apart) are more likely to be competitive, and one form that the rivalry takes is competition for mother's and father's attention.

Jealousy

What is jealousy? Could it be that it finds it origins in rivalry for the attention of mother or father? When you feel jealous do you feel that your relationship with a loved one is threatened? You feel that you no longer have exclusive rights to the other's love and attention?

Jealousy includes both the fundamental emotions of fear and anger. The fear comes from the threat of loss of love and all that the love means. Among many other things, love means protection and security, and insecurity is, as we have seen, a primary cause of fear. The anger component of jealousy results from feeling blocked in your effort to retain your position and security in the love and attention of the other. A sibling (or someone) has become a barrier between you and the source of unlimited love. The anger may be expressed toward the sibling, toward the parent, or, as in the example we discussed earlier, toward peers or playmates.

The example that we discussed of the 3-year-old girl who began attacking her playmates at nursery school is an example that can teach us something else. It tells us that even a 3-year-old is capable of inhibiting the anger she feels in the presence of the baby sister or the loving mother and father. Instead, the anger is displayed in the nursery school. It could be that the child is now more sensitive to the way teacher gives affection and attention to the other children. The child may perceive her playmates now as rivals thwarting her needs for affection and attention from the teachers. In the nursery school setting, the child's own inhibitions against anger expression and aggressive behavior were apparently not as strong as they were in the home.

Love among brothers and sisters is likely to have characteristics that are different from parent–child love or from love between friends. Usually, the strongest love is that between mother and child, father and child. The next strongest love is often that between siblings. Like parent–child love, love between most siblings is likely to be enduring, although it may take a stormy course for periods during early childhood. The storm may even get a little more tempestuous during adolescence, but the love endures. Even during periods of jealousy and rivalry one knows that the basic love is always there. One may take pride in one's friends, but one is even more likely to take pride in the accomplishments or achievements of brothers or sisters. Like parental love, sibling love can withstand temporary ups and downs because the love is there for many reasons, not the least of which is the close proximity and the shared experiences that have occurred over the years.

Romantic Love: An Example

Some of the research on romantic love has focused on passionate affection and sexual arousal (Hatfield, Schmitz, Cornelius, & Rapson, 1988). Although sexual attraction is an important component of romantic love, it is not the only one. The full explanation of romantic love involves an understanding of all the emotions that participate in this phenomenon and the way these emotions and sexual excitement influence thought and action. The complete story will not be written for some time to come. A real-life example may facilitate our understanding. The example is from the diary of John Henry Cliburn.

> The girl who captured my romantic interest appeared to me to be the most beautiful girl in the world. Her tall, slender body gave her beauty a special elegance. Her bright and easy smile gave it warmth and charm. Though it has been more than 40 years, I remember our first date vividly.
>
> I remember even more vividly the first time I kissed her. I was 19, she was 16. Just walking together and holding hands on a warm Mississippi evening was nothing short of exotic. The mockingbird song was more brilliant on such occasions and the magnolia blossoms more fragrant. At the end of one of these walks we stood quietly for a moment by a pecan tree. As I stood close and sensed all her loveliness, I seemed to have been magically transported into a fantasy world. The pleasures signaled by this beauty and charm were surely not available to me, I thought, except perhaps in my imagination, where I had enjoyed them before. Somehow I managed to act out part of my fantasy—I kissed her. Her lips were warmer and softer than the summer evening, and their sensual response made the earth beneath my feet seem uneven. The pecan and magnolia trees moved sideways and the

moonlit clouds on the horizon came closer. She smiled and the world righted itself and so began a love affair of a lifetime.

Perhaps no one can analyze with any great degree of certainty all the forces that changed my world during that seemingly magic moment. I can at least name some of them. There was interest so intense that it was truly excitement. There was sexual urge, there can be no doubt about that. It magnified my excitement, but it did not create it nor can it account for it altogether. For I had envisioned with this lovely person far more than sexual pleasure. My analysis of what might be in store would most assuredly not meet the standards of rigorous logic, but I seem to have had an intuitive grasp of the possibilities of a unique kind of sharing, of exploration, of family and children, a lively and enticing companionship. But be not deceived by the perspective that age has enabled. Sexual attraction was an imminent power on that warm evening in the Mississippi moonlight.

Although I had already studied biology, psychology, and the sociology of marriage and the family, I could not begin to envision all the trials and tribulations that we would have to live through in finishing our growing up, establishing professions and having children, and experiencing crises. I count it my greatest good fortune to be able to continue to enjoy the love that was enhanced and strengthened by all of these life experiences.

There was also joy on that evening. It was fun being together. Each of us seemed to have the effect of lowering the other's threshold for smiling and laughing.

There is no way to measure the joy that we have shared. There were many more lazy strolls hand in hand. There were the years we were both students at the same university, reunions after wartime separation, the births of children, our first real home the years scrambling for security in our professions, the year in Paris, the marvelous achievements of our children, the half-year in Moscow, the month in the mountain states, the voyage through China, and the increasingly satisfying evenings at home in the study or by the fire.

FIGURE 17-4. Romantic consummate love.

> But has it always been fun and games? No. Emphatically no! Experiencing the love between us was always fun, excitement, and joy. When we consider the love relationship, the relationship between two people who love each other, then we must allow for the intrusions of just about every emotion of which human beings are capable. But just as no one could claim my attention and affection with such power, so too could no one make me so angry. We knew we had differences going into the marriage, but they seemed small by comparison with the strength of our love. We had differences in timing, tastes, temperament, and choice of leisure activities.
>
> I am a scientist and at least some of my behavior is guided by a scientific attitude. Barbrellen is in theater, an actress and director, with the soul of an artist. I want to reason why. Barbrellen knows why intuitively and immediately. It took me a long, long time to appreciate how she could know so quickly how something was "just perfect" or "wouldn't do at all." Now we laugh at our differences or find them amusing more often than we quarrel about them. But many, many times they were the occasion for high anger.
>
> Our love relationship was also on occasion a source of fear. There were moments when I was afraid the relationship would end or that I would lose her. These moments were relatively rare but quite real.

If jealousy is born in the nursery, it achieves its full strength in a romantic love relationship. The first jealous moments may be experienced when the child feels that it is losing the attention and affection of the mother to a sibling. When these thoughts are joined with the passion of young love, they are indeed powerful. Jealousy includes both anger and fear. The anger comes from the thought that you have been neglected and betrayed. The fear comes from thoughts of the loss of your beloved, of love, and of self-esteem.

It will probably help us in our thinking about the phenomena of love if we remember the distinction between the experience of love and the love relationship. The experience of love should always be excitement and joy. The love relationship may include the full range of emotions, but for the love relationship to endure and enhance your life, it must include interest in each other as persons, pride in each other's achievements, and joy in sharing time together.

Summary

Love is basic and fundamental to human nature, but it is not a discrete emotion like joy or sadness. The development of affective bonds with parents, siblings, and a mate appear to be part of our evolutionary heritage. Love involves a social relationship, a strong attachment, an affectionate bond. Love is characterized by interest and joy, and a love relationship may run the full gamut of emotions.

There are several types of love relationships and love may be expressed differently in each of these. Romantic love includes sexual expression, sibling love does not. All types of love have some common elements: attachment, loyalty, devotion, protectiveness, and nurturance.

Suggested Readings

Berschied, E., & Peplau, L. A. (1983). The emerging science of relationships. In H. H. Kelly, E. Berschied, A. Christensen, J. H. Harvey, T. L. Huston, G. Levinger, E. McClintock, L. A. Peplau, & D. R. Peterson (Eds.), *Close relationships* (pp. 1–19). New York: W. H. Freeman.

An integrative review of research and theory on intimate relationships.

Coleman, C., & Ganong, L. H. (1985). Love and sex role stereotypes: Do macho men and feminine women make better lovers? *Journal of Personality and Social Psychology*, *49*(1), 170–176.

A study of the effects of gender and sex role orientation on the feelings and behaviors associated with love.

Dunn, J., & Munn, P. (1985). Becoming a family member: Family conflict and the development of social understanding. *Child Development*, *56*, 480–492.

Demonstrates the early emergence of sibling affection and conflict and of children's understanding of the emotions expressed in the family.

Hatfield, E., Schmitz, E., Cornelius, J., & Rapson, R. L. (1988). Passionate love: How early does it begin? *Journal of Psychology and Human Sexuality*, *1*(1), 35–51.

A review of theory and research on romantic or passionate love. Definition of passionate love. Discussion of the role of physiological arousal, positive and negative emotions.

Stenberg, R. (1985). A triangular theory of love. *Psychological Review*, *93*, 119–135.

A theory of love in which passion, intimacy, and commitment are the dynamic factors used in explaining the nature of the love relationship.

White, G. L., Fishbein, S., & Rutstein, J. (1981). Passionate love and the misattribution of arousal. *Journal of Personality and Social Psychology*, *41*, 56–62.

Studies examining the effect of nonsexual physiological arousal on romantic feelings and sexual attraction.

Epilogue

A recent paper on the evolutionary functions of emotions described them as "specialized states, shaped by natural selection, that increase fitness in specific situations" (Nesse, 1990, p. 261). The author argued, as have other scientists cited in this text, that the neural, behavioral, and experiential components of a specific emotion increase the ability of individuals to cope with the opportunities, challenges, and threats presented by the social and physical environment.

This text, having been influenced by an evolutionary-developmental perspective, has attempted to present theory and evidence that support the idea that emotions played a significant role in evolutionary adaptation and that they continue to play a crucial role in human development and in facilitating coping and adaptation in daily life. They accomplish this through their ability to organize and motivate cognitions and actions that are necessary for effective person–environment transactions.

Old notions that emotions are epiphenomenal, transient states that do not lend themselves to scientific inquiry have become unacceptable. These notions have been replaced by functionalist views of emotions that extend our knowledge of them by inspiring research on their characteristics and functions. Happily, this trend is gaining increasing support from neuroscientists who are establishing the foundation for understanding the functions of particular brain mechanisms and neural pathways that have special significance for emotions.

There is now a convergence of a variety of approaches on some central issues in emotion theory. For example, there is wide agreement on four important premises. First, expressions of emotions serve important communicative functions, especially apparent in early development but present at all ages. Second, emotion experiences influence perception, thought, and action. Third, emotions are central features of social bonds, such as attachment, and integral to the concepts temperament and personality. Fourth, knowledge of emotions and their functions at different ages is essential not only to understanding the development of the normal personality but also to the diagnosis and treatment of psychological disorders. A growing body of empirical research supports these premises on which emotion theories have converged.

The final word goes to the positive emotions. For a long time, psychologists have proposed that positive emotions have a salubrious effect on things ranging from good health to intellectual activities. This is no longer a matter of abstract theory. This text has presented substantial research supporting the notion that positive emotions enhance a variety of constructive psychological functions, including creativity and altruistic behaviors.

References

Abelson, R. P., & Sermat, V. (1962). Multidimensional scaling of facial expressions. *Journal of Experimental Psychology*, *63*(6), 546–554.

Abraham, K. (1968). Notes on the psycho-analytical investigation and treatment of manic-depressive insanity and allied conditions. In W. Gaylin (Ed.), *The meaning of despair* (pp. 26–49). New York: Science House. (Original work published 1911)

Adler, A. (1964). *Social interest: A challenge to mankind*. New York: Capricorn Books.

Ainsworth, M. D., Blehar, M. D., Waters, E., & Wall, S. (1978). *Patterns of attachment: A psychological study of the strange situation*. Hillsdale, NJ: Erlbaum.

Allport, G. W. (1955). *Becoming: Basic considerations for a psychology of personality*. New Haven: Yale University Press.

Allport, G. W. (1961). *Pattern and growth in personality*. New York: Holt, Rinehart & Winston.

Anshen, R. N. (1966). Credo perspectives: Their meaning and function. In E. W. Sinnott (Ed.), *The bridge of life* (pp. 7–17). New York: Simon & Schuster.

Antrobus, J. S., Singer, J. L., & Greenberg, S. (1966). Studies in the stream of consciousness: Experimental enhancement and suppression of spontaneous cognitive processes. *Perceptual and Motor Skills*, *23*(2), 399–417.

Ardrey, R. (1966). *The territorial imperative*. New York: Dell.

Argyle, N. (1972). Non-verbal communication in human social interaction. In R. A. Hinde (Ed.), *Non-verbal communication* (pp. 243–269). New York: Cambridge University Press.

Arnold, M. B. (1960a). *Emotion and personality: Vol. 1. Psychological aspects*. New York: Columbia University Press.

Arnold, M. B. (1960b). *Emotion and personality: Vol. 2. Neurological and physiological aspects*. New York: Columbia University Press.

Arnold, M. B. (1968). In defense of Arnold's theory of emotion. *Psychological Bulletin*, *70*, 283–284.

Asberg, M., Thoren, P., & Traskman, L. (1976). Serotonin depression—a biochemical subgroup within the affective disorders? *Science*, *191*, 478–480.

Ausubel, D. P. (1955). Relationships between shame and guilt in the socializing process. *Psychological Review*, *62*, 378–390.

Averill, J. R. (1968). Grief: Its nature and significance. *Psychological Bulletin*, *70*, 721–748.

Averill, J. R. (1969). Autonomic response patterns during sadness and mirth. *Psychophysiology*, *5*, 399–444.

Averill, J. R. (1983). Studies on anger and aggression: Implications for theories of emotion. *American Psychologist*, *38*, 1145–1162.

Azrin, N. H., Hutchinson, R. R., & McLaughlin, R. (1965). The opportunity for aggression as an operant reinforcer during aversive stimulation. *Journal of the Experimental Analysis of Behavior*, *8*, 171–180.

Baron, R. A. (1971a). Magnitude of victim's cues and level of prior anger arousal as determinants of adult aggressive behavior. *Journal of Personality and Social Psychology*, *17*, 236–243.

Baron, R. A. (1971b). Exposure to an aggressive model and apparent probability of retaliation from the victim as determinants of aggressive behavior. *Journal of Experimental and Social Psychology*, *7*, 343–355.

Bartlett, J. C., Burleson, G., & Santrock, J. W. (1982). Emotional mood and memory in young children. *Journal of Experimental Child Psychology*, *34*, 59–76.

Bartlett, E. S., & Izard, C. E. (1972). A dimensional and discrete emotions investigation of the subjective experience of emotion. In C. E. Izard (Eds.), *Patterns of emotions: A new analysis of anxiety and depression* (pp. 129–173). New York: Academic Press.

Beach, F. A. (1935). *Sex and behavior*. New York: Krieger.

Beck, A. T. (1967). *Depression*. New York: Harper & Row.

Beck, A. T. (1976). *Cognitive therapy and the emotional disorders*. New York: International Universities Press.

Becker, E. (1962). Toward a comprehensive theory of depression: A cross disciplinary appraisal of objects, games, and meaning. *Journal of Nervous and Mental Disease*, *57*, 281–304.

Belsky, J., & Most, R. K. (1981). From exploration to play: A cross-sectional study of infant behavior. *Developmental Psychology*, *17*, 630–639.

Benedict, R. (1934). *Patterns of culture*. Boston: Houghton Mifflin.

Benedict, R. (1946). *The chrysanthemum and the sword*. Boston: Houghton Mifflin.

Bergson, H. L. (1911). *Laughter—An essay on the meaning of the comic*. (C. Brereton, Trans.). New York: Macmillan.

Berkowitz, L. (1983). Aversively stimulated aggression: Some parallels and differences in research with animals and humans. *American Psychologist*, *38*, 1135–1144.

Berkowitz, L. (1990). On the formation and regulation of anger and aggression: A cognitive-neoassociationistic analysis. *American Psychologist*, *45*(4), 494–503.

Berscheid, E. (1982). Attraction and emotion in interpersonal relations. In M. S. Clark & S. T. Fiske (Eds.), *Affect and cognition* (pp. 37–78). Hillsdale, NJ: Erlbaum.

Bibring, E. (1968). The mechanism of depression. In W. Gaylin (Ed.), *The meaning of despair* (pp. 155–181). New York: Science House.

Block, J. (1957). Studies in the phenomenology of emotions. *Journal of Abnormal and Social Psychology*, *54*, 358–363.

Blumberg, S. H., & Izard, C. E. (1985). Affective and cognitive characteristics of depression in 10- and 11-year-old children. *Journal of Personality and Social Psychology*, *49*(1), 194–202.

Blumberg, S. H., & Izard, C. E. (1986). Discriminating patterns of emotion in 10- and 11-year-old children's anxiety and depression. *Journal of Personality and Social Psychology*, *51*(4), 852–857.

Bonanno, G. A., & Singer, J. C. (1990). Repressive personality style: Theoretical and methodological implications for health and pathology. In J. L. Singer (Ed.), *Repression and dissociation* (pp. 435–470). Chicago: The University of Chicago Press.

Boring, E. G. (1950). *A history of experimental psychology*. New York: Appleton-Century-Crofts.

Boss, M. (1963). *Psychoanalysis and daseinsanalysis* (Ludwig R. Lefebre, Trans.). New York: Basic Books.

Boucher, J., & Osgood, C. E. (1969). The pollyanna hypothesis. *Journal of Verbal Learning Behavior*, *8*, 1–8.

Bower, G. H., Gilligan, S. G., & Monteiro, K. P. (1981). Selectivity of learning caused by affective states. *Journal of Experimental Psychology: General*, *110*, 451–473.

Bower, T. G. R. (1971). The object in the world of the infant. *Scientific American*, *225*(4), 30–38.

Bower, T. G. R. (1974). *Development in infancy*. San Francisco: Freeman.

Bowlby, J. (1960). Grief and mourning in infancy and early childhood. *Psychoanalytical Study of Children*, *15*, 9–52.

Bowlby, J. (1961). Processes of mourning. *International Journal of Psychoanalysis*, *42*, 317–340.
Bowlby, J. (1963). Pathological mourning and childhood mourning. *Journal of the American Psychoanalytic Association*, *11*, 500–541.
Bowlby, J. (1969). *Attachment and loss: Vol. 1. Attachment*. New York: Basic Books.
Bowlby, J. (1973). *Attachment and loss: Vol. II. Separation, anxiety, and anger*. New York: Basic Books.
Bradburn, N. M. (1969). *The structure of psychological well-being*. Chicago: Aldine.
Brock, T. C., & Becker, L. A. (1962). "Debriefing" and susceptibility to subsequent experimental manipulations. *Journal of Experimental Social Psychology*, *2*, 314–323.
Bronson, G. W. (1972). Infants' reactions to unfamiliar persons and novel objects. *Monographs of the Society for Research in Child Development*, *37*(3, Serial No. 148).
Brownfield, C. A. (1966). Optimal stimulation levels of normal and disturbed subjects in sensory deprivation. *Psychologia*, *9*, 27–38.
Bugental, J. F. (1965). *The search for authenticity*. New York: Holt, Rinehart & Winston.
Bull, N. (1951). Experimental investigation of the body–mind continuum in affective states. *Journal of Nervous and Mental Disease*, *113*, 512–521.
Buss, A. H. (1966a). The effect of harm on subsequent aggression. *Journal of Experimental Research in Personality*, *1*, 249–255.
Buss, A. H. (1966b). Instrumentality of aggression, feedback and frustration as determinants of physical aggression. *Journal of Personality and Social Psychology*, *3*, 153–162.
Buss, A. H. (1979). *Self consciousness and social anxiety*. San Francisco: Freeman.
Campos, J. J., & Barrett, K. C. (1984). Toward a new understanding of emotions and their development. In C. E. Izard, J. Kagan, & R. B. Zajonc (Eds.), *Emotions, cognition, and behavior* (pp. 229–263). New York: Cambridge University Press.
Campos, J. J., Hiatt, S., Ramsay, D., Henderson, C., & Svejda, M. (1978). The emergence of fear on the visual cliff. In M. Lewis & L. A. Rosenblum (Eds.), *The development of affect: Vol. 1. Genesis of behavior* (pp. 149–182). New York: Plenum.
Campos, J. J., & Stenberg, C. (1981). Perception, appraisal, and emotion: The onset of social referencing. In M. E. Lamb & L. R. Sherrod (Eds.), *Infant social cognition: Empirical and theoretical considerations* (pp. 273–314). Hillsdale, NJ: Erlbaum.
Cannon, W. B. (1927). The James–Lange theory of emotions: A critical examination and an alternative theory. *American Journal of Psychology*, *39*, 106–124.
Cantor, J. R., Bryant, J., & Zillman, D. (1974). Enhancement of humor appreciation by transferred excitation. *Journal of Personality and Social Psychology*, *30*, 812–821.
Cantor, J. R., Zillman, D., & Bryant, J. (1975). Enhancement of experienced sexual arousement in response to erotic stimuli through misattribution of unrelated residual exciation. *Journal of Personality and Social Psychology*, *32*, 69–75.
Cantril, H. (1962). A transactional inquiry concerning mind (pp. 330–353). In J. M. Scher (Ed.), *Theories of the mind*. New York: The Free Press of Glencoe.
Carlsmith, J. M., & Gross, A. E. (1969). Some effects of guilt on compliance. *Journal of Personality and Social Psychology*, *4*, 321–322.
Cattell, R. B. (1946). *Description and measurement of personality*. San Francisco: Jossey-Bass.
Cattell, R. B., & Scheier, I. H. (1961). *The meaning and measurement of neuroticism and anxiety*. New York: Ronald Press.
Charlesworth, W. R. (1968). Cognition in infancy: Where do we stand in the mid-sixties? *Merrill-Palmer Quarterly*, *14*, 25–46.
Charlesworth, W. R. (1969). The role of surprise in cognitive development. In D. Elkind & F. Flavell (Eds.), *Studies in cognitive development* (pp. 257–314). London: Oxford University Press.
Charlesworth, W. R. (1974). General issues in the study of fear: Section IV. In M. Lewis & L. A. Rosenblum (Eds.), *The origins of fear* (pp. 254–258). New York: Wiley.

Charlesworth, W. R., & Kreutzer, M. A. (1973). Facial expressions of infants and children. In P. Ekman (Ed.), *Darwin and facial expression: A century of research in review* (pp. 91–168). New York: Academic Press.
Chevalier-Skolnikoff, S. (1973). Facial expression of emotion in nonhuman primates. In P. Ekman (Ed.), *Darwin and facial expression: A century of research in review* (pp. 11–89). New York: Academic Press.
Cheyne, J. A., & Walters, R. H. (1970). Punishment and prohibition: Some origins of self-control. In T. M. Newcomb (Ed.), *New directions in psychology* (Vol. IV, pp. 266–281). New York: Holt, Rinehart & Winston.
Church, J. (1966). *Three babies*. New York: Random House.
Cicchetti, D. (1990). The organization and coherence of socioemotional cognitive and representational development: Illustrations through a developmental psychopathology perspective on Down's syndrome and child maltreatment. In R. Thompson (Ed.), *Nebraska Symposium on Motivation, Vol. 36*. Lincoln, Nebraska: University of Nebraska Press.
Cohen, B., Izard, C. E., & Simons, R. F. (1986, October). *Facial and physiological indices of emotions in mother–infant interactions*. Paper presented at the Twenty-Sixth Annual Meeting of the Society for Psychophysiological Research, Montreal, Canada.
Coles, R. (1971). *Children of crisis: A study of courage and fear*. Boston: Little Brown.
Coll, C. G., Kagan, J., Reznick, J. S. (1984). Behavioral inhibition in young children. *Child Development*, *56*, 1005–1019.
Combs, A. W., & Snygg, D. (1959). *Individual behavior*. New York: Harper.
Constantinople, A. (1970). Some correlates of average level of happiness among college students. *Developmental Psychology*, *2*(3), 447.
Costello, C. G. (1972). Depression: Loss of reinforcers of loss of reinforcer effectiveness. *Behavior Therapy*, *3*, 240–250.
Costello, C. G. (1978). A critical review of Seligman's laboratory experiments on learned helplessness and depression in humans. *Journal of Abnormal Psychology*, *87*, 21–31.
Crozier, W. R. (1986). Individual differences in shyness. In W. H. Jones, J. M. Cheek, & S. R. Briggs (Eds.), *Shyness: Perspectives on research and treatment* (pp. 133–145). New York: Plenum.
Cummings, E. M., Zahn-Waxler, C., & Radke-Yarrow, M. (1981). Young children's responses to expressions of anger and affection by others in the family. *Child Development*, *52*, 1274–1282.
Cupchik, G. C., & Leventhal, H. (1974). Consistency between expressive behavior and the evaluation of humorous stimuli: The role of sex and self-observation. *Journal of Personality and Social Psychology*, *30*, 429–442.
Daniels, D., & Plomin, R. (1985). Origins of individual differences in infant shyness. *Developmental Psychology*, *21*(1), 118–121.
Darwin, C. R. (1872/1965). *The expression of emotions in man and animals*. Chicago: University of Chicago Press.
Darwin, C. R. (1877). A biographical sketch of an infant. *Mind*, *2*, 286–294.
Das, S. S. (1971). Grief and suffering. *Psychotherapy: Theory, Research, and Practice*, *8*(1), 8–9.
David, A., & Fahy, T. A. (1987). *Disgust: A further perspective*. Unpublished manuscript, the Maudsley Hospital, London.
Davis, A., & Dollard, J. (1940). *Children of bondage*. Washington, D.C.: American Council on Education.
Davis, J. (1970). Theories of biological etiology of affective disorders. *International Review of Neurobiology*, *12*, 145–175.
Davitz, J. R. (1970). A dictionary and grammar of emotion. In M. B. Arnold (Ed.), *Feelings and emotions* (pp. 251–258). New York: Academic Press.
Deglin, V. L. (1973). Clinical-experimental studies of unilateral electroconvulsive block. *Journal of Neuropathology and Psychiatry*, *11*, 1609–1621.
Deikman, A. (1971). Bimodal consciousness. *Archives of General Psychiatry*, *45*, 481–489.

Deikman, A. (1973). The meaning of everything. In R. E. Ornstein (Ed.), *The nature of human consciousness* (pp. 317–326). San Francisco: Freeman.

Dennis, W. (1960). Causes of retardation among institutional children: Iran. *Journal of Genetic Psychology*, *96*, 47–59.

DePaulo, B. M., Dull, W. R., Greenberg J. M., & Swain, G. W. (1989). Are shy people reluctant to ask for help? *Journal of Personality and Social Psychology*, *56*(5), 834–844.

Dickey, E. C., & Knower, F. H. (1941). A note on some ethnological differences in recognition of simulated expressions of the emotions. *American Journal of Sociology*, *47*, 190–193.

Diener, E., & Emmons, R. A. (1984). The independence of positive and negative affect. *Journal of Personality and Social Psychology*, *47*, 1105–1117.

Duffy, E. (1934). Emotion: An example of the need for reorientation in psychology. *Psychological Review*, *41*, 184–198.

Duffy, E. (1941). An explanation of "emotional" phenomena without the use of the concept "emotion." *Journal of General Psychology*, *25*, 283–293.

Duffy, E. (1951). The concept of energy mobilization. *Psychological Review*, *58*, 30–40.

Duffy, E. (1957). The psychological significance of the concept of "arousal" or "activation." *Psychological Review*, *64*, 265–275.

Duffy, E. (1962). *Activation and behavior*. New York: Wiley.

Dumas, G. (1932). La mimique des aveugles. *Bulletin de L'Academie de Medicine*, *107*, 607–610.

Dumas, G. (1948). *La vie affective*. Paris: Presses Universitaires de France.

Dunbar, F. (1954). *Emotions and bodily changes* (4th ed.). New York: Columbia University Press.

Duval, S., & Wicklund, R. A. (1972). *A theory of objective self-awareness*. New York: Academic Press.

Eibl-Eibesfeldt, I. (1971). *Love and hate: The natural history of behavior patterns*. New York: Holt, Rinehart & Winston.

Eibl-Eibesfeldt, I. (1972). Similarities and differences between cultures in expressive movements. In R. A. Hinde (Eds.), *Nonverbal communication* (pp. 297–311). Cambridge, MA: Cambridge University Press.

Ekman, P. (1964). Body position, facial expression, and verbal behavior during interviews. *Journal of Abnormal and Social Psychology*, *68*(3), 295–301.

Ekman, P. (1971). Universal and cultural differences in facial expression of emotion. In J. R. Cole (Ed.), *Nebraska Symposium on Motivation*. Lincoln, Nebraska: University of Nebraska Press.

Ekman, P. (1984). Expression and the nature of emotion. In K. Scherer & P. Ekman (Eds.), *Approaches to emotion* (pp. 319–343). Hillsdale, NJ: Erlbaum.

Ekman, P., & Friesen, W. V. (1982). Felt, false, and miserable smiles. *Journal of Nonverbal Behavior*, *6*(4), 238–252.

Ekman, P., & Friesen, W. V. (1986). A new pan-cultural facial expression of emotion. *Motivation and Emotion*, *10*, 159–168.

Ekman, P., Friesen, W. V., & Ellsworth, P. C. (1972). *Emotion in the human face*. New York: Pergamon Press.

Ekman, P., & Heider, K. G. (1988). The universality of a contempt expression: A replication. *Motivation and Emotion*, *12*, 303–308.

Ekman, P., Levenson, R. W., & Friesen, W. V. (1983). Autonomic nervous system activity distinguishes among emotions. *Science*, *221*(4616), 1208–1210.

Ellsworth, P. C. (1975). Direct gaze as a social stimulus: The example of aggression. In P. L. Pliner, L. Krames, & T. Alloway (Eds.), *Nonverbal communication of aggression* (pp. 53–75). New York: Plenum.

Ellsworth, P. C., & Smith, C. A. (1988). From appraisal to emotion: Differences among unpleasant feelings. *Motivation and Emotion*, *12*(3), 271–302.

Emde, R. (1980). Toward a psychoanalytic theory of affect. II. Emerging models of emotional development is infancy. In S. Greenspan & G. Pollock (Eds.), *Psychonanalysis and development, current perspectives* (pp. 85–112). Washington, DC: U. S. Government Printing Office.

Emde, R., Katz, E. L., & Thorpe, J. K. (1978). Emotional expression in infancy. II. Early deviations in Down's syndrome. In M. Lewis & L. Rosenblum (Eds.), *The development of affect* (pp. 351–360). New York: Plenum.

Emde, R., & Koenig, K. L. (1969). Neonatal smiling and rapid eye-movement states. *Journal of American Academy of Child Psychiatry, 8*, 57–67.

Engen, R., Levy, N., & Schlosberg, H. (1958). The dimensional analysis of a new series of facial expressions. *Journal of Experimental Psychology, 55*(5), 454–458.

Epstein, S. (1983). The unconscious, the preconscious, and the self-concept. In J. Suls & A. G. Greenwald (Eds.), *Psychological perspectives on the self* (Vol. 2, pp. 219–247). Hillsdale, NJ: Erlbaum.

Erickson, E. H. (1950). *Childhood and society*. New York: Norton.

Erickson, E. H. (1956). Growth and crises of the health personality. In C. Kluckhohn, H. A. Murray, & D. M. Schneider (Eds.), *Personality in nature, society, and culture* (2nd ed./rev., pp. 185–225). New York: Knopf.

Eron, L. D. (1987). The development of aggressive behavior from the perspective of a developing behaviorism. *American Psychologist, 42*(50), 435–442.

Exline, R. V., Ellyson, S. L., & Long, B. (1975). Visual behavior as an aspect of power role relationships. In P. Plines, L. Krames, & T. Alloway (Eds.), *Nonverbal communication of aggression* (pp. 21–52). New York: Plenum.

Eysenck, H. J. (1970). *The structure of human personality*. London: Methuen.

Fagan, J. F. (1980). The origins of facial pattern recognition. In M. Bornstein & W. Kessen (Eds.), *Psychological development from infancy* (pp. 83–113). Hillsdale, NJ: Erlbaum.

Faigan, H. (1953). *Childrearing in the Rimrock community with special reference to the development of guilt*. Unpublished doctoral dissertation, Radcliffe College.

Fair, C. M. (1969). *The dying self*. Middletown, CT: Wesleyan University Press.

Fantz, R. L. (1973). Pattern vision in newborn infants. In L. J. Stone, H. T. Smith, & L. B. Murphy (Eds.), *The competent infant* (pp. 314–316). New York: Basic Books.

Feigl, H. (1962). Mind–body, not a pseudo problem. In J. M. Scher (Ed.), *Theories of the mind* (pp. 572–581). New York: The Free Press of Glencoe.

Fenyes, G. (1967). Moral judgment and situations: Appropriateness for self-blame and resistance to temptation. (Doctoral dissertation, University of California). *Dissertation Abstracts, 78*(13), 1687–1683.

Feshbach, S., Stiles, W. G., & Bitner, E. (1967). The reinforcing effect of witnessing aggression. *Journal of Experimental Research in Personality, 3*, 133–139.

Fitts, W. H. (1971). *The self-concept and self-actualization: Studies on the self-concept and rehabilitation*. Dede Wallace Center, Nashville.

Forgas, J. P., & Bower, G. H. (1987). Mood effects on person-perception judgments. *Journal of Personality and Social Psychology, 53*(1), 53–60.

Forster, C. B. (1972). A functional analysis of depression. *American Psychologist, 28*, 857–871.

Fox, R., Aslin, R. N., Shea, S. L., & Dumais, S. T. (1980). Stereopsis in human infants. *Science, 207*(4428), 323–324.

Fox, N. A., & Davidson, R. J. (1986). Taste-elicited changes in facial signs of emotion and the asymmetry of brain electrical activity in human newborns. *Neuropsychologia, 24*, 417–422.

Fox, N. A., & Davidson, R. J. (1984). Hemispheric substrates of affect: A developmental model. In N. A. Fox & R. J. Davidson (Eds.), *The psychobiology of affective development* (pp. 353–381). Hillsdale, NJ: Erlbaum.

Fox, R., & McDaniel, C. (1982). The perception of biological motion by human infants. *Science, 218*, 486–487.

Frankl, V. E. (1962). *Man's search for meaning: An introduction to logotherapy*. A newly revised and enlarged edition of *From death-camp to existentalism* (I. Lasch, Trans.). Boston: Beacon Press.

Freedman, S. J., & Fraser, S. C. (1966). Compliance without pressure: The foot-in-the-door technique. *Journal of Personality and Social Psychology, 4*, 195–202.

Freedman, S. J., Gruebaum, H. U., & Greenblath, M. (1961). Perceptual and cognitive changes in sensory deprivation. In P. Solomon, P. E. Kubsansky, P. H. Leiderman, J. H. Mendelson, R. Trumbull, & D. Wexler (Eds.), *Sensory deprivation* (pp. 58–71). Cambridge, MA: Harvard University Press.

Freedman, J. L., Wallington, S. A., & Bless, E. (1967). Compliance without pressure: The effect of guilt. *Journal of Personality and Social Psychology*, *7*(2), 117–124.

Freud, S. (1930). *Civilization and its discontents* (J. Riviere, Trans.). New York: Jonathan Cape and Hanson Smith.

Freud, S. (1936). Inhibitions, symptoms, and anxiety. In J. Strackey (Ed.), *The standard edition of the complete psychological works of Sigmund Freud* (Vol. 20, pp. 77–175). London: Hogarth Press.

Freud, S. (1938). *The basic writings of Sigmund Freud* (A. A. Brill, Trans.). New York: Random House.

Freud, S. (1968). Mourning and melancholia. In W. Gaylin (Ed.), *The meaning of despair* (pp. 50–69). New York: Science House.

Frijda, N. H. (1970). Emotion and recognition of emotion. In M. B. Arnold (Ed.), *Feelings and emotions* (pp. 241–250). New York: Academic Press.

Frijda, N. H. (1986). *The emotions*. London: Cambridge University Press.

Frijda, N. H., & Phillipszoon, E. (1963). Dimensions of recognition of expression. *Journal of Abnormal and Social Psychology*, *66*, 45–51.

Fromm-Reichmann, F. (1953). An intensive study of twelve cases of manic-depressive psychosis. Final Report, Office of Naval Research Contract Nonr-751(00). Baltimore: Washington School of Psychiatry.

Fulcher, J. S. (1942). "Voluntary" facial expression in blind and seeing children. *Archives of Psychology*, *272*, 5–49.

Funkenstein, D. H., King, S. H., & Drolette, M. E. (1957). *Mastery of stress*. Cambridge: Harvard University Press.

Galin, D. (1976). Two modes of consciousness and two halves of the brain. In P. R. Lee, R. E. Ornstein, D. Galin, A. Deikman, & C. T. Tart (Eds.), *Symposium on consciousness* (pp. 26–66) (AAAS, 1974). New York: Viking.

Gambaro, S. (1967). Blood pressure relations to expressed and unexpressed anger in low guilt and high guilt subjects. *Disseration Abstracts*, *27*(9-B), 3284–3285.

Gasanov, G. G. (1974). Emotions, visceral functions, and limbic system. In G. G. Gasanov (Ed.), *Emotions and visceral functions*. Moscow: Elm Press.

Gazzaniga, M. S. (1989). Organization of the human brain. *Science*, *245*, 947–952.

Gellhorn, E. (1964). Motion and emotion: The role of proprioception in the physiology and pathology of the emotions. *Psychological Review*, *71*(6), 457–472.

Gellhorn, E. (1970). The emotions and the ergotropic and trophotropic systems. *Psychologische Forschung*, *34*, 48–94.

Gibson, E. J. (1969). *Principles of perceptual learning and development*. New York: Appleton-Century-Crofts.

Gibson, E. J. (1970). Visual perception: Depth, constancies, and cognition. *American Scientist*, *58*, 98–107.

Glueck, S., & Glueck, E. (1950). *Unraveling juvenile delinquency*. Cambridge, MA: Howard University Press.

Goodenough, F. L. (1932). Expressions of emotions in a blind–deaf child. *Journal of Abnormal and Social Psychology*, *27*, 328–333.

Goodman, L. S., & Gilman, A. (Eds.). (1970). *Pharmacological basis of therapeutics* (4th ed.). New York: Macmillan.

Gough, H. G., & Thorne, A. (1986). Positive, negative, and balanced shyness: Self-definitions and the reaction of others. In W. H. Jones, J. M. Cheek, & S. R. Briggs (Eds.), *Shyness: Perspectives on research and treatment* (pp. 205–225). New York: Plenum.

Gray, J. A. (1971). *The psychology of fear and stress*. New York: McGraw-Hill.

Hamburg, D. A. (1963). Emotions in the perspective of human evolution. In P. H. Knopp (Ed.), *Expression of the emotions in man* (pp. 300–317). New York: International Universities Press.

Harlow, H. F. (1971). *Learning to love*. San Francisco: Albion.

Harris, P. L. (1989). *Children and emotion: The development of psychological understanding*. Oxford, England: Basil Blackwell.

Hartman, H. (1969). Influence of symbolically modeled instrumental aggression and pain cues on aggressive behavior. *Journal of Personality and Social Psychology*, *11*, 280–288.

Hass, H. (1970). *The human animal*. New York: Putnam.

Hatfield, E., Schmitz, E., Cornelius, J., & Rapson, R. L. (1988). Passionate love: How early does it begin? *Journal of Psychology & Human Sexuality*, *1*(1), 35–51.

Hebb, D. O. (1949). *The organization of behavior*. New York: Wiley.

Hebb, D. O. (1955). Drives and CNS (conceptual nervous system). *Psychological Review*, *62*, 243–254.

Hebb, D. O. (1961). *The organization of behavior*. New York: Science Editions.

Hembree, E. A. (1986). *Individual differences and developmental changes in infants' emotion expressions during early mother–infant interaction*. Unpublished master's thesis, University of Delaware, Newark.

Henderson, D., & Gillespie, R. D. (1956). *A textbook of psychiatry*. London: Oxford University Press.

Himwich, H. E. (1962). Emotional aspects of mind: Clinical and neurophysiological analysis. In J. M. Scher (Ed.), *Theories of the mind* (pp. 145–180). New York: The Free Press.

Hinde, R. A., & Rowell, T. E. (1962). Communication by postures and facial expressions in the rhesus monkey (*Macaca mulatta*). *Proceedings of the Zoological Society of London*, *138*, 1–21.

Hoffman, M. L. (1981). Is altruism part of human nature? *Journal of Personality and Social Psychology*, *40*, 121–137.

Hoffman, M. L., & Saltzstein, H. D. (1967). Parent discipline and the child's moral development. *Journal of Personality and Social Psychology*, *5*, 45–57.

Hofstatter, P. R. (1955–1956). Dimensionen des mimischen ausdrucks. *Zeitschrift fuer Angewante und Experimentelle Psychologie*, *3*, 503–509.

Holt, R. R. (1967). Beyond vitalism and mechanism: Freud's concept of psychic energy. In J. H. Masserman (Ed.), *Science and psychoanalysis: Vol. 11. Concepts of ego* (pp. 1–41). New York: Grune & Stratton.

Holt, R. R. (1970). On the interpersonal and intrapersonal consequences of expressing or not expressing anger. *Journal of Consulting and Clinical Psychology* *35*(1), 8–12.

Holt, R. R. (1976). Drive or wish? A reconsideration of the psychoanalytic theory of motivation. In M. M. Gill & P. S. Holzman (Eds.), Psychology versus metapsychology: Psychoanalytic essays in memory of George S. Klein. *Psychological Issues*, *9*(4), 158–197.

Horner, M. S. (1972). Toward an understanding of achievement-related conflicts in women. *Journal of Social Issues*, *28*, 157–176.

Huebner, R. R., & Izard, C. E. (1988). Mothers' responses to infants' facial expressions of sadness, anger and physical distress. *Motivation and Emotion*, *12*(2), 185–196.

Hunt, J. McV. (1965). Intrinsic motivation and its role in development. In D. Levine (Ed.), *Nebraska Symposium on Motivation* (pp. 189–282). Lincoln: University of Nebraska Press.

Huxley, A. (1954). *The doors of perception*. New York: Harper & Row.

Hyland, M. E., Curtis, C., & Mason, D. (1985). Fear of success: Motive and cognition. *Journal of Personality and Social Psychology*, *49*(6), 1669–1677.

Hyson, M. C., & Izard, C. E. (1985). Continuities and changes in emotion expressions during brief separation at 13 and 18 months. *Developmental Psychology*, *21*(6), 1165–1170.

Isen, A. (1984). Toward understanding the role of affect in cognition. In R. Wyer & T. Srull (Eds.), *Handbook of social cognition* (pp. 179–236). Hillsdale, NJ: Erlbaum.

Isen, A. M., & Daubman, K. A. (1984). The influence of affect on categorization. *Journal of Personality*, *47*, 1206–1217.

Isen, A. M., Daubman, K. A., & Norwicki, G. P. (1987). Positive affect facilitates creative problem solving. *Journal of Personality and Social Psychology, 52*(6), 1122–1131.

Isen, A. M., & Shalker, T. E., Clark, M. S., & Karp, L. (1978). Affect, accessibility of material in memory, and behavior: A cognitive loop? *Journal of Personality and Social Psychology, 36*, 1–12.

Ittelson, W. H., & Kilpatrick, F. P. (1951). Experiments in perception. *Scientific American, 185*, 50–55.

Izard, C. E. (1965). Personal growth through group experience. In S. S. Tomkins and C. E. Izard (Eds.), *Affect, cognition, and personality* (pp. 200–241). New York: Springer.

Izard, C. E. (1971). *The face of emotion*. New York: Appleton-Century-Crofts.

Izard, C. E. (1972). *Patterns of emotions: A new analysis of anxiety and depression*. New York: Academic Press.

Izard, C. E. (1977). *Human emotions*. New York: Plenum.

Izard, C. E. (1978). On the ontogenesis of emotions and emotion–cognition relationships in infancy. In M. Lewis & L. A. Rosenblum (Eds.), *The development of affect* (pp. 389–413). New York: Plenum.

Izard, C. E. (1979). *The maximally discriminative facial movement coding system (Max)*. Newark: University of Delaware, Office of Instructional Technology.

Izard, C. E. (1984). The facets and interfaces of emotions. In R. Bell, J. L. Greene, & J. H. Harvey (Eds.), *Interfaces in psychology* (pp. 57–85). Lubbock, TX: Texas Tech Press.

Izard, C. E. (1990). Facial expressions and the regulation of emotions. *Journal of Personality and Social Psychology, 58*(3), 487–498.

Izard, C. E., & Blumberg, S. H. (1985). Emotion theory and the role of emotions in anxiety in children and adults. In A. H. Tuma & J. D. Maser (Eds.), *Anxiety and the anxiety disorders* (pp. 109–129). Hillsdale, NJ: Erlbaum.

Izard, C. E., Blumberg, S. H., & Oyster, C. K. (1985). Age and sex differences in the pattern of emotions in childhood anxiety and depression. In J. T. Spence & C. E. Izard (Eds.), *Motivation, emotion, and personality* (pp. 317–324). North-Holland: Elsevier Science Publishers B.V.

Izard, C. E., & Caplan, S. (1974). Sex differences in emotion responses to erotic literature. *Journal of Clinical and Consulting Psychology, 42*, 468.

Izard, C. E., Caplan, S., Walker, S., & Kotsch, W. E. (1977). *Changes in emotions in response to erotic literature and opposite-sex experimenter*. Unpublished manuscript.

Izard, C. E., Dougherty, F. E., Bloxom, B. M., & Kotsch, W. E. (1974). *The differential emotions scale: A method of measuring the subjective experience of discrete emotions*. Unpublished manuscript, Vanderbilt University, Department of Psychology, Nashville.

Izard, C. E., Dougherty, L. M., & Hembree, E. A. (1983). *A system for identifying affect expressions by holistic judgements (Affex)*. Newark: University of Delaware, Office of Instructional Technology.

Izard, C. E., & Haynes, O. M. (1988). On the form and universality of the contempt expression: A challenge to Ekman and Friesen's claim of discovery. *Motivation and Emotion, 12*(1), 1–16.

Izard, C. E., Hembree, E. A., Dougherty, L. M., & Spizirri, C. C. (1983). Changes in facial expressions of 2- to 19-month-old infants following acute pain. *Developmental Psychology, 19*(3), 418–426.

Izard, C. E., Hembree, E. A., & Heubner, R. R. (1987). Infants' emotion expressions to acute pain: Developmental change and stability of individual differences. *Developmental Psychology, 23*(10), 105–113.

Izard, C. E., Huebner, R. R., Risser, D., McGinnes, G., & Dougherty, L. (1980). The young infant's ability to produce discrete emotion expressions. *Developmental Psychology, 16*(2), 132–140.

Izard, C. E., & Hyson, M. C. (1986). Shyness as a discrete emotion. In W. H. Jones, J. M. Cheek, & S. R. Briggs (Eds.), *Shyness: Perspectives on research and treatment* (pp. 147–160). New York: Plenum.

Izard, C. E., & Malatesta, C. Z. (1987). Perspectives on emotional development I: Differential emotions theory of early emotional development. In J. D. Osofsky (Ed.), *Handbook of infant development* (2nd ed., pp. 494–554). New York: Wiley-Interscience.

Izard, C. E., Nagler, S., Randall, D., & Fox, J. (1965). The effects of affective picture stimuli on learning, perception and the affective values of previously neutral symbols. In S. S. Tomkins & C. E. Izard (Eds.), *Affect, cognition, and personality* (pp. 42–70). New York: Springer.
Izard, C. E., & Nunnally, J. C. (1965). Evaluative responses to affectively positive and negative facial photographs: Factor structure and construct validity. *Educational and Psychological Measurement*, *25*, 1061–1071.
Izard, C. E., & Schwartz, G. M. (1986). Patterns of emotion in depression. In M. Rutter, C. E. Izard, & P. B. Read (Eds.), *Depression in young people: Developmental and clinical perspectives* (pp. 33–70). New York: Guilford Press.
Izard, C. E., Spiegel, M., Alessio, G., & Kotsch, W. E. (1974). *Sex standards, sex experience, and emotion responses to imaging sexual intercourse*. Unpublished manuscript.
Izard, C. E., & Tomkins, S. S. (1966). *Affect and behavior: Anxiety as a negative affect*. In C. D. Spielberger (Ed.), Anxiety and behavior (pp. 81–125). New York: Academic Press.
Izard, C. E., Wehmer, G. M., Livsey, W., & Jennings, J. R. (1965). Affect, awareness, and performance. In S. S. Tomkins & C. E. Izard (Eds.), *Affect, cognition, and personality* (pp. 2–41). New York: Springer.
Jacobs, W. J., & Nadel, L. (1985). Stress-induced recovery of fears and phobias. *Psychological Review*, *92*(4), 512–531.
Jacobsen, R. H., Lahey, B. B., & Strauss, C. C. (1983). Correlates of depressed mood in normal children. *Journal of Abnormal Child Psychology*, *11*(1), 29–39.
James, W. (1890). *The principles of psychology* (Vol. 2). New York: Dover.
Janet, P. (1928). Fear of action as an essential element in the sentiment of melancholia. In M. L. Reymert (Ed.), *Feelings and emotions: The Wittenberg Symposium* (pp.297–309). Worcester, MA: Clark University Press.
Janis, I. L., Kagan, J., Mahl, G. F., & Holt, R. R. (1969). *Personality: Dynamics, development, and assessment*. New York: Harcourt, Brace, and World.
John, E. R. (1962). Some speculations on the psychophysiology of mind. In J. M. Scher (Ed.), *Theories of the mind* (pp. 80–121). New York: The Free Press of Glencoe.
Johnson, R. C., Ackerman, J. M., Frank, H., & Fionda, A. J. (1968). Resistance to temptation, guilt following yielding, and psychopathology. *Journal of Consulting and Clinical Psychology*, *32*, 169–175.
Johnson, R. C., Dokecki, P. R., & Mowrer, O. H. (1972). *Conscience, contract, and social reality: Theory and research in behavioral science*. New York: Holt, Rinehart & Winston.
Johnson, R. C., & Medinnus, G. R. (1965). *Child psychology: Behavior and development*. New York: Wiley.
Jolly, A. (1966). Lemur social behavior and primate intelligence. *Science*, *153*, 501–506.
Jones, W. H., & Carpenter, B. N. (1986). In W. H. Jones, J. M. Cheek, & S. R. Briggs (Eds.), *Shyness: Perspectives on research and treatment* (pp. 227–238). New York: Plenum.
Jones, W. H., Cheek, J. M., & Briggs, S. R. (Eds.). (1986). *Shyness: Perspectives on research and treatment*. New York: Plenum.
Jung, C. G. (1933). *Psychological types*. New York: Harcourt.
Kagan, J. (1971). *Change and continuity in infancy*. New York: Wiley.
Kagan, J., Kearsley, R. B., & Zelazo, P. R. (1978). *Infancy: Its place in human development*. Cambridge: Harvard University Press.
Kagan, J., Reznick, J. S., & Snidman, N. (1986). The physiology and psychology of behavioral inhibition in children. *Child Development*, *58*, 1459–1473.
Kagan, J., Reznick, J. S., & Snidman, N. (1988). Biological bases of childhood shyness. *Science*, *240*, 167–171.
Katz, P. K., & Ziegler, P. K. (1967). Self-image disparity: A developmental approach. *Journal of Personality and Social Psychology*, *5*, 186–195.
Kazdin, A. E., Esveldt-Dawson, K., Unis, A. S., & Rancurello, M. D. (1983). Child and parent

evaluations of depression and aggression in psychiatric inpatient children. *Journal of Abnormal Psychology*, *11*(3), 401–412.
Kelly, G. A. (1955). *The psychology of personal constructs* (Vol. I). New York: Norton.
Kety, S. S. (1970). Neurochemical aspects of emotional behavior. In P. Black (Ed.), *Physiological correlates of emotion* (pp. 61–72). New York: Academic Press.
Khanna, D. (1969). A critique of existential guilt. *Psychotherapy: Theory, research, and practice*, *6*(3), 209–211.
Kierkegaard, S. (1944). *The concept of dread* (W. Lowrie, Trans.). Princeton: Princeton University Press. (Original work published in 1844).
Kilty, K. M. (1969). On the relationship between affect and cognition. *Psychological Reports*, *25*, 215–219.
Kish, G. B. (1970). Cognitive innovation and stimulus seeking: A study of the correlates of the obscure figures test. *Perceptual and Motor Skills*, *30*, 95–101.
Kistiakovskaia, M. I. (1965). Stimuli evoking positive emotions in infants in the first months of life. *Soviet Journal of Psychiatry*, *3*, 39–48.
Klein, G. S. (1976). In M. M. Gill & P. S. Holzman (Eds.), *Psychology versus metapsychology: Psychoanalytic essays in memory of George S. Klein* (pp. 14–70). New York: International Universities Press.
Klerman, G. (1974). Depression and adaption. In R. Frieman & M. Katz (Eds.), *The psychology of depression: Contemporary theory and research* (pp. 127–156). Washington, DC: Winston and Sons.
Klinger, E. (1971). *Structure and functions of fantasy*. New York: Wiley-Interscience.
Koestler, A. (1964). *The act of creation*. New York: Macmillan.
Konner, M. (1982). Biological aspects of the mother–infant bond. In R. N. Emde & R. J. Harmon (Eds.), *The development of attachment and affiliative systems* (pp. 137–160). New York: Plenum.
Kovacs, M., & Beck, A. (1977). An empirical clinical approach towards a definition of childhood depression. In J. G. Schulterbrandt & A. Raskin (Eds.), *Depression in children: Diagnosis, treatment, and conceptual models* (pp. 1–25). New York: Raven Press.
Kraines, S. H. (1957). *Mental depressions and their treatment*. New York: Macmillan.
Kron, R. E., Stein, M., & Goddard, K. E. (1966). Newborn sucking behavior affected by obstetric sedation. *Pediatrics*, *37*, 1012–1016.
Kubie, L. S. (1974). The fallacious use of quantitative concepts in dynamic psychology. *Psychoanalytic Quarterly*, *16*, 507–518.
Kubie, L. S. (1961). Theoretical aspects of sensory deprivation. In P. Solomon, P. E. Kubsansky, P. H. Leiderman, J. H. Mendelson, R. Trumbell, & D. Wexler (Eds.), *Sensory deprivation* (pp. 208–220). Cambridge, MA: Harvard University Press.
Kummer, H. (1968). *Social organization of Hamadrya baboon*. Chicago: University of Chicago Press.
Lacey, J. I. (1967). Somatic response patterning in stress. Some revisions of activation theory. In M. H. Appley & R. Trumbull (Eds.), *Psychological stress: Issues in research* (pp. 14–44). New York: Appleton.
Lacey, J. I., & Lacey, B. C. (1970). Some autonomic central nervous system interrelationships. In P. Black (Ed.), *Physiological correlates of emotion* (pp. 205–227). New York: Academic Press.
Langsdorf, P., Izard, C. E., Rayias, M., & Hembree, E. (1983). Interest expression, visual fixation, and heart rate changes in 2- to 8-month-old infants. *Developmental Psychology*, *19*(3), 375–386.
Lanzetta, J. T., & Orr, S. P. (1986). Excitatory strength of expressive faces: Effects of happy and fear expressions and context on the extinction of a conditioned fear response. *Journal of Personality and Social Psychology*, *50*(1), 190–194.
Lazarus, R. (1968). Emotions and adaptation: Conceptual and empirical relations. In W. Arnold (Ed.), *Nebraska Symposium on Motivation* (pp. 175–270). Lincoln: University of Nebraska Press.
Lazarus, R. (1974). Cognitive and coping processes in emotion. In B. Weiner (Ed.), *Cognitive views of human motivation* (pp. 21–32). New York: Academic Press.

Lazarus, R. (1982). Thoughts on the relations between emotion and cognition. *American Psychologist*, *37*, 1019–1024.
Lazarus, R. (1984). On the primacy of cognition. *American Psychologist*, *39*(2), 124–129.
Le Boeuf, B. J., & Peterson, R. S. (1969). Social status and mating activity in elephant seals. *Science*, *163*, 91–93.
Leeper, R. W. (1948). A motivational theory of emotion to replace "emotion as disorganized response." *Psychological Review*, *55*, 5–21.
Leeper, R. W. (1965). Some needed developments in the motivational theory of emotions. In D. E. Levine (Ed.), *Nebraska Symposium on Motivation* (pp. 25–122). Lincoln: University of Nebraska Press.
Leventhal, H. (1982). The integration of emotion and cognition: A view from the perceptual-motor theory of emotion. In M. S. Clark & S. T. Fiske (Eds.), *Affect and cognition* (pp. 121–156). Hillsdale, NJ: Erlbaum.
Leventhal, H., & Chupchik, G. C. (1975). The informational and facilitative effects of an audience upon expression and the evaluation of humorous stimuli. *Journal of Experimental Social Psychology*, *11*, 363–380.
Leventhal, H., & Chupchik, G. C. (1977). *Sex differences in response to cartoons and slapstick movies*. Unpublished manuscript, University of Wisconsin, Madison.
Leventhal, H., & Mace, W. (1970). The effect of laughter on evaluation of a slapstick movie. *Journal of Personality*, *38*, 16–30.
Levine, R. A. (1973). *Culture, behavior and personality*. Chicago: Aldine.
Lewis, H. (1971). *Shame and guilt in neurosis*. New York: International Universities Press.
Lewis, M., & Rosenblum, L. A. (Eds.). (1978). *The development of affect*. New York: Plenum.
Lewis, M., Sullivan, M. W., Stanger, C., & Weiss, M. (1989). Self development and self-conscious emotions. *Child Development*, *60*, 146–156.
Lewinsohn, P. (1974). A behavioral approach to depression. In R. J. Friedman & M. Katz (Eds.), *The psychology of depression: Contemporary theory and research* (pp. 157–185). Washington, DC: Wiley.
Liberman, R. P., & Raskin, D. (1971). Depression: A behavioral formulation. *Archives of General Psychiatry*, *24*, 515–523.
Liddell, H. (1962). The biology of the "prejudiced" mind. In J. M. Scher (Ed.), *Theories of the mind* (pp. 203–240). New York: The Free Press of Glencoe.
Lindsley, D. B. (1951). Emotion. In S. S. Stevens (Ed.), *Handbook of experimental psychology* (pp. 473–516). New York: Wiley.
Lindsley, D. B. (1957). Psychophysiology and motivation. In M. R. Jones (Ed.), *Nebraska Symposium on Motivation* (pp. 44–105). Lincoln: University of Nebraska Press.
London, P. (1968). The major psychological disorders. In P. London & D. Rosenhan (Eds.), *Foundations of abnormal psychology* (pp. 391–426). New York: Holt, Rinehart & Winston.
London, P., Schulman, R. E., & Black, M. S. (undated manuscript). *Religion, guilt, and ethical standards*. University of Illinois.
Lorenz, K. (1965). *Evolution and modification of behavior*. Chicago: The University of Chicago.
Lorenz, K. (1966). *On aggression* (M. K. Wilson, Trans.). New York: Bantam Books.
Luria, A. R., & Vinogradova, I. S. (1959). An objective investigation of the dynamics of semantic systems. *British Journal of Psychology*, *50*, 89–105.
Lynd, H. M. (1961). *On shame and the search for identity*. New York: Science Editions.
Maas, J. W., & Mednieks, M. (1971). Hydrocortisone-mediated increase of norepinephrine uptake by brain slices. *Science*, *171*, 178–179.
Maher, B. A. (1966). *Principles of psychopathology*. New York: McGraw-Hill.
Maier, S. F. (1970). Failure to escape traumatic shock: Incompatible skeletal motor responses or learned helplessness? *Learning and Motivation*, *1*, 157–170.
Main, M., & George, C. (1985). Responses of abused and disadvantaged toddlers to distress in agemates: A study in the day care setting. *Developmental Psychology*, *21*(3), 407–412.
Major D. R. (1906). *First steps in neonatal growth*. New York: Macmillan.

Mandler, G. (1975). *Mind and emotions*. New York: Wiley.

Manstead, A. S. R., & Wagner, H. L. (1981). Arousal, cognition, and emotion: An appraisal of two-factor theory. *Current Psychological Reviews*, *1*, 39–54.

Marsella, A. J., Murray, M. P., & Golden, C. (1974). Ethic variations in the phenomenology of emotions, I. Shame. *Journal of Cross Cultural Psychology*, *5*, 312–328.

Marshall, A. G., & Izard, C. E. (1972a). Cerebral electrotherapeutic treatment of depressions. *Journal of Consulting and Clinical Psychology*, *42*(1), 193–197.

Marshall, A. G., & Izard, C. E. (1972b). Depression as a pattern of emotions and feelings: Factor-analytic investigations. In C. E. Izard, *Patterns of emotions: A new analysis of anxiety and depression* (pp. 237–254). New York: Academic Press.

Marshall, G. (1976). *The affective consequences of "inadequately explained" physiological arousal*. Unpublished doctoral dissertation, Stanford University.

Marx, J. L. (1985). "Anxiety peptide" found in the brain. *Science*, *227*, 934.

Maslach, C. (1979). Negative emotional biasing of unexplained arousal. *Journal of Personality and Social Psychology*, *37*(6), 953–969.

Maslow, A. (1971). *The farther reaches of human nature*. New York: Viking.

Matas, L., Arend, R., & Sroufe, L. (1978). Continuity of adaptation in the second year: The relationship between quality of attachment and later competence. *Child Development*, *49*, 547–556.

May, R. (1958). The origins and significance of the existential movement in psychology. In R. May, E. Angel, & H. F. Ellenberger (Eds.), *Existence: A new dimension in psychiatry and psychology* (pp. 3–36). New York: Basic Books.

McCary, J. L. (1973). *Human sexuality: Physiological, psychological and sociological factors*. New York: Van Nostrand.

McClelland, C. C. (1985). How motives, skills, and values determine what people do. *American Psychologist*, *40*, 812–825.

McDougall, W. (1908). *An introduction to social psychology*. London: Methuen.

McGhee, P. E. (1971a). Cognitive development and children's comprehension of humor. *Child Development*, *42*, 123–138.

McGhee, P. E. (1971b). Development of the humor response: A review of the literature. *Psychological Bulletin*, *76*, 328–348.

McGhee, P. E. (1974). Cognitive mastery and children's humor. *Psychological Bulletin*, *81*, 721–730.

McGrade, B. J. (1968). Newborn activity and emotional response at eight months. *Child Development*, *39*, 1247–1252.

McKennan, D. (1938). Violation of prohibitions. In H. A. Murray (Ed.), *Explorations in personality* (pp. 491–501). New York: Oxford University Press.

McNally, R. J. (1989). On "stress-induced recovery of fears and phobias." *Psychological Review*, *96*(1), 180–181.

Mead, M. (1956). Social change and cultural surrogates. In C. Kluckhohn, H. A., Murray, & D. M. Schneider (Eds.), *Personality in nature, society, and culture* (2nd ed., pp. 651–662). New York: Knopf.

Meade, M. (1950). Some anthropological considerations concerning guilt. In M. L. Reymert (Ed.), *Feelings and emotions* (pp. 362–373). New York: McGraw-Hill.

Meadows, C. M. (1968). *Joy in psychological and theological perspective: A constructive approach*. Unpublished doctoral dissertation, Princeton Theological Seminary, Princeton, NJ.

Meadows, C. M. (1975). The phenomenology of joy: An empirical investigation. *Psychological Reports*, *37*, 39–54.

Mellen, S. L. W. (1981). *The evolution of love*. San Francisco: Freeman.

Meskin, B., & Singer, J. L. (1974). Daydreaming, reflective thought and laterality of eye movements. *Journal of Personality and Social Psychology*, *30*(1), 64–71.

Milgram, S. (1963). Behavioral study of obedience. *Journal of Abnormal and Social Psychology*, *67*, 371–378.

Milgram, S. (1964). Group pressure and action against a person. *Journal of Abnormal and Social Psychology*, *69*, 137–143.
Milgram, S. (1965). Some conditions of bedience and disobedience to authority. *Human Relations*, *18*(1), 53–75.
Miller, D., & Swanson, G. (1956). The study of conflict. In M. Jones (Ed.), *Nebraska Symposium on Motivation* (pp. 137–173). Lincoln: University of Nebraska Press.
Miller, N. E. (1948). Studies of fear as an acquirable drive: I. Fear as motivation and fear-reduction as reinforcement in the learning of new responses. *Journal of Experimental Psychology*, *38*, 89–101.
Mineka, S., Davidson, M., Cook, M., & Keir, R. (1984). Observational conditioning of snake fear in rhesus monkeys. *Journal of Abnormal Psychology*, *93*(4), 355–372.
Modigliani, A. (1971). Embarrassment, facework and eye contact: Testing a theory of embarrassment. *Journal of Personality and Social Psychology*, *17*(1), 15–24.
Moore, B. S., Underwood, B., & Rosenhan, D. (1973). Affect and altruism. *Developmental Psychology*, *8*, 99–104.
Moore, B. W., Underwood, B., & Rosenhan, D. (1984). Emotion, self, and others. In C. E. Izard, J. Kagan, & R. Zajonc (Eds.), *Emotions, cognition, and behavior* (pp. 464–483). New York: Cambridge University Press.
Morris, D. (1968). *The naked ape: A zoologist's study of the human animal*. New York: McGraw-Hill.
Mosher, D. L. (1965). The interaction of fear and guilt in inhibiting unacceptable behavior. *Journal of Consulting Psychology*, *29*, 161–167.
Mosher, D. L. 1967). The learning of congruent and noncongruent social structures. *Journal of Social Psychology*, *73*, 285–290.
Mosher, D. L. (1968). Measurement of guilt in females by self-report inventories. *Journal of Consulting and Clinical Psychology*, *32*, 690–695.
Mosher, D. L., & Galbraith, G. G. (1970). Effects of sex guilt and sexual stimulation on the recall of word associations. *Journal of Consulting and Clinical Psychology*, *34*(1), 67–71.
Mosher, D. L., & Mosher, J. B. (1967). Guilt in prisoners. *Journal of Clinical Psychology*, *23*, 171–173.
Mowrer, O. H. (1960). *Learning theory and behavior*. New York: Wiley.
Mowrer, O. H. (1961). *The crisis in psychiatry and religion*. Princeton, NJ: Van Nostrand.
Murphy, G. (1958). *Human potentialities*. New York: Basic Books.
Murray, H. A. (1938). *Explorations in personality: A clinical and experimental study of fifty men of college age.*. New York: Oxford University Press.
Nasby, W., & Yando, R. (1982). Selective encoding and retrieval of affectively valent information: Two cognitive consequences of children's mood states. *Journal of Personality and Social Psychology*, *43*(6), 1244–1253.
Nathan, P. (1969). *The nervous system*. Philadelphia: Lippincott.
Nesse, R. M. (1990). Evolutionary explanations of emotions. *Human Nature*, *1*(3), 261–289.
Nicholas, O. L. (1966). Guilt as related to self-concept and personality adjustment. *Dissertation Abstracts*, *26*(7), 4080.
Nichols, R. C. (1978). Heredity and environment: Major findings from twin studies of ability, personality and interests. *Homo*, *29*, 158–173.
Nowlis, V. (1965). Research with the mood adjective check list. In S. S. Tomkins & C. E. Izard (Eds.), *Affect, cognition, and personality* (pp. 352–389). New York: Springer.
Nowlis, V. (1970). Mood: Behavior and experience. In M. B. Arnold (Ed.), *Feelings and emotions* (pp. 261–277). New York: Academic Press.
Nurnberger, J. I., & Gershon, E. S. (1984). Genetics of affective disorders. In R. M. Post & J. C. Ballenger (Eds.), *Neurobiology of mood disorders* (pp. 76–101). Baltimore: Williams & Wilkins.
Ogren, D. J., & Dokecki, P. R. (1972). Moral development and behavior disorders in young children. In R. C. Johnson, P. R. Dokecki, & O. H. Mowrer (Eds.), *Conscience, contract, and social reality: Research in behavioral science* (pp. 402–410). New York: Holt, Rinehart & Winston.
Ohman, A., & Dimberg, V. (1978). Facial expressions as conditioned stimuli for electrodermal responses: A case of "preparedness"? *Journal of Personality and Social Psychology*, *36*, 1251–1258.

Okle, E., & Mosher, D. L. (1968). Changes in affective states as a function of guilt over aggressive behavior. *Journal of Consulting Psychology*, *32*, 265–270.

Oliver, W. A., & Mosher, D. L. (1968). Psychopathology and guilt in heterosexual reformatory inmates. *Journal of Abnormal Psychology*, *73*, 323–329.

Olweus, D. (1980). The consistency issue in personality psychology revisited—with special reference to aggression. *British Journal of Social and Clinical Psychology*, *19*, 377–390.

Olweus, D. (1982). Development of stable aggressive reaction patterns in males. In R. Blanchard & C. Blanchard (Eds.), *Advances in the study of aggression* (Vol. 1, pp. 117–137). New York: Academic Press.

Orr, S. P., & Lanzetta, J. T. (1980). Facial expressions of emotion as conditioned stimuli for human autonomic responses. *Journal of Personality and Social Psychology*, *38*(2), 278–282.

Osgood, C. E. (1966). Dimensionality of the semantic space for communication via facial expressions. *Scandinavian Journal of Psychology*, *7*, 1–30.

Osgood, C. E. (1969). On the why and wherefore of E, P, and A. *Journal of Personality and Social Psychology*, *12*, 194–199.

Osgood, C. E., Suci, G. J., & Tannenbaum, P. H. (1957). *The measurement of meaning*. Urbana: University of Illinois Press.

Parke, R. D., & Slaby, R. G. (1983). The development of aggression. In P. H Mussen (Ed.), *Handbook of child psychology* (4th ed., pp. 547–641). New York: Wiley.

Peretz, D. (1970). Reaction to loss. In B. Schoenberg, A. C. Carr, D. Peretz, & A. H. Kutscher (Eds.), *Loss and grief; Psychological management in medical practice* (pp. 3–19). New York: Columbia University Press.

Perry, R. B. (1926). *General theory of value: Its meaning and basic principles constructed in terms of interest*. New York: Longmans, Green.

Perry, R. B. (1954). *Realms of value*. Cambridge, MA: Harvard University Press.

Persons, R. W. (1970a). Intermittent reinforcement, guilt, and crime. *Psychological Reports*, *26*, 421–422.

Persons, R. W. (1970b). The Mosher Guilt Scale: Theoretical formulation, research, and normative data. *Journal of Projective Techniques*, *34*, 266–270.

Persons, R. W., & Marks, P. A. (1969). Self-disclosure with recidivists: Optimum interviewer–interviewee matching. *Proceedings of the 77th Annual Convention of the American Psychological Association*, *4*, 531–543.

Peterfreund, E. (1971). Information, systems, and psychoanalysis: An evolutionary biological approach to psychoanalytic theory (with Jacob T. Schwartz). *Psychological Issues*, *7*, 1–39.

Peterson, D. R. (1967). The insecure child: Oversocialized or undersocialized? In O. H. Mowrer (Ed.), *Morality and mental health* (pp. 459–471). Chicago: Rand McNally.

Piaget, J. (1952). *The origins of intelligence in children* (M. Cook, Trans.). New York: International Universities Press. (Original work published 1932)

Piers, G., & Singer, M. S. (1953). *Shame and guilt: A psychoanalytic and cultural study*. Springfield: Charles C. Thomas.

Pilkonis, P. A., & Zimbardo, P. G. (1979). The personal and social dynamics of shyness. In C. E. Izard (Ed.), *Emotions in personality and psychopathology* (p. 133–160). New York: Plenum.

Plutchik, R. (1954). The role of muscular tension in maladjustment. *Journal of General Psychology*, *50*, 45–62.

Plutchik, R. (1962). *The emotions: Facts, theories, and a new model*. New York: Random House.

Plutchik, R. (1980). *Emotion: A psychoevolutionary synthesis*. New York: Harper & Row.

Plutchik, R., & Ax, A. F. (1967). A critique of determinants of emotional state by Schachter and Singer (1962). *Psychophysiology*, *4*, 79–82.

Podell, L., & Perkins, J. C. (1957). A Guttman scale for sexual experience—a methodological note. *Journal of Abnormal and Social Psychology*, *54*, 420–422.

Pope, K. S. (1977). *The stream of consciousness*. Unpublished doctoral dissertation, Yale University.

Pope, K. S., & Singer, J. L. (1976). Regulation of the stream of consciousness: Toward a theory of ongoing thought. In G. Schwartz & D. Shapiro (Eds.), *Consciousness and self regulation: Advances in research, Vol. II* (pp. 101–138). New York: Plenum.

Potegal, M. (1979). The reinforcing value of several types of aggressive behavior: A review. *Aggressive Behavior*, *5*, 353–373.

Prange, A., & Vitols, M. M. (1962). Cultural aspects of the relatively low incidence of depression in Southern Negroes. *International Journal of Social Psychiatry*, *8*, 104–112.

Pribram, K. H. (1970). Feelings as monitors. In M. B. Arnold (Ed.), *Feelings and emotions* (pp. 41–53). New York: Academic Press.

Puig-Antich, J. (1986). Psychobiological markers: Effects of age and puberty. In M. Rutter, C. E. Izard, & P. B. Read (Eds.), *Depression in young people: Clinical and developmental perspectives* (pp. 341–381). New York: Guilford.

Rado, S. (1968). Psychodynamics of depression from the etiologic point of view. In W. Gaylin (Ed.), *The meaning of despair* (pp. 96–107). New York: Science House. (Original work published 1928)

Rapaport, D. (1942). *Emotions and memory*. New York: Science Editions.

Rapaport, D. (1953). On the psychoanalytic theory of affects. *International Journal of Psychoanalysis*, *34*, 177–198.

Rapaport, D. (1960). On the psychoanalytic theory of motivation. In M. R. Jones (Ed.), *Nebraska Symposium on Motivation* (pp. 173–257). Lincoln: University of Nebraska Press.

Rapaport, D. (1961). *Emotions and memory*. New York: Science Editions. (Original work published 1942)

Rasa, O. A. E. (1969). Territoriality and the establishment of dominance by means of visual cues in *Domacentrus jenkinsi* (pices: pomacentridae). *Zeitscriet fur Tierpsychologie*, *26*, 825–845. (Cited by R. N. Johnson, *Aggression in man and animals*. Philadelphia: W. B. Saunders, 1972).

Reiss, I. L. (1967). *The social context of premarital sexual permissiveness*. New York: Holt, Rinehart & Winston.

Renninger, K. A., & Wozniak, R. H. (1985). Effect of interest on attentional shift, recognition, and recall in young children. *Developmental Psychology*, *21*(4), 624–632.

Rheingold, H. L. (1974). General issues in the study of fear: Section I. In M. Lewis & L. A. Rosenblum (Eds.), *Origins of fear* (pp. 249–253). New York: Wiley.

Richardson, L. F. (1960). Statistics of deadly quarrels. Pittsburgh: Boxwood.

Rodin, J., & Singer, J. L. (1976). Eye-shift, thought, and obesity. *Journal of Personality*, *44*(4), 594–610.

Rogers, C. R. (1951). *Client centered therapy*. Boston: Houghton Miffin.

Rogers, C. R. (1959). A theory of therapy, personality, and interpersonal relationships, as developed in the client-centered framework. In S. Koch (Ed.), *Psychology: Vol. 3. A study of a science* (pp. 184–256). New York: McGraw-Hill.

Rogers, C. R. (1961). *On becoming a person*. Boston: Houghton Mifflin.

Rosenhan, D., & London, P. (1970). *Foundations of abnormal psychology*. San Francisco: Holt, Rinehart & Winston.

Roseman, I. J. (1984). Cognitive determinants of emotions: A structural theory. In P. Shaver (Ed.), *Review of personality and social psychology: Vol. 5. Emotions, relationships, and health* (pp. 11–36). Beverly Hills, CA: Sage.

Rothbart, M. K. (1973). Laughter in young children. *Psychological Bulletin*, *80*, 247–256.

Rozin, P., & Fallon, A. E. (1987). A perspective on disgust. *Psychological Review*, *94*(1), 23–41.

Rubinstein, B. B. (1967). Explanation and mere description: A metascientific examinations of certain aspects of the psychoanalytic theory of motivation. In R. R. Holt (Ed.), *Motives and thought: Psychoanalytic essays in honor of David Rapaport*. (*Psychological Issues*. Monograph 18/19, *5*, 20–77.)

Rusalova, M. N., Izard, C. E., & Simonov, P. V. (1975). Comparative analysis of mimical and autonomic components of man's emotional state. *Aviation, Space, and Environmental Medicine*, *46*(9), 1132–1134.

Russell, J. A. (1980). A circumplex model of affect. *Journal of Personality and Social Psychology, 39*, 1161–1178.
Russell, J. A. (1983). Pancultural aspects of the human conceptual organization of emotions. *Journal of Personality and Social Psychology, 45*, 1281–1288.
Safer, M. A. & Leventhal, H. (1977). Ear differences in evaluating emotional tones of voice and verbal content. *Journal of Experimental Psychology: Human Perception and Performance, 3*, 75–82.
Sameroff, A. J. (1971). Respiration and sucking as components of the orienting reaction in newborns. *Psychophysiology, 7*(2), 213–22.
Sarason, S. B. (1966). The measurement of anxiety in children: Some questions and problems. In C. D. Spielberger (Ed.), *Anxiety and behavior* (pp. 63–80). New York: Academic Press.
Savitsky, J. C., & Izard, C. E. (1970). Developmental changes in the use of emotion cues in a concept formation task. *Developmental Psychology, 3*(3), 350–357.
Savitsky, J. C., & Sim, M. (1974). Trading emotions. Equity theory of reward and punishment. *Journal of Communication, 24*, 140–146.
Schachtel, E. G. (1959). *Metamorphosis*. New York: Basic Books.
Schachter, S. (1966). The interaction of cognitive and physiological determinants of emotional state. In C. D. Spielberger (Ed.), *Anxiety and behavior* (pp. 193–244). New York: Academic Press.
Schachter, S. (1971). *Emotion, obesity, and crime*. New York: Academic Press.
Schachter, S., & Singer, J. E. (1962). Cognitive, social, and physiological determinants of emotional states. *Psychological Review, 69*(5), 379–399.
Scher, J. M. (1962). Mind as participation. In J. M. Scher (Ed.), *Theories of the mind* (pp. 354–375). New York: The Free Press of Glencoe.
Schlosberg, H. S. (1941). A scale for the judgement of facial expressions. *Journal of Experimental Psychology, 44*, 229–237.
Schlosberg, H. S. (1952). The description of facial expressions in terms of two dimensions. *Journal of Experimental Psychology, 44.*, 229–237.
Schlosberg, H. S. (1954). Three dimensions of emotion. *Psychological Review, 61*, 81–88.
Schoenberg, B., Carr, A. C., Peretz, D., & Kutscher, A. H. (Eds.). (1970). *Loss and grief: Psychological management in medical practice*. New York: Columbia University Press.
Schultz, D. K. (1976). *Fantasy stimulation in the treatment of depressed psychiatric patients*. Unpublished doctoral dissertation, Yale University.
Schutz, W. (1967). *Joy: Expanding human awareness*. New York: Grove Press.
Schwartz, G. E. (1990). Psychobiology of repression and health: A systems approach. In J. L. Singer (Ed.), *Repression and dissociation* (pp. 405–434). Chicago: The University of Chicago Press.
Schwartz, G. E., Fair, P. I., Greenberg, P. S., Freedman, M., & Klerman, J. L. (1974). Facial expression and depression: An electromyographic study. *Psychosomatic Medicine, 36*, 458.
Schwartz, G. E., Fair, P. I., Salt, P. S., Mandel, M. R., & Klerman, J. L. (1976). Facial electromyography in the assessment of emotion. *Psychophysiology, 11*, 237.
Schwartz, G. M., Davidson, R. J., Maer, F., & Bromfield, E. (1973). *Patterns of hemispheric dominance in musical, emotional verbal, and spatial tasks*. Paper presented at the meetings of the Society for Psychophysiological Research, Galveston, TX.
Schwartz, G. M., Izard, C. E., & Ansul, S. E. (1985). The 5-month-old's ability to discriminate facial expressions of emotion. *Infant Behavior and Development, 8*, 65–77.
Scott, W. A. (1969). Structure of nature cognitions. *Journal of Personality and Social Psychology, 12*(4), 261–278.
Sears, R. R., Maccoby, E. E., & Levin, H. (1957). *Patterns of child rearing*. New York: Harper.
Seligman, M. E. P. (1975). *Helplessness: On depression development and death*. San Francisco: Freeman.
Seligman, M. E. P., & Maier, S. F. (1967). Failure to escape traumatic shock. *Journal of Experimental Psychology, 74*, 1–9.
Seligman, M. E. P., Maier, S. F., & Greer, J. (1968). The alleviation of learned helplessness in the dog. *Journal of Abnormal and Social Psychology, 73*, 256–262.

Seligman, M. E. P., & Peterson, C. (1986). A learned helplessness perspective on childhood depression: Theory and research. In M. Rutter, C. E. Izard, & P. B. Read (Eds.), *Depression in young people* (pp. 223–249). New York: Guilford.

Shagass, C. (1962). Explorations in the psychology of affect. In J. M. Scher (Ed.), *Theories of the mind* (pp. 122–144). New York: The Free Press of Glencoe.

Shaw, G. A., & De Mers, S. T. (1987). Relationships between imagery and creativity in high-IQ children. Imagination, *Cognition and Personality*, *6*(3), 247–262.

Sheaffer, C. I., Gold, S. R., & Henderson, B. B. (1987). Environmental influences on children's fantasy. *Imagination, Cognition and Personality*, *6*(2), 151–157.

Shiller, V., Izard, C. E., & Hembree, E. A. (1986). Patterns of emotion expression during separation in the Strange-Situation Procedure. *Developmental Psychology*, *22*, 378–382.

Silverman, C. (1968). *The epidemiology of depression*. Baltimore: Johns Hopkins Press.

Silverman, I. W. (1967). Incidence of guilt reactions in children. *Journal of Personality and Social Psychology*, 338–340.

Simonov, P. V. (1975). Higher nervous activity of man: Motivational-emotional aspects. Moscow: Izdatelstvo Nauka.

Singer, J. L. (1966). *Daydreaming: An introduction to the experimental study of inner experience*. New York: Random House.

Singer, J. L. (1973). *The child's world of make-believe: Experimental studies of imaginative play*. New York: Academic Press.

Singer, J. L. (1974). *Imagery and daydream methods in psychotherapy and behavior modification*. New York: Academic Press.

Singer, J. L. (1975). Navigating the stream of consciousness. *American Psychologist*, *30*, 727–738.

Singer, J. L. (1979). Affect and imagination in play and fantasy. In C. E. Izard (Ed.), *Emotions in personality and psychopathology* (pp. 13–34). New York: Plenum.

Singer, J. L. (Ed.). (1990). *Repression and dissociation*. Chicago: The University of Chicago Press.

Singer, J. L., & Antrobus, J. S. (1963). A factor analysis of daydreaming and conceptually related cognitive and personality variables. *Perceptual and Motor Skills, Monograph Supplement* (3-V17).

Sinnott, E. W. (1966). *The bridge of life*. New York: Simon & Schuster.

Sinsheimer, R. L. (1971, January–February). The brain of Pooh: An essay on the limits of the mind. *American Scientist*, 20–28.

Smilansky, S. (1968). *The effects of sociodramatic play on disadvantaged preschool children*. New York: Wiley.

Smith, C. A., & Ellsworth, P. C. (1985). Patterns of cognitive appraisal in emotion. *Journal of Personality and Social Psychology*, *48*, 813–838.

Snygg, D., & Combs, A. W. (1949). *Individual behavior*. New York: Harper.

Sogon, S., & Masutani, M. (1989). Identification of emotion from body movements: A cross-cultural study of Americans and Japanese. *Psychological Reports*, *65*, 35–46.

Solomon, R. I., Corbit, J. D. (1974). An opponent process theory of motivation: I. Temporal dynamics of affect. *Psychological Review*, *81*, 119–145.

Solomon, R. L., Turner, L. H., & Lessac, M. S. (1968). Some effects of delay of punishment on resistance to temptation in dogs. *Journal of Personality and Social Psychology*, *8*(3), 233–238.

Solomon, R. I., & Wynne, L. C. (1953). Traumatic avoidance learning: Acquisition in normal dogs. *Psychological Monographs*, *67*, (1–19, Whole No. 354).

Spencer, H. (1890). *The principles of psychology* (Vol. 1). New York: Appleton.

Spielberger, C. D. (1966). Theory and research on anxiety. In C. D. Spielberger (Ed.), *Anxiety and behavior* (pp. 3–22). New York: Academic Press.

Spielberger, C. D., Edwards, C. D., Lushene, R. F., Montuori, J., & Platzek, D. (1973). *STAIC: Preliminary manual*. Palo Alto, California: Consulting Psychologists Press.

Spielberger, C. D., Gorsuch, R. R., & Lushene, R. E. (1970). *State–trait anxiety inventory test manual for form X*. Palo Alto: Consulting Psychologists Press.

Spiro, M. (1949). *Ifaluk: A South Sea culture*. Unpublished manuscript, Human Relations Area Files, Yale University.
Spitz, R. A. (1945). Hospitalism: An inquiry into the genesis of psychiatric conditions in early childhood. *Psychoanalytic Study of the Child, 1*, 53–74.
Spitz, R. A. (1946). Hospitalism: A follow-up report. *Psychoanalytic Study of the Child, 2*, 113–117.
Spitz, R. A. (1965). *The first year of life*. New York: International Universities Press.
Spitz, R. A., & Wolf, K. M. (1946). The smiling response: A contribution to the ontogenesis of social relations. *Genetic Psychology Monographs, 34*, 57–125.
Spranger, J. M. (1928). *Lebensformen* (P. Pigors. Trans). New York: Steckert.
Sroufe, L. A., & Waters, E. A., & Matas, L. (1974). Contextual determinants of infant affective response. In M. Lewis & L. A. Rosenblum (Eds.), *The origins of fear* (pp. 49–72). New York: Wiley.
Sroufe, L. A., & Wunsch, J. P. (1972). The development of laughter in the first years of life. *Child Development, 43*, 1326–1344.
Stechler, G. (1964). The effect of medication during labor on newborn attention. *Science, 144*, 315–317.
Steiner, J. E. (1979). Human facial expressions in response to taste and smell stimulation. In *Advances in child development and behavior* (Vol. 13, pp. 257–294). New York: Academic Press.
Suomi, S. J. (1979). Genetic and maternal contributions to individual differences in rhesus monkey biobehavioral development. In N. A. Krasnagor, E. M. Blass, M. A. Hoffer, & W. P. Smotherman (Eds.), *Perinatal development: A psychobiological perspective* (pp. 397–420). New York: Academic Press.
Swann, W. B., Griffin, J. J., Predmore, S. C., & Gaines, B. (1987). The cognitive-affective crossfire: When self-consistency confronts self-enhancement. *Journal of Personality and Social Psychology, 52*(5), 881–889.
Switzer, D. K. (1968). A psychodynamic analysis of grief in the context of an interpersonal theory of self. *Dissertation Abstracts, 29*(3), 381.
Tart, C. T. (1973). States of consciousness and state-specific sciences. In R. Ornstein (Ed.), *The nature of human consciousness* (pp. 41–60). San Francisco: Freeman.
Tart, C. T. (1976). Discrete states of consciousness. In P. R. Lee, R. E. Ornstein, D. Galin, A. Deikman, & C. T. Tart (Eds.), *Symposium on Consciousness* (AAAS, 1974). New York: Viking.
Tellegen, A. (1982). *Brief manual for the differential personality questionnaire*. Unpublished manuscript, University of Minnesota, Minneapolis.
Tellegen, A. (1985). Structures of mood and personality and their relevance to assessing anxiety, with an emphasis on self-report. In A. H. Tuma & J. D. Maser (Eds.), *Anxiety and the anxiety disorders* (pp. 681–706). Hillsdale, NJ: Erlbaum.
Termine, N. T., & Izard, C. E. (1988). Infants' responses to their mothers' expressions of joy and sadness. *Developmental Psychology, 24*(2), 223–229.
Thompson, J. (1941). Development of facial expression of emotion in blind and seeing children. *Archives of Psychology, 37*, 5–47.
Thompson, J. G. (1988). *The psychobiology of emotions*. New York: Plenum.
Thompson, R. A., Lamb, M. E., & Estes, D. (1982). Stability of infant–mother attachment and its relationship to changing life circumstances in an unselected middle class sample. *Child Development, 53*, 144–148.
Tinbergen, N. (1968). On war and peace in animals and man. *Science, 160*, 1411–1418.
Tolman, E. C. (1932). *Purposive behavior in animals and men*. New York: Appleton-Century-Crofts.
Tomkins, S. S. (1962). *Affect, imagery, consciousness: Vol. 1. The positive affects*. New York: Springer.
Tomkins, S. S. (1963). *Affect, imagery, consciousness: Vol. 2. The negative affects*. New York: Springer.
Tonks, C. M., Paykel, E. S., & Klerman, G. L. (1970). Clinical depressions among Negroes. *American Journal of Psychiatry, 127*, 329–335.
Triandis, H. C., & Lambert, W. W. (1958). A restatement and test of Schlosberg's theory of emotions

with two kinds of subjects from Greece. *Journal of Abnormal and Social Psychology*, *56*, 321–328.

Tronick, E. Z. (1990). Emotions and emotional communication in infants. [Special issue]. *American Psychologist*, *42*(2), 112–119.

Unger, J. M. (1962). *On the development of guilt reactivity in the child*. Unpublished doctoral dissertation, Cornell University.

Vernon, J. A., McGill, T. E., Gulick, W. L., & Candland, D. K. (1961). The effect of human isolation upon some perceptual and motor skills. In P. Solomon (Ed.), *Sensory deprivation* (pp. 41–57). Cambridge, MA: Harvard Press.

Vine, I. (1973). The role of facial-visual signalling in early social development. In M. Von Cranach & I. Vine (Eds.), *Social communication and movement* (pp. 195–298). New York: Academic Press.

Wallace, J., & Sadalla, E. (1966). Behavioral consequences of transgression. I. The effects of social cognition. *Journal of Experimental Research in Personality*, *1*, 187–194.

Washburn, R. W. (1929). A study of the smiling and laughing of infants in the first years of life. *Genetic: Psychology Monographs*, *6*, 398–537.

Watson, D., Clark, L. A., & Carey, G. (1988). Positive and negative affectivity and their relation to anxiety and depressive disorders. *Journal of Abnormal Psychology*, *97*, 346–353.

Watson, J. B. (1919). *Psychology from the standpoint of a behaviorist*. Philadelphia: Lippincott.

Watson, J. B., & Raynor, R. (1920). Conditioned emotional reactions. *Journal of Experimental Psychology*. *3*, 1–14.

Weinberger, D. A. (1990). The construct validity of the repressive coping style. In J. L. Singer (Ed.), *Repression and dissociation* (pp. 337–386). Chicago: The University of Chicago Press.

Weiner, B. (1985). An attributional theory of achievement motivation and emotion. *Psychological Review*, *89*(4), 548–573.

Wenger, M. A. (1950). Emotion as a visceral action: An extension of Lange's theory. In M. L. Reymert (Ed.), *Feeling and emotions* (pp. 3–10). New York: McGraw-Hill.

Wessman, A. E., & Ricks, J. H. (1966). *Mood and personality*. New York: Holt, Rinehart & Winston.

Wheeler, J. A. (1974). The universe as home for man. *American Scientist*, *62*, 683–691.

Wheeler, L., & Caggiula, A. R. (1966). The contagion of aggression. *Journal of Experimental and Social Psychology*, *2*, 1–10.

White, B. L. (1975). *The first three years of life*. Englewood Cliffs, NJ: Prentice-Hall.

Whiting, J. W. M., & Child, I. L. (1953). *Child training and personality*. New Haven: Yale University Press.

Whybrow, P. C., Akiskal, H. S., & McKinney, W. T. (1984). *Mood disorders: Toward a new psychobiology*. New York: Plenum.

Willingham, C. (1963). *Eternal fire*. New York: Vanguard Press.

Wilson, W. R. (1979). Feeling more than we can know: Exposure effects without learning. *Journal of Personality and Social Psychology*, *37*, 811–821.

Witkin, H. A. (1949). Perception of body position and of the position of the visual field. *Psychology Monographs.*, *63*(7), 1–46.

Wolff, P. H. (1963). Observations on the early development of smiling. In B. M. Foss (Ed.), *Determinants of infant behavior* (pp. 113–134). New York: Wiley.

Wolff, P. H. (1966). The causes, controls, and organization of behavior in the neonate. *Psychological Issues*, *5*(1, Whole No. 17).

Wolpe, J. (1969). *The practice of behavior therapy*. New York: Pergamon Press.

Woodworth, R. S. (1938). *Experimental psychology*. New York: Henry Holt and Company.

Woodworth, R. S., & Schlosberg, H. S. (1954). *Experimental psychology*. New York: Holt.

Wright, S., & MacDonald, C. (1974). Review of behavioral treatment of depression. *Psychological Reports*, *34*, 1335–1341.

Wundt, W. (1896). *Outlines of psychology* (C. H. Judd, Trans.). New York: Stechert.

Wynne, L. C., & Solomon, R. L. (1955). Traumatic avoidance learning: Acquisition and extinction in dogs deprived of normal peripheral autonomic functioning. *Genetic Psychology Monographs*, *52*, 241–284.

Young, P. T. (1961). *Motivation and emotion: A survey of the determinants of human and animal activity*. New York: Wiley.

Zahn-Waxler, C., Radke-Yarrow, M., & King, R. A. (1979). Child rearing and children's prosocial initiations towards victims of distress. *Child Development*, *50*, 319–330.

Zajonc, R. B. (1980). Feeling and thinking: Preferences need no inferences. *American Psychologist*, *35*(2), 151–175.

Zajonc, R. B. (1984). On the primacy of affect. *American Psychologist*, *39*, 117–123.

Zigler, E., Levine, J., & Gould, L. (1967). Cognitive challenge as a factor in children's humor appreciation. *Journal of Personality and Social Psychology*, *6*, 332–336.

Zillman, D. (1971). Excitation transfer in communication-mediated aggressive behavior. *Journal of Experimental Social Psychology*, *7*, 419–434.

Zimbardo, P. G. (1969). *The human choices: Individuation, reason, and order vs. deindividuation, impulse, and chaos*. Unpublished manuscript, Stanford University.

Zimbardo, P. G. (1986). The Stanford shyness project. In W. H. Jones, J. M. Cheek, & S. R. Briggs (Eds.), *Shyness: Perspectives on research and treatment* (pp. 17–25). New York: Plenum.

Zimbardo, P., Pilkonis, P., & Norwood, R. (1974). *The silent prison of shyness*. Stanford University. (Paper distributed by Scott, Foresman College Division, Glenview, Illinois.)

Zuckerman, M. (1960). The development of an affect adjective check list for the measurement of anxiety. *Journal of Consulting Psychology*, *24*, 457–462.

Zuckerman, M. (1979). *Sensation seeking: Beyond the optimal level of arousal*. Hillsdale, NJ: Erlbaum.

Zuckerman, M. (1984). Sensation-seeking: A comparative approach to a human trait. *The Behavioral and Brain Sciences*, *7*(3), 413–471.

Zuckerman, M., & Wheeler, L. (1975). To dispel fantasies about the fantasy-based measure of fear of success. *Psychological Bulletin*, *82*, 932–946.

Author Index

Subject Index